IFIP Advances in Information and Communication Technology

677

Editor-in-Chief

Kai Rannenberg, Goethe University Frankfurt, Germany

Editorial Board Members

IFIP Advances in Information and Communication Technology

The IFIP AICT series publishes state-of-the-art results in the sciences and technologies of information and communication. The scope of the series includes: foundations of computer science; software theory and practice; education; computer applications in technology; communication systems; systems modeling and optimization; information systems; ICT and society; computer systems technology; security and protection in information processing systems; artificial intelligence; and human-computer interaction.

Edited volumes and proceedings of refereed international conferences in computer science and interdisciplinary fields are featured. These results often precede journal publication and represent the most current research.

The principal aim of the IFIP AICT series is to encourage education and the dissemination and exchange of information about all aspects of computing.

More information about this series at https://link.springer.com/bookseries/6102

Ilias Maglogiannis · Lazaros Iliadis ·
Antonios Papaleonidas ·
Ioannis Chochliouros
Editors

Artificial Intelligence Applications and Innovations

AIAI 2023 IFIP WG 12.5 International Workshops

MHDW 2023, 5G-PINE 2023, AIBMG 2023
and VAA-CP-EB 2023, León, Spain, June 14–17, 2023
Proceedings

 Springer

Editors
Ilias Maglogiannis ⓘ
University of Piraeus
Piraeus, Greece

Lazaros Iliadis ⓘ
Democritus University of Thrace
Xanthi, Greece

Antonios Papaleonidas ⓘ
Democritus University of Thrace
Xanthi, Greece

Ioannis Chochliouros
Hellenic Telecom Organization OTE
Athens, Greece

ISSN 1868-4238   ISSN 1868-422X (electronic)
IFIP Advances in Information and Communication Technology
ISBN 978-3-031-34173-1   ISBN 978-3-031-34171-7 (eBook)
https://doi.org/10.1007/978-3-031-34171-7

This Springer imprint is published by the registered company Springer Nature Switzerland AG
The registered company address is: Gewerbestrasse 11, 6330 Cham, Switzerland

Preface

WORKSHOPS of the 19th AIAI 2023

Artificial Intelligence (AI) is the core of the 4th Industrial Revolution. Its applicability keeps growing extremely fast, to include several diverse domains in our post-modern societies. The positive achievements of AI are amazing, and the expectations are continuously rising. However, each coin has two sides. There are also numerous potentially hazardous AI applications that call for immediate actions. Serious ethical matters have emerged (e.g., Privacy, Surveillance, Bias-Discrimination, Elimination of entire job categories) requiring corrective legislative actions. Moreover there has been a lot of discussion recently about the ChatGPT of Open AI.

The 19th *Artificial Intelligence Applications and Innovations* (AIAI) conference offered insight into all timely challenges related to technical, legal, and ethical aspects of intelligent systems and their applications. New algorithms and potential prototypes employed in diverse domains were introduced.

AIAI is a mature international scientific conference that has been held all over the world and it is well established in the scientific area of AI. Its history is long and very successful, following and spreading the evolution of intelligent systems.

The first event was organized in Toulouse, France in 2004. Since then, it has had a continuous and dynamic presence as a major global, but mainly European scientific event. More specifically, it has been organized in China, Greece, Cyprus, Australia, France, and Spain. It has always been technically supported by the International Federation for Information Processing (IFIP) and more specifically by the Working Group 12.5, which is interested in AI applications.

Following a long-standing tradition, this Springer volume belongs to the IFIP AICT Springer Series, and it contains the papers that were accepted and presented orally at the Workshops of the AIAI 2023 conference that were held as parallel satellite events.

The 19th AIAI was held during June 14–17, 2023, at the University of León, Spain. The diverse nature of the papers presented demonstrates the vitality of AI algorithms and approaches. It certainly proves the very wide range of AI applications as well.

The response of the international scientific community to the workshops organized under the auspices of the 19th AIAI call for papers was more than satisfactory, with 86 papers initially submitted. All papers were Single blind by at least two independent academic referees. Where needed, a third referee was consulted to resolve any potential conflicts. A total of 37 papers (43% of the submitted manuscripts) were accepted to be published in the AIAI 2023 workshops' proceedings volume.

Overall, six (6) workshops were organized under the auspices of AIAI 2023, as satellite events. As is described below, four (4) of them called for submissions of research papers to be published in the AIAI workshops' volume. The other two (2) were organized for the third time in a row and served as forums for presentation and discussion on hot timely AI-related potential applications in specific domains.

This Springer volume contains the original research papers that were accepted after passing through the peer review process to be presented orally at the following four (4) workshops that were organized under the framework of the AIAI 2023 conference:

- The **12th Mining Humanistic Data** Workshop (MHDW 2023)
- The **8th Workshop on 5G-Putting Intelligence to the Network Edge** (5G-PINE 2023)
- The **2nd Workshop on AI in Energy, Building and Micro-Grids** (AIBMG 2023)
- The **1st Workshop on Visual Analytics Approaches for Complex Problems in Engineering and Biomedicine** (VAA-CP-EB 2023).

Moreover, a brief presentation of the other two workshops is given.

The following paragraphs contain a brief description of the four (4) workshops with a call for research paper submissions.

- The 12th Mining Humanistic Data Workshop (MHDW 2023)

The 12th MHDW was organized by the University of Patras and the Ionian University, Greece. The Steering Committee consists of Spyros Sioutas, University of Patras, Greece, Ioannis Karydis and Katia Lida Kermanidis, Ionian University, Greece. The workshop aimed to bring together interdisciplinary approaches that focus on the application of innovative as well as existing artificial intelligence, data matching, fusion and mining, and knowledge discovery and management techniques to data derived from all areas of Humanistic Sciences.

- The 8th Workshop on 5G-Putting Intelligence to the Network Edge (5G-PINE 2023)

Coordinator: Ioannis Chochliouros, Hellenic Telecommunications Organization (OTE). The 8th 5G-PINE workshop was organized by the research team of the Hellenic Telecommunications Organization (OTE) in cooperation with many major partner companies. The 8th 5G-PINE Workshop was established to disseminate knowledge obtained from ongoing EU projects as well as from any other action of EU-funded research, in the wider thematic area of 5G Innovative Activities – Putting Intelligence to the Network Edge and with the aim of focusing on Artificial Intelligence in modern 5G telecommunications infrastructures. This should be achieved by emphasizing associated results, methodologies, trials, concepts, and/or findings originating from technical reports/deliverables, related pilot actions, and/or any other relevant 5G-based applications intending to enhance intelligence at the network edges.

- The 2nd Workshop on AI in Energy, Buildings and Micro-Grids (AIBMG 2023)

Coordinators: Iakovos Michailidis (CERTH Greece), Stelios Krinidis (IHU, CERTH, Greece), Elias Kosmatopoulos (DUTh, CERTH, Greece) and Dimosthenis Ioannidis (CERTH, Greece). Sustainable energy is hands down one of the biggest challenges of our times. As the EU sets its focus to reach its 2030 and 2050 goals, the role of artificial intelligence in the energy domain at building, district, and micro-grid level becomes prevalent. The EU and member states are increasingly highlighting the need to complement IoT capacity (e.g., appliances and meters) with artificial intelligence capabilities (e.g., building management systems, proactive optimization, prescriptive maintenance). Moreover, moving away from the centralized production schema of the grid, novel approaches are needed for the optimal management/balancing of local (or remote aggregated net metering) generation and consumption rather than only reducing energy consumption for communities.

The aim of the AIBMG Workshop was to bring together interdisciplinary approaches that focus on the application of AI-driven solutions for increasing and improving energy efficiency of residential and tertiary buildings without compromising the occupants' well-being. Applied directly to either the device, building, or district management system, the proposed solutions should enable more energy efficient and sustainable operation of devices, buildings, districts, and micro-grids. The workshop also welcomed cross-domain approaches that investigate how to support energy efficiency by exploiting decentralized, proactive, plug-n-play solutions.

- The 1st VAA-CP-EB Workshop on Visual Analytics Approaches for Complex Problems in Engineering and Biomedicine (VAA-CP-EB 2023)

Coordinators: Ignacio Díaz Blanco, Jose María Enguita Gonzalez, University of Oviedo, Spain.

Many problems in the fields of Biomedicine and Engineering involve huge volumes of data, and an extended spectrum of variables under highly complex underlying processes. Numerous factors influence their behavior, leading to common challenges in diagnosis, prognosis, estimation, anomaly detection, explainability, image analysis, or knowledge discovery.

Machine learning (ML) algorithms allow modeling of complex processes from massive data, being able to surpass humans in well-defined tasks. However, they are prone to error under changes in the context or in the problem's definition. Also, they are often "black box" models, which makes their integration with an expert's domain knowledge difficult. Humans, in turn, although less precise, can work with poorly posed problems, perform well on a wide range of tasks, and are able to find connections and improve responses through an iterative, exploratory process. Aiming to embrace both approaches, Visual Analytics (VA) has emerged in recent years as a powerful paradigm based on the integration of ML and human reasoning by means of data visualization and interaction for complex problem solving.

The two workshops that were organized for discussions and presentations of timely cases and algorithms in specific cases related to AI domains were the following:

- The 2nd Workshop on Defense Applications of AI (DAAI 2022)

The 2nd DAAI workshop was organized by the European Defense Agency (EDA), a European Union (EU) Organization. Defense and security systems are becoming more and more complicated and at the same time equipped with a plethora of sensing devices which collect an enormous amount of information both from their operating environment as well as from their own functioning. Considering the accelerating technology advancements of AI it is likely that it will have a profound impact on practically every segment of daily life, from the labor market to doing business and providing services. The security and defense sectors will not remain idle or unaffected by this technological evolution. On the contrary, AI is expected to transform the nature of the future defense and security domains, because by definition defense and security forces are highly dependent on (accurate) data and (reliable) information. The second Defense Applications of Artificial Intelligence (DAAI) Workshop aimed to present recent evolutions in artificial intelligence applicable to defense and security applications.

- The 3rd Workshop on AI and Ethics (AIETH 2022)

Coordinator: John Macintyre Co-Editor-in-Chief, AI and Ethics and Editor-in-Chief Neural Computing and Applications, University of Sunderland, UK.

The 3rd AIETH workshop was coordinated and organized by John Macintyre. It included short presentations from the panel members and an open Q&A session where the audience members were able to ask, and answer, important questions about the current and future development of Generative AI models. It aimed to emphasize the need for responsible global AI. The respective scientific community must be prepared to act preemptively and ensure that our societies will avoid the negative effects of AI and of 4th Industrial Revolution in general.

Panel Members:

- Larry Medsker, George Washington University, USA
- Peter Smith, University of Sunderland, UK
- Lee Club, Hong Kong
- Laura Illia, University of Fribourg, Switzerland

The following important questions will be raised and discussed.

✓ How should education systems and institutions respond to their students or their employees using LLMs and Generative AI?
✓ Are there ways that education systems and education institutions can embrace Generative AI as a positive part of the education process?
✓ Can LLMs or Generative AI tools be truly "creative"? If so, can they be considered as authors or creators of their outputs?
✓ How should LLMs and Generative AI tools be regulated? Should they be regulated at all?
✓ Should authors or creative artists be allowed to remove their material from the training data used to train Generative AI tools? Should their permission have been sought in the first place?
✓ How should the data used to train Generative AI tools be properly referenced and/or credited for their contribution to the output of the models?

✓ How will Generative AI develop? Where are these tools going, both technically, and societally? What impacts can we foresee, both good and bad?

✓ If such tools are found to have created harm, who is responsible for this harm and how should they be held to account?

June 2023

Ilias Maglogiannis
Lazaros Iliadis
Antonis Papaleonidas
Ioannis Chochliouros

Organization

Executive Committee

General Co-chairs

Ilias Maglogiannis   University of Piraeus, Greece
John Macintyre   University of Sunderland, UK
Manuel Dominguez   University of León, Spain

Program Co-chairs

Lazaros Iliadis   Democritus University of Thrace, Greece
Serafin Alonso   University of León, Spain

Steering Committee

Ilias Maglogiannis   University of Piraeus, Greece
Lazaros Iliadis   Democritus University of Thrace, Greece
Eunika Mercier-Laurent   University of Reims Champagne-Ardenne, France

Honorary Co-chairs

Nikola Kasabov   Auckland University of Technology, New Zealand
Vera Kurkova   Czech Academy of Sciences, Czech Republic

Organizing Co-chairs

Antonios Papaleonidas   Democritus University of Thrace, Greece
Antonio Moran   University of León, Spain

Advisory Co-chairs

George Magoulas   Birkbeck, University of London, UK
Paulo Cortez   University of Minho, Portugal
Plamen Angelov   Lancaster University, UK

Doctoral Consortium Co-chairs

Valerio Bellandi   Università degli Studi di Milano, Italy
Ioannis Anagnostopoulos   University of Thessaly, Greece

Publication and Publicity Co-chairs

Antonios Papaleonidas   Democritus University of Thrace, Greece

Anastasios Panagiotis Psathas	Democritus University of Thrace, Greece
Athanasios Kallipolitis	Hellenic Air Force (HAF)/University of Piraeus, Greece
Dionysios Koulouris	University of Piraeus, Greece

Liaison Chair

| Ioannis Chochliouros | Hellenic Telecommunications Organization (OTE), Greece |

Workshops Co-chairs

| Spyros Sioutas | University of Patras, Greece |
| Peter Hajek | University of Pardubice, Czech Republic |

Special Sessions and Tutorials Co-chairs

| Luca Magri | Politecnico di Milano, Italy |

Local Organizing/Hybrid Facilitation Committee

Anastasios Panagiotis Psathas	Democritus University of Thrace, Greece
Athanasios Kallipolitis	University of Piraeus, Greece
Dionysios Koulouris	University of Piraeus, Greece
Guzmán González Mateos	Universidad de León, Spain
Héctor Alaiz Moretón	Universidad de León, Spain
Ioanna-Maria Erentzi	Democritus University of Thrace, Greece
Ioannis Skopelitis	Democritus University of Thrace, Greece
José Ramón Rodriguez Ossorio	Universidad de León, Spain
Lambros Kazelis	Democritus University of Thrace, Greece
Leandros Tsatsaronis	Democritus University of Thrace, Greece
María del Carmen Benavides Cuéllar	Universidad de León, Spain
Maria Teresa García Ordás	Universidad de León, Spain
Natalia Prieto Fernández	Universidad de León, Spain
Nikiforos Mpotzoris	Democritus University of Thrace, Greece
Nikos Zervis	Democritus University of Thrace, Greece
Panagiotis Restos	Democritus University of Thrace, Greece
Raúl González Herbón	Universidad de León, Spain
Tassos Giannakopoulos	Democritus University of Thrace, Greece

Abstracts of Keynote/Invited Talks

Evolutionary Neural Architecture Search: Computational Efficiency, Privacy Preservation and Robustness Enhancement

Yaochu Jin ⓘ

Bielefeld University, Germany, University of Surrey, UK

Abstract. Evolutionary neural architecture search has received considerable attention in deep learning. This talk begins with a presentation of computationally efficient evolutionary neural architecture search algorithms by means of sampled training and partial weight sharing. Then, we introduce communication-efficient deep neural architecture search in a federated learning environment. Finally, a surrogate-assisted evolutionary search algorithm for neural architectures that are robust to adversarial attacks is described. The talk is concluded with a brief discussion of open questions for future research.

Interpretable-By-Design Prototype-Based Deep Learning

Plamen Angelov

Lancaster University, UK

Abstract. Deep Learning justifiably attracted the attention and interest of the scientific community and industry as well as of the wider society and even policy makers. However, the predominant architectures (from Convolutional Neural Networks to Transformers) are hyper-parametric models with weights/parameters being detached from the physical meaning of the object of modelling. They are, essentially, embedded functions of functions which do provide the power of deep learning; however, they are also the main reason for diminished transparency and difficulties in explaining and interpreting the decisions made by deep neural network classifiers. Some dub this the "black box" approach. This makes problematic the use of such algorithms in high-stakes complex problems such as aviation, health, bailing from jail, etc. where a clear rationale for a particular decision is very important and the errors are very costly. This motivated researchers and regulators to focus efforts on the quest for "explainable" yet highly efficient models. Most of the solutions proposed in this direction so far are, however, post-hoc and only partially address the problem. At the same time, it is remarkable that humans learn in a principally different manner (by examples, using similarities) and not by fitting (hyper-) parametric models, and can easily perform the so-called "zero-shot learning". Current deep learning is focused primarily on accuracy and overlooks explainability, the semantic meaning of the internal model representation, reasoning and decision making, and its link with the specific problem domain. Once trained, such models are inflexible to new knowledge. They cannot dynamically evolve their internal structure to start recognising new classes. They are good only for what they were originally trained for. The empirical results achieved by these types of methods according to Terry Sejnowski "should not be possible according to sample complexity in statistics and nonconvex optimization theory". The challenge is to bring together the high levels of accuracy with the semantically meaningful and theoretically sound and provable solutions. All these challenges and identified gaps require a dramatic paradigm shift and a radical new approach. In this talk, the speaker will present such a new approach towards the next generation of explainable-by-design deep learning. It is based on prototypes and uses kernel-like functions, making it interpretable-by-design. It is dramatically easier to train and adapt without the need for complete re-training; learning can start from few training data samples, explore the data space, detect and learn from unseen data patterns. Indeed, the ability to detect the unseen and unexpected and start learning this new class/es in real time with no or very little supervision is critically important and is something that no currently existing classifier can offer. This method was applied to a range of applications including but not limited to remote sensing, autonomous driving, health and others.

Intelligent Mobile Sensing for Understanding Human Behaviour

Oresti Baños Legrán

University of Granada, Spain

Abstract. Understanding people's behaviour is essential to characterise patient progress, make treatment decisions and elicit effective and relevant coaching actions. Hence, a great deal of research has been devoted in recent years to the automatic sensing and intelligent analysis of human behaviour. Among all sensing options, smartphones stand out as they enable the unobtrusive observation and detection of a wide variety of behaviours as we go about our physical and virtual interactions with the world. This talk aims at giving the audience a taste of the unparalleled potential that mobile sensing in combination with artificial intelligence offers for the study of human individual and collective behaviour.

Secure, Efficient and High-Performance Computing: A Computer Architecture Perspective

Tamara Silbergleit Lehman

University of Colorado Boulder, USA

Abstract. Distributed systems and new architectures introduce new sets of security risks. Microarchitectural attacks have presented many challenges in the computer architecture community and this talk will present a few of the methods that the Boulder Computer Architecture Lab (BCAL) has been studying in order to address these vulnerabilities. The talk will first introduce physical and microarchitectural attacks and why they are hard to mitigate. Then, the talk will introduce an efficient implementation of speculative integrity verification, Poisonivy, to construct an efficient and high-performance secure memory system. Finally, the talk will show how we can leverage emerging memory technologies such as near memory processing to defend and identify microarchitectural side-channel attacks. The talk will end by briefly introducing a new research direction that is investigating the Rowhammer attack impact on neural network accuracy running on GPUs and how we can leverage secure memory to protect the accuracy of the models.

How AI/Machine Learning Has the Power of Revolutionizing (for Good?) Cybersecurity?

Javier Alonso López

University of León,Spain

Abstract. As we already know, Machine Learning is already used in various cybersecurity tasks such as malware identification/classification, intrusion detection, botnet identification, phishing, predicting cyberattacks like denial of service, fraud detection, etc. However, during recent years there has been a revolution in machine learning, specifically, deep learning that creates not only an unbelievable opportunity to develop more effective solutions but also represents a new threat and a new tool to be used to attack and gain control over systems, organizations and even countries.

In this talk, we will overview the major applications of Machine Learning in the field of cybersecurity prevent attacks, but also how Machine Learning can be used to pose a threat. We will review the main advances of Deep Learning in the last 5 years and their application into Cybersecurity. Finally, we will discuss the possible future trends we can expect (I do not expect a high accuracy, but high recall :D) in the intersection of Deep Learning and Cybersecurity.

Contents

The 8th Workshop on 5G – Putting Intelligence to the Network Edge (5G-PINE)

6G-BRICKS: Developing a Modern Experimentation Facility for
Validation, Testing and Showcasing of 6G Breakthrough Technologies and
Devices   17
    Ioannis P. Chochliouros, John Vardakas, Kostas Ramantas, Sofie Pollin,
    Sylvie Mayrargue, Adlen Ksentini, Walter Nitzold, Md Arifur Rahman,
    Jimmy O'Meara, Ashima Chawla, Dimitrios Kritharidis,
    Vasileios Theodorou, Shuaib Siddiqui, Francisco Ibañez,
    Georgios Gardikis, Dimitris Diagourtas, Loizos Christofi,
    Alain Mourad, Didier Nicholson, Alexandros Kostopoulos,
    Anastasia S. Spiliopoulou, and Christos Verikoukis

ETHER: Energy- and Cost-Efficient Framework for Seamless Connectivity
over the Integrated Terrestrial and Non-terrestrial 6G Networks   32
    Lechosław Tomaszewski, Robert Kołakowski, Agapi Mesodiakaki,
    Konstantinos Ntontin, Angelos Antonopoulos, Nikolaos Pappas,
    Marco Fiore, Mohammadreza Mosahebfard, Simon Watts,
    Philip Harris, Chih-Kuang Lin, Ana Rita Santiago, Fotis Lazarakis,
    and Symeon Chatzinotas

Fetal ECG Extraction Based on Overcomplete ICA and Empirical
Wavelet Transform   45
    Theodoros Lampros, Nikolaos Giannakeas, Konstantinos Kalafatakis,
    Markos Tsipouras, and Alexandros Tzallas

Implementing Network Applications for 5G-Enabled Robots Through the
5G-ERA Platform   55
    Andreas Gavrielides, Marios Sophocleous, Christina C. Lessi,
    George Agapiou, Jakub Španhel, Adrian Lendinez, Renxi Qiu,
    and Dayou Li

Media Services in Dense, Static and Mobile Environments Leveraging
Edge Deployments   66
    Maria-Evgenia Xezonaki, N. Psaromanolakis,
    P. Konstantinos Chartsias, Konstantinos Stamatis,
    Dimitrios Kritharidis, Vasileios Theodorou, Christina Politi,
    Panagiotis Papaioannou, Christos Tranoris,
    Spyros Denazis, Ioanna Mesogiti, Eleni Theodoropoulou, Fotini Setaki,
    George Lyberopoulos, Nikos Makris, Paris Flegkas,
    Jesus Gutierrez Teran, Markos Anastassopoulos, and Anna Tzanakaki

Network Slicing vs. Network Neutrality – Is Consent Possible?   77
    Lechosław Tomaszewski and Robert Kołakowski

OASEES: An Innovative Scope for a DAO-Based Programmable Swarm
Solution, for Decentralizing AI Applications Close to Data Generation
Locations   91
    Ioannis P. Chochliouros, Michail -Alexandros Kourtis, George Xilouris,
    Wouter Tavernier, Enrique Areizaga Sanchez, Margarita Anastassova,
    Christian Bolzmacher, Nikolay Tcholtchev, Antonello Corsi,
    Panagiotis Trakadas, Marta Millet, Christos Xenakis, Adnan Imeri,
    Francesco Bellesini, Paride D'Ostilio, Albertos Markakis,
    Ihsan Bal Engin, Antonis Litke, Lucrezia Maria Quarato, Diego Cugat,
    Georgios Gardikis, Charilaos Zarakovitis, Stephane Bouilland,
    Zaharias Zaharis, Christina Lessi, Dimitrios Arvanitozisis,
    and Anastasia S. Spiliopoulou

Putting Intelligence into Things: An Overview of Current Architectures.   106
    Maria Belesioti, Ioannis P. Chochliouros, Panagiotis Dimas,
    Manolis Sofianopoulos, Theodore Zahariadis, Charalabos Skianis,
    and Enric Pages Montanera

Slicing Mechanism Deployment in 5G Networks for Robotic Use Cases   118
    Christina C. Lessi, George Tsiouris, George Agapiou, Renxi Qiu,
    Andreas Gavrielides, Konstantinos C. Lessis,
    and Ioannis P. Chochliouros

Smart5Grid Testing Strategy & Field Implementations for RT Wide Area
Monitoring of Interconnected Systems   126
    Ioannis P. Chochliouros, Dimitrios Brodimas, Nikolaos Tzanis,
    Michalis Rantopoulos, Daniel Shangov, Georgi Hristov, Atanas Velkov,
    Irina Ciornei, and Daniele Porcu

Techno-economic Analysis Highlighting Aspects of 5G Network
Deployments at Railway Environments 139
    Ioanna Mesogiti, Eleni Theodoropoulou, Fotini Setaki,
    George Lyberopoulos, Konstantinos Stamatis,
    Panteleimon Konstantinos Chartsias, Nikos Makris, Paris Flegkas,
    Jesús Gutiérrez, Christina Politi, Christos Tranoris,
    Markos Anastasopoulos, and Anna Tzanakaki

Use Cases Employing a Machine Learning Network Architecture 151
    Ioannis P. Chochliouros, John Vardakas, Christos Verikoukis,
    Md Arifur Rahman, Andrea P. Guevara, Robbert Beerten,
    Philippe Chanclou, Roberto Gonzalez, Charalambos Klitis,
    Pierangela Samarati, Polyzois Soumplis, Emmanuel Varvarigos,
    Dimitrios Kritharidis, Kostas Chartsias, and Christina Lessi

Use Cases for Network Applications to Enable Connected Intelligence 168
    Renxi Qiu, Dayou Li, Enjie Liu, Christina C. Lessi, George Agapiou,
    and Andreas Gavrielides

The 2nd Workshop on AI in Energy, Buildings and Micro-Grids (AIBMG)

A Guide to Visual Comfort: An Overview of Indices and Its Applications 183
    Christos Tzouvaras, Asimina Dimara, Alexios Papaioannou,
    Kanela Karatzia, Christos-Nikolaos Anagnostopoulos,
    Stelios Krinidis, Konstantinos I. Arvanitis, Dimosthenis Ioannidis,
    and Dimitrios Tzovaras

A Novel Social Collaboration Platform for Enhancing Energy Awareness 195
    Efstathia Martinopoulou, Asimina Dimara, Anastasia Tsita,
    Sergio Luis Herrera Gonzalez, Rafael Marin-Perez,
    Juan Andres Sanchez Segado, Piero Fraternali, Stelios Krinidis,
    Christos-Nikolaos Anagnostopoulos, Dimosthenis Ioannidis,
    and Dimitrios Tzovaras

Ensuring Reliability in Smart Building IoT Operations Through Real-Time
Holistic Data Treatment 207
    Aliki Stefanopoulou, Asimina Dimara, Iakovos Michailidis,
    Georgios Karatzinis, Alexios Papaioannou, Stelios Krinidis,
    Christos-Nikolaos Anagnostopoulos, Elias Kosmatopoulos,
    Dimosthenis Ioannidis, and Dimitrios Tzovaras

Realtime Multi-factor Dynamic Thermal Comfort Estimation for Indoor
Environments   219
    Georgia Tzitziou, Asimina Dimara, Alexios Papaioannou,
    Christos Tzouvaras, Stelios Krinidis,
    Christos-Nikolaos Anagnostopoulos, Dimosthenis Ioannidis,
    and Dimitrios Tzovaras

Self-protection of IoT Gateways Against Breakdowns and Failures
Enabling Automated Sensing and Control   231
    Alexios Papaioannou, Asimina Dimara, Iakovos Michailidis,
    Aliki Stefanopoulou, Georgios Karatzinis, Stelios Krinidis,
    Christos-Nikolaos Anagnostopoulos, Elias Kosmatopoulos,
    Dimosthenis Ioannidis, and Dimitrios Tzovaras

Semantic Interoperability for Managing Energy-Efficiency and IEQ:
A Short Review   242
    Christos Tzouvaras, Asimina Dimara, Alexios Papaioannou,
    Christos-Nikolaos Anagnostopoulos, Konstantinos Kotis,
    Stelios Krinidis, Dimosthenis Ioannidis, and Dimitrios Tzovaras

Treating Common Problems Observed During Smart Building Control
Real-Life Testing: Sharing Practical Experience   254
    Georgios Karatzinis, Iakovos Michailidis, Asimina Dimara,
    Aliki Stefanopoulou, Vasileios Georgios Vasilopoulos, Stelios Krinidis,
    Christos-Nikolaos Anagnostopoulos, Elias Kosmatopoulos,
    Dimosthenis Ioannidis, and Dimitrios Tzovaras

The 12th Workshop on Mining Humanistic Data (MHDW)

A Framework for Co-creation in Generic Educational Activities
Using Swarming   271
    Gregory Gasteratos, Eleni Vlachou, Panagiotis Gratsanis,
    and Ioannis Karydis

Analyzing User Reviews in the Tourism & Cultural Domain - The Case
of the City of Athens, Greece   284
    Tasos Papagiannis, George Ioannou, Konstantinos Michalakis,
    Georgios Alexandridis, and George Caridakis

Applying SCALEX scRNA-Seq Data Integration for Precise Alzheimer's
Disease Biomarker Discovery   294
    Aristidis G. Vrahatis, Konstantinos Lazaros, Petros Paplomatas,
    Marios G. Krokidis, Themis Exarchos, and Panagiotis Vlamos

Ensemble Machine Learning Models for Breast Cancer Identification 303
  Elias Dritsas, Maria Trigka, and Phivos Mylonas

EventMapping: Geoparsing and Geocoding of Twitter Messages in the
Greek Language 312
  Gerasimos Razis, Ioannis Maroufidis, and Ioannis Anagnostopoulos

Extracting Knowledge from Recombinations of SMILES Representations 325
  Christos Didachos and Andreas Kanavos

Forecasting Stock Market Alternations Using Social Media Sentiment
Analysis and Regression Techniques 335
  Christina Saravanos and Andreas Kanavos

Handwritten Word Recognition Using Deep Learning Methods 347
  Vasileios Lagios, Isidoros Perikos, and Ioannis Hatzilygeroudis

Local Maximal Equality-Free Periodicities 359
  *Mai Alzamel, Jacqueline W. Daykin, Christopher Hampson,
  Costas S. Iliopoulos, Zara Lim, and W. F. Smyth*

Readability Classification with Wikipedia Data and All-MiniLM
Embeddings 369
  *Elena Vergou, Ioanna Pagouni, Marios Nanos,
  and Katia Lida Kermanidis*

Using Siamese BiLSTM Models for Identifying Text Semantic Similarity 381
  Georgios Fradelos, Isidoros Perikos, and Ioannis Hatzilygeroudis

Water Quality Estimation from IoT Sensors Using a Meta-ensemble 393
  Gregory Davrazos, Theodor Panagiotakopoulos, and Sotiris Kotsiantis

**The 1st Workshop on "Visual Analytics Approaches for Complex
Problems in Engineering and Biomedicine" (VAA-CP-EB)**

An XAI Approach to Deep Learning Models in the Detection of DCIS 409
  Michele La Ferla

Conditioned Fully Convolutional Denoising Autoencoder for Energy
Disaggregation 421
  *Diego García, Daniel Pérez, Panagiotis Papapetrou, Ignacio Díaz,
  Abel A. Cuadrado, José Maria Enguita, Ana González,
  and Manuel Domínguez*

Principal Component Modes of Reservoir Dynamics in Reservoir
Computing. 434
    José María Enguita, Ignacio Díaz, Diego García,
    Abel Alberto Cuadrado, and José Ramón Rodríguez

Visual Analytics Tools for the Study of Complex Problems in Engineering
and Biomedicine. 446
    Ignacio Díaz, José M. Enguita, Abel A. Cuadrado, Diego García,
    and Ana González

Visualizing Cell Motility Patterns from Time Lapse Videos with Interactive
2D Maps Generated with Deep Autoencoders. 458
    Ana González, José María Enguita, Ignacio Díaz, Diego García,
    Abel Alberto Cuadrado, Nuria Valdés, and María D. Chiara

Author Index 469

The 8th Workshop on 5G – Putting Intelligence to the Network Edge (5G-PINE)

Preface to 5G-PINE 2023 Proceedings

The eighth 5G-PINE Workshop, following the great success, the wider market- and research-oriented impact and the good tradition of its predecessors, was established and organized in a concrete and efficient way to disseminate knowledge obtained from actual 5G EU-funded projects (mainly coming from the 5G-PPP/Horizon 2020 framework and the Horizon-JU-SNS framework, both covering 5G and "Beyond 5G" (B5G) aspects) as well as from other research actions in the wider thematic area of "5G Innovative Activities – Putting Intelligence to the Network Edge ("5G-PINE")" and with the aim of focusing upon Artificial Intelligence (AI) in modern 5G-oriented telecommunications infrastructures.

Based on its selected research papers that have promoted a highly competitive framework of reference in the modern 5G/B5G environment, the 8th 5G-PINE Workshop once again had a strong and deep impact on the broader context of the AIAI 2023 International Conference, which took place at the *School of Industrial, Computer Science and Aerospace Engineering* of the *University of León, León, Spain* (June 14–17, 2023). For once again, the preparatory work was mainly driven by the hard organizational effort, the dynamic coordination and the continuous supervision of Ioannis P. Chochliouros (Hellenic Telecommunications Organization S.A. - OTE, Greece) who has been the main organizer of the event for 8 subsequent years.

Support has also been provided by: Latif Ladid (President of IPv6 Forum and Researcher of SnT/University of Luxembourg, Luxembourg); George Lyberopoulos (COSMOTE Mobile Telecommunications S.A., Greece); Daniele Porcu (ENEL Global Infrastructure and Networks S.r.l., Italy) also coordinator of the 5G-PPP/Horizon 2020 project "Smart5Grid"; John Vardakas (Iquadrat Informatica S.L., Spain) also coordinator of the 5G-PPP project "MARSAL"; Pavlos Lazaridis (University of Huddersfield, UK); Zaharias Zaharis (Aristotle University of Thessaloniki, Greece); Slawomir Kukliński and Lechosław Tomaszewski (Orange Polska, Poland); Nancy Alonistioti (National and Kapodistrian University of Athens, Greece); Christina Lessi (Hellenic Telecommunications Organization S.A. - OTE, Greece); Oriol Sallent and Jordi Pérez-Romero (Universitat Politècnica de Catalunya, Spain); Christos Verikoukis (University of Patras, Greece and Industrial Systems Institute (ISI)/Athena Research Centre, Greece), also coordinator of the Horizon/JU-SNS project "6G-BRICKS"; and Michail-Alexandros Kourtis (National Centre for Scientific Research "DEMOKRITOS", Greece) also coordinator of the Horizon project "OASEES".

Special thanks also to Anastasia S. Spiliopoulou (Hellenic Telecommunications Organization S.A. - OTE), lawyer and IT expert, for her valuable support in a multiplicity of issues covering administration and technology.

Apart from the above members of the Workshop Organizing Committee, the entire process was also supported by more than 90 European experts, several of whom came from the relevant EU-funded H2020/5G-PPP and/or Horizon projects "Smart5GRID", "MARSAL", "5G-ERA", "OASEES" and "6G-BRICKS". These projects formed the "core" of the corresponding effort towards realizing a "joint" 5G-PINE 2023 Workshop, purely "5G/B5G"-oriented.

The 8th 5G-PINE Workshop promoted, *inter-alia*, the context of modern 5G network infrastructures and of related innovative services in a complex and highly heterogeneous underlying wireless communications ecosystem, strongly enhanced by the inclusion of cognitive capabilities and intelligence features, with the aim of significantly improving network management and orchestration. Furthermore, based upon the well-known Self-Organizing Network (SON) functionalities, the 8th 5G-PINE Workshop not only identified but also promoted network planning and optimization processes through Artificial Intelligence- (AI-) based tools, able to smartly process input data from the surrounding environment(s) and come up with extended knowledge that can be formalized in terms of models and/or structured metrics, to explicitly "depict" the network behavior to a satisfactory level. This allows, *among others*, in-depth and detailed knowledge to be gained about the whole underlying 5G ecosystem; also understanding of hidden "patterns", data structures and relationships in a diversity of (interactive) sectors and, ultimately; their use for more efficient network management to respond to a multiplicity of situations and requirements to provide new market offerings and/or solutions.

In parallel, related Key Performance Indicators (KPIs) were also discussed, evaluated and assessed to the extent possible, to demonstrate progress implicated by the ongoing – or even by the expected – 5G/B5G growth. Among the "core objectives" of the 5G-PINE 2023 Workshop was to support "delivery and implementation of intelligence" directly to the network's edge, by exploiting the emerging paradigms of Network Functions Virtualization (NFV), Software Defined Networking (SDN), Network Slicing (NS) and Edge Cloud Computing. Moreover, the workshop also supported promotion of rich virtualization and multi-tenant capabilities, optimally deployed close to the end-user(s) and, consequently, enhancing network and service opportunities towards establishing a competitive and innovative telecoms market with flavours to multiple verticals.

Among the pillars of the 8th 5G-PINE Workshop was the innovative background of the ongoing 5G-PPP/H2020 **"Smart5Grid"project**, where emphasis has been put on aspects coming for a very interesting use case with strong market impact, dealing with real-time wide-area monitoring of power interconnected systems between Greece and Bulgaria. The smart grid paradigm poses new challenges to communication networks, requiring a flexible and orchestrated network, slicing, and millisecond-level latency. In order for today's power distribution grids to be transformed into "evolved" smart grids that feature online monitoring data and to enable efficient, fast and secure operation, power distribution companies need new tools that will allow them to monitor and operate the distribution network and to maintain and increase reliability and Quality of Service (QoS).

The selected paper discusses the project's testing strategy and corresponding field implementations. In fact, integration of renewable energy sources in the electrical grid imposes several operational issues affecting energy markets as well as the transmission system operators; in this context, it is a matter of major importance not only to detect events but also to react in due time to prevent faults, as the latter may implicate outages for consumers or even permanent damage to the energy equipment. Within this scope, among the core issues of the paper has been the criticality of the role of Phasor Measurement

Units (PMUs) being able to provide readings of voltage, frequency and current. The work also discussed how the 5G network may assist in the transfer of the measurements with its low latency capabilities and high availability criteria. Based on a Smart5Grid project's dedicated use case, the concept of 5G enhanced wide area monitoring was presented, along with the associated field platform implementations both in Greece and Bulgaria. A complete list of defined Field Platform Validation Metrics (FPVM) was also elaborated with the equivalent targeted values, in order to create a framework for evaluating expected trials.

The 8th 5G-PINE Workshop also included the discussion of several important use cases employing a Machine Learning- (ML-) based architecture, as proposed by the ongoing 5G-PPP/H2020 **"MARSAL"project**. 5G mobile networks will soon be available to handle all types of applications and provide services to massive numbers of users, thus creating a complex and dynamic network ecosystem, where end-to-end (E2E) performance analysis and optimization will be "key" features to effectively manage the diverse requirements imposed by multiple vertical industries over the same shared infrastructure. To enable such a challenging vision, the MARSAL EU-funded project targets the development and evaluation of a complete framework for the management and orchestration of network resources in 5G and beyond, by utilizing a converged optical-wireless network infrastructure in the access and fronthaul/midhaul segments. In the network design domain, MARSAL targets the development of novel cell-free- (CF-) based solutions that allow significant scaling up of the wireless access points in a cost-effective manner, by exploiting the application of the distributed cell-free concept and of the serial fronthaul approach, while contributing innovative functionalities to the O-RAN project. In parallel, in the fronthaul/midhaul segments MARSAL aims to radically increase the flexibility of optical access architectures for beyond-5G Cell Site connectivity via different levels of fixed-mobile convergence. In the network and service management domain, the design philosophy of MARSAL is to provide a comprehensive framework for the management of the entire set of communication and computational network resources by exploiting novel ML-based algorithms of both edge and midhaul Data Centres by incorporating the Virtual Elastic Data Centres/Infrastructures paradigm.

Finally, in the network security domain, MARSAL aims to introduce mechanisms that provide privacy and security to application workload and data, aiming to allow applications and users to maintain control over their data when relying on the deployed shared infrastructures, while Artificial Intelligence and Blockchain technologies will be developed in order to guarantee a secured multi-tenant slicing environment.

The selected paper thus presented the essential MARSAL network architecture and discussed how the main experimentation scenarios have been mapped to the considered architecture. More specifically, the paper discussed: (i) Cell-Free networking in dense and ultra-dense hotspot areas by emphasizing two scenarios of use covering dense user-generated content distribution with mmWave fronthauling and also ultra-dense video traffic delivery in a converged fixed-mobile network, and; (ii) cognitive assistance, security and privacy implications covering a scenario of smart connectivity for next-generation sightseeing and another one for data security and privacy in multi-tenant infrastructures.

Moreover, the 8th 5G-PINE Workshop included discussion of the evolutionary progress of the ongoing 5G-PPP/H2020 **"5G-ERA"project**, which aims to develop an enhanced 5G experimentation facility and relevant Network Applications for third-party application developers to provide them with a 5G experimentation playground to test and qualify their respective applications. 5G-ERA addresses the new challenges to experimental facilities from vertical developers and designers in the field of robotic applications. Taking into account the present state of this project, three papers were accepted for presentation, due to their clarity and their pure innovative context:

One paper is about proposing an interesting slicing mechanism deployment in 5G networks, for robotic use cases. As robotics is a rapidly growing field, it will play an important role in automating many activities. However, the requirements that a robot may have for effective use can have large costs, depending on the nature of each specific scenario. Different demands on network resources lead to the need to implement flexible networks, able to guarantee the disposal of necessary resources in the most efficient and reliable way. To this aim, slicing is a network capability that can provide specific network characteristics and can be implemented in different 5G network domain elements (such as Radio Access Network (RAN), 5G Core or End-to-End). The paper presents a slicing mechanism that was implemented to be utilized for the needs of the use cases described in the 5G-ERA's context, dealing with solutions in sensitive sectors such as Public Protection and Disaster Relief (PPDR) and healthcare but also in demanding sectors such as transport and Industry 4.0. Thus, an advanced network architecture has been designed including a Slice Manager responsible for the direct communication with the packet core and requesting the proper – per case – slice, and also a Middleware which is an external network component communicating with the robots and knowing their needs for resources. In phase-1 of the project implementation, which is described in detail, slicing is focused on the packet core of the network that was integrated based on the 5G SA Rel.16 architecture.

A second paper is dedicated to the discussion of several appropriate use cases for Network Applications with the aim of "enabling connected intelligence". The corresponding work is based on the important role that robots perform in consuming digital infrastructures during the process of continual learning. A continuous leaning process is considered as the way to increase the level of autonomy for robots and also "pushes" the limits of their cognition. In this context, the future of connected robotics should be skillful in maximizing the Quality of Experience (QoE) for its vertical users rather than solely reacting to the QoS. Moreover, Network Applications and continual learning are combined with the aim of realizing the 6G vision. The paper is designed to discuss and promote use cases of Network Applications that need to be implemented for connected robots by steering digital transitions through human-centered data-driven technologies and innovations. Typical scenarios applied to robot continual learning have been identified and integrated into design patterns of network applications under connected intelligence. The paper's major innovation is the fact that the proposed approach practically serves as a "guide" for developing future Network applications to ground the idea of connected intelligence.

The third selected paper is dedicated to the discussion about implementing Network Applications for 5G-enabled robots through the 5G-ERA platform. Novel orchestration architectures for 5G networks have primarily focused on enhancing QoS, yet have neglected to address QoE concerns. Consequently, these systems struggle with intent recognition and E2E interpretability, thus resulting in the possibility of suboptimal control policies being developed. The 5G-ERA project has proposed and demonstrated an AI-driven intent-based networking solution for autonomous robots to address this issue. More specifically, the proposed solution employs a workflow consisting of four tools (i.e., Action Sequence Generation, Network Intent Estimation, Resource Usage Forecasting and OSM (Open Source Management and Orchestration) Control Policy Generation) to map an individual vertical action's intent to a global OSM control policy. The paper describes how the 5G-ERA platform enables the onboarding and control of 5G-enabled robots and how the platform's capabilities are demonstrated through the project's use cases. It also discusses how the use of semantic models and machine learning tools for 5G-enhanced robot autonomy can be incorporated into the 5G-ERA platform through the Intent-based, front-end Dashboard (IBD) component for better management.

An interesting part of the actual Workshop concerned the progress of the ongoing Horizon **"OASEES" project**, which aims to deliver a European, fully open-source, decentralized and secure Swarm programmability framework for edge devices and to leverage various AI/ML accelerators (FPGAs, SNNs, Quantum) while supporting a privacy-preserving Object ID federation process. A corresponding accepted paper was about the discussion of an innovative scope for a decentralized autonomous organization-(DAO-) based programmable swarm solution, for decentralizing AI applications close to data generation locations. As traditional linear models have proved to be ineffective due to stagnant decision-making and inefficient data federation, the pathway to European data sovereignty requires a sustainable and circular economy across diverse market sectors. In this scope, the EU-OASEES project has identified the need for a novel, inclusive and disruptive approach regarding the cloud-to-edge continuum and swarm programmability and also support for multi-tenant, interoperable, secure and trustworthy deployments.

The selected paper discusses actual challenges for the management and orchestration of edge infrastructure and/or services to exploit the potential of edge processing. The paper also discusses the concept and fundamental features of the OASEES approach, together with technology challenges that are to be covered by the intended system development. A set of several vertical edge applications with significant market impact is also discussed, dealing with: (i) a smart edge-connected node for the analysis of voice, articulation and fluency disorders in Parkinson's disease; (ii) coordinated recharging of an electrical vehicle (EV) fleet to support optimal operation of an electricity grid; (iii) a drone swarm over 5G for high mast inspection; (iv) swarm-powered intelligent structural safety assessment for buildings; (v) a robotic swarm-powered smart factory for I4.0; and (vi) smart swarm energy harvesting and predictive maintenance for wind turbines.

Furthermore, another remarkable area is the one correlated to the ongoing Horizon-JU-SNS **"6G-BRICKS" project.** Shifting towards B5G/6G implies a great diversity of challenges for the involved markets, especially via the creation of vast amounts of generated data and of related novel applications serving, in parallel, a great multiplicity of verticals. Such innovative services exceed the capabilities of existing 5G infrastructures for potential support of their corresponding KPIs and computational offloading, thus creating a new generation of smart networks. Towards fulfilling this ambitious target, the ongoing 6G-BRICKS project aims to deliver a new 6G experimentation facility building on the baseline of mature platforms coming from ongoing EU-funded activities and bringing breakthrough cell-free and RIS (Reconfigurable Intelligent Surface) technologies that have shown promise for B5G networks. These will be integrated in reusable, self-contained testbed nodes, to be deployed at two E2E 6G testbed sites in Belgium and in France and will be federated under a common set of Experimentation Tools, deployed under a common cloud node in Greece. Moreover, novel unified control paradigms based on Explainable AI and Machine Reasoning are explored. All enablers will be delivered in the form of reusable components with open APIs, termed "bricks". Finally, initial integrations with O-RAN are performed, aiming at the future-proofing and interoperability of 6G-BRICKS outcomes.

6G-BRICKS will be the first open 6G platform that combines cell-free, Open Air Interface (OAI) and RIS, while adopting the proven principles of softwarization, open Interfaces (O-RAN) and Open Source software stacks, putting future expansion and evolvability at its core. The corresponding selected paper presents the essential architectural structure of the 6G-BRICKS' facility and also discusses the various core objectives, simultaneously "identifying" diverse technical challenges and dedicated areas for future research. The paper also discusses and evaluates two fundamental use cases where the former examines the metaverse as an "enabler" of a modern workplace while the latter aims to focus on 6G Applications for serving Industry 4.0. This is done in parallel with a description of the intended Proofs of Concept (PoCs), which are expected to demonstrate strong market impact.

The scope of the approved works also included two interesting papers coming from the ongoing 5G-PPP/H2020 **"5G-VICTORI" project**, aiming to conduct large scale trials for advanced vertical use case verification, focusing on transportation, energy, media and factories of the future and cross-vertical use cases. 5G-VICTORI's platform aims to transform current closed, purposely developed and dedicated infrastructures into open environments where resources and functions are exposed to ICT and vertical industries, and can be accessed, shared on demand and deployed to compose very diverse sets of services in a large variety of ecosystems.

The first paper discusses a detailed techno-economic analysis highlighting aspects of 5G network deployments in railway environments. 5G and beyond networks will comprise versatile infrastructures consisting of multiple disaggregated pools of network, compute and storage resources, while network deployments are expected to appear in various (physical/vertical) environments as access network extensions of public networks or as Non-Public-Networks (NPNs). In many physical/vertical environments, the necessary network deployments may be very dissimilar to the wide-area public network ones, thus raising new deployment challenges. Such cases can be the railway environment or specific deployments along rivers or roads, where a variety of factors has to be taken into account (such as area specifics, technologies' deployment feasibility, traffic/usage forecasts considering long-term services roadmaps and, certainly, the associated costs). Consequently, network planning and dimensioning shall be tightly accompanied by the techno-economic analysis of the various deployment alternatives. Focusing upon fulfilling this challenge, the paper provides insights into 5G network deployments at railway environments as retrieved through macroscopic techno-economic analysis and demonstrates their applicability on the architectural concepts of the 5G-PPP 5G-VICTORI project. The work proposes a methodology framework as well as a tool for the techno-economic analysis of 5G/B5G network deployments at vertical facilities, enabling cost evaluation of various network technologies and deployment options by individually modeling, dimensioning and cost-analyzing the various network segments, while taking into account a plethora of critical technology-related parameters. Obtained results from the applicability of the tools in indicative railway vertical deployment scenarios provide interesting conclusions on the potential selection of alternative 5G technologies and deployments achieving higher cost efficiency. Flexible by nature, the tool can be further expanded.

The second paper has discussed media services in dense, static and mobile environments leveraging edge deployments. The media sector is one of the domains that is highly impacted by the 5G network principles and capabilities, especially in terms of service provisioning and performance in versatile environments. Simultaneously, the media sector is gradually becoming an integral part of transportation, as a variety of media services can be offered and also used to facilitate passengers' needs in various directions (especially infotainment and safety/security). The 5G-VICTORI project proposes the integration of Content Delivery Network- (CDN-) aided infotainment services in 5G network deployments to enable the uninterrupted delivery of such services with high quality to dense, static and mobile environments. The solution is deployed and evaluated in an experimentation setup in the lab and in operational railway environments. The deployment entails integration of multi-level CDN platforms with private 5G network deployments that include edge computing capabilities and edge caching on-board the train. Multi-level CDN capabilities are enabled via "data showers" installed at selected locations along the train route. The paper actually discusses the service KPIs as well as technical requirements and provides an overview of the proposed experimental deployment and performance evaluation results. Delivering a high-performance deployment for the corresponding and demanding verticals entails network planning based on various technologies and on the placement of compute resources in the right proximity to the end-user.

The 8th 5G-PINE Worksop also hosted a selected paper correlated to the broader scope introduced by the Horizon **"NEMO" project,** practically discussing various issues about putting intelligence into things and discussing an overview of current architectures. In the era of the Internet of Things (IoT), billions of sensors collect data from their environment and process it to enable intelligent decisions at the right time. However, transferring massive amounts of disparate data in complex environments is a complex and challenging issue. The conceived convergence of AI and IoT has breathed new life into IoT operations and human-machine interaction. Resource-constrained IoT devices typically need more data storage and processing capacity to build modern AI models. The intuitive solution integrates cloud computing technology with AIoT and leverages cloud-side servers' powerful and flexible processing and storage capacity.

This paper briefly introduces IoT and AIoT architectures in the context of cloud computing, fog computing and more. Going a step further, an overview of the NEMO EU-funded context is presented, by highlighting its specific concept and objectives. The project considers that intelligence needs to "move closer to the point of decision" and become an integral part of the AIoT meta-Operating System (mOS), supporting every activity, process and decision that ranges from ad hoc micro-cloud cluster self-organization to micro-services migration and intent-based programming. To facilitate knowledge easily and almost administrator-free instant deployment on any AIoT device, all mechanisms need to be integrated and connected, essential mOS tools and plug-ins installed as a (semi-)automated/standalone software package while ensuring interoperability, trust, cybersecurity and privacy. NEMO aims to establish itself as the "game changer" of the AIoT-Edge-Cloud Continuum by bringing intelligence closer to data, making AI-as-a-Service an integral part of self-organizing networks orchestrating micro-service execution. Its widespread penetration and massive acceptance will be achieved via new technology, pre-commercial exploitation components and liaison with open-source communities.

In a parallel approach, two papers coming from the ongoing Horizon-JU-SNS **"ETHER"project** were also accepted. ETHER will develop solutions for a Unified Radio Access Network (RAN) and for energy-efficient, AI-enabled resource management across the terrestrial, aerial and space domains, while creating the business plans driving future investments in the area.

The first paper provideS a detailed overview of various aspects originating from the ETHER project. Several use cases that have already been proposed for 5G networks cannot be facilitated by terrestrial infrastructure, due either to its small penetration in remote/rural areas or to the harsh propagation conditions due to the terrain. Indicative applications are forestry, mining, agriculture, semi-autonomous control of long-range vehicles, industrial services, logistics, asset tracking, telemedicine, beyond visual line-of-sight drone operations, and maritime insurance. Hence, such use cases necessitate the integration of terrestrial with non-terrestrial networks (NTNs), which gives rise to several challenges to overcome. Towards this, the ETHER project aims to provide a holistic approach for energy- and cost-efficient integrated terrestrial-non-terrestrial networks. To achieve this goal, ETHER develops solutions for a unified Radio Access Network and for AI-enabled resource management across the terrestrial, aerial and space domains, while creating the business plans driving future investments in the area. To that end, the paper discusses a series of "key" technologies that ETHER combines under a unique 3-Dimensional (3D) multi-layered architectural proposition that brings together: (i) user terminal antenna design and implementation for direct handheld access in the integrated network; (ii) a robust unified waveform; (iii) energy-efficient seamless horizontal and vertical handover policies; (iv) a zero-touch network/service management and orchestration framework; (v) a flexible payload system to enable programmability in the aerial and space layers; (vi) joint communication, compute and storage resource allocation solutions targeting E2E performance optimization leveraging novel predictive analytics; and (vii) energy-efficient semantics-aware information handling techniques combined with edge computing and caching for reduced latency across the distributed 3D compute/storage continuum. The 3D ETHER architecture and the targeted three use cases are also discussed (dealing with: horizontal handovers for delay-tolerant IoT applications; ETHER unified RAN for direct handheld device access in the Ka band; and ETHER architecture demonstration for air-space safety-critical operations), paving the way towards 6G networks.

The second paper is dedicated to discussion about assessing potential consent between network slicing and network neutrality, thus dealing with a critical issue of modern telecoms markets. Network Slicing (NS) is the inherent concept of the 5G network and beyond, ensuring dynamic and flexible use of resources, and is considered a fundamental enabler of the "Industry 4.0" vision. However, its widespread implementation today encounters barriers and faces challenges in the area of the regulatory and business ecosystem, among which the paradigm of "network neutrality" (NeN) is of key importance. The paper discusses and analyzes the various factors affecting the wide implementation of NS, that is: legal and political – including the European Union regulations on network neutrality, trends in the telecommunications market, technical conditions of NS in 5G networks and beyond, especially physical barriers, and the fundamental conflicts of interest between various business actors in the telecommunications market as well as the consequences of the dominant position of content providers over mobile operators enabled by the mentioned regulation. Based on the analysis of the above factors, it is concluded that NS has become a "hostage" of contradictory paradigms and visions that, if not revised, prevent sustainable development based on communication services implemented with the use of NS. The latter is an idea in whose development a lot of resources and effort have been invested – in the stages of conceptualization, research, trials, industrial standardization and harmonization of interoperability. Currently, it is faced with a combination of factors (paradigms, regulations, trends, business models, physical and technological barriers) creating multidimensional contradictions that prevent its wide implementation. Among them, the regulations concerning NeN are of key importance. Therefore, it is necessary to undertake a broad discussion towards the revision of the adopted paradigms and visions in order to "unlock" the opportunities for economic development dependent on the implementation of NS-based communication services.

Last but not least, the 8th 5G-PINE Workshop also included a detailed paper coming from research supported by the project **"Immersive Virtual, Augmented and Mixed Reality Center Of Epirus"(MIS 5047221),** which is implemented under the Action "Reinforcement of the Research and Innovation Infrastructure", funded by the Operational Programme "Competitiveness, Entrepreneurship and Innovation" **(NSRF 2014-2020)** and co-financed by Greece and the European Union. Continuous fetal heart monitoring during pregnancy can be crucial in detecting and preventing many pathological conditions related to fetal heart development. In particular, because of its potential to provide prenatal diagnostic information, the non-invasive fetal electrocardiogram (NI-fECG) has become the focus of several recent studies. Due to its higher temporal frequency and spatial resolution, NI-fECG makes possible the "beat-to-beat" monitoring of the Fetal Heart Rate (FHR) and allows for a deeper characterization of the electrophysiological activity (i.e., electrical conduction of the heart) through morphological analysis of the fetal waveform. However, acquisition of the fetal ECG from maternal abdominal recordings remains an open problem, mainly due to the interference of the much stronger maternal ECG. The paper proposes a novel hybrid method for accurate fetal ECG extraction based on Reconstruction Independent Component Analysis (R-ICA) and Empirical Wavelet Transform (EWT) enhancement. The RICA-EWT method was tested on of real signals acquired from pregnant women in different stages of labour. The results indicate its robustness and efficiency in different SNR levels

As mentioned above, the accepted papers focus upon several innovative findings coming directly from modern European research in the area, that is from: Four (-4-) 5G-PPP/H2020 projects coming from the current "Phase 3" (i.e., "Smart5Grid", "MARSAL", "5G-ERA" and "5G-VICTORI"); two (-2-) Horizon-JU-SNS projects (i.e., "6G-BRICKS"and "ETHER"); two (-2-) Horizon projects (i.e., "OASEES" and ""NEMO"); and one (-1-) NSRF 2014-2020 project between Greece and the EU. All the above projects cover a wide variety of technical and business aspects and explicitly promote options for growth and development in the respective market(s). All accepted papers are fully aligned to the objectives of the 8th 5G-PINE scope and purely introduce innovative features, able to "influence" 5G/B5G's effective deployment.

Organization

Co-chairs

Ioannis P. Chochliouros	Hellenic Telecommunications Organization S.A. (OTE), Greece
Latif Ladid	IPv6 Forum and University of Luxembourg, Luxembourg
George Lyberopoulos	COSMOTE - Mobile Telecommunications S.A., Greece
Daniele Porcu	ENEL Global Infrastructure and Networks S.r.l., Italy
John Vardakas	Iquadrat Informatica S.L., Spain
Pavlos Lazaridis	University of Huddersfield, UK
Zaharias Zaharis	Aristotle University of Thessaloniki, Greece
Slawomir Kukliński	Orange Polska & Warsaw University of Technology, Poland
Lechosław Tomaszewski	Orange Polska, Poland
Nancy Alonistioti	National and Kapodistrian University of Athens, Greece
Christina Lessi	Hellenic Telecommunications Organization S.A. (OTE), Greece
Oriol Sallent	Universitat Politècnica de Catalunya, Spain
Jordi Pérez-Romero	Universitat Politècnica de Catalunya, Spain
Christos Verikoukis	University of Patras, Greece and Industrial Systems Institute (ISI)/Athena Research Centre, Greece
Michail-Alexandros Kourtis	National Centre for Scientific Research "Demokritos", Greece
Anastasia S. Spiliopoulou	Hellenic Telecommunications Organization S.A. (OTE), Greece

Program Committee Members

Theodora Politi	Hellenic Telecommunications Organization (OTE), Greece
Anastasios Kourtis	National Centre for Scientific Research "Demokritos", Greece
Alexandros Kostopoulos	Hellenic Telecommunications Organization (OTE), Greece

Maria Belesioti	Hellenic Telecommunications Organization (OTE), Greece
Nina Mitsopoulou	Hellenic Telecommunications Organization (OTE), Greece
Eirini Vasilaki	Hellenic Telecommunications Organization (OTE), Greece
Michalis Rantopoulos	OTE/COSMOTE - Mobile Telecommunications S.A., Greece
Elina Theodoropoulou	COSMOTE - Mobile Telecommunications S.A., Greece
Konstantinos Filis	COSMOTE - Mobile Telecommunications S.A., Greece
Ioanna Mesogiti	COSMOTE - Mobile Telecommunications S.A., Greece
Fotini Setaki	COSMOTE - Mobile Telecommunications S.A., Greece
Sebastien Ziegler	Mandat International, Switzerland
Hicham Khalifé	Thales SIX GTS France SAS, France
Christos-Antonios Gizelis	Hellenic Telecommunications Organization (OTE), Greece
Konstantinos Ramantas	Iquadrat Informatica S.L., Spain
Betty Charalampopoulou	GeoSystems Hellas S.A., Greece
Ioannis Giannoulakis	Eight Bells Ltd., Greece
Emmanouil Kafetzakis	Eight Bells Ltd., Cyprus
George Kontopoulos	Eight Bells Ltd., Cyprus
Vaios Koumaras	Infolysis P.C., Greece
Marina Koulaloglou	Infolysis P.C., Greece
Nikolaos Vrionis	Infolysis P.C., Greece
Ioannis Neokosmidis	INCITES Consulting S.A.R.L., Luxembourg
Theodoros Rokkas	INCITES Consulting S.A.R.L., Luxembourg
Monique Calisti	Martel Innovate, Switzerland
Dimitrios Brodimas	Independent Power Transmission Operator, Greece
Nikolaos Tzanis	Independent Power Transmission Operator S.A., Greece
Ralitsa Rumenova	Entra Energy, Bulgaria
Verzhinia Ivanova	Entra Energy, Bulgaria
Daniel Shangov	Bulgarian Electricity System Operator (ESO EAD), Bulgaria
Georgi Hristov	VivaCom, Bulgaria
Atanas Velkov	VivaCom, Bulgaria

Irina Ciornei	University of Cyprus, Cyprus
Lenos Hadjidemetriou	University of Cyprus, Cyprus
Markos Asprou	University of Cyprus, Cyprus
Stamatia Rizou	Singular Logic Systems Ltd., Greece
Cedric Crettaz	Mandat International, Switzerland
Vishanth Weerakkody	University of Bradford, UK
Tilemachos Doukoglou	ACTA Ltd., Greece
Panayiotis Verrios	ACTA Ltd., Greece
Ioannis Patsouras	ACTA Ltd., Greece
Tinku Rasheed	TriaGnoSys GmbH, Germany
Rodoula Makri	National Technical University of Athens, Greece
Antonino Albanese	Italtel SpA, Italy
Elisa Jimeno	ATOS Spain S.A., Spain
Claus Keuker	Smart Mobile Labs AG, Germany
Fidel Liberal	Universidad del Pais Vasco/Euskal Herriko Unibertsitatea (EHU), Spain
Begoña Blanco	Universidad del Pais Vasco/Euskal Herriko Unibertsitatea (EHU), Spain
Jose-Oscar Fajardo	Universidad del Pais Vasco/Euskal Herriko Unibertsitatea (EHU), Spain
August Betzler	Fundació Privada i2CAT, Internet i Innovació Digital a Catalunya, Spain
Ehsan Ebrahimi-Khaleghi	Thales SIX GTS France SAS, France
George Agapiou	WINGS ICT Solutions, Greece
Velissarios Gezerlis	Hellenic Telecommunications Organization (OTE), Greece
Stelios Androulidakis	Hellenic Telecommunications Organization (OTE), Greece
Ioanna Papafili	Hellenic Telecommunications Organization (OTE), Greece
Konstantinos Chelidonis	Hellenic Telecommunications Organization (OTE), Greece
Dimitra Vali	Hellenic Telecommunications Organization (OTE), Greece
Christos Mizikakis	Hellenic Telecommunications Organization (OTE), Greece
Kelly Georgiadou	Hellenic Telecommunications Organization (OTE), Greece
Konstantina Katsampani	Hellenic Telecommunications Organization (OTE), Greece
Stephanos Chatzipantelis	Hellenic Telecommunications Organization (OTE), Greece

George Tsiouris	Hellenic Telecommunications Organization (OTE), Greece
George Goulas	Hellenic Telecommunications Organization (OTE), Greece
Dimitrios Mouroukos	Hellenic Telecommunications Organization (OTE), Greece
Daniele Munaretto	Athonet S.R.L., Italy
Nicola di Pietro	Athonet S.R.L., Italy
Antonis Georgiou	ACTA Ltd., Greece
Angelos Antonopoulos	NearBy Computing S.L., Spain
Nicola Cadenelli	NearBy Computing S.L., Spain
Dimitrios Tzempelikos	Municipality of Egaleo, Greece
Evridiki Pavlidi	Municipality of Egaleo, Greece
Donal Morris	RedZinc Services, Ireland
Luis Cordeiro	OneSource Consultoria Informatica, LDA, Portugal
Vitor Fonseca	OneSource Consultoria Informatica, LDA, Portugal
Panagiotis Kontopoulos	National & Kapodistrian University of Athens, Greece
Sotiris Nikoletseas	University of Patras, Greece
Vasilios Vlachos	University of Thessaly, Greece
Srdjan Krčo	DunavNET, Serbia
Luca Bolognini	Italian Institute for Privacy, Italy
Camilla Bistolfi	Telecom Italia Mobile, Italy
Konstantinos Patsakis	University of Piraeus, Greece
Robert Kołakowski	Warsaw University of Technology, Poland
Sonia Castro	ATOS IT Solutions and Services Iberia SL, Spain
Borja Otura	ATOS IT Solutions and Services Iberia SL, Spain
Nissrine Saraireh	Smart Mobile Labs AG, Germany
Oscar Carrasco	CASA Communications Technology SL, Spain
Antonello Corsi	Engineering-Ingegneria Informatica SpA, Italy
Stephanie Oestlund	University of Luxembourg, Luxembourg
Adam Flizikowski	IS-Wireless Pietrzyk Slawomir, Poland
Mike Iosifidis	Clemic Services S.A., Greece
George Fountakos	Telecommunications Engineer, Greece

6G-BRICKS: Developing a Modern Experimentation Facility for Validation, Testing and Showcasing of 6G Breakthrough Technologies and Devices

Ioannis P. Chochliouros[1]([⊠]) [iD], John Vardakas[2], Kostas Ramantas[2], Sofie Pollin[3], Sylvie Mayrargue[4], Adlen Ksentini[5], Walter Nitzold[6], Md Arifur Rahman[7], Jimmy O'Meara[8], Ashima Chawla[8], Dimitrios Kritharidis[9], Vasileios Theodorou[9], Shuaib Siddiqui[10], Francisco Ibañez[11], Georgios Gardikis[12], Dimitris Diagourtas[13], Loizos Christofi[14], Alain Mourad[15], Didier Nicholson[16], Alexandros Kostopoulos[1], Anastasia S. Spiliopoulou[1], and Christos Verikoukis[17]

[1] Hellenic Telecommunications Organization (OTE) S.A., 99 Kifissias Avenue, 15124 Maroussi-Athens, Greece
ichochliouros@oteresearch.gr
[2] Iquadrat Informatica SL, Barcelona, Spain
[3] Katholieke Universiteit Leuven, Leuven, Belgium
[4] Commissariat à L'Energie Atomique et aux Energies Alternatives, Paris, France
[5] EURECOM, Biot, France
[6] National Instruments Dresden GmbH, Dresden, Germany
[7] IS-Wireless, Piaseczno, Poland
[8] L.M. Ericsson Limited, Dublin, Ireland
[9] Intracom S.A. Telecom Solutions, Peania, Greece
[10] Fundació Privada i2CAT, Barcelona, Spain
[11] Brainstorm Multimedia SL, Valencia, Spain
[12] Space Hellas S.A., Athens, Greece
[13] Satways Ltd., Iraklio-Athens, Greece
[14] eBOS Technologies Limited, Nicosia, Cyprus
[15] InterDigital R&D France, Cesson-Cévigné, France
[16] Ektacom, Les Ulis, France
[17] Industrial Systems Institute (ISI) / Athena Research Center, Athens, Greece

Abstract. Shifting towards B5G/6G implicates for a great diversity of challenges for the involved markets, especially via the creation of vast amounts of generated data and of related novel applications serving a great multiplicity of verticals. Such innovative services exceed the capabilities of existing 5G infrastructures for potential support of their corresponding KPIs and computational offloading, thus creating a new generation of Smart Networks. Towards fulfilling this target, the 6G-BRICKS project aims to deliver a new 6G experimentation facility building on the baseline of mature platforms coming from ongoing EU-funded activities and bringing breakthrough cell-free (CF) and RIS technologies. We have presented the essential architectural structure of the above facility and assessed in detail the core objectives of the project, as these "identify" diverse technical challenges and

I. Maglogiannis et al. (Eds.): AIAI 2023 Workshops, IFIP AICT 677, pp. 17–31, 2023.
https://doi.org/10.1007/978-3-031-34171-7_1

dedicated areas for future research. In addition, we have discussed and evaluated the fundamental use cases together with their intended PoCs that are expected to demonstrate strong market impact.

Keywords: 5G · 6G · Artificial Intelligence (AI) · Cell-Free (CF) · CFmMIMO · Edge continuum · eXplainable AI (XAI) · Industry 4.0 · Machine Learning (ML) · MIMO · Metaverse · mmWave · O-RAN · Reconfigurable Intelligent Surfaces (RIS) · xApp · Zero-Touch service management

1 Introduction

Commercial deployments of 5G are now progressing worldwide, delivering new capabilities, improved performance and new applications for customers. For Mobile Network Operators (MNOs), a set of figures that are 5G-supported, including network slicing, disaggregation, and cloud-native design [1], are enabling the use of new applications and new business models [2]. The gradual shift to the full digitization of the real world is expected to create vast amounts of generated data and applications, like immersive communication, and holographic telepresence, while social experiences powered by Extended Reality (XR) will become our default way of communication in the near future. These emerging applications exceed the current and future capabilities of 5G networks, both in terms of Key Performance Indicators (KPIs) that must be supported and in terms of their requirements on an ultra-dense computational infrastructure, to support the required degree of computational offloading [3]. Thus, academia and industry have "shifted" their attention to the investigation of a new generation of Smart Networks capable of supporting such performance. The first results of these studies show that 6G networks will deliver efficiency clearly superior to 5G and satisfy evolving services and applications [4, 5] making them a key enabler for the intelligent digital society of 2030 [6].

More specifically, 5G kick-started a trend towards software-defined infrastructures (SDI) and Software Networks that replace "black boxes" (e.g., physical network functions, such as firewalls) with their softwarized equivalents, deployed at standards-based "Whitebox" Servers. This trend has gradually propagated to the RAN (Radio Access Network) via the O-RAN (Open-RAN) initiative [7] that delivers software implementations of the CU (Centralized Unit) and DU (Distributed Unit) components, while Software-Defined Radios (SDRs) allow softwarization principles to reach down to the low-PHY (Physical layer). While softwarization and open APIs (Application Programming Interfaces) have been adopted with the objective of promoting interoperability and reducing OPEX (Operating Expenses) and CAPEX (Capital Expenditure), they have also revolutionized experimentation platforms and testbeds. Open Source software [8] stacks and Common Off-the-Shelf (COTS) hardware can be leveraged to affordably build and scale-up testbeds that allow customization and experimentation on every aspect of 5G and Beyond (B5G) infrastructures. Still, the enormous complexity of the 5G standards and software stacks makes end-to-end (E2E) experimentation platforms extremely challenging to deploy, requiring interdisciplinary efforts and big investments in integration.

The 6G-BRICKS project [9] will deliver this vision, bringing together specialists that work on breakthrough 6G technologies from all architecture tiers, namely Cell-Free (CF) networking [10–12] and Reconfigurable Intelligent Surfaces (RIS) [13]. These technologies will be integrated in reusable, self-contained testbed nodes, to be deployed at two E2E 6G testbed sites (i.e.: Katholieke Universiteit Leuven (KU-L) in Belgium and Eurecom (EUR) / CEA-LETI in France). These will be federated under a common set of Experimentation Tools, deployed under a common Cloud node, offered by ATHENA/ISI in Greece.

2   6G-BRICKS: Essential Scope and Core Objectives

6G-BRICKS will be the first open 6G platform that combines cell-free, Open Air Interface (OAI) [14] and RIS, while adopting the proven principles of softwarization, open Interfaces (O-RAN), and Open Source software stacks, putting future expansion and evolvability at its core. However, experience from past 5G-PPP efforts [15] has shown that the enormous complexity of the standards and software stacks makes evolvability and scaling-out efforts extremely challenging, requiring interdisciplinary efforts and big investments in integration, by the involved market "actors". To this very challenging end, 6G-BRICKS intends to deliver the first open and programmable O-RAN Radio Unit (RU) for 6G networks, termed as the OpenRU, based on an NI USRP-based platform [16]. Further on, among the project's target is also to integrate the RIS concept into the OAI. The scheduled effort will lead to breakthrough experimentation tools, going well beyond the current Testing as-a-Service (TaaS) capabilities [17] of current initiatives and allowing experiments also on devices via O-RAN compliant xAPPs[1]. Thus, 6G-BRICKS aims to deliver a new 6G experimentation facility, building on the baseline of mature ICT-52 platforms [18], that bring breakthrough cell-free and RIS technologies, which have shown promise for growth in beyond 5G networks. Moreover, novel unified control paradigms based on Explainable AI (Artificial Intelligence) and Machine Reasoning are to be explored in detail. In our intended approach, all corresponding enablers will be delivered in the form of reusable components with open APIs, termed as "bricks". Initial integrations with O-RAN will also be performed, aiming for the future-proofing and interoperability of 6G-BRICKS outcomes.

6G-BRICKS' aim is so to offer a trusted, agile and evolvable 6G experimentation facility, effectively federating two experimentation platforms (one in Belgium and one in France) from previous 5G-PPP initiatives under a "Core Site" (in Greece) acting as the facility entry point and offering Public Cloud and experimentation services. This facility is expected to be accessible by third-party consortia, vertical application owners and experimenters from the vertical and component industry. It will showcase a

---

[1] An xApp is a software tool used by a RAN Intelligent Controller (RIC) to manage network functions in near-real time. The xApps are part of a RIC which is a central software component of the Open RAN architecture, being responsible for controlling and optimizing RAN functions and resources. These applications – or services –include functions like radio resource management, mobility management and security.

disaggregated Management Plane and Operations Support System (OSS) to support extendibility, evolvability and multi-tenancy, beyond centralized Cross-Domain Service Orchestrators (CDSOs) [19] and OSS / BSS systems, as in current 5G-PPP experimentation platforms. The corresponding 6G experimentation facility is shown in Fig. 1 and includes the following architectural tiers:

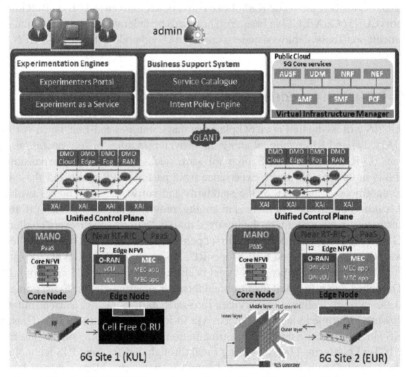

Fig. 1. 6G-BRICKS experimentation facility - General architecture.

Core Tier: It acts as the entry point to the facility, offering public cloud services to the 6G sites. Mature front-end elements and experimentation engine will be leveraged and deployed at the Core Site from the 5GMediaHUB project [20], delivering DevOps Driven Testing as-a-Service functionality allowing, in turn, test cases and validation testing workflows to be authored via standard DevOps tools. A unique testing tool based on Near-RT (Real-Time) RIC (RAN Intelligent Controller) are to be delivered giving experimenters access to low-level RRM (Radio Resources Management) and RAN slicing capabilities [21] via standardized xApps. In addition the Core Site will offer Business Support System (BSS) services to the 6G-BRICKS facility, allowing vertical application owners to upload their applications and Business Intents [22] (Service Level Objectives - SLOs).

A disaggregated Management Plane: It consists of a set of Domain Manager Orchestrators (DMOs) for each Cloud, Edge, and Network orchestration domain. The DMO layer, deployed at each facility sites, acts as a unified controllability framework aiming to provide the ability to enforce and propagate state-to-action mappings, automatically generating service objectives based on the SLOs (or business intents) submitted at the Business Layer. These actions are subsequently implemented by the infrastructure domain (e.g., RAN controller, SDN, VIM (Virtual Infrastructure Manager), etc.). Explainable AI (XAI) mechanisms [23] are leveraged for policy translation and unification. This breakthrough explainable architecture design supports end-to-end slicing [21], provides explainable feedback to experimenters for potential SLA (Service Level Agreement) breaches and facilitates a loose coupling with the Business Layer, avoiding bottlenecks.

The 6G Experimentation Platforms layer: Here, breakthrough 6G technologies are integrated in reusable, self-contained modules with O-RAN interfaces to ensure the openness and reusability of the developed components. At the KU-L site, a Distributed CF RAN is delivered, leveraging on the MARSAL [24] baseline work and also an O-RAN stack. The EUR site builds on the 5G-EVE [25] facility and the EUR OAI O-RAN stack, which will be integrated with a RIS platform from the RISE-6G project [26]. In both sites, UE (User Equipment) Farms will be deployed, i.e., a managed constellation of UE devices to be offered to experimenters, supporting virtualization and service placement at the device level, termed as the Deep Edge [27]. The UE farm may include: (i) 5G enabled remotely controlled smartphone devices, or; (ii) similarly specified clusters of Single Board Computers (e.g. Raspberry Pis) and Internet of Things (IoT) devices.

The project is structured around fulfilling several explicit objectives, all fully aligned to its novel strategic vision. These fundamental objectives are listed and briefly discussed/assessed as follows:

Objective 1: Delivering an evolvable 6G experimentation facility that will integrate breakthrough 6G technologies and will efficiently "federate" two well-established experimentation platforms – testbeds, under a common set of experimentation tools. The intended scope will be about: (i) Delivering an open Experimentation and Business Support layer with DevOps-driven testing and Zero-Touch service management capabilities [28], thus unlocking access to the facility for vertical owners and experimenters, and; (ii) supporting a managed UE farm layer, thus "pushing" computation down to the device tier.

Objective 2: Validate and showcase advanced use cases in holographic communication, metaverse and digital twinning, showcasing the benefits of 6G breakthrough technologies and architectures. Intended targeted actions will be about: (i) Demonstrating the technological feasibility of "better than 5G" KPIs in terms of capacity, reliability, location accuracy and energy efficiency; (ii) evaluating the effect of Network KPIs and Edge Continuum deployments [29] on extreme 6G Service KPIs [30], thus identifying bottlenecks and trade-offs, and; (iii) validating a set of Key Value Indicators (KVIs) [31], jointly defined with four ongoing ICT-52 baseline projects (i.e.: MARSAL [24], REINDEER [32], RISE-6G [26] and HEXA-X [33]).

Objective 3: Support fully disaggregated and software-defined infrastructures (SDIs) [34], adopting virtualization, Software-Defined Radio (SDR) and O-RAN interfaces to promote modularity and reusability of developed components. Intended targeted actions will be about: (i) Delivering open and reusable components ("bricks") for all technological domains, including USRP-based OpenRUs [16], O-RAN compliant CUs, DUs, as well as RIC and open DMO and PaaS (Platform as-a-Service) abstraction frameworks; (ii) offering programmable infrastructures at the compute domain and at the network domain, where physical resources (e.g., UEs) and virtual resources (e.g., slices, etc.) can be shared by multiple tenants/experimenters; (iii) hosting third party experiments and vertical applications, coming from corresponding future Open Calls, and; (iv) supporting RAN slicing and RRM down to the RU level, allowing low-level control from experimenters via xAPPs.

Objective 4: *Offer a fully decentralized management plane, supporting zero-touch orchestration of compute and communication resources based on XAI* [23]. Intended targeted actions will be about: (i) Defining and delivering a scalable architecture of DMOs, disaggregating the CDSOs of the State-of-the-Art (SoTA) facilities; (ii) implementing a Zero-touch policy engine that benefits from XAI and Machine Reasoning (MR) methods [35]; (iii) defining a XAI and MR for root cause analysis at DMO level, and; (iv) defining both XAI and MR to help experimenters to debug the tests run on 6G-BRICKS (including RAN and Cloud Edge Continuum platforms) and find solutions.

Objective 5: *Offer a Compute Continuum abstraction framework supporting a disaggregated wireless Xhaul.* Intended targeted actions will be about: (i) Delivering an interoperable continuum of solutions, comprising of Cloud, Edge and Far Edge/IoT device levels [36] as well as the disaggregated wireless X-HAUL systems [37] that link them (Fronthaul, Midhaul, Backhaul); (ii) offering a PaaS abstraction framework, exposing infrastructure resources via common and open APIs, following the Composable Infrastructures paradigm[2]; (iii) delivering Multi-agent Deep Reinforcement Learning (DRL) [27, 38] agents, driving automatic adaptations and joint optimizations to the end-to-end provisioning and connectivity layer to fluctuating user demand.

Objective 6: *Deliver breakthrough technologies towards a 6G RAN via Distributed Cell-Free and RIS.* Intended targeted actions will be about: (i) Integrating for the first time RIS and gNB (mmWave) to demonstrate and experiment with RIS technology using E2E service; (ii) devising and implementing a novel RIS controller to dynamically update RIS reflector configuration to support UE mobility; (iii) devising and implementing novel ML-based RIS control algorithms that predict user position and optimal RIS configuration; (iv) designing novel CF algorithms that distribute the computations in an optimal way (according to the respective use case); (v) implementing selected algorithms as software "Bricks"; (vi) designing novel multi-band algorithms that maximally exploit information gathered in different frequency bands; (vii) implementing a selection of these as software "Bricks"; (viii) designing and implementing novel Over-The-Air (OTA) synchronization algorithms [39] that minimize the signalling overhead while satisfying the stringent synchronization requirements for CFmMIMO (CF massive multiple Input Multiple Output) [40].

---

[2] Composable infrastructure is a framework that decouples device resources in order to treat them as services. Physical compute, storage and network fabrics are examples of device resources that can be treated as services.

Objective 7: Provide a secure and trusted Experimentation Facility for multiple concurrent tenants and experimentation platforms. To this aim, specific targeted actions will be about: (i) Supporting zero-trust establishment via the Software Defined Perimeter (SDP) paradigm [41]; (ii) offering VPN (Virtual Private Network) as-a-Service [42] for simplifying the establishment towards cross-site VPN encrypted tunnels, and ensuring future expansion towards experimentation sites outside the GEANT network; (iii) delivering a Security Orchestrator (SO) for the overall management of the security policies and configurations of the facility.

Objective 8: Maximise the impact expected to be created by the project to a great number of potential "actors"/recipients through wide means of dissemination, communication, standardisation and exploitation activities.

3 Use Cases

The 6G-BRICKS project is structured around two selected use cases (UCs) that are further to be developed, as discussed below. The former examines metaverse as an "enabler" of a modern workplace while the latter aims to focus on 6G Applications for serving Industry 4.0. Moreover, 6G-BRICKS intends to proceed to dedicated Proofs-of Concept (PoCs) for each separate UC so that not only to extend any corresponding market impact but also to increase adaptability in real scenarios of use and assess Business viability, especially in verticals. These UCs are briefly discussed in the following sections.

3.1 Use Case 1: Metaverse as an Enabler of a Modern Workplace

The Metaverse [43–45] is one of the emerging use cases, which is expected to "drive" the transition to B5G systems, as it requires KPI improvements by at least an order of magnitude. The Metaverse leverages of the latest advances in Extended Reality (XR) / Virtual Reality (VR) technologies to support social interactions in virtual spaces; this trend is well aligned with the ongoing digitalization of our societies and the digital transformation of businesses that place more and more emphasis on remote collaboration [46]. In this context, videoconferencing is a "key aspect" of the digital transformation, and disruptive technologies can make it even more compelling, helping mitigate limitations in terms of social interaction. Untethered VR [47] is already at the limit of 5G network capabilities, requiring extremely high downlink capacity (>100Mbps per device), and low latency (<5ms), to achieve impressiveness. The Metaverse further "pushes" the limits, allowing users to interact in 360 XR environments [48], while freely navigating in a Virtual Environment (VE). Recent advancements in the volumetric video domain allow to capture the user's volume in real time and insert the resulting hologram into these VEs, enabling multiple users to be co-present, together with others, in a 3D space while embodied in the own self-representation.

  This UC will demonstrate how network densification via distributed cell-free can make untethered Metaverse UCs a reality, offering acceptable quality of experience, and the ability of immersive social interactions (cf. Figure 2). Both scenarios adopt the Multi-point Control Unit (MCU) element [49], that is the application which handles

24   I. P. C. et al.

the real-time processing of "holograms" (i.e., the 3D representation of users), ensuring synchronization aspects and state consistency of the VE, and streaming a 360 VR Sphere of the VE to each participant. The MCU receives and transmits multiple MPEG (Moving Pictures Experts Group) 3D video streams with the volumetric videos. The (timestamped) incoming videos are decoded, processed accordingly, and converted into a fused volumetric video for the scene, thus providing a single stream to the client devices. This brings together specialists on breakthrough 6G technologies, such as cell-free networking, distributed processing and RIS, as well as adopting principles of modularity and softwarisation to deliver the first truly modular E2E 6G experimentation platform in Europe. 6G-BRICKS focuses upon structuring the various architecture tiers around the concept of "LEGO Bricks", delivering self-contained testbed nodes that can be reused across testbed infrastructures. This significantly lowers the barrier of entry to an E2E experimentation platform for specialists to bring their breakthrough technologies for validation and experimentation.

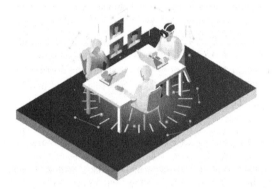

Fig. 2. 6G-BRICKS Use Case 1.

A first PoC will demonstrate an evolutionary "holoconference" scenario in a virtual meeting room, showcasing ultrahigh-speed with low-latency communication (uHSLLC) [50] that is made possible with distributed CF technologies. Holoconferencing is a special case of Social Virtual Reality (VR) platforms, where users can meet and cooperate with others, normally represented as virtual avatars, in a 3D environment [51]. This scenario will leverage on an innovative volumetric capture technique that uses conventional (and thus lower cost) cameras, hence promoting adoption by a wider audience. The Metaverse attendees will be represented by their avatars around a semicircular virtual meeting table.

A second PoC will deal with virtual team Building activities and will demonstrate a revolutionary scenario, showcasing ultrahigh data density (uHDD) communications and Joint Communication and Sensing enablers [52]. A much more advanced Volumetric Capture technology based on RGBD (Red-Green-Blue-Depth) cameras [53] will be offered, resulting in volumetric videos that involve point clouds, hence requiring much higher bandwidths in the uplink (UL) direction. Moreover, participants will be free to roam in a 3D environment, while interacting with their peers and completing a "team building" activity or puzzle, such as the very popular escape room challenge. In this scenario the VE is much larger and involves multiple 360 spheres (one per participant).

3.2 Use Case 2: 6G Applications for Industry 4.0

This UC aims to focus upon Industry 4.0 applications [54–56] and demonstrate how 6G enablers [57, 58] can contribute towards more efficient operators, leveraging autonomous robots, digital twinning and XR. Autonomous driving [59] and Digital Twins (DT) [60] are a rapidly growing market [61], particularly suitable for industrial applications [62] (cf. Figure 3). Yet, its actual impact to the operations heavily relies on the collection of high-volume data with low latency, which is something 6G can offer.

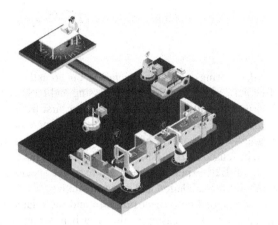

Fig. 3. 6G-BRICKS Use Case 2.

For the case of DT [63–65] a Tbps-level transmission rate is often required to meet the requirements on data volume for precise modeling, simulation and verification. Through fast iterative optimization and decision-making, digital entities can also be generated in centralized or distributed mode as required [66]. Security and privacy are also an important requirement; towards this, 6G networks also contribute [67] by supporting data storage, collection, processing, training, and modeling in both centralized and distributed architectures. Meanwhile, NGMN [68] considers autonomous robots [69, 70] and enhanced Machine Communication as one of the key 6G use-cases, reflecting the growth in collaborative robotics, and autonomous machines. The requirements concern mainly the extreme low-latency communications and high reliability to synchronize robots among them and with the remote controller. This UC is intended to be examined and validated via two dedicated PoCs, as briefly described below.

The PoC of this use case will show how 6G will support autonomous robots for industry 4.0 [71]. Autonomous robots are machines that can manage their tasks without the assistance of a human operator [72, 73]. They efficiently perform repetitive and complex tasks while requiring little to no downtime, which is ideal for continuous production. Autonomous robots help prevent human injury in the factory by holding and moving heavy items on the production line [74–76]. In addition, they can quickly analyze and choose the most efficient route to "pick and deliver" items in the factory based on incoming requests. The autonomous robot will move in the factory while having low-latency communication. It will move objects from position "A" to "B" according to the received request from a server.

The second PoC will show how 6G supports remote DT visualization through an Augmented Reality (AR) interface [77–79] by superposing SCADA data on the real object. This PoC will exploit AR to enable an inspection feature for discovering malfunctioning elements in indoor Oil and Gas systems [80, 81]. Potential malfunctions will be identified by close virtual inspection via the combination of several techniques [82]. Apart from being considerably flexible, virtual inspection is the most intuitive, straightforward and economical method for assessing the conditions of an industrial machinery.

4   Discussion

The 6G-BRICKS project brings together specialists on breakthrough 6G technologies, such as cell-free networking, distributed processing and RIS, as well as adopting principles of modularity and softwarisation to deliver the first truly modular E2E 6G experimentation platform in Europe. 6G-BRICKS focuses upon structuring the various architecture tiers around the concept of "LEGO Bricks", delivering self-contained testbed nodes that can be reused across testbed infrastructures. This significantly lowers the barrier of entry to an E2E experimentation platform for specialists to bring their breakthrough technologies for validation and experimentation.

In particular, the corresponding project platform and the related facilities will be used for validation testing and showcasing of the clear benefits and capabilities of 6G breakthrough technologies and devices. The 6G-BRICKS experimentation facility aims to serve a "dual role, "that is both as a playground for testing advanced vertical applications and for validation testing and showcasing of the clear benefits and capabilities of 6G breakthrough technologies and devices. Moreover, the scope is about delivering and testing new architecture principles, with multi-tenancy, disaggregated Operations Support Systems (OSS) and Deep Edge integration at the forefront.

In the present paper we have briefly presented the essential architecture of the intended experimentation facility and discussed its essential architectural tiers. As a step further we have not only discussed but in fact extended the 6G-BRICKS fundamental objectives, strongly affecting all potential dimensions of the expected technical progress of the project. These objectives practically "delineate" the forthcoming research and testing effort around several thematic domains (mainly CF and RIS), towards proposing innovative and fully validated 6G-oriented solutions.

Then we have presented the fundamental use cases that are to be deployed and evaluated during the course of the project. The first one is about the consideration and the effective inclusion of the Metaverse context as a practical enabler for realizing a modern workplace where we intend to demonstrate an evolutionary "holoconference" scenario in a virtual meeting room showcasing uHSLLC as well as distinct virtual team building activities, showcasing uHDD communications and sensing. The second UC is about the use of 6G applications in Industry 4.0 and is to be assed via two PoCs examining the inclusion of autonomous robots for the support of industrial processes and the development of digital twin visualization through an AR interface to allow inspection in indoor Oil and Gas systems.

Acknowledgments. This work has been performed in the scope of the *6G-BRICKS* European Research Project and has been supported by the Commission of the European Communities */HORIZON, Grant Agreement No.101096954.*

References

1. Shah, S.D.A., Gregory, M.A., Li, S.: Cloud-Native Network Slicing Using Software Defined Networking Based Multi-Access Edge Computing: A Survey. IEEE Access **9**, 10903–10924 (2021)
2. Saad, W., Bennis, M., Chen, M.: A Vision of 6G Wireless Systems: Applications, Trends, Technologies, and Open Research Problems. IEEE Network **34**(3), 134–142 (2020)
3. Ericsson: "XR and 5G: Extended reality at scale with time-critical communication", https://www.ericsson.com/en/reports-and-papers/ericsson-technology-review/articles/xr-and-5g-extended-reality-at-scale-with-time-critical-communication
4. Bhat, J.R., Alqahtani, S.A.: 6G Ecosystem: Current Status and Future Perspective. IEEE Access **9**, 43134–43167 (2021)
5. Akyildiz, I.F., Kak, A., Nie, S.: 6G and Beyond: The Future of Wireless Communications Systems. IEEE Access **8**, 133995–134030 (2020)
6. Seppo Yrjölä, S., Ahokangas, P., Matinmikko-Blue, M.: Value Creation and Capture From Technology Innovation in the 6G Era. IEEE Access **10**, 16299–16319 (2022)
7. O-RAN Alliance eV, https://www.o-ran.org/
8. Open Source, https://opensource.com/resources/what-open-source
9. 6G-BRICKS (Building Reusable testbed Infrastructures for validating Cloud-to-device breakthrough technologieS) Horizon-JU-SNS project, Grant Agreement No.101096954, https://6g-bricks.eu/
10. Chen, S., Zhang, J., Zhang, J., Björnson, E., and Ai, B: A Survey on User-centric Massive MIMO Systems. Digital Communications and Networks **8**(5), 695--719 (2022)
11. Ngo, H.Q., Ashikhmin, A., Yang, H., Larsson, E.G., Marzetta, T.L.: Cell-Free Massive MIMO Versus Small Cells. IEEE Trans. Wireless Commun. **16**(3), 1834–1850 (2017)
12. Ngo, H.Q., Ashikhmin, A., Yang, X., Larsson, E.G., and Marzetta, T.L.: Cell-Free Massive MIMO: Uniformly Great Service for Everyone. In: Proceedings of the 16th IEEE International Workshop on Signal Processing Advances in Wireless Communications (SPAWC'15), pp.201–205. IEEE (2015)
13. European Telecommunications Standards Institute (ETSI): Reconfigurable Intelligent Interfaces, https://www.etsi.org/technologies/reconfigurable-intelligent-surfaces
14. OpenAirInterface (OAI), https://openairinterface.org/
15. 5G Public Private Infrastructure (5G-PPP), https://5g-ppp.eu/
16. NI, https://www.ni.com/en-us/shop/wireless-design-test/what-is-a-usrp-software-defined-radio.html
17. Girardon, G., Costa V., Machado, R., Bernardino, M., Legramante, M., Basso, F.P., et *al.*: Testing as a Service (TaaS): A Systematic Literature Map. In: Proceedings of the 35th Annual ACM Symposium on Applied Computing (SAC'20), pp.1989–1996. ACM (2020)

18. 5G Public Private Infrastructure (5G-PPP): H2020-ICT52–2020: "5G-PPP Smart connectivity beyond 5G", https://5g-ppp.eu/5g-ppp-phase-3-6-projects/
19. Toumi, N., Bernier, O., Meddour, D.-E., Ksentini, A.: On cross-domain service function chain orchestration: an architectural framework. Comput. Netw. **187**, 107806–107823 (2021)
20. 5GMediaHUB ("5G Experimentation Environment for 3rd Party Media Services") 5G-PPP/H2020 Project, Grant Agreement No.101016714, https://www.5gmediahub.eu/
21. Chochliouros, I.P., Spiliopoulou, A.S., Lazaridis, P., Dardamanis, A., Zaharis, Z., Kostopoulos, A.: Dynamic Network Slicing: Challenges and Opportunities. In: Maglogiannis, I., Iliadis, L., Pimenidis, E. (eds.) AIAI 2020. AICT, vol. 585, pp. 47–60. Springer, Cham (2020). https://doi.org/10.1007/978-3-030-49190-1_5
22. European Telecommunications Standards Institute (ETSI) ETSI GR ENI 008 (V2.1.1) (2021–03) Experiential Networked Intelligence (ENI); InTent Aware Network Autonomicity (ITANA). https://www.etsi.org/deliver/etsi_gr/ENI/001_099/008/02.01.01_60/gr_ENI008v020101p.pdf
23. Jonathon Phillips, P., Hahn, C.A., Fontana, P.C., Yates, A.N., Greene, K., Broniatowski, D.A., Przybocki, M.A.: Four Principles of Explanable Artificial Intelligence (NISTIR 8312). National Institute of Standards and Technology (2021). https://nvlpubs.nist.gov/nistpubs/ir/2021/NIST.IR.8312.pdf
24. MARSAL ("Machine Learning-based Networking and Computing Infrastructure Resource Management of 5G and Beyond Intelligent Networks") 5G-PPP/H2020 project, Grant Agreement No.101017171, https://www.marsalproject.eu/
25. 5G-EVE ("5G European Validation platform for extensive trials") 5G-PPP/H2020 project, Grant Agreement No.815074, https://www.5g-eve.eu/
26. RISE-6G ("Reconfigurable Intelligent Sustainable Environments for 6G Wireless Networks") 5G-PPP/H2020 project Grant Agreement No.10101701, https://rise-6g.eu/
27. Yamansavascilar, B., Baktir, A.C., Sonmez, C., Ozgovde, A., and Ersoy, C.: DeepEdge: A Deep Reinforcement Learning based Task Orchestrator for Edge Computing (2021), https://arxiv.org/abs/2110.01863
28. European Telecommunications Standards Institute (ETSI): Zero-touch network and Service Management (ZSM). ETSI (2023), https://www.etsi.org/technologies/zero-touch-network-service-management
29. Rosendo, D., Costan, A., Valduriez, P., Antoniu, G.: Distributed intelligence on the Edge-to-Cloud Continuum: A systematic literature review. Journal of Parallel and Distributed Computing **166**, 71–94 (2022)
30. 5G Public Private Infrastructure (5G-PPP): 5G-PPP White Paper: "Beyond 5G/6G KPIs and Target Values" (2022), https://5g-ppp.eu/5g-ppp-white-paper-beyond-5g-6g-kpis-and-target-values/
31. 6G Infrastructure Association (6G-IA), Vision and Societal Challenges Working Group: White Paper: "What societal values will 6G address? Societal Key Values and Key Value Indicators analysed through 6G use cases" (2022), https://doi.org/10.5281/zenodo.6557534
32. REINDEER ("REsilient INteractive applications through hyper Diversity in Energy Efficient RadioWeaves technology") 5G-PPP/H2020 Project, Grant Agreement No.101013425, https://reindeer-project.eu/
33. HEXA-X ("A flagship for B5G/6G vision and intelligent fabric of technology enablers connecting human, physical, and digital worlds") 5G-PPP/H2020 Project, Grant Agreement No.101015956, https://hexa-x.eu/
34. Kandiraju, G., Franke, H., Williams, M.D., Steinder, M., and Black, S.M.: Software defined infrastructures. IBM Journal of Research and Development **58**(2/3), 2:1--2:13 (2014)

35. Čyras, K., Badrinath, R., Mohalik, S.K., Mujumdar, A., Nikou, A., Previti, A., Sundararajan, V., and Vulgarakis-Feljan, A.: Machine Reasoning Explainability (2020), https://arxiv.org/pdf/2009.00418.pdf,
36. Balouek-Thomert, D., Renart, E.G., Zamani, A.R., et al.: Towards a computing continuum: Enabling edge-to-cloud integration for data-driven workflows. The International Journal of High Performance Computing Applications 33(6), 1159–1174 (2019)
37. La Oliva, A.D., Costa-Pérez, X., Azcorra, A., Di Gigglio, A.: Xhaul: toward an integrated fronthaul/backhaul architecture in 5G networks. IEEE Wirel. Commun. 22(5), 32–40 (2015)
38. Arulkumaran, K., Deisenroth, M.P., Brundage, M., Bharath, A.A.: A Brief Survey of Deep Reinforcement Learning. IEEE Signal Process. Mag. 34(6), 26–38 (2017)
39. Xie, Z., and Xu, Y.: Research on OTA Optimization of Wireless Sensor Networks Based on CSMA/CA Improved Algorithm. In: Proceedings of the 2018 10th International Conference on Communications, Circuits and Systems (ICCCAS'18), pp.331–335. IEEE (2018)
40. Interdonato, G., Björnson, E., Ngo, H.Q., Frenger, P., Larsson, E.G.: Ubiquitous Cell-Free Massive MIMO Communications. EURASIP J. Wirel. Commun. Netw. 197, 1–13 (2019)
41. Lefebvre, M., Engels, D.W., and Nair, S.: On SDPN: Integrating the Software-Defined Perimeter (SDP) and the Software-Defined Network (SDN) Paradigms. In: Proceedings of the 2022 IEEE Conference on Communications and Network Security (CNS'22), pp.353–358. IEEE (2022)
42. Bhat, A.Z., Shuaibi, D.K.A., and Singh, A.V.: Virtual private network as a service - A need for discrete cloud architecture. In: Proceedings of the 2016 5th International Conference on Reliability, Infocom Technologies and Optimization (Trends and Future Directions) (ICRITO'16), pp.526–532. IEEE (2016)
43. J. Lee, J., Yeo, I., et al.: Metaverse Current Status and Prospects: Focusing on Metaverse Field Cases. In: Proceedings of the 2022 IEEE/ACIS 7th International Conference on Big Data, Cloud Computing, and Data Science (BCD'22), pp. 332–336. IEEE (2022)
44. Go, S.Y., Jeong, H.G., Kim, J.I., Sin, Y.Y.: Concept and Development of Metaverse. Korea Information Processing Society Review 28(1), 7–16 (2021)
45. Peng, H., Chen, P.-C., Chen, P.-H., Yang, Y.-S., Hsia, C.-C., et al.: 6G toward Metaverse: Technologies, Applications, and Challenges. In: Proceedings of the 2022 IEEE VTS Asia Pacific Wireless Communications Symposium (APWCS'22), pp.6–10. IEEE (2022)
46. Aslam, A.M., Chaudhary, R., Bhardwaj, A., Budhiraja, I., Kumar, N., Zeadally, S.: Metaverse for 6G and Beyond: The Next Revolution and Deployment Challenges. IEEE Internet of Things Magazine 6(1), 32–39 (2023)
47. Abari, O.: Enabling High-Quality Untethered Virtual Reality. In: Proceedings of the 1st ACM Workshop on Millimeter-Wave Networks and Sebsning Systems (mmNets'17), pp.1–49. ACM (2017)
48. Zucchi, S., Füchter, S.K., Salazar, G., and Alexander, K.: Combining immersion and interaction in XR training with 360-degree video and 3D virtual objects. In: Proceedings of the 2020 23rd International Symposium on Measurement and Control in Robotics (ISMCR'20), pp.1–5. IEEE (2020)
49. Cernigliaro, G., Martos, M., Montagud, M., Ansari, A., and Fernandez, S.: PC-MCU: point cloud multipoint control unit for multi-user holoconferencing systems. In: Proceedings of the 30th ACM Workshop on Network and Operating Systems Support for digital Audio and Video (NOSSDAV'20), pp.47–53. ACM (2020)
50. Bennis, M., Debbah, M., et al.: Ultrareliable and Low-Latency Wireless Communication: Tail, Risk, and Scale. Proc. IEEE 106(10), 1834–1853 (2018)
51. Langa, S.F., Montagud, M., Cernigliaro, G., Rivera, D.R.: Multi-party Holomeetings: Toward a New Era of Low-Cost Volumetric Holographic Meetings in Virtual Reality. IEEE Access 10, 81856–81876 (2022)

52. Alraih, S., Shayea, I., et al.: Revolution or Evolution? Technical Requirements and Considerations towards 6G Mobile Communications. Sensors (MDPI) **22**(3), 762 (2022)
53. Numan, N., Haar, F.T., and Cesar, P.: Generative RGB-D face completion for head-mounted display removal. In: Proceedings of the IEEE Conference on Virtual Reality and 3D User Interfaces Abstracts and Workshops (VRW'21), pp.109–116. IEEE (2021)
54. Standardization Council Industrie 4.0: The German Standardization Roadmap Industrie 4.0-Edition 4. Din & DKE (2020), https://www.sci40.com/english/publications/
55. Maier, M.: 6G as if People Mattered: From Industry 4.0 toward Society 5.0 (Invited Paper), In: Proceedings of the 2021 International Conference on Computer Communications and Networks (ICCCN), pp.1–10. IEEE (2021)
56. Xu, L.D., Xu, E.L., & Li, L.: Industry 4.0: state of the art and future trends. International Journal of Production Research **56**(8), 2941--2962 (2018)
57. Sigov, A., Ratkin, L., Ivanov, L.A., Xu, L.D.: Emerging Enabling Technologies for Industry 4.0 and Beyond. Inf. Syst. Front. (2022). https://doi.org/10.1007/s10796-021-10213-w
58. Liu, G., et al.: Vision, requirements and network architecture of 6G mobile network beyond 2030. China Communications **17**(9), 92–104 (2020)
59. Yurtsever, E., Lambert, J., Carballo, A., Takeda, K.: A Survey of Autonomous Driving: Common Practices and Emerging Technologies. IEEE Access **8**, 58443–58469 (2020)
60. Liu, M., Fang, S., Dong, H., Xu, C.: Review of digital twin about concepts, technologies, and industrial applications. J. Manuf. Syst. **58**(part B), 346–361 (2021)
61. Grand View Research, Inc.: Digital Twin Market Size Worth $26.07 Billion By 2025 with CAGR 38.2% - Digital Twin Market Growth & Trends (2022), https://www.grandviewresearch.com/press-release/global-digital-twin-market
62. Tao, F., Zhang, H., Liu, A., Nee, A.Y.: Digital Twin in Industry: State-of-the-Art. IEEE Trans. Industr. Inf. **15**(4), 2405–2415 (2019)
63. Han, B., Habibi, M.A., Richerzhagen, B., Schindhelm, K., Zeiger, F., Lamberti, F., Pratticò, F.G., Upadhya, K., Korovesis, C., Belikaidis, I.-P., Demestichas, P., Yuan, S., and Schotten, H.D.: Digital Twins for Industry 4.0 in the 6G Era (2022), https://arxiv.org/ftp/arxiv/papers/2210/2210.08970.pdf
64. Wang, T., Li, J., Deng, Y., Wang, C., Snoussi, H., Tao, F.: Digital twin for human-machine interaction with convolutional neural network. Int. J. Comput. Integr. Manuf. **34**(7–8), 888–897 (2021)
65. Fuller, A., Fan, Z., Day, C., Barlow, C.: Digital twin: Enabling technologies, challenges and open research. IEEE Access **8**, 108952–108971 (2020)
66. Huang, Z., Shen, Y., Li, J., Fey, M., and Brecher, C.: A survey on AI-driven digital twins in Industry 4.0: Smart manufacturing and advanced robotics. Sensors (MDPI) **21**(19), 6340 (2021)
67. Dang, S., Amin, O., Shihada, B., Alouini, M.-S.: What should 6G be? Nature Electronics **3**, 20–29 (2020)
68. Next Generation of Mobile Networks Alliance (NGMN): 6G Use Cases and Analysis – Version 1.0. NGMN (2022), https://www.ngmn.org/publications/6g-use-cases-and-analysis.html
69. Sakai, T., Nagai, T.: Explainable autonomous robots: a survey and perspective. Adv. Robot. **36**(5–6), 219–238 (2021)
70. Goel, R., and Gupta, P.: Robotics and Industry 4.0. In: Nayyar, A., Kumar, A. (eds) A Roadmap to Industry 4.0: Smart Production, Sharp Business and Sustainable Development. Advances in Science, Technology & Innovation, pp.157–169. Springer, Cham (2020), https://doi.org/10.1007/978-3-030-14544-6_9
71. Gonzalez-Aguirre, J.A., Osorio-Oliveros, R., Rodríguez-Hernández, K.L., Lizárraga-Iturralde, J., Morales Menendez, R., Ramírez-Mendoza, R.A., et al.: Service robots: trends and technology. Appl. Sci. (MDPI) **11**(22), 1070 (2021)

72. Bayram, B., İnce, G.: Advances in Robotics in the Era of Industry 4.0. In: Industry 4.0: Managing The Digital Transformation. SSAM, pp. 187–200. Springer, Cham (2018). https://doi.org/10.1007/978-3-319-57870-5_11

73. Javaid, M., Haleem, A., Singh, R.P., and Suman, R.: Substantial capabilities of robotics in enhancing industry 4.0 implementation. Cognitive Robotics 1, 58--75 (2021)

74. Hu, L., Miao, Y., Wu, G., Hassan, M.M., Humar, I.: iRobot-Factory: An intelligent robot factory based on cognitive manufacturing and edge computing. Futur. Gener. Comput. Syst. 90, 569–577 (2019)

75. Gualtieri, L., Rauch, E., Vidoni, R.: Emerging research fields in safety and ergonomics in industrial collaborative robotics: A systematic literature review. Robotics and Computer-Integrated Manufacturing 67, 101998–102001 (2021)

76. Parmar, H., Khan, T., Tucci, F., Umer, R., and Carlone, P.: Advanced robotics and additive manufacturing of composites: towards a new era in Industry 4.0. Materials and Manufacturing Processes 37(5), 1--35 (2021)

77. Schroeder, G.N., Steinmetz, C., Pereira, C.E., Muller, I., Garcia, N., Espindola, D., and Rodrigues, R.: Visualising the digital twin using web services and augmented reality. In: Proceedings of the 2016 IEEE 14th International Conference on Industrial Informatics (INDIN'16), pp.522–527. IEEE (2016)

78. Künz, A., Rosmann, S., Loria, E., Pirker, J.: The potential of augmented reality for digital twins: a literature review. In: Proceedings of the 2022 IEEE Conference on Virtual Reality and 3D User Interfaces (VR 2022), pp. 389–398. IEEE (2022)

79. Böhm, F., Dietz, M., Preindl, T., Pernul, G.: Augmented Reality and the Digital Twin: State-of-the-Art and Perspectives for Cybersecurity. Journal of Cybersecurity and Privacy (MDPI) 1, 519–538 (2021)

80. Yu, L., Yang, E., Ren, P., Luo, C., Dobie, G., Gu, D., and Yan, X.: Inspection Robots in Oil and Gas Industry: a Review of Current Solutions and Future Trends. In: Proceedings of the 2019 25th International Conference on Automation and Computing (ICAC'19), pp.1–6. IEEE (2019)

81. MarketWatch: Inspection Robotics in Oil and Gas Market Share by 2031 (2023) https://www.marketwatch.com/press-release/inspection-robotics-in-oil-and-gas-market-share-by-2031-2023-03-24

82. Hajjaj, S.S.H., Khalid, I.B.: Design and Development of an Inspection Robot for Oil and Gas Applications. International Journal of Engineering & Technology 7(435), 5–10 (2018)

ETHER: Energy- and Cost-Efficient Framework for Seamless Connectivity over the Integrated Terrestrial and Non-terrestrial 6G Networks

Lechosław Tomaszewski[1]([✉]) [ID], Robert Kołakowski[1,2] [ID], Agapi Mesodiakaki[3] [ID],
Konstantinos Ntontin[4] [ID], Angelos Antonopoulos[5] [ID], Nikolaos Pappas[6] [ID],
Marco Fiore[7,8] [ID], Mohammadreza Mosahebfard[9,10] [ID], Simon Watts[11],
Philip Harris[12] [ID], Chih-Kuang Lin[12] [ID], Ana Rita Santiago[13] [ID],
Fotis Lazarakis[14] [ID], and Symeon Chatzinotas[4] [ID]

[1] Orange Polska S.A., ul. Obrzeżna 7, 02-691 Warszawa, Poland
lechoslaw.tomaszewski@orange.com
[2] Warsaw University of Technology, ul. Nowowiejska 15/19, 00-665 Warszawa, Poland
[3] Aristotle University of Thessaloniki, 10th km Thessalonikis, Thermis 57001, Greece
[4] SnT, University of Luxembourg, 29 Avenue J.F. Kennedy,
Luxembourg 1855, Luxembourg
[5] Nearby Computing, Travessera de Gracia 18, 3o/3a, 08021 Barcelona, Spain
[6] Linköping University, Campus Valla, Linköping 58183, Sweden
[7] IMDEA Networks Institute, Aven. Mar Mediterraneo 22, 28918 Madrid, Spain
[8] Net AI, 1-4 Atholl Crescent, Edinburgh, Scotland EH3 8HA, UK
[9] i2CAT Foundation, Calle Gran Capità 2-4, Edifici Nexus I, 08034 Barcelona, Spain
[10] Polytechnic University of Catalunya, C. Jordi Girona 31, 08034 Barcelona, Spain
[11] Avanti Communications, One Ariel Way, White City, London W12 7SL, UK
[12] Collins Aerospace, Penrose Wharf Business Centre, Cork T23 XN53, Ireland
[13] Ubiwhere, Travessa Senhor das Barrocas, 38, 3800-075 Aveiro, Portugal
[14] National Centre for Scientific Research "Demokritos", Neapoleos 88,
153 41 Agia Paraskevi, Greece

Abstract. Several use cases already proposed for 5G networks cannot be facilitated by terrestrial infrastructure, either due to its small penetration in remote/rural areas or the harsh propagation conditions due to the terrain. Indicative applications include forestry, mining, agriculture, semi-autonomous control of long-range vehicles, industrial services, logistics, asset tracking, telemedicine, beyond visual-line-of-sight drone operations, and maritime insurance. Hence, such use cases necessitate the integration of terrestrial with non-terrestrial networks, which gives rise

ETHER project has received funding from the Smart Networks and Services Joint Undertaking (SNS JU) under the European Union's Horizon Europe research and innovation programme under Grant Agreement No. 101096526. Views and opinions expressed are however those of the author(s) only and do not necessarily reflect those of the European Union. Neither the European Union nor the granting authority can be held responsible for them.

to several challenges to overcome. The project ETHER aims to provide a holistic approach for energy- and cost-efficient integrated terrestrial-non-terrestrial networks. To achieve this goal, ETHER develops solutions for a unified Radio Access Network and for Artificial Intelligence-enabled resource management across the terrestrial, aerial, and space domains while creating the business plans driving future investments. To that end, this paper discusses a series of key technologies that ETHER combines under a unique 3-Dimensional (3D) multi-layered architectural proposition that brings together: i) user terminal antenna design and implementation for direct handheld access in the integrated network, ii) a robust unified waveform, iii) energy-efficient seamless horizontal and vertical handover policies, iv) a zero-touch network/service management and orchestration framework, v) a flexible payload system to enable programmability in the aerial and space layers, vi) joint communication, compute, and storage resource allocation solutions targeting at end-to-end network performance optimisation leveraging novel predictive analytics, and vii) energy-efficient semantics-aware information handling techniques combined with edge computing and caching for reduced latency across the distributed 3D compute/storage continuum. The 3D ETHER architecture and the targeted use cases are also discussed, paving the way toward 6G networks.

Keywords: 5G · 6G · terrestrial · non-terrestrial · mobile network · satellite · GEO · MEO · LEO · HAPS · drone · UAV · Ka band · handheld terminal · unified RAN · MANO · ZSM · NFV · SDN · MEC · cloud continuum · vertical handover · horizontal handover · MIoT · eMBB · URLLC · semantic communications · aviation · safety · IoT

1   Introduction

1.1   Background and Related Work

Although the deployment of 5th Generation (5G) networks is currently ongoing, research on the 6th Generation (6G) use cases that can be facilitated by such networks has already been initiated. One important problem not expected to be solved by 5G networks is the ubiquitous coverage, especially in remote areas. This is due to the fact that the straightforward solution of heavily densifying Terrestrial Networks (TNs) with small cells is prohibitive both in terms of cost and energy consumption. In addition, in terms of revenues, such a strategy is not viable for Mobile Network Operators (MNOs) for remote/rural areas that have a low density of users. Therefore, non-urban areas are generally undercovered – in terms of either supported Quality of Service (QoS) or service availability in general. In particular, several rural applications of growing social and economic importance, such as telemedicine, agriculture/forestry, shipping and freight tracking, cannot be appropriately served.

A fundamental requirement of 6G networks is to provide unlimited access on the globe, covering land, sea, and sky [1]. This is achieved through Non-Terrestrial Networks (NTNs) in the mobile communication ecosystem. However, while the direction of efforts initially was to integrate non-3rd Generation Partnership Project (3GPP) NTNs with a 5G System (5GS), the 6G is characterised by a unified access composed of TN and NTN [2]. 3GPP has been working on NTN integration since 2017. The vision of a few satellite use cases has been defined [3] together with delay Key Performance Indicators (KPIs) targets for various orbits satellites (and the latter have been further incorporated to the general service requirements of 5GS [4]). The issues of the New Radio (NR) support for NTNs [5] and solution proposals [6] have been analysed and reported. Currently, 3GPP identifies Low-Earth Orbit (LEO), Medium-Earth Orbit (MEO), Geostationary Earth Orbit (GEO), and High Elliptical Orbit (HEO) satellites, drones, and High Altitude Platform Systems (HAPSs) among the NTN platforms; 5GS is required to support both 3GPP and non-3GPP NTN access nodes [4,7]. The new study on satellite access in 5GS [8] with new use cases, i.a., store-and-forward operation, delay-tolerant Internet of Things (IoT) data collection, drones with satellite access, is at an early stage.

Several advancements regarding the identification of requirements, challenges, and enabling technologies for the efficient integration of TN with NTN have also been proposed by academia. Novel architectural solutions are being proposed, such as a Space-Air-Ground Integrated Network (SAGIN) focused on supporting ubiquitous coverage and expected 6G services [9] or Civil Aircraft-Assisted (CAA)-SAGIN [10] aiming to reduce launching costs of airborne communications platforms by installing base stations and relays on already operating civil aircraft. The TN-NTN integration is expected to aggravate the complexity of the service management and orchestration due to the mobility and heterogeneity of the NTN infrastructure [11]. Potential solutions to these issues have been proposed and include the usage of hierarchical multi-layered management architecture with global and local controllers to reduce the complexity of network control [12] or exploitation of specific enablers within service management and orchestration framework such as Temporospatial Software-Defined Networking (SDN) [13,14] – enhanced SDN concept facilitating application-driven network control based on the location, motion, and orientation of assets in space.

Among different Horizon 2020/Horizon Europe projects, several are dedicated to various aspects of NTN access. In particular, the EU-KR project "5G-ALLSTAR" [15] has demonstrated multiple access based on TN and satellite links, providing 50 Mbps expected user data rate, 10 ms latency and 99.999% reliability, especially to support critical applications. The project "SaT5G" has developed and demonstrated a cost-effective plug-and-play solution to integrate satellites with SDN, Network Function Virtualisation (NFV) and Multi-access Edge Computing (MEC)-enabled 5G networks [16]. At the beginning of 2023, three other projects started. The project "Hexa-X II" [17] will work on the European 6G vision from use cases, services and requirements for 6G, through platform and system design, to proofs of concepts. The project "5G-STARDUST"

[18] is aimed at a fully integrated 5G-NTN autonomous system for enabling ubiquitous radio access through, *i.a.*, deeper TN and NTN integration, unified radio interfaces, Artificial Intelligence (AI)-driven management, and O-RAN architecture. The project "6G-NTN" [19] plans to design and validate key technical enablers for the integration of NTN and TN components into 6G. Moreover, the project "TRANTOR" [20] targets the in-orbit validation of a complete satellite value chain involving automated management of satellite resources across multiple bands, satellites, and orbits, and a converged radio access network. Furthermore, concerning European Space Agency (ESA)-related projects, the "5G-GOA project" [21] investigates direct radio access of User Equipment (UE) devices via satellites, while the objective of the "5G-LEO" project is to extend the OpenAirInterface5G software to support non-GEO satellite systems [22].

1.2 Motivation, Pillars, and Objectives

Despite the abundance of literature works and projects related to TN-NTN integration, there is a lack of an architectural framework that deals with efficient smart management of the numerous resources of the highly heterogeneous and dynamic 3-Dimensional (3D) network to support diverse foreseen use cases in an automated, "zero-touch" way. Also, the proposed solutions have not provided adequate schemes to robustly meet the QoS requirements for constrained avionic communications and networking. ETHER (sElf-evolving terrestrial/non-Terrestrial Hybrid nEtwoRks) aspires to close this gap and provide a complete roadmap for a multilayered 3D flexible and sustainable unified Radio Access Network (RAN) architecture that leverages proposed essential air interface technical innovations and manages its resources in an automated way via data-driven methods. To achieve that, the project relies on the following pillars:

I. Unified RAN advancements that enable broadband connectivity from every corner of the world, even with handheld devices and in challenging frequency bands, such as the Ka band;

II. Intelligent management of the 3D network resources for meeting predefined KPIs, allowing the network to self-adapt to rapidly evolving traffic conditions and situations on the ground without human intervention;

III. A distributed 3D computing and caching continuum enabling the reduction of response delays by alleviating congestions towards cloud data center.

ETHER will address the pillars above by targeting the following objectives:

1. Provide solutions for a unified and sustainable RAN for the integrated TN and NTN (Pillar I) – direct access of user devices (particularly handheld ones, e.g., smartphones), from aerial and space platforms, like HAPS and LEO satellites, in mmWave bands, *i.e.*, the Ka band; development of a unified waveform for the hybrid TN/NTN continuum; development of seamless horizontal/vertical handover procedures between the same and different Radio Access Technologies (RATs) without any service disruption, while targeting high energy efficiency.

2. Provide an AI-based framework for the self-evolving network slicing management and orchestration of the integrated network and the onboarded services, automatically adjusting its management policies and allocated resources based on *stimuli* corresponding to unknown environments and situations (Pillar II) – full, zero-touch, predictive analytics learning-based automation of the integrated 3-layer network resources under highly dynamic and complex conditions.

3. Architect a viable, highly energy- and cost-efficient, flexible integrated TN/NTN 6G network offering seamless and continuous connectivity (Pillars I, II, and III) – flexible and scalable multi-layered architecture relying on flexible payloads (connectivity, compute, and storage resources) on board NTN platforms, employing an SDN cross-layer distributed controller placement-based approach, for intelligent network management and orchestration.

4. Demonstrate the effectiveness of ETHER solutions by experimentation activities targeting practical applications (Pillars I, II, and III) – showcasing the technical innovations of ETHER, relevant to key use cases arising from societal needs, through in-lab emulations.

5. Identify the key benefits that will drive the investment in the integration of NTNs with TNs (Pillars I, II, and III) – driving forces behind involvement and investments towards the integration of NTNs into existing TNs on the grounds of reduced costs and revenue opportunities.

2 ETHER Architecture Overview and Technological Enablers

2.1 ETHER Architecture

The ETHER system architecture is presented in Fig. 1. The heterogenous 3D architecture is composed of terrestrial, aerial, and satellite access layers integrated with a common 5GS Core Network (CN) [23]. To provide End-to-End (E2E) control and automation of network and service management, which extends to all network domains – from the radio access through transport to the CN, the hierarchical ETHER Management and Orchestration (MAN is envisioned. The domain MANOs will expose standardised functionalities through Application Programming Interfaces (APIs) covering domain complexities, namely the satellite ones (especially in complex multi-orbit, multi-system networks). The integrated terrestrial/aerial/space orchestrator, ETHER MANO, capable of interfacing the 5GS CN, will enable a single telecom network to make use of both TN and NTN assets in an optimal and seamless manner. Regarding service orchestration, the envisioned framework will integrate and extend existing advanced edge orchestration platforms for cloud-native service life cycle management, introducing novel interfaces, features and functionalities to efficiently exploit the mix of cloud/edge computational capabilities offered by the ETHER infrastructure. In addition, one of the main goals of ETHER is to design an edge platform—based on open-source solutions. This will enable the Edge-for-AI concept, *i.e.*, the execution of AI/optimisation algorithms in a closed-loop.

ETHER envisions a cross-domain SDN architecture with distributed SDN controllers across all three layers. In particular, due to the challenging conditions and limited capabilities in fast-moving platforms such as LEOs and drones, the placement of distributed controllers is considered in GEOs and HAPSs, and the coordination of the rest of the components of each layer through them or the terrestrial domain. ETHER also adopts the communication network softwarisation based on NFV to allow efficient and flexible provisioning of services and network on demand. Given that satellite networks use different dedicated hardware, adopting the NFV concept in the satellite layer will enable better support of beyond 5G and 6G requirements as well as seamless integration with TN via the use of standard 3GPP network interfaces in the satellite network. Through the proliferation of softwarised 3GPP TN functional solutions in the commodity hardware-based NTN domains, the deployment of satellite systems and their components will be faster and more cost-efficient.

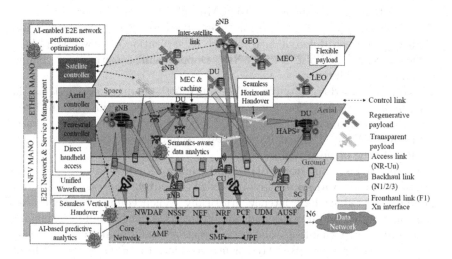

Fig. 1. High-level 3D multi-layered ETHER architecture.

2.2   Technological Enablers

To realise the vision of a 3D unified TN-NTN, several enabling technologies are essential [24–27]. ETHER targets the following innovations (*cf.* Fig. 1):

1. **Integrated architecture** composed of terrestrial, aerial (HAPSs, drones), and satellite (LEO, MEO, and GEO) access layers integrated with a common CN, with distributed SDN-based transport and storage/compute capabilities in each layer. Virtualisation- and softwarisation-based architecture is expected to provide network reconfiguration flexibility (flexible NTN nodes payload) to accommodate the changing service demand. The unified, multi-layered RAN will provide seamless handovers to support service continuity. The distributed

computing and storage capabilities will enable the ETHER nodes to pre-process and store large sets of information for elastic delay-tolerant services, which contribute to latency reduction below 5 ms.

2. **Direct handheld terminal access in the Ka band from LEO satellites** enabled by integrated antennas instead of external 20–50 cm square flat panels, and distributed beamforming from LEO swarms. In the case of antennas integrated with UE, the compact phase array antennas (compatible with the size constraints of handheld devices, able to target satellites' trajectory through electrical beamsteering, and providing the gain for sufficient radio link budget) will be designed and fabricated. The link budget will be further enhanced through distributed beamforming from a virtual large array of multiple LEO satellites.

3. **Uniform waveform design for high channel impairment robustness** to provide context-aware waveform adaptation. For different communication scenarios, an Machine Learning (ML)-based decision on whether to apply either Orthogonal Frequency-Division Multiplexing (OFDM) or Orthogonal Time Frequency Space (OTFS) multiplexing scheme will be used, including trade-offs between different factors, such as saturation of power amplifiers, sufficient Signal to Noise Ratio (SNR), Doppler shift sensitivity, or channel estimation complexity.

4. **Flexible payloads** of satellite nodes, which is the ability to orchestrate the satellite hosts resources for proper service provisioning. To this end, the interface between orchestration systems and satellite payloads should be defined, exploiting Software-Defined Radio (SDR) technology for free adaptation of payload to the orchestrated service.

5. **Data analytics, edge computing and caching for low-latency energy-efficient aerial and space layers** – edge computing and caching have the potential to reduce E2E latency drastically. When equipped with processing capabilities, aerial nodes and satellites can take the communication and networking functionalities from ground stations and eliminate unnecessary round-trip control signals delays, hence reducing the E2E delays. Utilising the semantics of information [28, 29] in NTNs combined with edge computing and caching will further increase the efficiency and reduce the E2E latency without affecting the amount of conveyed information. The development of caching schemes and cooperative computing techniques will be enabled.

6. **Horizontal/vertical handovers** – efficient handovers, inter-layer and intra-layer, respectively, are crucial for seamless connection continuity. While 5GS supports two basic mechanisms – with and without control by CN [30], the project will balance a variety of handover criteria in hybrid TNs/NTNs, leveraging the process autonomy with AI-based algorithms, in order to consider proactively the E2E context and network evolution over time (including latency, rate, traffic, satellites trajectory) as well as minimisation of handovers-related energy consumption.

7. **Automated MANO for the integrated network** – resource-constrained and highly changing satellite systems are capable of serving a large number of heterogeneous users in a single coverage area. Integration of current operational MANO technologies, designed for TN, with NTN infrastructure, remains a technological challenge. Dynamic and constant path reconfiguration becomes crucial for connection sustainability. The project will advance the following aspects: unified management and orchestrator framework for satellite systems and aerial platforms (able to manage satellite mobility and its intermittent connectivity with ground systems) and AI-based adaptive resource orchestration optimisation mechanism for service provisioning (able to cope with the diverse latency, computing and operational requirements of TN and NTN UE access).

8. **E2E integrated TN and NTN performance optimisation** – contemporary communication networks evolve towards "networks of networks" with constantly growing complexity, thus making the E2E performance optimisation of such a complex network a challenging task. Integration of NTNs imposes the additional challenges and constraints associated with the components belonging to the aerial and space layers for performance optimisation of communication, computation, and storage resources. Particularly, the project will focus on low-complexity algorithms for energy-efficient user association, traffic routing, Virtual Network Function (VNF) placement and caching, with regard to the constraints imposed by terrestrial/aerial/space layers and required QoS. In addition, the project will elaborate the efficient predictive analytics for E2E service-level network optimisation through algorithms that target capacity prediction needed for demands of specific applications and ensure QoS guarantees.

3   Demos of ETHER Architecture and Technologies

To prove the effectiveness of the ETHER vision, three use cases showcasing the capabilities of the developed system mechanisms and related enablers will be demonstrated. The planned tests involve the aspects of delay-tolerant IoT communication (Sect. 3.1), unified RAN access for handheld UEs (Sect. 3.2) and air-space safety-critical operations (Sect. 3.3). All of the above-mentioned subjects align with the 3GPP study documents related to NTN use cases.

3.1   UC1: Horizontal Handovers for Delay-Tolerant IoT Applications

Important future applications will require global connectivity even in distant rural and offshore areas. In such areas, a significant part of UEs will be dedicated to typical Massive Machine Type Communications (mMTC) applications exploiting Narrow Band IoT (NB-IoT) technology. Such delay-tolerant applications can be efficiently deployed using LEO satellites and be supported by regenerative and flexible payloads offering diverse services at different points in time. Nonetheless, two major issues should be tackled: service link discontinuity due to the low density of LEO constellations and a limited number of available feeder links between satellites and the ground, which necessitates the implementation of regenerative payload architecture, and a store-and-forward mechanism for both User Plane (UP) and Control Plane (CP). Therefore, it is essential to provide solutions such as discontinuous NB-IoT backhauling, standard 3GPP interfaces for service providers to use the same LEO constellations and mobility management mechanisms. This use case aims to demonstrate the provisioning of the NB-IoT service by a low-density constellation of LEO satellites. Due to the constant satellite constellation changes, efficient horizontal handovers (*cf.* Fig. 2) are crucial. Service continuity is planned to be maintained by the ground NFV MANO that will coordinate the ETHER flexible payload among the satellites to provide the correct services to the UEs on time (perform activation/deactivation of services, status and context exchange between the satellites, *etc.*). Two other IoT services will also be deployed in parallel to prove the ability of the developed flexible payload solution to autonomously manage software-based payloads and propagate their status among the satellites. Such capability enables the provisioning of global connectivity, ultimately contributing to the reduction of vendor and technology lock-in as well as market growth.

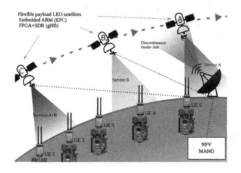

Fig. 2. Horizontal handovers for latency-tolerant IoT services.

3.2 UC2: ETHER Unified RAN for Direct Handheld Device Access in the Ka Band

The currently used sub-6 GHz bands are envisioned to be supplemented by mmWave ones, offering much larger bandwidths but more susceptible to blockages. Deployment of 100% mmWave broadband coverage with TN is not economically feasible, so the coverage by both TN and NTN platforms will be used with necessary UE handovers to provide service continuity.

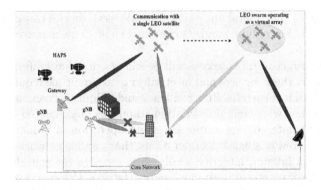

Fig. 3. Overview of unified RAN demonstration.

The primary objective of this use case is to demonstrate TN to NTN handover operation triggered by the intelligent algorithms maximising energy efficiency under the constraints of time, availability, power, capacity and flow conservation aspects. In this scenario (*cf.* Fig. 3), the handheld UE connected to TN moves towards the area with poor TN coverage. Based on the coverage measurement data reported by UE (TN and NTN platforms), the ETHER algorithms will trigger the handover operation and, in the case of NTN connection, select OFDM or OTFS modulation depending on the Doppler spread and its impact on performance. The ability to access the Ka band by the handheld UEs directly will massively contribute to the ubiquitous access to broadband communication for terrestrial users, even in distant rural areas.

3.3 UC3: ETHER Architecture Demonstration for Air-Space Safety-Critical Operations

One of the key aspects of the integration of TN and NTN networks is conformance with the emerging aviation and space standardisation proposed, *e.g.*, by EUROCONTROL or European Union Aviation Safety Agency (EASA). The specific domain needs will imply diverse requirements related to mobi-

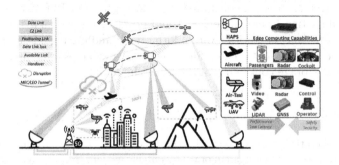

Fig. 4. Air-space safety-critical application within ETHER framework.

lity management (horizontal and vertical handovers), service continuity maintenance (transmission redundancy), QoS enforcement, fault management, service
performance, *etc.*

The main target of this use case will be safety-critical aircraft operations. In
order to support these services and meet safety goals, multiple requirements have
to be met, which involve reliability, resiliency and ubiquity of communication system, conformance with emerging aviation standards, *e.g.*, related to Air Traffic
Services (ATS) data communications, remote operation of unmanned aircraft,
future reduced crew or single pilot operations, that provide network-specific KPIs
(communication latency, integrity, availability, *etc.*). In the considered scenario
(*cf.* Fig. 4), one or several aircraft move across the area with coverage provided by
TN and LEO satellites. Therefore, multilink features and handover procedures
(both horizontal and vertical) leveraging unified waveform and access technology
will be exploited. Additionally, a smart multi-link capability will be deployed in
the network layer to manage dissimilar data links and ensure service performance maintenance. The evaluation of the ETHER solutions will be supported
by the MEC framework capabilities to deploy aviation-domain applications supporting safety-critical aircraft operations, and then assist with the collection of
KPIs vital for pertaining service-continuity (latency, backhaul performance, data
synchronisation, application mobility across the network, *etc.*). The trialled enablers are expected to contribute to the safety of aircraft operations and mitigate
potential risks such as human injuries or property/environmental damage.

4   Conclusions

In this paper, the ETHER project was presented, which targets an integrated 3D
architecture consisting of the terrestrial, aerial, and space layers. Its objectives
were discussed together with main ETHER technology enablers. In addition, the
three use cases targeted by the project were analysed. Key technological enablers
include the design of a user antenna for direct handheld access, the design of
a robust unified waveform for the integrated network, seamless energy-efficient
horizontal and vertical handovers, a zero-touch network/service management and
orchestration framework to automatically adapt to rapidly varying traffic load
conditions, a flexible payload system to enable programmability in the aerial
and space layers, resource allocation solutions targeting at E2E network performance optimisation leveraging efficient and novel predictive analytics schemes,
and energy-efficient semantics-aware information handling techniques combined
with edge computing and caching for reduced latency across the distributed 3D
compute and storage continuum of the 3D architecture.

References

1. Next Generation Mobile Networks (NGMN) Alliance: 6G Drivers and Vision
(Apr 2021). https://www.ngmn.org/wp-content/uploads/NGMN-6G-Drivers-and-
Vision-V1.0_final.pdf. Accessed 22 May 2023

2. Guidotti, A., Vanelli-Coralli, A., Schena, V., Chuberre, N., Jaafari, M.E., Puttonen, J., et al.: The path to 5G-Advanced and 6G Non-Terrestrial Network systems. arXiv (Sep 2022). 10.48550/ARXIV.2209.11535

3. 3GPP: Study on using Satellite Access in 5G; Stage 1. Technical Report TR 22.822, ver. 16.0.0, 3rd Generation Partnership Project (Jun 2018)

4. 3GPP: Service requirements for the 5G system; Stage 1. Technical Standard TS 22.261, ver. 19.2.0, 3rd Generation Partnership Project (Mar 2023)

5. 3GPP: Study on New Radio (NR) to support non-terrestrial networks. Technical Report TR 38.811, ver. 15.4.0, 3rd Generation Partnership Project (Sep 2020)

6. 3GPP: Solutions for NR to support non-terrestrial networks (NTN). Technical Report TR 38.821, ver. 16.2.0, 3rd Generation Partnership Project (Apr 2023)

7. 3GPP: Unmanned Aerial System (UAS) support in 3GPP. Technical Standard TS 22.125, ver. 17.6.0, 3rd Generation Partnership Project (Apr 2022)

8. 3GPP: Study on satellite access - Phase 3. Technical Report TR 22.865, ver. 1.0.0, 3rd Generation Partnership Project (Mar 2023)

9. Cui, H., Zhang, J., Geng, Y., Xiao, Z., Sun, T., Zhang, N., et al.: Space-air-ground integrated network (SAGIN) for 6G: Requirements, architecture and challenges. China Communications 19(2), 90–108 (Feb 2022). 10.23919/JCC.2022.02.008

10. Li, S., Chen, Q., Meng, W., Li, C.: Civil aircraft assisted space-air-ground integrated networks: An innovative NTN of 5G and beyond. IEEE Wirel. Commun. **29**(4), 64–71 (2022). 10.1109/MWC.204.2100207

11. Giordani, M., Zorzi, M.: Non-terrestrial networks in the 6G era: challenges and opportunities. IEEE Network **35**(2), 244–251 (2021). 10.1109/mnet.011.2000493

12. Ma, T., Qian, B., Qin, X., Liu, X., Zhou, H., Zhao, L.: Satellite-terrestrial integrated 6G: An ultra-dense LEO networking management architecture. IEEE Wirel. Commun., 1–8 (Dec 2022). 10.48550/10.1109/MWC.011.2200198

13. Barritt, B., Eddy, W.: Service management & orchestration of 5G and 6G non-terrestrial networks. In: 2022 IEEE Aerospace Conference (AERO), pp. 1–11 (Mar 2022). 10.1109/AERO53065.2022.9843390

14. Barritt, B., Eddy, W.: Temporospatial SDN for aerospace communications. In: AIAA SPACE 2015 (Aug 2015). 10.2514/6.2015-4656

15. 5G-ALLSTAR: 5G AgiLe and fLexible integration of SaTellite And cellulaR. [Website]. https://5g-allstar.eu. Accessed 22 May 2023

16. SaT5G: ST Engineering iDirect and Avanti Communications Play Integral Roles in Successful Integration of 5G Core Network into Live Satellite Network. [Website]. https://www.idirect.net/news/sat5g-st-engineering-idirect-and-avanti-communications-play-integral-roles-in-successful-integration-of-5g-core-network-into-live-satellite-network/. Accessed 22 May 2023

17. Hexa-X II: A Holistic Flagship Towards The 6G Network Platform And System, To Inspire Digital Transformation, For The World To Act Together In Meeting Needs In Society And Ecosystems With Novel 6G Services. [Website]. https://hexa-x-ii.eu. Accessed 22 May 2023

18. 5G-STARDUST: Satellite and Terrestrial Access for Distributed, Ubiquitous, and Smart Telecommunications. [Website] https://www.5g-stardust.eu. Accessed 22 May 2023

19. 6G Non-Terrestrial Networks. [Website]. https://www.6g-ntn.eu. Accessed 22 May 2023

20. TRANTOR: 5G+ evoluTion to mutioRbitAl multibaNd neTwORks. [Website]. https://www.trantor-he.eu/. Accessed 22 May 2023

21. 5G-GOA: 5G-enabled Ground segment technologies Over the Air demonstrator. [Website]. https://artes.esa.int/projects/5ggoa. Accessed 22 May 2023

22. 5G-LEO: OpenAirInterface^TM extension for 5G satellite links. [Website]. https:// artes.esa.int/projects/5gleo. Accessed 22 May 2023

23. 3GPP: System architecture for the 5G System (5GS). Technical Standard TS 23.501, ver. 18.1.0, 3rd Generation Partnership Project (Apr 2023)

24. Al-Hraishawi, H., Chougrani, H., Kisseleff, S., Lagunas, E., Chatzinotas, S.: A survey on nongeostationary satellite systems: the communication perspective. IEEE Commun. Surv. Tutorials 25(1), 101–132 (1st quarter 2023). 10.1109/COMST.2022.3197695

25. Azari, M.M., Solanki, S., Chatzinotas, S., Kodheli, O., Sallouha, H., Colpaert, A., et al.: Evolution of non-terrestrial networks from 5G to 6G: A survey. IEEE Commun. Surv. Tutorials 24(4), 2633–2672 (4th quarter 2022). 10.1109/COMST.2022.3199901

26. Marrero, L.M., Merlano-Duncan, J.C., Querol, J., Kumar, S., Krivochiza, J., Sharma, S.K., et al.: Architectures and synchronization techniques for distributed satellite systems: a survey. IEEE Access 10, 45375–45409 (2022). 10.1109/ACCESS.2022.3169499

27. Kodheli, O., Lagunas, E., Maturo, N., Sharma, S.K., Shankar, B., Montoya, J.F.M., et al.: Satellite communications in the new space era: A survey and future challenges. IEEE Communications Surveys & Tutorials 23(1), 70–109 (Oct 2021), doi: 10.1109/COMST.2020.3028247

28. Kountouris, M., Pappas, N.: Semantics-empowered communication for networked intelligent systems. IEEE Communications Magazine 59(6), 96–102 (Jun 2021), doi: 10.1109/MCOM.001.2000604

29. Pappas, N., Abd-Elmagid, M., Zhou, B., Saad, W., Dhillon, H.: Age of Information: Foundations and Applications. Cambridge University Press (Feb 2023), doi: 10.1017/9781108943321

30. 3GPP: Procedures for the 5G System (5GS); Stage 2. Technical Standard TS 23.502, ver. 18.1.1, 3rd Generation Partnership Project (Apr 2023)

Fetal ECG Extraction Based on Overcomplete ICA and Empirical Wavelet Transform

Theodoros Lampros[1]([✉]), Nikolaos Giannakeas[1], Konstantinos Kalafatakis[1], Markos Tsipouras[2], and Alexandros Tzallas[1]

[1] Deparment of Informatics and Telecommunication, University of Ioannina, Arta, Greece
{grgiannakeas,k.kalafatakis,tzallas}@uoi.gr
[2] Deparment of Electrical and Computer Engineering, University of Western Macedonia, Kozani, Greece
mtsipouras@uowm.gr

Abstract. Continuous fetal heart monitoring during pregnancy can be crucial in detecting and preventing many pathological conditions related to fetal heart development. In particular, because of its potential to provide prenatal diagnostic information, the noninvasive fetal electrocardiogram (NI-fECG) has become the focus of several recent studies. Due to its higher temporal frequency and spatial resolution, NI-fECG makes possible the "beat-to-beat" monitoring of the Fetal Heart Rate (FHR) and allows for a deeper characterization of the electrophysiological activity (i.e. electrical conduction of the heart) through morphological analysis of the fetal waveform. However, acquisition of the fetal ECG from maternal abdominal recordings remains an open problem, mainly due to the interference of the much stronger maternal ECG. This paper proposes a novel hybrid method for accurate fetal ECG extraction based on Reconstruction Independent Component Analysis (R-ICA) and Empirical Wavelet Transform (EWT) enhancement. The RICA-EWT method was tested on of real signals acquired from pregnant women in different stages of labour. The results indicate its robustness and efficiency in different SNR levels.

Keywords: Fetal ECG extraction · Reconstruction ICA · Empirical Wavelet Transform · Fast Fourier Transform · Wavelet Thresholding

1 Introduction

Non-invasive fetal electrocardiography (NI-FECG) uses electrodes placed on the mother's abdomen to detect and record the electrical activity of the fetal heart. This technique can provide information about the fetal heart rate, rhythm, and overall cardiac health without requiring invasive procedures. NI-FECG is a relatively safe and non-invasive technique that poses no significant risk to the mother or fetus. It can be performed at any stage of pregnancy and is often used to monitor the fetal heart rate during labour and delivery and assess fetal well-being in high-risk pregnancies.

© IFIP International Federation for Information Processing 2023
Published by Springer Nature Switzerland AG 2023
I. Maglogiannis et al. (Eds.): AIAI 2023 Workshops, IFIP AICT 677, pp. 45–54, 2023.
https://doi.org/10.1007/978-3-031-34171-7_3

The extraction of a non-invasive fetal electrocardiogram (NI-FECG) involves the processing and analysis of the electrical signals recorded by the electrodes placed on the mother's abdomen. There are various algorithms used for NI-FECG extraction. Template Subtraction [1], Blind Source separation (BSS) [2], Adaptive Filtering [3], and Artificial Neural Networks [4] have been proposed in the literature. To denoise and enhance the extracted fetal ECG, some of the most common approaches are Empirical Mode Decomposition (EMD) [5], Wavelet-Based denoising (WD) [6], and Extended Kalman Smoothing (EKS) [7]. Hybrid algorithms [8, 9] combine multiple methods to improve the accuracy and reliability of the extracted features.

One of the most popular algorithms for fetal ECG extraction is Independent Component Analysis (ICA). However, ICA enforces a hard orthonormality constraint on the data, which makes it difficult to learn overcomplete features. In addition, ICA is sensitive to whitening. In the case of multichannel, nonstationary, and nonlinear signals such as abdominal ECG recordings, these properties make it challenging to scale ICA to high-dimensional data. Overcomplete ICA refers to using more basis functions than inputs to represent a signal. This approach can be useful in cases where the signal is complex or has a high degree of variability. By using more basis functions than inputs, an overcomplete representation can capture more detailed features and variations in the signal, which can be beneficial for fetal ECG extraction.

The Empirical Wavelet Transform (EWT) [10] is a signal processing technique that decomposes a signal into a set of localized oscillatory components. It is a data-driven approach that does not rely on predefined basis functions but instead adapts to the local features of the signal. The EWT is based on the Hilbert transform, a mathematical operation that allows for the extraction of the amplitude and phase components of a signal. The EWT works by iteratively filtering the signal into a set of bands, using the Hilbert transform to extract the amplitude and phase components, and applying a local frequency estimation to obtain a set of oscillatory components.

This work focuses on providing a robust system for extracting the NI-FECG from abdominal recordings and estimating the Fetal Heart Rate (FHR). For this reason, we employ a modified version of ICA called Reconstruction ICA (R-ICA) [11] to extract overcomplete representations of multichannel abdominal recordings, signal Quality Indices to verify the quality of the extracted fetal component and denoising and enhancement using the Empirical Wavelet Transform (EWT).

2 Materials and Methods

The proposed methodology consists of two distinct processing pipelines. For the fetal ECG extraction stage, the abdominal signal, which consists of four channels, is separated in overcomplete modes, i.e., five, six, and seven Independent Components using R-ICA. Fetal-specific signal Quality Indices evaluate the fetal components in each mode, and the best raw fetal ECG is selected for further processing. In the denoising stage, the short-time Fourier transform (STFT) represents the frequency content of the ex-tracted fECG; then the EWT decomposes the signal into Intrinsic Mode Functions (IMF) and undesired artifacts, such as baseline wander, and high-frequency noise is removed. Figure 1 (a) and (b) illustrate the proposed method.

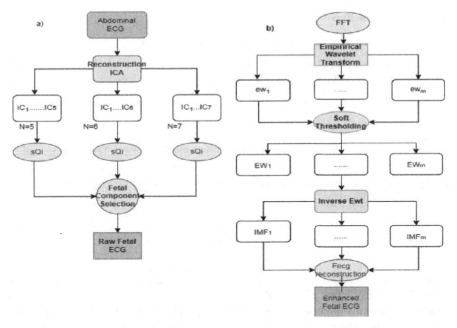

Fig. 1. (a) Fetal ECG extraction, (b) Fetal ECG denoising

2.1 Dataset

To evaluate the performance of our algorithms, we used set A of Physionet Challenge 2013 (Fig. 2) [12]. The data consist of a collection of 74 one-minute, four-channel non-invasive FECGs sampled at 1 kHz, obtained from multiple sources using a variety of instrumentation with differing frequency response, resolution, and configuration. The length of the individual signals is 1 min with a sampling frequency of 1 kHz and a resolution of 12 bits. Set A consists of reference annotations validated by experts and indicates the positions of the individual R-peaks. A total of 38 recordings from the dataset were used for this study.

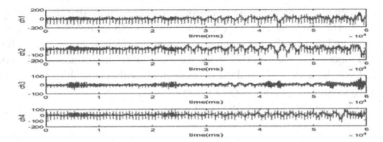

Fig. 2. Example of records in the Challenge Dataset (record a014).

2.2 FECG Extraction

The standard ICA optimization problem can be formulated as

$$min \sum_{i=1}^{M} \sum_{j=1}^{K} g(W_J x^i) \tag{1}$$

$$\text{Subject to} WWT = I, \tag{2}$$

where W is the weight matrix and g is a nonlinear convex function. The orthonormality constraint in Eq. 2 makes ICA difficult to learn overcomplete representations of data. Reconstruction ICA replaces the hard orthonormality criterion with a soft reconstruction cost, as shown in Eq. 3

$$min \frac{1}{m} \sum_{i-1}^{M} W^T W x^i + \lambda \sum_{i=1}^{M} \sum_{j=1}^{K} g(W_J x^i) \tag{3}$$

where λ is a scaling constant, which can determine the relative importance of two terms above. This reconstruction penalty, allows the algorithm to learn sparse representations on the data without whitening, when W is overcomplete. In this work we used the R-ICA algorithm to separate the 4-channel abdominal mixture into 5, 6 and 7 Independent Components. We did not extract a larger number of components as we observed that increasing the number of components to more than seven caused redundancy in our extracted data. Figure 3 shows an example of our extraction approach.

2.2.1 Signal Quality Indices

To select the best IC corresponding to the fetal ECG and assess the separation algorithm's accuracy, we used specific signal Quality Indices presented below.

- Approximate entropy (AppEn): AppEn is a common-use feature for quantifying irregularity in time series data with no knowledge about the system. Larger values correspond to more complexity and irregularity in the data.
- Spectral entropy: Spectral entropy, based on Shannon entropy, can quantify the regularity or uncertainty of the power spectrum during a specific period. Higher irregularity in Spectral entropy indicates a more uniform power spectrum distribution (Fig. 4).
- bSQi [12]: The bSQi index uses the detection of QRS complexes by 2 detection algorithms and detects the percentage of common strokes in algorithms. The QRS detection algorithms used on this work are the Pan-Tompkins algorithm, modified for fetal QRS detection [14], and the maxsearch algorithm available in Open-Source Electrophysiological Toolbox (OSET) [15].
- kSQi: fourth moment (kurtosis) of signal.

2.3 FECG Denoising

The fECG component obtained by the R- ICA method is not completely noise-free. It still contains several types of noise, such as electrode artifacts, baseline wander, and other

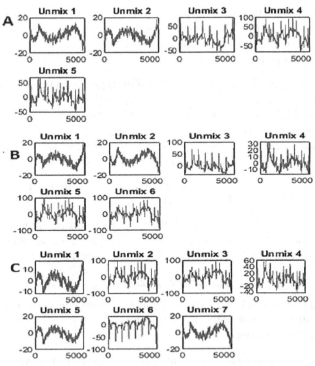

Fig. 3. Results of the R-ICA algorithm. The 4-channel abdominal signal is separated into A = 5, B = 6, and C = 7 extracted components. This is shown to better represent the fetal component of interest.However, increasing the number of extracted features can result in producing redundant signals.

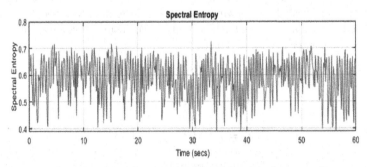

Fig. 4. Spectral Entropy (SE) from an extracted fetalECG can be interpreted as a measurement of the time uncertainty in frequency domain. In the power spectrum of EEG signals, when the spectrum peak is narrow, its entropy value is small. It indicates that the signal has an obvious concussive rhythm.A more uniform distribution of spectral entropy in the frequency domain indicates a higher quality fetal signal.

high frequency noise that can be attributed to maternal ECG interference. To remove such artifacts that can affect FHR estimation, we used the Empirical Wavelet Transform (EWT) combined with a soft thresholding function. The steps of our proposed demising algorithm are described below.

1 Compute the Fast Fourier Transform (FFT) of the input signal to obtain its frequency spectrum
2 Segment the FFT spectrum by finding all the local maxima and obtaining the segmentation boundaries according to their distance
3 Construct adaptive wavelet filter banks according to the detected boundaries
4 Threshold the empirical wavelets according to the soft thresholding function [16]

$$\hat{C}_i(t) = \left\{ \begin{array}{c} sign((c_i(t))[|c_i(t)| - \lambda], \ |c_i(t)| \geq \lambda \\ 0, , \ |c_i(t)| < \lambda \end{array} \right\} \tag{4}$$

where i and t are positive integers, $c_i(t)$, is the component obtained after decomposition, $\hat{C}_i(t)$ is the de1noised version of $c_i(t)$, λ is the threshold corresponding to $c_i(t)$, and $sign()$ is the sign function. The threshold λ is calculated as [17]:

$$\lambda = b\sigma_i \sqrt{2lnN} \tag{5}$$

5 Perform the Inverse EWT to compute the Intrinsic Mode Functions (IMF'S).
6 Select the IMF's that contain the useful signal information.
7 Reconstruct the input signal.

In this work, we decomposed the input fetal ECG into 10 IMF's. An example of the denoising process is presented in Fig. 5.

3 Results

R-peak detection was performed using the JQRS detector [14], with the following parameters: 0.5 detector threshold, 1.5-s window size, 150-ms refractory period. We evaluated our proposed methodology using the Sensitivity (SE), Positive Predictive Value (PPV), Accuracy (ACC), and F1 score (F1) metrics:

$$SE = TP/(TP + FN). \tag{6}$$

$$PPV = TP/(TP + FP). \tag{7}$$

$$ACC = TP/(TP + FP + FN). \tag{8}$$

$$F1 = (2*SE*PPV)/(SE + PPV). \tag{9}$$

Where TP stands for True Positive, FP for False Positive and FN for False Negative. The results are shown in Table 1.

We also compared our results with our previous work [19] and recent works published in the same Dataset. To test our previously presented algorithm, we used the same metrics and QRS detector parameters as in this work for consistency. We can see from Table 2 that our proposed system offers an improvement from our previous work and other recent works that were tested on the Challenge Dataset.

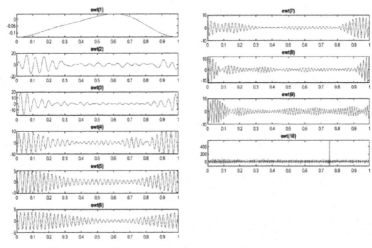

Fig. 5. Empirical Wavelets produced from EWT. The first IMF represents the signal baseline wander, while IMF's 2 to 9 are wave harmonics related to Power Line Interferences. Finally, most of the signal information is contained in IMF 10.

Table 1. Results of our method in the Challenge Dataset. 38 one minute recordings from the dataset were included in this study. The variable Q stands for the number of extracted components from the abdominal mixture in which the fetal ECG was more accurately represented. SNR levels range from -2 to -18 dB, indicating various noise levels in the input signals.

RECORD	Q	ACC(%)	F1(%)	PPV(%)	SE(%)	SNR
a01	5	98.62	99.31	100.00	98.62	−11.28
a02	6	78.75	88.11	100	78.75	−17.94
a03	6	78.91	88.21	100	78.91	−12.28
a04	5	93.08	96.41	99.18	93.80	−9.57
a05	6	84.38	91.53	100.00	84.38	−10.66
a06	6	98.45	99.22	100.00	98.45	−9.76
a07	5	85.23	92.03	86.99	97.69	−12.28
a08	6	92.75	96.24	92.75	100.00	−14.39
a09	6	77.40	87.26	87.60	86.92	−18.12
a010	6	96.05	97.98	98.84	97.14	−10.41
a011	7	73.79	84.92	95.54	76.43	−17.35
a012	5	80.28	89.06	96.61	82.61	−11.61
a013	6	78.18	87.76	82.69	93.48	−10.63
a014	6	81.68	89.92	95.54	84.92	−0.15
a015	7	82.11	90.18	100	82.11	−9.82
a016	6	97.01	98.48	100	97.01	−11.74
a017	7	71.92	83.67	86.78	80.77	−13.19
a018	6	86.57	92.80	98.31	87.88	−2.69

(continued)

Table 1. (*continued*)

RECORD	Q	ACC(%)	F1(%)	PPV(%)	SE(%)	SNR
a019	5	72.73	84.21	96.55	74.67	−18.66
a020	7	81.38	89.73	86.76	92.91	−7.61
a021	5	78.99	88.26	93.97	83.21	−2.90
a022	6	94.56	97.20	98.58	95.86	−12.79
a023	6	79.10	88.33	92.98	84.13	−3.06
a024	6	80.30	89.08	92.17	86.18	−8.11
a025	5	80.00	88.89	91.53	86.40	−2.31
a026	5	81.08	89.55	92.31	86.96	−5.12
a029	4	72.18	83.84	94.12	75.59	5.65
a032	6	83.54	91.03	91.95	90.13	−11.47
a037	5	97.01	98.48	100	97.01	−13.74
a043	6	84.30	91.48	91.19	91.77	−11.32
a046	6	75.69	86.17	89.34	83.21	−9.88
a055	6	77.42	87.27	90.91	83.92	−2.81
a059	5	93.21	96.49	94.38	98.69	−9.39
a062	6	78.34	87.86	90.44	85.42	−13.28
a064	5	86.93	93.01	88.67	97.79	−7.60
a070	6	76.33	86.58	82.17	91.49	−5.93
a071	7	75.00	85.71	85.71	85.71	−3.81
AVERAGE		83.33	90.71	93.64	88.40	−7.45

Table 2. Comparative Results from other studies tested on the same Dataset. ACC, SE, PPV, and F1 values shown are average values reported for all recordings tested.

Author(s)	ACC (%)	F1(%)	PPV(%)	SE(%)
Panigrahy et al. [20]	84.89	91.82	92.18	91.47
DaPoian et al. [21]	Not reported	77.50	77.00	78.00
Jaros et.al [22]	68.25	75.68	81.31	72.60
Barnova et.al [23]	78.47	84.62	87.90	82.06
Previous work [19]	74.35	84.95	93.16	79.19
This work	83.33	90.71	94.64	88.40

4   Discussion

In this work, we presented a robust automated methodology for accurately extracting the Non-Invasive fetal ECG from multichannel abdominal recordings. We evaluated our system in many signals from different sources with different acquisition protocols and varying Signal to Noise Ratios (SNR). Results show that our method offers several advantages in the fECG extraction and the denoising stage.

As is evident from our presented results, an overcomplete representation of a noisy, nonlinear, and nonstationary signal, such as the abdominal ECG mixture, can lead to a more robust and more precise extraction of the fetal component of interest, even when presented with input data that vary in acquisition protocols and SNR levels. The R-ICA algorithm performed consistently both in low and high SNR scenarios. Furthermore, the EWT algorithm combined with a soft threshold function can represent the extracted fECG component subbands more helpfully than other signal decomposition algorithms, such as the Empirical Mode Decomposition (EMD) or Wavelet De-composition.

While our approach is effective in accurate fetal ECG extraction and FHR estimation, three limitations should be considered in real-world applications. First, in the extraction stage, the optimal number of the overcomplete basis of the input signal needs to be automatically determined to prevent the R-ICA model from overfitting and to produce redundant features. Also, while the EWT algorithm provides an improved signal decomposition, each mode's number of modes and frequency boundaries need to be pre-set. This is always difficult due to a lack of prior knowledge about the analyzed signal. Future work will focus on using machine learning methods to address these issues. Specifically, we plan to implement an Artificial Neural Network (ANN) using our signal Quality indices as predictive features, which will be able to classify the fetal ECG quality in several overcomplete modes of the input mixture and select the optimal level of separation.

Acknowledgements. We acknowledge the support of this work by the project "Immersive Virtual, Augmented and Mixed Reality Center Of Epirus" (MIS 5047221) which is implemented under the Action "Reinforcement of the Research and Innovation Infrastructure", funded by the Operational Programme "Competitiveness, Entrepreneurship and Innovation" (NSRF 2014–2020) and co-financed by Greece and the European Union (European Regional Development Fund).

References

1. Liu, H., Chen, D., Sun, G.: Detection of Fetal ECG R Wave from Single-Lead Abdominal ECG Using a Combination of RR Time-Series Smoothing and Template-Matching Approach. IEEE Access **7**, 66633–66643 (2019)
2. Ghazdali, A., Hakim, A., Laghrib, A., Mamouni, N., Raghay, S.: A new method for the extraction of fetal ECG from the dependent abdominal signals using blind source separation and adaptive noise cancellation techniques. Theoretical Biology and Medical Modelling, 12(1) (2015)
3. Liu, S. J., Liu, D. L., Zhang, J. Q., Zeng, Y. J. Extraction of fetal electrocardiogram using recursive least squares and normalized least mean squares algorithms. 2011 3rd International Conference on Advanced Computer Control (2011).
4. Zhong, W., Liao, L., Guo, X., Wang, G.: A deep learning approach for fetal QRS complex detection. Physiol. Meas. **39**(4), 045004 (2018)
5. Li, H., Wang, X., Chen, L., Li, E.: Denoising and R-Peak Detection of Electrocardiogram Signal Based on EMD and Improved Approximate Envelope. Circuits Syst. Signal Process. **33**(4), 1261–1276 (2013). https://doi.org/10.1007/s00034-013-9691-3
6. Wang, Y., Fu, Y., & He, Z. (2018). Fetal Electrocardiogram Extraction Based on Fast ICA and Wavelet Denoising. 2018 2nd IEEE Advanced Information Management, Communicates, Electronic and Automation Control Conference (IMCEC)

7. PANIGRAHY, D., SAHU, P.K.: Extraction of fetal electrocardiogram (ECG) by extended state Kalman filtering and adaptive neuro-fuzzy inference system (ANFIS) based on single channel abdominal recording. Sadhana **40**(4), 1091–1104 (2015). https://doi.org/10.1007/s12 046-015-0381-7

8. Taha, L.Y., Abdel-Raheem, E.: Fetal ECG Extraction Using Input-Mode and Output-Mode Adaptive Filters With Blind Source Separation. Can. J. Electr. Comput. Eng. **43**(4), 295–304 (2020)

9. Liu, G., Luan, Y.: An adaptive integrated algorithm for noninvasive fetal ECG separation and noise reduction based on ICA-EEMD-WS. Med. Biol. Eng. Compu. **53**(11), 1113–1127 (2015). https://doi.org/10.1007/s11517-015-1389-1

10. Gilles, J.: Empirical Wavelet Transform. IEEE Trans. Signal Process. **61**(16), 3999–4010 (2013)

11. Le, Q.V., Karpenko, A., Ngiam, J., Ng, A.Y.: ICA with Reconstruction Cost for Efficient Overcomplete Feature Learning. Neural Information Processing Systems **24**, 1017–1025 (2011)

12. https://physionet.org/content/challenge-2013/1.0.0/

13. Li, Q.J., Mark, R.G., Clifford, G.D.: Robust heart rate estimation from multiple asynchronous noisy sources using signal quality indices and a Kalman filter. Physiol. Meas. **29**(1), 15–32 (2008)

14. Andreotti, F., Grasser, F., Malberg, H., Zaunseder, S.: Non-invasive Fetal ECG Signal Quality Assessment for Multichannel Heart Rate Estimation. IEEE Trans. Biomed. Eng. **64**(12), 2793–2802 (2017)

15. Sameni, R.: The Open-Source Electrophysiologicall Toolbox (OSET)(2010).

16. Li, C., Xu, F., Yang, H., Zou, L.: A rolling element bearing fault feature extraction method based on the EWT and an arctangent threshold function. J. Mech. Sci. Technol. , 01–16 (2022). https://doi.org/10.1007/s12206-022-0306-4

17. Donoho, D.L.: De-noising by soft-thresholding. IEEE Trans. Inf. Theory **41**(3), 613–627 (1995)

18. Andreotti, F., Behar, J., Zaunseder, S., Oster, J., Clifford, G.D.: An open-source framework for stress-testing non-invasive foetal ECG extraction algorithms. Physiol. Meas. **37**(5), 627–648 (2016)

19. Lampros, T., Kalafatakis, K., Violaris, I. G., Giannakeas, N., Tzallas, A. T., & Tsipouras, M.G.: Fetal Heart Beat detection based on Empirical Mode Decomposition, Signal Quality Indices and Correlation Analysis. Bioinformatics and Bioengineering (2020)

20. Panigrahy, D., Sahu, P.K.: Extraction of fetal ECG signal by an improved method using extended Kalman smoother framework from single channel abdominal ECG signal. Australas. Phys. Eng. Sci. Med. **40**(1), 191–207 (2017). https://doi.org/10.1007/s13246-017-0527-5

21. Da Poian, G., Bernardini, R., Rinaldo, R.: Separation and Analysis of Fetal-ECG Signals From Compressed Sensed Abdominal ECG Recordings. IEEE Trans. Biomed. Eng. **63**(6), 1269–1279 (2016)

22. Jaros, R., Martinek, R., Kahankova, R., Koziorek, J.: Novel Hybrid Extraction Systems for Fetal Heart Rate Variability Monitoring Based on Non-Invasive Fetal Electrocardiogram. IEEE Access **7**, 131758–131784 (2019)

23. Barnova, K., Martinek, R., Jaros, R., Kahankova, R., Behbehani, K., Snasel, V.: System for adaptive extraction of non-invasive fetal electrocardiogram. Appl. Soft Comput. **113**, 107940 (2021)

Implementing Network Applications for 5G-Enabled Robots Through the 5G-ERA Platform

Andreas Gavrielides[1]([✉]) [ID], Marios Sophocleous[1] [ID], Christina C. Lessi[2],
George Agapiou[3] [ID], Jakub Špaňhel[4] [ID], Adrian Lendinez[5], Renxi Qiu[5] [ID],
and Dayou Li[5]

[1] eBOS Technologies Ltd., Arch. Makariou III and Mesaorias 1, 2090 Lakatamia, Nicosia,
Cyprus
andreasg@ebos.com.cy
[2] Hellenic Telecommunications Organization (OTE) S.A., 99, Kifissias Avenue, 15124
Maroussi, Athens, Greece
[3] WINGS ICT Solutions, Nea Smymi, 189, Siggrou Avenue, 17121 Athens, Greece
[4] Faculty of Information Technology, Brno University of Technology, Brno, Czech Republic
[5] School of Computer Science, University of Bedfordshire, Luton, UK

Abstract. Novel orchestration architectures for 5G networks have primarily
focused on enhancing Quality of Service, yet have neglected to address Quality of
Experience concerns. Consequently, these systems struggle with intent recognition
and End-to-End interpretability, resulting in the possibility of suboptimal control
policies being developed. The 5G-ERA project has proposed and demonstrated an
AI-driven intent-based networking solution for autonomous robots to address this
issue. Specifically, the proposed solution employs a workflow consisting of four
tools - Action Sequence Generation, Network Intent Estimation, Resource Usage
Forecasting, and OSM Control Policy Generation - to map an individual vertical
action's intent to a global OSM control policy. The paper describes how the 5G-
ERA platform enables the onboarding and control of 5G-enabled robots and how
we demonstrate the platform's capabilities through the project's use cases.

Keywords: 5G · Intent-based networking · Enhanced robot autonomy ·
5G-ERA · Machine Learning · Semantic models · autonomous robots

1 Introduction

In recent years, 5G technology has gained significant attention from both the scientific
and industrial communities. Its advantages are particularly attractive to various sectors,
including the robotics industry. However, current innovative 5G orchestration architectures have primarily been designed for service delivery [1–3] without vertical-specific
knowledge. These architectures rely on information models to manage the life cycle of
services and resources [3, 4], which are based on the concept of Anaemic Domain Models

© IFIP International Federation for Information Processing 2023
Published by Springer Nature Switzerland AG 2023
I. Maglogiannis et al. (Eds.): AIAI 2023 Workshops, IFIP AICT 677, pp. 55–65, 2023.
https://doi.org/10.1007/978-3-031-34171-7_4

[5] optimized for creating, reading, updating, and deleting (CRUD) services in a procedural style. Consequently, implicit intents of the services are not considered, leading orchestrators to prioritize Quality of Service (QoS) over Quality of Experience (QoE). This results in inherited problems for orchestration systems, such as intent recognition and End-to-End (E2E) interpretability, potentially creating ineffective control policies [6]. While some existing 5G vertical applications have partially addressed this issue by limiting the number of technology stacks, the robotic vertical typically requires components from multiple vendors with various technology stacks. Therefore, a solution that maintains intent recognition and maps user requirements into measurable network KPIs is necessary for 5G experimental facilities involving multiple technology stacks [7–10].

The implementation of intent-based networking (IBN) is becoming increasingly essential for realizing the full potential of 5G-Enhanced Robot Autonomy (5G-ERA). IBN is a network architecture that leverages machine learning algorithms and artificial intelligence to provide automated network management, policy enforcement, and security, among other functions. In the context of 5G-ERA, IBN is utilized to streamline the deployment of Network Applications, which are tailored for specific vertical use cases such as Public Protection and Disaster Relief (PPDR), transport, healthcare, and industry 4.0.

The Intent-based, front-end Dashboard (IBD) is crucial in facilitating the onboarding and utilization of the associated Network Applications. It provides an intuitive interface for users to visualize and manage network resources and configure policies, among other functions. This allows users to easily understand the behaviour of the network, which in turn enables them to make informed decisions regarding the deployment and management of Network Applications.

Moreover, the IBD provides a unified view of the entire network infrastructure, which is crucial for ensuring the seamless integration of the various network components. This includes the middleware, which serves as a platform for hosting the Network Applications, and the edge computing infrastructure, enabling real-time data processing and analysis.

In summary, the paper expands on how the IBD is a critical component of the IBN [11] architecture for 5G-ERA use cases. It facilitates the onboarding and utilization of Network Applications by providing an intuitive interface for managing network resources, monitoring network performance, and configuring policies. By providing a unified view of the entire network infrastructure, it enables users to make informed decisions regarding the deployment and management of Network Applications, thereby maximizing the potential of 5G-ERA.

2   5G-Enabled Autonomous Robots: An Intent-Based Networking Paradigm

The objective of intent-based networking for autonomous robots is to enhance the QoE of 5G orchestrators for vertical applications [12]. In order to achieve optimal experience for individual 5G-based autonomous robots, it is crucial to specify and allocate resources required by the connected intelligence optimally. The intent-based networking technique [13–17] predicts the need for intelligence based on the intents. It specifies policies for individual applications to ensure efficient management, topology, placement, and resource optimization within 5G and cloud environments. Connected intelligence in autonomous use cases requires dynamic and repeated shifting of computing and storage among robots, edges, and the central cloud. To facilitate this process, partial information will be replicated among Network Services (NSs) deployed in different locations.

The challenge of deploying robotic applications at a large scale with robust capabilities to react to real-world scenarios is a persistent issue. The concept of deployable robotics involves enhancing the ability of robots to be deployed effectively in real-world environments. Currently, this ability is constrained by the fragmented nature of robot intelligence and limited scalability. To overcome these limitations, a paradigm of transparent knowledge, connected intelligence, and scalable skills must be formulated. Autonomous operation with the ability to handle unexpected situations is a key characteristic of deployable robotics under this framework.

To tailor NSs under intent-based networking, different configurations of Virtual Network Functions (VNFs) and slices are required [18–20]. The creation of slices, at the level of complexity of the use cases, is still problematic for existing testbeds. 5G experimental facilities must be adapted towards a cloud-native approach for efficient service delivery on enhanced robot autonomy. Meanwhile, intent-based networking also enhances the existing NSs using a cloud-native approach with respect to the scalability, availability and feature velocity of the NSs as expected by autonomous robots. Therefore, the development of intent-based networking fills the gaps between existing 5G product vision and cloud-native deployment required by the robot autonomy enhancement. Overall, the development of intent-based networking for autonomous robots reveals how operational processes of essential robotic capabilities can be integrated into a rich domain model supporting advanced orchestration.

In the 5G-enabled Non-Public Networks (NPNs) context, a middleware implemented through the Platform as a Service (PaaS) paradigm facilitates intent-based networking. This allows for creating customized virtual network platforms for specific vertical applications rather than requiring vertical applications to conform to the network infrastructure. By adopting this approach, the management of network resources can be optimized, leading to an enhanced QoE for users. For instance, this methodology could facilitate 5G-enhanced robot autonomy by enabling the offloading of learning tasks in a multi-domain multi-administration environment.

3   The 5G-ERA Platform as a Network Application Facilitator

The IBD is an important component of the 5G-ERA project, as it enables the use of Semantic & Machine Learning (ML) tools for better network resource management. While each robot vendor may have an existing User Interface (UI) for controlling and communicating with their robots, there is no existing UI for the 5G-ERA's unique ML tool for resource usage prediction based on the user's intent as described by Sophocleous et al. [21].

3.1 Benefits of Intent-Based Networking

The 5G-ERA envisions an intent-based networking dashboard (IBD) that can offer significant benefits to users in effectively managing and optimizing their Network Applications. Our IBD provides users with a user-friendly interface to visualize and control their various Network Applications on the network infrastructure.

One of the main advantages of an intent-based networking dashboard is that it provides users with a single view of their Network Applications, irrespective of the underlying infrastructure. This allows users to manage their Network Applications more efficiently without worrying about the complexities of the infrastructure. For example, they can easily create, delete, or modify Network Applications or adjust the QoS settings for each application without having to deal with the technical details of the network infrastructure.

In addition to the benefits mentioned earlier, an intent-based networking dashboard can offer users several other advantages.

Firstly, it can provide an intuitive and customizable interface that allows users to interact with their Network Applications in a way that makes sense to them. This means that users can quickly and easily access the information that they need without having to navigate through complex menus or interfaces. Furthermore, a customizable interface means that users can tailor the dashboard to their specific needs, which can increase their efficiency and productivity. Secondly, an intent-based networking dashboard can enable users to automate certain tasks related to managing their Network Applications. Thirdly, an intent-based networking dashboard can provide users with insights into how their Network Applications are being used [22]. This can be particularly valuable for organizations with multiple departments or locations using the same network infrastructure. By providing detailed analytics and reporting, an intent-based networking dashboard can help users identify usage patterns, monitor resource utilization, and allocate resources more effectively.

Overall, our IBD will be a valuable tool for users who need to manage and optimize their Network Applications. By providing a user-friendly interface, it can enable users to achieve their business objectives more effectively and efficiently.

3.2 Functionalities Offered by the 5G-ERA Paradigm

The IBD's original design and functionalities were described by Sophocleous et al. [21]. To accommodate the needs of the Network Applications users and developers, we have incorporated a number of additional functionalities described in this section.

The IBD features a grid that provides robot-task information and allows users to view the number of tasks executed by the robot fleet and sort their task status by date. The IBD approach used in 5G-ERA is visualized in Fig. 1. A basic control grid has been implemented for the cloud/edge times in the topology, enabling users to easily view the number of clouds and their current status in terms of activity for supporting the robot fleet.

Through the IBD, users will be informed on what actions are in each action sequence loaded in the knowledge base and visualize the company topology and the action sequences with their respective relationships among robots and tasks. Through the IBD

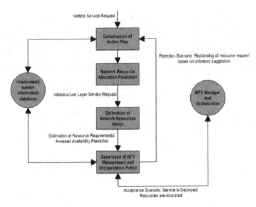

Fig. 1. Workflow of developed tools for intent-based management

and access control implementation, the system administrator can view, delete and modify existing middleware policies. This is necessary to change the way the middleware plans and works.

A critical feature implemented is the ability to onboard models for middleware entities such as robots, edge, clouds, tasks, instances etc. [23], with their relationships. This will allow the system administrator to create and provision new robots, edges etc., into the middleware database.

By implementing a control grid for Network Applications, the user can view the onboarding process and information about the project's Network Applications, as well as the associated Robot Operating System (ROS) version and distribution. This control grid will also provide users with the information they may require, such as the Network Application distribution, what type of application the Network Application can be used for (e.g., perception, navigation) and the Network Application ID (for example, face recognition).

Finally, through implementing a control grid for the robots, users in this section of the IBD have a table that describes the basic control grid for Robots like onboarding, ID, ROS version, and distribution, as well as if the robot is online or offline.

4 5G-ERA Use Cases

As part of the 5G-ERA project [24], pertinent Network Applications will be prototyped for each selected use case [33]. This will confirm the innovative capabilities of the project's experimental facilities and showcase the advancements achieved in 5G-Enhanced Robot Autonomy across various vertical sectors. The project has identified four specific vertical sectors, namely PPDR, transport, healthcare, and industry 4.0, as the focus of its use cases.

4.1 Use Case 1: Public Protection and Disaster Relief (PPDR)

The 5G-ERA project is designing a novel Network Application specifically facilitating autonomous PPDR services in unstructured environments. This use case has been carefully chosen to showcase the technological advancements made possible by 5G communication solutions and demonstrate their potential to serve as gateways between existing legacy technologies and cutting-edge communication solutions.

The primary objective of this use case is to enable close-to-seamless handover and switch capabilities between Edges [25] (i.e., the peripheral network elements) and Mobile Operators. Achieving this objective requires developing robust communication solutions that can seamlessly integrate and switch between different network environments, providing uninterrupted services to the end users. The use case specifications are summarized in Fig. 2.

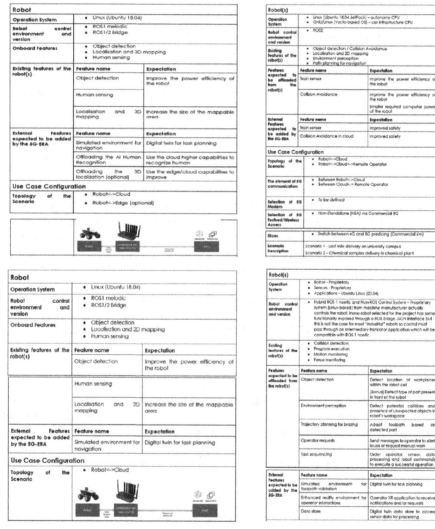

Fig. 2. 5G-ERA Use Cases Specifications: Use Case 1 (upper left side), Use Case 2 (upper right side). Use Case 3 (bottom left side), Use Case 4 (bottom right side) [33].

This use case seeks to address the challenges of unstructured environments in the context of PPDR services. By leveraging the advanced capabilities of 5G communication solutions, the Network Application currently being finalized, facilitates the deployment of autonomous PPDR services that can operate in diverse and unpredictable environments. The IBD, under continuous updates, provides the functionality required to support the Network Application associated and deliver edge simultaneous localization and mapping (SLAM) services driven by localization and mapping and the central cloud SLAM service for feature optimization and support of semantic maps based on global knowledge. Additionally, the provision of an intervention service that will provide troubleshooting and emergent interventions is also facilitated through the IBD.

4.2 Use Case 2: 5G Enhanced Semi-autonomous Transport

The primary goal of this use case is to enable robots to operate in teleoperated and semi-autonomous modes with the help of 5G technology [26]. By leveraging the capabilities of 5G communication solutions, this use case demonstrates the potential for efficient and reliable communication between robots and the transport infrastructure.

The Network Application currently under development supports semi-autonomous transport operations, providing enhanced real-time decision-making and navigation capabilities. The use of lightweight onboard unit virtualization techniques enables the creation of a flexible and scalable fog environment capable of adapting to the changing needs of the transport domain. The role of the IBD is to support the various data flows and QoS to map several data streams from sources such as sensors and video streaming, as well as facilitate the security of the Network Applications' endpoints to preserve sensitive and confidential data.

This use case showcases the potential of 5G technology to reduce service creation time and enhance the capabilities of the transport sector. By leveraging 5G communication solutions, the Network Application will enable seamless communication and collaboration between robots and the transport infrastructure, leading to more efficient and reliable transport operations. The use case specification is summarized in Fig. 2.

4.3 Use Case 3: 5G Enhanced Healthcare Robots

The 5G-ERA project features a use case focused on designing and developing a new Network Application that supports various data flows with different priorities and QoS. The primary goal of this use case is to enable the mapping of multiple data streams, including sensor data, alerts, and video streaming, while demonstrating the security of Network Application endpoints and data streams to protect sensitive and confidential data.

The Network Application developed under this use case will enable robots to carry supporting materials on behalf of healthcare workers, depending on their level of autonomy. Using 5G technology will allow for efficient and reliable communication between the robots and healthcare infrastructure, enabling the robots to carry out their tasks safely and effectively [27–29].

One of the key aspects of this use case is demonstrating the security of the Network Applications endpoints and their data streams. To achieve this, the Network Application leverages the capabilities of 5G technology to ensure that sensitive and confidential data is protected at all times. The Network Application also supports the mapping of data flows with different priorities and QoS, allowing for efficient and effective communication between the robots and healthcare infrastructure. Additionally, the IBD will ensure that the Network Application endpoints are secured, ensuring that sensitive and confidential data are preserved. The IBD supports the various data flows that will be generated and prioritize the mapping of such streams coming from sensors, video streaming, etc. Through the IBD, users will be able to use the local and task planning services, which serve the purpose of planning the tasks based on local information and the edge task planning services, which in turn plan the tasks integrated with a smart environment. Finally, by providing a central cloud planning service, the IDB facilitates the feature and semantic maps optimization based on global knowledge and semantic-based task planning. The use case specifications are summarized in Fig. 2.

Overall, this use case contributes significantly to the 5G-ERA project's [24] goal of advancing the state-of-the-art in 5G-Enhanced Robot Autonomy. By showcasing the practical applications of 5G technology in the healthcare sector, this use case demonstrates the potential for robots to provide valuable support to healthcare workers during times of crisis while also ensuring that sensitive and confidential data is protected at all times.

4.4   Use Case 4: 5G-Remote Assistance for Manufacturing Process

Finally, the 5G-ERA project [24] features a use case that focuses on enabling an interface between the Robot Operating System – Industry (ROS-I) [30] and an industrial production cell. The primary goal of this use case is to leverage Industry 4.0 techniques and the 5G-ERA middleware to support the deployment of highly flexible and robust manufacturing for both small and medium-sized enterprises (SMEs) and large-scale fabricators.

To demonstrate the potential of this use case, the project uses a brazing cell, showcasing how the algorithms for human-robot learning control [31, 32] can be employed for collaborative output tasks. Using these algorithms, the use case demonstrates how the project achieves seamless communication between robots and human operators, enabling the production cell to be highly flexible and responsive to changing demands.

One of the key advantages of this use case is that it enables the deployment of highly flexible and robust manufacturing for both SMEs and large-scale fabricators. By leveraging Industry 4.0 techniques and the 5G-ERA middleware, the use case aims to create a seamless interface between the production cell and the ROS-I system, enabling the production cell to be responsive to changing demands. The IBD will serve a variety of services coming from the Network Application associated with this use case, including the brazing robot operation through the task planning based on the brazing process specification, the edge operation planning services, the central cloud service tasked with optimising features and semantic maps based on global knowledge, the learning service tasked with updating a dense and semantic map proactively as well as updating the robot skills set thus improving the accuracy and autonomy level. The features of this use case are supported by the connection of an external dashboard located at the premises of the use case provider. The specifications concerning this use case are summarized in Fig. 2.

Overall, this use case will contribute significantly to the 5G-ERA project's [24] goal of advancing the state-of-the-art in 5G-Enhanced Robot Autonomy. By showcasing the potential of Industry 4.0 techniques and the 5G-ERA middleware to enable highly flexible and robust manufacturing, this use case will demonstrate how robots can be integrated seamlessly into industrial production processes, enhancing productivity and efficiency.

5 Conclusions

The 5G-ERA project aims to showcase the potential of 5G and semantic models in achieving enhanced robot autonomy across various vertical sectors. Using machine learning tools in conjunction with the intent-based networking dashboard (IBD) will enable the development of cloud-native connected robotics that can utilize 5G and 6G resources. The IBD serves as a crucial component of the project by providing a platform for onboarding and utilization of Network Applications while simultaneously monitoring and optimizing QoE key performance indicators (KPIs) set for each use case.

Demonstrating the project's use cases can validate the functionalities of the IBD and the associated network applications. Developing a reference design for connected robotics that can leverage 5G resources and the scalability of the communication interface for ROS can facilitate the mass deployment of cloud-native connected robotics.

Using semantic models and machine learning tools in 5G-enhanced robot autonomy will pave the way for new and innovative applications in various sectors. The 5G-ERA project is a significant step towards achieving this goal and can contribute significantly to advancing robotics technology.

Acknowledgements. This project has received funding from the European Union's Horizon 2020 research and innovation programme under the Grant Agreement No 101016681.

References

1. Open-source Management and Orchestration (OSM). https://osm.etsi.org/. Accessed 01 May 2020
2. Cloudify. https://cloudify.co/. Accessed 01 May 2020
3. Trakadas, P.; Karkazis, P.; Leligou, H.C, et. al.: Comparison of management and orchestration solutions for the 5G Era. J. Sens. Actuator Netw. 4(9), (2020)
4. OSM Experience with NFV architecture, interfaces and information models (May 2018). https://osm.etsi.org/wikipub/index.php/Release_notes_and_whitepapers. Accessed 01 May 2020
5. Anaemic Domain Models, M. Fowler. https://martinfowler.com/bliki/AnemicDomainModel.html. Accessed 01 May 2020
6. Desot, T., Portet, F., Vacher, M.: Towards end-to-end spoken intent recognition in smart home. In: Chioreanu, I., Stan, A., Burileanu, D., (Eds.) Speech Technology and Human-Computer Dialogue: 10th International Conference, SpeD 2019, Timisoara, Romania, October 18–19, 2019, Revised Selected Papers (pp. 1–8) (2019)

7. Soldani, D., Rajatheva, R., Liyanage, M., Liyanage, C., Seneviratne, A.: 5G mobile systems for healthcare. In: Proceedings of the 2017 IEEE 85th Vehicular Technology Conference (VTC Spring) (pp. 1–5). IEEE (2017). https://doi.org/10.1109/VTCSpring.2017.8108602

8. Lv, Z., Qiao, L., Wang, Q.: Cognitive robotics on 5G networks. ACM Trans. Internet Technol. 21(4), Article 92, 18 (2021). https://doi.org/10.1145/3414842

9. Yu, H., Lee, H., Jeon, H.: What is 5G? Emerging 5G mobile services and network requirements. Sustainability **2017**, 9 (1848). https://doi.org/10.3390/su9101848

10. Raunholt, T., Rodriguez, I., Mogensen, P., Larsen, M.: Towards a 5G mobile edge cloud planner for autonomous mobile robots. In: Proceedings of the 2021 IEEE 94th Vehicular Technology Conference (VTC2021-Fall) (pp. 01–05). IEEE (2021). https://doi.org/10.1109/VTC2021-Fall52928.2021.9625208

11. Abbas, K., Khan, T.A., Afaq, M., Song, W.-C.: Network slice lifecycle management for 5G mobile networks: an intent-based networking approach. IEEE Access **9**, 80128–80146 (2021). https://doi.org/10.1109/ACCESS.2021.3084834

12. Gramaglia, M., Serrano, P., Banchs, A., Costa-Pérez, X., Gutierrez-Estevez, D., Sciancalepore, V.: Flexible connectivity and QoE/QoS management for 5G networks: the 5G NORMA view. In: 2016 IEEE International Conference on Communications Workshops (ICC) (pp. 373–379). Kuala Lumpur, Malaysia (2016). https://doi.org/10.1109/ICCW.2016.7503816

13. ETSI GR NFV-IFA 022 V3.1.1 (2018–04) Network Functions Virtualisation (NFV) Release 3; Management and orchestration; Report on management and connectivity for multi-site services

14. Femminella, M., Nencioni, G., Garroppo, R.G., Gonzalez, A.J., Helvik, B.E., Procissi, G.: Orchestration and control in software-defined 5G networks: research challenges. Wireless Commun. Mobile Comput. **2018**, 6923867 (2018). https://doi.org/10.1155/2018/6923867

15. ETSI White Paper on Developing Software for Multi-Access Edge Computing, https://www.etsi.org/images/files/ETSIWhitePapers/etsi_wp20ed2_MEC_SoftwareDevelopment.pdf. Accessed 01 May 2020

16. Beshley, M., et al.: Customer-oriented quality of service management method for the future intent-based networking. Appl. Sci. **10**(22), 8223 (2020). https://doi.org/10.3390/app10228223

17. Zheng, X., Leivadeas, A., Falkner, M.: Intent-Based Networking management with conflict detection and policy resolution in an enterprise network. Comput. Netw. **219**, 109457 (2022). https://doi.org/10.1016/j.comnet.2022.109457

18. Leivadeas, A., Falkner, M.: VNF Placement Problem: a multi-tenant intent-based networking approach. In: Proceedings of the 24th Conference on Innovation in Clouds, Internet and Networks and Workshops (ICIN) 2021 (pp. 143–150). IEEE (2021). https://doi.org/10.1109/ICIN51074.2021.9385553

19. Paganelli, F., Paradiso, F., Gherardelli, M., Galletti, G.: Network service description model for VNF orchestration leveraging intent-based SDN interfaces. In: Proceedings of the 2017 IEEE Conference on Network Softwarization (NetSoft) (pp. 1–5). IEEE (2017). https://doi.org/10.1109/NETSOFT.2017.8004210

20. Rafiq, A., Mehmood, A., Ahmed Khan, T., Abbas, K., Afaq, M., Song, W.-C.: Intent-based end-to-end network service orchestration system for multi-platforms. Sustainability **12**(7), 2782 (2020). https://doi.org/10.3390/su12072782

21. Sophocleous, M., et al.: AI-Driven intent-based networking for 5G enhanced robot autonomy. In: Maglogiannis, I., Iliadis, L., Macintyre, J., Cortez, P. (eds) Artificial Intelligence Applications and Innovations. AIAI 2022 IFIP WG 12.5 International Workshops. AIAI 2022. IFIP Advances in Information and Communication Technology, vol 652. Springer, Cham (2022). https://doi.org/10.1007/978-3-031-08341-9_6

22. Khalid, O., Khan, I.A., Abbas, A.: Insights into software-defined networking and applications in fog computing. In: Zomaya, A., Abbas, A., Khan, S., Zomaya, A.Y. (eds.) Fog Computing: Theory and Practice. First published: 25 April 2020. Chapter 16 (2020). https://doi.org/10.1002/9781119551713.ch16

23. Sahni, Y., Cao, J., Jiang, S.: Middleware for multi-robot systems. In: Ammari, H.M. (ed.) Mission-Oriented Sensor Networks and Systems: Art and Science. SSDC, vol. 164, pp. 633–673. Springer, Cham (2019). https://doi.org/10.1007/978-3-319-92384-0_18

24. 5G-ERA. 5th sssgeneration enhanced robot autonomy. european commission. https://5g-era.eu/, 2021–2024

25. Monir, N., et al.: Seamless handover scheme for MEC/SDN-based vehicular networks. J. Sens. Actuator Netw. 11, 9 (2022). https://doi.org/10.3390/jsan11010009

26. Hakak, S., et al.: Autonomous vehicles in 5G and beyond: a survey. Veh. Commun. 39, 100551 (2023). https://doi.org/10.1016/j.vehcom.2022.100551ss

27. Devi, D.H., et al.: 5G technology in healthcare and wearable devices: a review. Sensors 23, 2519 (2023). https://doi.org/10.3390/s23052519

28. Siriwardhana, Y., Gür, G., Ylianttila, M., Liyanage, M.: The role of 5G for digital healthcare against COVID-19 pandemic: opportunities and challenges. ICT Express, 7(2), 244–252 (2021). ISSN 2405–5595. https://doi.org/10.1016/j.icte.2020.10.002

29. Huseien, G.F., Shah, K.W.: A review on 5G technology for smart energy management and smart buildings in Singapore. Energy AI 7, 100116 (2022). ISSN 2666–5468. https://doi.org/10.1016/j.egyai.2021.100116

30. Siurana, J.L., Dimas, M., Barrientos, A., Pairet, È., Pujol, M.: ROS-Industrial: towards an open and scalable industry 4.0 automation system. In: Jeschke, S., Brecher, C., Song, H., Rawat, D.B. (eds.) Industrial Internet of Things. Volume 67 of the book series "Advances in Intelligent Systems and Computing". Springer International Publishing, pp. 491–503 (2017). https://doi.org/10.1007/978-3-319-42559-7_38

31. Schaal, S.: Learning robot control. In: Arbib, M.A. (ed.) The Handbook of Brain Theory and Neural Networks, 2nd edn., pp. 983–987. MIT Press, Cambridge, MA (2002)

32. Schaal, S., Atkeson, C.G.: Learning control in robotics. IEEE Robot. Autom. Mag. 17(2), 20–29 (2010). https://doi.org/10.1109/MRA.2010.936957

33. Špaňhel, J., Kapinus, M., Dobeš, P., Materna, Z., Juránek, R., Klepárník, P.: Reference NetApps for 5G-ERA - Initial version. In: D4.3, 5th Generation Enhanced Robot Autonomy, European Commission, 30 June 2022

Media Services in Dense, Static and Mobile Environments Leveraging Edge Deployments

Maria-Evgenia Xezonaki[1] ⓘ, N. Psaromanolakis[1], P. Konstantinos Chartsias[1],
Konstantinos Stamatis[1], Dimitrios Kritharidis[1], Vasileios Theodorou[1],
Christina Politi[2], Panagiotis Papaioannou[2], Christos Tranoris[2], Spyros Denazis[2],
Ioanna Mesogiti[3]([⊠]) ⓘ, Eleni Theodoropoulou[3], Fotini Setaki[3],
George Lyberopoulos[3], Nikos Makris[4], Paris Flegkas[4], Jesus Gutierrez Teran[5],
Markos Anastassopoulos[6], and Anna Tzanakaki[6]

[1] Intracom Telecom S.A, Athens, Greece
[2] University of Patras, Patras, Greece
[3] COSMOTE Mobile Telecommunications S.A, Athens, Greece
imesogiti@cosmote.gr
[4] Department of Electrical and Computer Engineering, University of Thessaly, Volos, Greece
[5] IHP - Leibniz-Institut Für Innovative Mikroelektronik, Frankfurt, Germany
[6] National and Kapodistrian University of Athens, Athens, Greece

Abstract. The media sector is one of the domains that are highly impacted by the 5G network principles and capabilities, in terms of service provisioning and performance in versatile environments. At the same time the media sector is gradually becoming an integral part of transportations, as a variety of media services can be offered and used to facilitate passengers' needs in various directions, especially infotainment and safety/security. The 5GPPP 5G-VICTORI project proposes the integration of Content Delivery Network-aided infotainment services in 5G network deployments to enable the uninterrupted delivery of such services with high quality to dense, static and mobile environments. The solution is deployed and evaluated in an experimentation setup in lab and in operational railway environments. This paper discusses the service Key Performance Indicators and technical requirements and provides an overview of the proposed experimental deployment and performance evaluation results.

Keywords: 5G · Content Delivery Networks · CDN · Edge Computing · vertical services · railways

1 Introduction

The explosive growth in the demand for broadband and mobile services goes hand in hand with the radical proliferation of media services of various purposes and types; while the media sector has been identified as a vertical industry being highly impacted by the enhanced mobile broadband capabilities of 5G and beyond networks. At the same time, the media sector is gradually becoming an integral part of transportations, as a variety

© IFIP International Federation for Information Processing 2023
Published by Springer Nature Switzerland AG 2023
I. Maglogiannis et al. (Eds.): AIAI 2023 Workshops, IFIP AICT 677, pp. 66–76, 2023.
https://doi.org/10.1007/978-3-031-34171-7_5

of media-related services (especially infotainment and safety/security related) can be provided to passengers for performing various tasks in versatile situations.

A number of projects and programmes (EU, national funded etc., e.g. 5G-PPP Project 5G-PICTURE [1], 5G-MEDIA [2], 5G-SOLUTIONS [3], 5GMediaHUB [4], 5G-ZORRO[5]) are focusing on the technical realization of CDN (Content Delivery Network) concepts and principles for the provisioning of infotainment media services, and their deployment over 5G infrastructures.

To this end, 5G-PPP 5G-PICTURE project [1] delivered a 5G infrastructure paradigm able to support a wide variety of vertical services, including infotainment services at railway environment over mmWave wireless access deployed along the tracks. 5G-PICTURE solution enabled services, among others, such as railway on-board multimedia entertainment / infotainment services and telecommunication services at ultra-dense hotspots (e.g. stadiums) with huge traffic demands and extreme irregular and seasonal characteristics.

Focusing on the media sector, 5G-PPP 5G-MEDIA project [2], presented an agile programming, verification and orchestration platform for services, and the development of network functions and applications to be deployed over large-scale media service deployments. The innovative components of the platform have been exploited for the delivery of ultra-high-definition (UHD) media over CDNs. 5G-MEDIA provided Media Service Providers with the ability to build flexible and adaptable media distribution service chains, made up of virtualized functions, and deliver UHD media content over 5G network infrastructures to end-users. Moreover, 5G-PPP 5G-SOLUTIONS project [3] aims to prove and validate 5G infrastructures in delivering use cases of significant vertical domains including the media industry. As media services distributed through multiple CDNs need to be shielded from content delivery degradation and outages, the project leverages the ETSI 5G MEC architecture capabilities by introducing caching of popular content at the network edge. Using active monitoring by smart proxies paired to gNB (5G access nodes) in combination with enhanced client-side analytics, the project provides a solution to predictively decide to switch to alternative CDNs or to cache content, in order to prevent degradation or improve the QoS (Quality of Service).

Considering extending large scale architectures for the support of media services, 5G-PPP 5GMediaHUB project [4] aims to accelerate the testing and validation of innovative 5G-empowered media applications and NetApps from 3rd parties through an open, integrated experimentation facility. The project builds an elastic, secure and trusted multi-tenant service execution and NetApps development environment and leverages 5G technologies to explore its applicability as media distribution network. Emphasis is placed on CDN-aided multi-domain content caching deployments and its evaluation. In addition, 5G-PPP 5GZORRO project [5], envisions the 5G Long Term Evolution and its capability to deliver diverse vertical applications, including media applications. 5G services are envisioned to be deployed over logically segmented and geographically distributed virtualized infrastructure resources, which can be allocated flexibly according to traffic or user-generated requirements. For instance, content popularity dynamics present significant variations in the context of flash crowd scenarios e.g., video sharing in stadiums, sharing breaking news live feed, etc. In such cases, 5G-ZORRO introduces a novel approach based on leveraging upon 3rd party resources to support scalable, pervasive vCDN services (live and/or VoD).

In this landscape, the 5G-PPP 5G-VICTORI project [6] is extending existing 5G experimentation facilities towards adopting a novel solution for the integration of CDN-aided infotainment services in 5G network deployments to enable the uninterrupted delivery of such services with high quality to static and mobile users. The project puts focus on delivering two implementation paradigms, available for experimentation at railway operational sites (as indicative environments of high mobility) in Greece and Germany. This paper presents the implementation paradigm at an experimental railway facility in Patras, Greece, and discusses the initial evaluation results.

This paper is organized as follows: Sect. 2 presents the requirements and KPIs of media services vertical in various dense, static and mobile environments and discusses the high-level 5G network deployment options. In Sect. 3, the 5G-VICTORI network deployment paradigm is described, on top of which a multi-level CDN service is deployed, especially addressing the specific challenges and characteristics of operational railway environments. The next section describes the lab setup in which the paradigm was initially validated and presents the obtained performance evaluation results. Finally, conclusions are drawn.

2   Media Services and Requirements in 5G-VICTORI

2.1   Overview of Vertical Service Requirements and KPIs

Media services constitute the most representative category of the enhanced Mobile Broadband (eMBB) profile of 3GPP standardized services [7]. Versatile factors determine the requirements and Key Performance Indicators (KPIs) set for the underlying networks to fulfill (e.g. format, purpose and scope of service, interactivity, type of terminal device, environment etc.). In general, the most critical requirement for infotainment services is to provide high data rate at various availability levels.

At the same time, in modern railway transportations, there is a demand for novel services addressing various end-users and versatile rail operations. These services, collectively denoted as Future Railway Mobile Communication System services (FRMCS), correspond to applications for passengers, critical services and emergency services for stakeholders engaged in train operation, as well as complementary services related to optimization of train operation ([3, 5]). FRMCS services are typically categorized into "Business", "Performance" and "Critical" services.

In particular, "Business services" refer to communication and broadband connectivity services provided to passengers located at railway facilities, i.e. at the train stations/ platforms, on-board. These services include infotainment (e.g. internet, Video on Demand (VoD), linear TV services, etc.), digital mobility, travel information services etc. These services are in the focus of this paper. At this point, the media and the transportation vertical sectors' interests come together and their requirements need to be converged in 5G and beyond network deployments. In this landscape, 5G-VICTORI aims to provide a cross-vertical deployment paradigm for (CDN-aided) VoD (Video on Demand) and near-real time, linear TV services. These services pose the following high-level requirements (aligned with [9]):

- Support for High-resolution Real-time Video Quality of video content/ TV streaming channels, implying jitter limits below 40 ms, end-to-end latency below 100ms and guaranteed data rates of 5-10Mbps per stream.
- Considering the access network capacity, aggregate data rates should be at least 150-500Mbps for the support of CDN "data shower" capability. This KPI will be further analyzed explained in Sect. 3.2. Assuming also all FRMCS service categories as mentioned in [10], in cases that this is not possible to have coverage along the tracks, data rates of 1–1.5 Gbps are required at places where the train resides for some time, e.g. at platforms, train depots, etc.
- Low Channel/Stream Switching time, corresponding to the time between the triggering of channel switching and the presentation of the new channel on screen; typically to be under the 1–2 s, corresponding to end-to-end network latency below 150ms.
- Total Wagon User Density accounting for 100–300 users per train (peak time) at large, highly congested trains.
- Seamless service provisioning to train wagons at high speeds is required, reflecting the vertical specific requirement for mobility at trains velocity (reaching 100 km/h and in cases 250 km/h), for all services provided on-board.
- Service Availability on board the train, wherever it resides along the tracks (and at station platforms); with "Business" services being highly tolerant to low availability levels.
- Service deployment time-that is the time required for deploying all CDN components over the 5G infrastructure through its orchestration layer and verifying initial connectivity between them- should be less than 90 min (adhering to 5GPPP targets for 5G networks).

2.2 Network Deployment Requirements and Options

Radio access network planning in railway environments needs to take into consideration the fact that area characteristics along the railway tracks may vary between areas that are remote, isolated, with challenging terrain for radio coverage (e.g. mountainous, with tunnels, long straight track-segments etc.) and metropolitan areas (e.g. with high buildings, tunnels, lots of curves, etc.). Considering also the access network capacity requirements, along the tracks and in cases that this is not possible, at places where the train resides for some time, e.g. at platforms, train depots, etc. it becomes obvious that, there is no single solution to address such environment.

Currently, private GSM-R (Global System for Mobile Communications – Railway) networks serve part of the railway communication needs – mainly the Rail-critical services- while public and on-board WiFi networks provide connectivity for "business" services. To meet the service requirements and KPIs, novel architectural solutions and network deployment options tailored to the railway environment need to be considered. The fact that most services are consumed in the railway facilities, and most of them are only relevant in this environment, makes non-public network (NPN) deployments [11] a candidate deployment option, as long as service continuity is ensured for services (especially of "Business" type) consumed across private and public networks.

Other factors may as well lead to extending public networks to the railway facilities as another deployment option. In these cases, a distributed core network deployment allowing service deployment and processing at edge compute resources, and traffic offloading at Mobile Edge Computing (MEC) network elements can serve well the purpose of meeting the service performance requirements (especially for low latency), while optimizing public network utilization and performance. Moving one step further, for services that are consumed or/and processed at train level, the inclusion of on-board edge resources in the distributed network and service deployment setup can be considered.

Leveraging these concepts, the 5G-VICTORI project has proposed three deployment options for the case of the railway vertical network [12]:

- Option 1: NPN (as autonomous edge): that considers a silo 5G Core Network (5GCN) deployed at central premises of the vertical facility.
- Option 2: NPN with distributed data plane – multiple edges: including a 5GCN deployed at central premises of the vertical and several UPFs and application servers deployed at several sites of the vertical facility.
- Option 3: Fully disaggregated 5G architecture: including a 5GCN deployed at central premises of the vertical, UPFs and application servers deployed at several sites of the vertical facility, and disaggregated RAN (Radio Access Network) segment.

Considering the logical network design and configuration, the performance requirements and the diversity of the complete FRMCS services necessitates the adoption of the 5G network slicing - at service and tenant level. The 3GPP distinction of services to uRLLC (ultra-Reliable Low Latency), and eMBB (enhanced Mobile Broadband), can be considered as basis for network layer slicing, over either a single private network deployment or a distributed public one.

3 Media Services Deployment for 5G-VICTORI

3.1 5G Network Deployment

Considering the CDN services as well as the deployment requirements and challenges related to the railway environment, 5G-VICTORI has proposed a disaggregated, layered experimentation framework ([12, 13]) extending the 5G-VINNI experimentation facility in Patras (Patras5G) [14], along a railway track in the area of Patras, Greece.

Access and Transport Network: A straight forward access network deployment option is the installation of gNBs providing coverage along the tracks and at platforms. Besides that, 5G-VICTORI solution includes a multi-technology dense transport network providing transport coverage along the tracks to support disaggregated RAN options. Transport aggregation is also considered.

An on-board train installation is also foreseen. This comprises: (1) 5G CPEs on-board the train allowing connectivity of the train systems to the 5G networks, (2) on-board compute servers for on-board application processing, data storage etc., and (3) on-board WiFi connectivity to end-users. The on-board train installation has two purposes: (1) to allow connectivity of the train systems to the 5G network and (2) to provide services to end-users.

However, key assumption for the "Business" services is that there can be service coverage gaps along the tracks, attributed either to the lack of RAN nodes or to unavailability of RAN nodes due to prioritization of other traffic. In this case asynchronous services can rely on high-data rate access network connectivity at train stations and platforms.

Edge Computing: For the deployment of services, cloud compute resources are available at the central cloud infrastructure of the Patras5G facility (University of Patras premises). Also, to achieve high network performance and to optimize resource utilization, edge and far edge computing are integrated as MEC (Mobile Edge Computing) in the Patras5G facility using the aforementioned deployment options. The NPN option is supported via the deployment of the complete 5GCN close to the vertical premises. The implementation is based on the Patras 5G Autonomous Edge, which is a portable "box", ideal for on-premise 5G deployments, containing everything from the 5G NR and 5GCN and service orchestration on a virtualized environment based on OpenStack.

Last mile edge computing is considered on-board the train, to provide the necessary storage and compute capabilities for asynchronous "business" services. Virtualization of the edge resources allows them being used for various applications/services and integrated at various layers with the rest of the multi-technology, multi-layer network setup. In practice, virtualized edge resources can be integrated with the non-3GPP last-mile transport and WiFi access connectivity layer for hosting part of the asynchronous applications, enabling service delivery temporarily, during the periods that 5G access network coverage is unavailable.

Network Management, Orchestration and Slicing: Adhering to the 5G-VICTORI architecture, a network management and service orchestration layer operates on top of the aforesaid facility, to ensure that services are delivered across the edges ([12, 13]). This layer is based on Open Source MANO (OSM) and Openslice ([15, 16]), and it assumes automated deployment of services and multiple customized-slices over the complete infrastructure (access, transport and core). In the specific setup, this layer follows the Network Slice as a Service (NSaaS) paradigm.

In the context of 5G-VICTORI railway use case, compute and network resources are included in the orchestration layer instance. The CDN components are managed as 3rd party virtual network functions (VNFs) with the necessary Network Service Descriptors (NSDs) by the service orchestration layer, thus automated deployment of these services across the distributed compute resources is supported, along with creation of an end-to-end slice.

3.2 CDN Deployment

In this context, 5G-VICTORI aims to showcase that it is possible to provide - through a multi-stage caching CDN platform - continuous TV and VoD content to railway passengers as they move between train stations, without full 5G coverage along the tracks. In other words, to showcase how the combination of the advanced, multi-stages CDN platform with the 5G-enabled "data shower" when available, can alleviate delays and content gaps occurring when content is delivered directly from the existing content origins. This implies having a multi-stage CDN platform with appropriate caching capabilities. The CDN platform provided is comprising 3 CDN stages (considered as 3-stages linear application graph) implemented by 3 CDN application components:

1. the Central CDN Server serving as a point of connection to various sources/ TV/ VoD providers etc., mainly responsible for receiving the (CDN) Source Content and preparing it to be delivered.
2. the Main CDN Server serving as the main caching point that receives content from the Central CDN server and provides the necessary functionalities and elements to support the content delivery (storage and streaming) to end users. This is also called Train Station CDN Cache/ Server.
3. the Edge CDN Server providing the last mile caching server that receives content from the Main CDN server. This is also called Train CDN Cache/Server.

In this linear application graph of the 3 CDN components, the most delay and data-rate critical interface -which determines the overall CDN service performance - is that between the Edge CDN server and the Main CDN server. Connectivity to this interface is provided over a 5G slice.

The media content can be either of VoD type (e.g. pre-stored content that can be stored at UoP cloud) or live TV pulled by the CDN from a niche content origin extending a commercial TV platform. The Content Origin platform comprises an Origin, an OTT (Over The Top) Encoder and Headend equipment with interfaces that provide access to a number of linear TV channels for the CDN platform. The latter requires interconnectivity between the 5GCore site and the content origin. Apparently, the delays occurring over this interconnection link actually constitute the problem to be solved by the 3 stages CDN platform. In this context, the CDN service is the vertical service under evaluation/ validation in the context of 5G-VICTORI, and the content origin is the necessary counterpart of the service to prove its operation/ performance.

The purpose of the operation of CDN in a "data shower" fashion in the railway environment consists in ensuring that the Train CDN Cache is updated with popular content (not yet acquired) each time the train reaches a train station, i.e. whenever the train resides in 5G network coverage. This can be either VoD content that was not completely transferred during the previous stop due to its size, or live content that was shown during the train's trip from one stop to another and shall be stored on the train to be played as time-shifted (delayed by some minutes). This update should be performed in a pull-based manner, i.e. the Train CDN Cache requesting content from the Train Station CDN Cache, so that when leaving the station, the Train CDN Cache contains as much popular content as possible (from the previous stop's available download).

Apparently, the necessary aggregate data rate required between the Train CDN Cache and the Train Station CDN Cache is a function of the number of channels to be provided to end-users, of the time the train resides at a train station and of the time it takes to the train to arrive to the next station with available connectivity (and Train Station CDN Cache). For instance, assuming, 3–10 TV channels of 7-10 Mbps data rate, about 3–5 min stop time at the train station, 10–15 min time between the two train station, the necessary data rate of the Train CDN Cache – Train Station CDN Cache ranges between 150-500 Mbps.

The proposed deployment scenarios assume that the central CDN Server is deployed at the central facility premises. At the MEC level, the Main CDN server (packaged as VNFs) is deployed and provides the necessary functionalities and elements to support the content delivery (storage and streaming) to end users. An additional Edge (CDN) server is deployed at the train on-board compute resources. The Edge (CDN) server is responsible for preloading and caching large amounts of content and serving the passengers even during disconnection periods. The Content Origin point(s) is located at central facility premises, (i.e. as a video streaming server hosting VoD content) to emulate local streaming services, and remotely to emulate a Content Origin point of a real CDN network deployment.

As the train approaches the station, the on-board 5G-CPE connects to the available 5G RAN in order to download streaming content in a "data shower" fashion to the Edge server -which is deployed at the on-board computer resources of the train-, with the aid of the aforementioned CDN multi-level solution.

The CDN service deployment for the demonstration activities of 5G-VICTORI project, across the remote premises of the TV source, the central regional cloud facilities, the local railway premises or the Central Train Station, and the Train is presented in Fig. 1. The underlying 5G network infrastructure the 5G network functions deployment is also presented along with the interfaces, the 5G slices and the CDN application flow.

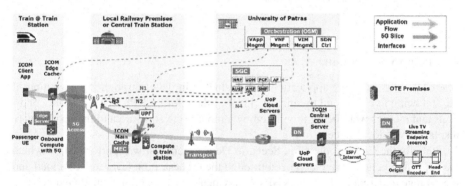

Fig. 1. Deployment blueprint for CDN service in static and mobile environments

4   Experimental Setup and Results

4.1 Lab CDN Deployment

For the deployment and evaluation of the different services of the above use case, the first testing phases took place in a lab setup. Remote configuration and testing of the application at the Patras5G facility was feasible. The CDN solution is containerized and the Central CDN server and the Main CDN Server (Train Station Cache) were deployed in NFV-compatible format at and Patras5G Cloud facility. The lab setup was also connected to external TV streaming content source provided by a remote niche

(CDN) Content Origin platform in Athens. The Edge CDN server (Train Cache) was deployed on a laptop connected to a 5G-CPE and through that it was connected to the Main CDN server /cache over the NPN 5G network deployed at UoP lab. An eMBB slice (meeting the relevant requirements) was configured for this session. The same laptop also emulated the end user/passenger UE.

The access network configuration in the Patras experimentation setup is the following: Frequency Band: n78, Bandwidth: 100 MHz, subcarrier spacing 20 kHz, 4x4 MIMO, TDD, UL/DL modulation 256 QAM/256 QAM. The setup for the lab testing along with the different facilities of the deployment is illustrated in Fig. 2.

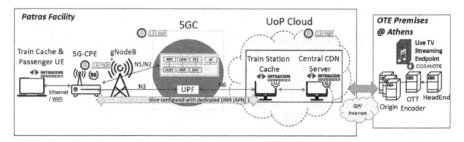

Fig. 2. The setup for the lab testing of the CDN scenario

4.2 Performance Results

The CDN (data shower) application was evaluated in detail through the execution of the following five tests and the measurement of the relevant KPIs. The network conditions and metrics were being monitored by a monitoring software and the results were displayed on a local screen.

Initially the CDN Application Scenario Deployment test was performed, in which the CDN components were deployed through the orchestration layer at UoP cloud and the average time required for the VNFs deployment was measured. It shall be noted that the low application deployment time, < 90 min, is a key target KPI which was measured from the difference between the timestamps of the application deployment request and the application deployment completion. From the results, a service deployment time of 5.36 min was achieved.

After the deployment of the CDN components, initial connectivity between all of them was verified and evaluated. The link between the Edge CDN cache and the Main CDN cache was measured, as well as the data rate between the Central CDN server and the Main DCN cache (despite deployed as VNFs at the same facility in the context of lab testing). An average of around 95 Mbps was measured using iperf tool and/or computed by the volume of transferred data in a specific amount of time.

Moving on the synchronization of the Main CDN cache with the latest linear TV content from the central CDN server, the performance of the Periodic Update functionality was measured. End-to-end 5G network latency was measured around 35ms on average on a high-bandwidth slice.

The next step was to evaluate the data shower mechanism from the Main CDN cache to the Edge CDN cache; which was also verified. The CDN (data shower) scenario experimentation was complemented with performance measurement of Content Distribution to passengers onboard. An average of around 75 Mpbs was measured using iperf tool, resulting in the transfer of approximately 2.5 GB of content in 4 min on the train and therefore adequate content onboard to serve passengers for almost 38 min after the loss of connectivity. The content was measured to be distributed with an approximate data rate of 88.36 Mbps to the passengers.

5 Conclusions

This paper has provided an overview of the media service requirements and KPIs, and their relation to FRMCS "business" services category as an indicative media-transportation cross-vertical use case. These applications have been used as a basis for the definition of system specifications of the 5G-VICTORI solution. Delivering a high-performance deployment for these demanding verticals entails network planning based on various technologies and on the placement of compute resources at the right proximity to the end user.

To this end, specifications have been nailed down to an experimentation deployment for testing and performance evaluation of services in operational railway environment in the area of Patras, Greece. The deployment entails integration of multi-level CDN platforms with private 5G network deployments that include edge computing capabilities and edge caching on-board the train. Multi-level CDN capabilities are enabled via "Data Showers" at selected locations along the train route. Initial lab testing activities have validated the applicability of such extensions to the railway environment, taking under consideration the time trains reside/ wait at platforms, the number of stations between platforms and the time it takes the train to move between platforms, the Video on Demand (VoD) as well as semi-real time TV streaming service requirements.

Acknowledgements. The research leading to these results has received funding from the European Union's Framework Programme Horizon 2020 under grant agreement (1) No. 857201 and project name "5G-VICTORI: VertIcal demos over Common large scale field Trials fOr Rail, energy and media Industries".

References

1. 5G-PPP Project 5G-PICTURE. http://www.5g-picture-project.eu/. Accessed Mar 2023
2. 5G-PPP Project 5G-MEDIA. https://5g-ppp.eu/5g-media/. Accessed Mar 2023
3. 5G-PPP Project 5G-SOLUTIONS. https://5gsolutionsproject.eu/. Accessed Mar 2023
4. 5G-PPP Project 5GMediaHUB. https://www.5gmediahub.eu/. Accessed Mar 2023
5. 5G-PPP Project 5G-ZORRO. https://www.5gzorro.eu/. Accessed Mar 2023
6. 5G-PPP Project 5G-VICTORI. https://www.5g-victori-project.eu/. Accessed Mar 2023
7. 3GPP, TR 22.863: Feasibility study on new services and markets technology enablers for enhanced mobile broad-band; Stage 1, Rel. 14
8. 3GPP TR 22.890: Study on supporting railway smart station services, Rel 17

9. 3GPP TS 22.289: Mobile communication system for railways; Stage 1, Rel. 17
10. UIC, International union of railways: future railway mobile communication system user requirements specification v5.0. February 2020. https://uic.org/IMG/pdf/frmcs_user_require ments_specification-fu_7100-v5.0.0.pdf. Accessed Mar 2023
11. Mahmood, K., Gavras, A., Hecker, A.: Non-public-networks - state of the art and way forward. Zenodo (2022). https://doi.org/10.5281/zenodo.7230191
12. 5G-VICTORI Deliverable D2.4: 5G-VICTORI end-to-end reference architecture. April 2022, https://www.5g-victori-project.eu/wp-content/uploads/2022/05/2022-04-11-D2.4-5G-VICTORI-end-to-end-reference-architecture.pdf
13. Mesogiti, I., et al.: 5G-VICTORI: future railway communications requirements driving 5G deployments in railways. In: Maglogiannis, I., Macintyre, J., Iliadis, L. (eds.) AIAI 2021. IAICT, vol. 628, pp. 21–30. Springer, Cham (2021). https://doi.org/10.1007/978-3-030-791 57-5_2
14. Tranoris, C., Denazis, S.: Patras 5G: an open source based end-to-end facility for 5G trials, ERCIM NEWS, Special Theme 5G, Number 117, April 2020
15. Christos Tranoris: Openslice: an opensource OSS for delivering network slice as a service. February 2021, https://arxiv.org/abs/2102.03290. Accessed Mar 2020
16. Openslice, Open source, operations support system. http://openslice.io. Accessed Mar 2020

Network Slicing vs. Network Neutrality – Is Consent Possible?

Lechosław Tomaszewski[1]([⊠]) and Robert Kołakowski[1,2]

[1] Orange Polska S.A., ul. Obrzeżna 7, 02-691 Warszawa, Poland
lechoslaw.tomaszewski@orange.com
[2] Warsaw University of Technology, ul. Nowowiejska 15/19, 00-665 Warszawa, Poland

Abstract. Network Slicing (NS) is the inherent concept of the 5G network and beyond, ensuring dynamic and flexible use of resources, considered also a fundamental enabler of the "Industry 4.0" vision. However, its widespread implementation today encounters barriers, among which the paradigm of "network neutrality" is of key importance. This paper discusses the various factors affecting the wide implementation of NS: legal and political – including the European Union regulation on network neutrality, trends in the telecommunications market, technical conditions of NS in 5G networks and beyond, especially physical barriers, and the fundamental conflicts of interest between various business actors in the telecommunications market as well as consequences of a dominant position of content providers over mobile operators enabled by the mentioned regulation. Based on the analysis of the above factors, it is concluded that NS has become a hostage of contradictory paradigms and visions that, if not revised, prevent sustainable development based on communication services implemented with the use of NS.

Keywords: 5G · 6G · network slicing · network neutrality · net neutrality · regulation · eMBB · URLLC · MIoT · QoS · QoE · Internet access · mobile service · specialised service · Industry 4.0 · energy · efficiency · sustainability · spectrum · capacity · physical limit · digital transformation · market position imbalance · MNO · hyperscaler · OTT

1 Introduction

Network Slicing (NS) is the concept behind 5G System (5GS) [1] and beyond. On the technical side, a lot of effort has gone into it, from research to industry standardisation. Today, however, NS has to face challenges in the area of

ETHER project has received funding from the Smart Networks and Services Joint Undertaking (SNS JU) under the European Union's Horizon Europe research and innovation programme under Grant Agreement No. 101096526. Views and opinions expressed are however those of the author(s) only and do not necessarily reflect those of the European Union. Neither the European Union nor the granting authority can be held responsible for them.

the regulatory and business ecosystem. The goal of the paper is to discuss the aspects of Network Neutrality (NeN) regulations and their potential impact on the telecommunication network ecosystem implementing NS technology. The paper is structured as follows. In Sect. 2, the motivation of the paper together with an outline of recent developments in the mobile network ecosystem is presented. Section 3 discusses the European Union (EU) NeN regulation and other political factors impacting the NS implementation. In Sect. 4, the key global telecommunication market trends and forecasts are outlined. Section 5 provides the technological issues related to NS and relevant in the context of NeN principles implementation. Section 6 presents the existing conflicts of interest in the business ecosystem. Section 7 is devoted to the discussion on the key challenges, threats, obstacles, and open issues for NS, triggered or intensified due to the NeN regulations. Section 8 summarises and concludes the paper.

2   Motivation

The monetisation of telecom operators' resources has always been an issue of interest. Unused fixed network infrastructure has been offered in the form of leased lines (analogue or digital), copper links or dark fibers, Local Loop Unbundling (LLU) or BitStream Access (BSA) offers, collocation of third-party equipment in the operator's premises – voluntarily or under regulatory pressure. The widespread deployment of mobile networks has opened up new models of inter-operator collaboration and resource sharing: roaming (national/international), Mobile Virtual Network Operator (MVNO) on top of Mobile Network Operator's (MNO's) resources, Multi-Operator Radio Access Network (MORAN) – shared radio access infrastructure, Multi-Operator Core Network (MOCN) – MORAN with spectrum sharing, or GateWay Core Network (GWCN) – spectrum and entire infrastructure sharing except for databases of subscribers.

Mobile networks up to 3G were in fact mobile telephony networks with value-added services, including access to the Internet Protocol (IP) network. Along with the 4G network, the "All IP" paradigm was implemented, *i.e.*, the separation of access to the IP network from communication services built on top of generic access mechanisms. However, the 4G network is a universal, general-purpose network with a unified User Plane (UP) architecture for the entire spectrum of diverse services with often conflicting requirements, thus, it is unable to provide traffic handling to be satisfactory for all competing services. The application of the "All IP" rule was disruptive to the previous business model [2] and revealed a fundamental conflict of interests of business actors in the roles of service provider and access provider operating a general-purpose network. The experience of 4G networks has proven the need to diversify traffic processing according to the specific requirements of the service or application.

NS has emerged as a concept initially introduced with PlanetLab (a federation of overlay networks testbed resources distributed over the globe and offering the ability to slice the resources for services experimentation worldwide) [3], later reinvented by Next Generation Mobile Networks (NGMN) [1] as an inherent feature requested from (at that time) future 5GS to support fundamentally the vision of "Industry 4.0", and then adopted by 3rd Generation Partnership Project (3GPP). Starting in 2016, NS was a hot topic and attracted interest from numerous research projects, in particular those sponsored by EU under the Horizon 2020 calls. There is no unified vision of NS; they are located between the extremes of "separate complete single-purpose communication network, either isolated or interconnected with other complete networks" and "federation of multiple application-tailored communication networks on top on shared network control mechanisms". While the first one resembles the "Network Service" concept according to European Telecommunications Standards Institute (ETSI) Network Function Virtualisation (NFV) [4], *i.e.*, an isolated communication solution implemented in a virtualisation platform with all 5GS Control Plane (CP) features deployed per slice, the latter one is followed by the 3GPP approach in which implemented are application-specific User Plane Functions (UPFs) and necessary control mechanisms as add-ons to generic 5GS CP [5]. However, it can be stated that NS is about adapting a service traffic processing chain architecture to the specific requirements of the service while optimising the use of resources, and with regard to spatial distribution and dynamics of traffic demand [6].

The ability to implement NS is directly conditioned by the deployment of a 5G network in the Stand-Alone (SA) architecture (rare, so far). The 3GPP standardisation of NS in 5GS is still under development (in the scope of currently ongoing Release 18), and there yet remain open issues [7]. Nevertheless, MNOs with clear conviction identify NS among the top benefits of the 5G technology (44% of indications) [8]. However, the expected benefits can be precluded by often-overlooked non-technical obstacles, which will be discussed in this paper.

3   Legal, Regulatory and Political Conditions for Network Slicing in the European Union and Associated States

The fundamental concept associated with NS is the principle of NeN, intuitively understood as the "transparency" of the network for the transmitted data, both technical (equal treatment of all Internet communications) and in terms of the fundamental freedom of speech (no discrimination or filtering out of any content). However, there is no single universally accepted definition of NeN [9]. Within the European Economic Area (EEA), *i.e.*, EU and associated states – Liechtenstein, Iceland and Norway, under the banner of NeN, the Open Internet Access Regulation (OIAR) has been implemented [10]. Its basic principles include: (i) obligation for public Internet Access Services (IASs) providers to treat all traffic equally, without discrimination, restriction or interference, and irrespective of the sender and receiver, content, applications, services, or terminal equipment; (ii) reasonable traffic management measures: transparent, non-discriminatory, proportionate, commercial considerations-agnostic and based on objectively different technical Quality of Service (QoS) requirements of specific categories of traffic, without specific content monitor and maintained only for a necessary period of time; (iii) prohibition of traffic management measures going beyond the above, in particular, to block, slow down, alter, restrict, interfere with, degrade or discriminate between specific content, applications or services, or specific categories thereof.

The only listed exceptions for the latter are, in the case and for the duration of necessity: (i) providing compliance with EU or national law; (ii) preservation of network integrity and security; (iii) prevention of impending network congestion and mitigation of existing exceptional or temporary one, with equal treatment of equivalent categories of traffic. Finally, providers of IASs to the public may offer or facilitate services optimised to QoS requirements for specific content, applications, or services, or a combination thereof, as long as the network capacity is sufficient to provide these services in addition to any IASs, not as a replacement for IASs and without the detriment of IASs availability or general quality for end users.

Pursuant to the provisions of OIAR, the Body of European Regulators for Electronic Communications (BEREC) has issued implementation guidelines regarding the obligations of National Regulatory Authorities (NRAs) resulting from OIAR [11]. In addition, detailed expanded interpretations of the general provisions of OIAR have been added. In particular, equalisation of end users and content/application providers in terms of their rights as consumers of IASs has been stated. Networks outside the scope of OIAR are explicitly defined: non-public or for predetermined/closed user groups, e.g., corporate, Internet access in restaurants, etc., private Machine-to-Machine (M2M) networks. Similarly, outside the scope of OIAR are access services for terminals, which by their nature are used to communicate with a limited number of endpoints, e.g., e-book readers, or M2M terminals. However, sub-Internet services, i.e., restricting access to some communications services or applications (e.g., video streaming) or enabling access to only a predefined part of the Internet (e.g., particular websites), are considered as being in scope of OIAR. In the area of traffic treatment equality, the IP interconnect is excluded from the scope. It is also explained that equal treatment does not imply the same network performance/QoS experience by all end users. In the area of reasonable traffic management, it is acceptable, for optimisation of the overall transmission quality and user experience, to use necessary, suitable, and appropriate traffic management measures that differentiate between objectively different and QoS requirements-justified categories of traffic, within thereof similar treatment has to be provided. It is also allowed to prioritise the traffic related to network management/control over the rest. In the area of beyond reasonable traffic management, it is acceptable to use lossless compression that is transparent to the end user, but it is forbidden to use network mechanisms to force the communication service provider to degrade its service quality, e.g., to lower the resolution of video transmission. When discussing the three admissibility conditions for the principles of reasonable traffic management violation, it was clearly stated that congestion management can be done on a general basis, independent of applications, and only for exceptional cases – the recurrent and more long-lasting network congestion cannot justify the OIAR-allowed exception. Congestion management should not be used as a substitute for network capacity expansion.

The group of services beyond IAS (i.e., NeN rule) is named specialised services (SpSs) by BEREC. Their offering is limited by the OIAR restrictions mentioned above, which are aimed at ensuring the continued availability and general

QoS of IAS. They are subject to verification by NRAs (the detailed guidelines for such a process are described) whether the application could be provided over IAS at the specific and objectively necessary QoS level or they are defined to unacceptably circumvent the provisions regarding traffic management measures applicable to IAS, discussed above. In particular, a simple prioritisation of traffic over IAS or comparable traffic violates OIAR provisions. SpS and IAS traffic fractions can be logically separated when using the same network resources (with static/dynamic reservation or without it). However, any detriment of the general quality of IAS for end users due to SpSs is unacceptable. Therefore, NRAs will also validate the network capacity in terms of its ability to support QoS of SpSs without negative impact on QoS of IAS. In mobile networks, featuring more difficult to anticipate users and traffic volumes mobility, if the overall negative impact of SpSs is unavoidable, minimal, and limited to a short duration, it should not be considered as a detriment for IAS QoS. If persistent perceptible decreases in IAS performance are detected, *e.g.* there is a statistically significant difference between performance before and after SpS is introduced, NRAs' intervention is required. Voice over LTE (VoLTE) and IPTV services are listed as undisputed examples of SpS; Virtual Private Network (VPN) service potentially contradicts the SpSs definition because it can provide Internet access via a remote gateway.

In addition to the law and regulatory policy related to the field, the telecommunications sector in EU is also influenced by other policies or is subject to ones on the digital future for Europe, clean energy and energy union, climate change, and European Green Deal [12]. In addition, due to the energy intensity of the telecommunications industry, it is additionally affected by the crisis in the energy carriers market initiated in 2021 and then intensified by the geopolitical situation after Russia's attack on Ukraine in 2022 (war and mutual economic sanctions between the aggressor and EU).

4   Key Trends in the Telecommunications Market

According to the latest forecasts [13], in the coming years, there will be a dynamic superseding of older technologies by 5G, including the currently dominant Long Term Evolution (LTE) – 4G; at the same time, the sharp growth in traffic volume will continue with the increase in demand for mobile broadband services and migration to voice services based on IP/IP-Multimedia Subsystem (IMS) technology (cf. Table 1). In parallel, the share of smartphones among the mobile terminals used will increase: from 6.2 billion (75%) in 2021 to 7.4 billion (84%) in 2025 [8], additionally stimulated by such initiatives as "Smartphones for All" under the auspices of the International Telecommunication Union (ITU)/United Nations Educational, Scientific and Cultural Organization (UNESCO) Broadband Commission for Sustainable Development, aimed at providing the ability to access the Internet services through a smartphone to another 3.4 billion people by 2030 [14]. It should also be mentioned that the structure of demand for services is systematically changing. In the case of video streaming (62%), music streaming (56%), live sports (36%), gaming (36%), cloud storage (55%), and digital security (57%), the indicators in brackets refer to the percentage of contract mobile subscribers who have added or are interested in adding the respective services to their subscriptions [8].

The above phenomena are supported by MNOs, not only by network expansion. The continuous increase in traffic is associated with the common policy of Average Revenue Per User (ARPU) defence (to save the flat ARPU trend or at least mitigate its decline) in a very competitive market – by raising the monthly data volume allowances in post-paid plans, introducing unlimited plans, enhancing QoS – especially through elevated data speeds, which additionally stimulate consumption. The mobile data traffic growth is additionally sustained by premium features like carrying over unused data to the next month, group data allowance sharing, or plans with a subscription of Over-the-Top (OTT) services with zero-rating: entertainment – Video on Demand (VoD), gaming, streaming of live TV or music; connectivity – social media, messaging, audio or video calls; and other – e-books access or map and traffic applications [15].

Table 1. Selected indicators characterising the forecasted global market of mobile networks (based on [13]).

Indicator	Unit	2022	2028
Mobile subscriptions (total)	billion	8.4	9.2
Mobile subscriptions (5G)	billion	1.0	5.0
Mobile subscriptions (LTE)	billion	5.2	3.6
Mobile data traffic per smartphone	GB per month	15	46
Global total mobile network data traffic	EB per month	115	453
Global 3G/4G/5G Fixed Wireless Access (FWA) data traffic	EB per month	25	128
Global mobile 5G data traffic	EB per month	15	225
Global mobile 2G/3G/4G data traffic	EB per month	75	100
Global video traffic (1)	EB per month	90	324
Broadband Internet of Things (IoT) and Critical IoT (4G/5G) connections	billion	1.4	3.3
Broadband IoT and Critical IoT (4G/5G) share in overall IoT	–	50%	60%
Global population coverage with 5G networks	–	30%	85%
VoLTE subscriptions	billion	4.8	7.7

(1) Both social media and VoD.

The described trends have a significant impact on the problem of powering mobile networks. In 2018, based on the clearly exponentially decreasing trend during the period 2010–2017, the energy efficiency indicator of transmitted mobile data in Finland was expected (least squares fit-based estimation model) to fall to 0.017 kWh/GB in 2022 [16]. However, based on the pilot data collection by Finnish Traficom [17], the average mobile data energy efficiency in 2022 was still at the level of 0.12 kWh/GB, $i.e.$ 7× higher than foreseen. Nokia reports up to even 90% energy savings ($i.e.$, 10× lower consumption) with 5GS compared to legacy networks [18]. Hence, assuming the 5G and non-5G traffic distribution and global monthly data volume according to Table 1, it would mean an approximate global annual energy consumption level of 141 TWh in 2022 and 246 TWh in

2028, or average global power consumption by mobile networks of about 16 GW in 2022 and 28 GW in 2028. These figures consider only the data transmitted over the mobile networks and do not include the energy consumed by the IT systems hosting the OTT service platforms. For comparison, the global electric energy consumption in 2022 was about 27,000 TWh, while the global generation capacity was about 8500 GW and has grown since 2012 by about 48% [19]. During the same period, the worldwide mobile data traffic has increased 133.5-fold [13,20]! While the computational model used here is very simplified, even the orders of magnitude give an idea of the scale of the problem.

5   Technological Considerations Related to Network Slicing

NS is associated with multiple technical and technological aspects.

5GS in its SA architecture variant provides support for NS *per se*. The entire signalling between User Equipment (UE) and Public Land Mobile Network (PLMN) takes place in the context of an individual Network Slice Instance (NSI), identified by Single-Network Slice Selection Assistance Information (S-NSSAI), composed of 8-bit Slice/Service Type (SST) and additional 24-bit slice differentiator [5,21], so the potential capacity of this numbering is almost 4.3 billion NSIs! SSTs can take a value of either 128 3GPP standardised classes or one of 128 "private" classes inside PLMN. Currently, only 5 classes have been standardised: 3 basic ITU classes – Enhanced Mobile Broadband (eMBB), Ultra-Reliable Low-Latency Communication (URLLC), and Massive Internet of Things (MIoT) - equal to Massive Machine Type Communications (mMTC) by ITU, extended with Vehicle to Everything (V2X), and High-Performance Machine-Type Communications (HMTC). UE can be attached to up to 8 different NSIs at the same time. The visions of the future 6G System (6GS) assume much denser and narrower SST differentiation, *e.g.*, Human-Centric Services (HCS), Multi-Purpose Services (MPS), reliable eMBB, Mobile Broadband Reliable Low Latency (MBRLLC), Massive Ultra-Reliable Low Latency Communication (mURLLC) [22] or hybrids of basic ITU classes: URLLC-mMTC, mMTC-eMBB, and URLLC-eMBB [23].

Adaptation of NSI template to the service requirements is performed through flexible shaping of the UP chain and CP ability to accommodate slice-specific control mechanisms (*e.g.*, network data analytics or UE authentication) through its Service-Based Architecture (SBA) and exposure of CP functionality to higher-level systems (*e.g.*, vertical industry environment) [5]. GSM Alliance (GSMA) works on standardisation of interoperable NS templates at the level of their QoS definitions [24]. 5GS supports QoS through End-to-End (E2E) QoS flows, characterised by, *i.a.*, 5G QoS Identifier (5QI) mechanism. The standardised 5QI values include the flow priority, guaranteed/non-guaranteed bit rate attribute, required packet delay budget/error rate, and maximum data burst volume; for guaranteed bit rate flows, maximum/guaranteed rate values can be defined [5].

For radio access, the capacity of spectrum resources is the fundamental issue. Radio spectrum is a scarce good, subject to national and international management coordination. It is agreed to open more bands for use by mobile networks as well as there emerge various modes of band sharing: dynamic spectrum sharing (between different systems, *e.g.*, 4G and 5G, for smooth transition), licensed shared access (primary, incumbent users allow other users – other MNOs or vertical industries – to share their resources), and license-exempt access [25]. However, the traffic capacity of radio channels, *i.e.*, the quest for more and more spectrally efficient modulations, under the pressure of ever-growing demand for data rate, is not physically unlimited. The maximum errorless channel capacity in the presence of noise is bounded by the Shannon-Hartley theorem [26]. Additionally, the expected future mobile networks frequency range stretches from GHz up to sub-THz and THz bands. While the lower bands can be quite efficiently used, the higher frequencies suffer from high penetration loss, poor propagation characteristics, and very high losses due to channel attenuation and scattering [27], which require compensation by much more expensive and energy-intensive amplifiers. Hence, real-life deployments in higher bands are a challenge due to the short operation range (typically up to 200 m). Furthermore, the scope of usable frequency bands for each network cell is also reduced by the standard network planning procedures aiming to reduce cross-cell interference. Moreover, operation in THz bands requires specifically crafted transceivers [28], further questioning their exploitability in large-scale commercial deployments.

The future Radio Access Network (RAN) infrastructure is expected to rely heavily on Software-Defined Radio (SDR). To handle the increasing data rates, the techniques that enable the improvements of the spectral efficiency of the transmission and coverage have to be applied, including gradually more advanced coding schemes, higher order and more complex modulations, increasing order of Multiple Input, Multiple Output (MIMO) systems, beam management mechanisms, RAN slicing specific support (*e.g.*, scheduler-level algorithms), *etc.* Implementation of these methods together with the increasing volume of processed data, however, will require significantly higher compute power on the SDR side. Other technology-specific factors will need to be improved, such as, *e.g.*, Signal to Noise Ratio (SNR) for higher order modulation schemes [29]. The energy aspect is especially important in the context of the green networking paradigm, promoted by the EU, and resulting energy efficiency targets. The technological enhancements will require significant energy investments on both network and UE side (additionally constrained by the battery size in the majority of devices) to operate efficiently and provide the throughput gains to the end user, at the same time contradicting the energy saving trends.

6   Conflicts of Interests and Contradictions

The adoption of NeN principles will raise multiple contradictory challenges for IAS providers, particularly MNOs, to tackle. Some major identified conflicts of interest and contradictory requirements are discussed below.

The digital world to which the mobile networks contribute claims to be "virtual" (so "dematerialised"), but it is responsible for the consumption of 10% of the electricity produced worldwide and 4% of CO_2 emissions (almost double the civilian air sector), while the streaming technology alone produces 1% of global CO_2 emission. A single Google search power consumption is equal to a light bulb left on for 35 min, while an e-mail with a big attachment is the equivalent of 24 h of lighting [30]. The digital revolution has specific energy and environmental costs that have only been increasing so far. While the pressure to reduce emissions related to terrestrial and aerial transportation, energy losses in buildings, and inefficient heat and lighting sources is everyday now, no one questions the paradigm of the ongoing and developing digital revolution in which the amount of data produced, processed and stored is growing exponentially, generating an obvious energy cost. It should be emphasised that this is happening even before the massive implementation of Artificial Intelligence (AI), which is announced in the future, especially as an inherent component of 6GS [22,23]. On the other hand, the content providers accelerate the development of new services and increase quality – thereby, data volume demand. As of today, the 6 players consume the majority of the global OTT traffic: Google (20.99%), Facebook (15.39%), Netflix (9.39%), Apple (4.18%), Amazon (3.68%), and Microsoft (3.32%) [31]. Additionally, the mechanisms of auto-playing of the next video or commercials drive OTT providers' revenues, stimulating passive network traffic consumption having to be supported by Internet Providers, i.a., MNOs, at their cost. While the entry into the use of quantum computers with computing performance 1000× greater than supercomputers, at the same power consumption, is predicted, this technology will be used in central server rooms due to the requirements of powering and sterility of working conditions. This will deepen the imbalance between OTT providers and operators of virtualised, distributed networks based on commodity hardware, serving the OTT traffic.

The NeN approach principles will impose on IAS providers, in the face of a steady increase in traffic, the obligation to constantly improve the network capacity to accommodate OTT's services, which requires progressive investments in the infrastructural assets. In the current business setting, however, the OTT providers are the primary beneficiaries of the service hyperscalers, while the IAS providers pay for the delivery of the OTT traffic to the end customers [31]. Therefore, new business models shall emerge to facilitate financial contributions from the major traffic generators to the IAS providers that will enable a fair split of costs and gains of the OTT services upscaling. To this end, the NS paradigm can be efficiently exploited as it would allow the adoption of different pricing policies per OTT service.

The area of focus for NeN is the provision of services without deterioration of QoS. It has to be noted, however, that from the end customer point of view, the parameter that portrays the quality for the service consumer is Quality of Experience (QoE). In general, performing the mapping between the QoE and QoS is service type dependent and requires thorough studies of factors related to human perception. Several successful biological constraints have been well studied and can be leveraged to optimise resource usage, *e.g.* image and audio compression algorithms. As principles of NeN do not consider QoE as a target, which can lead to severe resource overspending. An example of such a common case is a very high-quality video streaming (4K and higher resolution) consumed via a handheld device. With the limited resolution of the human eye, perception is dependent mostly on the viewing distance and to a lesser extent on the display size [32]. For the relative viewing distances higher typical for smartphones, the sensitivity to spatial losses is low, *i.e.*, 480p video is seen almost as sharp as HD video [32], which questions the rationale for constant improvement of the resolution of the transferred video (4K, 8K) in some cases.

7 Discussion

Based on the analysis of considerations in the previously described areas as well as the mutual influence between them, some general observations can be made.

NS has been proposed and then included in the standardisation as a fundamental feature of 5GS, which is to be further developed in 6GS. Its mass implementation was assumed, and the basic mechanisms to support it are those of differentiated processing of individual traffic fractions, QoS management, and traffic prioritisation. While the wired part of PLMN can theoretically be expanded without any obstacles, the bottleneck that forces hard competition between individual traffic fractions is frequency resources – both those at the disposal of individual MNOs and general ones.

NeN rules in EU mandate equal, non-discriminatory treatment of all fractions of the traffic. The use of QoS management mechanisms is theoretically possible, in a proportional manner, but the use of prioritisation of access to resources for a class of SpSs, seemingly not subject to the NeN rigour, in practice would inevitably lead to the impermissible degradation of IAS QoS. The available frequency resources are not unlimited, and MNOs, under their licenses, may only divide them between IAS traffic and SpSs traffic.

Both the forecasts regarding traffic volumes and the number of smartphone users – terminals generating traffic dominated by the ever-growing fraction associated with streaming – predict continuous growth. As the NeN rules equalise the rights of end users and content providers (OTTs), they gain a privileged position over IAS providers. However, the position of MNOs among IAS providers becomes extremely difficult here: any expansion of network capacity can be immediately consumed by ever-increasing OTT traffic. Blocking radio resources for future SpSs would be a form of protection against charges of QoS degradation of IAS services, but it would be economically absurd (freezing resources so that they do not bring benefits) and an abandonment of optimisation of the use of resources from their flexible allocation.

In its current form, NeN prioritises maintenance of QoS for the consumers of the typical, overwhelming eMBB traffic (streaming, social media, gaming, *etc.*) over other types of services. The NS paradigm, largely extends the spectrum of the latter, enabling MNOs to offer SpSs such as, *e.g.*, safety-critical services requiring very high NSI availability, reliability, and resilience. Considering the network resource limitations and potential rapid changes in their usage (due to users' mobility, time of day, and other special circumstances such as *e.g.*, sports events, concerts, *etc.*), maintaining the required service level for the eMBB consumers can potentially affect the performance of services in which interruption has critical consequences (injury, death, environmental or property damage, *etc.*).

NS-based SpSs were and still are envisioned as enablers of the "Industry 4.0" vision. The services tailored for drones, telemedicine, transportation, agriculture and forestry, public security, and many other applications, with guaranteed QoS, would be of great social and economic importance as well as a business opportunity for MNOs being currently under extremely high market pressure. However, under the conditions imposed by NeN, such services can practically only be provided by MNOs not offering IAS. Nevertheless, even then, effective spectrum management in the spectrum sharing model may be impossible if MNO offering the privileged IAS is the co-user of the shared band.

Due to physical constraints of spectrum capacity and energy consumption, the ever-growing variety of OTT services, especially those related to entertainment, and their elevated QoS requirements, will be near-to-impossible for MNOs to handle in the long run. The raising pressure for networks' energy efficiency further aggravates this issue, as it requires MNOs to reduce power consumption, which will also impact the total system capacity.

In the case of road traffic, there is general agreement that there must be privileged, emergency vehicles to which other participants must give way. The economic, social, ecological, and climatic consequences of unrestricted motorisation are commonly discussed. The sense of certain ways of using cars is questioned, and pros/cons of individual and collective transportation are also compared. In the case of digital virtual reality, which leaves a deep footprint in physical reality (*e.g.*, related to energy or raw materials consumption), the paradigm of the unlimited digital revolution and unlimited production, transmission, and consumption of data applies, and the footprint is continuously growing. Therefore, the question must be asked whether the "digital revolution" has turned into "digital greed". It will be appropriate to consider the sustainable use of the Internet and whether all uses of digital reality (*e.g.*, telemedicine and entertainment), which is also a set of limited resources, are of equal social value and importance, also whether unrestricted mobile access to entertainment services, cannibalising other applications due to being privileged, is socially and economically justified.

In summary, it can be stated that NS is an idea, which consumed a lot of effort and resources during its development – in the stages of conceptualisation, research, trials, industrial standardisation, and harmonisation of interoperability. Currently, it is faced with a combination of factors (paradigms, regulations, trends, business models, physical and technological barriers) creating multidimensional contradictions preventing its wide implementation. Among them, the regulation concerning NeN is of root and key importance. Therefore, it is necessary to undertake a broad discussion towards the revision of the adopted paradigms and visions in order to unlock the opportunities for economic development, dependent also on the implementation of NS-based communication services. Care should also be taken to balance the market position of the telecommunications business actors in the context of sustainable development and exploitation of the planet's resources, as is the case of other sectors of the economy and industry.

8   Conclusions

This paper discusses the issue of the regulatory and business environment for the possibility of providing communication services based on NS, perceived as an enabler for the "Industry 4.0" vision. The basic features of the EU regulation concerning NeN have been presented, as well as other political factors affecting NS. Trends in the telecommunications market have been analysed; in particular, the continued unstoppable increase in traffic, driven mainly by OTT providers, placed by the NeN regulation in a dominant position over IAS providers, including MNOs. Technical conditions of NS in PLMNs have been discussed, especially physical barriers blocking unlimited traffic growth. Attention has also been drawn to the fundamental conflicts of interest between various business actors in the telecommunications market.

Based on the above considerations, a general conclusion is formulated that in view of the fundamental contradiction of the NeN, digital revolution, sustainable and socially responsible growth, and business fairness paradigms, until they are revised, the widespread implementation of communication services based on NS, and thus the realisation of the "Industry 4.0" vision are currently impossible.

References

1. Next Generation Mobile Networks (NGMN): 5G White Paper (Feb 2015). https://ngmn.org/wp-content/uploads/NGMN_5G_White_Paper_V1_0.pdf. Accessed 22 May 2023
2. Kukliński, S., Tomaszewski, L., Kozłowski, K., Pietrzyk, S.: Business models of network slicing. In: 2018 9th International Conference on the Network of the Future (NOF), pp. 39–43 (Nov 2018). https://doi.org/10.1109/NOF.2018.8597858
3. PlanetLab: An open platform for developing, deploying, and accessing planetary-scale services. [Website]. http://www.planet-lab.org/. Accessed 22 May 2023
4. ETSI: Network Functions Virtualisation (NFV); Architectural Framework. Group Specification ETSI GS NFV 002 V1.2.1, European Telecommunications Standards Institute (Dec 2014). https://www.etsi.org/deliver/etsi_gs/NFV/001_099/002/01.02.01_60/gs_nfv002v010201p.pdf
5. 3GPP: System architecture for the 5G System (5GS). Technical Standard TS 23.501, ver. 18.1.0, 3rd Generation Partnership Project (Apr 2023)
6. Chochliouros, I.P., Spiliopoulou, A.S., Lazaridis, P., Dardamanis, A., Zaharis, Z., Kostopoulos, A.: Dynamic network slicing: challenges and opportunities. In: Maglogiannis, I., Iliadis, L., Pimenidis, E. (eds.) Artificial Intelligence Applications and Innovations. AIAI 2020 IFIP WG 12.5 International Workshops, pp. 47–60. Springer International Publishing, Cham (Jun 2020). https://doi.org/10.1007/978-3-030-49190-1_5

7. Tomaszewski, L., Kołakowski, R.: Mobile services for smart agriculture and forestry, biodiversity monitoring, and water management: challenges for 5G/6G networks. Telecom **4**(1), 67–99 (2023). https://doi.org/10.3390/telecom4010006

8. GSM Alliance (GSMA): The Mobile Economy 2022 (Feb 2022). https://www.gsma.com/mobileeconomy/wp-content/uploads/2022/02/280222-The-Mobile-Economy-2022.pdf. Accessed 22 May 2023

9. Gadringer, S.: Network neutrality in the european union: a communications policy process analysis. Internet Histories **4**(2), 178–195 (2020). https://doi.org/10.1080/24701475.2020.1749807

10. European Parliament and Council: Regulation (EU) 2015/2120 of the European Parliament and of the Council of 25 November 2015 laying down measures concerning open internet access and retail charges for regulated intra-EU communications and amending Directive 2002/22/EC and Regulation (EU) No 531/2012 (Text with EEA relevance). Official Journal of the European Union, L 310, pp. 1–18 (26 Nov 2015). https://eur-lex.europa.eu/eli/reg/2015/2120/2020-12-21

11. BEREC: BEREC Guidelines on the Implementation of the Open Internet Regulation. BoR (22) 81, pp. 1–55 (09 Jun 2022). https://www.berec.europa.eu/sites/default/files/files/document_register_store/2022/6/BoR_%2822%29_81_Update_to_the_BEREC_Guidelines_on_the_Implementation_of_the_Open_Internet_Regulation.pdf

12. Council of the the European Union and the European Council: Policies. [Website]. https://www.consilium.europa.eu/en/policies. Accessed 22 May 2023

13. Ericsson: Ericsson Mobility Report (Nov 2022). https://www.ericsson.com/4ae28d/assets/local/reports-papers/mobility-report/documents/2022/ericsson-mobility-report-november-2022.pdf. Accessed 22 May 2023

14. Vodafone: The Broadband Commission for Sustainable Development and Vodafone urge action to connect 3.4 bn people with smartphones by 2030. [Website] (Sep 2021). https://www.vodafone.com/news/planet-news/broadband-commission-vodafone-urge-action-connect-people-smartphones. Accessed 22 May 2023

15. Basile, V., Casahuga, G., Lippautz, M., Mukhija, P., Bhatia, A.: Evolving pricing of mobile tariff plans; Be dynamic or lose (Oct 2019). https://www.adlittle.com/sites/default/files/viewpoints/adl_pricing_mobile_tariffs-min.pdf. Accessed 22 May 2023

16. Pihkola, H., Hongisto, M., Apilo, O., Lasanen, M.: Evaluating the energy consumption of mobile data transfer-from technology development to consumer behaviour and life cycle thinking. Sustainability **10**(7) (Jul 2018). https://doi.org/10.3390/su10072494

17. Traficom: First study on the energy consumption of communications networks. [Website] (Nov 2022). https://www.traficom.fi/en/news/first-study-energy-consumption-communications-networks. Accessed 22 May 2023

18. Nokia: Nokia confirms 5G as 90 percent more energy efficient. [Website] (Dec 2022). https://www.nokia.com/about-us/news/releases/2020/12/02/nokia-confirms-5g-as-90-percent-more-energy-efficient/. Accessed 22 May 2023

19. International Energy Agency: Electricity market report 2023 (Feb 2023). https://www.iea.org/reports/electricity-market-report-2023. Accessed 22 May 2023

20. Digital News Asia: Mobile data traffic to grow 13-fold from 2012–2017: Cisco (Feb 2013). https://www.digitalnewsasia.com/digital-economy/mobile-data-traffic-to-grow-13fold-from-2012-2017-cisco. Accessed 22 May 2023

21. 3GPP: Numbering, addressing and identification. Technical Standard TS 23.003, ver. 18.1.0, 3rd Generation Partnership Project (Mar 2023)

22. Yazar, A., Doğan Tusha, S., Arslan, H.: 6G vision: an ultra-flexible perspective. ITU J. Future Evolving Technol. **1**(1), 121–140 (2020). https://doi.org/10.52953/IKVY9186

23. Corici, M.I., et al.: On the road to 6G: drivers, challenges and enabling technologies. White Paper v1.0, Fraunhofer Fokus (Nov 2021). https://cdn0.scrvt.com/fokus/137064883186fe80/9a009606e5a4/6g-sentinel-white-paper.pdf

24. GSMA: Generic Network Slice Template. Official Document NG.116, ver. 7.0, GSMA (Jun 2022). https://www.gsma.com/newsroom/wp-content/uploads/NG.116-v7.0.pdf

25. Moussaoui, M., Bertin, E., Crespi, N.: Telecom business models for beyond 5G and 6G networks: Towards disaggregation? In: 2022 1st International Conference on 6G Networking (6GNet), pp. 1–8 (Jul 2022). https://doi.org/10.1109/6GNet54646.2022.9830514

26. Shannon, C.E.: Communication in the presence of noise. Proc. IEEE **86**(2), 447–457 (1998). https://doi.org/10.1109/JPROC.1998.659497. reprinted from the Proceedings of the IRE, 37(1), 10–21, (Jan 1949),

27. Kokkoniemi, J., Lehtomäki, J., Juntti, M.: Measurements on penetration loss in terahertz band. In: 2016 10th European Conference on Antennas and Propagation (EuCAP), pp. 1–5 (Apr 2016). https://doi.org/10.1109/EuCAP.2016.7481176

28. Tripathi, S., Sabu, N.V., Gupta, A.K., Dhillon, H.S.: Millimeter-wave and terahertz spectrum for 6G wireless. In: Wu, Y., Singh, S., Taleb, T., Roy, A., Dhillon, H.S., Kanagarathinam, M.R., De, A. (eds.) 6G Mobile Wireless Networks. CCN, pp. 83–121. Springer, Cham (2021). https://doi.org/10.1007/978-3-030-72777-2_6

29. Coudert, D., Nepomuceno, N., Rivano, H.: Wireless backhaul networks: Minimizing energy consumption by power-efficient radio links configuration. Research Report RR-6752, INRIA (Feb 2009). https://hal.inria.fr/inria-00344344/document/. Accessed 22 May 2023

30. Pitron, G.: L'enfer numérique. Voyage au bout d'un like (Digital Hell: Journey to the End of a Like). Les Liens Qui Liberent, Paris (Sep 2021)

31. Fierce Wireless: "It's not fair" cry Orange, DT, Telefonica, Vodafone about hyperscaler traffic. [Website] (Mar 2023). https://www.fiercewireless.com/wireless/its-not-fair-cry-orange-dt-telefonica-vodafone-about-hyperscaler-traffic. Accessed 22 May 2023

32. Berger, J.: Quality evaluation of streaming video on mobile networks. White Paper 8SQ-AR, Rohde & Schwarz (Aug 2018). https://scdn.rohde-schwarz.com/ur/pws/dl_downloads/premiumdownloads/premium_dl_brochures_and_datasheets/premium_dl_whitepaper/White_Paper__Quality_Evaluation_of_Streaming_Video_on_Mobile_Networks_5215-4369-92_v0100.pdf. Accessed 22 May 2023

OASEES: An Innovative Scope for a DAO-Based Programmable Swarm Solution, for Decentralizing AI Applications Close to Data Generation Locations

Ioannis P. Chochliouros[1]([✉])[iD], Michail -Alexandros Kourtis[2], George Xilouris[2], Wouter Tavernier[3], Enrique Areizaga Sanchez[4], Margarita Anastassova[5], Christian Bolzmacher[5], Nikolay Tcholtchev[6], Antonello Corsi[7], Panagiotis Trakadas[8], Marta Millet[9], Christos Xenakis[10], Adnan Imeri[11], Francesco Bellesini[12], Paride D'Ostilio[13], Albertos Markakis[14], Ihsan Bal Engin[15], Antonis Litke[16], Lucrezia Maria Quarato[17], Diego Cugat[18], Georgios Gardikis[19], Charilaos Zarakovitis[20], Stephane Bouilland[21], Zaharias Zaharis[22], Christina Lessi[1], Dimitrios Arvanitozisis[1], and Anastasia S. Spiliopoulou[1]

[1] Hellenic Telecommunications Organization (OTE) S.A., 99 Kifissias Avenue, 15124 Maroussi-Athens, Greece
ichochliouros@oteresearch.gr
[2] National Center for Scientific Research "Demokritos", Athens, Greece
[3] IMEC—Department of Information Technology, Ghent University, Ghent, Belgium
[4] Fundacion Tecnalia Research & Innovation, Derio, Spain
[5] Commissariat à L'Energie Atomique et aux Energies Alternatives, Paris, France
[6] Fraunhofer Gesellschaft Zur Forderung der Angewandten Forschung EV, Munich, Germany
[7] Engineering – Ingegneria Informatica SpA, Rome, Italy
[8] National & Kapodistrian University of Athens, Athens, Greece
[9] Robotnik Automation SLL, Barcelona, Spain
[10] Inqbit Innovations Srl, Bucharest, Romania
[11] Infrachain SBL, Luxembourg, Luxembourg
[12] Emotion Srl, Le Galatina, Italy
[13] ASM Terni SpA, Terni, Italy
[14] Adrestia Erevnitiki Idiotiki Kefalaiouxiki Etaireia, Iraklio, Greece
[15] Senso Engineering BV, Groningen, The Netherlands
[16] Infili Technologies S.A., Athens, Greece
[17] SCM Group SpA, Rimini, Italy
[18] CapGemini Engineering, Barcelona, Spain
[19] Space Hellas S.A., Athens, Greece
[20] Axon Logic, Athens, Greece
[21] Fondation Hopale, Berck Sur Mer, France
[22] Aristotle University of Thessaloniki, Thessaloniki, Greece

Abstract. As traditional linear models have proved to be ineffective in perspective of the stagnant decision-making and inefficient data federation, the pathway onwards a European data sovereignty dictates for a sustainable and circular economy across diverse market sectors. In this scope, the EU-funded OASEES project

I. Maglogiannis et al. (Eds.): AIAI 2023 Workshops, IFIP AICT 677, pp. 91–105, 2023.
https://doi.org/10.1007/978-3-031-34171-7_7

has identified the need for a novel, inclusive and disruptive approach regarding the cloud to edge continuum and swarm programmability and also supporting multi-tenant, interoperable, secure and trustworthy deployments. In the present paper we discuss actual challenges for the management and orchestration of edge infrastructure and services to exploit the potential of edge processing. Then we discuss the concept and fundamental features of the OASEES approach together with technology challenges that are to be covered by the intended system development. We also discuss, in brief, a set of several vertical edge applications with significant market impact.

Keywords: 5G · AI · blockchain · cloud hosting · compute continuum · DAO · decentralized applications · edge computing · edge processing · edge sharing · enhanced platform awareness · ML · MLOps · swarm computing · secure edge

1 Introduction

The huge increase in device connectivity and produced data has resulted in the extended growth of diverse intelligent processing services to create insights and exploit data in a multi-modal manner. At present, the most powerful data processing – as it is observed in various systems – takes place in a centralized way at the cloud and this offers the opportunity and the capability not only to scale but also to allocate involved and available resources both on demand and efficiently. Centralized data processing [1] actually occurs when all data is collected to a single centralized storage area and processed upon completion by a single computer with often very large architectures in terms of memory, processor and storage. All of the data is saved/stored in a centralized data storage system. Protection level decisions and authorised access are the responsibility of the respective system administrator. In this context, centralized processing can so offer several distinct benefits for the involved "actors" as, among others: it helps in reducing the cost as there is no emphasis on more hardware and machines to be involved; it can provide more enhanced data security, and; the data and the program on each information system are independent to other information systems, thus extending security and trust. Cloud hosting [2] makes applications and websites accessible by using dedicated cloud resources. Unlike traditional hosting processes, the respective solutions are not deployed on a single server; instead, a network of connected virtual and physical cloud servers does host the application – or the website – ensuring greater elasticity and scalability. "Key features" of this context may implicate for: (i) applications and solutions being deployed on a cloud network rather than an on-premises, single server; (ii) resources can be scalable to user needs; (iii) involved entities/organizations only pay for the resources they use, and; (iv) solutions are automated and controlled using Application Programming Interfaces (APIs), web portals and mobile applications. This also offers flexibility and reliability: for the former, as traditional hosting services offer limited bandwidth, cloud hosting scales to accommodate traffic spikes or seasonal demands; for the latter, hardware failures do not cause downtime because sites and applications are hosted on a network of server; thus, traffic travels across separate network interfaces, where it is segregated and secured.

However, centralized processing and cloud hosting although they have been widely used and deployed in numerous systems, bound – and up to a certain extent "limit" – their services and/or applications to operate in a resource restricted manner, relying most of times on large single entities to offer: (i) authentication; (ii) data storage; (iii) data processing; (iv) connectivity, and; (v) vendor-locked environments for development and orchestration. This significantly limits the users from their data governance and even identity management [3, 4], as it prevents them from efficiently managing their identities and access, restricts their visibility into identities and access privileges and does not help them to implement any of the necessary controls for preventing potential inappropriate or risky access. Data governance implicates for the sum of policies, processes, standards, metrics, and roles being able to ensure that data is used effectively to help an entity to realize its objectives. Data governance establishes the responsibilities and processes which ensure that the data being used is not only of high quality but is also secure. As such, it defines who takes what actions, on what data, in which situations and what methods are in use. On the other hand, an identity management (IdM) system prevents unauthorized access to systems and resources, helps prevent exfiltration of protected data and raises alerts and alarms when access attempts are made by unauthorized users or programs, whether from inside or outside the entity's perimeter. IdM includes polices and technologies to properly identify, authenticate and authorize people, groups of people, or software applications through attributes (including user access rights and restrictions based on their identities). Similarly, existing solutions for edge device authentication [5–7] require a centralized entity to trust them and authenticate them, rendering a non-portable identification paradigm.

2   Challenges for a More Efficient Edge Processing

Over the past years and following the fast progress of the underlying IT and network infrastructures (especially within the "5G and beyond" context), several platforms and/or related solutions, also including open-source- based ones, have been emerged focusing primarily on the management and orchestration of edge infrastructure and services [8–11]. However, in order to fully exploit the potential of edge processing [12], a need has been raised towards proposing for a "more holistic solution" by embracing the entire compute continuum [13] (the compute continuum allows the exploitation of hybrid IoT-Edge-Cloud infrastructures with great flexibility while guaranteeing high-performance) as well as by including central infrastructures (public clouds and networks) and smart devices. In fact, edge processing occurs when the computation of data is carried out directly in the smart sensor node or at the gateway of the network, intending to save power consumption and ensure that data is kept confidential, thus allowing involved "actors" to analyze critical information at the node level and reduce anomaly detection time(s). The idea is to "put" basic computation as close as possible to the physical system, making the involved IoT (Internet of Things) device as "smart" as possible. In this context edge processing can implicate for several benefits such as: (i) confidentiality, as data is not sent to the cloud and is locally stored on the device or the other equipment used; (ii) cost reduction, as latency and throughput of high-volume time-series asset data can be optimized - in fact, reducing the amount of useless machine data sent and stored in the cloud leads to significant benefits as it enables real-time distributed applications and simultaneously eliminates the need for complex systems; (iii) lower latency, implicating that a minimal delay in the repair of equipment is essential for assets which are assessed as mission-critical.

Under the previously discussed framework and with the purpose of meeting performance, cost and/or potential legal requirements, cloud resources are nowadays moving toward the edge of the network to "bridge the gap" between resource-constrained devices and distant but powerful cloud Data Centres (DCs). Edge computing [14, 15] is an emerging computing paradigm which refers to a range of networks and devices at or near the user. Edge (which implicates for both edge devices and the network edge) is about processing data closer to where data is being generated, enabling processing at greater speeds and volumes, leading to greater action-led results and experiences in real time. The wide adoption of the recently coined fog and edge computing paradigms alongside conventional cloud computing creates a novel scenario, known as the "cloud continuum" [16], where services may benefit from the overall set of resources to optimize their execution. To operate successfully, such a cloud continuum scenario demands for novel management strategies, enabling a coordinated and efficient management of the entire set of resources, from the edge up to the cloud, designed in particular to address key edge characteristics, such as mobility, heterogeneity and volatility. While recent studies propose that the future of cloud computing [17] will be distributed and heterogeneous [18], there is a lack of open management frameworks to address this sort of dispersion and heterogeneity. Commercial solutions for hybrid core/edge management, such as Azure Edge Stack [19] indeed exist, but these are usually "closed", restricted to specific deployment scenarios and only provided as managed services (i.e., not suitable for private (fully on-premises) deployments).

Another essential "gap" to deal with is related to the ease of access from the point of view of the data scientists and engineers. Public clouds already provide user-friendly abstractions (notebooks, simplified administration interfaces, graphical workflow designers, etc.) to data experts, so that the latter can concentrate on the management of the data and the selection and optimization of the ML (Machine Learning) / AI (Artificial Intelligence) algorithms, rather than on the management of the physical and virtual resources which are needed and committed. This is actually a feature missing from existing edge orchestration solutions [20]. Edge orchestration [21–23] is a term that describes the use of an "Edge Orchestrator" to manage, automate and coordinate the flow of resources between multiple types of devices, infrastructure and network domains at the edge of a network. Edge orchestration allows businesses and organizations to efficiently route data resources so that to avoid potential bottlenecks, reduce latency and scale their network as needed, per case. The goal of edge orchestration in a network is about establishing more intelligence to the network in which real-time network events, traffic or other dynamic requests can be handled automatically, at the edge of the network. This eases the effective deployment of resources and allows near-instantaneous provisioning of network services. It can also help reallocation of network resources across multiple devices or other sort of equipment used.

Furthermore, security is a similarly important aspect [24, 25] as edge infrastructures can be highly dynamic, involving ad-hoc onboarding of edge nodes and smart devices, possibly under different status of ownership (e.g., in multi-actor environments). In such a volatile context, in order to guarantee data privacy and availability (here data availability means that information shall be accessible to authorized users) there is a need to continuously verify the integrity of both infrastructure and services across the considered compute continuum [26].

3 "OASEES" Concept: Features and Technology Challenges

Following to the various challenges and trends discussed in the previous section, the ongoing OASEES [27] project aims to deliver and promote a European, fully open-source, decentralized and secure Swarm programmability framework for edge devices and leveraging various AI/ML accelerators (Field Programmable Gate Arrays [28] (FPGAs), Spiking Neural Networks [29] (SNNs), Quantum [30]), while supporting a privacy preserving Object ID federation process [31]. More specifically, OASEES will be built leveraging existing open-source edge orchestration solutions and intends to be capable of:

- *Managing the lifecycle of services across the compute continuum* [32, 33] by orchestrating heterogeneous resources in the cloud, WAN (Wide Area Network), edge and smart device domains. Resources from Central Processing Units (CPUs), Graphics Processing Units (GPUs), NPUs, FPGAs bespoke chips (e.g., for Spiking Neural Networks [34] acceleration) and Quantum processors [35] are to be pooled and jointly managed to optimize ML at the edge, for maximum performance and energy efficiency. While the focus is expected to be on managing the edge and smart device domains, adaptors to popular public clouds will also be integrated, for supporting end-to-end (E2E) services with the appropriate Quality of Service (QoS) guarantees at WAN network level (i.e., core- edge interconnect).
- *Promoting the development of decentralized ML/AI edge services* [36] by means of an SDK (Software Development Kit) and in the form of Decentralized Applications [37] (DApps) in a user-friendly notebook-style abstractions for data scientists and engineers. DApps can operate autonomously, typically through the use of smart contracts, that run on a decentralized computing, blockchain or other distributed ledger system. The "serverless" fashion for Swarm deployment will make use of distributed ML platform capabilities and a Distributed Data Fabric; this will essentially realise the vision of Decentralized Artificial Intelligence as-a-Service [38] (DAIaaS), an essential component towards a smarter Internet of Everything (IoE). DAI is a model that allows for the isolation of processing without the downside of aggregate knowledge sharing. By virtue, it enables the user to process information independently, among varying computing apparatuses or devices. In doing so, one can achieve different results and then analyze the knowledge, creating new solutions to a problem which a centralized AI system would not be able to.
- *Supporting multi-actor/multi-domain deployments*, by: (i) enforcing security and trustworthiness; (ii) enabling the federation with peer OS instances [39] in other administrative domains (multi-domain operation) and; (iii) fostering monetization by advertising/trading capabilities and resources in third-party Marketplaces (including

the Marketplace of the European Open Science Cloud (EOSC) [40]; EOSC's ambition is to provide European researchers, innovators, companies and citizens with a federated and open multi-disciplinary environment where they can publish, find and re-use data, tools and services for research, innovation and educational purposes).

OASEES has identified specific research topics and corresponding challenges which it aims to directly "address" as briefly discussed in the following sections:

Programmable Frameworks for Swarm and Edge Computing: The existing management and orchestration frameworks landscape [41] is scattered in systems focusing either on cloud management, NFV MANO [42] (Network Functions Virtualization Management and Orchestration), Software Defined Networking- (SDN) based network control [43] or IoT-focused edge platforms [44]. OASEES' aim is to reconcile and "go beyond" existing control systems and APIs into an open programmable Swarm framework so that to enable an IoT-to-edge-to-cloud continuum where services can be developed, benefiting from: (i) an IoT-to-edge-to-cloud infrastructure model enabling to characterize a wide variety of related resources, building further on existing State-of-the-Art (SotA) such as OCCI [45]; (ii) a de/composable service model based on SotA such as TOSCA [46] enabling to characterize which components require performance profiling and/or allow hardware acceleration, which components require security measures (monitoring, anomaly detection, etc.), or what particular reliability or QoS-based control loops. Composability in the service model of OASEES also means that services can recursively build upon each other – this will enable one service to serve as an intelligence or data-processing component for another; (iii) a security- and intelligence-aware SDK enabling lifecycle management and asymptotic orchestration of data rich services. To this aim, OASEES' target is to employ a transactional model for the lifecycle of services, which can enable partial provisioning, migration, roll-back and or tear-down of individual components while ensuring service integrity.

Support for Heterogeneous Dynamic Infrastructure: **Enhanced Platform Awareness** (EPA) [47] is a well-known capability of recent resource management and orchestration systems either in the context of Virtual Machines - VMs (e.g., OpenStack, Open Source Management (OSM)) or in the context of Containers [48]. The challenge here is that cloud computing resources are becoming increasingly heterogeneous and, at the same moment, are distributed widely in across smaller DCs at multiple locations. This trend points to a rapidly increasing adoption of accelerators in the near future. Thus OASEES will enable the discovery and pooling of edge platform acceleration capabilities to create a holistic view of all the different capabilities available in the distributed edge environment and, ultimately, to optimize placement decisions. This can be achieved by leveraging the proposed OASEES agents operating over these heterogeneous infrastructures, platforms and smart devices and collecting device capability information to be stored in OASEES' central repository. OASEES will run customizable optimization algorithms to select the best mapping of the service demands on the physical infrastructure.

Edge Infrastructure Sharing and Monetization: A core OASEES' attribute is also the "sharing" of services across distributed edge-based infrastructures [49], purely suggesting a cross-layer orchestration mechanism between involved network, computation and storage services as already identified by the ETSI MEC Industry Specification Group

(ISG) [50]. In this scope, the Mosaic 5G initiative [51] has already proposed some APIs allowing for an easier cross-domain orchestration of services and federated resource management, while other initiatives work towards achieving a cross-infrastructure collaboration but focusing on more specific layers [52]. The evolution and proliferation of software defined infrastructures allows access and configuration of services through well-defined APIs; to this aim, OASEES intends to combine existing and SotA technologies and techniques so that to develop an E2E cross-domain service sharing framework [53], to achieve optimal resource management/consumption. The developed framework will allow third-party service providers to offer their services through a service marketplace. This capability can be perfectly aligned with the "neutral host" paradigm [54], which has lately become an attractive business model, expanding to 5G/6G infrastructures.

AI-Enabled Data Processing for Hyper-Distributed Applications: Numerous of analytics processes, varying from factory automations to autonomous vehicle operations or safety-critical applications rely on the continuous, low-latency flow and processing of data to generate results within a short timeframe. Especially in production environments with continually evolving data, a deployed ML model is "bound" to degrade in quality without a constant feed of new data feeds, as the assumptions on which it was developed may become less valid with time [55]. Although edge computing seems to be an attractive alternative for such cases, the majority of the existing computing techniques (used in the cloud and/or on premises) are usually not directly applicable to the edge, due to the diversity of computing sources, lack of resource management and distribution of data. However, the provision of the necessary abstraction layers practically "brings" AI tasks "closer" to the source, thus overcoming the most common culprits of cloud computing while, at the same time, benefiting from the enhanced privacy and inherent scalability of distributed edge approaches. Based on this approach, OASEES aims to rely on secure data spaces for storage and privacy-preserving ML technologies (i.e., Federated Learning [56]), allowing users to train and share their models without compromising the sovereignty of their data. Moreover, the edge analytics services shall benefit from increased trust and faster response times to changing environmental conditions (concept/data drifts) through the adoption of MLOps (ML Operations) principles [57] for continuous monitoring, treating ML assets consistently with all other software assets within a Continuous Integration/Continuous Deployment (CI/CD) environment.

Trustworthy and Secure Edge: The highly distributed and heterogeneous nature of the OASEES infrastructure and operating environment dictates architectural design around a form of "Zero-Trust" Architecture [58], as only trustworthy and secure edge nodes shall be authorized to participate. This implicates for deployment of a "mixture" of existing and cutting-edge technologies, such as Trusted Computing attestation [59] and cloud-native secure identities with SPIFFE (Secure Production Identity Framework for Everyone) [60]. The attestation capability of OASEES ensures that only nodes with a trusted hardware, firmware and Operating System (OS) environment shall be used, which prevents from hardware supply chain attacks, bootkits, rootkits and malware. The cloud-native secure identity of a workload is bound to the attestation of the underlying hosting infrastructure, ensuring that only secure and trusted services can participate in the workload.

Blockchain-Backed IoT Governance: The multi-party smart contract deployed on top of blockchain technology [61] sustains the deployment of heterogeneous and dynamic architecture to help orchestrate processes and workflows in the OASEES. Blockchain as a decentralized distributed database enables sharing of trustworthy information among different nodes part of a certified network. Its main technological features are decentralization, availability, information immutability and non-repudiation properties. It considerably improves trust over data processing. OASEES intends to present an agile architecture and supports heterogeneous technological devices that enable easy integration of blockchain technology. The edge and cloud components of OASEES will generate and process different information. Blockchain and smart contracts will serve as a software connector among various architectural components by enabling exchanging a particular set of information in a trustworthy manner. With the help of the smart contract, it will enable decentralized autonomous software agents (Self-Sovereign Identity (SSI) [62]) to play a role in certifying edge and cloud devices, which further can be identified in a decentralized manner by using the notion of a Decentralized Identifier (DID) [63]. That will enable authorizing information exchange as an independent decision-maker, based on specific data sharing policy, performing service automation according to specified requirements. This also covers the management aspect of edge and cloud devices in a decentralized autonomous organization (DAO) way [64], fostering trusted data processing.

4   Use Cases and Pilot Deployments

OASEES has identified the need for a novel, inclusive and disruptive approach regarding the cloud to edge continuum and swarm programmability. To increase expected impact, the project has identified six distinct use cases related to different verticals, as briefly discussed in the following sections. The common features of all proposed approaches is the fact the OASEES proposes: (i) agile and secure architectures for collaborative smart nodes with decentralized or swarm intelligence, which build on European strengths in embedded sensors and devices and wireless communication, both non-cellular and mobile 5G networks; (ii) appropriate programming environments for smart edge-connected nodes and dynamic groups of nodes across the device-edge-cloud continuum, which reduce the complexity of programming and maintenance; (iii) dynamic open environments and tools, which stimulate open architectures and interfaces, interoperability and avoiding vendor-lock-in, and open source where appropriate, and; (iv) solutions to further strength Europe's position in the market of next generation smart systems (sensors and devices) integrated in an evolving IoT and cyber-physical ecosystems with strong capacities at the edge. The proposed use cases are discussed as follows:

Smart Edge-Connected Node for the Analysis of Voice, Articulation and FluencyDisorders in Parkinson Disease: OASEES will develop and test an innovative smart edge-connected sensor, which will be the basis of an interactive and intelligent wearable for the acoustic analysis of voice in Parkinson Disease (PD). Voice alterations and oral communication disorders, especially in articulation, are present in 40–80% of patients with PD. Instrumented voice analysis allows an early identification of these distortions in order to design or adapt supportive interventions. It also allows the identification of changes in voice parameters for predicting the worsening of disease. OASEES will develop an intelligent edge device capable of sensing, recording and analysing patients' utterances, as well as providing smart, adaptive and personalized guidance on rhythm and intonation. The aim is to develop a system usable both in rehabilitation centres during sessions with therapists and at home. The edge devices will operate and be monitored over the OASEES DAO [65], supporting real-time monitoring of the health information in a trusted and private manner, while allowing the medical practitioner to take the crucial decisions. The devices will operate in the form of swarm and be able to be updated automatically and also leverage the AI edge accelerators for advanced processing and insights.

Electrical Vehicles (EVs) Fleet Coordinated Recharging to Support Optimal Operation of Electricity Grid: In a power infrastructure power network congestions can occasionally take place in the operated electricity grid, which may be dealt with or without any grid reinforcement by leveraging on mobilizing flexibility and stabilization services from local energy consumption stationary (including smart home consumption IoT flexible devices, smart substation devices for decentralized grid monitoring, smart EV recharging stations) and on-the-move-assets (EV fleets).

Electricity produced by renewable sources (photovoltaics - PVs) is usually fed into the low voltage (LV) electricity network and most is consumed by energy customers (i.e. houses, offices, etc.). However, surplus of generated power would generate reverse power flows through the LV distribution network substation which is generally designed to handle only unidirectional electricity flows, thus reverse flows may generate significant issues. To avoid this abnormal operation, electrical vehicles can be offered a dedicated EV fleet platform to "match" their EV charging needs with proper network time and space requirements. This use case will demonstrate the capability of deploying and coordinating in a scalable yet near real-time way the operation and management of swarms of IoT-based devices (e-vehicles), which will be coordinated and programmed through the OASEES SDK and orchestration platform. The involved EV fleet operator and respective EV drivers community manager will optimize EVs' recharging schedule to "address" local technical requirements from the electricity grid operator, in presence of local congestion or local planned or unplanned maintenance of electricity grid branches. The respective pilot will also include smart stationary assets such as smart meters, and smart recharging stations. The EVs will be requested to be charged when surplus of PV generated power is available, with a view to increase the share of self-consumption. The charger will be hence communicating with EV driver and with car battery management system to predict if the requested flexibility will be available in due time.

Drone Swarm over 5G for High Mast Inspection: Autonomous drone inspections can provide tower companies with the data and insights they need to expand their infrastructure. OASEES autonomous drone software will gather high resolution aerial data and generate accurate 3D models and a 360-degree panoramic view of a potential antenna's location. Stakeholders shall be able to: see exactly what is in the line of sight from the location; identify potential obstructions, and; establish the distance from nearby existing antennae. This data can be easily and inexpensively acquired locally – but can be shared anywhere in the world. The process of acquiring local permits is made dramatically easier when accurate data is shared between tower companies and local regulators. In dense urban areas, tower companies may not be able to develop an entirely new site; in urban environments, tower companies must adapt their existing site to the 5G network needs. Autonomous drone inspections will allow companies to see exactly what that existing equipment is and determine how to utilize the site profitably for the 5G network rollout. A successful operation of drone swarms in a self-organized manner requires the integration of the networking and computational systems, which until now have been mostly investigated in isolation. To this aim, OASEES will integrate the DAO paradigm for the self-organized operation of a drone swarm, which will rely on the tight consolidation of the networking (5G-RedCap [66], 6LoWPAN (IPv6 over Low-Power Wireless Personal Area Networks)) [67, 68] and edge acceleration technologies (i.e.: SNN). Each of these two systems shall benefit from the presence of the other: for instance, the networking system should be able to find better transmission channels towards neighbors and/or better end-to-end paths towards faraway drones. The SNNs in this case will serve as a power efficient accelerator technology mounted in the drone, to provide fast and accurate detection of mast defects.

Swarm Powered Intelligent Structural Safety Assessment for Buildings: The structural condition of critical infrastructures is usually inferred by processing data from local sensors (mostly accelerometers and laser deformation sensors). There are already in use decision support software (DSS) that collect the structural data and help in decision making in critical times (such as post-earthquake, strong winds, heavy snows, etc.). Currently, the collection of the sensor data takes place in the customer's premises. The data are then transferred to a remote DSS for post-processing and decision making, which is inefficient and causes several practical problems, including data privacy concerns and, most importantly, increased response time. It would be highly beneficial to migrate to a distributed DSS architecture, with components both at the edge and the central cloud. This use case will exploit already installed sensor networks which are feeding data to their DSS. This shall imply for the necessary hardware upgrades and adaptations at the sensor locations, modifications in the local network infrastructure as well as (possible) adaptations to the data acquisition protocols. OASEES will be integrated by: (i) installing the respective edge devices close to the sensors, and; (ii) composing and deploying a distributed DSS application via the use of a dedicated SDK. The sensor data will be locally pre-processed at the edge and then the product will be forwarded to the cloud for high-level monitoring and dissemination. This approach is expected to yield a much more robust system, higher reliability, as well as less dependence on human intervention.

Robotic Swarm Powered Smart Factory for I4.0: In this case, it shall be developed a fully automated system for the production of furniture in all stages of processing, that is: from the standard panel to the assembly of the cabinet where the operator is assisted by industrial anthropomorphic robots for dangerous and low added value tasks, by collaborative robots in the final stages of assembly, insertion of hardware, glue dispensing and finishing, in a safe way, without any need for fences or other barriers, and AMR (Autonomous Mobile Robots) self-driving for flexible interconnections between different cells and islands. In OASEES, the focus of this use case would be the finishing (sanding) machine, designed to satisfy medium and large companies that require the highest quality: this will deal with sanding of "complex" geometry pieces of furniture (e.g. doors) via an automatic sanding system based on the application of a collaborative anthropomorphic robot. The aim will be about implementing an automated manufacturing process for semi-finished wood panels to be transferred from one station to the sanding machine and from there to the other station via AGVs (Automated Guided Vehicles), coordinated and programmed by the OASEES orchestrator and SDK for line supervision, relieving human operators from burdensome tasks. The essential part in this process is the incorporation of DAO functionality for HITL (Human in the Loop) [69, 70] decision making for I4.0.

Smart Swarm Energy Harvesting and Predictive Maintenance Wind Turbines: Today, the maintenance of wind farms represents a cost of 20% of the total project and this is a determining factor for the viability and durability of the asset. Of major importance are issues about inspection of wind turbine blades and, correspondingly, detection of possible anomalies so that to optimize the operation and maintenance of the turbines. BAMS (Blade Acoustic Monitoring System) is a new system for such sort of inspection and predictive maintenance of wind turbine blades, which is also portable, non-intrusive and independent from the manufacturer. It can "listen" to the wind turbine, acquire the acoustic signals produced when the wind interacts with the blades and detect and identify faults in them, thus improving the performance and operational reliability of the wind turbine. BAMS can detect abnormal operations in the blades such as structural failures, wear, ice, corrosion, or dirt. The key enabler in the seamless integration of smart energy renewable systems to existing infrastructure is smart metering. Blockchain can provide the backend for distributed data structures to securely store transactions in a decentralized manner. In OASEES, novel IoT based meters will be implemented to support on-the-fly programmability. The device swarm will be based upon IoT sound transducer (microphones) applied to wind turbines. The main goal is to extend the capabilities of BAMS, to be able to function as an IoT device in swarm mode. This will allow the simultaneous capture and processing of data from a considerable number of wind turbines thus creating a BAMS network. All the acquired data will be transmitted to the cloud, processed securely, and analyzed using machine learning algorithms so that the sensors are able to learn from each other (improved calibration, noise suppression, etc.), and to improve and obtain better metrics while optimizing the failure prediction on the blades of the wind turbine.

5   Overview

The Open Source community will also be invited to leverage its capabilities for building and managing innovative edge services. The project scope envisions a holistic approach for edge data processing, aiming to disrupt current practices which heavily rely on non-European cloud AI data processing, and "push" AI training and inference at the edge of the network, while being vertical agnostic.

In particular, OASEES targets several specific measurable objectives, each one associated with one – or more – key results, which are in turn accompanied with a set of capabilities and KPIs to be validated during project duration. These are about: (i) designing a decentralized, agile and secure architecture for collaborative smart nodes at the edge, supporting heterogeneous device communication, backed by the DAO paradigm integration; (ii) building a secure, trustworthy and decentralized edge ecosystem with native device support for a portable digital identity that does not depend on any centralized authority; the related device identity will be a new class of identifier that fulfils requirements for persistence, global resolvability, cryptographic verifiability and decentralization; (iii) structuring rapid development kits (RDKs) for an open programmable framework across different smart edge nodes, while incorporating efficient cloud-to-edge continuum intelligence across heterogeneous target environments; (iv) demonstrating the framework and programmability toolkit in a set of six different vertical use cases and evaluating the benefits across different sectors; (iv) maximizing business impact of the expected results and fostering the creation of an open-source community around the proposed, per case, solutions, engaging a diverse set of stakeholders, to support market viability.

OASEES will be capable to operate in multi-instance (multi-domain) configurations and the corresponding system shall enable the user to: (i) discover and select available platforms, services and capabilities pertinent to their needs; (ii) develop AI services as well as automate lifecycle management operations; (iii) deploy and manage AI workflows across the compute continuum; (iv) configure service performance constraints; (v) interactively explore data and exercise MLOps; (vi) verify the integrity of infrastructure and services across the continuum.

Acknowledgments. This work has been performed in the scope of the *OASEES* European Research Project and has been supported by the Commission of the European Communities */HORIZON, Grant Agreement No.101092702.*

References

1. Gabriel, T., Cornel-Cristian, A., Arhip-Calin, M., Zamfirescu, A.: Cloud storage. A comparison between centralized solutions versus decentralized cloud storage solutions versus decentralized cloud storage solutions using Blockchain technology. In: Proceedings of the 54th International Universities Power Engineering Conference (UPEC'19), pp. 1–5. IEEE (2019)
2. IBM, What is cloud hosting. https://www.ibm.com/cloud/learn/what-is-cloud-hosting
3. Leskinen, J.: Evaluation criteria for future identity management. In: Proceedings of the 11th International Conference on Trust, Security and Privacy in Computing and Communications (TrustCom'12), pp. 801–806. IEEE (2012)
4. Thakur, M.A., Gaikwad, R.: User identity and access management trends in IT infrastructure - an overview. In: Proceedings of the 2015 International Conference on Pervasive Computing (ICPC'15), pp. 1–4. IEEE (2015)
5. Zareen, M.S., et *al.*: Artificial intelligence/machine learning in IoT for authentication and authorization of edge devices. In: Proceedings of the 2019 International Conference on Applied and Engineering Mathematics (ICAEM'19), pp. 220–224. IEEE (2019)
6. Vorakulpipat, C., et *al.*: Comprehensive-factior authentication in edge devices in smart environments: a case study. In: Proceedings of the 11th International Conference on Control, Automation and Information Sciences (ICCAIS'22), pp. 391–396. IEEE (2022)
7. Lu, Y., Wang, D., et *al.*: Edge-assisted intelligent device authentication in cyber-physical systems. IEEE Internet Things J. **10**(4), 3057–3070 (2023)

8. Castellano, G., Esposito, F., Risso, F.: A service-defined approach for orchestration of heterogeneous applications in cloud/edge platforms. IEEE Trans. Netw. Serv. Manag. **16**(4), 1404–1418 (2019)

9. Taleb, T., Samdanis, K., Mada, B., Flinck, H., Dutta, S., Sabella, D.: On multi-access edge computing: A survey of the emerging 5G network edge cloud architecture and orchestration. IEEE Commun. Surv. Tutor. **19**(3), 1657–1681 (2017)

10. Sonmez, C., et *al.*: Fuzzy workload orchestration for edge computing. IEEE Trans. Netw. Serv. Manag. **16**(2), 769–782 (2019)

11. Ranjan, A., Guim, F., Chincholkar, M., Ramchandran, et *al.*: Convergence of edge services & edge infrastructure. In: Proceedings of the 2021 IEEE Conference on Network Function Virtualization and Software Defined Networks (NFV-SDN'21), pp. 96–99. IEEE (2021)

12. Loghin, D., Ramapantulu, L., Teo, Y.M.: Towards Analyzing the performance of hybrid edge-cloud processing. In: Proceedings of the 2019 IEEE International Conference on Edge Computing (EDGE'19), pp. 87–94. IEEE (2019)

13. Risso, F.: Creating an edge-to-cloud computing continuum: status and perspective. In: Proceedings of the 3rd International Conference on Embedded and Distributed Systems (EDiS'22), p 4. IEEE (2022)

14. Accenture, Edge computing. https://www.accenture.com/bg-en/insights/cloud/edge-computing-index

15. Shi, W., Cao, J., Zhang, Q., Li, Y., Xu, L.: Edge computing: Vision and challenges. IEEE Internet Things J. **3**(5), 637–646 (2016)

16. Masip-Bruin, H., Marín-Tordera, E., et *al.*: Managing the cloud continuum: lessons learnt from a real fog-to-cloud deployment. Sensors (MDPI) **21**(9), 2974 (2021)

17. Dietrich, M., Facca, F.M.: Cloud computing in Europe: landscape analysis, adoption challenges and future research and innovation opportunities. Horizon Cloud (2022). https://www.h-cloud.eu/?wpdmdl=4541&ind=1645025986562

18. John, W., Sargor, C., Szabo, R., Awan, A.J, Padala, C., Drake, E., et *al.*: The future of cloud computing. Ericsson Technol. Rev. **2020**, 1–13 (2020)

19. Microsoft Azure Stack Edge. https://azure.microsoft.com/en-us/products/azure-stack/edge/

20. StackPath LLC, What is edge orchestration? https://www.stackpath.com/edge-academy/what-is-edge-orchestration/

21. Hossain, M.D., Sultana, T., Hossain, M.A., Huh, E.-N.: Edge orchestration based computation peer offloading in MEC-enabled networks: a fuzzy logic approach. In: Proceedings of the 15th International Conference on Ubiquitous Information Management and Communication (IMCOM'17), pp. 1–7. IEEE (2017)

22. Wu, Y.: Cloud-edge orchestration for the internet of things: architecture and AI-powered data processing. IEEE Internet Things J. **8**(16), 12792–12805 (2021)

23. Petri, I., Rana, O., Zamani, A.R., Rezgui, Y.: Edge-cloud orchestration: strategies for service placement and enactment. In: Proceedings of the 2019 IEEE International Conference on Cloud Engineering (IC2E'19), pp. 67–75. IEEE (2019)

24. Waguie, F.T., Al-Turjman, F.: Artificial intelligence for edge computing security: a survey. In: Proceedings of the 2022 International Conference on Artificial Intelligence in Everything (AIE'22), pp. 446–450. IEEE (2022)

25. Xiao, Y., Jia, Y., Liu, C., Cheng, X., Yu, J., Lv, W.: Edge computing security: state of the art and challenges. Proc. IEEE **107**(8), 1608–1631 (2019)

26. Pujol, V.C., Raith, P., Dustdar, S.: Towards a new paradigm for managing computing continuum applications. In: Proceedings of the 2021 IEEE Third International Conference on Cognitive Machine Intelligence (CogMI'21), pp. 180–188. IEEE (2021)

27. OASEES ("Open Autonomous programmable cloud appS and smart EdgE sensors") Horizon project, Grant Agreement No. 101092702. https://oasees-project.eu/

28. Kim, J.-Y.: FPGA based neural network accelerators. Adv. Comput. **122**, 135–165 (2022)
29. Yamazaki, K., Vo-Ho, V.-K., Bulsara, D., Le, N.: Spiking neural networks and their applications: a review. Brain Sci. **12**(7), 863 (2022)
30. Abdelgaber, N., Nikolopoulos, C.: Overview on quantum computing and its applications in artificial intelligence. In: Proceedings of the 2020 IEEE 3rd International Conference on Artificial Intelligence and Knowledge Engineering (AIKE'20), pp. 198–199. IEEE (2020)
31. Li, Z., Sharma, V., Mohanty, S.P.: Preserving data privacy via federated learning: challenges and solutions. IEEE Consum. Electron. Mag. **9**(6), 8–16 (2020)
32. European Technology Platform for High Performance Computing (ETP4HPC): ETP4HPC Strategic Research Agenda. https://www.etp4hpc.eu/sra.html
33. Balouek-Thomert, D., Gibert Renart, E., et al.: Towards a computing continuum: enabling edge-to-cloud integration for data-driven workflows. Int. J. High Perform. Comput. Appl. **33**(6) 1159–1174 (2019)
34. Chen, Q., Gao, C., Fang, X., Luan, H.: Skydiver: a spiking neural network accelerator exploiting spatio-temporal workload balance. IEEE Trans. Comput. Aided Des. Integr. Circuits Syst. **41**(12), 5732–5736 (2022)
35. Biamonte, J., Wittek, P., Pancotti, N., Rebentrost, P., Wiebe, N., Lloyd, S.: Quantum machine learning. Natures **549**(7671), 195–202 (2017)
36. Mahmood, Z.: Fog Computing: Concepts, Frameworks and Technologies. Springer, Cham (2018). https://doi.org/10.1007/978-3-319-94890-4
37. Johnston, D.: The General Theory of Decentralized Applications, Dapps. (2013). https://git hub.com/DavidJohnstonCEO/DecentralizedApplications
38. Moralis Academy, What is Decentralized AI? The Relationship Between Blockchain and AI. https://academy.moralis.io/blog/what-is-decentralized-ai-the-relationship-between-blockchain-and-ai
39. European Commission, Open Science. https://research-and-innovation.ec.europa.eu/strategy/strategy-2020-2024/our-digital-future/open-science_en
40. European Open Science Cloud (EOSC). https://eosc-portal.eu/
41. Vaquero, L.M., Cuadrado, F., Elkhatib, Y., Bernal-Bernabe, J., et al.: Research challenges in nextgen service orchestration. Futur. Gener. Comput. Syst. **90**, 20–38 (2019)
42. European Telecommunications Standards Institute (ETSI): ETSI GS NFV-MAN 001 V1.1.1 (2014–12): "Network Functions Virtualisation (NFV); Management and Orchestration". https://www.etsi.org/deliver/etsi_gs/nfvman/001_099/001/01.01.01_60/gs_nfv-man001v010101p.pdf
43. Kreutz, D., Ramos, F.M.V., Veríssimo, P.E., Rothenberg, C.E., et al.: Software-defined networking: a comprehensive survey. Proc. IEEE **103**(1), 14–76 (2015)
44. Zhao, Y., Wang, W., Li, Y., Meixner, C.C., et al.: Edge computing and networking: a survey on infrastructures and applications. IEEE Access **7**, 101213–101230 (2019)
45. Metsch, T., Edmonds, A., Parák, B.: GFD-R.184 Open Cloud Computing Interface - Infrastructure. Open Grid Forum (OGF), OCCI Working Group, European Commission (2011)
46. OASIS Topology and Orchestration Specification for Cloud Applications (TOSCA) Technical Committee (TC). https://www.oasis-open.org/committees/tc_home.php?wg_abbrev=tosca
47. Villarreal Pelegrino, J.: An Introduction to Enhanced Platform Awareness (EPA) capabilities in OpenStack (2020). https://www.juliosblog.com/a-quick-introduction-to-enhanced-platform-awareness-epa-capabilities-in-openstack/
48. Intel, Enhanced Platform Awareness in Kubernetes Application Note (2017). https://networkbuilders.intel.com/solutionslibrary/enhanced-platform-awareness-in-kubernetes-application-note

49. Dustdar, S., Murturi, I.: Towards distributed edge-based systems. In: Proceedings of the 2020 IEEE Second International Conference on Cognitive Machine Intelligence (CogMI'20), pp. 1–9. IEEE (2020)
50. Sabella, D.: MEC: standards and industry associations around edge computing. In: Sabella, D. (ed.) Multi-access Edge Computing: Software Development at the Network Edge, pp. 19–56. Springer, Cham (2021). https://doi.org/10.1007/978-3-030-79618-1_2
51. Wiranata, F.A., Shalannanda, W., Mulyawan, R., Adiono, T.: Automation of virtualized 5G infrastructure using mosaic 5G operator over kubernetes supporting network slicing. In: Proceedings of the 2020 14th International Conference on Telecommunication Systems, Services, and Applications (TSSA'20), pp. 1–5. IEEE (2020)
52. Valcarenghi, L., Martini, B., Antevski, K., et al.: A framework for orchestration and federation of 5G services in a multi-domain scenario. In: Proceedings of the Workshop on Experimentation and Measurements in 5G (EM-5G'18), pp. 19–24 (2018)
53. Addad, R.A., Taleb, T., Bagaa, M., et al.: Towards modeling cross-domain network slices for 5G. In: Proceedings of the 2018 IEEE Global Communications Conference (GLOBECOM'18), pp. 1–7. IEEE (2018)
54. Froehlich, A.: An introduction to neutral host networks using private 5G. TechTarget (2023). https://www.techtarget.com/searchnetworking/tip/An-introduction-to-neutral-host-networks-using-private-5G
55. Yan, M.M.W.: Accurate detecting concept drift in evolving data streams. ICT Express **6**(4), 332–338 (2020)
56. Bonawitz, K., Eichner, H., Grieskamp, W., Huba, D., et al.: Towards Federated Learning at Scale: System Design. Cornell University (2019). https://arxiv.org/abs/1902.01046
57. MLOps. https://ml-ops.org/content/mlops-principles
58. Rose, S., Borchert, O., Mitchell, S., Connelly, S.: NIST Special Publication 800-207: "Zero-Trust Architecture". National Institute of Standards and Technology (NIST) (2020). https://nvlpubs.nist.gov › NIST.SP.800-207.pdf
59. Trusted Computing Group: Where Trust Begins – Protecting the Connected Ecosystem (2023). https://trustedcomputinggroup.org/resource/where-trust-begins/
60. Secure Production Identity Framework for Everyone (SPIFFE). https://spiffe.io/
61. McKinsey & Company: What is Blockchain? (2022). https://www.mckinsey.com/featured-insights/mckinsey-explainers/what-is-blockchain
62. Bosch GmbH: Digital identity – enabling secure collaboration with blockchain technology (2023). https://www.bosch.com/stories/self-sovereign-identities/
63. World Wide Web Consortium (W3C): W3C Recommendation: "Decentralized Identifiers (DIDs) v1.0" (2022). https://www.w3.org/TR/did-core/
64. Buterin, V.: DAOs, DACs, DAs and More: An Incomplete Terminology Guide [Blog post]. Ethereum Foundation Blog (2014). https://blog.ethereum.org/2014/05/06/daos-dacs-das-and-more-an-incomplete-terminology-guide/
65. Hassan, S.: Decentralized autonomous organization. Internet Policy Review **10**(2), 1–10 (2021)
66. EverythingRf: What is 5G RedCap? (2020). https://www.everythingrf.com/community/what-is-5g-reduced-capability-or-5g-redcap
67. Bertenyi, B.: 5G evolution: what's next? IEEE Wirel. Commun. **28**(1), 4–8 (2021)
68. McGee, K., Collier, M.: 6LoWPAN forwarding techniques for IoT. In: Proceedings of the 2019 IEEE 5th World Forum on Internet of Things (WF-IoT'19), pp. 888–893. IEEE (2019)
69. Google: Human-in-the-Loop Overview. https://cloud.google.com/document-ai/docs/hitl
70. Bisen, V.S.: What is Human in the Loop Machine Learning: Why and How Used in AI? (2020). https://medium.com/vsinghbisen/what-is-human-in-the-loop-machine-learning-why-how-used-in-ai-60c7b44eb2c0

Putting Intelligence into Things: An Overview of Current Architectures

Maria Belesioti[1], Ioannis P. Chochliouros[1(✉)], Panagiotis Dimas[2],
Manolis Sofianopoulos[2], Theodore Zahariadis[1,2], Charalabos Skianis[1,2],
and Enric Pages Montanera[1,2]

[1] Hellenic Telecommunications Organization (OTE) S.A., 99 Kifissias Avenue, 15124
Maroussi-Athens, Greece
{mbelesioti,ichochliouros}@oteresearch.gr
[2] COSMOTE Mobile Telecommunications S.A., Athens, Greece

Abstract. In the era of the Internet of Things (IoT), billions of sensors collect data from their environment and process it to enable intelligent decisions at the right time. However, transferring massive amounts of disparate data in complex environments is a challenging issue. The convergence of Artificial Intelligence (AI) and the Internet of Things has breathed new life into IoT operations and human-machine interaction. Resource-constrained IoT devices typically need more data storage and processing capacity to build modern AI models. The intuitive solution integrates cloud computing technology with AIoT and leverages cloud-side servers' powerful and flexible processing and storage capacity. This paper briefly introduces IoT and AIoT architectures in the context of cloud computing, fog computing and more. Finally, an overview of the NEMO [1] concept is presented. The NEMO project aims to establish itself as the "game changer" of AIoT-Edge-Cloud Continuum by bringing intelligence closer to data, making AI-as-a-Service an integral part of self-organizing networks orchestrating micro-service execution.

Keywords: Internet of Things (IoT) · Artificial Intelligence (AI) · AIoT · AIoT-Edge-Cloud

1 Introduction

The rapid development and implementation of intelligent IoT, cloud and edge technologies have enabled various technological advances in different areas of life. The main goal of IoT technology is to simplify processes in various fields, increase the efficiency of systems (technology and/or specific processes) and, ultimately, improve the quality of life. Towards fulfilling this challenge, sustainability has become a vital issue for those who see the dynamic development of IoT technologies being able to provide various valuable benefits. However, this rapid development must be carefully monitored and evaluated from the sustainability perspective to "limit" harmful effects and ensure innovative use and limited world resources. Considering the strengths and weaknesses of IoT technology, this requires considerable research effort in the current sense. The present paper aims to contribute to understanding the impacts of the current technological advances related to sustainable corporate development in the IoT and edge computing era.

Published by Springer Nature Switzerland AG 2023
I. Maglogiannis et al. (Eds.): AIAI 2023 Workshops, IFIP AICT 677, pp. 106–117, 2023.
https://doi.org/10.1007/978-3-031-34171-7_8

The era of the Industry 4.0 revolution begins with the development of intelligent sensors technology to integrate AI-based systems used in real-time applications [2]. Smart sensors are a topic that contributes to increased production and sales in various industries [3]. These advantages are especially evident when commercially available technologies are used effectively. Additionally, sensors may "react" differently in different environments. They can provide data of varying quality that can mislead the respective underlying model's decisions and lead to classification errors if the corresponding model needs to be more robust. AI-based systems designed to solve a single classification challenge are labour-intensive and costly; even a single misclassification scenario is costly in this scope. Cloud and edge computing are essential technologies in the computing continuum for efficient data management "closer to its source" rather than sending raw data to data-centres [4]. These trends, therefore, require a "shift" towards the technical and business convergence of the previously formally separated cloud, edge and IoT domains.

The Internet of Things fundamentally aims to change diverse sectors of our society and economy. However, realizing the vision of IoT requires data processing (stream, static, or both) in a "sweet spot" in the edge cloud continuum. Far-edge/sensors produce data and actuate; edge/fog consists of "heterogeneous intermediate devices" where data can be processed; cloud facilities deliver unlimited processing capabilities, while all of them jointly (and supported by resources/services/data orchestration) constitute the edge-cloud continuum. In this context, future IoT platforms will have to manage processes in multi-stakeholder, multi-cloud, federated and large-scale IoT ecosystems.

"Key" challenges are related to the fact that such platforms (encompassing operating systems, up to applications) will have to jointly leverage the continuous progress of multiple enabling technologies such as, for example, 5G/6G networking, privacy and security, distributed computing, artificial intelligence, trust management, autonomous computing, distributed/innovative applications, data management, etc. Moreover, they must facilitate intelligent (autonomous) orchestration of physical/virtual resources and tasks by realizing them at the "optimal location" within the considered ecosystem (e.g., closer to where data is produced). This implies that resource-aware, frugal AI is needed to facilitate self-awareness and decision support across the heterogeneous ecosystem. Finally, it is also imperative that resource management considers the carbon footprint of the ecosystem, uses data and tasks efficiently and also leverages multi-owner heterogeneous renewable energy sources.

The next section of the paper provides an overview of the related work in this field, while Sect. 3 explains the layers of the IoT and AIoT architectures. Section 4 refers exclusively to the framework of the ongoing NEMO EU-funded project, highlighting its specific concept and objectives. Finally, Sect. 5 concludes the scope of the paper.

2 Related Work

With the rapid development of technology, the number of IoT devices has increased dramatically. However, due to its limited resources, it can run out of capacity when processing computationally intensive and time-sensitive applications. As such, compute offloads that use cloud and network edge nodes for processing and analyzing data are emerging, so edge computing has recently started receiving much attention [5]. It supports cloud-like computing at the network edge by providing compute and network resources along the path between data sources and cloud data centres [6]. Fog computing [7] and mobile edge computing [8] are two well-known edge computing paradigms. Fog computing focuses on the infrastructure side and is typically deployed at the edge of the core network. Mobile edge computing, on the other hand, focuses on the mobile user side and is typically deployed within the wireless access network. To this respect, many offload algorithms for edge computing have been proposed with different offload criteria.

Chen et al. focus on performance in terms of the average number of beneficial cloud computing users and the average amount of computational effort across the system [9]. They designed a distributed computing offload algorithm to improve the wireless access efficiency of computing offload in the mobile edge cloud computing environment. At the same time, many computational offload algorithms have been proposed to reduce service delays, including both network and computational delays. Using the Markov decision process, Liu et al. [10] formulated a power-constrained delay minimization problem for mobile edge computing systems and proposed an efficient one-dimensional search algorithm. Further on, Yang et al. proposed a Multi-Dimensional Search and Adjustment (MDSA) method for connecting computation partitioning and resource allocation to reduce the average delay of latency-sensitive applications on mobile edge clouds [11]. Youselfpour et al., aiming to reduce service delay for IoT applications, proposed interesting delay-minimizing guidelines for fog-capable devices in [12]. Zhang et al. studied the problem of allocating computing resources in a three-tier IoT fog network [13], focusing on performance from a utility perspective.

At the same time, Liu et al. explored the appearing tradeoffs between latency and reliability in mobile edge computing offloading [14], while Li et al. researched the offloading problem related to heterogeneous real-time activities in fog systems as well as the resource allocation investigating the compromise between high throughput and high task completion rate [15].

3   Internet of Things (IoT) and AIoT Architectures

This section provides a brief overview of the overall IoT architecture and edge computing in terms of related paradigms. IoT technology acquires global perception in a ubiquitous connected environment using sensors, wired and wireless networks and cloud computing. The IoT architecture is widely recognized as a tri-tier, consisting of three layers, as indicatively shown in the figure below; the respective layers are the perception layer, network layer and application layer (Fig. 1).

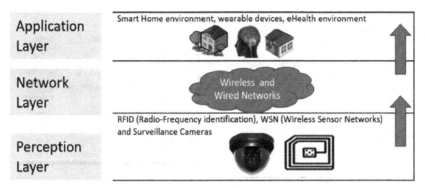

Fig. 1. Three-layered architecture [16]

The perception layer, also known as the physical layer, includes diverse technologies and devices (such as sensors and actuators) according to the requirements of the intended applications per case. These devices are used for sensing and gathering information in the form of data, so that to enable comprehensive awareness of the surrounding environment(s). The network layer is the most standardized of the three IoT levels. Here, the devices existing at the perception level can communicate by using IoT gateways, wireless fidelity (Wi-Fi), Access Points (APs) and Base Stations (BS) for data transmission. The communication can be either short-range or long-range using various communication protocols such as, for example, Bluetooth, ZigBee, Sigfox, Long Range Radio (LoRa) and Narrowband IoT (NB-IoT). The data generated in the perception layer must be quickly and with accuracy transmitted to the server through the network layer and exactly. Within the application layer all the applications using IoT technology are defined. This layer can provide countless applications such as industrial control, urban management, smart agriculture and smart farming. This layer corresponds to the control level and the IoT decision layer.

However, the above three-tier architecture has been proved "insufficient" due to the fast-growing IoT requirements. Considering that, ITU-T [17] proposed a four-layer architecture introducing an additional layer, namely the support layer (also known as transport layer), between the network layer and the application layer (cf. Figure 2a).

The new tier has been proposed because of the deficiencies in the 3-tier architecture and, more specifically, in order to enhance security in the architecture of IoT. In the prior approach, information is sent directly to the network layer of the three-tier architecture, so threats are more likely to appear. In the four-tier architecture, information is sent to the support layer and received by the perception layer. The support layer has two specific roles: to ensure the information is sent by genuine users and protected from threats. There are many ways to verify the authenticity of information. The most commonly used method is authentication, implemented with a pre-shared secret, key and password. The support layer's second task is sending information to the network layer. Radio- or wire-based is the medium for transferring information from the support layer to the network layer. Various attacks, such as Denial of Service (DoS) attacks, malicious insiders, and unauthorized access, can affect this layer [20].

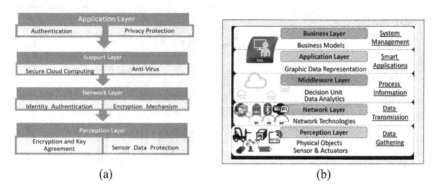

(a)   (b)

Fig. 2. (a): Four-layer IoT Architecture [18]; (b): Five-layer IoT Architecture [19]

The previously explained four-tier architecture has played an essential role in IoT development and approval. However, since security and storage issues continued, researchers have proposed a subsequent 5-layer architecture to secure the IoT [21]. Similar to previous architectures, there are three layers named perception layer, network layer, and application layer and two additional layers named middleware and business layers (cf. Figure 2b). This 5-tier proposed architecture meets multiple novel IoT technology requirements.

The processing layer, or the middleware layer, collects and processes the information sent by the network layer. Here, meaningless information is removed, and valuable information is extracted. This procedure solves the big data issue in the IoT domain since a large amount of information is received, thus impacting the IoT ecosystem's performance. The business layer is considered the "manager" of the system. The function of this specific layer is the management of IoT applications and intended services. Based on the volume of accurate data received from lower layers, it effectively analyzes such data. This layer can also determine how information is created, stored and modified, simultaneously managing users' privacy.

3.1   Fundamentals of Artificial Internet of Things

The artificial intelligence of things is enabled by combining IoT [22] and artificial intelligence techniques [23]. IoT is defined as any device that can be interconnected – e.g. sensors – and collect data in real-time [24]. This relevance is revealed by processing the acquired data using artificial intelligence models, especially machine learning (ML) or, in some cases deep learning (DL), to analyze the collected data and extract valuable information for decision-making ([25, 26]).

Combining AI and IoT results in Artificial Intelligence of Things (AIoT) which, in turn, enables building more efficient IoT operations thus enhancing human-machine interaction and data management and analytics. IoT is considered the spine of the system, while artificial intelligence is the system's brain. AIoT is revolutionary and beneficial for both types of technology since artificial intelligence evaluates IoT through machine learning capabilities and IoT artificial intelligence through connectivity, signalling and data exchange. As IoT networks spread across large industries, there will be a large amount of human-centric, machine-generated data [27]. This can support data analytics solutions that can "add value" to all data forms generated by IoT. Several IoT systems are designed for simple event control, but other events are much more complex, and IoT can be used for analytics purposes. AIoT elaborates on this context for preparing the appropriate steps to make this process happen. With intelligent tools on, edge devices are capable of observing their surroundings, perceiving data and finally making the best decision(s); and the most important is that all of these procedures can be implemented with the minor human intervention. Artificial intelligence transforms AIoT devices into intelligent machines capable of performing self-centred analysis and independent operations rather than mere messengers providing information to a control centre [28].

Regarding data analytics, with the combination of machine learning with IoT networks and systems, AIoT can create "learning machines". This can be applied to enterprise and industrial data, controlling IoT data such as the network edge and automating tasks in the connected workplace. Real-time data is critical to all AIoT applications and solutions. In particular, there are four main areas where AIoT is expected to have a significant impact: wearables, smart homes, smart cities and smart industry. Other fields are also currently expanding, requiring dynamic solutions that can be solved with AI, for example, sustainability [29], health [30], communication systems [31], data protection [32], electric vehicles [33] and power systems [34].

3.2 Overview of AIoT Architecture

Similar to IoT, AIoT also assumes a 3-tier architecture, this time from a computational perspective. The three layers are now cloud, fog and edge computing as illustrated in Fig. 3.

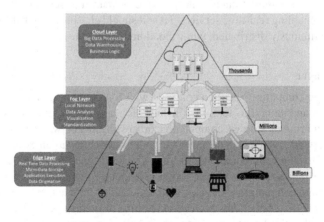

Fig. 3. AIoT layered architecture [35]

The Edge computing layer can be considered as the perception layer in IoT architecture. It supports control and execution via sensors and actuators, enhancing AIoT system's behaviour, overall perception and cognitive abilities. Fog computing is embedded in the fog nodes (i.e. hubs, routers, gateways) within the network; finally, the cloud computing layer supports application services per the IoT application layer. The fog and cloud computing layers have vast computational resources, access to considerable amounts of data and are primarily concerned with empowering AIoT systems with learning and reasoning capabilities.

3.2.1 Edge Layer

Edge networks are often powered by specific computing and storage capabilities. The bottom edge nodes are responsible for receiving data from the end-devices of the perception layer and returning control flows to the devices over wireless interfaces [36]. The upper-edge servers use the received data to perform computational tasks, which, in cases of augmented complexity, can also be outsourced to higher-level servers with more powerful computational capabilities. Other edge server functions include authentication, authorization, offloading and storing data exchanged across the networks. This type of edge computing can reduce latency and provide continuous service while at the same time protecting data security and privacy. This has practical value for several AIoT applications such as agriculture, ships and smart grids where the internet could be more practically stable.

Edge layer resources are scarce compared to traditional cloud computing. This makes edge computing flexible and scalable, delivering various services anywhere between end-users and the cloud. Edge computing is usually viewed as an "extension" of cloud platforms and, in some scenarios, can work effectively, independently or in conjunction with cloud platforms. In this sense, edge computing refers to providing computing power to edge devices close to sensors and actuators. The emergence of edge computing depends on migrating computational tasks to the edge of the cloud, succeeding proximity to sensors or actuators, thus reducing the pressure of data transfer and the end-to-end (E2E) latency enabling real-time services. Here it should also be noted that fog and edge nodes are continuously distributed, while cloud nodes are not.

3.2.2 Fog Layer

The term "edge computing" is often confused with fog computing in literature [37] or is perceived as an "umbrella" term that includes fog as well. In fact, fog computing is responsible for bringing storage, computation, processing and networking capacity to the edge of the network, which is in the proximity of devices acting as an extension of and a "supplement" to cloud computing. Although fog nodes (routers, switches, gateways and wireless access points) are functioning similarly to cloud computing, fog computing can provide real-time collaborative services with less latency for numerous interconnected IoT devices as well as better data protection in terms of security and privacy since data can be held within the Local Area Network (LAN). Fog computing can provide real-time collaborative services with less latency for numerous interconnected IoT devices via distributed fog nodes [38].

3.2.3 Cloud Layer

The cloud enables AIoT corporations to have virtual computational resources instead of physical ones. The Cloud computing layer is a service-oriented architecture that provides flexible, scalable, elastic and reliable resources (such as computing, storage, and networking), enabling various AIoT applications and reducing information technology overhead for end-users and ownership costs. Real-time data is sent from distributed sensors and devices to remote cloud centres over the internet for processing and storage. However, cloud centres are usually built in remote locations far away from the end-user, thus causing delays in data transmission. With the increased number of IoT devices, the cloud cannot "meet" latency and data protection requirements, especially regarding latency-sensitive and privacy-sensitive applications [39]. AI can perform such tasks, and it is located in two places within an IoT ecosystem (i.e., centre and edge). AI deployments in centres traditionally generate predictive analytics or even anomaly detection. So far, AI deployments have mostly had a secondary function of reducing the amount of data entering the cloud.

4 NEMO Concept Leveraging IoT

The Internet of Things can offer new and improved services and applications based on knowledge of the environment and the entities it contains. Millions of micro-suppliers could be created, formulating a highly fragmented market with new business opportunities able to offer commercial services. In this respect, the ongoing NEMO EU-funded project considers that intelligence needs to "move closer to the point of decision" and become an integral part of the AIoT meta-Operating System (mOS), supporting every activity, process and decision that ranges from ad-hoc micro-cloud cluster self-organization to micro-services migration and intent-based programming. To facilitate knowledge easily and almost without administrator instant deployment on any AIoT device, all mechanisms need to be integrated and connected, essential mOS tools and plug-ins installed as a (semi-)automated/standalone software package while ensuring interoperability, trust, cybersecurity and privacy.

Under this framework the NEMO project [1] aims to "drive" the IoT-Edge-Cloud continuum to the next generation by offering flexible, multi-path 5G/IoT connectivity and a lightweight micro-services' mesh migration/execution to ensure horizontal and vertical scalability. NEMO will pursue a close collaboration among semi-autonomous IoT nodes, IoT fog clusters, far-edge and near-edge cloud, and national and federated cloud infrastructures. Following a flexible collaboration model, new generation AIoT nodes will be equipped with intelligence to function in a semi-autonomous mode, reducing the latency and performing many complex operations locally without transporting raw data. Furthermore, federated on-device learning, data sovereignty, and trusted, explicitly attested (edge) cloud nodes will "bring" AI to environments with limited network coverage. The NEMO core functionality will be offered by an AI-based meta-Orchestrator, which will automatically, and in real-time, re-configure the mOS set-up at each node (either IoT, Edge, Cloud, ad-hoc or hybrid Clouds) so that the end-to-end federation operates optimally, matching the applications' Service Level Objectives (SLOs) and the policies set by the mOS administrators (Fig. 4).

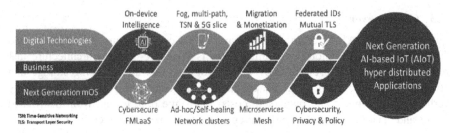

Fig. 4. NEMO Concept

This effort will be highly related to security, regulation and legal restrictions. In this respect, new security and policy enforcement capabilities in the form of plug-in modules that comply with the terms of the Linux Security Modules (LSM) will be built for better protection against malicious code, cyberattacks or unintentional misconfigurations. Capabilities that go far beyond traditional smart contracts, such as data sharing and introducing innovative contractual perspectives as microservices, will consider the energy consumption and the costs of processing, storage, network/transmission, and cooling for providing optimal end-to-end services.

5 Conclusion

The Internet of Things is driving a significant transformation with the help of technologies such as 5G, fog computing and artificial intelligence to create new applications with specific requirements and greater flexibility and efficiency. This paper surveyed on several fundamental concepts (including IoT, AI and edge computing) and how these have managed to move the frontiers of AI away from the cloud network edge. Guided by these concepts, the paper also explores the general AIoT architecture and the integration that facilitated the corresponding rapid development. Connecting Edge Computing, IoT, and AI creates a new paradigm for edge intelligence with specific vertical industries such as smart agriculture, smart energy management, smart media and cultural experiences to exploit this innovative feature, also emphasizing the integration of substantial new data streams from machines and sensors.

This paper has so provided a comprehensive insight into the IoT and AIoT architectures, being able to promote on-edge intelligence. Specifically, first, our work has presented a short review of the related background and then the most known architectures. Based on these concepts, the paper has further outlined open challenges and future directions of AIoT in the context of the NEMO concept, aiming to have direct impact on several use cases of market importance.

Acknowledgements. Part of this paper has been based on the context of the "NEMO" ("*Next Generation Meta Operating System*") Project. This project has received funding from the EU Horizon Europe research and innovation Programme under Grant Agreement No. 101070118.

References

1. NEMO, Horizon EU - funded project, GA No.101070118. https://meta-os.eu/
2. Peres, R.S., Jia, X., Lee, J., Sun, K.A.W.J.: Industrial artificial intelligence in industry 4.0 - systematic review, challenges and outlook. IEEE Access **8**, 220121–220139 (2020). https://doi.org/10.1109/ACCESS.2020.3042874
3. Ramamurthy, H., Prabhu, B.S., Gadh, R., Madni, A.M.: Wireless industrial monitoring and control using a smart sensor platform. IEEE Sens. J. **7**(5), 611–618 (2007) https://doi.org/10.1109/JSEN.2007.894135
4. The European Cloud, Edge and IoT Continuum Initiative (2023). https://eucloudedgeiot.eu/the-eu-vision-on-the-cei-continuum/
5. Shi, W., Dustdar, S.: The promise of edge computing. Computer **49**(5), 78–81 (2016). https://doi.org/10.1109/MC.2016.145
6. Shi, W., Cao, J., Zhang, Q., Li, Y., Xu, L.: Edge computing: vision and challenges. IEEE Internet Things J. **3**(5), 637–646 (2016)
7. Bonomi, F., Milito, R., Zhu, J., Addepalli, S.: Fog computing and its role in the internet of things. In: Proceedings of the ACM 1st Ed. of the MCC Workshop on Mobile Cloud Computing (MCC'12), pp. 13–16. ACM (2012)
8. Abbas, N., Zhang, Y., Taherkordi, A., Skeie, T.: Mobile edge computing: a survey. IEEE Internet Things J. **5**(1), 450–465 (2018)
9. Chen, X., Jiao, L., Li, W., Fu, X.: Efficient multi-user computation offloading for mobile-edge cloud computing. IEEE/ACM Trans. Network. **24**(5), 2795–2808 (2016). https://doi.org/10.1109/TNET.2015.2487344
10. Liu, J., Mao, Y., Zhang, J., Letaief, K.B.: Delay-optimal computation task scheduling for mobile-edge computing systems. In: Proceedings of the 2016 IEEE International Symposium on Information Theory (ISIT'16), pp. 1451–1455. IEEE (2016)
11. Yang, L., Liu, B., Cao, J., Sahni, Y., Wang, Z.: Joint computation partitioning and resource allocation for latency sensitive applications in mobile edge clouds. In: Proceedings of the 2017 IEEE 10th International Conference on Cloud Computing (CLOUD'17), pp. 246–253. IEEE (2017)
12. Yousefpour, A., Ishigaki, G., Jue, J.P.: Fog Computing: towards minimizing delay in the internet of things. In: Proceedings of the IEEE International Conference on Edge Computing (EDGE'17), pp. 17–24. IEEE (2017)
13. Zhang, H., Xiao, Y., Bu, S., Niyato, D., Yu, F.R., Han, Z.: Computing resource allocation in three-tier IoT fog networks: a joint optimization approach combining stackelberg game and matching. IEEE Internet Things J. **4**(5), 1204–1215 (2017)
14. Liu, J., Zhang, A.Q.: Offloading schemes in mobile edge computing for ultra-reliable low latency communications. IEEE Access **6**, 12825–12837 (2018)
15. Li, L., Guan, Q., Jin, L., Guo, M.: Resource allocation and task offloading for heterogeneous real-time tasks with uncertain duration time in a fog queueing system. IEEE Access **7**, 9912–9925 (2019)
16. Mashal, I., Alsaryrah, O., Chung, T.Y., Yang, C.Z., Kuo, W.H., Agrawal, D.P.: Choices for interaction with things on internet and underlying issues. Ad Hoc Netw. **28**, 68–90 (2015)
17. International Telecommunication Union – Telecommunication Standardization Sector (ITU-T): Recommendation Y4000/Y.2060 (06/12): Overview of the Internet of Things (2012). https://www.itu.int/rec/T-REC-Y.2060-201206-I
18. Burhan, M., Rehman, R.A., Khan, B., Kim, B.-S.: IoT elements, layered architectures and security issues: a comprehensive survey. Sensors (MDPI) **18**(9), 2796. https://doi.org/10.3390/s18092796

19. Antão, L., Pinto, R., Reis, J., Gonçalves, G.: Requirements for testing and validating the industrial internet of things. In: Proceedings of the 2018 IEEE International Conference on Software Testing, Verification and Validation Workshops (ICSTW'18), pp. 110–115. IEEE (2018)
20. Sanzgiri, A., Dasgupta, D.: Classification of insider threat detection techniques. In: Proceedings of the 11th Annual Cyber and Information Security Research Conference (CISRC'16), pp. 1–4. ACM (2016). https://doi.org/10.1145/2897795.2897799
21. Sethi, P., Sarangi, S.R.: Internet of things: architectures, protocols, and applications. J. Electr. Comput. Eng. 1–25 (2017). https://doi.org/10.1155/2017/9324035
22. Viel, F., Silva, L.A., Valderi Leithardt, R.Q., Zeferino, C.A.: Internet of things: concepts, architectures and technologies. In: Proceedings of the 2018 13th IEEE International Conference on Industry Applications (INDUSCON'18), pp. 909–916. IEEE (2018). https://doi.org/10.1109/INDUSCON.2018.8627298
23. Sopelsa Neto, N.F., et al.: A study of multilayer perceptron networks applied to classification of ceramic insulators using ultrasound. Appl. Sci. 11(4), 1592 (2021). https://doi.org/10.3390/app11041592
24. Leithardt, V., Santos, D., Silva, L., Viel, F., Zeferino, C., Silva, J.: A solution for dynamic management of user profiles in IoT environments. IEEE Lat. Am. Trans. 18(7), 1193–1199 (2020). https://doi.org/10.1109/TLA.2020.9099759
25. Stefenon, S.F., Kasburg, C., Nied, A., Klaar, A.C.R., Ferreira, F.C.S., Branco, N.W.: Hybrid deep learning for power generation forecasting in active solar trackers. IET Gener. Transm. Distrib. 14(23), 5667–5674 (2020)
26. Kasburg, C., Stefenon, S.F.: Deep learning for photovoltaic generation forecast in active solar trackers. IEEE Lat. Am. Trans. 17(12), 2013–2019 (2019)
27. Guo, T., Yu, K., Aloqaily, M., Wan, S.: Constructing a prior-dependent graph for data clustering and dimension reduction in the edge of AIoT. Futur. Gener. Comput. Syst. 128, 381–394 (2021)
28. Xiong, Z., Cai, Z., Takabi, D., Li, W.: Privacy threat and defense for federated learning with non-i.i.d. data in AIoT. IEEE Trans. Ind. Inform. 18(2), 1310–1321 (2022). https://doi.org/10.1109/TII.2021.3073925
29. Muniz, R.N., et al.: Tools for measuring energy sustainability: a comparative review. Energies (MDPI) 13(9), 2366 (2020). https://doi.org/10.3390/en13092366
30. da Silva, L.D.L., Pereira, T.F., Leithardt, V.R.Q., Seman, L.O., Zeferino, C.A.: Hybrid impedance-admittance control for upper limb exoskeleton using electromyography. Appl. Sci. (MDPI) 10(20), 7146 (2020). https://doi.org/10.3390/app10207146
31. Kaur, J., Khan, M.A., Iftikhar, M., Imran, M., Emad Ul Haq, Q.: Machine learning techniques for 5G and beyond. IEEE Access 9, 23472–23488 (2021). https://doi.org/10.1109/ACCESS.2021.3051557
32. Lopes, H., Pires, I.M., Sánchez San Blas, H., García-Ovejero, R., Leithardt, V.: PriADA: management and adaptation of information based on data privacy in public environments. Computers (MDPI) 9(4), 77 (2020). https://doi.org/10.3390/computers9040077
33. Pinto, H., Américo, J., Leal, O., Stefenon, S.: Development of measurement device and data acquisition for electric vehicle. Revista Gestão Inovação e Tecnologias 11(11), 5809–5822 (2021). https://doi.org/10.7198/geintec.v11i1.1203
34. Stefenon, S.F., Furtado Neto, C.S., Coelho, T.S., Nied, A., Yamaguchi, C.K., Yow, K.-C.: Particle swarm optimization for design of insulators of distribution power system based on finite element method. Electr. Eng. 104(2), 615–622 (2021). https://doi.org/10.1007/s00202-021-01332-3
35. Permutive (2023). https://support.permutive.com/hc/en-us/articles/360012435279

36. Xiao, Y., Jia, Y., Liu, C., Cheng, X., Yu, J., Lv, W.: Edge computing security: state of the art and challenges. Proc. IEEE **107**(8), 1608–1631 (2019). https://doi.org/10.1109/JPROC.2019.2918437

37. Abbas, N., Zhang, Y., Taherkordi, A., Skeie, T.: Mobile edge computing: a survey. IEEE Internet Things J. **5**(1), 450–465 (2018). https://doi.org/10.1109/JIOT.2017.2750180

38. Bonomi, F., Milito, R., Natarajan, P., Zhu, J.: Fog computing: a platform for internet of things and analytics. In: Bessis, N., Dobre, C. (eds.) Big Data and Internet of Things: A Roadmap for Smart Environments. SCI, vol. 546, pp. 169–186. Springer, Cham (2014). https://doi.org/10.1007/978-3-319-05029-4_7

39. Zhou, Z., Chen, X., Li, E., Zeng, L., Luo, K., Zhang, J.: Edge intelligence: paving the last mile of artificial intelligence with edge computing. Proc. IEEE **107**(8), 1738–1762 (2019). https://doi.org/10.1109/JPROC.2019.2918951

Slicing Mechanism Deployment in 5G Networks for Robotic Use Cases

Christina C. Lessi[1]([✉]), George Tsiouris[1], George Agapiou[2], Renxi Qiu[3], Andreas Gavrielides[4], Konstantinos C. Lessis[2], and Ioannis P. Chochliouros[1]

[1] Hellenic Telecommunications Organization (OTE) S.A., 99 Kifissias Avenue, 15124 Maroussi, Athens, Greece
clessi@oteresearch.gr
[2] WINGS ICT Solutions, 189, Siggrou Avenue, 17121 Athens, Greece
[3] School of Computer Science, University of Bedfordshire, Luton, UK
[4] eBOS Technologies Ltd., Arch. Makariou III and Mesaorias 1, 2090 Lakatamia, Nicosia, Cyprus

Abstract. Robotics is a rapidly growing field that is set to play an important role in automating many activities. The requirements that a robot can have for effective use can have large appeals. For example, in the case of its use for transport applications where it moves between people and vehicles, it is necessary to connect to a network with extremely low latency so that its reaction is immediate. In contrast, applications such as video transmission and recording and sending data require high throughput. The different demands on network resources lead to the need to implement flexible networks that can guarantee the necessary resources in the most efficient and reliable way. Slicing is a network capability that can provide specific network characteristics and can be implemented in different 5G network domain elements such as Radio Access Network (RAN), 5G Core or end-to-end. This paper presents the slicing mechanism that was implemented to be utilized for the needs of the use cases described in the 5G-ERA research project. In phase 1 of the implementation, which is described, slicing is focused on the packet core of the network that was integrated based on 5G SA Rel. 16 architecture.

Keywords: Slicing · 5G networks · Management and Orchestration · Middleware · Standalone architecture · Slice Manager · API · 5QI · Allocation and Retention Priority

1 Introduction

5G-ERA is a European funded research project that focuses on integrating vertical knowledge into the existing 5G testing framework to improve Quality of Experience (QoE) for customers which are targeting vertical sectors such as transport, healthcare, Public Protection and Disaster Relief (PPDR), and Industry 4.0 [1]. These sectors require high data transmission and processing and offer demanding services that could be integrated in a 5G network taking advantage from its capabilities in order to implement robotic collective intelligence approaches.

© IFIP International Federation for Information Processing 2023
Published by Springer Nature Switzerland AG 2023
I. Maglogiannis et al. (Eds.): AIAI 2023 Workshops, IFIP AICT 677, pp. 118–125, 2023.
https://doi.org/10.1007/978-3-031-34171-7_9

The use case analysis [2, 3] proved that several types of services are required. For example, in the PPDR use case that is proposed by 5G-ERA, the robot should be able to transmit a large amount of data since it should be able to send video streaming and data collected from sensors. At the same time, the reliability of the network should be high, because the robot, due to the emergency situation in which it is called upon to contribute, must communicate without interruptions with the control center. In the healthcare use case high data transmission is required, as well as high reliability. However the mobility, which is the ability of a moving user to send and receive data, is not high, since the robot is not expected to move very fast. The transport sector does not require high data transmission, but the network should support high location accuracy and availability when the robot is moving. Finally in Industry 4.0 network reliability seems to be essential, unlike throughput which is not critical.

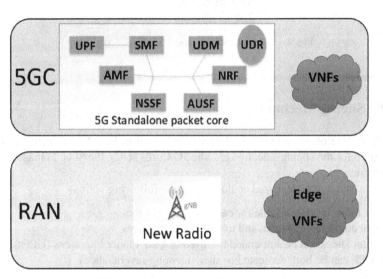

Fig. 1. 5G-ERA high level architecture

In order to manage network resources optimally and provide the QoS that is needed, the slicing feature is important. 5G Rel. 16 architecture [4] which is used in 5G-ERA (Fig. 1.) is able to support, by using network slicing, new network services [5, 6] such as:

- Enhanced Mobile Broadband (eMBB), which offers high bandwidth and is ideal to be used in cases where a large amount of data should be transferred
- Ultra-Reliable and Low Latency Communications (URLLC), which supports data transmission with lower delay than the 4G technology or the other types of services
- Massive Machine Type Communications (mMTC), which is used when large number of devices should used at the same time

Slicing is a network capability that can provide specific network characteristics optimally, based on the end users demands [7, 8]. For instance, there could be network slices that provide high bandwidth, others that ensure the low latency or high reliability. Slicing could be implemented in RAN or in 5G Core or in end-to-end network infrastructure.

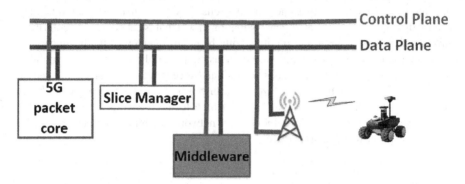

Fig. 2. Network components in 5G-ERA ecosystem

2   The Slicing Mechanism

The architecture of the network deployed is presented in Fig. 2. The components that will be used for the slicing selection are: the 5G Core (5GC), the Slice Manager and the Middleware.

The testbed that is deployed could support the following options:

- One or more slices available for each subscribed robot
- A robot could be registered and use one or more slices
- Different slices can be associated to different User Planer Functions (UPFs).
- One UPF can be both dedicated or shared among several slices

The phase 1 slicing mechanism design focuses on the 5G Core slicing. Several slices are configured in the 5G Core (which is implemented based on the 5G SA Rel. 16 architecture) supporting different types of services. One of these slices is defined as the default slice where a robot will be registered for the first time it gets access to the network. If the slice is not the preferred one, then a slice selection mechanism will be activated. The flow diagram of the mechanism is presented in Fig. 3:

Multiple user profiles are configured in the packet core. These profiles contain provisioning of information about the users, the access and session management data, the network slices etc. Even though the user profiles are not the same as slices, for the mechanism that is designed each user profile will be mapped to a specific slice:

user profile (1) = slice profile (1)
user profile (2) = slice profile (2)
user profile (3) = slice profile (3)

Therefore, according to the above implementation, it is ensured that the reference to a specific user profile coincides with the reference to a specific slice.

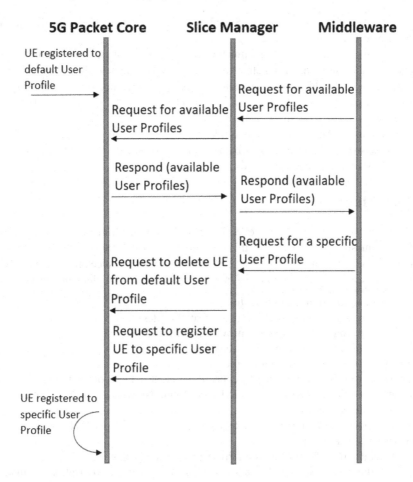

Fig. 3. Slicing flow diagram

The component that will trigger the mechanism described above is the Middleware which will send the request for slice change. More specifically, the Middleware will send a message to the slice manager to get information about the available user profiles. Then, the slice manager will send the request to the packet core and the packet core will respond with the list of user profiles which will be forwarded to the Middleware. In this list, the slices characteristics are not provided. Only the user profile name will be included: eg. UserProfile1 (UserProfile characteristics will be pre-installed in Middleware). Middleware will choose the proper user profile based on the needs of the robot for the specific use case and inform the slice manager. The slice manager will then send a request to delete User Equipment (UE) from the default UserProfile and re-register in in a new one.

The slicing mechanism described above has been tested by using a Teltonika TRB500 [9] Customer Premises Equipment (CPE). The use of this CPE was preferred since its operation is the same as the one of the robots that are used in 5G-ERA. TRB500 was initially registered in Slice1. Then, Slice2 was manually requested and after a CPE reboot, it was connected to slice2.

The slicing mechanism that is implemented is currently static. TRB500 is not able to request a slice automatically nether to be registered to the new slice without reboot. An external user should request for a slice change by interfering with Middleware and then UE should terminate the Protocol Data Unit session (PDU session) and restart a new one. Even though the mechanism is not dynamic, it could offer the advantages of the slicing feature. The UE is able to use the resources it requires, reliably and secured, while the network operator is able to manage the network resources optimally, offering to each UE only the resources it needs.

3 Slice Manager

As it was shown in Fig. 3, the Slice Manager is a component directly connected to the 5G Core requesting slice changing. It is built in Java using the Spring Boot Framework [10], while its southbound interface is used to interact with the slice plugins deployed in 5G testbed. Application programming interfaces (APIs) were implemented in order to:

- get the authentication token from the 5G Core
- retrieve the complete list of Provisioned Data Profiles
- retrieve information on a specific provisioned Profile
- delete an existing Provisioned Data Profile
- create a new Provisioned Data Profile
- replace an existing Provisioned Data profile or creates a new one if it doesn't exist
- retrieve the rule for a specific Public Land Mobile Network (PLMN) of an existing provisioned data profile
- create a new rule or replace an existing one for a specific PLMN for an existing Provisioned Data Profile
- delete an existing PLMN rule for a Provisioned Data Profile
- replace the policy data profile associated to an existing Subscription Permanent Identifier (SUPI)
- replace the provisioned data profile associated to an existing SUPI

The Slice Manager plays an important role in the designed mechanism since it is the component responsible for the slice management. Additionally, it receives the information from the middleware about the specific slice that the robot needs based on the Use Case requirements. As it is illustrated in Fig. 3, Slice Manager is the component that lets the Middleware to access the services offered by the packet core, translating the messages that both packet core and Middleware send and receive through the through a REST API it includes. These messages include important information about slices such as the Allocation and Retention Priority (ARP) and the 5G QoS Identifier (5QI) [11, 12].

4 The Middleware in the Proposed Slicing Mechanism

Middleware is a component in 5G-ERA infrastructure which is responsible to address the needs of vertical developers. Network Applications, Machine Learning (ML) tools and Artificial intelligence (AI) algorithms will be installed in Middleware. However, it will be used for additional purposes such as to optimise teleoperators' experience in handling unknown vertical applications, aggregate optimised vertical requests to the Open Source MANO (OSM) autonomously and request slices for the interconnected robots.

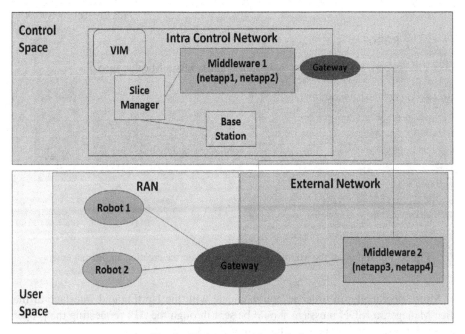

Fig. 4. Slicing control logical view

The Middleware will be implemented in two different places within the 5G-ERA infrastructure. The first implementation will be done centrally (Middleware2 in Fig. 4), where it will be possible for different networks to access and utilize Network Applications and the services it provides. The second implementation will be done at the edge (Middleware1 in Fig. 4), bringing the services closer to the user. More specifically, the second implementation of the Middleware will be local to the specific network infrastructure from which it will be leveraged. This choice was made with the aim of being able to offer services with different needs. For example, if a service has a requirement for low delays, it should necessarily be offered by the local middleware, in contrast to services that do not have such a requirement and can be offered by the central middleware, saving physical resources. In Fig. 4 the slicing control logic is presented. Middleware1 is installed in the edge layer of the network infrastructure, communicating with Slice Manager which is installed close to 5G Core, and Middleware2 which is a centralized component. Middleware1 will be synchronised with Middleware2 offering services that require low latency.

This local Middleware will be used in the slicing mechanism and its integration should focus not only on the demonstration of the standardised API for the Network Application developers, but also on the deployment of the proper interface to interconnect with the Slice Manager, allowing UEs to access 5G resources by using the required slice [13]. As it is presented in Fig. 5, Middleware will include several REST APIs to let it communicate with all the main components of the 5G-ERA infrastructure.

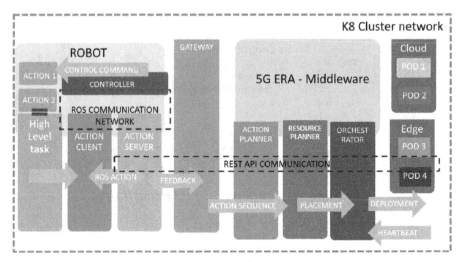

Fig. 5. Illustration of the Middleware end-to-end service creation and management

More specifically, in order to communicate with the Northbound Interface of the Slice Manager, a JSON message should be sent through the API requesting the proper slice as it is presented in the flow diagram of Fig. 3.

5   Conclusion

In this paper the slicing mechanism that was deployed for the needs of 5G-ERA project was presented. The use cases of 5G-ERA propose solutions in sensitive sectors such as PPDR and healthcare, but also in demanding sectors such as transport and Industry 4.0. The requirements that users have from the network are very diverse and it is important to be able to provide the necessary services in a reliable and efficient manner. Therefore, slicing is an important feature provided by the network to achieve this service offering.

The mechanism that was designed and presented in this paper focused on the packet core slicing, where several slices were designed. An advanced network architecture was designed, including a Slice Manager, which is responsible for the direct communication with the packet core, requesting the proper slice, and a Middleware, which is an external network component, communicating with the robots and knowing their needs for resources. Middleware is the component that drives the slice change process by asking from the slice manager a specific slice.

Currently, as it is the phase 1 of slicing mechanism deployment, this mechanism could be considered as a static one. Robots will be able to use one slice based on their needs and change it, if it is required, but the process is not taking place autonomously and robots should be rebooted in order to reconnect to the new slice. However, it is a mechanism that offers the advantages of slicing in better resources management and services availability.

Acknowledgments. This work has been performed in the scope of the *5G-ERA* European Research Project and has been supported by the Commission of the European Communities (*Grant Agreement No. 101016681*).

References

1. 5G-ERA project. https://www.5g-era.eu
2. Lessi, C., Agapiou, G., Sophocleous, M., Chochliouros, I., Qiu, R., Androulidakis, S.: The use of robotics in critical use cases: the 5G-ERA Project solution. In: AIAI 2022: Artificial Intelligence Applications and Innovations. AIAI 2022 IFIP WG 12.5 International Workshops, pp. 148–155 (2022). https://doi.org/10.1007/978-3-031-08341-9_13
3. 5G-ERA D1.1. (2021). Use case scenarios definition and evaluation specification. https://5g-era.eu
4. 3GPP TR 21.916 V1.0.0 (2020–12) Release 16. https://portal.3gpp.org/desktopmodules/Spe cifications/SpecificationDetails.aspx?specificationId=3493
5. SRS Project (2013). http://wiki.ros.org/srs_public
6. KnowRob Project (2014). http://knowrob.org
7. NGMN Alliance: Description of network slicing concept. Next Generation Mobile Networks Alliance (2016). https://ngmn.org/wp-content/uploads/160113_NGMN_Network_Sli cing_v1_0.pdf
8. 3GPP TS 28 530: 5G Management and orchestration; Concepts, use cases and requirements. V15.0.0, November (2018)
9. https://teltonika-networks.com/products/gateways/trb500
10. https://spring.io/
11. ETSI TS 123 502 V16.12.0 (2022–03): 5G Procedures for the 5G System (5GS) (3GPP TS 23.502 version 16.12.0 Release 16), March (2022). https://www.etsi.org/deliver/etsits/123500 123599/123502/16.12.0060/ts123502v161200p.pdf. Accessed Feb (2023)
12. 3GPP: Study on new services and markets technology enablers. 3GPP TS 22.891. European Telecommunications Standards Institute (ETSI), technical report version 14.2.0. (14 Sep 2016)
13. 5G-ERA D4.1: 5G-ERA Middleware initial version (2022). https://5g-era.eu

Smart5Grid Testing Strategy & Field Implementations for RT Wide Area Monitoring of Interconnected Systems

Ioannis P. Chochliouros[1](✉)(iD), Dimitrios Brodimas[2], Nikolaos Tzanis[2],
Michalis Rantopoulos[1], Daniel Shangov[3], Georgi Hristov[4], Atanas Velkov[4],
Irina Ciornei[5], and Daniele Porcu[6]

[1] Hellenic Telecommunications Organization (OTE) S.A., 99 Kifissias Avenue, 15124
Maroussi-Athens, Greece
ichochliouros@oteresearch.gr
[2] Independent Power Transmission Operator S.A., Athens, Greece
[3] Bulgarian Electricity System Operator ESO EAD, Sofia, Bulgaria
[4] Vivacom (Bulgarska Telekomunikatsionna Kompaniya EAD), Sofia, Bulgaria
[5] University of Cyprus, Nicosia, Cyprus
[6] Enel Global Infrastructure and Networks Srl, Rome, Italy

Abstract. The integration of renewable energy sources in the electrical grid imposes several operational issues for the energy markets and the transmission system operators, in particular. It is of great importance not only to detect events, but also to react in time to prevent faults in the transmission system that could lead to outages for the consumers or even to permanent damage to the energy equipment. Towards this scope, the criticality of the role of the Phasor Measurement Units (PMUs) which provide readings of voltage, frequency and current, is explained in this paper. It is also discussed how the 5G network may assist in the transfer of the measurements with its low latency capabilities and high availability criteria. Based on a Smart5Grid project's dedicated use case, the concept of 5G enhanced wide area monitoring is presented along with the associated field platform implementations both in Greece and Bulgaria. A complete list of defined Field Platform Validation Metrics is also elaborated with the equivalent targeted values.

Keywords: 5G · energy vertical ecosystem · latency · Network Applications · network slicing · smart-grid · wide area monitoring (WAM) · network functions virtualization (NFV) · synchrophasor · Phasor Measurement Unit (PMU)

1 Introduction

Current electrical grids consist of large and interconnected power systems which have served well modern societies in providing the necessary power supply of electricity. However, factors such as the growing demand, fast depletion of energy sources, unreliability and impact on the environment must be responded to in a vision of the future. The

© IFIP International Federation for Information Processing 2023
Published by Springer Nature Switzerland AG 2023
I. Maglogiannis et al. (Eds.): AIAI 2023 Workshops, IFIP AICT 677, pp. 126–138, 2023.
https://doi.org/10.1007/978-3-031-34171-7_10

smart grid is a new paradigm shift that combines the electricity, information, and communication infrastructures to create a more reliable, stable, accessible, flexible, clean, and efficient electric energy system. The smart grid can be considered as a modern electric power grid infrastructure for enhanced efficiency and reliability through automated control, high-power converters, modern communications infrastructure, sensing and metering technologies, and modern energy management techniques based on the optimization of on-demand, energy and network availability. A smart grid uses digital technology to improve reliability, security, and efficiency of the electric system from large generation, through the delivery systems to electricity consumers and a growing number of distributed-generation and storage resources [1]. Thus, a smart grid brings the power of networked, interactive technologies into an electricity system, giving both utilities and consumers exceptional control over energy use, improving power grid operations and, ultimately, reducing costs to consumers. So far, the communication networks dedicated for the needs of power control and automation were handled by the Transmission Systems Operators (TSOs), whereas telecom operators played almost no role in the power grids communication infrastructure. This is expected to change in the era of smart grid [2, 3] with the latter being the basis of smart energy and assessed as an important factor for promoting economic and social coordination as well as sustainable development. It can also provide strong support for a better life, cleaner environment and a more harmonious society.

Fifth Generation (5G) Networks will be an important enabler for the development of smart grid technologies [4]. The smart grid business, as one of the senior representatives of the vertical industry, has brought a lot of challenges to the communication network with its rich and diverse business types and differentiated industry needs. The advantages of 5G over earlier generations include higher data rate and low communication latency, improved security and reliability, low power consumption, and ability to connect a higher number of devices. As a consequence, 5G networks can very efficiently deal with several among the smart grid-related challenges faced by utility companies, such as connecting a vast number of sensors and providing ubiquitous coverage with high security and reliability [5, 6]. Furthermore, the 5G networks are able not only to propose but also to establish and make operational a new service-based architecture with advanced wireless technologies to deliver innovative business use-cases requiring low latency, increased capacity, high reliability and flexibility to satisfy the needs of different services [7, 8]. In this respect, the adaptation of 5G in the energy vertical will allow the grid to integrate to the dynamics of renewable energy and distributed generation [9, 10].

Solar and wind power tend to become prevalent in the near future [11], demanding more efficient monitoring and control mechanisms. Towards this direction, 5G networks will assist smart grids to control easier bi-directional power flows and support distributed energy resources. The 5G Networks capabilities providing low latency, large bandwidth, ultra high reliability and massive connection "match" the service requirements of the smart grids [12]. As one of the unconventional 5G technologies, the network slicing technology can divide the physical network into several independent, isolated and demand-based logical networks, which can ensure the efficient customization and smooth-going of various service needs. In this scope, 5G network technology can process and integrate network resources according to different user needs and scene characteristics and provide users with exclusively customized services. Three key sets of Network Slices [13, 14] in 3GPP have been defined for 5G Networks: massive Machine Type Communications (mMTC) for efficient monitoring of remote equipment, ultra-Reliable and Low Latency Communication (uRLLC) for handling of time-bounded traffic data and enhanced Mobile Broadband (eMBB) for handling of higher amounts of data in densely populated areas. These features along with the flexibility of the 5G Networks technology could enable a significant shift for the smart grid's communication layer.

The present paper is composed by several distinct sections: Sect. 1 identifies the strong innovative correlation between the 5G capabilities and smart grid's service requirements. Section 2 provides an overview of the concept of Smart5Grid and highlights its functional architecture with its 3 distinct layers. Section 3 discusses the respective use case 4 (UC#4), focusing on its conceptual descriptions, its proposed services related to UC-specific Network Applications and the inclusion of 5G technology. It also gives a high level view of the field implementations for the Greek and Bulgarian sides and illustrates the main network components. Section 4 depicts UC#4's Testing Strategy by reviewing the Field Platform Validation Metrics (FPVMs) developed for its needs. Section 5 serves as an overview.

2   The Smart5G Concept and Functional Architecture

The Smart5Grid EU-funded project [15] faces all the above challenges by providing an innovative, open and 5G enabled experimentation platform for the benefit of the energy market vertical [16]. Synoptically, Smart5Grid's aim is to assist the integration of modern energy grids to 5G network resources. This will be achieved through the open experimentation platform and the associated newly created Network Applications [17].

A Network Application is a piece of software that interacts with the control plane of a mobile network by consuming the exposed Application Programmable Interfaces (APIs), e.g., northbound APIs of 5G core and RAN Intelligent Controller (RIC), and edge computing APIs, in a standardized and trusted manner to compose services for the vertical industries. Network Applications can provide services to vertical applications, either as an integrated part within the vertical application or by exposing APIs (called business APIs). The Network Applications allow developers to concentrate on building the applications that are specific to the vertical domain on which they concentrate their expertise, while leveraging the features and performance that 5G networks offer. Network Applications enable them to do so by creating an abstraction of the complexities of the 5G network into a set of requirements, captured formally in a Network Application descriptor. The corresponding ecosystem is more than the introduction of new vertical applications that have interaction capabilities. It refers to the need for a separate middleware layer to simplify the implementation and deployment of vertical systems on a large scale.

Smart5Grid constitutes a step forward in the integration of energy grids with the latest innovations in virtualization and communication technologies that 5G, brings [18, 19]. Thus, Smart5Grid may be regarded as an ecosystem where professionals from various fields such as Telco experts, Software Developers, ICT integrators, Institute Researchers and Energy operators, work interactively towards the goal of utilizing the opportunities offered by the 5G Networks. Smart5Grid is one of the 19 European selected projects to deal with "5G innovations for verticals with third party services & Smart Connectivity beyond 5G" [20]. In concrete, the project responds to the dedicated 5G-PPP ICT-41-2020 Call [21]. The main common objective of the nine selected projects funded under the this Call is to provide 5G open experimental platforms that attract and provide opportunities for SMEs and developers to test Network Applications for specific vertical sectors and to create open-source repositories of such applications for wide use and towards standards development.

Four real-life scenarios will be demonstrated targeting to the Renewable Energy Sources (RES) production and distribution [22]. UC#1 in Italy deals with fault-detection and self-healing of the power distribution grids. UC#2 in Spain considers the critical issue of workers' safety in High-Voltage (HV) power substations. UC#3 in Bulgaria demonstrates a millisecond level precise distributed generation monitoring for a wind, hydro and photovoltaic power plant. UC#4 monitors in real-time the wide-area transmission grids between the borders of Greece and Bulgaria.

Smart5Grid leverages on network slicing (NS) [23–25] which refers to partitioning of one physical network into multiple virtual networks, each architected and optimized for a specific application/service. Specifically speaking, a network slice is a virtual network that is created on top of a physical network in such a way that it gives the illusion to the slice tenant of operating its own dedicated physical network with its own Service Level Agreements (SLAs) [26]. This is particularly beneficial for the Network Requirements fulfilment of the newly developed Network Applications thus enhancing the features of the proposed smart grids. Additionally, NS due to its ability to support differentiated service scenarios, can be viewed as the main enabler that will help smart grid actors to significantly reduce the Total Cost of Ownership (TCO) at power communication networks.

The Smart5Grid platform [27] aims to provide a common place for application developers and consumers within the vertical market of energy grid applications. In order to achieve this goal, Smart5Grid will develop a list of thoroughly tested Network Applications hosted in the Open Service Repository (OSR), made available for consumers to use. Figure 1 depicts the Smart5Grid Functional Architecture which is logically divided into three distinct layers, briefly discussed as follows:

- *Platform:* this layer provides the User Interface (UI) with the developers. The UI is the entry point of users to the Smart5Grid facility and consists also a web application that manages the authentication and authorization of users. Also, it provides access to the services of the exposed APIs of the Open Service Repository and the Validation & Verification (V&V) framework, which are the other components of the upper layer. The OSR enables 3rd Party developers and experimenters to register their Network Applications and Virtual Network Functions (VNFs) [28]. The V&V Framework realizes the testing process which provides guarantees on the correct performance of the Network Applications to the consumers. The Verification part specifically ensures that the Network Application packages and all its components are well formed and syntactically correct. The Validation part performs tests on live instances of Network Applications guaranteeing performance with the required levels [29].

- *NFV (Network Functions Virtualization):* The NFV/Telco layer contains the Management & Orchestration (M&O) Framework [30–31] and the NFV/Telco Infrastructure. The M&O Framework is responsible of managing the end-to-end lifecycle of a Network Application deployment and provides services to cover all aspects of the complete lifecycle including onboarding, instantiation, scaling and termination. The NFV/Telco infrastructure part is inseparable and equally important as the M&O Framework. It consists of the computing and the network infrastructure. The computing infrastructure deploys the software components in the form of containers that constitute a Network Application and can be centrally located or at the edge of the network in order to fulfill low latency requirements. Networking infrastructure consists of the telco network components in both the access/core domains, orcherstrated to meet demands of the Network Applications.
- *Energy:* The Energy Infrastructure layer is positioned at the bottom of the Smart5Grid architecture, containing the grid components that connect to the Network Applications. It is an equally important layer as the upper layer parts, composed of heterogeneous sets of devices from across the generation, transmission, distribution and consumption network segments. It may also contain other energy devices such as cameras and sensors which may provide measurements to the Network Applications. The Telco Network acts as an intermediary domain between the Energy part and the NFV Infrastructure where the Network Applications are placed.

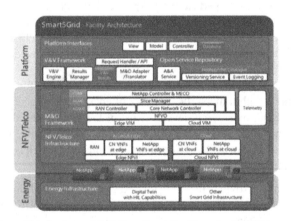

Fig. 1. Smart5Grid Functional Architecture [27, 32]

3   UC#4: Real-Time Wide Area Monitoring – Field Platform Implementations

The scope of UC#4 is the Real-Time (RT) Wide Area Monitoring (WAM) of the interconnection power flow between Greece and Bulgaria. This is achieved by leveraging the advantages that the 5G Telecommunication Networks provide. The monitoring process is executed from the newly established Regional Security Coordinator (RSC) in Thessaloniki, Greece. The role of the RSC is to promote regional cooperation and to support the strengthening of the neighbouring power systems in the region. Towards this goal, the RT monitoring of power flows between the countries is of great importance.

The continuous expansion of the European high penetration rate of the Distributed Energy Resources (DERs) significantly increases the complexity of the power system thus making its RT operation and control functions difficult to handle. As the number of connected DERs increases, inverter-connected devices dominate, leading to lack of physical inertia. The lack of inertia results in significant variations in the Rate of Change of Frequency (RoCoF), resulting in critical changes in the dynamic behaviour of the system. This challenge makes the existence of a WAM essential for the stability of the entire interconnected European power system [33, 34]. WAM systems leverage the high accuracy of the PMUs combined with the ultra-low latency and high availability of modern telecommunication networks.

A Phasor Measurement Unit, also called as a PMU[1] – or a synchrophasor – is a key tool used on electric systems to improve operators' visibility into what is happening throughout the vast grid network [35–37]. A PMU is a device that measures a quantity called a phasor and it is considered as a most robust device that can enhance the observability of modern power systems [38, 39]. The data originating from several PMUs, placed in a wider area of monitoring are gathered by the Phasor Data Concentrators (PDCs) devices. Those concentrators are responsible for the synchronization of the measurements of the different PMUs according to their timestamp and the forwarding of the synchronized measurements to the next level PDCs. Several layers of PDCs intervene between the PMUs and the SCADA (Supervisory Control and Data Acquisition) system[2] [40] of the transmission system operator (TSO). From the communication point of view, the PMUs and the PDCs are connected with optical fiber with each other ensuring that the data will arrive on time to the destination and that there will not be any security breach or data leakage. However, this architecture only permits central, predefined and cumbersome implementation of wide-area monitoring and control (WAMC) strategies, even if the PMU data can be used in a variety of combinations according to the grids graph [41]. In addition, the installation of a new PMU and its connectivity with the rest of the system is a costly and troublesome procedure for the TSO. Therefore it is essential to optimize the number and installation location of PMUs [37].

Wide-area monitoring protection and control [42] has been proposed to solve the problems and limitations of SCADA [43, 44]. Providing time synchronized data of power system operating states, Wide Area Monitoring Systems (WAMS) can play a crucial role in next generation smart grid protection and control. Such systems help secure efficient energy transmission as well as reliable and optimal grid management.

In a WAMS, the sensor nodes are the basic parts of the implementation of information sensing and communication. Compared to other wireless network, the WAMS

---

[1] PMU was first invented in Virginia Tech in 1988 to measure phasors of voltage and current, frequency and real/reactive power in real-time. PMUs have been continuously enhanced and are now deployed in substations.

[2] The most common task of SCADA is the state estimation of the power grid, which depends on unsynchronized and slow measurements.

is a specific application oriented network, which has characteristics of large size and dynamic topology. A WAMS usually uses a multi-level hierarchical communication network with reliability, RT responsiveness, scalability, and reliability, to integrate all these components together. The main component of WAMC is the PMU that can facilitate the RT computing and synchronized phasor measurement of voltage and current in a power grid [45]. PMUs can achieve precision and accuracy by using the Global Positioning System (GPS), which have precise reference timing signals. This timing is used to achieve the synchronized measurement of voltage and current phasors. PMU's utilization has increased rapidly to improve the monitoring of the power grid [46]. This process purely implicates for a new quality of insight into the dynamic behaviour of the electric power network and the corresponding values are increasing because of more dynamic requirements for the system caused by renewable power infeed such as wind, solar and energy trade.

To this part, the integration of 5G network can assist by ensuring the same network performance as the optical fiber in terms of low-latency, high-speed and zero data loss communication that previous generations of wireless networks could not offer [47]. Additionally, the virtualization and the edge computing that the 5G brings as an attribute [48], offer a new view of the possibility to deal with the PDC as a virtualized instance (vPDC) that can be deployed in any general purpose of the node instead of a monolithic and expensive device [49]. Smart5Grid tries to fill in this gap by proposing a flexible wide area monitoring framework based on the deployment of vPDC instances across the grid enabled by 5G communication channels. This framework envisions to provide a comprehensive view of the power grid's condition and allow the operators to take coordinated actions to prevent cascading failures and blackouts and drastically increase reliability and resilience of power grids [50].

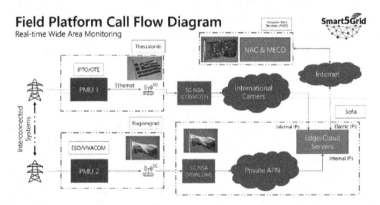

Fig. 2. Smart5Grid-Field Platform Call Flow Diagram for UC#4

Figure 2 depicts a high level overview of the field platform currently implemented for the integration of the PMUs through separate 5G NSA (Non-Standalone) networks [51]. One of the main challenges of this setup is the topology of the 2 PMUs involved, since they are placed in neighboring countries (i.e., in Greece and Bulgaria), served by COSMOTE and VIVACOM, *respectively.* The *"Greek side of the Demo"* is often referred to the Network part connecting the Greek PMU with the edge/cloud Server in Sofia. Correspondingly, the *"Bulgarian side of the Demo"* is often referred to the Network part connecting the Bulgarian PMU with the edge/cloud server in Sofia. The Setup Diagram can be considered as a "zoom-in" in "Fig. 1-Smart5Grid Platform" highlighting in the *Energy* and the *NFV/Telco* domains.

The PMUs at each site "gather" online measurements such as voltage, current and frequency of the interconnected power systems and forward those readings to the 5G gateway routers through an Ethernet connection. The 5G gateway routers at each site are provided with 5G-enabled SIM (Subscriber Identity Module) cards from each network operator and have both successfully established 5G connectivity. Specific port forwarding configuration is programmed at each 5G gateway router so that forwarding the measurements to the edge/cloud server is successfully established. The involvement of 5G NSA communication networks from COSMOTE and VIVACOM ensures the critical low latency and high availability. On the edge/cloud server side at VIVACOM's premises in Sofia, Bulgaria, specific security configurations are established in order to allow the reception of the PMU measurements. The edge/cloud server hosts the virtual machine (VM) where the Kubernetes cluster with the Network Application is placed. Involved network components are briefly listed below:

Interconnected Systems: These are the power interconnection lines between the Greek TSO's (IPTO) substation in Thessaloniki and the Bulgarian TSO's (ESO) substation in Blagoevgrad.

PMUs: Both are located at the HV network between Greece and Bulgaria and the vPDC is connected by using 5G NSA networks, needed for this critical operation.

5G NSA Networks: For both sides of the intended Demo, networks of COSMOTE and VIVACOM shall be utilized, correspondingly. Site surveys have been performed to verify the availability of 5G Network Coverage. However, a "criticality" issue that has been faced is the lack of 5G Core Network (CN).

International Carriers: Various interconnection scenarios of the Greek site to the edge/cloud server at Bulgaria are currently under evaluation with respect to the network latency requirements. At the time of writing this paper, the optimal routing is considered as the "Roaming Scenario" which exploits the commercial 5G Network Roaming Agreement between COSMOTE and VIVACOM. In this scenario, a VIVACOM SIM card is connected at the 5G gateway router at the Greek side, thus forwarding related data through the international carriers to the edge/cloud server in Sofia. In this way it is achieved the "shortest travel" between Thessaloniki and Sofia.

Edge/Cloud Server: It is installed on the virtual machine at VIVACOM's cloud server in Sofia. It hosts the Network Application created for the RT WAM scenario. The VM hosts a Kubernetes cluster, managed by the Network Application Controller. The role of the Network Application is to collect the measurements from the PMUs and provide live monitoring of the wide area between the borders of Greece and Bulgaria to the TSOs [22]. It is composed of 3 Virtual Network Functions (VNFs):

(i) *Virtual Phasor Data Concentrator (vPDC) Service*: The vPDC receives and time-synchronizes phasor data from the two PMUs, to produce an RT, time-aligned output data stream. The vPDC is to synchronize the measurements according to their timestamp, to be comparable to each other. The C37.118 protocol [52] will be used to collect data from the PMUs. The vPDC may also transmit the combined data to other applications which can perform the tasks of archiving, visualization or control. Upon successful reception of the PMUs' measurements, the vPDC performs data integrity checking and validation, by means of the data status flag and time quality of PMUs.

(ii) *Wide Area Monitoring (WAM) Service:* This service aims to present several status indicators and visualization features of the PMUs such as: a map indicating the device's current location; the device's name, address, model, serial number and firmware version; the nominal grid frequency (Hz) and the current reporting speed (fps); the phase diagram with voltage/current vectors displayed (updated in near RT); voltage magnitude and angle difference monitoring, derived from historical data.

(iii) *Advisory Service:* here the main task is to propose the remedial actions for RT operation to both TSOs. Additionally, it intends to provide advisory indications for RT operation to both TSOs and ex-post analysis provision in case of severe event occurrence in the grid.

4   Testing Strategy – Definition of FPVMs

A complete list of "Field Platform Validation Metrics" (FPVMs) is developed and presented as discussed below for the Scope of RT WAM. The choice of the Metrics and the Targeted Values is a task requiring combined effort from a variety of partners coming from different backgrounds, that is: Energy operators (TSOs), telco operators, ICT providers, research institutes and application developers. The term "FPVM" may be considered as a "hyper-set" of Key Performance Indicators (KPIs) consisting of: Core Network KPIs such as network latency; Application KPIs such as application packet loss, or; a combination of these such as closed loop latency [53].

The final choice of the FPVMs depends on three main factors. Firstly, they must satisfy the network requirements as they have been already elaborated during the works of Smart5Grid's D2.1 [54]. This has to be achieved with a clear statement on what enforcements the 5G Networks will offer to the intended UC#4. Secondly, a mapping between Network KPIs and Application KPIs has to be performed in order to provide newly formed FPVMs that "best describe" the field implementations features. Thirdly, the availability of resources to measure the metrics on field; the latter, is a particularly crucial factor, since 5G commercial networks are utilized for the Greek and Bulgarian sides of the scheduled demos. This imposes significant constraints regarding the live measurements as expected to be available from the involved Telco Operators. The FPVMs for RT Wide Area Monitoring are as follows:

Network Latency (in msec): Total time required for the PMU measurements to reach the vPDC service (i.e., the absolute waiting time for the vPDC to receive the measurements) [44]. A targeted value is of <40.

End-to-End (E2E) Latency (in msec): E2E latency, or one trip time (OTT) latency, refers to the time it takes from when a data packet is sent from the transmitting end to when it is received at the receiving entity. A targeted value is of <200.

Closed Loop Latency (in msec): It consists of the E2E Latency in addition to the time the TSOs are notified of a possible fault in the power network.

Delay Jitter (in msec): It is a measure of the variation in latency over time. A targeted value is of 5, approx.

Application (vPDC) Packet Loss (in %): It refers to packets not reaching their destination after being discarded by the vPDC component. (Targeted value: <0.1).

Communication Service Availability (in %): It is the amount of time the E2E application is properly delivered according to the specified performance metrics, over the amount of time the that is expected to deliver the E2E Network Application [54]. A targeted value is of >99.999%.

Communication Service Reliability (in %): Reliability is defined [54] as the percentage value of the amount of sent network layer packets successfully delivered to a given node within the time constraint required by the targeted service, divided by the total number of sent network layer packets. A targeted value is of >99.999%.

Device Density (in devices/km): It is the maximum number of PMU devices per unit area under which the specified reliability should be achieved [54]. A targeted value is 1.

5   Overview

The adaptation of 5G networks is an important enabler for the development of smart grid technologies. In particular, 5G supports inclusion of many innovative features also including network slicing for the provision of specific services tailored to specific needs. The Smart5Grid project is a modern research initiative facing such challenges and serving dedicated energy verticals upon the consideration of a modern architecture. Our work is structured around one specific use case dealing with RT WAM of the interconnection power flow between Greece and Bulgaria. More specifically, we assess the important role performed by PMUs in parallel with 5G NSA networks upon a roaming-based scenario and then we discuss the related field platform implementations by assessing the roles of the involved networks components. To facilitate future trials we also define a set of KPIs under the term "Field Platform Validation Metrics" giving a complete performance overview of the field implementations and we set corresponding targeted values.

Acknowledgments. This work has been performed in the scope of the *Smart5Grid* European Research Project and has been supported by the Commission of the European Communities /5G-PPP/H2020, *Grant Agreement No.101016912.*

References

1. U.S. Department of Energy: The Smart Grid: An Introduction. U.S. Department of Energy (2008). http://www.oe.energy.gov/1165.htm
2. Ekram, H., Zhu, H., Poor, V.: Smart Grid Communications and Networking, pp. 1–27. Cambridge University Press, Cambridge (2012). https://assets.cambridge.org/97811070/14138/frontmatter/9781107014138_frontmatter.pdf
3. Refaat, S.S., Ellabban, O., Bayhan, S., Abu-Rub, H., et al.: Smart Grid Architecture View. Smart Grid and Enabling Technologies. Wiley-IEEE Press, Hoboken (2021)
4. Borgaonkar, R., Jaatun, M.G.: 5G as an enabler for secure IoT in the smart grid: invited paper. In: Proceedings of the SA'19 Conference, pp.1–7. IEEE (2019). https://doi.org/10.1109/SA47457.2019.8938064
5. Hui, H., Ding, Y., et al.: 5G Network-based Internet of Things for demand response in smart grid: a survey on application potential. Appl. Energy **257**, 113972–113986 (2020)
6. Ahmadzadeh, S., et al.: A review on communication aspects of demand response management for future 5G IoT-based smart grids. IEEE Access **9**, 77555–77571 (2021)
7. Cosovic, M., Tsitsimelis, A., et al.: 5G mobile cellular networks: enabling distributed state estimation for smart grids. IEEE Commun. Mag. **55**(10), 62–69 (2017)
8. Leligou, H.C., Zahariadis, T., et al.: Smart grid: a demanding use case for 5G technologies. In: Proceedings of the PerCom'18 Workshops, pp. 2025–220. IEEE (2018)
9. Chen, J., Zhu, H., Chen, L., et al.: 5G enabling digital transformation of smart grid: a review of pilot projects and prospect. In: Proceedings of the ICCC'21 Conference Workshops, pp. 353–357. IEEE (2021)
10. Abrahamsen, F.E., et al.: Communication technologies for smart grid: a comprehensive survey. Sensors (MDPI) **21**, 8087 (2021). https://www.mdpi.com/1424-8220/21/23/8087
11. IRENA (International Renewable Energy Agency): Global energy transformation: a roadmap to 2050. IRENA (2019). https://www.irena.org/-/media/Files/IRENA/Agency/Publication/2018/Apr/IRENA_Report_GET_2018.pdf
12. The Third Generation Partnership Project (3GPP): 3GPP TS 22.261 V17.2.0 (2020–03): Technical Specification Group Services and System Aspects; Service requirements for the 5G system; Stage 1 (Release 17) (2020). https://www.3gpp.org/ftp/Specs/archive/22_series/22.261/
13. Liu, R., Hai, X., Du, S., et al.: Application of 5G network slicing technology in smart grid. In: Proceedings of the ICBAIE'21 Conference, pp. 740–743. IEEE (2021)
14. Li, W., Liu, R, Dai, Y., Cai, H., Fan, J., Li, Y.: Research on network slicing for smart grid. In: Proceedings of ICEIEC'20 Conference, pp. 107–110. IEEE (2020)
15. Smart5Grid 5G-PPP/H2020 Project (GA No.101016912). https://smart5grid.eu/
16. NRG5 Project: Deliverable 1.2: NRG-5 Reference Architecture and Functional Decomposition (2018). http://www.nrg5.eu/wp-content/uploads/2019/01/Deliverable-D1.2-compressed.pdf
17. 5G-PPP Software Network Working Group: "NetApp: Opening up 5G and beyond networks – 5G-PPP projects analysis" (White Paper) (2022). https://5g-ppp.eu/wp-content/uploads/2022/10/Software-Network-WG-Network-Applications-2022.pdf
18. European Telecommunications Standards Institute: ETSI GS NFV 002 V1.2.1 (2014–12): Network Functions Virtualisation (NFV); Architectural Framework. ETSI (2014). https://www.etsi.org/deliver/etsi_gs/NFV/001_099/002/01.02.01_60/gs_nfv002v010201p.pdf
19. European Telecommunications Standards Institute: ETSI GR NFV-IFA 029 V3.3.1 (2019-11): Network Functions Virtualisation (NFV) Release 3; Architecture; Report on the Enhancements of the NFV architecture towards "Cloud-native" and "PaaS". ETSI (2019). https://www.etsi.org/deliver/etsi_gr/NFV-IFA/001_099/029/03.03.01_60/gr_NFV-IFA029v030301p.pdf

20. The 5G Public Private Partnership (5G-PPP): Phase 3.6: 5G Innovations and Beyond 5G. https://5g-ppp.eu/5g-ppp-phase-3-6-projects/
21. European Commission: 5G PPP - 5G innovations for verticals with third party services. https://ec.europa.eu/info/funding-tenders/opportunities/portal/screen/opportunities/topic-det ails/ict-41-2020
22. Porcu, D., et al.: 5G communications as "enabler" for smart power grids: the case of the Smart5Grid project. In: Maglogiannis, I., Macintyre, J., Iliadis, L. (eds.) AIAI 2021. IAICT, vol. 628, pp. 7–20. Springer, Cham (2021). https://doi.org/10.1007/978-3-030-79157-5_1
23. Afolabi, I., Taleb, T., Samdanis, K., Ksentini, A., Flinck, H.: Network slicing and softwariza-tion: a survey on principles, enabling technologies, and solutions. IEEE Commun. Surv. Tutor. **20**(3), 2429–2453 (2018)
24. Alotaibi, D.: Survey on network slice isolation in 5G networks: fundamental challenges. Procedia Comput. Sci. **182**, 38–45 (2021)
25. Papageorgiou, A., Fernández-Fernández, A., et al.: On 5G network slice modelling: Service resource-, or deployment-driven? Comput. Commun. **149**, 232–240 (2020)
26. Chochliouros, I.P., Spiliopoulou, A.S., Lazaridis, P., Dardamanis, A., Zaharis, Z., Kostopou-los, A.: Dynamic network slicing: challenges and opportunities. In: Maglogiannis, I., Iliadis, L., Pimenidis, E. (eds.) AIAI 2020. AICT, vol. 585, pp. 47–60. Springer, Cham (2020). https://doi.org/10.1007/978-3-030-49190-1_5
27. Porcu, D., Castro, S., Otura, B., Encinar, P., Chochliouros, I., et al.: Demonstration of 5G solutions for smart energy grids of the future: a perspective of the Smart5Grid project. Energies (MDPI) **15**(3), 839 (2022). https://doi.org/10.3390/en15030839
28. Abdelwahab, S., Hamdaoui, B., Guizani, M., Znati, T.: Network function virtualization in 5G. IEEE Commun. Mag. **54**(4), 84–91 (2016)
29. Smart5Grid project: Deliverable 3.1: Interim Report for the development of the 5G network facilities (2022). https://smart5grid.eu/dissemination-activities/deliverables/
30. European Telecommunications Standards Institut: ETSI TS 128 533 V15.4.0 (2020–03): 5G; Management and orchestration; Architecture framework (3GPP TS 28.533 version 15.4.0 Release 15). ETSI (2020). https://www.etsi.org/deliver/etsi_ts/128500_128599/128533/15. 04.00_60/ts_128533v150400p.pdf
31. The Third Generation Partnership Project: 3GPP TS 28.530 V17.4.0 (2023-03): Management and orchestration of networks and network slicing; Concepts, use cases and requirements (Release 17)". 3GPP (2023). https://www.3gpp.org/ftp/Specs/archive/28_series/28.530/
32. Smart5Grid project: Deliverable 2.2.: Overall Architecture Design, Technical Specifications and Technology Enablers (2022). https://smart5grid.eu/dissemination-activities/deliverables/
33. Appasani, B., Mohanta, D.K.: A review on synchrophasor communication system: commu-nication technologies, standards and applications. Protect. Control Mod. Power Syst. **3**(1), 1–17 (2018). https://doi.org/10.1186/s41601-018-0110-4
34. Zacharia, L., Asprou, M., Kyriakides, E.: Measurement errors and delays on wide area control based on IEEE Std C37.118.1-2011: impact and compensation. IEEE Syst. J. **14**(1), 422–432 (2020)
35. Nuqui, R.F., et al.: Phasor measurement unit placement techniques for complete and incomplete observability. IEEE Trans. Power Deliv. **20**(4), 2381–2388 (2005)
36. Abdullah Sufyan, M.A.,Zuhaib, M., Rihan, M.: Optimal PMU placement for smart grid: a technical case study. In: Proceedings of the INDICON'20 Conference, pp. 1–7. IEEE (2020)
37. Sefid, M., Rihan, M.: Optimal PMU placement in smart grid: an updated review. Int. J. Smart Grid Clean Energy **8**(1), 59–69 (2019)
38. Sexauer, J., Javanbakht, P., Mohagheghi, S.: Phasor measurement units for the distribution grid: necessity and benefits. In: Proceedings of the 2013 IEEE PES Innovative Smart Grid Technologies Conference (ISGT'13), pp. 1–6. IEEE (2013)

39. Tlusty, J., et *al.*: The monitoring of power system events on transmission and distribution level by the use of phasor measurements units (PMU). In: Proceedings of CIRED 2009 Conference - Part 1, pp. 1–4. IET (2009)
40. Rahman, M.A., et *al.*: Formal analysis for dependable supervisory control and data acquisition in smart grids. In: Proceedings of the DSN'16 Conference, pp. 263–274. IEEE (2016)
41. Chaudhuri, N.R.: Wide-area monitoring and control of smart energy cyber-physical systems (CPS). In: Song, H., Shrinivasan, R., Sookoor, T., Jeschke, S. (eds.) Smart Cities: Foundations, Principles and Applications, pp. 155–180. Wiley, Hoboken (2017). https://onlinelibrary.wiley.com/doi/10.1002/9781119226444.ch6
42. Singh, A.K.: Smart grid wide area monitoring, protection and control. Int. J. Comput. Res. **2**(7), 553–584 (2012)
43. Jiaping, L., et *al.*: Wide-area monitoring protection and control of future power system networks. In: Proceedings of the WARTIA'14 Conference, pp. 903–905. IEEE (2014)
44. Song, H., Srinivasan, R., Sookoor, T., Jeschke, S.: Wide-area monitoring and control of smart energy cyber-physical systems (CPS). In: Smart Cities: Foundations, Principles, and Applications, pp. 155–180. Wiley, Hoboken (2017). https://doi.org/10.1002/9781119226444.ch6
45. Wache, M., Murray, D.: Application of phasor measurement units in distribution networks. In: Proceedings of CIRED 2013 Conference, pp. 1–4. IET (2013)
46. Mohanta, D.K., Murthy, C., and Roy, D.S.: A brief review of phasor measurement units as sensors for smart grid. Electr. Power Comp. Syst. **44**(4), 411–425 (2016)
47. Taveras Cruz, A.J., Aybar-Mejía, M., et *al.*: Implications of 5G technology in the management of power microgrids: a review of the literature. Energies (MDPI) **16**(4) (2023). https://doi.org/10.3390/en16042020
48. Hassan, N., Yau, K.-L.A., Wu, C.: Edge computing in 5G: a review. IEEE Access **7**, 127276–127289 (2019)
49. Tzanis, N., et *al.*: Optimal relocation of virtualized PDC in edge-cloud architectures under dynamic latency conditions. In: Proceedings of ICECET'22 Conference, pp. 1–6. IEEE (2022)
50. Shafiullah, G.M.,Oo, A.M.T., Shawkat Ali, A.B.M., Wolfs, P.: Smart grid for a sustainable future. Smart Grid Renew. Energy **4**(1), 23–34 (2013)
51. Darah, D.: 5G NSA vs. SA: how does each deployment mode differ? TechTarget (2023). https://www.techtarget.com/searchnetworking/feature/5G-NSA-vs-SA-How-does-each-deployment-mode-differ
52. International Institute of Electrical and Electronic Engineers: IEEE Standard for Synchrophasor Measurements for Power Systems (IEEE C37.118.1-2011). https://standards.ieee.org/standard/C37_118_1-2011.html
53. 5G-PPP: White Paper: Service performance measurement methods over 5G experimental networks (2021). https://5g-ppp.eu/wp-content/uploads/2021/06/Service-performance-measurement-methods-over-5G-experimental-networks_08052021-Final.pdf
54. Smart5Grid project: Deliverable 2.1: Elaboration of UCs and System Requirements. https://smart5grid.eu/dissemination-activities/deliverables/

Techno-economic Analysis Highlighting Aspects of 5G Network Deployments at Railway Environments

Ioanna Mesogiti[1]([⊠]) [iD], Eleni Theodoropoulou[1], Fotini Setaki[1],
George Lyberopoulos[1], Konstantinos Stamatis[2], Panteleimon Konstantinos Chartsias[2],
Nikos Makris[3], Paris Flegkas[3], Jesús Gutiérrez[4], Christina Politi[5], Christos Tranoris[5],
Markos Anastasopoulos[6], and Anna Tzanakaki[6]

[1] COSMOTE Mobile Telecommunications S.A., Athens, Greece
imesogiti@cosmote.gr
[2] Intracom Telecom S.A., Peania, Greece
[3] Department of Electrical and Computer Engineering, University of Thessaly, Volos, Greece
[4] IHP - Leibniz-Institut Für Innovative Mikroelektronik, Frankfurt, Germany
[5] University of Patras, Patras, Greece
[6] National and Kapodistrian University of Athens, Athens, Greece

Abstract. 5G and beyond networks will comprise versatile infrastructures consisting of multiple disaggregated pools of network, compute and storage resources, while network deployments are expected to appear in various (physical/vertical) environments as access network extensions of public networks or as Non-Public-Networks. In many physical/vertical environments, the necessary network deployments may be very dissimilar to the wide area public network ones, raising new deployment challenges. Such cases can be the railway environment or specific deployments along rivers or roads. In these cases, the various network deployment alternatives, in terms of technologies and topologies, shall take into account various factors such as area specifics, technologies' deployment feasibility, traffic/usage forecasts considering long-term services roadmaps and, certainly, the associated costs. In this context, network planning and dimensioning shall be tightly accompanied by the techno-economic analysis of the various deployment alternatives. This paper provides insights of 5G network deployments at railway environments as retrieved through macroscopic techno-economic analysis and demonstrates their applicability on the architectural concepts of the 5G-PPP 5G-VICTORI project.

Keywords: 5G · Railway Vertical · Transport Network · Wireless-Optical Convergence · Techno-economic · Fronthaul · Backhaul

1 Introduction

5G and beyond access network deployments are expected to coexist with physical environments that belong to vertical industries as network extensions of public networks or as Non-Public-Networks (NPNs). In many cases, these upgraded environments may

© IFIP International Federation for Information Processing 2023
Published by Springer Nature Switzerland AG 2023
I. Maglogiannis et al. (Eds.): AIAI 2023 Workshops, IFIP AICT 677, pp. 139–150, 2023.
https://doi.org/10.1007/978-3-031-34171-7_11

be very dissimilar to the wide area coverage deployments of existing public networks, raising new challenges in the deployment of the networks.

At the same time, it is a fact that 5G and beyond network services will pose stringent coverage and data rate requirements to access network segments. For transport network segments it will be necessary to support high-capacity Macro Sites (MS), dense layers of high capacity Small Cells (SCs), or/and versatile disaggregated Radio Access Network (Cloud/Distributed/Open RAN) setups. For this purpose, the transport network needs to be equipped with mechanisms to support flexible and scalable RAN deployments, and to converge fronthaul (FH) and backhaul (BH) traffic of various functional splits (FS). This is usually carried out using a common infrastructure that comprises various wireless and optical technologies [1].

A number of research projects have addressed the development of next generation transport network technologies. In this context, the 5G-XHaul [2] and 5G-PICTURE [3] projects proposed converged optical-wireless network solutions capable of supporting flexible splitting options, while the 5G-PICTURE project [3] further aimed at delivering a paradigm shift, by "disaggregating" hardware and software components across domains wirelessly or/and optically interconnected. 5G-VICTORI [4] aims at showcasing and evaluating the applicability of disaggregated 5G network deployments on versatile vertical environments, namely railway and smart cities.

Delivering 5G network deployments to meet the service requirements of railway and smart city environments is not a straightforward task. In practice, many factors need to be considered, such as area specifics, deployment feasibility, long-term service roadmaps, traffic demand and growth patterns/forecasts, as well as infrastructure availability, scaling capabilities and the associated costs. The scaling capabilities and the identification of these costs need to also consider the various deployment phases (over time), in order to estimate the critical, high-cost factors and to extract deployment guidelines at early network planning stages. Performing techno-economic analyses is an equally complex task, the underlying reasons being many and versatile depending on the scope, scale, system, technologies in focus, etc. An overview of the versatility of techno-economic analyses in the 5G era is provided in [5].

This paper proposes a methodology for the techno-economic evaluation of large-scale 5G and beyond network deployments, aiming to identify cost optimizations and to investigate various technological aspects and critical parameters at early stages towards delivering economically viable and sustainable deployments. The methodology is based on previous studies' fully parameterized expandable Techno-Economic analysis tools [6, 7, 14] that reflect the concepts of 5G deployments. The tool has been applied in the case of real network deployments at a railway environment, and the results confirm their capabilities and usage potential.

The paper is organized as follows: Sect. 2 presents a methodology and a tool for performing techno-economic analyses in the context of 5G and beyond networks. In Sect. 3, the beyond 5G architectural principles are applied to the railway vertical environment. The next section presents an application of the tool in modeling and dimensioning an indicative (though realistic) railway vertical facility deployment, followed by cost assessment of various deployment scenarios. A number of network deployment alternative scenarios are identified and evaluated from a techno-economic perspective. Finally, conclusions are drawn.

2 Techno-economic Analysis Methodology and Tool

In the context of 5G-VICTORI, a methodology for performing technoeconomic analysis of 5G deployments has been implemented [11] (leveraging [6]) as a fully parameterized tool tailored for vertical network deployments. These allow the estimation of the critical, high-cost factors and the extraction of deployment guidelines at early network planning stages through comparative analysis of multiple deployment scenarios. The innovative nature of the methodology and the tool lies in the modeling of versatile 5G network technologies and architectural/ deployment options while considering the railway vertical premises specificities, as well as rules and assumptions resembling usage/operation conditions in the most realistic way. The methodology that was implemented with the techno-economic analysis tool (see Fig. 1) comprises the following steps:

1 Definition of the vertical premises: coverage area (as distance or as surface) and modelling of the vertical premises environment specifics, in this case considering the deployment at a railway area along the tracks and on platforms.
2 Definition of the service scenarios in terms of coverage area/routes, traffic demand to be served, services to be provided etc. and their scaling over years.
3 Definition of the access and transport deployment blueprint, providing a general model of alternative RAN/BH/FH/MEC (Mobile Edge Computing)/5G Core Network (5G CN or CN) options that can co-exist in a deployment.
4 Definition of the scaling rules for each technology and the dimensioning rules for each segment. In practice this includes:
   a. RAN dimensioning: as access network nodes' elements calculation based on capacity and coverage increase over years; considering access radio units capacity, gNB (5G nodeB) disaggregation model, etc.
   b. Transport segments dimensioning: as capacity and required links calculation considering various FS, various transport aggregation levels, various transport technologies link capacity/range/hops, etc.
   c. Edge segment dimensioning: as compute resources calculation considering the application services and Network Functions requirements, loading factors, etc.
   d. Core segment placement and dimensioning of UPFs (User Plane Function) to serve the Edges.
5 Definition of the cost information and cost scaling rules for all elements that are modelled/analyzed.
6 Definition of deployment scenarios in terms of technologies, including usage of various FS, wireless/optical technologies, MEC, RAN disaggregation, etc.
7 Application of common Cash Flow Model, which leads to automatically calculated Capital Expenses/Operational Expenses (CAPEX/OPEX) breakdown, as well as the Total Cost of Ownership (TCO) estimation, on per technology/equipment/segment basis. In practice, CAPEX/OPEX breakdown and TCO are calculated, taking into account, equipment- and fiber deployment- specific costs, labor costs, operations and maintenance, as well as additional financial figures such as Weighted Average Cost of

Capital (WACC) and Tax Deduction (%equipment cost). The Yearly Total Cost (YTC) has been calculated by harmonizing the sum - each CAPEX has to be annualized, splitting the investment by the appropriate *amortization period (AP)*:

$$YTC = \sum_{i=1}^{N} \frac{CAPEX_i}{AP_i} + \sum_{j=1}^{M} OPEX_j$$

where $CAPEX_i$ and $OPEX_j$ are the i-th component and j-th component of CAPEX and OPEX respectively.

8 Iteration of all steps for the various scenarios and collection of analytical, comparative cost results, in order to identify key factors influencing cost and extract deployment recommendations.

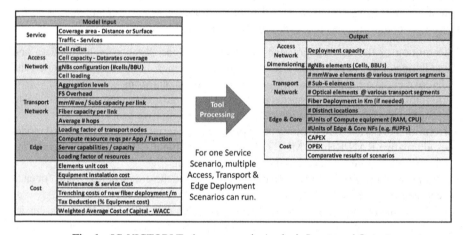

Fig. 1. 5G-VICTORI Techno-economic Analysis Inputs and Outputs

3   5G Vertical Deployment Aspects

3.1   5G-VICTORI Deployment Blueprint

5G-VICTORI has adopted the infrastructure disaggregation concepts and the baseline principles of the physical and logical/functional architecture of 5G networks. More specifically, the 5G architecture considers an integrated optical and wireless network topology and infrastructure to support jointly backhauling of SCs/MSs and fronthauling of various FSs (as defined in [8]) of Remote Radio Units (RRUs). The access transport links are aggregated at various levels using optical network technologies and the traffic is forwarded to the backbone optical transport network. In particular, we distinguish the following transport network segments:

- Transport access, providing connectivity from the access network nodes to the 1st level aggregation sites;

- Transport aggregation, aggregating transport access links at COs (Central Offices);
- Transport core, providing connectivity between COs to the CN.

Compute resources are present at various physical and logical locations of the network for hosting applications and/or network services such as Virtual Base Band Units (vBBUs) [12]. These are indicated as edge (close to the location of or collocated with a MS), (at COs), or central clouds (at CN).

Leveraging these concepts, the project has proposed three deployment options for the case of the railway vertical network [9]:

- Option 1: NPN (with autonomous edge): that considers a silo 5G CN deployed at central premises of the vertical facility.
- Option 2: NPN with distributed data plane – multiple edges: including a 5GCN deployed at central premises of the vertical and several UPFs and application servers deployed at a number of specific sites of the vertical facility.
- Option 3: Fully disaggregated 5G architecture: including a 5G CN deployed at central premises of the vertical, UPFs and application servers deployed at a number sites of the vertical facility, and disaggregated RAN segment.

The principles and these deployment options are reflected in a general deployment blueprint that is modelled with the techno-economic tool. The blueprint includes also the support of multiple hierarchical transport network comprising the aforementioned three segments, i.e. the access, the aggregation and the core transport segment.

To model the case of the extension of access network nodes on-board the trains [10], the blueprint considers the option of last-mile transport segment. The overall blueprint that has been used in 5G-VICTORI techno-economic analysis is depicted in Fig. 2.

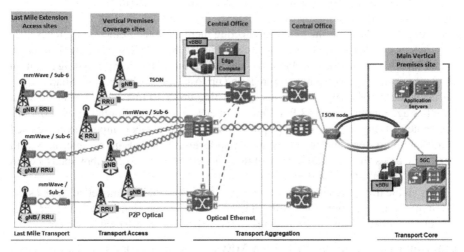

Fig. 2. 5G-VICTORI Physical Architecture Blueprint

3.2 Network Modeling, Dimensioning and Deployment Aspects

Access Network Deployment Dimensioning. The RAN deployment at railway vertical premises, will comprise (1) a dense layer of small range access network nodes (RRUs and Small Cell gNBs) to serve the high traffic demand at specific hotspot areas of the vertical premises, and (2) a macro layer of access network nodes for maximizing coverage over the wider vertical premises area. The RRU and gNBs are modelled by the cell capacity, the cell data rates expected at the cell-edge (deriving from communication service-driven radio network planning), and the expected loading factor. For the RRUs and gNBs various FS options are considered. The access network deployment dimensioning is based on service driven radio network planning and forecasts of traffic demand density – especially over a hotspot area.

5G Transport Network Deployment Modeling. The 5G data plane architecture considers an integrated optical and wireless network topology and infrastructure to support jointly BH of gNBs, and FH of various FSs of RRUs to BBUs. The 5G-VICTORI transport access deployment options are related to the usage of different FSs (ranging from eCPRI (evolved Common Public Radio Interface) A to E options) [13], to the usage of various wireless and optical technologies and other deployment specificities.

In particular, mmWave (millimeter Wave) and Sub-6 links are considered for BH and/or FH providing ~1 Gbps (Gigabits/sec) average data rates per link; depending highly on the spectrum (frequency, bandwidth) and the clutter. MmWave links are implemented by pairs of transceivers, while links' capacity scales by adding new pairs of transceivers and/or by adding capacity software keys up to the 10Gbps per transceiver depending on the equipment specifications. Sub-6 links scale by adding new pairs of transceivers. The wireless transport connections may consist of one or multiple hops.

P2P (Point-to-Point) Optical Ethernet connections for BH/FH links at 10 Gbps are also included as an alternative technology in the model. Scaling of these links is performed by adding interfaces and connecting them to Optical Ethernet switches.

These access transport links are aggregated at 1st level at COs (edge sites), and then at 2nd level at a Main Vertical Premises site where the CN resides. At 1st aggregation level we consider mmWave hubs aggregating up to 10 links, Elastic Time-Shared Optical Network (TSON) [9] components aggregating up to 10 links and Optical Ethernet switches aggregating up to 48 P2P Optical Interfaces with the limitation of 100 Gbps aggregate capacity in two 100 Gbps ports. We consider TSON components to be used at transport core segments to aggregate, at 2nd level, (Optical) Ethernet interfaces with flexible degrees of aggregation (reaching aggregation of 12×10 Gbps interfaces to 100 Gbps optical Ethernet) [9].

For all the transport segments, other deployment specifics are modelled, such as the maximum link utilization, the loading factor for the aggregation nodes interfaces, the existence of fiber deployment – Greenfield (GF)/Brownfield (BF) scenarios, etc.

Usage and Placement of vBBUs and MEC. Compute resources are considered at various physical and logical locations of the network for hosting applications and/or network services such as vBBUs and UPFs. These are indicated as Edge Compute located at COs. Similarly, to large scale deployments' common practice, it is assumed that COs host the transport aggregation equipment.

By modifying the deployment options and the relevant model parameters, different access network, access transport and aggregation transport deployment scenarios can be defined, dimensioned and evaluated.

4   Techno-economic Evaluation of 5G Network Deployments

The stepwise methodology was used to perform a techno-economic assessment for a 5-year timeframe of the various network deployments at a railway vertical premises in the Athens-Patras railway area. As example deployment area we consider the total distance of the railway tracks between the two main stations (ends in Athens and Patras), and the surface of all platforms between these two ends. Traffic and service demand is facilitated by additional information such as the number of platforms, the number of trains that are simultaneously in operation, the number of passengers per train, etc. The vertical facility characteristics are summarized in Fig. 3.

In the railway area under study, we consider 100% coverage along the tracks and at the platforms from the 1st year, and a cell overlapping factor of 10%, given the criticality of train automation services. The traffic demand is considered initially as 1.5 Gbps peak on train reaching 4 Gbps peak on train the 5th year, and initially 3 Gbps peak data rate at each platform reaching 10 Gbps at each platform the 5th year.

Area under study		Railway tracks
Railway Area	Km of tracks	208000
Platforms	#Platforms	15
	Platform Area m^2	12000
	Total Platform surface	180000
Trains	# Trains in operation per day	10
	Increase of #trains	5%
	#Trains Operating/ Total #Trains	90%
	# Passengers per Train	300
	Total Passengers = Users *2	16000
	Average Users per train	417
Deployment related	Average MS radius (m)	1000
	Average SC radius (m)	70
	Average distance to cabinet (m)	13900
	#COs	15

Fig. 3. Railway Vertical Facility Assumptions

4.1   Techno-economic Analysis Scenarios

For the techno-economic analysis, multiple network deployment scenarios were analyzed along the lines of the afore-described network modeling capabilities (summarized in Table 1). Scenario Set 1 considers the level of existing fiber deployment and usage of various FS (Set 1). We consider that fiber deployment is already existing at platforms towards ISPs. However, not all platforms are directly interconnected via fiber. Scenario set 1 BF options refer to the existence of fiber deployment along the tracks for 100% to 50% of the MSs deployed along tracks. This set assumes GF vs BF scenarios in pure optical deployments. Scenario Set 2 analyses the level of usage of optical vs wireless technologies at various transport aggregation segments and for various FS.

Table 1. Deployment Scenario Sets under evaluation.

Optical Transport Deployment (Set 1 Scenarios)		
BF - 100	Existing fiber deployment @ Platforms: 100% Existing fiber deployment along tracks: 100%	eCPRI A
		eCPRI IID/IU
		eCPRI E
BF - 50	Existing fiber deployment @ Platforms: 100% Existing fiber deployment along tracks: 50%	eCPRI A
		eCPRI IID/IU
		eCPRI E
GF	Existing fiber deployment @ Platforms: 100% Existing fiber deployment along tracks: 0%	eCPRI A
		eCPRI IID/IU
		eCPRI E
Transport Network Technologies Mix (Set 2 Scenarios)		
Only Optical	Access Transport: P2P optical	eCPRI A
	Aggregation Transport: Optical Ethernet Switching 50% & TSON 50%	eCPRI IID/IU
	Optical Scenarios BF - 100%, BF - 50%, and GF correspond to Scenarios of Set 0	eCPRI E
Only Wireless	Access Transport: Wireless:	eCPRI A
	Along Tracks: 30%Sub-6, 20% + 50% mmWave, At Platforms: 80%Sub6, 20%mmWave	eCPRI IID/IU
	Aggregation Transport: mmWave 50% & TSON 50%	eCPRI E
Optical-Wireless	Access Transport Wireless:	eCPRI A
	Along Tracks: 20%Sub-6, 30% + 10% mmWave, 40% P2P optical	eCPRI IID/IU
	At Platforms: 40%Sub6, 20%mmWave, 40% P2P optical Aggregation Transport: mmWave 40%, Optical Switching 20%, TSON 40%	eCPRI E
Edge Offloading Options (Set 3 Scenarios)		
Decentralised	vBBU Processing at Edge: 100% Application offloading at Edge: 70%	eCPRI A
		eCPRI IID/IU
		eCPRI E
Completely Centralised	Completely Centralised Deployment (vBBUs and App. Processing at Main site)	eCPRI A
		eCPRI IID/IU
		eCPRI E
Only vBBU Processing	vBBU Processing at Edge: 100% App. Offloading at Edge: 0%	eCPRI A
		eCPRI IID/IU
		eCPRI E

Scenario Set 3 deals with the level of decentralization of traffic and Network Functions (Set 3). We consider edge deployment at the railway platforms, with scenarios ranging from: (1) completely decentralized (vBBU processing and application offloading is performed at Edge – only internet traffic is routed via a main UPF node); to (2) partially decentralized (only vBBU processing at Edge while all traffic is served by a central UPF); to (3) completely centralized (all vBBU and application traffic processed centrally).

Finally, a 4th scenario analyses the deployment of gNBs or RRUs on poles along the tracks vs the deployment of access network nodes on-board trains; in which case practically, we consider wireless access transport nodes as an additional hop to deployment option 1 (evaluated with Scenario Set 2). We consider FS A/B (following eCPRI split naming). Essentially, we evaluate the cost benefits incurred by the decrease of the access network nodes number for the on-board deployment, and the cost overheads incurred by densification and extension of the access transport along the tracks compared to the trackside deployment; i.e. scenario 4 compared to FS A/B scenarios of Set 2.

4.2   Techno-economic Analysis Results

Through the comparative evaluation of costs, broken down per network segment, critical network deployment factors were revealed. The comparative results for Scenario Sets 1–3 are presented in Fig. 4. In particular, the 1st set of scenarios focus on the evaluation of a GF optical network deployment compared to various BF options. The results revealed that the fiber deployment cost is an extremely critical factor of the total cost, although the criticality is very location/deployment dependent, e.g. digging/trenching costs, etc.

Considering the selection of optical-wireless technologies (Scenario Set 2 results), the comparative analysis results revealed that the cost of deployment is highly influenced by the selection of the transport network technologies, by the existence of fiber deployment and by the selection of the FS at gNBs. In practice, in areas where fiber deployment is already existing, using wireless technologies increases the cost significantly from 50% to even 145% depending on the level of wireless technologies usage and on the FS scheme, due to the current capacity vs cost relation of these technologies. However, considering the cases of no fiber deployment, it could be cost efficient to use wireless technologies even with low level FS. In the case of partial existing fiber deployment, the scenarios shall be carefully analyzed, since the cost efficiency of wireless technologies depends highly on the FS scheme.

Considering the BBU processing and application offloading at Edge (Set 3), the results indicated that the centralized or decentralized deployment of vBBU processing have no impact on the TCO for CPRI schemes A to IID, while the TCO increases by 80% for eCPRI E when vBBU deployment is centralized compared to the decentralized case. The impact of application offloading at the edge is also marginal in terms of cost, however this will depend on the estimated traffic generated by the specific applications.

Last but not least, the Track-to-Train network deployment versus that on-board (5G) is evaluated from the techno-economic perspective (Scenario 4). In the Athens-Patras railway case, the cost of the RAN decreases by 76% in the case of the on-board deployment compared to the trackside one, while the cost of the access transport is almost 10 times greater in the case of the on-board deployment compared to that of the trackside.

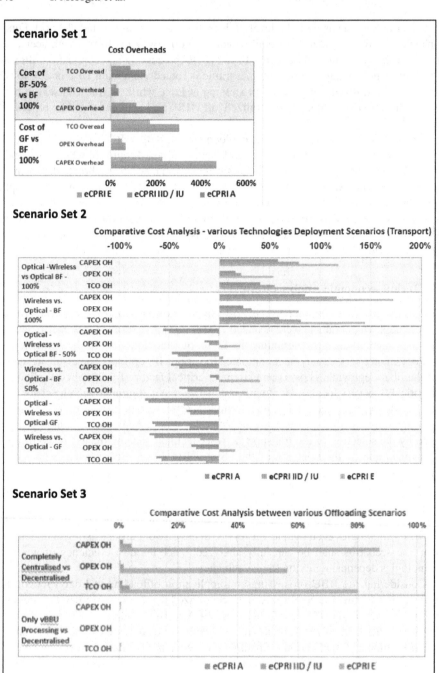

Fig. 4. Techno-economic analysis results

Considering the total costs of the Track-to-Train network deployment versus that on-board (5G) (Scenario 4 versus Scenario set 2), CAPEX is almost doubled, and OPEX is also increased significantly in scenario 4. However, eventually, the TCO in the pure on-board deployment is increased only by 50% compared to the trackside deployment. The access transport cost overhead depends highly on the radio emission characteristics of the equipment and the clutter along the tracks. Thus, in real network deployments, this analysis shall be carefully performed for the different wireless access transport equipment alternatives.

4.3 Overview of Results

A Techno-economic analysis is useful for quick and coarse evaluation of a large number of scenarios of network dimensioning and rollout. Analysis of longer-term scenarios can also provide insights related to future-proofness od deployment and to securing investments. The more accurate the pricing information, the more accurate and valuable the results of the analysis. To this end, the cost and cost models of the equipment are critical factors, making analysis highly sensitive to the cost assumptions, which are highly influenced by the Business-to-Business agreements, the target equipment volumes, the maturity level of the product, etc. However, unitary equipment costs cannot provide safe conclusions about network deployment. Instead, equipment cost and scaling information shall be associated also with 5G network deployment options such as the usage of MEC, the use of various FS and the placement of associated vBBUs. Apparently, the deployment environment and restrictions should also be taken under consideration. For this purpose, techno-economic tools capable of modelling such technical aspects prove to be useful.

In the indicative railway vertical case under study, the exemplary cost analysis has revealed the following:

- The fiber deployment along the tracks is a big cost share, so that premises with existing fiber deployments, are commercially advantaged.
- Wireless systems is a valid transport network alternative to optical transport, with the performance and cost efficiency of these technologies increasing over the years – compared to past deployment analyses [6].
- The selection of eCPRI scheme shall come hand in hand with the deployment distribution and technologies selection decision.

5 Conclusions

In this paper, we propose a methodology framework and a tool for the techno-economic analysis of 5G and beyond network deployments at vertical facilities. The methodology enables the cost evaluation of various network technologies and deployment options, by modeling, dimensioning and cost-analyzing individually of the various network segments while taking into account a plethora of critical technology-related parameters. Results from the applicability of the tools in indicative railway vertical deployment scenarios provide interesting conclusions on the potential selection of alternative 5G technologies and deployments achieving higher cost efficiency. Flexible by nature, the tool can be further expanded to include additional technologies, more complex deployment options as well as business factors, to enable the investigation of cost-efficient high performance network deployments as well as deeper understanding and familiarization with the disaggregated network architectures.

Acknowledgements. The research leading to these results has received funding from the European Union's Framework Programme Horizon 2020 under grant agreement No. 857201 and project name "5G-VICTORI - VertIcal demos over Common large scale field Trials fOr Rail, energy and media Industries".

References

1. Gavras, A., Bulakci, Ö., et al.: 5G PPP Architecture Working Group - View on 5G Architecture, Version 4.0. Zenodo (2021). https://doi.org/10.5281/zenodo.5155657
2. 5G-PPP Project 5G-XHaul. http://www.5g-xhaul-project.eu/. Accessed Mar 2023
3. 5G-PPP Project 5G- PICTURE. http://www.5g-picture-project.eu/. Accessed Mar 2023
4. 5G-PPP Project 5G-VICTORI. https://www.5g-victori-project.eu/. Accessed Mar 2023
5. Oughton, E.J., Lehr, W.: Surveying 5G techno-economic research to inform the evaluation of 6G wireless technologies. IEEE Access **10**, 25237–25257 (2022). https://doi.org/10.1109/ACCESS.2022.3153046
6. Mesogiti, I., et al.: Macroscopic and microscopic techno-economic analyses highlighting aspects of 5G transport network deployments. Photon Netw. Commun. **40**(3), 256–268 (2020). https://doi.org/10.1007/s11107-020-00912-w
7. Mesogiti, I., et al.: Techno-economic aspects of 5G transport network deployments. In: Tzanakaki, A., et al. (eds.) ONDM 2019. LNCS, vol. 11616, pp. 118–129. Springer, Cham (2020). https://doi.org/10.1007/978-3-030-38085-4_11
8. 3GPP, TS 23.501. System Architecture for the 5G System; Stage 2, Rel. 15
9. 5G-VICTORI Deliverable D2.4: 5G-VICTORI end-to-end reference architecture (2022). https://www.5g-victori-project.eu/wp-content/uploads/2022/05/2022-04-11-D2.4-5G-VICTORI-end-to-end-reference-architecture.pdf
10. Karamichailidis, P., Makris, N., Flegkas, P., Tzanakaki, A., et al.: Session management across heterogeneous wireless technologies in a rail transport environment. In: CAM'21: IEEE 5G for Connected and Automated Mobility (2021)
11. 5G-VICTORI Deliverable D3.7: 5G-VICTORI Use Case Assessment (2023)
12. Nikaein, N.: Processing radio access network functions in the cloud: critical issues and modeling. In: Proceedings of the 6th International Workshop on Mobile Cloud Computing and Services, 11 September 2015, Paris, France (2015)
13. Larsen, L.M.P., Checko, A., Christiansen, H.L.: A survey of the functional splits proposed for 5G mobile crosshaul networks. IEEE Commun. Surv. Tutor. **21**(1), 146–172, Firstquarter 2019 (2019). https://doi.org/10.1109/COMST.2018.2868805
14. di Giglio, A., Pagano, A.: Scenarios and economic analysis of fronthaul in 5G optical networks. J. Lightwave Technol. (JLT) **2018** (2018)

Use Cases Employing a Machine Learning Network Architecture

Ioannis P. Chochliouros[1]([✉]) [iD], John Vardakas[2], Christos Verikoukis[2],
Md Arifur Rahman[3], Andrea P. Guevara[4], Robbert Beerten[4], Philippe Chanclou[5],
Roberto Gonzalez[6], Charalambos Klitis[7], Pierangela Samarati[8], Polyzois Soumplis[9],
Emmanuel Varvarigos[9], Dimitrios Kritharidis[10], Kostas Chartsias[10],
and Christina Lessi[1]

[1] Hellenic Telecommunications Organization (OTE) S.A., 99 Kifissias Avenue, 15124
Maroussi, Athens, Greece
ichochliouros@oteresearch.gr
[2] Iquadrat Informatica SL, Barcelona, Spain
[3] IS-Wireless, Piaseczno, Poland
[4] Katholieke Universiteit Leuven, Leuven, Belgium
[5] Orange S.A., Paris, France
[6] NEC Laboratories Europe GmbH, Heidelberg, Germany
[7] eBOS Technologies Limited, Nicosia, Cyprus
[8] Universita Degli Studi Di Milano, Milan, Italy
[9] Institute of Communications and Computer Systems (ICCS), Athens, Greece
[10] Intracom S.A. Telecom Solutions, Peania, Greece

Abstract. 5G mobile networks will soon be available to handle all types of applications and to provide services to massive numbers of users. In this complex and dynamic network ecosystem, an end-to-end performance analysis and optimisation will be "key" features to effectively manage the diverse requirements imposed by multiple vertical industries over the same shared infrastructure. To enable such a challenging vision, the MARSAL EU-funded project [1] targets the development and evaluation of a complete framework for the management and orchestration of network resources in 5G and beyond by utilizing a converged optical-wireless network infrastructure in the access and fronthaul/midhaul segments. In this paper, we present the network architecture of the MARSAL, as well as how the experimentation scenarios are mapped to the considered architecture.

Keywords: 5G · Cell-free (CF) · distributed cloud · network automation · machine learning (ML) · secure multi-tenancy

1 Introduction

Communication networks currently undergo a high number of structural and functional changes that are associated with the need to support current and future demands (e.g., mobile traffic is expected to grow three-fold within 2025, as a result of predicted 10

© IFIP International Federation for Information Processing 2023
Published by Springer Nature Switzerland AG 2023
I. Maglogiannis et al. (Eds.): AIAI 2023 Workshops, IFIP AICT 677, pp. 151–167, 2023.
https://doi.org/10.1007/978-3-031-34171-7_12

million devices per km^2 and 100 billion devices worldwide), and with the commitment for the provision of ultra-low latency and reliability [2]. With the advancement of technology, the communication nodes will be inseparable from human social activities. To truly realize the diverse connection and interaction needs "at any-time and anywhere", future networks need to have specific characteristics, such as: Omnipresence (covering air, ground, space and sea); All-in-one (Internet of Everything); Omniscience (with the help of various sensors), and All-purpose (based on big data and deep learning). The same circumstances are also forecasted for other fields, such as Industry 4.0, health sectors, manufacturing industries, and autonomous industries, where revolutionary changes are underway. Another major challenge of the future 6G networks is to reach climate goals by reducing CO_2 emissions. This will be achieved through improved operational and management efficiency and energy consumption reduction [3, 4].

To tackle these challenges, several steps should be taken from the perspective of network concepts and technological aspects, to ensure economic developments, reliability and increased energy efficiency [5]. Key advances are required both at the network design and network management levels, as well as at the network security level to accommodate highly dynamic traffic demand, achieve energy reduction and provide cost-effective multi-level resource pooling in a secured way. Specifically, the network should support multiple distributed edge nodes and a multitude of access points (APs) coordinated by entities in a low-cost and near-zero latency manner. A unified and hierarchical infrastructure is essential to provide intelligent management of communication, computation and storage resources. The incorporation of efficient Machine-Learning (ML) algorithms [6] can further improve network efficiency. Additionally, infrastructure sharing is a sustainable way of lowering the network's capital and operating expenditures. Furthermore, support of multiple tenants is the key enabler of the new sharing economy business models in the telecommunication industry. Novel mechanisms for resourceful and efficient management of shared networks are necessary to enable a plethora of use-cases and industry verticals targeted in beyond-5G (B5G) and 6G systems [7–11].

In this context, MARSAL proposes a novel converged optical-wireless configuration based on the Cell-Free (CF) concept that targets flexible connectivity of a massive number of Radio Units (RUs) and aims to unlock the potential of user-centric CF deployments in 6G networks, while aligned with the O-RAN initiative [12]. The paper is organized as follows: In Sect. 2, we present the MARSAL overall architecture. Section 3 presents use cases enabling cell-free networking in dense and ultra-dense hotspot areas. Section 4 presents use cases for cognitive assistance, as well as security and privacy implications. Each experimentation scenario is mapped to the MARSAL architecture. We built on our previous paper [13], where we presented the main use cases and the involved stakeholders. Our innovation is focused on how these use cases are applied to our proposed ML network architecture.

2   Network Architecture

The proposed approach is illustrated in Fig. 1 and consists of an evolved 3GPP NG-RAN [14, 15] that is extended with emerging CF technologies, and of an innovative optical transport domain that deploys a distributed edge infrastructure with Data Centres (DCs) structured in 2 tiers, featuring Regional Edge and Radio Edge nodes.

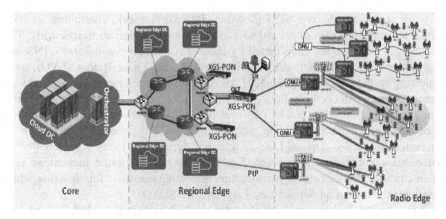

Fig. 1. The MARSAL network architecture

At the radio edge, the proposed radio network configuration is based on two radio access solutions. The first solution is based on the interconnection of multiple RUs (Radio Units) with the DU (Distributed Unit) via a bus configuration (upper right part of Fig. 1). This approach aims at addressing the most pressing CF limitations, as well as dealing with the fact that the clustering literature only considers disjoint RU clusters, even when multiple Central Processing Unit (CPU) nodes are assumed; thus, this novel approach will allow deployment of CF networks in beyond 5G RANs (Radio Access Networks) [16–18], based on the utilization of dynamic cluster-formation algorithms. The dynamic feature of such RU clustering algorithms is based on the CF CPU fragmentation in multiple DUs, a procedure that triggers the support of distributed computation and coordination between RUs and between DUs. Under this networking configuration, clusters of RUs, connected to multiple DUs, jointly address inter-DU and RU-DU coordination for the first time, while also considering fronthaul and midhaul constraints. The optimal cooperation levels between RUs and DUs and between DUs can be guaranteed through the application of dynamic adaptability algorithms of the involved entities' coordination levels.

The second solution for MARSAL's radio edge is based on a mmWave Hybrid Fronthaul for CF networks. Wireless CF Massive MIMO fronthauling solutions have been already proposed in the literature [19–21] targeting efficient interconnection of multiple APs to the CPU, by considering CF-based network configurations [22]. MARSAL's novel Hybrid MIMO fronthauling approach targets to provide support to CF networks through advanced beamforming solutions. In this way, the various RU topologies can be supported, where RUs can be reassigned to different DUs on demand. For the provision of this point-to-multipoint (PtMP) connectivity, MARSAL targets a new design of a mmWave radio node, by utilizing an RFIC (Radio Frequency Integrated Circuit) mmWave beamforming transceiver and phased-array antenna module [23]. As in the first radio-edge solution, MARSAL's mmWave Hybrid fronthaul approach also considers inter-DU coordination, targeting to introduce the interface for direct interconnection of DUs for the first time.

At the regional node, two SDN (Software Defined Network) controllers are considered, for managing the optical and wireless networking resources, respectively. The controllers at the edge are coordinated by the Network-Slicing-as-a-Service (NSaaS) subsystem at the core-tier Network Function Virtualization Orchestrator (NFVO), communicating via the OR-Vi interfaces [24]. Thus, intelligent traffic management and load balancing among PtP (Point to Point) and PtMP traffic via the appropriate scheduling of the two SDN controllers can be implemented, while improved power consumption can be achieved via traffic rerouting and shutting down individual SFP-OLTs (Small-Formfactor Pluggable – Optical Line Terminals[1]) during light loads. Additionally, the implementation of predictive slice reconfiguration that provides traffic fluctuations' prediction can trigger slice reconfiguration, thus increasing statistical multiplexing while minimizing the impact on Service Level Agreement (SLAs).

At the core, the orchestrator is integrated to the NFV infrastructure [25, 26] and supports coordinated resource allocation for MEC (Multi-access Edge Computing) applications [27] and network functions by coordinating two diverse management and orchestration subsystems (i.e., the NFVO and the MEC Application Orchestrator (MEAO)) [24]. Moreover, MARSAL aims at achieving self-driven and closed-loop autonomy for the Virtual Elastic Infrastructure to enable dynamic orchestration and management of networking and computing resources. To this end, MARSAL incorporates a distributed approach that involves Analytic Engines (AEs) at all tiers of the Edge infrastructure, and Decision Engines (DEs) in the two Core-Tier orchestration subsystems, targeting to overcome the isolation and underutilization of resources deployed at Edge nodes, through resource sharing.

For the network security pillar of MARSAL, three main contributions are considered in the overall architecture. Firstly, the solution for private and secure exchange of data among tenants through decentralized framework for confidentiality and trust that is based on novel data privacy representation techniques that are integrated into a smart contract platform. Secondly, the solution for ensuring data security through different policies and distributed storage of the data. Finally, the solution for network security protection through two different technologies that allow the analysis of the data transferred by the network in real time. Thus, MARSAL do not limit itself to the typical network security (also covered using accelerated hardware ML), but it also aims at protecting the data stored in the cloud, allowing secure multi-party computation and distributed data storage, while also it allows the cooperation among tenants by allowing them to automatically sign smart contracts and share data in a privacy preserving way.

---

[1] An SFP is a compact, hot-pluggable network interface module format used for both telecommunication and data communications applications. An SFP interface on networking hardware is a modular slot for a media-specific transceiver, such as for a fiber-optic cable or a copper cable. A GPON (Gigabit Ethernet Passive Optical Network) SFP module transmits and receives signals of different wavelengths between the OLT at the "Central Office" side and the ONT (Optical Network Terminal) at the end-users' side. GPON SFPs utilize both the upstream data and downstream data by means of Optical Wavelength Division Multiplexing (WDM).

3   Cell-Free Networking in Dense and Ultra-dense Hotspot Areas

During high-popularity events, both indoors and outdoors, a large number of users tend to stream high volumes of content from multiple handheld devices, thus creating a heavy burden to the network infrastructure both in the uplink and in the downlink. In Cell-Free massive MIMO (Multiple Input Multiple Output) [28, 29], users are simultaneously served by multiple cooperating APs (with a low number of antennas) instead of associating each user terminal to a specific cell of a gNB (next generation NodeB) equipped with a large number of antenna elements. Thus eliminating cell boundaries, which can significantly reduce or even eliminate inter-cell interference and significantly improve user fairness. Therefore, the canonical cell-free mMIMO (massive MIMO) [30, 31] shows 2.5X improvement over small cell in terms of per-user UL (Uplink) network throughput and it can achieve 95%-likely user throughputs of 4 Mbits/s and a mean throughput up to 8 Mbits/s on a 20 MHz bandwidth [32, 33]. This makes cell-free networking, an emerging 6G technology, extremely suitable for hotspot areas, as it can offer seemingly infinite capacity and fully mitigates the problem of cell-edge users having lower data rates. Like 5G the Small-Cell Network (SCN) with the concept of non-cooperative base stations (BSs) can only serve up to 200-m cell-radius, reduce power in signal transmission up to 10 Watts, and achieve the mean spectral efficiency 3 Mbits/s. Network densification through small-cell deployments, even with cellular Massive MIMO, are outperformed by Cell-Free Massive MIMO [34]. This is because of the interference generated by the neighboring cells and increasing numbers of uncoordinated and lightly loaded small cells in the network; an in-depth analysis of small cell deployments is provided in [35]. We will overcome the Inter-Cell Interference (ICI) problem [36] and uncoordinated deployment of such SCN by the distributed cell-free RAN solution of MARSAL where the dynamic adaptability algorithm will enable RU-DU and DU-DU coordination. Such a coordinated solution can further improve the system capacity/spectral efficiency of future 6G networks.

3.1   Dense User-Generated Content Distribution with MmWave Fronthauling

The main objective of this scenario is to demonstrate and evaluate MARSAL's cell-free RAN in terms of increased sum capacity and user fairness gains, and the adaptivity of dynamic clustering and RRM (Radio Resource Management) mechanisms in managing connectivity resources in a dynamic environment with varying hotspots areas. Furthermore, an additional objective of this scenario is to evaluate the Hybrid MIMO Fronthaul [37] in terms of its ability to offer dynamic fronthaul connections.

This experimentation scenario shows the potential of deploying Cell-Free algorithms in 6G networks with massive AP deployments [38], named now RU under O-RAN architecture. Here the MARSAL innovations focus on distributed processing, with clusters of RUs and DUs coordinating via fronthaul links. In this experimentation scenario, we evaluate the performance of dynamic data driven clustering algorithm. This scenario will also explore and evaluate the effect of inter-DU cooperation on Spectral Efficiency [39] and propose dynamic adaptability of the coordination levels jointly addressing RU-DU and DU-DU coordination, for the first time. The Cell-Free vRAN (virtualised RAN) components in this experimentation scenario will validate the design of cell-free enabled vO-DU, Cell-Free MAC (Medium Access Control) scheduler, PHY (Physical layer). Moreover, it will also validate the appropriate modification of the CP (Control Plane) protocols and O-RAN specified interfaces (i.e., E2, O1) [12, 40], to support practical cell-free operation [41] and fully distributed processing.

The investigated experimental scenario represents an event with a high density of users and APs. It can be an indoor venue (e.g., a concert) or an outdoor setting (e.g., a football stadium). During this kind of event, it is common for dense UGC (User Generated Content) to be streamed by spectators via their handheld devices and consumed locally in real-time (RT). Moreover, there may be users with very different requirements: for instance, a UAV (Unmanned Aerial Vehicle) controlled by law enforcement or security agent vs. a regular user/spectator. In general, this use case is characterized by high user density and the users generate much traffic.

In this scenario, RUs will be interconnected with O-DU (ORAN DU) [12] nodes serving the users in a coordinated manner. Furthermore, MARSAL's Hybrid MIMO fronthaul solution [42] will be leveraged for the interconnection of O-RUs (ORAN Radio Units) and O-DUs. The performance of the cell-free NG-RAN (Next Generation RAN) will be evaluated via pre-recorded video content that will be uploaded and downloaded by UEs (User Equipments) to/from a video streaming MEC application (app) deployed at the Regional Edge node, to emulate Dense UGC streaming both in the uplink and in the downlink (DL) direction.

To support the abovementioned experimentation scenario, MARSAL CF NG-RAN will include cell-free clustering solutions, mmWave fronthaul and a CF MAC scheduler as part of the vRAN to provide CF mMIMO support in the MARSAL architecture. The cell-free vRAN, especially the vO-DU and vO_CU-UP will be deployed as VNFs (Virtual Network Functions) at the radio edge data centre. The mmWave transport network will be providing distributed cell-free coordination amongst the VNFs deployed in radio edge DCs (data centers) and regional edge DCs. A MEC platform be deployed both at the regional and radio edge DCs and a pre-recorded video will be used during the PoC (Proof-of-Concept) evaluation. Moreover, Near-RT RIC (RAN Intelligent Controller) will be hosted at the regional edge DCs, and it will relate to the XGS-PON (10 Gigabit Symmetrical - Passive Optical Network) of the MARSAL architecture.

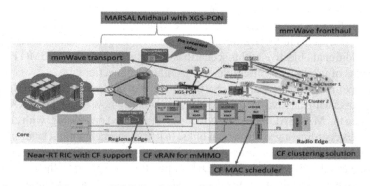

Fig. 2. Overview of the dense UGC distribution with mmWave fronthauling scenario, mapped into the MARSAL architecture

Figure 2 depicts the mapping of this scenario into the MARSAL architecture. To deploy the cell-free vRAN solution on the radio edge data centre we can consider the higher and lower layer split suggested by 3GPP [43], O-RAN [12], and Small Cell Forum [44]. Such flexible split options together with the utilization of a converged optical wireless network will allow us to deploy the cell-free vRAN solution in a cost-effective manner for future 6G networks. Furthermore, the O-RAN Alliance [45] introduces a near Real-Time RAN Intelligent Controller (RT-RIC), which implements radio resource management, measurement, and telemetry.

The proposed configuration deploys the vO_CU-UP and vO-DU at the Radio Edge, while the vO_CU-CP near-RT RIC is deployed at the Regional Edge. The split inside the physical layer will simplify the data mapping by limiting the required associated control messages and it will also allow us to enable transport bandwidth scalability based allowing usage of a higher number of antennas without asking for extra transport bandwidth. The O-RAN compliant vO-CU and vO-DU components are incorporated in the form of RAN Virtual Network Functions, while the APs serve as the O-RUs [46].

3.2   Ultra-dense Video Traffic Delivery in a Converged Fixed-Mobile Network

This scenario showcases MARSAL's solution towards Fixed-Mobile Convergence (FMC) in an ultra-dense indoors context like campus, stadium, malls, etc. Mobile clients served by a distributed Cell-Free RAN will be sharing the Optical Midhaul [47] with third party fixed clients. The Fixed-Mobile Convergence in an Ultra-dense indoors scenario will be operated based on two operation modes, that is Fixed operation (Passive Optical LAN (Local Area Network)) and Mobile operation (small/pico cell with optionally Distributed Antenna System - DAS), respectively. The mobile clients served by a distributed cell-free RAN will be sharing the Optical Midhaul with third party FTTH (Fiber-to-he-Home) clients. The optical fiber access equipment (Optical Line Terminal - OLT) will relate to PON and PtP interfaces where the Network urbanism organization, e.g., OLT and CU co-localized and DU at the end face of the optical termination.

Here we would like to highlight the motivation of this work by considering the 5G status and the 6G needs. So first, 5G carriers and equipment are emitted and localized at the regular antenna locations with previous generations (2G/3G/4G). The pressure of coverage based on the requirements of the regulator is the main reason to have such deployment engineering rules. Concerning the mobile backhaul, 5G deployment coincides with a massive use of optical fiber to achieve the required backhaul throughput up to 10GEth. The fixed access network is based on PtP topology to achieve the connectivity between antenna site and the first aggregation node (central office). Due to the fact that in parallel of 5G, FTTH is under deployment, we have more and more central offices equipped with OLT shelf. 5G backhauling could be addressed either by direct PtP connection to aggregation switch/router or through OLT PtP ports & cards. To address the increase of 6G cells, the preferred fixed technology to collect multiple spots is the PtMP also named PON based on "tree" fiber infrastructure. 6G transport challenges concern the coordination between RAN and FAN (Radio & Fixed Access Networks) networks to address throughput, latency, availability issues.

MARSAL's distributed cell-free RAN Radio Unit is deployed based on a Serial Fronthaul topology [48, 49]. The Serial Fronthaul allows a large number of cell-free APs to be interconnected in a bus topology, significantly increasing Spectral Efficiency, but with minimal cabling requirements. The technology of transmission considered to support serial fronthaul is Wavelength Division Multiplexing (WDM) [50]. A passive fiber network infrastructure is preferred using passive optical multiplexer. Serial Fronthauling is considered an ideal solution for indoor venues.

Secondly, in this scenario, Radio Edge nodes, that host the vRAN elements, are interconnected via PtP and PtMP (PON technology like G-PON (gigabit capable) and XGS-PON (10 gigabit capable)) midhaul links with the Regional Edge. The Regional Edge nodes, interconnected in a WDM ring topology, will host the Near-RT RIC and vCU_CP VNFs. The SDN-Transmission controller and Near-RT RIC SDN function will also be deployed at the Regional Edge nodes. The performance of this scenario will be evaluated via pre-recorded 4K/HDR (High Dynamic Range) video that will be uploaded and downloaded by UEs to/from a video streaming MEC application deployed at the Regional Edge node. Fixed clients will be included as well in this scenario that will be served by the same infrastructure via PtMP (PON) links sharing capacity with the Radio Edge node.

To support this experimentation scenario, we include an Optical Access Network to serve the connectivity between radio edge data centers and cell sites equipped with DUs and RUs. We also propose coordination between the controllers dedicated to Fixed and Radio access networks. Figure 3 depicts the mapping of the scenario into the MARSAL architecture. It must be noted that we also use existing and next-generation PON technologies, to take advantage of their lower CAPEX (due to higher reuse of commodity Fiber-to-the-x (FTTx) equipment) and shared OPEX options, to demonstrate 5G midhaul and backhaul traffic over PON [51]. The PON solution also provides a management interface to the network operators. When used for mobile networks, PONs already make use of a Dynamic Bandwidth Allocation (DBA) algorithm to prioritize certain flows [52]. The development of network slicing could be proposed by dynamic creation/edition/deletion of slice instances.

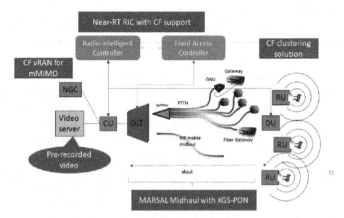

Fig. 3. Overview of the ultra-dense video traffic delivery in a converged fixed-mobile network scenario, mapped into the MARSAL architecture

This scenario demonstrates an on-the-fly reconfiguration of the PON DBA parameters, to be managed from an SDN controller in coordination between fixed and radio networks, used for mid- and back-haul of 5G traffic with integrated RU/DU. We also consider PTPv2 (Precision Time Protocol v2) and SyncE (Synchronous Ethernet) protocols (transportation over the different transport domain mentioned above will be demonstrated). To support this demonstration, video services of various flavors (e.g., downstream HD/4K streams and/or conversational video) will be selected as representative vertical services that the Edge and Core DCs will also host the 5G NFs (e.g., the 5G Core VNFs) [53], while resource sharing will be accomplished via MARSAL's innovative MEO. This will allow disaggregating the AR (Augmented Reality), scene analysis, and activity recognition application functions in multiple tiers (i.e., Regional Edge, Radio Edge, on-device).

4 Cognitive Assistance and Security and Privacy Implications

The introduction of B5G/6G networks for cognitive assistance in a multi-tenant environment, without assuming trust, will raise security concerns that need to be addressed [52]. In fact, many security and privacy implications are inherent in applications that process personal data and Personally Identifiable Information (PII) as per the GDPR regulations [54], including video streams with users' field of view and tracked location. Hence, privacy and security mechanisms that guarantee the isolation of slices and ensure collaboration of participants in multi-tenant B5G/6G infrastructures without assuming trust, need to be developed and demonstrated. Hereof, to ensure the end-to-end security in 6G, AI techniques will also play a critical role in protecting the network, user equipment, and vertical industries from unauthorized access and threats [11, 55–57]. Besides, blockchain is envisioned as another key technology in 6G privacy/security given its decentralized operation, immutability, and enhanced security [58, 59].

The effectiveness of the MARSAL solutions in B5G/6G Cognitive Assistance will be demonstrated as discussed in Sect. 4.1, below. By bringing state-of-the-art technologies in a novel way, MARSAL aims to address security- and privacy-related issues in B5G/6G networks, while optimizing user experience and enhancing confidentiality and trustworthiness.

4.1 Cognitive Assistance and Smart Connectivity for Next-Generation Sightseeing

5G introduced real-time, interactive, Next-Generation Internet (NGI) applications [60] that support human-centered interaction via novel interfaces (e.g., vision and haptics) including augmented reality applications. However, as it has been described in the previous section, current 5G networks do not have the capabilities to unleash the full potential of these applications due to, e.g., the required huge data throughputs and low latency for scene analysis and activity recognition. In this context, this experimentation scenario motivates the need for going beyond 5G through a high-level definition of two real-time, interactive, cloud-native applications for B5G/6G outdoors sightseeing. Through the use of AR – a technology that superimposes a computer-generated image on a user's view of the real world, thus providing a composite view – these types of applications will support cognitive-assistance and human-centered interaction features.

Before moving forward to the description of the scenario, let us briefly define the key concepts involved from a user perspective. First, cognitive assistance is "*a systematic approach to increasing human intellectual effectiveness*" [61] that assumes "*computational assists to human decision making are best when the human is thought of as a partner in solving problems and executing decision processes, where the strengths and benefits of machine and humans are treated as complementary co-systems*" [62]. Second, human-centered computing is a computer system engineering methodology that uses a combination of methods from computer science, social science, and management studies to understand and model work practice, technology use, and technology gaps. Its objective is developing computer systems that fit human capabilities and practices by exploiting/improving AI programming methods [63, 64].

To support these applications while respecting the correct performance of others, operators must provide a flexible network architecture capable of adapting to the demand. So, this experimentation scenario puts the focus on how to cope with the challenging requirements imposed by the operation of the proposed applications while keeping the SLAs of the rest of applications running in parallel. Load balancing according to priority services will be implemented at the same time MEC approaches will be conducted to lighten the network burden of the AR applications and leverage the use of edge computing nodes.

In this scenario, the deployment of two real-time and interactive cloud-native applications for outdoors sightseeing supporting human-centered interaction via 3D cameras is envisioned in the MARSAL's multi-tenant Elastic Edge Infrastructure. These applications would be offered to users equipped with untethered AR glasses. Both applications would endure an enhanced strolling experience by showing overlaid information relevant to their surroundings (APP#1) and enabling virtual artifacts manipulation (APP#2), while considering background traffic from other applications and services.

The MARSAL's elastic edge infrastructure includes a MEC platform that is deployed at Regional Edge, and Radio Edge Data Centres and Centralized orchestrators (i.e., the MEO and NFVO) which are deployed at a Core-tier Data Centre. It must be noted that the Edge and Core Data Centres also host the network functions (e.g., the Core VNFs) while resource sharing is accomplished via MARSAL's innovative MEO. In the targeted scenario an enhanced strolling experience with overlaid information relevant to their surroundings and activities (e.g., restaurant ratings, nearest ATMs or bus-stations, touristic information, etc.) is offered to users equipped with untethered, 5G-enabled AR glasses. Specifically, an AR sightseeing application applies real-time video analytics on the user's field-of-view to detect user intent or activity, and offers visual guidance in the form of relevant information that is optically super-imposed. Furthermore, at certain attraction points IoT nodes equipped with novel interfaces (i.e., 3D cameras) and 5G connectivity is deployed to facilitate interaction with the user. A Cognitive Assistance application encourages the user to manipulate in real-time the virtual representation of an artefact, projected at their AR glasses. Gesture recognition will be implemented via real-time analysis of the 3D camera stream, while the application offers cognitive visual guidance, superimposing information at the users' field of view explaining how the exhibit (or artefact) is used in real time. Both applications rely on MARSAL's Virtual Elastic Infrastructure to optimize and disaggregate their AR, scene analysis and activity recognition application functions in multiple tiers (i.e., Regional Edge, Radio Edge, on-device). It has to be noted that the aim of this scenario is to showcase and evaluate MARSAL's innovations and sub-systems in the smart connectivity context, thus off-the-self 3D cameras (e.g., Intel Realsense) and AR glasses are used in a controlled lab-based environment.

The MARSAL framework has defined the following tests:

Demonstrate and evaluate the capabilities of the MEO to derive the optimal placement of the (containerized) application functions at the Radio Edge or Regional Edge DCs, achieving optimized distribution of latency budgets. The computational requirements and latency constraints of application functions will be derived from at the applications' manifest files. This results in imperceptible latency of the untethered AR applications, comparable to tethered AR, which are validated by user tests.

Demonstrate the collaborative interaction of the MEC system with the 5G UPF (User Plane Function) for real-time inter-DC traffic steering for load balancing purposes, evaluating the effect on resource utilization. Unbalanced demand is emulated in the coverage area of certain Regional Edge nodes, and the ability of the MEC system to uniformly re-direct traffic will be showcased.

Demonstrate the Analytic and Decision engines of MARSAL's Self-Driven infrastructure, and evaluate their ability derive accurate context representations and successfully drive the NFVO and MEO. Evaluate their effectiveness in achieving a set of objectives, related to SLA requirements (e.g., which of the two AR applications to prioritize) and cost considerations (e.g., related to OPEX, energy costs, etc.).

4.2 Data Security and Privacy in Multi-tenant Infrastructures

The goal of this scenario is to demonstrate and evaluate MARSAL's privacy and security mechanisms [65]. These guarantee the isolation of slices and ensure collaboration of participants in multi-tenant 6G infrastructures without assuming trust. These mechanisms will also be evaluated in terms of their ability to mitigate the increased privacy risks of NGI applications that process Personally Identifiable Information (PII). To this end, this scenario aims to demonstrate the application of security and privacy mechanisms in four different layers, namely: *secure and private sharing of information among tenants*; *legal security using smart contracts*; *security of the data stored in the cloud*, and *security of the final users*. The development of each of the different layers presents different challenges ranging from the implementation of smart contracts among different tenants to the real time analysis of network data to allow the protection of the final users in a timely manner.

In MARSAL we approach the security and privacy in 6G networks in a holistic way. Contrary to the previous scenarios, offering a solution tailored for the MARSAL architecture, now we present a modular design to offer four different layers of security and privacy that could be applied in very different contexts. This scenario assumes a multi-tenant infrastructure with one MNO (Mobile Network Operator) and two MVNOs (Mobile Virtual Network Operators), each serving an OTT (Over-The-Top) application provider. MARSAL's technology ensures the isolationon of the different slices while offering the possibility of collaboration among different tenant [66]. To this end, the aim is to demonstrate how the usage of smart contracts can be paired with the private representation of data [67], allowing the sharing of information among different tenants and the owner of the infrastructure that can be interested in the optimization of different ML models.

Moreover, the scenario also covers the security (and privacy) at different levels of the MARSAL architecture. First, we consider how policies can be used to safely store data in the cloud (either at the core or the edge of the network), testing different allocation strategies that ensure the perpetual security of the data. Then, we move our focus to the network intending to investigate how the browsing patterns of users can be analysed in real time so that to alert final users against malicious behaviours they may have before they get in trouble.

The different components of the demonstrator provide security and privacy to many parts of the MARSAL architecture, as depicted in Fig. 4. In the backend, we provide both, security to the data stored in the computing nodes and to the information shared among different tenants to improve the performance of the slicing infrastructure. Then, the Network Infrastructure Security is directly applied to the network equipment by using the SDN paradigm. Finally, a thread detection engine able to protect the final users will be demonstrated by collecting network data at the edge that can then be processed in the backend.

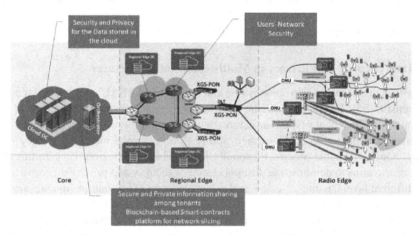

Fig. 4. Overview of the data security and privacy in multi-tenant infrastructures scenario, mapped into the MARSAL architecture

The main components of the demonstrator are:

• *Secure and Private Information Sharing among tenants and Blockchain-based Smart-contracts platform for network slicing:* The first two components are in charge of allowing secure information sharing among tenants. Both the algorithms for the secure and private information sharing and the smart-contract platform will be closely related and acting together with the Orchestrator to provide a better slicing with the collaboration of the different tenants.

- *Security and Privacy for the Data stored in the Cloud:* The third component defines the policies to ensure the data is stored in a secure and private way. As such, this component is an intrinsic part of cloud storage.
- *Users' Network Security:* Provide security to the final users from the network is a complex task that requires the collaboration of different parts of the network. In MARSAL, this security layer will involve the Data Centers on the regional edge and the network equipment placed on the regional edge.

5 Discussion

In this paper, we presented the main architectural components of MARSAL, as well as how the applied use cases are mapped into the proposed architecture.

In particular, the *first domain* is focused on *cell-free networking in dense and ultra-dense hotspot areas.* The first experimentation scenario considers *dense User-Generated Content (UGC) distribution with mmWave fronthauling.* The main objective of this scenario is to demonstrate and evaluate MARSAL distributed cell-free RAN in terms of increased capacity and spectral efficiency gains, and the adaptivity of dynamic clustering and RRM mechanisms in managing connectivity resources in a dynamic environment with varying hotspots areas. The second experimentation scenario investigates *ultra-dense video traffic delivery in a converged fixed-mobile network.* This showcases MARSAL's solution towards Fixed Mobile Convergence in an ultra-dense indoors context. Mobile clients served by a distributed Cell-Free RAN will be sharing the Optical Midhaul with third party FTTH clients.

The *second domain* is focused on *cognitive assistance and its security and privacy implications in 5G and Beyond.* The third experimentation scenario is about *cognitive assistance and smart connectivity for next-generation sightseeing.* In this scenario, the deployment of two real-time and interactive cloud-native applications for outdoors sightseeing supporting human-centered interaction via 3D cameras is envisioned in the MARSAL's multi-tenant elastic edge Infrastructure. These applications would be offered to users equipped with untethered AR glasses. Both applications would endure an enhanced strolling experience by showing overlaid information relevant to their surroundings and enabling virtual artifacts manipulation, while considering background traffic from other applications and services. The fourth experimentation scenario addresses *data security and privacy technical challenges in multi-tenant infrastructures.* We approach security and privacy in 6G networks in a holistic way. We present a modular design to offer four different layers of security and privacy that could be applied in very different contexts.

Our future work is focused on the evaluation process, as well as on a set of preliminary targeted KPIs. It should be noted here that these KPIs will be under continuous reconsideration. Furthermore, we will focus on the network architecture specifications, the requirements of management and security components, as well as the finalisation of MARSAL architecture.

Acknowledgments. The paper has been based on the context of the *"MARSAL" ("Machine Learning-Based, Networking and Computing Infrastructure Resource Management of 5G and*

Beyond Intelligent Networks") Project, funded by the EC under the Grant Agreement (GA) No.101017171.

References

1. MARSAL ("Machine Learning-based Networking and Computing Infrastructure Resource Management of 5G and Beyond Intelligent Networks") 5G-PPP/H2020 project, Grant Agreement No.101017171. https://www.marsalproject.eu/
2. Cisco, Cisco Visual Networking Index: Forecast and Trends, 2017–2022 White Paper (2019)
3. Ericsson Mobility Reports. https://www.ericsson.com/en/mobility-report/reports/november-2019
4. Chen, S., Liang, Y.-C., Sun, S., et al.: Vision, requirements, and technology trend of 6g: how to tackle the challenges of system coverage, capacity, user data-rate and movement speed. IEEE Wirel. Commun. **27**(2), 218–228 (2020)
5. Chochliouros, I.P., et al.: Energy efficiency concerns and trends in future 5G network infrastructures. Energies (MDPI) **14**(17), 5932 (2021). https://doi.org/10.3390/en14175392
6. Boutaba, R., Salahuddin, M., Limam, N., Ayoubi. S.: A comprehensive survey on machine learning for networking: evolution, applications and research opportunities. J. Internet Serv. Appl. **9**(1), 1–99 (2018)
7. Bhat, J.R., lqahtani, S.A.: 6G ecosystem: current status and future perspective. IEEE Access **9**, 43134–43167 (2021)
8. Nawaz, F., Ibrahim, J., et al.: A review of vision and challenges of 6g technology. Int. J. Adv. Comput. Sci. Appl. **11**(2), 1–7 (2020)
9. David, K., Berndt, H.: 6G vision and requirements: is there any need for beyond 5G? IEEE Veh. Technol. Mag. **13**(3), 72–80 (2018)
10. Shafin, R., Liu, L., et al.: Artificial intelligence-enabled cellular networks: a critical path to beyond-5G and 6G. IEEE Wirel. Commun. **27**(2), 212–217 (2020)
11. Jiang, W., Han, B., Habibi, M.A., et al.: The road towards 6G: a comprehensive survey. IEEE Open J. Commun. Soc. **2**, 334–366 (2021)
12. Open Radio Accees Network Alliance e.V. (O-RAN). https://www.o-ran.org/
13. Kostopoulos, A., Chochliouros, I.P., et al.: Experimentation scenarios for machine learning-based resource management. In: Maglogiannis, I., Iliadis, L., Macintyre, J., Cortez, P. (eds.) AIAI-2022, AICT, vol. 652, pp. 120–133. Springer, Cham (2022)
14. The 3rd Generation Partnership Project (3GPP): NG-RAN Architecture. https://www.3gpp.org/news-events/2160-ng_ran_architecture
15. The 3rd Generation Partnership Project (3GPP): Technical Specification (TS) 38.801 V14.0.0 (2017-03): Study on new radio access technology; Radio access architecture and interfaces (Release 14). 3GPPP (2017)
16. Saha, R.K., Nanba, S., Nishimura, K., Kim, Y.-B., Yamazaki, K.: RAN architectural evolution framework toward 5G and beyond cellular-an overview. In: Proceedings of the IEEE PIMRC'18, pp. 592–593. IEEE (2018). https://doi.org/10.1109/PIMRC.2018.8580833
17. Agarwal, V., Sharma, C., Shetty, R., Jangam, A., Asati, R.: A journey towards a converged 5G architecture & beyond. In: Proceedings of the IEEE 5GWF'21, pp. 18–23. IEEE (2010). https://doi.org/10.1109/5GWF52925.2021.00011
18. Niknam, S., Roy, A., Dhillon, H.S., et al.: Intelligent O-RAN for beyond 5G and 6G wireless networks. In: Proceedings of the 2022 IEEE Globecom Workshops (GC Wkshps), pp. 215–220. IEEE (2022). https://doi.org/10.1109/GCWkshps56602.2022.10008676

19. Demirhan, U., Alkhateeb, A.: Enabling cell-free massive MIMO systems with wireless millimeter wave fronthaul. IEEE Trans. Wirel. Commun. **21**(11), 9482–9496 (2022). https://doi.org/10.1109/TWC.2022.3177186
20. Wang, D., Zhang, C., Du, Y., Zhao, J., et *al.*: Implementation of a cloud-based cell-free distributed massive MIMO system. IEEE Commun. Mag. **58**(8), 61–67 (2020)
21. Bjornson, E., Sanguinetti, L.: Scalable cell-free massive MIMO systems. IEEE Trans. Commun. **68**(7), 4247–4261 (2020)
22. Blandino, S., et *al.*: Multi-user hybrid MIMO at 60 GHz using 16-antenna transmitters. IEEE Trans. Circuits Syst. I: Regular Papers **66**(2), 848–858 (2019)
23. Zhang, D., Wang, Y., Li, X., Xiang, W.: Hybridly connected structure for hybrid beamforming in mmWave massive MIMO systems. IEEE Trans. Commun. **66**(2), 662–674 (2018). https://doi.org/10.1109/TCOMM.2017.2756882
24. European Telecommunications Standards Institute (ETSI): ETSI GR MEC-017 V1.1.1 (2018-02): Mobile Edge Computing (MEC); Deployment of Mobile Edge Computing in an NFV environment. ETSI (2018)
25. European Telecommunications Standards Institute: ETSI GS NFV 002 V1.2.1 (2014-12): Network functions virtualisation (NFV); architectural framework. ETSI (2014). https://www.etsi.org/deliver/etsi_gs/NFV/001_099/002/01.02.01_60/gs_nfv002v010201p.pdf
26. European Telecommunications Standards Institute (ETSI): ETSI GR NFV 001 V1.3.1 (2021-03): Network Functions Virtualisation (NFV); Use Cases. ETSI (2021)
27. European Telecommunications Standards Institute (ETSI): Multi-access Edge Computing (MEC). https://www.etsi.org/technologies/multi-access-edge-computing
28. Chataut, R., Akl, R.: Massive MIMO systems for 5G and beyond networks - overview, recent trends, challenges, and future research direction. Sensors (MDPI) **20**(10), 2753 (2020). https://doi.org/10.3390/s20102753
29. Zhang, P., Willems, F.M.J.: On the downlink capacity of cell-free massive MIMO with constrained fronthaul capacity. Entropy (MDPI) **22**(4), 418 (2020)
30. Interdonato, G., et *al.*: Ubiquitous cell-free massive MIMO communications. EURASIP J. Wirel. Commun. Netw. **1**, 1–13 (2019)
31. Elhoushy, S., Ibrahim, M., Hamouda, W.: cell-free massive MIMO: a survey. IEEE Commun. Surv. Tutor. **24**(1), 492–523 (2022)
32. Ngo, H.Q., Ashikhmin, A., et *al.*: Cell-free massive MIMO versus small cells. IEEE Trans. Wirel. Commun. **16**(3), 1834–1850 (2017)
33. Ngo, H.Q., Ashikhmin, A., et *al.*: Cell-free massive MIMO: uniformly great service for everyone. In: Proceedings of the IEEE SPAWC'15, pp. 201–205. IEEE (2015)
34. Liu, W., Han, S., Yang, C.: Energy efficiency comparison of massive MIMO and small cell network. In: Proceedings of the IEEE GlobalSIP'14, pp. 617–621. IEEE (2014)
35. Mowla, M.M., Ahmad, I., et *al.*: A green communication model for 5G systems. IEEE Trans. Green Commun. Network. **1**(3), 264–280 (2017)
36. Hamza, A.S., Khalifa, S.S., Hamza, H.S., Elsayed, K.: A survey on inter-cell interference coordination techniques in OFDMA-based cellular networks. IEEE Commun. Surv. Tutor. **15**(4), 1642–1670 (2013)
37. Femenias, G., Riera-Palou, F.: Cell-free millimeter-wave massive MIMO systems with limited fronthaul capacity. IEEE Access **7**, 44596–44612 (2019)
38. Kassam, J., Castanheira, D., et *al.*: A review of cell-free massive MIMO systems. Electronics (MDPI) **12**(4), 1001 (2023). https://doi.org/10.3390/electronics12041001
39. Zhang, J., et *al.*: Spectral and energy efficiency of cell-free massive MIMO systems with hardware impairments. In: Proceedings of the IEEE WCSP'17, pp. 1–6. IEEE (2017)
40. Open Radio Access Network Alliance e.V. (O-RAN): O-RAN Alliance Specifications. https://www.o-ran.org/specifications

41. Vardakas, J.S., Ramantas, K., Vinogradov, E., et *al.*: Machine learning-based cell-free support in the O-RAN architecture: an innovative converged optical-wireless solution toward 6G networks. IEEE Wirel. Commun. **29**(5), 20–26 (2022)
42. Rommel, S., Thiago Raddo, R., Monroy, I.T.: The fronthaul infrastructure of 5G mobile networks. In: Proceedings of the IEEE CAMAD'18, pp. 1–6. IEEE (2018)
43. The 3rd Generation Partnership Project (3GPP). https://www.3gpp.org/
44. Small Cell Forum (SCF). https://www.smallcellforum.org/
45. Open Radio Access Network Alliance e.V. (O-RAN): O-RAN Architecture Description: Technical Specification (TS) O-RAN.WG1.OAD-R003scription-v08.00 (2023). https://orandownl oadsweb.azurewebsites.net/specifications
46. MARSAL Project: Deliverable 2.1: Description and definition of targeted PoCS (2021). https://www.marsalproject.eu/wp-content/uploads/2021/09/D2.1-Marsal-final.pdf
47. Pfeiffer, T.: Next generation mobile fronthaul and midhaul architectures. J. Opt. Commun. Network. **7**(11), B38–B45 (2015)
48. Furtado, L., Fernandes, A., Ohashi, A., Farias, F., Cavalcante, A., Costa, J.: Cell-free massive MIMO deployments: fronthaul topology options and techno-economic aspects. In: Proceedings of the EuCAP'22, pp. 1–5. IEEE (2022). https://doi.org/10.23919/EuCAP53622.2022.9768969
49. Farias, F., et *al.*: Cost- and energy-efficient backhaul options for heterogeneous mobile network deployments. Photon Netw. Commun. **32**(3), 422–437 (2016). https://doi.org/10.1007/s11107-016-0676-6
50. Song, D., Zhang, J., Xiao, Y., Wang, X., Ji, Y.: Energy optimization with passive WDM based fronthaul in heterogeneous cellular networking. In: Proceedings of the IEEE ACP'18, pp. 1–3, IEEE (2018)
51. Levi, D.: The Case for Using PON for 5G Fronthaul. Lightwave (2020). https://www.lightwaveonline.com/5g-mobile/article/14188094/the-case-for-using-pon-for-5g-fronthaul
52. Hexa-X Project: Deliverable 1.2: Expanded 6G vision, use cases and societal values – including aspects of sustainability, security and spectrum (2021). https://hexa-x.eu/wp-content/uploads/2021/05/Hexa-X_D1.2.pdf
53. The 3rd Generation Partnership Project (3GPP): Technical Specification (TS) 23.501 V18.0.0 (2022–12): System architecture for the 5G System (5GS); Stage 2 (Release 18). 3GPP (2022)
54. European Union: Regulation (EU) 2016/679 of the European Parliament and of the Council of 27 April 2016 on the protection of natural persons with regard to the processing of personal data and on the free movement of such data, and repealing Directive 95/46/EC (General Data Protection Regulation - GDPR). Off. J. **L119**, 1–88 (2016)
55. Letaief, K.B., Chen, W., Shi, Y., Zhang, J., Zhang, Y.-J.A.: The roadmap to 6G: AI empowered wireless networks. IEEE Commun. Mag. **57**(8), 84–90 (2019)
56. Zong, B., et *al.*: 6G technologies: key drivers, core requirements, system architectures, and enabling technologies. IEEE Veh. Technol. Mag. **14**(3), 18–27 (2019)
57. Zhang, Z., Xiao, Y., et *al.*: 6G wireless networks: vision, requirements, architecture, and key technologies. IEEE Veh. Technol. Mag. **14**(3), 28–41 (2019)
58. Sekaran, R., Patan, R., et *al.*: Survival study on blockchain based 6G-enabled mobile edge computation for IoT automation. IEEE Access **8**, 143453–143463 (2020)
59. Dai, Y., Xu, D., Maharjan, S., Chen, Z., He, Q., et *al.*: Blockchain and deep reinforcement learning empowered intelligent 5G beyond. IEEE Netw. **33**(3), 10–17 (2019)
60. European Commission: The Next Generation Internet initiative. https://digital-strategy.ec.europa.eu/en/policies/next-generation-internet-initiative
61. Engelbart, D.C.: Augmenting Human Intellect: A Conceptual Framework. Menlo Park, CA (1962)
62. National Research Council: Complex Operational Decision Making in Networked Systems of Humans and Machines: A Multidisciplinary Approach. National Academies Press (2014)

63. National Aeronautics and Space Administration (NASA). https://www.nasa.gov/centers/ames/research/technology-onepagers/hc-computing.html

64. Sebe, N.: Human-centered Computing. In: Nakashima, H., et *al.* (eds.) Handbook of Ambient Intelligence and Smart Environments, pp. 349–370. Springer, Boston (2010)

65. Ayala-Romero, J.A., Garcia-Saavedra, A., Gramaglia, M., Costa-Perez, X., Banchs, A., Alcaraz, J.J.: vrAIn: A deep learning approach tailoring computing and radio resources in virtualized RANs. In: Proceedings of MobiCom'19, pp. 1–16. ACM (2019)

66. García-Durán, A., Niepert, M.: Learning graph representations with embedding propagation. In: Advances in Neural Information Processing Systems, vol. 30, pp. 5119–5130 (2017)

67. Liu, J., Liu, Z.: A survey on security verification of blockchain smart contracts. IEEE Access **7**, 77894–77904 (2019)

Use Cases for Network Applications to Enable Connected Intelligence

Renxi Qiu[1]([✉]), Dayou Li[1], Enjie Liu[1], Christina C. Lessi[2], George Agapiou[3,4], and Andreas Gavrielides[5]

[1] University of Bedfordshire, University Square, Luton LU1 3JU, UK
Renxi.Qiu@beds.ac.uk
[2] Hellenic Telecommunications Organization (OTE) S.A., Marousi, Greece
[3] WINGS ICT Solutions, 189, Siggrou Avenue, 17121 Athens, Greece
[4] WINGS ICT Solutions, 99 Kifissias Avenue, 15124 Maroussi, Athens, Greece
[5] eBOS Technologies Ltd., Arch. Makariou III and Mesaorias 1, 2090 Lakatamia, Nicosia, Cyprus

Abstract. Robots are expected to be more intelligent in consuming digital infrastructures during the process of continual learning. The future of connected Robotics should be skillful in maximizing Quality of Experience (QoE) for its vertical users rather than solely reacting to Quality of Service (QoS). The paper provides a detailed use case specification and a network softwarization paradigm for realizing the 6G vision of connected intelligence. It serves as a guidance for developing future network applications to ground the idea of the connected intelligence.

Keywords: Connected intelligence · Robotics · 6G use cases · Network Softwarization · Design Patterns

1 Introduction

Connected intelligence [1] is an essential 6G vision and critical for robot continual learning [2]. An effective solution which connecting intelligence must be scalable to networks and at the same time personalized to vertical applications. The contradictory requirements are one of the main barriers on grounding the 6G vision into use cases within robotics and other verticals. The paper presents realistic scenarios for deploying robot continual learning in real world environments under connected intelligence. It demonstrates the potential of realizing the 6G vision under a new network softwarization framework called 5G-ERA middleware [3]. The use cases of the new network applications enable a native integration between AI and network to address the scalability and the transparency issue for both robotics and 6G networking at the same time.

© IFIP International Federation for Information Processing 2023
Published by Springer Nature Switzerland AG 2023
I. Maglogiannis et al. (Eds.): AIAI 2023 Workshops, IFIP AICT 677, pp. 168–177, 2023.
https://doi.org/10.1007/978-3-031-34171-7_13

2   Background

2.1   Network Applications

Network Applications is defined as "a set of services that provide specific functionalities to the verticals and their associated use cases" [4]. It is a separate middleware layer and common services to simplify the implementation and deployment of autonomous robots on a large scale [5]. With the Middleware embracing the service-based architecture and cloud-native design paradigms, the Network Applications, like 5G-ERA Middleware [6], can be utilized to translate current state-of-the-art robots deployed mainly for local applications towards large-scale robot deployment under a Platform as a Service paradigm.

2.2   Robot Continual Learning

Learning is an essential capability of autonomous robots and the driving force behind the deployment of 6G connected intelligence. In the past decade, the success of robot learning is pre-dominantly within a data-driven paradigm. A robot's continuous leaning are considered be the way to increase the level of autonomy for robots and push the limit of its cognition [7]. Learning at the post-deployment stage is crucial for deployable robotics, although this is hard to be implemented due to the limited human supervision available, also known as the small sample problem. Hybrid intelligence [8] suggested the sharing of symbolic knowledge and data-driven knowledge among robots and the use of the shared intelligence as the "additional" supervision to compensate for the small samples. The consensus in the community is that symbolic knowledge is more suitable for problems that need abstract reasoning; data-driven knowledge is better for problems that need interacting with the world or extracting patterns from massive, disordered data [9]. Together, the pair may cover the continuous learning problem. Although the ways towards their integration have been largely fruitless, reality is always far more miserable than our expectations.

To realize the 6G vision. Network applications and continual learning are combined in the paper to build up potential use cases of robot applications under the Connected Intelligence.

3   Network Applications Under the 5G-ERA Middleware

5G-ERA is an ecosystem and development environment for robot developers to build large scale distributed robotics; at the same time for network service provider to deliver the services more efficiently [3]. The 5G-ERA Middleware is allowing robots from different vertical sectors to use 5G and 6G digital skills to enhance their autonomy. The Middleware is a virtual platform between vertical applications managed by Robot Operating System - ROS [10] and 5G infrastructure managed by orchestrators such as OSM [11]. It realizes the intent-based network using cloud-native design. The 5G-ERA Middleware can be instantiated in the core network either in the Edge Machines or in the cloud. The implementation allows Robots to request the instantiation of the cloud-native resources that will support the execution of the task. The main components of the Middleware are:

- Gateway – It redirects the traffic across the Middleware system meaning rerouting to the microservices within the system. It also handles the authentication and authorization process.
- Action Planner – Integrating the semantic knowledge of the vertical into resource planning and knowledge recommendation. It is also part of the vertical level life cycle management implemented by Middleware.
- Resource Planner – is responsible for testbed level resource placement.
- Orchestrator – It orchestrates the process of the deployment of the distributed vertical applications. It is responsible for the vertical level lifecycle management of the deployed services.
- Redis Interface – Is the backend for synchronization. It allows the users to retrieve, insert and update data from/into the Redis-Server

The 5G-ERA Middleware is developed under the Platform as a Service (PaaS) paradigm to integrate the robotic applications and networking facility. It allows connecting the robots to the cloud-native systems to maximize the capabilities of the 5G networks by simplifying the design and the deployment processes of dynamic offloading critical tasks from the robots to the external Cloud or Edges. At the same time, recommending the potential knowledge and resources to robots for connected intelligence. The Middleware provides a flexible and intelligent selection of the needed actions and resources to integrate with the semantic knowledge.

4 Use Case Scenarios

The use case presented in the paper is focused on deployment of robot for continual learning under the connected intelligence. Robot deployment includes all the steps, processes, and activities that are required to make a robot adapted to its intended real-world environment. In a lab-environment, robots can learn and adapt but require detailed support and guidance. The construction of the environment is hardly to be scaled into deployment under real-world settings due to limited supervision and unexpected situations. The following scenarios will showcase the use cases of the network applications under the distributed real-world settings on tackling unexpected situations; adapt continuously and verified in the real-world by additional AI services sharing by the networks.

4.1 Scenario 1: Knowledge is not Known to the Robot but Already Available in the Cloud

The use case under the scenario is for Network Applications to address an unexpected situation of robot manipulation by making pro-active analogies. By default, knowledge is not synchronised (connected) among the robots and the cloud. In this specific scenario, skills such as open caps have already been defined in the cloud (with actions such as Pull, Flip, and Twist); although part of them (Flip and Twist) are designed by third parties, hence not yet known by the robot. At the same time, robot does not have a concept of "twisting", therefore cannot retrieve the knowledge without additional intervention.

To link the fragmented knowledge, the use cases of the network applications are defined step by step:

1) Samples (pictures and videos) from this unexpected situation will be collected by the robot and uploaded to Edge for help. Meanwhile, the robot will try to explain the corresponding circumstance for as much as possible (e.g., this is a bottle opening task in a kitchen, tried to pull with no success). This contextual information will be transferred together with the raw data samples to the Edge.

2) An 5G-ERA middleware will have already been deployed within the Edge to personalise the connected intelligence for current robot settings. It could make analogies based on the situation:

3) The information broker inside the task planner will analyse the context and make recommendations based on a multi-objective ranking system. A group of AI "experts" which are trained simultaneously within the Edge on current robot settings will track the spatial and temporal relationships of the tasks. They are designed to improve the precision of the recommendation. References of potentially useful knowledge will be retrieved from the cloud by the broker.

4) Recommendation raised by the task planner will be confirmed either semi-autonomously or fully autonomously by the deployed robot. This is similar to videos recommended by YouTube, they may or may not be relevant to the ongoing task. The mechanism is used to filter and prioritise relevant knowledge sets from the recommendations.

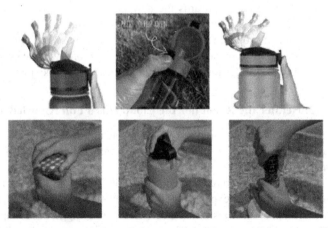

Fig. 1. Samples of recommended meta dataset. Top: Meta-sample-set-A on flip open caps; Bottom: Meta-sample-set-B on twister open caps

- In semi-autonomous mode, the recommended knowledge will be visualized and confirmed by the human operator under enhanced/mixed reality. As shown in Fig. 1, Meta-sample-set-A contains procedure knowledge for flipping open caps

is rejected; Meta-sample-set-B on twister open will be accepted. Alternatively, the recommended knowledge can be meta-tested using the samples submitted by robots for compatibility check. Similar to video playback, this is a process of experience replay. Users can cancel the replay, confirm, or reject at any time. The decision will be remembered by AI "experts" to further improve the broker in the 5G-ERA middleware.

- In a fully autonomous mode, the recommended knowledge will be meta-tested for similarity, similar as above. It must be noted that experience replay is not necessary to be accurate. In this example, both flip open and twist open models could be considered as compatible to the live samples after the replay.

(5) Until now, pre-designed meta-models with some specific knowledge have been selected for the ongoing task. The task is reduced to a standard Few-shots Learning problem. New design patterns presented in the next section will be applied to integrate local data and cloud meta models for solutions towards the targeted problem.

It should be noted that, even after the verification, the proposed solutions can still be wrong. Trial-and-error must be carried out further by robots in the field to reject unrealistic recommendations.

Within the scenario, the knowledge is distributed between the robot and the cloud. The intelligence of the robot and the cloud are connected by a meta-based computational approach online. The scenario is a direct example of knowledge sharing through connected intelligence. Compared to centralised knowledge systems with predefined ontology, adding new but unstructured knowledge in the centralised system is very hard. Any attempts to adapt ontology towards the new knowledge require strong a generalisation. Therefore, the scalability of a centralised knowledge architecture is limited. The distributed approach proposed illustrated in this scenario use analogies rather than induction or deduction, therefore there is little need of the ontology or the generalisation. Meta-models are used as bridges for synchronising expected and unexpected situations.

4.2 Scenario 2: Neither the Robot nor the Cloud Has a Full Knowledge

Under the scenario, skill for the specific robot task has not been defined locally in the robot or globally on the cloud. It needs to be programmed live through learning-by-demonstration.

In this case, there is either no recommendation from the AI "experts", or all recommendations were rejected. The expected skill is not available on the cloud, some kind of meta-based learning-by-demonstration would need to be triggered. Compared to the traditional learning-by-doing approach. The meta-based demonstration will be focused on a structured way of reusing prior knowledge for fast learning. Meta-models will be dynamically generated to align the unexpected scenes with known skills. The process of the scenario is summarized as follows:

1) AI "Experts" on Edge will further analyse the context and provide recommendations of generic knowledge such as "Grasp", "Navigate" and "Release". That knowledge was established beforehand as generic skills towards novel situations. To this end,

the model selection from the pre-learned meta-learning models is first realized by measuring the similarity between the new task scene and the previous scenes used for meta training. Thanks to the meta-learning representation, the similarities be-tween different scenes could be obtained given scene images or frames. Specifically, for the first trial several scene images are collected and imputed to the Edge, and several (e.g., three) models with the highest similarity scores are selected, with which the robot tries to complete the given task, simultaneously yielding scene frames. Subsequently, we can further obtain an optimal model based on the frames for the next trial.

2) Following the same routine as scenario 1, the robot will learn the new manipulation tasks using limited demonstration through prior knowledge and verified by trial-and-error. More specifically, if the optimal model selected from the last step cannot enable the robot to complete the task successfully, the model could be improved by adding the new scene data into the meta-training dataset, through a trial-by-error process. In this way, the robot would be able to handle the new task situations.

3) Finally, both the robot and the cloud will be synchronized with the new knowledge of "twisting" for future use in other robots. The meta-based knowledge representation enables the new skill to be reused as part of the connected intelligence.

Scenario 2 is illustrated by the Fig. 2. Meta knowledge will be retrieved by the 5G-ERA middlware for fast learning and knowledge synchronization. As part of the learning protocol defined in the lab, declarative knowledge for manipulation such as "Grasp", "Navigate" and "Release" will be dynamically recognized by meta-learning for knowledge synchronization. Hence reuse of the models is not limited to the original designer, but also the third-party manipulation models.

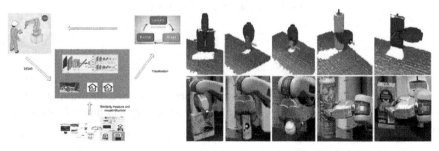

Fig. 2. Left: a learning-by-demonstration iteration & Right: meta-samples for PR2 "Grasp", grasp-meta-model can be generated accordingly

Under the scenario, new knowledge is generated by restructuring and reorganising existing knowledge on declarative level. The transparency enabled by meta-learning helps the skills to be aligned between known and unknown situations.

5 Design Patterns for Robot Continual Learning Under the Connected Intelligence

To realize the proposed scenarios into use cases, design patterns for meta learning are implemented to align live data captured by the robot into the pre-defined declarative knowledge. From a knowledge sharing perspective, meta-learning is used as a synchronization protocol between new observation and old experience. From the AI perspective, analogies are generated computationally. The processes defining Network Applications on continual learning under the connected intelligence are reflected by the following design patterns:

Knowledge Update Pattern (Supervised)
Meta-model A will be updated by some "small samples" from domain B via the meta-testing. A revised knowledge meta-model AB is generated.

This is a common approach applied in the few-shot learning (Fig. 3).

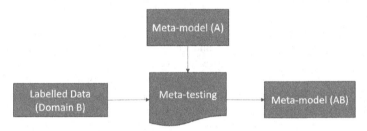

Fig. 3. Knowledge update pattern

Experience Replay Pattern
Experience of A will be replayed for recognizing some unlabeled data from domain B. Knowledge in domain A and domain B are shared within the meta-model (AB) (Figs. 4 and 5).

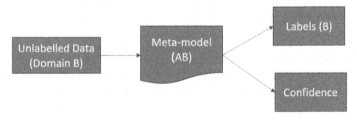

Fig. 4. Experience replay pattern

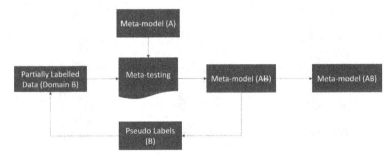

Fig. 5. Knowledge update pattern (semi-supervised):

Knowledge Update Pattern (Semi-supervised)

In an unexpected situation with-out a human supervisor, captured live data are not fully understood by the AI, therefore they can only be partially labelled. Semi-supervised meta-learning will be applied in the pattern. Intermediate models will be constructed to search for pseudo labels of the unlabeled data so that the model can generalize well on the labelled data. The pattern is formulated as a nested optimization problem to identify optimal share be-tween knowledge in domain A and domain B.

Analogy Pattern

Analogies are based on similarity checks between unknown domain B and existing domain A via experience replay. Analogies are used by 5G-ERA middlware for recom-mending knowledge sets without a pre-defined ontology. It leads to abstract knowledge and reasoning for sharing knowledge and connecting intelli-gence. The pattern shows similarity of unexpected B and priori experience A. An analogy between A and B will be produced if the similarity is high (Fig. 6).

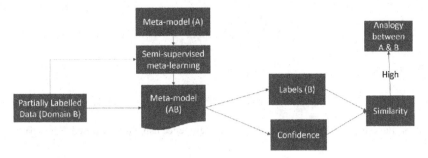

Fig. 6. Analogy pattern

Knowledge Aggregation

Labelled data and meta-models will be aggregated using the Knowledge update pattern (semi-supervised) for unexpected situations, or Knowledge update pattern (supervised) at expected situations (Fig. 7).

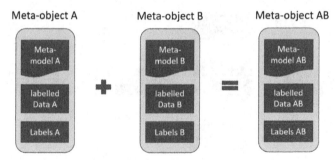

Fig. 7. Knowledge Aggregation

Combining the design patterns for the connected intelligence a distributed machine learning platform will be constructed. The reference design is illustrated in Fig. 8. It is delivered by 5G-ERA PaaS middleware for network computing fabric from the resource orchestration perspective. The personalized AI to the distributed robotics is delivered under the proposed deign patterns towards continual learning.

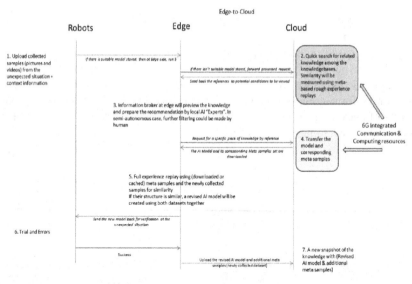

Fig. 8. Edge-to-Cloud pipeline for connected intelligence using the proposed design pattern.

6   Conclusion and Future Work

With 5G and 6G communication, Cloud Computing, and distributed AI coming together to facilitate the 6G vision, how we collaborate, connect, and interact under 6G is to be further clarified.

The paper is designed to discuss and promote use cases of Network Applications that need to be implemented for connected robots by steering digital transitions through human-centered data-driven technologies and innovations. Typical scenarios applied to the robot continual learning are identified and integrated into design patterns of network applications under connected intelligence. It will lead to technology to scale up network enhanced robot deployment in broader domains and enable frictionless integration of network and communication concepts into native robot design and how various communities work together to develop these novel solutions.

Acknowledgement. The work in this paper is sponsored by the EU H2020 project "5G Enhance Robot Autonomy" under grant agreement number 101016681.

References

1. Sefidcon, A., et al.: The network compute fabric – advancing digital transformation with ever-present service continuity. Ericsson Technol. Rev. **2021**(7), 2–11 (2021). https://doi.org/10.23919/ETR.2021.9904679(2021)
2. Lesort, T., et al.: Continual learning for robotics: definition, framework, learning strategies, opportunities and challenges. Inf. Fusion **58**, 52–68 (2020), ISSN 1566-2535, https://doi.org/10.1016/j.inffus.2019.12.004
3. Qiu, R., et al.: Intent-based deployment for robot applications in the 5g-enabled non-public-network. ITU J. Future Evolving Technol. 4(1), 209–220 (2023). https://doi.org/10.52953/AYMI1991
4. 5GASP, "5GASP definition of a NetApp" (2021). https://community.5gasp.eu/index.php/2021/07/12/what-is-a-netapp/
5. Bessem, S., et al.: Network applications: opening up 5G and beyond networks. Zenodo (2022). https://doi.org/10.5281/zenodo.7123919
6. 5G-ERA, 5G-ERA GitHub Repository (2023). https://github.com/5g-era
7. Hospedales, T., et al.: Meta-learning in neural networks: a survey. IEEE Trans. Pattern Anal. Mach. Intell. **01**, 1, 5555 (2021). https://doi.org/10.1109/TPAMI.2021.3079209
8. Bekkum, et al.: Modular design patterns for hybrid learning and reasoning systems a taxonomy, patterns and use cases. Appl. Intell. **51,** 6528–6546 (2021). Doi: https://doi.org/10.1007/s10489-021-02394-3
9. Sun, R., et al.: Artificial intelligence: connectionist and symbolic approaches. In: International Encyclopedia of the Social & Behavioral Sciences (2000). https://doi.org/10.1016/B0-08-043076-7/00553-2
10. Quigley, M., et.al.: ROS: an open-source Robot Operating System. In: Workshops at the IEEE International Conference on Robotics and Automation (2009)
11. ETSI OSM, Open source Management and Orchestration (MANO) https://osm.etsi.org/

The 2nd Workshop on AI in Energy, Buildings and Micro-Grids (AIBMG)

2nd Workshop on AI in Energy, Buildings and Micro-Grids (AIBMG 2023)

Sustainable energy is hands down one of the biggest challenges nowadays. As the EU sets its focus to reach its 2030 and 2050 goals, the role of artificial intelligence (AI) in the energy domain at building, district and micro-grid level becomes mandatory. The EU and member states are increasingly highlighting the need to complement IoT capacity (e.g. appliances and meters) with artificial intelligence capabilities (e.g. building management systems, proactive optimization, prescriptive maintenance, etc.). Moreover, moving away from the centralized production schema of the grid, novel approaches are needed for the optimal management/balancing of local (or remote aggregated net metering) generation and consumption rather than only reducing energy consumption for communities.

The 2nd AIBMG Workshop brought together interdisciplinary approaches that focus on the application of AI-driven solutions for increasing and improving energy efficiency of residential and tertiary buildings without compromising the occupants' well-being. Either applied directly to the device, building or district management system, the proposed solutions should enable more energy efficient and sustainable operation of devices, buildings, districts and micro-grids.

Topics of interest covered by the 2nd AIBMG 2023 included but were not limited to: AI-based energy management applications at building and district level; Smart digital building renovation solutions; AI-based assessment in smart-grid systems; Predictive modelling for energy consumption and indoor comfort; Prescriptive modelling for building asset maintenance; Non-Intrusive Load Monitoring (NILM)/energy disaggregation; Smart decentralized energy solutions; Grey- and black-box data-driven user profiling; Ontologies, ontology matching and alignment in the energy domain; Anomaly detection and data filtering; Visual analytics and recommendation systems. Accepted papers focus on the application of AI solutions to various aspects of the energy domain, from energy efficiency, edge computing, awareness, semantic interoperability, comfort modelling and more.

Organization of AIBMG 2022

Organizing Committee

Iakovos Michailidis	Centre for Research and Technology Hellas (CERTH)/Democritus University of Thrace (DUTH), Greece
Stelios Krinidis	International Hellenic University (IHU)/Centre for Research and Technology Hellas (CERTH), Greece
Elias Kosmatopoulos	Democritus University of Thrace (DUTH)/Centre for Research and Technology Hellas (CERTH), Greece
Dimosthenis Ioannidis	Centre for Research and Technology Hellas (CERTH), Greece

Program Committee

Christos Korkas	Democritus University of Thrace (DUTH)/Centre for Research and Technology Hellas (CERTH), Greece
Aliki Stefanopoulou	Centre for Research and Technology Hellas (CERTH)/Democritus University of Thrace (DUTH), Greece
Petros Tzallas	Centre for Research and Technology Hellas (CERTH), Greece
Georgia Tzitziou	Centre for Research and Technology Hellas (CERTH), Greece
Christos Tsaknakis	Centre for Research and Technology Hellas (CERTH), Greece
Alexios Papaioanou	Centre for Research and Technology Hellas (CERTH), Greece
Efi Martinopoulou	Centre for Research and Technology Hellas (CERTH), Greece
Napoleon Bezas	Centre for Research and Technology Hellas (CERTH), Greece
Asimina Dimara	Centre for Research and Technology Hellas (CERTH), Greece
Athanasios Moustakas	Centre for Research and Technology Hellas (CERTH)
Christos Timplalexis	Centre for Research and Technology Hellas (CERTH), Greece

Less Energy > Smarter Buildings

PRECEPT and **Smart2B** have received funding from the European Union's Horizon 2020 research and innovation programme under grant agreement No 958284 and No. 101004152 respectively

A Guide to Visual Comfort: An Overview of Indices and Its Applications

Christos Tzouvaras[1,2(✉)], Asimina Dimara[2,3], Alexios Papaioannou[3,4],
Kanela Karatzia[1], Christos-Nikolaos Anagnostopoulos[2], Stelios Krinidis[3,4],
Konstantinos I. Arvanitis[1], Dimosthenis Ioannidis[3], and Dimitrios Tzovaras[3]

[1] Watt and Volt S.A., Athens, Greece
{ch.tzouvaras,k.karatzia,k.arvanitis}@watt-volt.gr
[2] Department of Cultural Technology and Communication, Intelligent Systems Lab,
University of the Aegean (UoA), Mytilene, Greece
canag@aegean.gr
[3] Information Technologies Institute (ITI), Centre for Research Technology Hellas
(CERTH), Thessaloniki, Greece
{adimara,alexiopa,krinidis,djoannid,Dimitrios.Tzovaras}@iti.gr
[4] Management Science and Technology Department, International Hellenic
University (IHU), Kavala, Greece

Abstract. The COVID-19 pandemic has impacted the lives of millions of people around the world. During this period, many nations have imposed strict "stay at home" restrictions to mitigate the spread of the virus. Consequently, people spent more time at home, and the topic of their comfort and well-being in indoor environments came to the forefront. Prompted by the lack of clarity surrounding the topic of visual comfort, this paper aims to provide a detailed guide on visual comfort, its affecting factors, the way it is assessed and its assessment indices. As it became obvious, visual comfort depends on a lot of factors, is studied through many different lenses, has a variety of indices, and most importantly, is perceived differently from person to person.

Keywords: Visual comfort · Visual comfort indices · Visual comfort estimation

1 Introduction

As Aruga et al. state in [1], during the emergence of COVID-19, several nations imposed strict lockdown rules that forbade people from leaving their houses unless they needed to acquire basic necessities, resulting in a dramatic increase in the amount of time people spent indoors. In [2], Choi et al. argue that social distancing methods, while vital to restrict the virus's transmission, raise the chances of loneliness, isolation, and anxiety. As a result, the individual's experience in an indoor environment came into the limelight as a critical factor in their health, comfort, and well-being, which are key aspects of Indoor Environmental

© IFIP International Federation for Information Processing 2023
Published by Springer Nature Switzerland AG 2023
I. Maglogiannis et al. (Eds.): AIAI 2023 Workshops, IFIP AICT 677, pp. 183–194, 2023.
https://doi.org/10.1007/978-3-031-34171-7_14

Quality (IEQ) according to Rohde et al. [3]. The overall experience of the user in an indoor environment, hereinafter referred to as "comfort", is determined by the user's thermal, acoustic, and visual comfort.

The American Society of Heating, Refrigerating, and Air-Conditioning Engineers (ASHRAE) defines thermal comfort as the mental state in which contentment with the thermal environment is conveyed [4]. N. Djongyang et al. [5] add that its evaluation incorporates various inputs impacted by physical, physiological, psychological, and other aspects. Furthermore, Rindel JH defines acoustic comfort as a notion that can be distinguished by the lack of undesirable sound and chances for auditory activities without disturbing other people [6]. Similarly to thermal comfort, Rindel JH highlights the subjective nature of the concept of acoustic comfort by noting that acoustic comfort for an individual is tied to the individual not only as a receiver of sound but also as a generator of sound. Visual comfort shares the subjective nature of the concepts of thermal and acoustic comfort while its definition and quantitative determination of are less standardised than those of thermal and acoustic comfort because they are dependent on various external factors such as the amount of available external sunlight, the glazing and screens that "filter" it, the indoor environment (optical properties of walls), and, of course, the visual task itself [7].

While researching the topic of increasing comfort and well-being in indoor environments, two high-level observations were made. Firstly, in order to improve indoor acoustic comfort, some form of major building intervention, such as installing insulation material [8], prefabricated wall modules [9], or false ceilings [10], must take place during the construction or renovation of a building. As a result, the focus shifted to the topics of thermal and visual comfort, where minor interventions can lead to significant results. Secondly, while extensive review literature can be found on the topic of thermal comfort [11–16], the user's visual comfort is a topic that stands in need of further review. When searching "'thermal comfort' in buildings" on the Google Scholar platform, one can find more than 28,700 search results from 2017 to this day. On the other hand, search results for the keywords "'visual comfort' in buildings" are only 12,800. Moreover, many of these results represent research that includes both topics of thermal and visual comfort.

These facts led to the rough estimation that only one-third of the research effort dedicated to the topic of thermal comfort has been dedicated to the topic of visual comfort. Further research revealed that this deficiency in the literature lies not only in the volume of work but also in the clarity of the topics within it. Within this context, in this paper, a thorough examination and review of the literature surrounding the topic of visual comfort will be attempted to provide a detailed guide on visual comfort.

The rest of the paper is structured as follows: In Sect. 2, an overview of the factors that affect the resident's visual comfort will be presented along with the factors that are taken into consideration when assessing visual comfort. Section 3, presents eight of the most prominent visual comfort indices corresponding to the previously mentioned assessment factors. Finally, in Sect. 4, conclusions are drawn regarding this work, the state of the visual comfort literature and the future endeavours of the authors.

2   Visual Comfort Definition

According to the European standard EN 12665 [17], visual comfort is defined as a subjective condition of visual well-being induced by the visual surroundings. In this section, the key elements that affect visual comfort will be presented, along with the factors that are taken into account when assessing visual comfort. This description aims to assist in a better understanding of the main visual comfort indices that will be presented in the next section.

2.1   Factors Affecting Visual Comfort

As stated previously, the perception of visual comfort is highly subjective, differing between individuals since it depends on various factors including the physiology of the human eye, the spectral emission of the light source and the physical quantities describing the amount of light and its distribution in space [18].

The Physiology of the Human Eye: As Grzeczkowski et al. point out in [19] visual processing occurs in the eye and more than 30 visual cortical regions, which account for one-third of the neocortex. At each one of these regions, there are variations that may affect visual processing between individuals. Moreover, according to F. W. Campbell and R. W. Gubisch's research [20], numerous reasons can account for the differences in findings between physical and psychophysical techniques of judging optical quality including the optical function of the fundus as a poor optical screen or a smooth mirror as well as the light dispersion in optical media.

The Spectral Emission of the Light Source: Visible light is light that can be seen with the naked eye. Estimates of the range of wavelengths visible to the human eye vary, but the lower end of the range is around four hundred manometers (400 nm) which correspond to a frequency of about seven hundred and fifty terahertz (750×10^{12} Hz). The upper end of the range is around seven hundred manometers (700 nm), corresponding to a frequency of about four hundred and thirty terahertz (430×10^{12} Hz). In well-lit environments, the photopic luminosity function $V(\lambda)$ best represents the human eye's sensitivity to visible light at different wavelengths [21]. This function models the ratio of the energy of a light source of the wavelength to which the eye is most sensitive (λ_{max}) to the energy of a light source of wavelength λ that elicits the same reaction in the test subject. The function was based on test data acquired from a variety of laboratories using a variety of approaches [22].

In low-light conditions, the sensitivity of the human eye to visible light at different wavelengths changes, and is best represented by the scotopic luminosity function, based on measurements obtained by US scientists George Wald and B.H Crawford. This is due to the way the rods and cones in the retina of the eye function. Cones are generally utilized for daylight vision. They are not extremely sensitive to changes in light intensity, but they can distinguish between red, blue, and green wavelengths. Night vision is dominated by rods. They are significantly more sensitive to light than cones (and far more numerous), but far less sensitive to colour. They have a peak sensitivity of five hundred and seven manometers (507 nm) in the blue section of the visible light spectrum and are not especially sensitive to red light. As a consequence, the scotopic luminous efficiency curve is shifted towards the blue end of the spectrum [22]. The photopic (black) and scotopic (green) luminosity functions can be observed in the below Fig. 1 [23].

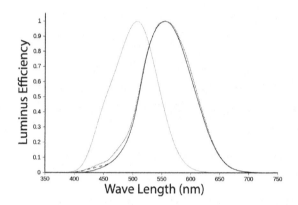

Fig. 1. The photopic and scotopoic luminosity functions

The Physical quantities describing the amount of light and its distribution in space:

I Luminous flux (Φ), also referred to as luminous power, describes the total radiance emitted by a light source as perceived by the human eye and is measured in lumens (lm):

$$\Phi = k_m \int_{380}^{780} V(\lambda)\phi_{e,\lambda}(\lambda)d\lambda \tag{1}$$

where k_m, $V(\lambda)$ and $\phi_{e,\lambda}(\lambda)$ are a constant of maximum photopic luminous efficacy of radiations, the spectral luminous efficiency in photopic vision, and the spectral concentration of radiant flux measured in watts per nanometer.

II The luminous intensity (I) represents the luminous flux (Φ) emitted within a certain angle in a three-dimensional space, and its unit, the candela (cd), is defined as lumens per steradian (lm/sr):

$$I = \frac{\Phi}{\Omega} \tag{2}$$

where Ω is the solid angle, measured in steradians (sr).

III Illuminance E is defined as the total luminous flux incident on a surface in lumens per square meter (lm/m^2). It is a measure of how well the incident light illuminates the surface. The SI unit of illuminance is lux (lx):

$$E = \frac{I \cos \theta}{d^2} \tag{3}$$

where θ and d are the angle of incidence (the angle between the light and the normal to the illuminated surface) and the distance from the light source to the target point in meters (m) respectively.

IV The amount of luminous intensity that passes through (or is emitted by) a certain area from a certain angle is described by luminance (L). Luminance indicates how bright an emitting or reflecting area appears by using the solid angle of a human's eye as a metric of the spatial light distribution. The SI luminance unit is candela per square meter (cd/m^2):

$$L = \frac{d^2 \Phi}{d\Sigma d\Omega_\Sigma \cos \theta_\Sigma} \tag{4}$$

where $d^2 \Phi$ is the luminous flux in lumens leaving the area $d\Sigma$ in any direction contained within the solid angle $d\Omega_\Sigma$ and θ_Σ is the angle between normal to $d\Sigma$ and the specified direction.

V The accumulated luminous intensity (I) applied to a certain area during a given time period is referred to as Luminous Exposure (H). In other words, it is the illuminance (E) per unit of time in seconds. The unit of Luminus Exposure is, therefore, $lx \times s$ (Fig. 2):

$$H = E \times t \tag{5}$$

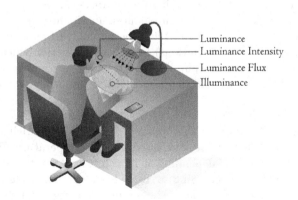

Luminance
Luminance Intensity
Luminance Flux
Illuminance

Fig. 2. Visual representation of L, I, Φ and E

2.2   Assesment Factors of Visual Comfort

The EN 12464-1 lighting standard [24] states that a person's ability to perceive and perform a visual activity quickly, safely, and comfortably depends greatly on the amount of light and how it is distributed in the task area and the surrounding environment. Visual comfort is often investigated by assessing factors that reflect the relationship between human needs and the light environment. According to [25] some of these factors are the amount of light, the uniformity of light, the quality of light in the rendering of colours and the prediction of the risk of glare for the occupants

The Amount of Light: According to the definitions of the physical quantities of light that were presented in Sect. 2.1, the physical quantity that is utilized to measure the amount of light reaching a certain surface is Illuminance (E) (3). The EN 12464-1 lighting standard [24] defines in clause 5 the minimum illuminance values, referred to as "maintained illuminance" (E_m), that must be maintained over the task area for various interiors and tasks. These values were determined considering, psychophysiological aspects such as visual comfort and well-being, requirements for visual tasks, visual ergonomics, practical experience, safety, and economy. Specifically, for office spaces, as Ballarini et al. note in [26], according to the EN 12464-1 lighting standard, the amount of light required to perform visual tasks in office settings should be 500 lx.

The Uniformity of Light and Luminance Distribution: [27] indicates that the luminance distribution in the field of vision influences the eye's adaptation level and its capacity to adjust to different degrees of darkness and light, which affects the visibility of the task and visual comfort. Poor luminance distribution can result in suboptimal visual conditions. Too high luminances can cause glare, too high luminance contrasts can induce fatigue due to frequent eye re-adaptation, and too low luminances and low luminance contrasts can create a dull and uninspiring working environment. A well-balanced luminance distribution, on the other hand, results in visual acuity (sharpness), contrast sensitivity (detection of small relative brightness variations), and ocular function efficiency (such as accommodation, convergence, pupillary contraction, eye movements, etc.). In conclusion, the task area should be illuminated as uniformly as possible.

Colour Appearance and the Quality of Light in Rendering Colours: A lamp's "colour appearance" relates to the apparent colour (chromaticity) of the light emitted. It is quantified by its correlated colour temperature (T_{CP}). T_{CP} is measured in Kelvin (K) and depending on its value, light is referred to as "warm", "intermediate" and "cool" according to Table 1. Colour rendering is also critical for visual comfort and performance. The colour rendering of a light source refers to its ability to correctly display the colours of different objects compared to an ideal or natural light source [28]. Natural colour rendering aids in a sense of well-being and is crucial when it comes to accurately recognizing safety colours. Boyce et al. mention in [29] that daylight is more likely to lead to optimal visual performance compared to electric light sources. The reason for this lies in both the tendency of daylight to be delivered in high quantities, but also in the wide spectrum that exists in daylight during different times, seasons, and climatic conditions guaranteeing optimal colour rendering.

Table 1. Lamp colour appearance groups

Colour appearance	*Correlated colour temperature TCP (K)*
Warm	below 3300 K K
Intermediate	3300 to 5300 K K
Cool	above 5300 K K

The Prediction of the Risk of Glare for Occupants: The European standard EN 12665 [17] defines "glare" as a state of vision in which there is discomfort or loss in the ability to perceive details or items, induced by an unsatisfactory distribution or range of luminance, or severe contrasts. CIE (International Commission on Illumination), in its International Lighting Vocabulary, [30] classifies glare into two categories:

1. Disability Glare, defined as "glare that impairs the vision of objects without necessarily causing discomfort"
2. Discomfort Glare, defined as "glare that causes discomfort without necessarily impairing the vision of objects"

Disability glare is seldom an issue in interior environments, but is commonly caused by oncoming vehicle headlights at night and in the day by sunlight. The experience of annoyance or pain induced by high levels of luminance in the field of view is known as discomfort glare. Discomfort glare, by definition, does not impair visual performance but does inflict discomfort. The desire for a model to assess whether a lighting installation will end up causing discomfort glare has resulted in the emergence of a number of empirical prediction systems in various countries, including the Visual Comfort Probability (VCP) system in North America. Given the trade hindrance created by different discomfort glare forecast methods in different countries and the overall lack of variation between them in terms of prediction accuracy, the CIE developed a consensus system. This system, known as the "Unified Glare Rating" system (UGR) [31], will be presented in the next chapter.

3   Visual Comfort Indices

In this section, eight of the most prominent visual comfort indices will be presented corresponding to the assessment factors presented in Sect. 2.2.

Daylight Factor, DF: This index describes the ratio of internal illumination E_{inside} at a given point to external horizontal illumination $E_{outside}$ [32].

$$DF = \frac{E_{inside}}{E_{outside}} \times 100\% \tag{6}$$

This index is the most straightforward and widely used way to assess the daylight permitted indoors by a window, since it indicates the prospective illuminance within a room in the worst-case scenario, under overcast sky conditions when there is less external daylight, offering a static metric that does not fluctuate with time or building direction [33].

Useful Daylight Illuminance, UDI: This index was derived in response to DF to include the wide range of light levels present in a visual plane. UDI, defines the range of useful daylight as $100lx-2000lx$ [34]. Levels less than 100 lx are generally regarded as insufficient, while levels greater than 2000 lx are likely to cause visual or thermal discomfort, or both. In [26] the authors define two further categories of UDI, supplementary UDI, UDI_s, when daylight illuminance ranges between 100 and 500 lx and autonomus UDI, UDI_a, when daylight illuminance ranges between 500 and 2500 lx.

Daylight Autonomy, DA: This index is defined as the percentage of the year when a minimum illuminance threshold is met by daylight alone. The level of illuminance is specified by referenced documents for lighting such as the IESNA Lighting Handbook [35] and is defined as the amount of daylight illuminance required for that specific task over the occupied times of the year. DA addresses the need for a long-term approach to the assessment of the visual environment.

$$DA = \frac{\sum_i \kappa_i \times t_i}{\sum_i t_i} \quad \epsilon[0,1] \quad \kappa_i = \begin{cases} 1 & E_{daylight} > E_{lim} \\ 0 & E_{daylight} < E_{lim} \end{cases} \tag{7}$$

DA, Similarly with UDI, is also divided into further more specialized indices, spatial DA, DAs, and continuous DA, DA_c. DAs introduces a spatial element to DA. It was introduced by the Illuminating Engineering Society (IES) and is used to evaluate if a certain fraction of space receives a sufficient amount of daylight during a certain fraction of the year. According to [26] a minimum threshold of 300 lx should be maintained for at least 95% of the occupied time $(sDA_{300|95\%})$, while a minimum illuminance of 500 lx should be maintained for at least 50% of the time. In [32] the authors point out that the value added by sDA to DA is that it provides a single value that describes the daylight illuminance over the space in question. In contrast to spatial DA, continuous DA, DA_c, considers fractional levels of illuminance that might not be enough to independently illuminate a fraction of space, but still contribute to its luminosity. For example, if the required maintained illuminance for a specific fraction of space is 500 lx, and the current illuminance is 300 lx, this level of illuminance is completely ignored when calculating sDA. On the other hand, DA_c credits this level of illuminance as $300/500 = 60\%$.

Annual Sun Exposure (ASE): DA, like *UDI*, does not provide an upper limit for daylight illumination. Excessive amounts of sun exposure can lead to discomfort and suboptimal visual performance. As a result, a new daylight index by the name of Annual Sun Exposure (*ASE*) was created to describe the maximum fraction of space that should receive a certain amount of sunlight during a certain time period. The U.S. Green Building Council (USGBC) advise in LEED v4 [36] that during 250 occupied hours, no more than 10% of the space in question should receive more than 1000 lx.

Colour Rendering Index (CRI): The rendering ability of a light source is measured by its (*CRI*). The appropriate name for the value often referenced as "*CRI*" in commercial lighting products is *CIE R_a*, "*CRI*" being a general term and *CIE R_a* being the international standard colour rendering index. The highest attainable *CIE R_a* value is 100, which would only be assigned to a source whose spectrum is equal to that of daylight [37]. According to the EN 12464-1 lighting standard [24], lamps possessing a colour rendering index of less than 80 should not be utilized in areas where people work or remain for extended periods of time.

Illuminance Uniformity (U): The EN 12464-1 lighting standard [24] defines *U* as the ratio of minimum illuminance to average illuminance in a visual plane.

Unified Glare Rating (UGR): Many indices have been developed over the years for individual countries to evaluate the discomfort caused by glare, such as the British Glare Index (*BGI*) and the CIE Glare Index (*CGI*). However, a unified glare index based on commonly accepted parameters was needed. This resulted in the development of the "Unified Glare Rating" (*UGR*) [31].

$$UGR = 8\log_{10}[\frac{0.25}{L_b}\sum\frac{L^2\omega}{p^2}] \qquad (8)$$

where p is the position index, ω is the solid angle, L is the illuminance towards the observer's eyes and L_b is the background illuminance.

Daylight Glare Probability (DGP): Despite the many benefits of daylight for the health, wellness, and productivity of users, too much exposure to daylight can cause glare and disturb the user. Wienold and Christoffersen [38] proposed a new index, the Daylight Glare Probability (*DGP*), which uses the probability that a person is disturbed as a glare metric. *DGP* is a function of the vertical eye illuminance as well as the luminance of the glare source, its solid angle, and its position index.

$$DGP = 5.87 \times 10^{-5}E_v + 0.098\log_{10}[1 + \sum_{i=1}^{n}\frac{L_{s,i}^2 \times \omega_{s,i}}{E_v^{1.87} \times p_i^2}] + 0.16 \qquad (9)$$

where E_v is the vertical eye illuminance, $L_{s,i}$ is the luminance of the source, $\omega_{s,i}$ the solid angle between the observer and the source, and p is the position index.

4   Conclusions

In this short study, an effort was made to provide a guide to the topic of visual comfort in indoor environments. The authors attempted to present this topic holistically prompted by the lack of clarity in the literature, beginning with the factors that affect visual comfort, continuing with the way it is assessed, and finally presenting its assessment indices. As it became obvious, visual comfort depends on a lot of factors, is studied through many different lenses, has a variety of indices, and most importantly, is perceived differently from person to person. The authors aim to continue this work, defining a holistic practical approach to determining the appropriate index to assess visual comfort and proposing innovative AI models to optimise the visual comfort of users in indoor spaces.

Acknowledgment. This work is partially supported by the PRECEPT project, funded by the EU H2020 under Grant Agreement No. 958284.

References

1. Aruga, K., Islam, M.M., Jannat, A.: Does staying at home during the COVID-19 pandemic help reduce CO_2 emissions? Sustainability **13**(15), 8534 (2021). https://doi.org/10.3390/su13158534
2. Choi, K.R., Heilemann, M.V., Fauer, A., Mead, M.: A second pandemic: mental health spillover from the novel coronavirus (COVID-19). J. Am. Psychiatr. Nurses Assoc. **26**(4), 340–343 (2020). https://doi.org/10.1177/1078390320919803
3. Rohde, L., Larsen, T.S., Jensen, R.L., Larsen, O.K.: Framing holistic indoor environment: definitions of comfort, health and well-being. Indoor Built Environ. **29**(8), 1118–1136 (2020). https://doi.org/10.1177/1420326X19875795
4. ANSI/ASHRAE Standard 55. Thermal Environment Conditions for Human Occupancy (2004)
5. Djongyang, N., Tchinda, R., Njomo, D.: Thermal comfort: a review paper. Renewable Sustainable Energy Rev. **14**(9), 2626–2640 (2010), ISSN 1364–0321, https://doi.org/10.1016/j.rser.2010.07.040
6. Rindel, J.: Acoustical comfort as a design criterion for dwellings in the future (2002)
7. Sicurella, F., Evola, G., Wurtz, E.: A statistical approach for the evaluation of thermal and visual comfort in free-running buildings, Energy Build. **47**, 402–410 (2012). https://doi.org/10.1016/j.enbuild.2011.12.013. ISSN 0378–7788
8. Kumar, D., Alam, M., Zou, P.X.W., Sanjayan, J.G., Memon, R.A.: Comparative analysis of building insulation material properties and performance. Renewable Sustainable Energy Rev. **131**, 110038 (2020). https://doi.org/10.1016/j.rser.2020.110038, ISSN 1364-0321
9. Tsirigoti, D., Giarma, C., Tsikaloudaki, K.: Indoor acoustic comfort provided by an innovative preconstructed wall module: sound insulation performance analysis. Sustainability **12**(20), 8666 (2020). https://doi.org/10.3390/su12208666
10. Francesco, L., et al.: Acoustic false ceiling in wide rooms, realized by an innovative textile system (2015)
11. Zhao, Q., Lian, Z., Lai, D.: Thermal comfort models and their developments: a review. Energy Built Environ. **2**(1), 21–33 (2021). https://doi.org/10.1016/j.enbenv.2020.05.007. ISSN 2666–1233

12. Lai, D., Lian, Z., Liu, W., Guo, C., Liu, W., Liu, K., Chen, Q.: A comprehensive review of thermal comfort studies in urban open spaces. Sci. Total Environ. **742**, 140092 (2020). https://doi.org/10.1016/j.scitotenv.2020.140092. ISSN 0048-9697

13. Lai, D., Liu, W., Gan, T., Liu, K., Chen, Q.: A review of mitigating strategies to improve the thermal environment and thermal comfort in urban outdoor spaces. Sci. Total Environ. **661**, 337–353 (2019). https://doi.org/10.1016/j.scitotenv.2019.01.062. ISSN 0048–9697

14. R. de Dear, J. Xiong, J. Kim, B. Cao, A review of adaptive thermal comfort research since 1998. Energy Build. **214**, 109893 (2020). https://doi.org/10.1016/j.enbuild.2020.109893. ISSN 0378-7788

15. Ma, N., Aviv, D., Guo, H., Braham, W.W.: Measuring the right factors: a review of variables and models for thermal comfort and indoor air quality, Renewable and Sustainable Energy Rev. **135**, 110436 (2021). https://doi.org/10.1016/j.rser.2020.110436. ISSN 1364-0321

16. Zhang, W., Wu, Y., Calautit, J.K.: A review on occupancy prediction through machine learning for enhancing energy efficiency, air quality and thermal comfort in the built environment. Renewable Sustainable Energy Rev. **167**, 112704 (2022), https://doi.org/10.1016/j.rser.2022.112704. ISSN 1364-0321

17. EN 12665. Light and lighting - Basic terms and criteria for specifying lighting requirements. Brussels, Belgium: European Committee for Standardization (2011)

18. Carlucci, S., Causone, F., De Rosa, F., Pagliano, L.: A review of indices for assessing visual comfort with a view to their use in optimization processes to support building integrated design. Renewable Sustainable Energy Rev. **47**, 1016–1033 (2015). https://doi.org/10.1016/j.rser.2015.03.062. ISSN 1364–0321

19. Grzeczkowski, L., et al.: About individual differences in vision. Vision Res. (2017). http://dx.doi.org/10.1016/j.visres.2016.10.006

20. Campbell, F. W., Gubisch, R. W., (1966), Optical quality of the human eye. The Journal of Physiology, 186 https://doi.org/10.1113/jphysiol.1966.sp008056.

21. Tyndall, E.P.T., Gibson, K.S.: Visibility of radiant energy equation. J. Opt. Soc. Am. **9**, 403–403 (1924)

22. https://www.technologyuk.net/science/measurement-and-units/luminous-intensity-and-photometry.shtml

23. Luminous efficiency function. (2022, October 21). In Wikipedia.https://en.wikipedia.org/wiki/Luminous_efficiency_function

24. European Committee for Standardization (CEN). EN 12464–1, Light and Lighting. Lighting of Work Places. Part 1: Indoor Work Places; CEN: Brussels, Belgium (2011)

25. Bhattarai, H.: Infusing energy efficient illumination design to retrofit existing infrastructures - a case of energy efficient illumination design of multipurpose hall at Jigme Namgyel Engineering College. J. Sci. Technol. Eng. Res. **2**(2), 89–100 (2021). https://doi.org/10.53525/jster.1035864

26. Ballarini, I., De Luca, G., Paragamyan, A., Pellegrino, A., Corrado, V.: Transformation of an Office Building into a Nearly Zero Energy Building (nZEB): implications for thermal and visual comfort and energy performance. Energies **12**(5), 895 (2019). https://doi.org/10.3390/en12050895

27. Carlucci, S., Causone, F., De Rosa, F., Pagliano, L.: A review of indices for assessing visual comfort with a view to their use in optimization processes to support building integrated design, Renewable and Sustainable Energy Reviews **47**, 1016–1033 (2015). https://doi.org/10.1016/j.rser.2015.03.062. https://www.sciencedirect.com/science/article/pii/S1364032115002154, ISSN 1364–0321

28. Color rendering. (2023, February 27). In Wikipedia. https://en.wikipedia.org/wiki/Color_rendering
29. Boyce, P., Hunter, C., Howlett, O.: The benefits of daylight through windows. Rensselaer Polytechnic Institute, Troy, New York (2003)
30. Commision Internationale de L'Eclairage (CIE), colour rendering, CIE S 017:2020 ILV: International Lighting Vocabulary, CIE, Viena (2020). https://doi.org/10.25039/s017.2020
31. Discomfort glare in interior lighting. CIE Technical Committee 3–13. CIE 117–1995. 1995
32. Khele, I., Szabó, M.: A Comprehensive Review of the Indoor Visual Comfort Indices and the Effect of Semi-Transparent Building-Integrated Photovoltaics on the Visual Comfort Indoors. Available at SSRN: https://ssrn.com/abstract=4090232 or https://doi.org/10.2139/ssrn.4090232
33. Acosta, I., Munoz, C., Campano, M.A., Navarro, J.: Analysis of daylight factors and energy saving allowed by windows under overcast sky conditions. Renewable Energy **77**, 194–207 (2015). https://doi.org/10.1016/j.renene.2014.12.017. ISSN 0960–1481
34. Nabil, A., Mardaljevic, J.: Useful daylight illuminance: a new paradigm for assessing daylight in buildings. Lighting Res. Technol. - Lighting Res Technol. **37**, 41–59 (2005). https://doi.org/10.1191/1365782805li128oa
35. IESNA. The lighting handbook. ninth ed. New York (USA): Illuminating Engineering Society of North America (2000)
36. U.S. Green Building Council (USGBC). LEED v4. https://www.usgbc.org/leed/v4
37. Colour rendering index (2022, November 27). https://en.wikipedia.org/wiki/colour_rendering_index
38. Wienold, J., Christoffersen, J.: Evaluation methods and development of a new glare prediction model for daylight environments with the use of CCD cameras. Energy Build. **38**(7), 743–757 (2006)

A Novel Social Collaboration Platform for Enhancing Energy Awareness

Efstathia Martinopoulou[1], Asimina Dimara[1,2(✉)], Anastasia Tsita[1],
Sergio Luis Herrera Gonzalez[3], Rafael Marin-Perez[4],
Juan Andres Sanchez Segado[4], Piero Fraternali[3], Stelios Krinidis[1,5],
Christos-Nikolaos Anagnostopoulos[2], Dimosthenis Ioannidis[1],
and Dimitrios Tzovaras[1]

[1] Information Technologies Institute (ITI), Centre for Research Technology
(CERTH), Thessaloniki, Greece
{emartini,adimara,krinidis,djoannid,Dimitrios.Tzovaras}@iti.gr,
a.tsita@ti.gr
[2] Department of Cultural Technology and Communication, Intelligent Systems Lab,
University of the Aegean (UoA), Mytilene, Greece
canag@aegean.gr
[3] Politecnico di Milano, 20133 Milano, Italy
{sergioluis.herrera,piero.fraternali}@polimi.it
[4] Department of Research and Innovation, Odin Solutions, 30009 Murcia, Spain
{rmarin,jasanchez}@odins.es
[5] Management Science and Technology Department, International Hellenic
University (IHU), Kavala, Greece

Abstract. Building managers and stakeholders should begin establishing cultures and practices that encourage collaborative impact toward energy awareness. In this context, a novel social collaboration platform is suggested provisioning best practices and recommendations for energy-efficient user actions. The platform is equipped with social collaboration tools that will link relevant parties via direct or indirect communication using sound, video, text, and context-aware knowledge. Moreover, it provides support for recommendations, prescriptions, and identification of best practices for proactivity, as well as best practices and proposals for energy efficiency and the well-being of building occupants. Furthermore, the platform provides search functionality that allows quick access to the preferred content regarding the posts and users and also provides filter options for locations and building groups that enhance the scalability of the system.

Keywords: Collaboration Platform · Energy awareness · Energy practices

1 Introduction

There has never been a more crucial time for a dedicated and global focus on the demand side of the energy equation [1]. Energy efficiency and energy savings are important due to the unpredictability of supply, high prices, and the

I. Maglogiannis et al. (Eds.): AIAI 2023 Workshops, IFIP AICT 677, pp. 195–206, 2023.
https://doi.org/10.1007/978-3-031-34171-7_15

pressing climate goals. Governments and European Union (EU) are responding with various actions, such as launching demand-reduction campaigns and creating targeted grants (such as The European Green Deal and Fit for 55) [2]. Energy ministers from around the world met at the IEA's recent 7th Annual Global Conference on Energy Efficiency [3] and declared that all governments, industry, enterprises, and stakeholders should strengthen their action on energy efficiency. They also agreed that demand-side management action and energy efficiency have a particularly important role to play now that global energy prices are high and volatile, hurting households, industries, and entire economies.

Effective marketing can prompt individuals to consume less energy. For instance, some researchers' estimates indicate that residential sector behaviour adjustments might save up to 20% of household energy demand [4]. According to another estimation, a large country like India has the potential to save between 3.4 and 10.2 TWh of energy by 2030 through lifestyle changes [5]. Furthermore, campaigns can have a wide range of effects regarding the energy saved, according to the IEA's 2021 report [6]. Even outside of the current energy crisis, IEA modelling emphasizes the significance of behavioural changes for attaining net zero goals [6].

Nonetheless, individuals and entire companies are unlikely to actively conserve energy or operate in a generally eco-friendly manner unless they are aware of the issue and its consequences. Towards this matter, energy awareness refers to a person's knowledge of energy's nature, production and characteristics as well as their awareness of energy consumption and conservation [7]. Moreover, energy awareness entails being aware of the energy consumption of various home appliances, their efficiency, and how certain activities impact energy use. Many things influence energy awareness like energy usage visibility. Building managers and stakeholders should begin establishing cultures and practices that encourage collaborative impact toward energy awareness. Having ways to track collective impact may meaningfully unite individuals around a common goal to share knowledge and practices, and work together, ultimately unleashing the group's potential at scale and producing real impact.

Within this context, a novel social collaboration platform for enhancing energy awareness (SCOPE) is suggested provisioning best practices and recommendations for energy-efficient user actions. The platform is equipped with social collaboration tools that will link relevant parties via direct or indirect communication using sound, video, text, and context-aware knowledge. Moreover, it provides support for recommendations, prescriptions, and identification of best practices for proactivity, energy efficiency and the well-being of building occupants. Via this social collaboration network, third parties will be able to share ideas and best practices. The platform also includes events and social networking to create communities that foster a more pleasant and connected community environment.

The remainder of the paper is structured as follows: Sect. 2 presents the methodology followed to build the social collaboration platform, including requirements and design approach. Section 3, presents the implementation of the platform and how the requirements are met. Finally, Sect. 4 summarizes the main findings.

2   Methodology

2.1   Requirements

The SCOPE's defined functional and non-functional criteria are outlined in this section.

The functional requirements addressed are:

- The SCOPE shall adhere to the General Data Protection Regulation (GDPR) guidelines for data collection, transmission, processing, and storage included in the EU regulation [8].
- The SCOPE must anonymously track users' pertinent actions while utilizing the application. The platform should keep track of every section users are visiting throughout a session, as well as any actions performed that are pertinent for the analysis of the platform's impact on their behaviour.
- The SCOPE should facilitate stakeholder communication and social engagement so they can exchange knowledge, expertise, and best practices regarding running buildings efficiently.

The Non-functional requirements addressed are:

- The SCOPE interface should be simple to use, and all messages should be easy to understand without using any obscure technical terms. Some of the users could have a medium to high degree of digital literacy. To enhance platform adoption, the user interface must be inviting and the messaging must be understandable.
- SCOPE platform should support Personal Computers (PCS), tablets, and even mobile phones. The platform interface should be responsive and adapt to the different device interaction modes. The platform may be used both at home and on the go. Mobile devices are the best for delivering notifications, while the best way to see charts and data is on tablets or computer monitors.
- The SCOPE must permit secure data flow among its components while protecting user privacy. A security and privacy platform should be used to handle communication with other modules.

2.2   Design Approach

It was crucial to develop a generic front-end layout that correlates to a flexible structure and workflow at the backend to construct a scalable, component-based user interface. The SCOPE's current architecture should be able to: (a) support scaling as a system architecture, including the back-end; (b) enable the interface components to accommodate more content and functionalities without "breaking" visually (e.g., affecting the functionality of responsiveness); (c) and without requiring significant changes to the platform's current architecture.

Moreover, the hierarchy of the data management workflow had to be defined in such a way that incorporates all the application functionalities for several pilot testing sites (e.g., various countries) in the same manner. All users, regardless of the specific characteristics of their pilot, building or residence, should be able to follow the same flow in order to succeed in the same goals using the application. It was also important that for similar actions, a similar flow should be followed by the user, regardless of differences in users' specifications and settings (e.g., different language). High-fidelity prototypes of the user interface (Mock-Ups) were used as the appropriate tool to support the user interface (UI) design process, first to illustrate various ways to implement the preliminary requirements given and explore the possibilities and limitations in a realistic manner.

Primarily, mock-ups enabled direct communication between the individuals involved in the platform's design and development through an iterative approach. The design and development team was able to develop ideas, pinpoint issues or gaps, and come up with questions, insights, and sound proposals based on such a typical and simple design output, which most people are familiar with and can easily understand. As identified issues could be immediately put under validation or consideration for additional research or dialogue among people involved in the social collaboration platform and its dependencies, such a process could also support emerging questions on the system architecture of the platform. The Mock-ups design went through two significant iterations. The general content and the primary user goals were established first. As a result, the hierarchy, menu, and functionalities were divided into pages.

The majority of the elements in terms of content and functionality were established during the initial mock-ups. Emerging concerns were gradually resolved, and a second version of mock-ups was finished by a continuous refinement and brainstorming on specific design visualization (components, navigation, etc.). In this text, they are shown and described. It is crucial to remember that solution could be made as a result of a new set of specific requirements, technical constraints, new insights, etc., even though an effort was made to deliver a complete design that is both adequate and necessary to match the project objectives as well as concrete and clear enough to support the development team. Throughout the platform's front-end development, a few small extra UI design considerations were made.

2.3   Architecture Overview

The SCOPE includes several applications that interact with one another and share data over secure, predefined channels. The SCOPE components are divided into groups for the front- and back-end, as well as a selection of tools for interfacing with external applications. The overall SCOPE architecture along with the main components are depicted in Fig. 1. The Simple Mail Transfer Protocol (SMTP) is used to send mail to the users (e.g., forgot password process). The firebase CMS is used to facilitate the communication between the mobile version and SCOPE. The SCOPE Data Base (DB) is used to save specifications and dependencies of the SCOPE. The Building Management System (BMS) is used to get energy-saving recommendations for users. The edge device is the gateway for retrieving indoor consumption data.

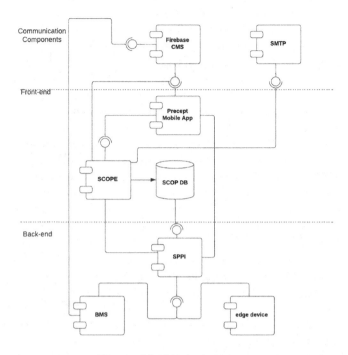

Fig. 1. SCOPE Architecture

Backend Architecture. As described in Sect. 2.3, the main components that SCOPE communicates with are the Security and Privacy Platform Integration (SPPI), the BMS and the edge to retrieve sensor data. The SCOPE's SPPI platform is a crucial component and provides some of the main functionalities like:

- Identity management, based on Keyrock ID-Manager [9], this component gives an API that allows executing numerous activities needed by the app. It also serves as a secure channel for communication.
- Data storage for current events (Broker FIWARE Orion-LD [10]).
- Archive of previous data (Historical Component [11]).
- A system for user authentication.
- User data access control (authorization with DCapBAC [11]).

One of the most important functionalities is the login process. During the login process, the SCOPE must access the SPPI, namely the Keyrock ID-Manager component, to authenticate the user in the system and retrieve his/her information. Figure 2 depicts how a user logs into the system and retrieves his/her identity information via the SCOPE.

Another important process is the access to real-time and historical data. The SCOPE must communicate with the SPPI to access real-time and historical data. This process is depicted in Fig. 3.

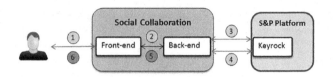

Fig. 2. SCOPE - Login process data flow

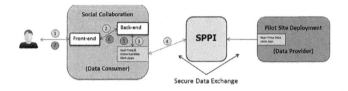

Fig. 3. SCOPE - Data flow from sensors to GUI

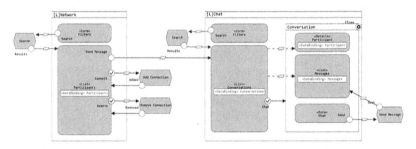

Fig. 4. SCOPE - IFML design of the Network and the Chat pages)

Front-end Architecture. The frontend architecture describes the principles followed to build both the mobile and web platforms of the SCOPE.

1. Mobile application. A strategy that has gained popularity in recent years for the implementation of the mobile version is used for the SCOPE mobile version. This strategy involved breaking the program down into different parts: web applications with Responsive Web Design (RWD) that handle the business logic and native client applications for each platform that wrapped the web applications and provided access to all native features.
2. Web application. The design of the SCOPE is going to be presented in Sect. 3. Indicatively, a user interaction of the SCOPE using Interaction Flow Modelling Language (IFML) will be presented. Figure 4 depicts the IFML design of the Network and the Chat pages.

3   Implementation

In this section, the implementation of the SCOPE will be presented. The main dashboard (login page) is depicted in Fig. 5. From this page, users may log in and then navigate to the main menu.

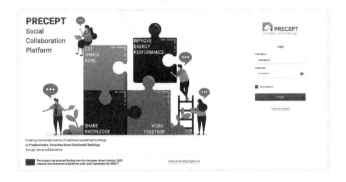

Fig. 5. The Login Page

The main menu is depicted in Fig. 6. The main dashboards of the social collaboration platform are Network, Chat, DIY tutorials, News and events, Notifications, My Account, and the About page.

3.1 Platform Sections and User Interfaces

Newsfeed. The NewsFeed page (Fig. 7) is the main page of the SCOPE platform that enables the transfer of knowledge and energy-related content between end users. The fundamental components of this page are the posts that allow the exchange of content, namely text, links, images, and/or videos under predefined energy-related topics. All users can respond to a post with remarks or show appreciation and can report a user if a post or message is deemed improper. The number of votes and replies for each post should be evident to all users, enabling the traceability of more accepted posts and encouraging the adoption of energy-effective solutions in terms of household energy. Furthermore, the SCOPE provides search functionality that allows quick access to the preferred content regarding the posts and users and also provides filter options regarding countries and building groups that enhance the scalability of the system. Sorting by the number of votes permits the more pronounced content to be presented in front, thus encouraging the participation and involvement of end users.

Network. The network page stores user accounts from all application pilot sites and allows them to connect. Users can utilize the search functionality or filter options to navigate through the network accounts or search for specific users. To ensure that no private information is visible to non-appropriate users, the only information available for each user is the username and the country. Before proceeding with a connection request, the user can examine the connection candidate's newsfeed activity to ensure that they share similar interests. By accepting a connection invitation, the connected users can start communicating with each other by enabling one-to-one private conversations. In the UI design, the network page is divided into the following tabs to facilitate navigation: (i) Search; (ii) My Connections; and (iii) Connection Invitations.

Fig. 6. The SCOPE menu

Fig. 7. SCOPE- Newsfeed Page

Do It Yourself (DIY). The DIY (Fig. 9) page provides educational material and is managed by the system administrator. The content here can be videos or instructions that provide guidance for hardware or software equipment, e.g., sensor placement, installation, and troubleshooting. This page inherits properties from the Newsfeed page, and each post can be related to an energy tag describing the post content. Apart from the energy tag, a post includes a title, a description, and complementary content such as videos and images.

News and Events. The News & Events page contains posts about actions taken by the Administration team, including newsletters and upcoming events. Each post is created by the administrator and is visible to all users. It consists

Fig. 8. SCOPE- Network

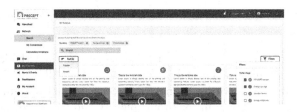

Fig. 9. SCOPE- DIY Tutorials

of a title, a mini-description, full-context text, images, and associated tags that enhance searchability.

Notifications. Notifications are automated messages that are produced by the system and inform users about their activity and the outcome of their actions. On this page, a smart table stores the notification history in chronological order, as well as the person who triggered the alert. The notifications include alerts generated by the chat page when a new message arrives at a chatroom, the network when a user accepts a connection request or notifications from the Administration team about newly posted items. Apart from the above, the user can sort the notifications by date, message, or user and mark some notifications as unread to further examine them at a later time. The most recent notifications are also presented through a fixed shortcut in the header to keep users informed.

Chat. The SCOPE also supports a chat module (Fig. 10) that allows either private one-to-one conversations or group chats among users. By default, each registered user will be enrolled in a predetermined group chat created for the pilot to which he or she belongs. More specifically, users of the same pilot are typically confronted with similar climate conditions; hence, there is an interplay among them and sharing practices that best suit them. Along with group chats, each user can initiate a one-to-one conversation with another user only if they have established a connection. The supported forms of messaging comprise text (images, video, and text). To enhance the protection of users in the SCOPE, each user can report a message if the content is regarded as abusive.

Fig. 10. SCOPE- Chat

My Account. My account page provides information about the logged-in user, including the username, an optional profile picture that will be visible to network users, and building information, namely the country, pilot, building, and group the user belongs to. Apart from the profile picture and password, the other information can only be changed by the system administrator at the user's request.

About. The about page is a welcoming page that contains content about the Precept project, under which SCOPE has been developed.

3.2   Energy Awareness Tabs

Energy awareness tags (Fig. 11) are predefined tags that allow users to categorise content more effectively. The initial setup includes the following categories: (i) Precept System; (ii) Energy Savings; (iii) Comfort Levels; (iv) Energy Efficiency; (v) Proactiveness; which are depicted in Fig. 11, and can be expanded by the administrator by adding new categories. Hence, only energy-related content will be posted in the SCOPE, and energy tags will serve as quick filtering options.

As a result, to restrict the content to being energy-related, users must tag their posts with the above topics before making them public. More specifically, the content associated with the "comfort levels" tag will provide discussions about techniques that increase comfort levels and well-being, as well as allow users to share information about specific building characteristics such as humidity, temperature levels, air quality, etc. Using the energy savings tag, methods, and recommendations for reducing costs will be returned. In the energy efficiency tag, users will discuss alternative energy-efficient solutions and equipment to perform household tasks. In the proactiveness tag, smart solutions and prescriptions will be displayed. Along with the above, posts from the Precept system will be filtered to allow quick access to content posted by the system administrator.

Furthermore, by exploiting the BMS system and monitoring data, posts will be shown to the user with average consumption encouraging them to consume less energy. Within the same perspective, general energy recommendations and prescriptions will be pushed to the users at the notifications tab.

Fig. 11. Energy Tags

4   Conclusions

To summarise, a novel social and collaboration platform has been developed to enhance energy awareness and buildings' proactiveness. A set of developed tools allows the dissemination of knowledge and practices towards effective energy management. Collaborative environments, the grouping of individuals that share the same needs, and the formation of social bonds can improve energy engagement as well as provide first-hand knowledge about energy. In future work, the system will be further evaluated to quantify acceptance measures through pilot production and questionnaires.

Acknowledgements. This work is partially supported by the PRECEPT project funded by the EU H2020 under Grant Agreement No. 958284.

References

1. Stavrakas, V., Flamos, A.: A modular high-resolution demand-side management model to quantify benefits of demand-flexibility in the residential sector. Energy Convers. Manage. **205**, 112339 (2020)
2. The European Green Deal and Fit for 55 Insights on the revision of the Renewable Energy Directive and Energy Efficiency Directive. https://kpmg.com/xx/en/home/insights/2021/11/the-european-green-deal-and-fit-for-55.html
3. 7th annual global conference on energy efficiency: welcome remarks and opening plenary. https://www.iea.org/events/7th-annual-global-conference-on-energy-efficiency-welcome-remarks-and-opening-plenary
4. Zangheri, P., Serrenho, T., Bertoldi, P.: Energy savings from feedback systems: A meta-studies' review. Energies **12**(19), 3788 (2019)
5. Sun, H., et al.: Energy efficiency: the role of technological innovation and knowledge spillover. Technol. Forecast. Social Change **167**, 120659 (2021)
6. Depledge, J., Saldivia, M., Peñasco, C.: Glass half full or glass half empty?: the 2021 Glasgow Climate Conference. Climate Policy **22**(2), 147–157 (2022)

7. Silva, P.V.B.C., et al.: Energy awareness and energy efficiency in internet of things middleware: a systematic literature review. Annal. Telecommun. **78**, 1–17 (2022)
8. The general data protection regulation. https://www.consilium.europa.eu/en/policies/data-protection/data-protection-regulation/
9. Identity Manager GE - keyrock. https://keyrock.docs.apiary.io/#
10. Orion-LD - FIWARE NGSI-LD Context Broker. https://hub.docker.com/r/fiware/orion-ld
11. Marin-Perez, R., et al.: PLUG-N-HARVEST architecture for secure and intelligent management of near-zero energy buildings. Sensors **19**(4), 843 (2019)

Ensuring Reliability in Smart Building IoT Operations Through Real-Time Holistic Data Treatment

Aliki Stefanopoulou[1,2], Asimina Dimara[1,3(✉)], Iakovos Michailidis[1,2], Georgios Karatzinis[1,2], Alexios Papaioannou[1,4], Stelios Krinidis[1,4], Christos-Nikolaos Anagnostopoulos[3], Elias Kosmatopoulos[1,2], Dimosthenis Ioannidis[1], and Dimitrios Tzovaras[1]

[1] Centre for Research adn Technology Hellas (CERTH), Information Technologies Institute (ITI), Thessaloniki, Greece
`{alikstef,adimara,michaild,gkaratzi,alexiopa,krinidis,kosmatop,djoannid,`
`Dimitrios.Tzovaras}@iti.gr`
[2] Department of Electrical and Computer Engineering, Automatic Control Systems and Robotics, Democritus University of Thrace (DUTh), Xanthi, Greece
[3] Department of Cultural Technology and Communication, Intelligent Systems Lab, University of the Aegean (UoA), Mytilene, Greece
`canag@aegean.gr`
[4] Management Science and Technology Department, International Hellenic University (IHU), Kavala, Greece

Abstract. Efficient smartification in buildings pre-requires highly reliable data. Modern AI applications consider real-time emergent responsiveness, which renders control safety of outmost importance. A number of sensors and other devices are installed that retrieve data on energy consumption, indoor conditions, and other information. By analyzing this data, smart home devices are able to customise user experiences while optimizing energy use while enhancing security in a real-time manner. In this paper, a holistic data treatment framework for Smart Building IoT applications is presented. The proposed framework considers a multifactorial anomaly detection and treatment. The implemented functional filtering pipeline consists of statistical filtering rules for detecting, recognizing and mitigating the most common anomalies observed in the historical data. First a methodology for estimating missing data values based on available data is considered. Moreover, an outlier detection and healing mechanism is also integrated to improve the accuracy and reliability of the analysed results. The results showcase that the clean data are of better quality for further exploitation.

Keywords: Data treatment · Data healing · Data filtering · AI Operational Safety · Real-time data reliability

1 Introduction

Smart homes are equipped with a plethora of sensors and devices that gather information about users' behaviour, energy consumption, indoor and outdoor

I. Maglogiannis et al. (Eds.): AIAI 2023 Workshops, IFIP AICT 677, pp. 207–218, 2023.
https://doi.org/10.1007/978-3-031-34171-7_16

environmental conditions and others. As a result, the potential of optimizing and understanding their operation through big data analysis is tremendous [1]. Smart building systems leverage the available amount of historical data to optimize energy use, and improve security while offering customized user experience by evaluating this data [2]. Smart home systems enable real-time operations management, especially during emerging phenomena, by regulating controllable settings in order to offer more personalized user satisfaction by gathering information on residents' preferences, habits, and actions [3]. Overall, big data has immense potential for smart home applications, and as the Internet of Things (IoT) technology develops further, more sophisticated big data exploitation in this field is anticipated.

Pushing sensorial data streams in IoT networks can be difficult for a variety of reasons, such as:

- Constraints due to Security: To save energy and reduce costs, IoT devices frequently use low-power highly-secure wireless technologies like Bluetooth, Zwave or Zigbee. Due to the inherent bandwidth limitations of these technologies, it might be difficult to send huge data streams to cloud servers or other devices [4].
- Handling Big-Data: Network congestion may occur in centralized IoT networks as a result of multiple devices attempting to push data streams at once. Delays, packet loss, and other problems may result from this, which may reduce the network's dependability [4].
- High latency for Real-time Control applications: High bandwidth is frequently needed for IoT applications to ensure prompt answers, especially when close-to real-time control frequency is employed. Pushing sensor data streams to cloud servers or other devices, however, might cause large latencies, especially if the network is busy or the devices are spread out far away [5].
- IoT device power limitations: Since many IoT devices rely on batteries or other low-power energy sources for power, this can restrict the amount of data streams they can push. Data transmission can use a lot of power, especially if the device is far from the closest access point or gateway [5].

Additionally, utilizing raw sensory data to extract reliable insights and provide data-intensive services may cause various issues that arise when operating with unprocessed or unstructured data deriving from the IoT applications [6]. Likewise, raw data collected directly by IoT devices may contain errors, duplicates or even large gaps. This can lead to inaccurate analysis and decision-making if the data is not cleaned, healed or corrected before the analysis process. IoT devices generate data in different formats, semantics and structures, making it challenging to integrate and analyze the data effectively [7]. This can require significant effort to normalize the data before it can be analyzed. This can overwhelm storage and processing resources and make it challenging to analyze the data in a timely and cost-effective manner. Finally, IoT data is often generated in real-time and at high speeds, which can make it challenging to store and process the data quickly enough to support real-time analysis and decision-making [6].

Additionally, environmental sensors rely on a reliable and stable network connection to transmit data. If the network is down or has low signal strength, the data transmission may be interrupted or delayed [8]. Environmental sensors need a stable power source to operate correctly. If the battery or power supply is running low, the sensor may not transmit data for a long period of time as required or may provide inaccurate readings [9]. Data corruption can occur during data transmission, especially when using wireless transmission methods. This can be due to various factors such as network interference, weak signals, or incompatible protocols.

Within this context, in this paper a holistic data treatment framework in Smart IoT Monitoring is suggested. A set of guidelines and procedures that outline how to manage and analyze data in a structured and systematic way is followed. It is a series of steps that helps to ensure that the data is reliable, consistent, and valid, and can be used for artificial intelligence models. The procedure includes removing errors, inconsistencies, and duplicates. This task also includes tasks such as data validation and data transformation. Moreover, a technique is involved to estimate missing data values based on the available data. Eventually, there are data points that are significantly different from other data points in the dataset, and they can have a significant impact on the analysis results. In the suggested pipeline an outlier healing is performed to identify and deal with these points while improving the accuracy and reliability of the analysis results.

The remainder of the paper is structured as follows: Sect. 2 addresses the methodology followed for data treatment. In Sect. 3, the type of problems that are detected in raw data streams are described. Section 4 presents the followed mitigation mechanisms that were implemented while Sect. 5 summarizes the key findings and their significance.

2 Data Treatment

Gathering and organizing unprocessed measured information can be challenging and typically involves several redundancies before it's ultimately stored in the central database. The process of obtaining measurement data involves multiple stages, such as triggering digital sensory equipment, interacting with local gateway brokers, harmonizing data points locally, and transmitting the received data-message to the designated database entity through the cloud server middleware platform. Each of these stages requires distinct devices and local firmware to manage data-messages locally. However, filtered data and cleansed datasets may increase the performance of data-intensive models and mechanisms for forecasting and situation assessment. Data cleansing is an integral part of the preprocessing level, considered of great importance before start trusting the information extracted from this same data.

As expected, the data collected from a deployed digital infrastructure (i.e., sensory equipment at the pilot sites (various countries)), may be found prune to such anomalies. After the preliminary evaluation process results, specific types of anomalies are observed in the measured time series, which render the implementation of filtering rules necessary. The implemented functional filtering pipeline, consists of statistical filtering rules for detecting, recognizing and mitigating the most common anomalies observed in the historical data, as illustrated in Fig. 1.

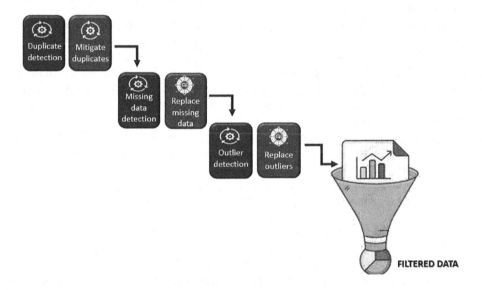

Fig. 1. Data-Filtering pipeline

2.1   Data Granularity

A sampling frequency of the sensory equipment at least equal to 5 min will result in retrieving detailed data and enable the representation of physical metrics that present almost equivalent inertia. In specific, physical metrics like indoor temperature, humidity, CO_2 saturation can be adequately represented based on a 5-minute sampling frequency even when the existing HVAC devices are fully operating (and apparently affecting their evolution through time). In addition, the inertia of metrics like energy consumption and illuminance levels are mostly affected by the control cycle frequency, which is usually set to 15 min, rendering 5-min sampling adequate once more.

3 Types of Anomalies Observed/Detected

3.1 Duplicate Data

Duplicate records are a frequent problem in centralized data management platforms, which can cause a variety of issues. In such platforms, data from multiple sources is collected, processed, and stored in a central database, making it easier to access and analyze. However, as data is collected from different sources, it is possible that the same data may be recorded multiple times, resulting in duplicate records. In the context of centralized data management platforms, duplicate records can lead to several problems. Firstly, redundant data can increase the size of the database and make it more challenging to manage. This can result in slower performance and increased storage costs, as well as difficulties in ensuring data accuracy. Moreover, duplicate records can cause data inconsistencies, leading to faulty overlaps and duplicated timestamps for the same physical metric. For instance, suppose data from two sources is recorded with slightly different timestamps, but they refer to the same physical event. In that case, duplicate records may lead to confusion about which data is accurate and which data should be discarded. This, in turn, can lead to inaccurate analysis and incorrect conclusions, which can have far-reaching consequences. Therefore, it is essential to have proper mechanisms in place to identify and remove duplicate records from the database. This can involve implementing unique identifiers for each data point, establishing data validation rules, or using automated tools to identify and remove duplicates. By doing so, centralized data management platforms can ensure data accuracy, improve performance, and prevent potential issues resulting from duplicate records.

3.2 Missing Data

There is a plethora of sensors and there exist various communication protocols and various types of sensors even of the same protocol. Each sensor reports data in a different way. Specifically, there are event-based sensors that report data when the monitored event changes status or at a predefined time interval (e.g., motion sensor reports a value every 5 min or in between if the status of the monitored room changes from absence to presence and vice versa). There are triggered-based sensors that report a value only when the status of the reported value changes, otherwise, they report nothing (i.e., door window sensor sends a value when the state of the window changes from open to close and vice versa). Other sensors are value-based and report their state if the current value is ± a default value (e.g., a temperature sensor sends temperature only if the current temperature is ± 0.02 than the previous value). Other sensors are time-based and they report a value every time interval that is set by default (e.g., an illuminance sensor reports a value every 1 min). Finally, there are constant sensors that report data constantly (i.e., energy analyser reports a value non-stop). As a result, when pushing data at a pre-defined time interval (e.g., 5 min for the monitoring) some values will be missing, as the sensor is asleep (e.g., no-event, no status change, no trigger). Furthermore, there are technical issues that prevent a sensor from sending data (e.g., poor WiFi signal, no sensor battery).

3.3   Outliers

Outliers are extreme values that deviate significantly from the average or typical values in a dataset. In a timeseries, outliers can occur due to various reasons, such as measurement errors, data corruption, or unusual events. These outliers can have a significant impact on data analysis, as they can skew the overall trends and patterns in the timeseries. Therefore, it is important to identify and handle outliers appropriately. Extraordinary data, not-following the same underlying pattern with the other data-points of the same timeseries and context, were also observed in our case, fortunately with low density, after the aforementioned two detection layers. Following up the mitigated duplicates and missing data replacement, a statistical rule for detecting the outlier data was implemented based on the rolling average of a well-defined time-window in the past. To detect low density outliers the following filtering rule, which depends on the quality of the recent past values, could be applied. In specific, to detect if a sample s_t at the tth timestep is an outlier, the implemented filter uses the past $h = 20$ samples of every physical metric respectively $S_h = s_{t-k} | k = 1, 2, \ldots, h$. Equation 1 is used to calculate the rolling average value of the specific timeseries.

$$\mu_h = E[S_h] = \frac{1}{h} \sum_{k=1}^{h} s_{t-k} \tag{1}$$

From the same subset the standard deviation is also calculated as presented in Eq. 2.

$$var_h = \frac{1}{h} \sum_{k=1}^{h} (\mu_h - s_{t-k})^2 \tag{2}$$

Finally, based on the calculations above, it is possible to define two threshold levels which decide if the s_t sample is an outlier. In particular, if $|s_t - \mu_h| \geq 2var_h$ then s_t is considered an outlier, as represented in Fig. 2, and its contribution will be omitted from the rolling average and variance calculations for its successor values (future values of the same timeseries).

4   Mitigation Mechanisms Implemented

4.1   Missing Data

As mentioned above, when trying to retrieve sensor data during a specific time interval there might be some missing values. The same occurs even if data were saved locally (e.g., at .csv format file, .json file format, local database). Consequently, specific guidelines have been established for both real-time and historical data to address this issue. Initially, a value that is not reported from any type

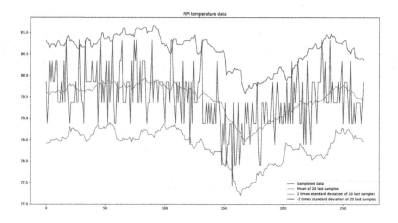

Fig. 2. Indicative indoor temperature outlier detection rule.

of the existing monitoring sensors and devises was selected to be posted when there is not a reporting value and cannot be somehow retrieved from the past (e.g., last temperature value was 3 d ago), this value was set equal to "-999". As a result, a value equal to "-999" at the retrieved Gateway .json automatically indicates that the sensor is currently operating normally but it did not report any data now and recently. If this problem insists for a long period for the same sensor, it indicates that there is a problem either with the sensor or with its default specifications and needs to be checked.

Furthermore, a value was selected to indicate that if there is no reporting value and the sensor is dead (not operating), this value was set equal to "None". Nonetheless, for all the missing values different missing data handling was followed for the historical and real time data based on the type of the sensor. Specifically, for the historical data, as the values are saved as time series, specific imputation and machine learning techniques were followed. Initially, the frequency was resampled [10] for all the saved values based on the biggest existing time interval. For example, if there were historical temperature values every half an hour, all data sets were resampled to a half an hour interval. Afterwards, the methodology followed was based on the monitored value.

For each day in the data sample, for temperature and humidity, if the missing values were less than 10% of the total daily, data interpolation and extrapolation was applied for the missing values [11]; else, "-999" was posted. For illuminance and motion detection, gaps were replaced with previous value if the gaps were more than 10% of the total daily data; else, "-999" was posted. For all energy qualities the gaps were replaced with "-999". For the real time data, a buffer was used on the local Gateway to keep past values. Therefore, if the sensor was properly operating but did not report a value for the last 2 h, the saved past value is posted. If the sensor does not report a value more than two hours, "-999" is posted. If the sensor is not operating then "None" is posted. Generally, for real time data there are no missing values posted except if there is a problem with the sensor or the network itself. All the above are summarized in Tables 1 and 2.

Table 1. Summary of methods utilized per variable for historical data

Variable	Missing values handling
Temperature	Interpolation and extrapolation
Humidity	Interpolation and extrapolation
Illuminance	Fill none with previous value
CO2	−999
Motion detection	Fill none with previous value
Energy meters	−999
Smart plugs	−999

Table 2. Summary of methods utilized per variable for real-time data

Variable	Missing values handling
Temperature	• Post previous value (sensor is alive) • None (sensor is not communicating)
Humidity	• Post previous value (sensor is alive) • None (sensor is not communicating)
Illuminance	• Post previous value (sensor is alive) • None (sensor is not communicating)
CO2	• Post previous value (sensor is alive) • None (sensor is not communicating)
Motion detection	• Post previous value (sensor is alive) • None (sensor is not communicating)
Energy meters	• -999 (sensor is alive) • None (sensor is not communicating)
Smart plugs	• -999 (sensor is alive) • None (sensor is not communicating)

4.2   Outliers

For the mitigation of the missing values in the datasets, a Neural Network (NN) with a Gated Recurrent Unit (GRU) [13] was utilized. The Gated Recurrent Unit is an advancement of the simple Recurrent Neural Network. To solve the vanishing gradient problem of a standard feed forward Recurrent Neural Network,

Gated Recurrent Units make use of an update gate and reset gate. These gates are two vectors which decide what information should be passed to the output. What's special about them is that they can be trained to keep information from long ago, without washing it through time or removing information which is irrelevant to the prediction [12]. The key distinction between simple Recurrent Neural Networks and Gated Recurrent Units is that the latter supports gating of the hidden state. This means that there are dedicated mechanisms for when a hidden state should be updated and when it should be reset. For instance, if the first token is of great importance the network learns not to update the hidden state after the first observation. Likewise, the network learns to skip irrelevant temporary observations. Lastly, it learns to reset the latest state whenever needed [12]. A Gated Recurrent Unit, at each timestamp t, takes an input X_t and the hidden state $H_{(t-1)}$ from the previous timestamp $t-1$. Later it outputs a new hidden state H_t which is again passed to the next timestamp.

To train the GRU models, the filtered historical and monitoring data from each pilot were utilized. Specifically, three models were created for each pilot, with each model designed to heal a particular data type. The models were trained using a set of features, which are as follows:

Table 3. Training results

Model	Mean Squared Error	Mean Absolute Error
Greece Indoor Temperature	0.015	0.0301
Greece Indoor Relative Humidity	0.0021	0.0350
Greece Indoor Carbon Dioxide	0.000176	0.0048
Germany Indoor Temperature	0.0030	0.0421
Germany Indoor Relative Humidity	0.0106	0.0816
Germany Indoor Carbon Dioxide	0.0011	0.0097
England Indoor Temperature	0.0012	0.0248
England Indoor Relative Humidity	0.0032	0.0488
England Indoor Carbon Dioxide	0.0021	0.0423
Spain Indoor Temperature	5.211E-12	1.84E-06
Spain Indoor Carbon Dioxide	0.005	0.0341
Spain Indoor Relative Humidity	0.0023	0.0075

– ("Indoor Temperature [C]", "Year", "Month", "Day", "Hour", "Minutes", "week-day"), for the training of the Indoor Temperature imputation models,
– ("Indoor Relative Humidity [%]", "Year", "Month", "Day", "Hour", "Minutes", "weekday"), for the training of the Indoor Relative Humidity Imputation models,

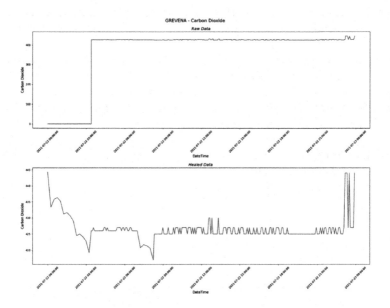

Fig. 3. Healed Carbon Dioxide data for the Greek pilot.

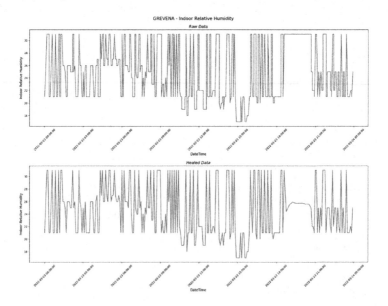

Fig. 4. Healed Indoor Relative Humidity data for the Greek pilot.

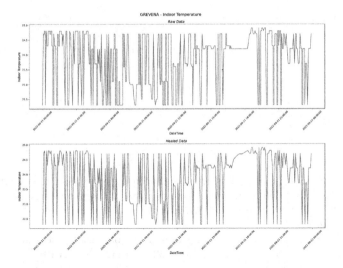

Fig. 5. Healed Indoor Temperature data for the Greek pilot.

- ("Carbon Dioxide [ppm]", "Year", "Month", "Day", "Hour", "Minutes", "week-day"), for the training of the Carbon Dioxide Imputation models.

All the previously mentioned models utilized a lookback period of 100 samples and 5 lagged values. This resulted in the input layer having a shape of (None, 100, 12). The second layer added to the models was an Encoder Bidirectional GRU Layer, which had a "tanh" activation function. Following that, the third layer added to the models was a Repeat Vector Layer. The fourth layer was a Decoder Bidirectional GRU Layer, which also had a "tanh" activation function. Finally, the output layer was a Time Distributed Dense Layer with a "linear" activation function. During training, the "adam" optimizer was used, and the loss function was "mean squared error". The models were trained for 20 epochs. The accuracy of the trained models is summarized in Table 3.

The imputation results for all the pilot sites are depicted in Figs. 3, 4 and 5.

5   Conclusions

In summary, raw data generated by IoT devices can be challenging to work with due to various issues such as errors, duplicates, and inconsistencies. To address these challenges, a holistic data treatment framework is proposed for Smart IoT Monitoring. The suggested pipeline includes removing errors, inconsistencies, and duplicates, as well as data validation and transformation. Missing data values can be estimated using available data, and outlier healing techniques can be used to identify and deal with data points that are significantly different from other data points in the dataset. By following these procedures, the accuracy and reliability of analysis results can be improved, and decision-making can be supported with more confidence.

Acknowledgements. This work is partially supported by the PRECEPT project funded by the European Union's Horizon 2020 under Grant Agreement No. 958284 https://www.precept-project.eu/ and the SMART2B https://smart2b-project.eu/ project funded by the European Union's Horizon 2020 under Grant Agreement 101023666.

References

1. Qolomany, B., et al.: Leveraging machine learning and big data for smart buildings: a comprehensive survey. IEEE Access **7**, 90316–90356 (2019)
2. King, J.: Energy impacts of smart home technologies. Report A1801 (2018)
3. Dimara, A., et al.: NRG4-U: a novel home energy management system for a unique loadprofile. Energy Sources, Part A: Recovery, Utilization Environ. Effects **44**(1), 353–378 (2022)
4. Zhao, X., et al.: Reliable IoT storage: minimizing bandwidth use in storage without newcomer nodes. IEEE Commun. Lett. **22**(7), 1462–1465 (2018)
5. Hiller, J., et al.: Secure low latency communication for constrained industrial IoT scenarios. In: 2018 IEEE 43rd Conference on Local Computer Networks (LCN). IEEE (2018)
6. Sadeeq, M.M., et al.: IoT and Cloud computing issues, challenges and opportunities: a review. Qubahan Acad. J. **1**(2), 1–7 (2021)
7. Krishnamurthi, R., et al.: An overview of IoT sensor data processing, fusion, and analysis techniques. Sensors **20**(21), 6076 (2020)
8. Dimara, A., et al.: Self-healing of semantically interoperable smart and prescriptive edge devices in IoT. Appl. Sci. **12**(22), 11650 (2022)
9. Almusaylim, Z.A., Zaman, N.: A review on smart home present state and challenges: linked to context-awareness internet of things (IoT). Wireless Netw. **25**, 3193–3204 (2019)
10. Liu, S., Yuan, Y., Yu, J., She, D., Wang, K.: On-the-fly interpolation of continuous temperature-dependent thermal neutron scattering data in RMC code. In: EPJ Web of Conferences, EDP Sciences, vol. 247 (2021)
11. One Click LCA Ltd., «One Click LCA,»[En línea]. Available: https://www.oneclicklca.com/
12. Dey, R., Salem, F.M.: Gate-variants of Gated Recurrent Unit (GRU) neural networks. In: 2017 IEEE 60th International Midwest Symposium on Circuits and Systems (MWSCAS), Boston, MA, USA, 2017, pp. 1597–1600. https://doi.org/10.1109/MWSCAS.2017.8053243
13. Li, C., Xiao, F., Fan, Y.: An approach to state of charge estimation of lithium-ion batteries based on recurrent neural networks with gated recurrent unit. Energies **12**(9), 1592 (2019)

Realtime Multi-factor Dynamic Thermal Comfort Estimation for Indoor Environments

Georgia Tzitziou[1], Asimina Dimara[1,2(✉)], Alexios Papaioannou[1,3],
Christos Tzouvaras[2,4], Stelios Krinidis[1,3], Christos-Nikolaos Anagnostopoulos[2],
Dimosthenis Ioannidis[1], and Dimitrios Tzovaras[1]

[1] Information Technologies Institute (ITI), Centre for Research
Technology (CERTH), Thessaloniki, Greece
{tzitzioug,adimara,alexiopa,krinidis,djoannid,Dimitrios.Tzovaras}@iti.gr
[2] Department of Cultural Technology and Communication, Intelligent Systems Lab,
University of the Aegean (UoA), Mytilene, Greece
canag@aegean.gr
[3] Management Science and Technology Department, International Hellenic
University (IHU), Kavala, Greece
[4] WATT AND VOLT, Anonimi Etairia Ekmetalleysis, Enallaktikon Morfon
Energeias, Athens, Greece
ch.tzouvaras@watt-volt.gr

Abstract. Thermal comfort models are mathematical representations
that simulate the thermal environment and predict human comfort based
on various factors such as air temperature, air velocity, relative humidity,
and radiation heat transfer. These models are used to design and evaluate heating, ventilation, and air conditioning systems, buildings, and
outdoor spaces. The main issue when exploiting predicted mean vote
(PMV) and predicted percentage of dissatisfied (PPD) and model for
thermal comfort estimation is how to estimate clothing insulation and
metabolic rate as accurately as possible. In this paper, a novel approach
for calculating thermal comfort is presented that combines algorithms
to enhance the precision of existing approaches. Experimental results
showcase the suggested method is more accurate than other approaches.

Keywords: Thermal comfort · Indoor environmental conditions ·
Personal factors

1 Introduction

Looking at people's daily lives, their timeless connection with the residence they
have chosen to live in may be observed. One of the main factors influencing
this interaction's quality is the thermal sensation inside the residence. In recent
years, the factors that influence the internal temperature of a building and how
they are taken into account to give us thermal comfort have been studied to a

© IFIP International Federation for Information Processing 2023
Published by Springer Nature Switzerland AG 2023
I. Maglogiannis et al. (Eds.): AIAI 2023 Workshops, IFIP AICT 677, pp. 219–230, 2023.
https://doi.org/10.1007/978-3-031-34171-7_17

large extent [1]. The importance of thermal comfort is extended even in early building stages like the design phase till further stages like renovation.

Thermal comfort, as defined by ISO standard 7730 [2], is the state of being satisfied with one's thermal environment. Thermal comfort models are mathematical representations that simulate the thermal environment and predict human comfort based on various factors such as air temperature, air velocity, relative humidity, and radiation heat transfer. These models use different methods and algorithms to estimate thermal comfort and are used to design and evaluate heating, ventilation, and air conditioning (HVAC) systems, buildings, and outdoor spaces. Some common thermal comfort models include the PMV (Predicted Mean Vote) and PPD (Predicted Percentage of Dissatisfied), the Adaptive model, and the Transfer Function model [3].

The research community is continually seeking the best thermal comfort model for estimating the ideal living conditions in buildings. Fanger's *PMV* model (*PredictedMeanVote*) is widely considered one of the most comprehensive and accurate thermal comfort models available. There are several reasons why the *PMV* model is considered better than other models [4]:

– Accounts for many factors that affect thermal comfort, such as air temperature, air velocity, relative humidity, and clothing insulation. This makes the *PMV* model more accurate and relevant compared to models that consider only a few factors.
– It is widely used and accepted in the residential sector and is established as the standard for the prediction of thermal comfort under the International ISO 7730 standard [2].
– It is relatively easy to use, with clear instructions for estimating the *PMV* index and thermal comfort based on index values.
– Has been proven to reliably estimate human thermal comfort in a wide range of situations, making it a dependable tool for evaluating and planning HVAC systems, buildings, and outdoor spaces.

These elements combine to make *PMV* an effective and trustworthy tool for forecasting thermal comfort, and these are some of the reasons why it is seen to be superior to other models. Based on ASHRAE, a fast and high-accuracy function has been developed that calculates the predicted mean vote (*PMV*) and the predicted percentage of satisfied (PPD) [5, 6].

The input variables of the model, such as dry bulb air temperature, mean radiant temperature, average air speed, and relative humidity, can be measured accurately through sensor installation. However, there are no standard real-time methods to calculate the metabolic rate and clothing insulation of people habiting inside the building. The temperature inside a building greatly affects the type of clothing one wears [7]. Furthermore, the variation in clothing insulation values is attributable to the fact that what we wear is influenced by factors other than temperature, such as gender, age, and cold and heat tolerance [7]. In addition, temperature plays an important role in the determination of metabolic rate [7]. The behavior of building occupants is difficult to predict, model, or calculate due to the complexity of humans. Furthermore, the absence of established standards and protocols for data collection, as well as the precision of data, pose difficulties in the field of building occupant research [8].

As a result, the main issue when exploiting the *PMV* and *PPD* model for thermal comfort estimation is how to estimate clothing insulation and metabolic rate as accurately as possible. Within this context, the aim of this paper is to present a novel approach by fusing widely used methodologies [7], one for the determination of clothing insulation and one for the determination of metabolic rate. The main objective is to mitigate the error in estimating personal factors by taking into account as many factors as possible, such as indoor and outdoor conditions.

The remainder of this paper is organized as follows: In Sect. 2 the way the thermal comfort is estimated is suggested, highlighting a novel approach for estimating the personal factors. Section 3 presents the experiment set up along with the results. Finally, in Sect. 4, conclusions are drawn.

2   Methodology

In this section, a novel approach for calculating thermal comfort is presented that combines algorithms to enhance the precision of existing approaches. A tool that would provide real-time, practical, and accurate thermal comfort estimation is suggested.

2.1   Thermal Comfort Inference

As addressed in the Introduction, Fanger's Predicted Mean Vote (*PMV*) and Predicted Percentage of Dissatisfied (*PPD*) model is widely used to estimate thermal comfort. The models are specified through a set of equations that are outlined below [9,10]:

$$PPD = 100 - 95 \cdot e^{-(0.03353 \cdot PMV^4 + 0.2179 \cdot PMV^2)} \tag{1}$$

$$PMV = (0.303 \cdot e^{-0.036 \cdot M} + 0.028) \cdot L \tag{2}$$

$$L = M - W \tag{3}$$

$$M - W = C + R + E_{sk} + (C_{res} + E_{res}) \tag{4}$$

$$C = f_{cl} \cdot h_c \cdot (T_{cl} - T_a) \tag{5}$$

$$R = \sigma \cdot \varepsilon_{cl} \cdot f_{cl} \cdot F_{vf} \cdot \left[(T_{cl} + 273.15)^4 - (T_r + 273.15)^4 \right] \tag{6}$$

$$C_{res} + E_{res} = 0.014 \cdot M \cdot (34 - T_a)$$
$$+ 0.0173 \cdot M \cdot (5.87 - P_a) \tag{7}$$

$$E_{sk} = 3.05 \cdot (5.73 - 0.007 \cdot M - P_a) + 0.42 \cdot (M - 58.15)) \tag{8}$$

All the used variables are briefly explained in Table 1 [13]. Finally, to estimate the thermal comfort based on the above equations the factors needed to estimate real-time PMV are [12]:

$$PMV = f(T_a, RH, I_{cl}, M), \tag{9}$$

where T_a refers to room temperature, RH refers to room humidity, I_{cl} and M refer to clothing insulation and metabolic rate respectively.

Room environmental conditions (i.e., T_a, RH) may be retrieved from indoor temperature and humidity sensors while estimating the personal factors may be proven to be a thorny problem [12]. Even though values for the personal factors may be retrieved from the ASHRAE table, an estimation of I_{cl} and M values based solely on the ASHRAE table may generate a significant mistake during thermal comfort estimation [14, 15]. As a result, another approach for estimating personal factors should be followed.

Table 1. PMV and PPD variables

Variable	Meaning	Unit
W	external work	W/m^2
M	metabolic rate (internal energy production)	W/m^2
C	heat loss by convection	W/m^2
R	heat loss by thermal radiation	W/m^2
E_{sk}	heat loss by evaporation from the skin	W/m^2
C_{res}	sensible heat loss due to respiration	W/m^2
E_{res}	heat loss by evaporation from the skin	W/m^2
T_{cl}	clothing surface temperature	$^\circ C$
T_a	ambient air temperature (indoor)	$^\circ C$
h_c	heat transfer coefficient	$W/m^2 \cdot K$
V_a	air velocity	m/s
f_{cl}	clothing area factor	clo
ε_{cl}	emmisivity of clothing	
F_{vf}	view factor between the body and the surrounding	
σ	Stefan Boltzmann constant [11]	$W/m^2 \cdot K^4$
T_r	radiant temperature	$^\circ C$
P_a	partial vapour pressure	P_a
RH	relative humidity	$\%$
I_{cl}	thermal insulation of clothing	clo

2.2   Clothing Insulation Estimation

Indoor temperature is an essential factor in clothing worn inside buildings, as suggested by the non-linear regression relationship between clothing insulation and indoor temperatures based on feedback observations in [7]. In this paper [7], an equation is used to calculate the insulation of clothing based on the temperature inside a room:

$$Cl_{T_{in}} = f(T_a) = 89.279(T_a)^{-1.592} \tag{10}$$

Additionally, the influence of season on clothing insulation is significant in determining thermal comfort, as individuals require different levels of insulation in their clothing to maintain comfort in different seasons [18]. During colder seasons, individuals require more insulation to keep warm, while during warmer seasons, individuals require less insulation to avoid overheating [21]. There are some standard values that correspond to each season, such as the 'Typical summer indoor clothing' equal to 0.5 and the 'Typical winter indoor clothing' equal to 1.0. A year is separated into four periods on the basis of seasonality. Each season is represented by average clothing insulation and the clothing insulation by season Cl_s is depicted in Fig. 1.

Fig. 1. Cl_s: Average clothing insulation by season values

The insulation value of clothing can also be expressed as representative of a particular clothing ensemble as a function of the outdoor temperature [18].

$$Cl_{T_{out}} = 2.1 \cdot 10^{-5}T_{out}^3 + 8 \cdot 10^{-4}T_{out}^2 - 0.0282T_{out} + 0.8167 \tag{11}$$

where T_{out} is the outdoor temperature expressed in ^oC. This equation is determining the Icl insulation of clothing based on real-time values.

There is a method that combines the $Cl_{T_{in}}$ and the Cl_s to estimate total clothing insulation as [12]:

$$I_{cl} = wCl_s + (1 - w)Cl_{T_{in}}, \tag{12}$$

this method was tested in real-life environments and has proven to be accurate enough. Nonetheless, this method may produce a significant error during periods of time when the outdoor temperature is extremely high or low than the average seasonal outdoor temperatures (e.g., during spring outdoor temperatures can be more than 25 °C or less than 10 °C). As a result, in this paper, we suggest a new method that will "correct" this specific error by combining all temperature factors. The insulation value of clothing is:

$$I_{cl} = aCl_s + bCl_{T_{in}} + (1 - a - b)Cl_{T_{out}}. \tag{13}$$

During an experimental phase, the values of a and b were set to $a = 0.5$ and $b = 0.25$.

Finally, when estimating the clothing insulation of a person in motion, it is important to account for the dynamic nature of the insulation, which is affected by both the individual's activity level and the air speed around them. As per the ISO 7730 standard, it is necessary to correct for these factors [2]. Similarly, the ASHRAE 55 Standard provides a correction equation for body movement for activities with a metabolic rate of 1.2 met or higher, expressed as:

$$I_{cl} = I_{cl}(0.6 + \frac{0.4}{met}), \tag{14}$$

2.3   Metabolic Rate

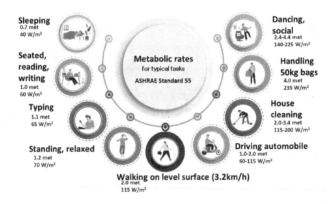

Fig. 2. Metabolic rates for typical tasks ASHRAE Standard 55 [17]

The metabolic rate that corresponds to the ideal level of comfort ranges from 84.8 W/m² to 89.9 W/m². This range is determined based on occupants' feedback who reported feeling thermally comfortable during a survey [16]. According to the ASHRAE metabolic rate table in Fig. 2, this range of activity is classified as low-level activity, similar to activities such as standing or relaxing. It appears that low-level activities are more feasible in a household setting, while more strenuous activities such as cleaning the house are not so frequent [16]. As a result, the metabolic rate could be set to low-level activities (that is, 70–80 W/m² or 1.2 *met*), such as standing and relaxed activities. During the night, the activity can be set to sleep (that is, 40 W/m² or 0.7 *met*).

2.4   Overall System

The overall conceptual architecture of the system suggested in Sect. 2 is depicted in Fig. 3. The sensors push real-time indoor environmental conditions to be utilized for both thermal comfort and clothing insulation estimation. The date and time are utilized for the estimation of metabolic rate and clothing estimation. In addition, outdoor conditions are utilized for clothing insulation. It may be observed how clothing insulation is estimated through a multifactor process.

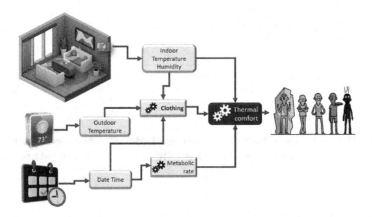

Fig. 3. Thermal comfort estimation conceptual architecture

3   Results

In this section, the results of the suggested methodology of thermal comfort estimation will be presented. Initially, how the experiment was set up will be discussed. Finally, experimental results will be showcased in the last subsection.

3.1   Experiment Set up

To test the suggested methodology as described in Sect. 2, data from the CERTH.ITI smart-home were exploited [19]. Data from a temperature humidity sensor (i.e., [20]) were retrieved. Values from a specific room for a year (i.e., temperature, humidity) were utilized for the tests (Fig. 4).

The average values during the tested period are presented in Table 2.

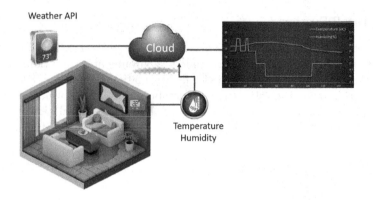

Fig. 4. Thermal comfort set up experiment

Table 2. Data-set average values

Month	Average Indoor Temperature °C	Average Indoor Humidity %	Average Outdoor Temperature °C
January	17.96	28	8.5
February	18.23	29.11	10.7
March	20.23	30.3	14.3
April	22.5	27.5	18.6
May	22.5	32.3	17.3
June	25.1	34.5	17.9
July	26.2	33.6	20.1
August	28.1	38.8	20.8
September	27	23.8	18.5
October	24.3	20.5	17.3
November	22.96	27.1	15.7
December	23.4	28.6	10.1

3.2   Experimental Results

In this section, some indicative results will be presented, one for each season. In the following graphs, real-time values of indoor and outdoor temperatures from the CERTH.ITI smart-home [19], along with the values of the PMV calculated with the two methods will be presented. $PMVold$ value based on Equation (12) and the $PMVnew$ value based on Eq. (13). The graph for each of the four seasons (i.e., Spring, Summer, Fall, and Winter), depicts a representative day from each season. When analyzing the following graphs two facts must be considered. First, the indoor temperature tends to stay more constant than the outdoor temperature and therefore closer to the average seasonal temperature, for reasons such as insulation of the building, heating and cooling systems, and solar radiation. Second, in terms of the thermal sensation scale in Fig. 5, as the *PMV* value is closer to 0 there is a better thermal sensation, and it is expected that in the summer season, it tends to go higher, where in the winter season it is lower.

Fig. 5. Thermal Sensation Scale

Figure 6 depicts values from April 13th, 2022 during the spring season. Outdoor temperatures may be observed to fall below average spring temperatures (e.g., average below 12 ^{o}C). As a result, the line of the PMV value calculated with the new equation is lower than the other, meaning that the resident is feeling colder. While the outdoor and indoor temperature increases, the deviation between the two PMV values is smaller.

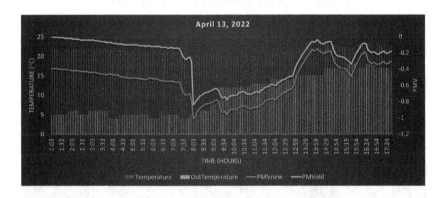

Fig. 6. Thermal comfort comparison for Spring

Figure 7 shows values from July 13th, 2022 during the summer season. On this day, outdoor temperatures are very close to indoor ones. So, here the fact that the PMV values calculated with the new equation are closer to 0, means that there is a better thermal sensation compared to the old one, as expected.

Following up, in the winter season, Fig. 8 depicts the data values for the day of December 28, 2022. The first thing that becomes apparent is that the line based on the old equation takes values higher than 0, which is in contrast to previous acknowledgments.

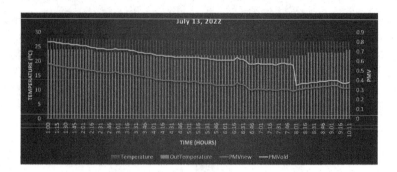

Fig. 7. Thermal comfort comparison for Summer

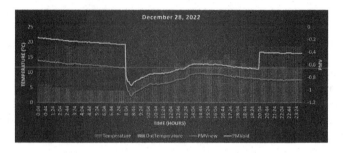

Fig. 8. Thermal comfort comparison for Winter

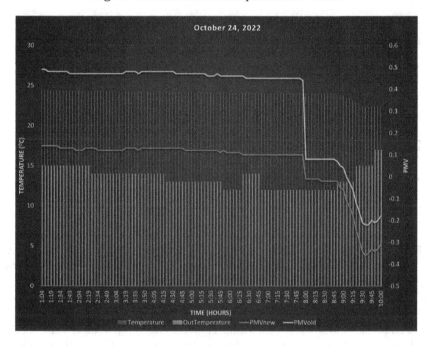

Fig. 9. Thermal comfort comparison for Fall

Finally, during the fall season, Fig. 9 depicts the values from October 24th, 2022. In this case, outdoor temperature values are far below the indoor ones and this leads to the conclusion that the line base on the new equation is more accurate.

4   Conclusions

In general, thermal comfort is an important factor in building occupants' behavior, which is difficult to predict, model, or calculate due to the complexity of humans. In this paper, a novel approach for calculating thermal comfort was presented that combines algorithms to enhance the precision of existing approaches. The proposed methodology was tested in real-time environments and has proven to be accurate enough.

The analyses of the graphs lead to the conclusion that when the outdoor and indoor temperatures are close, the new PMV values are more comparable to the optimum thermal sensation. Furthermore, the old method may produce a significant error in the thermal comfort calculation when the outdoor temperature is extremely higher or lower than the average seasonal outdoor temperature and consequently the indoor temperatures.

In summary, the proposed approach has shown promising results and could have significant implications for improving building occupant comfort and energy efficiency. However, to further improve the accuracy and applicability of the method, additional steps such as conducting validation tests in different settings, integrating the methodology with building automation systems, incorporating other factors that impact thermal comfort, and considering user feedback and perception should be taken into account.

Acknowledgements. This work is partially supported by the PRECEPT project funded by the EU H2020 under Grant Agreement No. 958284.

References

1. Sansaniwal, S.K., Mathur, J., Mathur, S.: Review of practices for human thermal comfort in buildings: present and future perspectives. Int. J. Ambient Energy **43**(1), 2097–2123 (2022)
2. ISO, ISO7730: 7730: Ergonomics of the thermal environment analytical determination and interpretation of thermal comfort using calculation of the PMV and PPD indices and local thermal comfort criteria. Management 3(605), e615 (2005)
3. OpenAI: Thermal Comfort Models. OpenAI (2023). openai.com/thermal-comfort-models/
4. Lourenço Niza, I., Broday, E.E.: Development of thermal comfort models over the past years: a systematic literature review. Int. J. Ambient Energy **43**(1), 8830–8846 (2022)
5. ANSI and ASHRAE, Thermal Environmental Conditions for Human Occupancy. Atlanta (2020)

6. Tartarini, F., Schiavon, S.: Pythermalcomfort: a Python package for thermal comfort research. SoftwareX **12**, 100578. Elsevier BV (2020). Crossref, https://doi.org/10.1016/j.softx.2020.100578

7. Dimara, A., Timplalexis, C., Krinidis, S., Tzovaras, D.: A dynamic convergence algorithm for thermal comfort modelling. In: Tzovaras, D., Giakoumis, D., Vincze, M., Argyros, A. (eds.) ICVS 2019. LNCS, vol. 11754, pp. 680–689. Springer, Cham (2019). https://doi.org/10.1007/978-3-030-34995-0_62

8. Harputlugil, T., de Wilde, P.: The interaction between humans and buildings for energy efficiency: a critical review. Energy Res. Soc. Sci. **71**, 101828 (2021)

9. Dimara, A., Krinidis, S., Tzovaras, D.: Comfit: a novel indoor comfort inference tool, 165–170 (2021)

10. Krinidis, S., et al.: Multi-criteria HVAC control optimization. In: 2018 IEEE International Energy Conference (ENERGYCON). IEEE (2018)

11. Peeters, L., et al.: Thermal comfort in residential buildings: comfort values and scales for building energy simulation. Appl. Energy **86**)(5), 772–780 (2009)

12. Dimara, A., et al.: NRG4-U: a novel home energy management system for a unique loadprofile. Energy Sources Part A: Recov. Utilization Environ. Effects **44**(1), 353–378 (2022)

13. Oğulata, R.T.: The effect of thermal insulation of clothing on human thermal comfort. Fibres Textiles Eastern Europe **15**(2), 67–72 (2007)

14. Havenith, G., Holmér, I., Parsons, K.: Personal factors in thermal comfort assessment: clothing properties and metabolic heat production. Energy Build. **34**(6), 581–591 (2002)

15. Luo, M., et al.: Human metabolic rate and thermal comfort in buildings: the problem and challenge. Build. Environ. **131**, 44–52 (2018)

16. Dimara, A., et al.: Optimal comfort conditions in residential houses. In: 2020 5th International Conference on Smart and Sustainable Technologies (SpliTech). IEEE (2020)

17. Arendt, K.: Influence of external walls' thermal capacitance on indoor thermal comfort (2013)

18. Schiavon, S., Lee, K.H.: Dynamic predictive clothing insulation models based on outdoor air and indoor operative temperatures. Build. Environ. **59**, 250–260 (2013). https://doi.org/10.1016/j.buildenv.2012.08.024

19. ITI Smart Home CERTH.ITI. https://smarthome.iti.gr/

20. Tuya ZigBee Temperature and Humidity Sensor. https://www.expert4house.com/en/smart-home/sensors-and-detectors/tuya-zigbee-temperature-and-humidity-sensor

21. Kwon, J.Y., Choi, J.: Clothing insulation and temperature, layer and mass of clothing under comfortable environmental conditions. J. Physiol. Anthropol. **32**(1) (2013). https://doi.org/10.1186/1880-6805-32-11

Self-protection of IoT Gateways Against Breakdowns and Failures Enabling Automated Sensing and Control

Alexios Papaioannou[1,2], Asimina Dimara[1,3(✉)], Iakovos Michailidis[1], Aliki Stefanopoulou[1], Georgios Karatzinis[1], Stelios Krinidis[1,2], Christos-Nikolaos Anagnostopoulos[3], Elias Kosmatopoulos[1], Dimosthenis Ioannidis[1], and Dimitrios Tzovaras[1]

[1] Information Technologies Institute (ITI), Centre for Research Technology (CERTH), Thessaloniki, Greece
{alexiopa,adimara,michaild,alikstef,gkaratzi,krinidis,
kosmatop,djoannid,Dimitrios.Tzovaras}@iti.gr
[2] Management Science and Technology Department, International Hellenic University (IHU), Kavala, Greece
[3] Department of Cultural Technology and Communication, Intelligent Systems Lab, University of the Aegean (UoA), Mytilene, Greece
canag@aegean.gr

Abstract. Smart home IoT technologies have provided a new level of overall degrees of control freedom over modern homes. The core of such a system is an edge device. In this paper, a CNN-based LSTM-Autoencoder method is presented to detect anomaly points in five critical operating parameters of an edge device while managing its perpetual operation. This proposed method is based on a hybrid model using 1D-CNN layers in the encoder layer and LSTM layers in the decoder layer. Experiments were conducted using real data from Raspberry Pi devices. Compared to other state-of-the-art methods, the proposed approach had a remarkable accuracy close to 0.996 and an execution time of 312 ms.

Keywords: Smart Home devices · IoT protection · Error Analysis · Failure Diagnosis

1 Introduction

A smart home refers to an automation system that interlinks our devices and appliances to automate particular chores and is often able to be operated from a distance (remotely). Sprinklers, cameras, sensors, power switches and home security systems may all be programmed using a smart home system, along with other domestic appliances like air conditioners and heaters [1]. Smart homes have enough functional flexibility and capacity to become energy-efficient and reduce carbon footprint through automation; saving also valuable programming time and waste of money. The first generation of smart homes focused more on

© IFIP International Federation for Information Processing 2023
Published by Springer Nature Switzerland AG 2023
I. Maglogiannis et al. (Eds.): AIAI 2023 Workshops, IFIP AICT 677, pp. 231–241, 2023.
https://doi.org/10.1007/978-3-031-34171-7_18

automation and remote control than intelligence [2]. A decade ago, all that was required to qualify as a smart home was an automated - usually rule-based environment - where you could automatically control simple operations e.g., blinders, lights, etc. with your smartphone or program your thermostat to recall your preferred temperature.

Nowadays, there is an entirely new degree of control freedom over household appliances, thanks to smart home IoT technology [3]. The entire functioning of smart applications can be fully automated, advancing many steps when compared to the simplistic switching/regulation of home equipment. IoT has emerged thanks to ongoing advances in micro-processing systems, interoperable connectors, open communication protocols that transform ordinary homes into smart ones. Sensors, actuators, control hubs, communication networks, and other hardware components make up the smart home system [4]. As a result, a variety of sensors are utilized to gather information about the indoor environment.

Such a system (Fig. 1 [5]), apart from the sensors, includes a Gateway or edge device (e.g., Rasberry Pi (Rpi), mini PC). The edge gateway device is the core of the system and the one responsible for retrieving and pushing all IoT devices data to a selected end-point. As a result, its operation should be perpetual while short failures and drop-downs must be detected soon to recover the system. If the edge device is not operating properly the IoT network will fail to fulfil its purpose. Within this context, it is really important to detect edge devices' breakdowns and failures as soon as possible, even proactively, to take informative recovery actions.

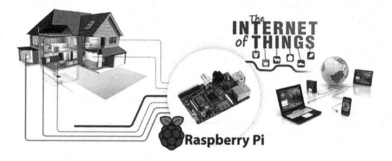

Fig. 1. Smart home IoT conceptual architecture

To detect malfunctions at the IoT network edge, an error analysis or error detection technique must be applied. Finding unusual occurrences or observations that drastically depart from the majority of the data is known as anomaly detection [6]. Anomalies for time series are categorized into three categories in the literature: point anomaly, contextual Anomaly and collective Anomaly [7]. There are various techniques and methodologies for data detection like reconstruction error, prediction error and dissimilarity [8]. Moreover, there are a plethora of models like Autoregressive Moving Average, Recurrent Neural Networks, Long short-term memory and Variational Autoencoders [9].

In the present study, to ensure that an edge will be operating smoothly and that the end-user will be informed to take some actions to prevent breakdowns, self-protection of IoT edges against breakdowns and failures is performed. In this perspective, an innovative CNN-based LSTM-Autoencoder is presented in this paper to detect anomaly points in five critical operating parameters of an edge device.

The remainder of the paper is set up as follows: Sect. 2 analyzes the methodology followed in the current study, highlighting the anomalies detection method utilized. Section 4 discusses the results during an experimental phase while the findings are summarized in the last section.

2   Methodology of Autoencoder-Based Anomaly Detection

2.1   LSTM Autoencoder

An autoencoder is a type of neural network that aims to extract a compressed representation from input data. It is an unsupervised method, although it is trained using supervised learning methods, referred to as self-supervised. Normally it consists of encoder layers that receive data from the input layer and compress them into the latent space and decoder layers which decompresses the output from the encoder and transmits them to the output layer [10]. The encoder layer can be described in detail using the following equation:

$$h_i = f_\theta(x) = s(\sum_n^{j=1} W_{ij}^{input} x_j + b_{input}), \tag{1}$$

where x is the input vector with $x \in \mathbb{R}^d$, θ is the parameters $\{W^{input}, b^{input}\}$, W is the encoder weight matrix with dimension $m * d$, $(m < d)$ and b is the bias.

Following, the decoder layer can be described:

$$x_i' = g_\theta'(h) = s(\sum_n^{j=1} W_{ij}^{hidden} h_j + b_{hidden}), \tag{2}$$

where the parameter set of the decoder is $\theta = \{W^{hidden}, b^{hidden}\}$.

LSTM is a special type of RNN, consisting of a number of interconnected units at each level, introduced by Hochreiter and Schmidhuber in 1997 [14]. It consists of one or more interconnected memory cells, input, output and forget gates. The main concept of the LSTM is described in the following equations:

$$i^t = \sigma(W^i x^t + V^i h^{t-1} + b^i), \tag{3}$$

$$f^t = \sigma(W^f x^t + V^f h^{t-1} + b^f), \tag{4}$$

$$o^t = \sigma(W^o x^t + V^o h^{t-1} + b^o), \tag{5}$$

$$c^t = f^t \odot c^{t-1} + i^t \odot \tanh(W^c x^t + V^c h^{t-1} + b^c), \qquad (6)$$

$$h^t = o^t \odot \tanh(c^t), \qquad (7)$$

where t is the time step, h^t the hidden state at time t, x^t the data at time t, h^{t-1} the hidden state at previous time, i^t the input gate, f^t the forget gate, o^t the output gate and c^t is a memory cell. Additionally, $W \in \mathbb{R}^{d*k}$, $V \in \mathbb{R}^{d*d}$, $b \in \mathbb{R}^d$, σ is the sigmoid function, $\odot$ denotes the element-wise product and k is a hyper-parameter that represents the dimensionality of hidden vectors.

2.2 CNN-Based LSTM-Autoencoder

CNN is a feed-forward deep neural network that is most commonly used in a variety of applications such as image and video recognition, image classification and recommender systems [15]. CNN which is used to analyze visual imagery does not directly support sequence input due to the 2D structure. However, 1D-CNN is capable of reading across sequence input and identifying the key features.

A hybrid model using 1D-CNN layers in the encoder layer and LSTM layers in the decoder layer is presented in this paper. Figure 2, illustrates the proposed methodology. Two 1D-CNN modules were used in the Encoder layer with 64 filters each one and kernel size of one time step. The first CNN reads through the input sequence and projects the observations onto feature maps. The second CNN module performs the same functionality on the feature maps exported by the first layer, attempting to recognize any notable features.

Subsequently, a 1D Max pooling layer was applied to the feature maps, keeping 1/4 of the values with the largest signal. A flatten layer was added to convert the output from the pooling layer to a single vector that then can be used as input to the decoding process. The decoder layer included two LSTM modules with 128 units each one. The output from the LSTM modules was used as input in the Time Distributed and Dense layer which exports the reconstructed time series. Finally, the real time series and the reconstructed time series for each feature are compared, and if the deviation exceeds a predetermined threshold, the point is classified as an anomaly point.

2.3 Framework of Anomaly Detection

The framework used for anomaly detection points using AEs consists of two phases; the training and the detection phase. The training phase includes:

- Data preprocessing: Five features regarding the IoT device were selected including, the CPU usage and temperature, the disk usage, the virtual memory usage and the power consumption of the device. Missing values or outliers were replaced with previous values and a scaling method was applied in order to pre-scale all the features into a specific interval. In this paper, the Standardization method was used to shift the distribution of data to have a mean

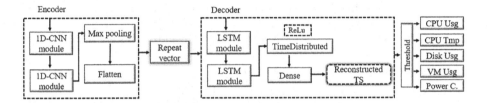

Fig. 2. Proposed CNN-Based LSTM-Autoencoder

of zero and a standard deviation of one. The following equation describes the method

$$X_{scaled} = \frac{X - mean}{StandardDeviation}. \qquad (8)$$

Subsequently, the scaled data is then transformed into [samples, time steps, and features] in order to be used as input in the autoencoder.

– Autoencoder training: Output data from the preprocessing phase is used as input in the training phase. For the proposed autoencoder the Adam optimizer was used to minimize the average reconstruction error [11]. Additionally, the mean squared error was used as a loss function.

The detection phase includes the execution of the autoencoder and the calculation of the error between the actual and predicted time series. The error is calculated using the mean absolute error (MAE) of the predicted value, $\hat{x}$ and the true one x [12]:

$$MAE = \sum_{i=1}^{D} |x - \hat{x}|. \qquad (9)$$

Additionally, a threshold value had to be set to classify the data as normal or anomaly points. In this paper as the output of the MAE follows a normal distribution the following equation was used to calculate the threshold value [13].

$$Threshold\_value = mean(MAE) + confidence\_interval * std(MAE) \qquad (10)$$

3   Results

In this section, the devices which were used to collect the dataset are described as well as the used dataset and the evaluation metrics. Additionally, the experimental results along with a comparison to the state-of-art methods are presented.

Table 1. Raspberry Pi 4 Model B specifications

Processor	Broadcom BCM2711, quad-core Cortex-A72 (ARM v8) 64-bit SoC @ 1.5 GHz
Memory	4 GB LPDDR4
Connectivity	2.4 GHz and 5.0 GHz IEEE 802.11b/g/n/ac wireless LAN, Bluetooth 5.0, BLE Gigabit Ethernet 2 × USB 3.0 ports 2 × USB 2.0 ports.
GPIO	Standard 40-pin GPIO header (fully backwards-compatible with previous boards)
Video & sound	2 × micro HDMI ports (up to 4Kp60 supported) 2-lane MIPI DSI display port 2-lane MIPI CSI camera port 4-pole stereo audio and composite video port
Multimedia	H.265 (4Kp60 decode); H.264 (1080p60 decode, 1080p30 encode); OpenGL ES, 3.0 graphics
SD card support	Micro SD card slot for loading operating system and data storage
Input power	5V DC via USB-C connector (minimum 3A1) 5V DC via GPIO header (minimum 3A1) Power over Ethernet (PoE)-enabled (requires separate PoE HAT)
Environment	Operating temperature 0–50°C

3.1 Experiment Setup, Evaluation Metrics, and Dataset

Measurements from 4 Raspberry Pis (Rpis) 4 Model B (Table 1) were collected at regular 10-s intervals which described normal and anomaly events. Furthermore, 4 Smart Wall Plugs Fibaro were utilized to measure energy consumption (Table 2). The smart plug was utilized to monitor the energy consumption (Fig. 3). Different residential and working areas were used for the experiment. Totally, 35,630 total data points were collected, including data on the CPU temperature (C), CPU usage (%), disk usage (%), virtual memory usage (%), and power consumption (W) of which 400 were labeled as anomaly points. Statistics for the used features are illustrated in Table 3.

Table 2. Smart Wall Plug Fibaro - type E/F FGWPE-102 — FGWPF-102 specifications

Power supply:	230 V AC, 50/60 Hz
Rated load current:	11 A
Power consumption:	up to 1.6 W
Power output (for resistive load):	2.5 kW
In accordance with EU standards:	RED 2014/53/EU
	RoHS 2011/65/EU
Operational temperature:	0–40 °C
To be used with E or F type (Schuko) sockets:	CEE 7/16 - max load 2.5 A
	CEE 7/17 - max load 11A
	Dual type plugs E/F
Radio protocol:	Z-Wave
	Z-Wave+ (firmware 3.2 or higher)
Radio frequency:	868.4 or 869.8 MHz EU;
	869.0 MHz RU;
Radio transmit power:	up to −10 dBm (EIRP)
Range:	up to 50 m outdoors
	up to 30 m indoors
	up to 40 m indoors (firmware 3.2 or higher)
	(depending on terrain and building structure)
Dimensions: (D x H):	43 × 65 mm

Due to the difficulty in observing anomalies in a normal operation of an RPi, various types of anomalies were simulated based on [10]. In order to find any power consumption anomalies, more tests were conducted and the results revealed that anomalies exist at power consumption greater than 6 W.

Table 3. Dataset Statistics

Stats	CPU Usage	CPU Temperature	Disk Usage	Virtual Memory Usage	Power Consumption
Mean	1.457	54.22	5.516	13.145	2.48
Std.	0.5137	1.596	0.042	0.406	0.262
Min.	0.64	48.558	5.50	12.20	0.4
25%	1.22	53.436	5.50	13.10	2.2
50%	1.35	54.023	5.50	13.40	2.5
75%	1.62	54.917	5.60	13.60	2.7
Max.	42.10	64.183	5.80	15.70	4.8

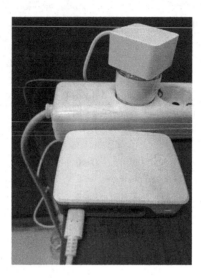

Fig. 3. Experimental setup

Precision, recall, accuracy and f-score were used to evaluate the performance of the proposed model. The f-score is an evaluation metric that combines the precision and recall of a classifier. The formulas used to calculate the evaluation metrics are provided below:

$$accuracy = \frac{TP + TN}{TP + TN + FP + FN}, \tag{11}$$

$$precision = \frac{TP}{TP + FP}. \tag{12}$$

$$recall = \frac{TP}{TP + FN}, \tag{13}$$

$$f - score = \frac{2 * precision * recall}{precision + recall}, \tag{14}$$

where TP, FP, TN, FN are abbreviations for True Positive, False Positive, True Negative, and False Negative.

3.2 Experimental Results

In this subsection, a comparison of the proposed method with state-of-the-art methods including AE-LSTM with one layer in the encoder and decoder layer, isolation-forest (IF) [16], one-class SVM (OCSVM) [17], local outlier factor (LOF) [18] and DBSCAN [19] is presented.

Table 4 illustrates that all models achieved high precision, recall, and f-score, indicating that they were able to detect the majority of anomaly points while keeping the number of false positives low. Additionally, the results showed that the proposed method outperformed the other algorithms, achieving an accuracy of 0.996, a precision of 0.956, a recall of 0.886 and an f-score of 0.896. The proposed method had the longest execution time when compared to other state-of-the-art methods, but 312 ms is more than enough time for the system to be informed and the necessary adjustments to be made.

Table 4. Comparison of the proposed model with state-of-the-art methods.

Model	Accuracy	Precision	Recall	f-score	Execution time (msec)
Isolation Forest (IF)	0.963	0.877	0.749	0.804	129 ms
One-Class SVM (OCSVM)	0.972	0.912	0.678	0.787	214 ms
Local Outlier Factor (LOF)	0.961	0.901	0.729	0.780	135 ms
DBSCAN	0.959	0.871	0.748	0.806	217 ms
LSTM → LSTM	0.984	0.927	0.762	0.834	237 ms
2*CNN → 2*LSTM	**0.996**	**0.956**	**0.886**	**0.896**	**312 ms**

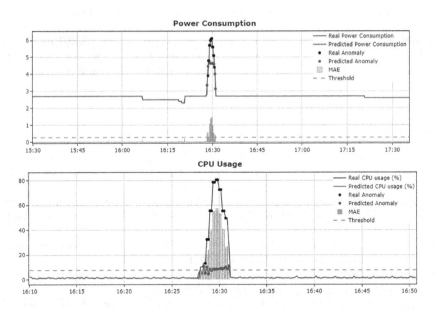

Fig. 4. Real and reconstructed time series for power consumption and cpu usage using the proposed method

Figure 4, depicts the results for two variable, power consumption and cpu usage of the Rpi device. The red lines illustrate the reconstructed power consumption and cpu usage, respectively for each diagram. The nearly horizontal lines (blue lines) represent the data which were collected from the Rpi when it was operating normally. Any deviation from those two lines denotes an anomaly point, and the values obtained are therefore regarded as malfunctions. Last but not least, there are bar plots for each variable that display the reconstruction error using the MAE metrics and lines that show the threshold value chosen using the method presented in Sect. 2.3. As it can be observed, the majority of anomaly points can be found using the proposed method at the start of the error phase.

4   Conclusions

This paper proposed a CNN-based LSTM-Autoencoder method to detect anomaly points in five critical operating parameters of an edge device. The proposed method is based on a hybrid model using 1D-CNN layers in the encoder layer and LSTM layers in the decoder layer. Compared to other state-of-the-art methods, the proposed approach had a remarkable accuracy close to 0.996 and an execution time of 312 ms.

In terms of future work, it will be interesting to use techniques to reduce execution time while retaining high accuracy using quantization techniques with 8 or 6-bit integers. In addition, more simulations can be conducted to create more samples at anomaly points to improve recall, precision and f-score.

Acknowledgements. This work is partially supported by the PRECEPT project funded by the European Union's Horizon 2020 under Grant Agreement No. 958284 and the SMART2B project funded by the European Union's Horizon 2020 under Grant Agreement 101023666.

References

1. Marikyan, D., Papagiannidis, S., Alamanos, E.: A systematic review of the smart home literature: a user perspective. Technol. Forecast. Soc. Chang. **138**, 139–154 (2019)
2. Sovacool, B.K., Furszyfer, D.D., Rio, D.: Smart home technologies in Europe: a critical review of concepts, benefits, risks and policies. Renew. Sustain. Energy Rev. **120**, 109663 (2020)
3. Maalsen, S., Sadowski, J.: The smart home on FIRE: amplifying and accelerating domestic surveillance. Surveillance Soc. **17**(1/2), 118–124 (2019)
4. Stolojescu-Crisan, C., Crisan, C., Butunoi, B.-P.: An IoT-based smart home automation system. Sensors **21**(11), 3784 (2021)
5. Vujović, V., Maksimović, M.: Raspberry Pi as a sensor web node for home automation. Comput. Electr. Eng. **44**, 153–171 (2015)
6. Ren, H., et al.: Time-series anomaly detection service at Microsoft. In: Proceedings of the 25th ACM SIGKDD International Conference on Knowledge Discovery and Data Mining (2019)
7. Braei, M., Wagner, S.: Anomaly detection in univariate time-series: a survey on the state-of-the-art. arXiv preprint arXiv:2004.00433 (2020)
8. Tang, Y., et al.: Integrating prediction and reconstruction for anomaly detection. Pattern Recogn. Lett. **129**, 123–130 (2020)

9. Thudumu, S., Branch, P., Jin, J., Singh, J.J.: A comprehensive survey of anomaly detection techniques for high dimensional big data. J. Big Data **7**(1), 1–30 (2020). https://doi.org/10.1186/s40537-020-00320-x

10. Dimara, A., et al.: Self-healing of semantically interoperable smart and prescriptive edge devices in IoT. Appl. Sci. **12**(22), 11650 (2022). https://doi.org/10.3390/app122211650

11. Kingma, D.P., Ba, J.: Adam: a method for stochastic optimization. arXiv preprint arXiv:1412.6980 (2014)

12. Gensler, A., Henze, J., Sick, B., Raabe, N.: Deep Learning for solar power forecasting-an approach using AutoEncoder and LSTM neural networks. In: 2016 IEEE International Conference on Systems, Man, and Cybernetics (SMC), pp. 002858–002865. IEEE, October 2016

13. Wang, B., Shi, W., Miao, Z.: Confidence analysis of standard deviational ellipse and its extension into higher dimensional Euclidean space. PLoS ONE **10**(3), e0118537 (2015)

14. Hochreiter, S., Schmidhuber, J.: Long short-term memory. Neural Comput. **9**(8), 1735–1780 (1997)

15. Li, Z., Liu, F., Yang, W., Peng, S., Zhou, J.: A survey of convolutional neural networks: analysis, applications, and prospects. IEEE Trans. Neural Netw. Learn. Syst. (2021)

16. Liu, F.T., Ting, K.M., Zhou, Z.H.: Isolation forest. In: 2008 Eighth IEEE International Conference on Data Mining, pp. 413–422. IEEE, December 2008

17. Schölkopf, B., Platt, J.C., Shawe-Taylor, J., Smola, A.J., Williamson, R.C.: Estimating the support of a high-dimensional distribution. Neural Comput. **13**(7), 1443–1471 (2001)

18. Breunig, M.M., Kriegel, H.P., Ng, R.T., Sander, J.: LOF: identifying density-based local outliers. In: Proceedings of the 2000 ACM SIGMOD International Conference on Management of Data, pp. 93–104 (2000)

19. Ester, M., Kriegel, H.P., Sander, J., Xu, X.: A density-based algorithm for discovering clusters in large spatial databases with noise. In: Proceedings of the 2nd International Conference on Knowledge Discovery and Data Mining (KDD-96), pp. 226–231 (1996)

Semantic Interoperability for Managing Energy-Efficiency and IEQ: A Short Review

Christos Tzouvaras[1,2], Asimina Dimara[2,3(✉)], Alexios Papaioannou[3,4], Christos-Nikolaos Anagnostopoulos[2], Konstantinos Kotis[2], Stelios Krinidis[3,4], Dimosthenis Ioannidis[3], and Dimitrios Tzovaras[3]

[1] WATT AND VOLT, Anonimi Etairia Ekmetalleysis, Enallaktikon Morfon Energeias, Athens, Greece
ch.tzouvaras@watt-volt.gr
[2] Department of Cultural Technology and Communication, Intelligent Systems Lab, University of the Aegean (UoA), Mytilene, Greece
{canag,kotis}@aegean.gr
[3] Information Technologies Institute (ITI), Centre for Research Technology Hellas (CERTH), Thessaloniki, Greece
{adimara,alexopa,krinidis,djoannid,Dimitrios.Tzovaras}@iti.gr
[4] Management Science and Technology Department, International Hellenic University (IHU), Kavala, Greece

Abstract. With the rise of the Internet of Things and Smart Home industries, there is a real opportunity to increase the energy efficiency of buildings and improve the indoor experience of their occupants. However, as these industries continue to grow, so does the number of data sources in the energy sector in recent years. This can lead to suboptimal exploitation of these data and even to dualities and misunderstandings. As a result, semantic interoperability in the energy sector is now more necessary than ever. Combining event processing to handle data quantities, semantics to manage numerous data streams, and background ontologies will increase prompt identification of all information. In this context, this short review aims to explore state-of-the-art semantic ontologies and their utilization in the energy sector, with an additional emphasis on the indoor environment and air quality. Furthermore, a semantically enriched framework for a smart home will be proposed.

Keywords: Semantics · Energy sector · Energy efficiency · Energy management · Indoor Environmental Quality

1 Introduction

The recent invasion of Ukraine by Russia brought the issue of Europe's dependence on external energy sources once again into the limelight. In response, the European Commission presented the REPowerEU [1] plan, which includes

I. Maglogiannis et al. (Eds.): AIAI 2023 Workshops, IFIP AICT 677, pp. 242–253, 2023.
https://doi.org/10.1007/978-3-031-34171-7_19

"saving energy" as a critical point of action. Energy savings can of course be achieved by adjusting the public's mindset and tendencies when it comes to how much energy they consume. However, significant energy savings can also be achieved by increasing the energy efficiency of the building stock, which has been one of the go-to demand-side measures over the past decades. This particularly applies to Europe, where 49% of the building stock was built before 1970 [2], which naturally results in higher energy losses and consumption.

Energy flexibility is a more recent form of a demand-side solution that builds on energy efficiency measures, offering the ability to adapt load and generation based on weather conditions, user preferences, and energy network capabilities [3]. Nevertheless, the interventions to increase the energy efficiency of the building stock should not affect the health, comfort and well-being of building users, which are key aspects of Indoor Environmental Quality (IEQ) according to Rohde et al. [4]. Standards and proper communication workflows are essential for these energy efficiency and flexibility interventions to avoid overlaps and create integrated solutions since they can include a variety of data sources such as traditional demand-response (DR) schemes, behind-the-meter distributed energy resources (DER) like on-site generation, thermal and battery storage, and electric vehicles [3].

Furthermore, the rapid growth in Building Information Model (BIM) and Digital Twin (DT) technologies, and their increasing integration into Building Energy Management Systems (BEMS), combined with the fact that Artificial Intelligence (AI) models are consistently deployed at both the building and the grid levels, introducing additional data sources (electricity meters, IoT equipment, etc.), renders the call for interoperability at both syntactic and semantic levels, increasingly acute.

In order to achieve interoperability between all systems, management and automation levels, certain semantic and syntactic requirements must be met [5]. In [6] the authors propose an initial novel implementation of a semantic digital twin technique for smart buildings while observing, monitoring, and optimizing comfort levels along with energy consumption. The idea behind the suggested semantic digital twin strategy is to reuse existing related semantic models to express integrated knowledge for both the physical and digital twins of smart buildings. The Semantic Digital Twin's prototype is being used to highlight analytics and comfort with visualization (SDT). Yet, real-time actuation of semantically annotated real building assets as well as semantically integrated real-time sensor data is also exhibited.

As stated in [7] the capacity of computer systems to exchange data with explicit, formal, agreed and shared meaning is known as semantic interoperability. In order to enable machine-computable automated reasoning, inference, knowledge discovery, and data federation amongst information systems, semantic interoperability is necessary. Returning to the example of the Digital Twins interoperability provides meaning to the content of all data. This is achieved by providing data (metadata) that describes the meaning of the main data content and is transmitted along with the main data content as a holistic information package. These metadata links each element of the main data content to a shared vocabulary and its associated links to an ontology, enabling machine interpretation, inference, and logic [7].

Within this context, this short review endeavors to review semantic interoperability in the context of the energy sector with a particular focus on IEQ. This is achieved by examining whether and to what extent semantics are utilized in the energy and IEQ sectors while presenting the most prevalent ontologies for each case. Finally, the aim is to suggest an applied solution for a semantically enriched smart home.

The remainder of this paper is structured as follows: Sect. 2 presents the state of semantic interoperability in the energy sector in terms of smart control and data management, IoT, smart cities, and the latest research. Section 3 describes the role of semantics in the IEQ and the air quality of interior spaces. Section 4 proposes a new semantically enriched edge architecture. Section 5 presents the challenges that hinder semantic interoperability in the energy and IEQ sectors. While Sect. 6 section contains the conclusions of this work.

2   Semantics in the Energy Sector

As already mentioned, the rapid introduction of new data sources in the energy sector, such as Demand Response (DR) and other flexibility services, Renewable Energy Sources (RES), Digital Twins (DT), Building Energy Management systems (BEMS), Artificial Intelligence (AI algorithms), etc., create an overwhelming amount of data. As Rahman and Hussain emphasize in [19] it is important to convert this raw data into information, then knowledge and finally actionable wisdom utilizing semantics.

2.1   Semantics for Smart Control and Data Management

In recent years, there has been an increasing deployment of BEMS to increase energy efficiency and decrease the energy consumption of buildings, as well as coordinate and deploy energy flexibility services. The operation of BEMS is based on the communication and synergy between automation-level technologies and management-level components, by exploiting high-quality data [5].

Dimara et al. [5] emphasize the utility of an intermediate semantic layer between the automation and management levels of a BEMS, to promote interoperability and provide semantic meaning to raw data from various sources with the objective of extracting knowledge. Some of the main energy-related ontologies can be found below:

- The DogOnt ontology was originally meant for home automation equipment but was later expanded to include all the components of an indoor IoT system [8].
- The PowerOnt ontology refers to the power that electrical devices and appliances consume in smart homes. This ontology is usually integrated with DogOnt [9].
- The SESAME ontology addresses the energy profile of the user, automation, representing meter data and energy pricing [10].

- The BASont ontology is utilized during a variety of the Building Automation System's (BAS) lifecycle's phases, such as design, operation, and refurbishment [11].
- The ThinkHome ontology addresses the critical aspects of analyzing the energy profile of residential buildings by gathering knowledge related to energy providers and their trading conditions, climate conditions, users, spatial knowledge, automation networks, and finally, indoor comfort [12].
- Smart Appliances REFerence (SAREF) ontology utilizes the ETSI TS 103 267 framework [13] to facilitate synergies between other standards and protocols [14].
- The SAREF4ENER ontology is an extension of SAREF and aims to increase the interoperability between smart components of a household and maximize energy efficiency and efficiency in DR schemes participation [15].
- The Generic Ontology of Energy Consumption Households describes a household in terms of energy consumption (appliances), energy production (RES), energy storage (BESS), and consumption profile of the user [16].
- The DEHEMS ontology aims to maximize the volume and quality of data available from home appliances by utilizing a taxonomy that includes the properties of an electric appliance [17].
- The ComfOnt ontology acts as a knowledge base for both energy savings and improvement of IEQ. [18] This ontology is described in detail in Sect. 3.1.

2.2   Semantics for the Internet of Things

In [19] the authors emphasize the heterogeneous and dynamic nature of IoT systems due to the integration of various IoT equipment with vast heterogeneity in devices, hardware, software, requirements, protocols, data formats, etc. This heterogeneity prevents not only the maximum exploitation of the available data but also the further development and deployment of IoT systems.

Technical and syntactic interoperability is not enough for the correct operation of IoT systems. Assuming that in the example of such a system, data can be transmitted from one component to another (technical interoperability) and one component is aware of what type of data to expect from the other (syntactic interoperability), these data still do not have any meaning for the various components. To better understand this point, assuming a smart home system, let T_{EXT} be the outdoor temperature and T_{DHW} be the temperature of domestic hot water (DHW). Both of these temperature values are measured in Celsius ($°C$) and can be transmitted from one component of the system to another. However, with no semantic values, these temperatures can be misidentified and lead to faults in the system's operation.

Despite the apparent need for semantic interoperability within IoT ecosystems, as Ganzha et al. mention in [20], the implementation of semantic practices is almost entirely limited within the scientific community. The authors continue to investigate the ontologies of various sectors and conclude that there is a lack of high-level ontology standardization and guidelines, as in each sector and in some cases organizations, different ontologies and standards are utilized.

Finally, the authors warn that due to the "additional effort" required to make them compatible, the abundance of domain- and use-case-specific ontologies may in and of itself provide difficulties when developing interoperable solutions inside and across domains.

2.3 Smart City Ontologies

As stated in [21] a smart city is an urban ecosystem with social, technological, and digital aspects, aiming to improve its inhabitants' quality of life. The recent deluge of available urban data from different smart city services led De Nicola and Villani [21] to review the various ontologies of different smart city sectors utilized to build the foundation for optimal smart city services.

Some of these sector-specific ontologies include a semantic web model that enables the formation and customization of virtual communities [22], ontologies revolving around emergency situations such as natural or anthropogenic disasters and are utilized for the optimal operation of emergency responders, the management and planning during these situations, the exchange of information and knowledge, and spatiotemporal changes during these events [23–28], ontologies aiming to connect smart cities with the industry and business sector, add value propositions, store transaction data, and execute contracts among others [21].

In the context of the energy sector in smart cities, the ontologies presented in Sect. 2.4 are naturally prevalent. Additionally, in [21] the authors include the Energy Knowledge Graph (EKG) ontology model, which is used to conceptualize microgrids, their components as well as the relationships between them, and classify smart energy services related to specific scenarios. In addition, the Generic Ontology for a Prosumer-Oriented Smart Grid collects knowledge regarding different aspects of the smart grid from the generation of power, energy consumption and the climate to the relationships between prosumers and energy providers.

2.4 Semantics in the Energy Sector Latest Research

As already mentioned, the plethora of data from various decentralized sources with different granularities, formats, protocols, etc., can lead to suboptimal utilization of these data and even dualities and misunderstandings. As Wu et al. point out in [29] a new decentralization-oriented BEMS could lead to major benefits in terms of energy consumption and emission reduction. The authors also note that due to the overwhelming amount of data, researchers tend to utilize data-driven techniques such as AI, which, however, can lead to unreliable and irreplicable results, since the data are extremely project specific and the energy sector has many interdependencies with various other sectors. On these projects, interoperability is limited to its technical and syntactic forms focusing more on message transmission, while semantic interoperability is often neglected.

To address these issues, Wu et al. created new ontology models focused on the interdependencies between energy consumption and variables from third-party sectors such as climate variables. To achieve this the authors follow a knowledge-driven approach by building systematic semantics for decentralized households and converting data generated from the household to Linked Data so as to facilitate the semantic integration with third-party sector data over the web. To validate their findings the authors conduct a test case by analysing household energy consumption and production (PV production, refrigerator/freezer energy consumption, and grid energy import) against temperature data. They finally conclude that climate data may be beneficial for data-oriented models.

In [30] Li and Hong take a knowledge-focused approach to the topic of energy flexibility in buildings. They propose EFOnt (an Ontology for Energy Flexibility of buildings), the first known domain-oriented ontology focused on building energy flexibility to be utilized as a tool for standardizing knowledge co-development and optimizing the integration of different energy efficiency applications. EFOnt gathers all the necessary terminologies and semantic components on the topic of building energy flexibility and creates hierarchical semantic relationships between them while providing an open-source, technology-agnostic, and extensible foundation for shared knowledge for the scientific community and industry backed by the highly interoperable semantic web.

3 Semantics for the Indoor Environmental Quality

3.1 Semantics for Indoor Comfort

A smart home is a home where various smart IoT devices create an ecosystem to enable energy efficiency, improve safety measures, provide ease to the inhabitants during everyday tasks and enhance their feeling of comfort and well-being [31]. However, as stated in [32], there is a lack of scientific work dedicated to standardizing indoor comfort semantic metrics.

To this end, Spoladore et al. [32] continue to propose ComfOnt, a set of domain ontologies that leverages the work done during three Italian research projects, with the aim of adding value to the sector of domain ontologies describing knowledge necessary to facilitate smart home services, including comfort semantics. ComfOnt can be utilized to describe the comfort conditions in the indoor environment and continue to actuate processes to increase the well-being and/or safety of occupants, based on its interpretation of reasoning processes. At the same time, ComfOnt, as a knowledge base, serves smart home inhabitants with suggestions regarding their energy-consuming activities, acting as the foundation for both IEQ improvement and energy consumption reduction. For the purposes of this subsection, ComfOnt will be examined through its comfort managing qualities.

ComfOnt is then validated serving as the knowledge base of the prototypical DECAM smart home management application, directed toward the elderly to assist them in living more independently, with the ability to extend its utilization for all smart home occupants. When it comes to comfort, the occupants have a clear view of the indoor environment conditions (temperature, humidity, illuminance, and CO_2 concentration) as illustrated in (Fig. 1). And have the ability to adjust and save their preferences according to their specific needs/impairments, while their presence is detected and adjustments to the environment are made in advance.

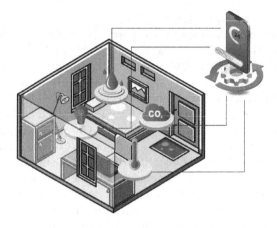

Fig. 1. ComfOnt's temperature, humidity, CO_2, and illuminance sensors.

In [33] a similar ontology framework is developed to optimize the comfort of cruise cabin guests via a mobile application, called Smart Cabin. This framework utilizes IoT sensors and actuators to take real-time action to improve the passengers' indoor experience based on occupancy, health requirements, preferences, activities, and feedback. Semantic web technologies are deployed to enable the knowledge exchange between these heterogeneous devices as well as their sharable and machine-understandable representation and visualization. Smart Cabin is based on four pillars; smart devices, the smartphone application, the knowledge base including the domain ontologies (Passenger's status ontology, Passenger's preferences ontology, ontology including the activities performed by a passenger, Cabin and devices ontology) and finally middleware Java program.

Eleftheriou et al. [34] follow a semantic digital twin approach. The authors demonstrate a semantic digital twin prototype oriented towards optimizing comfort levels, saving energy, analytics and visual comfort metrics visualization by efficiently providing integrated knowledge to decision-making components via the digital twin.

Their approach is founded on four layers; the physical twin layer contains the monitored room and its assets, both physical properties and smart devices, IoT equipment and actuators. The digital twin layer consists of the virtual room, as well as its assets and virtual sensors. The virtual room is an accurate digital representation of the monitored room and its assets, while the virtual sensors are utilized to simulate and visualize data streams in order to optimize decision-making processes and in some cases control the actual sensors. The service layer facilitates all the monitoring, actuation, optimization and scheduling processes. Finally, the semantic layer enables the knowledge exchange between the previously mentioned layers by semantically enriching data and information for the optimal operation of the system.

3.2   Semantics for Indoor Air Quality

When discussing the well-being of indoor spaces occupants, one should not neglect to take indoor air quality into account. According to the World Health Organization's (WHO) ambient air quality database [35] 90% of people around the world breathe polluted air, causing the deaths of 7 million people each year, mainly in low-income countries where immediate action is required. With the rapid growth of smart home and IoT technologies, there is a real opportunity to improve the indoor air quality of residents. However, as stated in [36], due to the inconsistent, blurry and vague nature of the data on the topic of air quality and the uncertainty when specifying the "degree of pollution", conventional ontologies are not optimal for the job. Neither are type-1 fuzzy logic systems (T1FS) that are shown to perform poorly on this topic.

To address this deficiency of the previously mentioned ontologies, the authors of [36] propose a new IoT-based method to assess indoor air quality, utilizing type-2 fuzzy logic systems (T2FS) to extract knowledge from the vague data, with promising results. In [37] the authors attempt to tackle the lack of modeling between sensor-acquired environmental health data and their association with medical terminology by semantically enriching data streams and extracting patterns from medical terminology and coding systems.

In [38] Jude et al. developed an ontology for proactive indoor air quality monitoring and control, as well as an indoor air quality index that was generated utilizing said ontology, which was then validated in a real-world case study in Durban, South Africa, to facilitate reasonable decision-making to improve IEQ. This ontology is developed utilizing the "Methontology" ontology engineering method [39] and enables a proactive framework to proactively warn the users when critical levels of indoor pollutants tend to rise to dangerous levels.

4   Proposed Approach

In [40] a new semantically enriched edge IoT is suggested (SEDGE). The SEDGE architecture adheres to the web of things (WoT) architecture requirements to minimize ambiguity and promote interoperability between diverse edge devices and other external systems (Fig. 2). The term "WoT" refers to the W3C standards for REST, RDF, and HTTP, which promote the effective communication and use of IoT network components. Edge devices are serialized in JSON-LD format and are semantically defined in a human-readable and machine-understandable representation that includes semantic metadata about them. The descriptions are built on common vocabularies and ontologies, which enables external systems to interpret the functionalities of various cooperating and interacting edge devices in a consistent way. With a WoT scripting API, edge devices are made visible and accessible to the web, allowing users to access the given interactions.

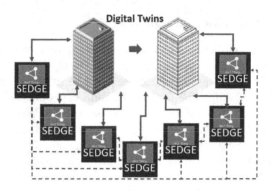

Fig. 2. SEDGE WoT to Digital Twin architecture

5 Discussion in Challenges for Managing Energy-Efficiency and IEQ

There are a few challenges when it comes to semantics in the energy sector. One challenge is that the energy sector is constantly evolving, so it can be difficult to agree on a single definition for certain terms. Another challenge is that the energy sector can be quite complex, so it can be difficult to communicate complex concepts clearly and accurately. Additionally, the energy sector can be quite political, so it can be difficult to agree on certain terms or policies. As a result, the ontologies will have to be constantly updated with new entities.

Furthermore, there are a few challenges in semantics for indoor comfort. One challenge is that people often have different definitions of what "comfort" means. Another challenge is that there is no one-size-fits-all definition of comfort since what feels comfortable to one person may not feel comfortable to another person. Additionally, the definition of comfort can change depending on the weather, the time of day, and other factors. Likewise, well-known semantics like SAREF could be extended to include comfort and IED entities.

6 Conclusions

In this short study, an attempt was made to review the current state of semantic interoperability in the energy sector. A thorough examination of the utilization of semantics and ontologies of the energy sector revealed that despite the variety of ontologies available, there is still a lack of semantic interoperability standardization, since many of these ontologies are developed on a case-by-case basis and often are abandoned. This issue was shown to be even more prevalent on the topic of IEQ and air quality, where the data are more blurry and vague. However, the rapid growth of the IoT industry in combination with the emerging prevalence of semantics in the research community allows an optimistic view of semantic interoperability in the energy sector.

Acknowledgment. This work is partially supported by the PRECEPT project, funded by the EU H2020 under Grant Agreement No. 958284.

References

1. https://commission.europa.eu/strategy-and-policy/priorities-2019-2024/ european-green-deal/repowereu-affordable-secure-and-sustainable-energy-europe. en#saving-energy
2. https://www.euronews.com/green/2022/12/09/europes-energy-crisis-in-data-which-countries-have-the-best-and-worst-insulated-homes
3. Li, H., Hong, T.: A semantic ontology for representing and quantifying energy flexibility of buildings. Adv. Appl. Energy **8**, 100113 (2022). ISSN 2666-7924, https://doi.org/10.1016/j.adapen.2022.100113
4. Rohde, L., Larsen, T.S., Jensen, R.L., Larsen, O.K.: Framing holistic indoor environment: definitions of comfort, health and well-being. Indoor Built Environ. **29**(8), 1118–1136 (2020). https://doi.org/10.1177/1420326X19875795
5. Dimara, A., Anagnostopoulos, C.-N., Kotis, K., Krinidis, S., Tzovaras, D.: BEMS in the era of internet of energy: a review. In: Maglogiannis, I., Macintyre, J., Iliadis, L. (eds.) AIAI 2021. IAICT, vol. 627, pp. 465–476. Springer, Cham (2021). https://doi.org/10.1007/978-3-030-79150-6_37
6. Anagnostopoulos, C.-N.: Saving Energy with Comfort: A Semantic Digital Twin Approach for Smart Buildings (2022)
7. Semantic interoperability, 14 February 2022. Wikipedia https://en.wikipedia.org/wiki/Semantic_interoperability
8. Bonino, D., Corno, F.: DogOnt - ontology modeling for intelligent domotic environments. In: Sheth, A., et al. (eds.) ISWC 2008. LNCS, vol. 5318, pp. 790–803. Springer, Heidelberg (2008). https://doi.org/10.1007/978-3-540-88564-1_51
9. Tayur, V.M., Suchithra, R.: A comprehensive ontology for Internet of Things (coIoT). In: 2019 Second International Conference on Advanced Computational and Communication Paradigms (ICACCP). IEEE (2019)
10. Fensel, A., et al.: Sesame-s: semantic smart home system for energy efficiency. Informatik-Spektrum **36**(1), 46–57 (2013)
11. Ploennigs, J., Hensel, B., Dibowski, H., Kabitzsch, K.: BASont - a modular, adaptive building automation system ontology. In: IECON 2012–38th Annual Conference on IEEE Industrial Electronics Society, Montreal, QC, Canada, pp. 4827–4833 (2012). https://doi.org/10.1109/IECON.2012.6389583
12. Reinisch, C., Kofler, M.J., Kastner, W.: ThinkHome: a smart home as digital ecosystem. In: 4th IEEE International Conference on Digital Ecosystems and Technologies. IEEE (2010)
13. Appliances, S.: Smartm2m; smart appliances; reference ontology and onem2m mapping (2017)
14. Daniele, L., den Hartog, F., Roes, J.: Created in close interaction with the industry: the smart appliances REFerence (SAREF) ontology. In: Cuel, R., Young, R. (eds.) FOMI 2015. LNBIP, vol. 225, pp. 100–112. Springer, Cham (2015). https://doi.org/10.1007/978-3-319-21545-7_9
15. Haghgoo, M., et al.: SARGON-smart energy domain ontology. IET Smart Cities **2**(4), 191–198 (2020)
16. Kott, J., Kott, M.: Generic ontology of energy consumption households. Energies **12**(19), 3712 (2019)

17. Shah, N., Chao, K.-M., Zlamaniec, T., Matei, A.: Ontology for home energy management domain. In: Cherifi, H., Zain, J.M., El-Qawasmeh, E. (eds.) DICTAP 2011. CCIS, vol. 167, pp. 337–347. Springer, Heidelberg (2011). https://doi.org/10.1007/978-3-642-22027-2_28

18. Spoladore, D., et al.: ComfOnt: a semantic framework for indoor comfort and energy saving in smart homes. Electronics 8(12), 1449 (2019)

19. Rahman, H., Hussain, M.I.: A comprehensive survey on semantic interoperability for Internet of Things: state-of-the-art and research challenges. Trans Emerging Tel Tech. 31, e3902 (2020). https://doi.org/10.1002/ett.3902

20. Ganzha, M., Paprzycki, M., Pawlowski, W., Szmeja, P., Wasielewska, K.: Semantic technologies for the IoT - an inter-IoT perspective. In: 2016 IEEE First International Conference on Internet-of-Things Design and Implementation (IoTDI), Berlin, Germany, pp. 271–276 (2016). https://doi.org/10.1109/IoTDI.2015.22

21. De Nicola, A., Villani, M.L.: Smart city ontologies and their applications: a systematic literature review. Sustainability 13(10), 5578 (2021). https://doi.org/10.3390/su13105578

22. Maret, P., Laforest, F., Lanquetin, D.: A semantic web model for ad hoc context-aware virtual communities application to the smart place scenario. In: Proceedings of the 16th International Conference on Enterprise Information Systems (ICEIS), Lisbon, Portugal, 27–30 April 2014, vol. 2, pp. 591–598 (2014)

23. De Nicola, A., Melchiori, M., Villani, M.L.: Creative design of emergency management scenarios driven by semantics: an application to smart cities. Inf. Syst. 81, 21–48 (2019)

24. Kurte, K., Potnis, A., Durbha, S.: Semantics-enabled spatio-temporal modeling of earth observation data: an application to flood monitoring. In: Proceedings of the 2nd ACM SIGSPATIAL International Workshop on Advances on Resilient and Intelligent Cities, Chicago, IL, USA, 5 November 2019, pp. 41–50 (2019)

25. Elmhadhbi, L., Karray, M.H., Archimède, B.: A modular ontology for semantically enhanced interoperability in operational disaster response. In: Proceedings of the 16th International Conference on Information Systems for Crisis Response and Management-ISCRAM 2019, Valencia, Spain, 19–22 May 2019, pp. 1021–1029 (2019)

26. Chehade, S., Matta, N., Pothin, J.B., Cogranne, R.: Handling effective communication to support awareness in rescue operations. J. Contingencies Crisis Manag. 28, 307–323 (2020)

27. The Empathi Ontology. https://shekarpour.github.io/empathi.io

28. Benaben, F., et al.: An AI framework and a metamodel for collaborative situations: application to crisis management contexts. J. Contingencies Crisis Manag. 28, 291–306 (2020)

29. Wu, J., Orlandi, F., AlSkaif, T., O'Sullivan, D., Dev, S.: A semantic web approach to uplift decentralized household energy data. Sustain. Energy Grids Netw. 32, 100891 (2022). ISSN 2352-4677, https://doi.org/10.1016/j.segan.2022.100891

30. Li, H., Hong, T.: A semantic ontology for representing and quantifying energy flexibility of buildings. Adv. Appl. Energy 8, 100113 (2022), ISSN 2666-7924, https://doi.org/10.1016/j.adapen.2022.100113

31. Gunge, V.S., Yalagi, P.S.: Smart home automation: a literature review. Int. J. Comput. Appl. 975, 8887 (2016)

32. Spoladore, D., Mahroo, A., Trombetta, A., Sacco, M.: ComfOnt: a semantic framework for indoor comfort and energy saving in smart homes. Electronics 8(12), 1449 (2019). https://doi.org/10.3390/electronics8121449

33. Mahroo, A., Spoladore, D., Nolich, M., Buqi, R., Carciotti, S., Sacco, M.: Smart cabin: a semantic-based framework for indoor comfort customization inside a cruise cabin. In: Yang, X.-S., Sherratt, S., Dey, N., Joshi, A. (eds.) Fourth International Congress on Information and Communication Technology. AISC, vol. 1041, pp. 41–53. Springer, Singapore (2020). https://doi.org/10.1007/978-981-15-0637-6_4
34. Eleftheriou, O., Dimara, A., Kotis, K., Anagnostopoulos, C.-N.: Saving Energy with Comfort: A Semantic Digital Twin Approach for Smart Buildings (2022)
35. Ambient air pollution database, World Health Organization (WHO). https://www.who.int/data/gho/data/themes/topics/topic-details/GHO/ambient-air-pollution
36. Ghorbani, A., Zamanifar, K.: Type-2 fuzzy ontology-based semantic knowledge for indoor air quality assessment. Appl. Soft Comput. **121**, 108658 (2022). ISSN 1568-4946, https://doi.org/10.1016/j.asoc.2022.108658
37. Silva, M., Felipe, L.: <Semantic Enrichment of Sensor Data: A Case Study in Environmental Health>. Goiânia, 2021. 112p. MSc. Master's Degree Monograph. Programa de Pós-Graduação em Ciência da Computação (PPGCC), Instituto de Informática (INF), Universidade Federal de Goiás
38. Adeleke, J.A., Moodley, D.: (2015) An ontology for proactive indoor environmental quality monitoring and control. In: Proceedings of the 2015 Annual Research Conference on South African Institute of Computer Scientists and Information Technologists (SAICSIT '15). Association for Computing Machinery, New York, Article 2, 1–10 (2015). https://doi.org/10.1145/2815782.2815816
39. Fernández-López, M., Gomez-Perez, A., Juristo, N.: METHONTOLOGY: from ontological art towards ontological engineering. In: Engineering Workshop on Ontological Engineering (AAAI97) (1997)
40. Dimara, A., et al.: Self-healing of semantically interoperable smart and prescriptive edge devices in IoT. Appl. Sci. **12**(22), 11650 (2022)

Treating Common Problems Observed During Smart Building Control Real-Life Testing: Sharing Practical Experience

Georgios Karatzinis[1,2], Iakovos Michailidis[1,2], Asimina Dimara[1,3(✉)],
Aliki Stefanopoulou[1,2], Vasileios Georgios Vasilopoulos[1,2], Stelios Krinidis[1,4],
Christos-Nikolaos Anagnostopoulos[3], Elias Kosmatopoulos[1,2],
Dimosthenis Ioannidis[1], and Dimitrios Tzovaras[1]

[1] Information Technologies Institute (ITI), Centre for Research and Technology
Hellas (CERTH), Thessaloniki, Greece
{gkaratzi,michaild,adimara,alikstef,vvasilop,krinidis,kosmatop,djoannid,
Dimitrios.Tzovaras}@iti.gr
[2] Department of Electrical and Computer Engineering, Automatic Control Systems
and Robotics, Democritus University of Thrace (DUTh), Xanthi, Greece
[3] Department of Cultural Technology and Communication, Intelligent Systems Lab,
University of the Aegean (UoA), Mytilene, Greece
canag@aegean.gr
[4] Management Science and Technology Department, International Hellenic
University (IHU), Kavala, Greece

Abstract. Building energy management systems (BEMSs) have attracted much attention in recent years due to their potential to reduce overall energy consumption, reduce electricity bills, improve the efficiency of the electricity network and effectively manage renewable energy exploitation. However, testing the efficiency of such mechanisms in a real-life setup is not trivial, due to different unexpected incidents caused by the Building Automation and Control System (BACS) itself or by human participants who do not always conform to the experiment constraints, rendering comparability and conclusions extraction a quite tricky process. Maintaining tests' credibility is a multi-factor problem which the simulation tests are fail to emulate, limiting the transferability of simulation-based results into real-life practise. In this work, we present a conceptualized framework for real-life smart building control testing, that presents useful suggestions towards maintaining testing credibility, ensuring solid performance evaluation outcomes and reliability. Finally, the current work is a collection of practical lessons learnt during BEMS performance testing activities.

Keywords: Building Energy Management · Practical Experience · Building Automation and Controls · Real-Life Problems

© IFIP International Federation for Information Processing 2023
Published by Springer Nature Switzerland AG 2023
I. Maglogiannis et al. (Eds.): AIAI 2023 Workshops, IFIP AICT 677, pp. 254–265, 2023.
https://doi.org/10.1007/978-3-031-34171-7_20

1   Introduction

The building sector is inevitably a major energy consumer that causes almost 40% of the world's energy consumption, 40% of greenhouse gas emissions, and 70% of electricity usage [21]. The high amount of energy needed in buildings (residential and commercial) is directly connected with heating-cooling loads, domestic hot water, lighting, electrical appliances, and indirectly with insufficient insulation. The directives of the European Commission and legislative proposals set specific energy reduction goals in this direction. With the 2030 Climate Target Plan, the Commission proposes to increase the EU's ambition to reduce greenhouse gas emissions to at least 55% below 1990 levels by 2030 [5] which is a substantial increase compared with the previously defined target of at least 40% [1].

The aforementioned transition of energy systems has led to the intensified interest in smart grid technologies and implementations to minimize overall energy consumption, reduce electricity bills, improve the efficiency of the electricity network and effectively manage renewably generated energy [8]. Smart buildings can be realized as independent entities capable of managing their own operations to maintain residents' comfort while minimizing energy consumption. There is a trade-off between the concepts of energy consumption reduction and comfort improvement, as their objectives can be in conflict with each other. The main principal components that consist a smart building are: a) monitoring system to have a perception of its environment; b) communication system to connect devices; c) energy management system (EMS) to conduct energy-related decisions; d) intelligent management control system (IMCS) or, energy management control system (EMCS), with learning capabilities to formulate an optimization criterion and subsequently apply actions encapsulating total energy consumption, total energy generation, user thermal comfort, and maximum available flexibility; e) grid connection and communication to adjust load profiles of building consorting the balanced operation of the grid;

Numerous studies have been presented in the literature describing trends, risks and benefits of the Internet of Things (IoT) technologies in buildings [14], approaches that have been applied for building energy prediction [4], intelligent controllers towards sustainable buildings [19], the incorporation of machine learning and deep learning techniques [18] and artificial intelligence in energy management systems improvement [2].

However, real-world challenges arise when applying these control strategies in building energy management systems outside the deterministic simulation environment safety. Apart from tuning difficulties, there are barriers connected with handling noisy data, the needs for a large amount of data and a long time for training operations, high number of control parameters or high computational load, increased complexity in large-scale systems, and occasionally human expertise requirements. On top of these key barriers that have to be investigated and resolved, there are high operational costs on the electricity bill until acceptable control matching, while also there is an increased risk for potential catastrophic transients. Hence, there are multi-faceted and multi-level limitations that need to be considered in real-world applications and subsequently during control evaluation tests. Within this context, key challenges for real-life smart building control evaluation tests presenting useful suggestions and usual practices towards achieving sustainable building energy management are suggested. The value of this study may also be extended by considering the emulation of similar incidents within an appropriate simulation environment to test the BEMS evaluation outcomes' robustness as well.

The rest of the manuscript is organized as follows: Sect. 2 presents real-life challenges for monitoring, analysis and control solutions in BEMS, while also potential credibility breaching points are defined. Section 3 extends further the identification of challenges presenting incidents occurred in real-life experiments and concludes suggesting mitigation actions towards real-life smart building control evaluation tests. Finally, Sect. 4 summarizes the main findings of this work in the direction of sustainable building energy management.

2   Real-Life Challenges and Potential Credibility Breaching Points

Building control systems monitor and control the indoor climatic conditions in buildings ensuring their operational performance as well as the safety and comfort of occupants. Undoubtedly, a key challenge for the efficient integration of a BEMS is the design of an effective and reliable control strategy. These strategies could be either conventional or intelligent-based control systems. A wide range of state-of-the-art approaches in intelligent-based control systems for energy and comfort management in smart building has been presented in [20] taking into consideration different aspects and parameters. The class of intelligent control can be categorized in: a) Learning methods, b) Model-based predictive control method, and c) Agent-based control systems.

Conventional Controllers: Standard control schemes that include thermostats, proportional-integral (PI) and proportional-integral-derivative (PID) approaches. Thermostats are mostly utilized for heating or cooling to a set point temperature but they may generate oscillations leading to wastage of energy in residential buildings [22]. PI and PID controllers are closed loop/feedback controls that are more efficient than thermostats [7]. However the lack of direct knowledge of the system and the proper gains' selection is a demanding task, otherwise the entire controlled system can be unstable. Thus, the controller parameters are tuned at a particular operating range with constant gains. Under noisy data and non-linear processes, large time delays occur.

Learning Methods: This class of controllers incorporates the concept of artificial intelligence alleviating the need for detailed models. Fuzzy logic controllers embody multi criteria strategies within expert knowledge where linguistic rules are generated using the system's observations and the designer's knowledge.

Fuzzy based approaches have been applied for heating purposes maximizing indoor thermal comfort capitalizing energy efficiency [9]. A more recent work presents a fuzzy based approach for cost, energy consumption and peak-to-average ratio reduction [11]. Artificial neural network (ANN) approaches are also used to bridge the gap between energy efficiency and indoor thermal comfort in buildings [3]. Reinforcement learning (RL) is also used for building energy management as the most prominent machine learning approach for control problems [16]. In RL methods the agent learn optimal actions using interaction with the system environment. Compared with MPC, RL is potentially model-free algorithm that takes advantage of real-time and historical data. Also, adaptive neuro-fuzzy inference systems are used combining the merits of fuzzy logic and neural networks for tasks such as building energy forecasting for cooling loads [6].

Model-based Predictive Control Method: This approach can cope with input/output signal constraints in multi-input and multi-output (MIMO) systems enabling the commands to use their full ability to set temperature limits for thermal comfort. Model predictive control (MPC) algorithms use nonlinear global optimization to manage the energy systems. In MPC, the system dynamics are reflected by a time-varying state space model derived from the energy system simulation model. MPC is based on a repeated real-time optimization of a mathematical system model impending disturbances (occupancy information, price tariffs, solar radiations) predicting the future system behavior that is considered within the optimization process. To carry out the control performance and optimization in BEMS, the MPC may be connected with a comprehensive model that is created in TRNSYS, EnergyPlus, Dymola or Matlab. An MPC approach for a combined thermal and electric energy system in a residential single-family building has been presented in [12]. This is the most popular approach for BEMS for shifting loads during peak hours with an ability to adapt to unexpected disturbances, including dynamic modelling and occupancy predictions. Also, it exploits better the thermal mass of building than conventional methods and shifting operations can be handled within a definite period. However, a challenging task is to select a suitable model while also some of the main limitations to be addressed are parameter tuning, choosing the cost function, and reformulating the optimal control problem.

Agent-based Control Systems: This is a burgeoning area of research that simulates the behavior and co-evolution of system components to explore complex adaptive systems (agents). The agents are distributed in the environment working on their assigned individual objectives with predefined behavior programs. However, they are capable of communicating with each other and with the environment. Agents have both perceiving and affecting qualities and they can be employed for modeling complex problems. Multi-agent systems (MAS) have been applied in energy management systems [13]. There is a need for open information exchange platforms between attached agents and the electrical appliances. Another issue is related with the huge amount of information associated with the process resulting in slow decision making. Lastly, an open challenge is the assignment of agents to components as each agent needs to have a perception of which component is the one that they are responsible for. Table 1 presents a qualitative comparison of the open challenges for different involved control approaches in BEMS.

During the development of control strategies, the need for simulation tools is emerged to establish a clear, continuous and effective interaction with the buildings. Simulation platforms characterized as white box models offer a physical energy model of the building presenting its dynamic thermal behavior. These physical models are fully explainable and they use detailed building information considering different heat transfer models (conduction, radiation and convection) between building envelop and its surroundings. Well-known simulation packages are the EnergyPlus, TRNSYS (Transient System Simulation Tool), Dymola which supports the Modelica modeling language, DOE-2 and the less used Matlab/ SIMULINK. Mathematical equations of heat and mass balance and all the energy transfer processes are used to create the system, leading to highly accurate models as most of the energy transfer processes are mapped into development of the building energy systems modeling structure [10]. Data-driven models or black box models are simpler but less accurate that the white box ones as they utilize less or no physical information of buildings. They use regression analysis

Table 1. Comparative analysis of the challenges emerge in control strategies

Family of Controllers	Challenges	Indicative Works
Conventional	Proper gain selection. Strictly bounded with system modelling. Inaccurate results due to sensitivity of controllers. Poor performance in noisy and non-linear processes.	[7,22]
Learning-based	Need for lots of data especially in Fuzzy, ANN and ANFIS approaches. In particular Fuzzy and hybrid-fuzzy methods have human expert knowledge relation for the principal elements of the system like membership functions definition. Training efforts are high in ANN based approaches. Scalability issues in RL methods when learning and acting in high-dimensional state (and action) spaces. Also, a proper system environment has to be constructed and reward engineering actions are required. In Multi-Agent RL, each agent may only have partial information of the environment making real-life application difficult.	[3,6,9,11,16,23]
MPC	Complexity of modeling and algorithmic tuning. Training and data collection efforts are high. Parameter tuning, choosing the cost function, and reformulation of the optimal control problem are needed.	[12,15]
Agent-based	Needs open information exchange platforms between attached agents and the electrical appliances. Huge amount of information associated with the process resulting in slow decision making. An open challenge is the assignment of agents to components. Real scale implementation difficulties due to the the involvement of humans and requirement for advanced information system.	[13]

based on historical data between output of net energy consumption and inputs such as solar, wind, occupancy behavior and equipment scheduling information. They are adaptable for buildings without the need for detailed physical parameters, but they can be time consuming to record the variables in long term simulations. Data-driven approaches include ANN, recurrent neural networks (RNN), regression methods, support vector machines (SVM) and extreme gradient boosting (XGBoost) among others. The last simulation class is referred to hybrid models that try to leverage the advantages and limitations of both physical (white box) and statistical (black box) models, thus named grey box models. They simplify the description of the building heat transfer process, regarding modelling and calibration, and simulate building energy demand. Resistance- capacitance (RC) thermal network represents this modelling approach. An analytical description of physical energy and data-driven models in building energy prediction has been presented in [4].

Clearly, monitoring and analysis operations are not separated from building energy control. Data acquisition from adequate number of devices is critical for the whole operation. It is important to ensure that IoT applications and networks are available at any time to establishing proper monitoring, control and fault-tolerance mechanisms that enhance robustness [14]. The interruption of constantly operating services may lead to catastrophic results. Data collection, storage and processing is a crucial requirement, especially when there are multiple heterogeneous connected sensors and devices. As a result of the Big Data, proper approaches are required to reduce traffic in information flow. Also, algorithms for cleaning raw and/or missing data are needed to improve data quality including feature engineering to extract informative knowledge. Failure management and prioritization of tasks is a backup plan for communication downtime assisting in the direction of security reasons. From the user's side, analysed and simplified data have to be visualized in forms of charts and animations through Graphic User Interface (GUI) to enable user-in-the-loop inserting a closed interaction and feedback regarding comfort acceptance. This serves, also, as a useful information for online calibration of the control algorithm. Occupancy patterns, personalized comfort behaviors and different occupancy profiles can be inserted in the computational optimization methods to enhance both energy efficiency and the occupants' comfort conditions term [17]. Optimal sensor localization secures misleading data collection and assists the diagnostic ability of the BEMS.

Summarizing, the challenges and open issues regarding monitoring, analysis and control are:

Monitoring and Analysis Challenges

- Development of a real-time data collection framework which stores, process and updates data from all available sensors and devices to have a clear perception of the under examination BEMS. Data cleaning and feature engineering are mandatory processes to extract informative knowledge feeding with appropriate data the predictive models.

- The IoT framework should integrate all available devices, sensors and networks to ensure managing uninterrupted data exchange. The integration of heterogeneous systems, data analytic tools and user-friendly GUI in the IoT system is crucial.
- Development of machine learning-based forecasting approaches for energy load prediction, energy consumption estimation, indoor temperature, weather conditions, energy prices and occupant's consumption behavior for the monitoring stage.

Control Test Challenges

- Define a control strategy that does not violate the global objectives and constraints of building energy management. There is a general balance or a trade-off between energy reduction and thermal comfort. The comfortable conditions should be maintained while moving towards energy efficiency ensuring. Also there are other constraints that should not be violated like the capacity of energy sources and energy storage systems, waiting time of appliances, constraints related with demand response, reactive power support limits while also maintaining operational temperatures within limits.
- The control schemes should be adaptable, effective, easily tunable and transferable to be applied from already evaluated simulated scenarios to real-life buildings integrated into smart energy systems. These characteristics are even more important when there is limited time in performing real-life experiments. The ability to learn from limited number of samples is crucial for convergence, stability and performance reasons. Also, the controller has to deal with delays in sensor measurements or actuators providing a robust method that manages uncertainty in the problem. Practically, the control method should be able to learn inherently the dynamics of the building regarding these induced delays and their relationship. Also, the control action should be applied with the lowest latency.

3   Real-Life Practise Experience: Lessons Learnt from a Spanish and a Greek Testbed

In this section we extend further the task of identifying challenges in BEMS, from a practical perspective, presenting malfunctions occurred during real-life experiments. The indicative malfunctioning incidents are from two different cases, i.e., an office (located in Greece) and a residential apartment case (located in Spain). Both are fully retrofitted with Adaptable/Dynamic Building Envelopes (ADBE) façade. The only heating source (no central heating system nor other supportive heating components) for the apartment was two controllable electric heaters

(1.5kW maximum power each) coupled with remotely controllable smart plugs. In the office case, a central heating system takes place already and one controllable electric heater is added with 2kW maximum power. Control actions follow a switch ON/OFF configuration.

In those cases, the goal was to minimize tuning efforts of real-time experiments presenting a framework that avoids potential catastrophic transients and high operational costs on the electricity bill. Usually, model assisted online approaches are used that last days or weeks leading to severe tuning efforts, energy waste or potential catastrophic transients. Thus, it was decided to use the simulation output tests from the, already validated, simulation model in an offline learning manner, rendering control set-points, energy consumption and indoor temperature together; to ultimately tune the controllers' gains. The control model considered mixed fuzzy approach to allow smooth switching across different operational areas. The tuning setup considered the intelligent management control system module to optimize the applied control policy in an energy-efficient and thermally comfortable manner at the same time. Following an episodic approach, i.e., repeating an indicative simulative week (over a 5-day horizon) considering Spanish and Greek autumn weather conditions at every tuning iteration, the tuning process required less than 100 iterations. The reason for doing so was to eventually consider exogenous noise in the tuning process, according to the fluctuation of the weather conditions during these five simulation days. Details about the simulation tests and controller pre-training and specifications are not provided here. In this work, the objective is to present the conceptualization adopted towards a framework for real-life smart building control evaluation tests and the usual practices that arise upon these tests.

For this reason, we present indicative malfunctions that occurred. The first two incidents have been presented in the office case and the third one has been observed in the residential apartment case. Note that the desired temperature in all cases has been derived on the basis of occupancy profiles. In the office case, the desired temperature is extremely low other than working hours as any heating system was forbidden to operate.

- **Incident 1:** The office includes a central heating system that is already in place, as mentioned above. The occupants increased its set-point higher than the desired temperature that the control method of the remotely electric heater operates. Thus, as depicted in Fig. 1 the remotely controlled device has been activated only for a short period of time during early morning.

- **Incident 2:** This is a scenario where control signal is sent but it was never applied on the remotely controlled device located in office (see Fig. 2). This scenario performed during weekend where central heating system was shut down. Unfortunately, an occupant turned off the smart device that was in standby mode and the control signals never applied to change the status of the device.

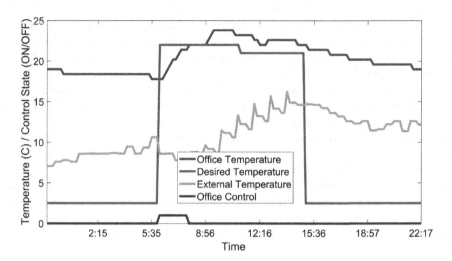

Fig. 1. Incident 1 - Office case

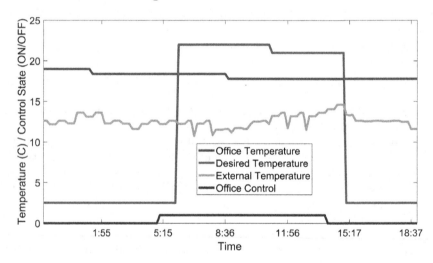

Fig. 2. Incident 2 - Office case

– **Incident 3:** In this case, there are two controllable devices, one located in the living room and the other located in an adjacent smaller room. Slightly after 14:01, a communication error occurs (Fig. 3), the control method is unable to communicate with the devices, the status of devices remains the same as prior to communication fault and subsequently the room temperature exceeds the desired temperature level leading to energy waste and potential catastrophic transients if left for unacceptable time frame.

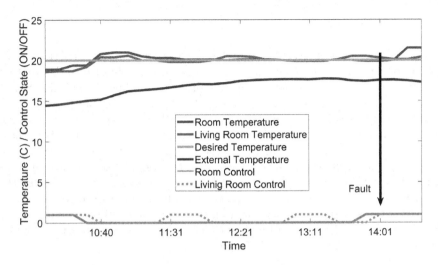

Fig. 3. Incident 1 - Residential apartment case

Based on the above depicted examples of incidents and aligned with the already defined challenges in building energy control applications, the following usual practices are added:

Common Mitigation Practices

- Integration of heterogeneous components is needed in cases where conventional appliances co-exist with smart ones. Especially when the conventional heating systems are not automated.
- Use non-intrusive sensors in optimal locations. Conceivable division of spaces into sub-areas to place sensors in the centre of these sub-areas. Otherwise, sensing devices close to windows or doors or to distant places will lead to misleading measurements. Smart meters, smart plugs and devices if possible to be hidden or not reachable. This is mainly for hotels, hospitals, offices, municipality buildings, public buildings and utilities.
- Mitigation actions should be foreseen when communication system and thus monitoring and control is down. Automated notifications are needed to alarm both users and building managers. At the same time a safe mode of control actions based on the last weather predictions and indoor measurements in relation with similar days in terms of occupancy profile is needed to operate in a conservative function. This is mandatory when control actions have been sent to smart plugs prior to communication interruption as the state of the devices will remain unchanged during the downtime. In the meantime the user should be able to verify locally via the GUI if the safe mode operates based on comfort desirability, otherwise a universal local signal of deactivation of all remotely controllable devices is essential to avoid catastrophic conditions accepting thermal comfort penalty.

4   Conclusions

To sum up, the building sector is responsible for a significant portion of the world's energy consumption and greenhouse-gas emissions, which has led to the need for energy reduction goals and the development of smart building technologies. Smart buildings are capable of managing their operations to maintain comfort while minimizing energy consumption, but there is a trade-off between energy consumption reduction and comfort improvement. In this paper, through an analysis of these challenges, useful suggestions and usual practices are presented to achieve sustainable building energy management. However, it is important to acknowledge that further investigation and resolution of key barriers are necessary to fully realize the potential of smart building technology. By considering multi-faceted and multi-level limitations during control evaluation tests, we can continue to improve the efficiency and sustainability of building energy management systems, ultimately contributing to a more sustainable future.

Acknowledgements. This work is partially supported by the PRECEPT project funded by the European Union's Horizon 2020 under Grant Agreement No. 958284 https://www.precept-project.eu/ and the Plug-N-Harvest https://www.plug-n-harvest.eu/ project funded by the European Union's Horizon 2020 under Grant Agreement 768735.

References

1. Directive (eu) 2018/844 of the European parliament and of the council of 30 May 2018 amending directive 2010/31/eu on the energy performance of buildings and directive 2012/27/eu on energy efficiency (text with eea relevance). OJ L **156**, 75–91 (1962018)
2. Aguilar, J., Garces-Jimenez, A., R-Moreno, M., García, R.: A systematic literature review on the use of artificial intelligence in energy self-management in smart buildings. Renew. Sustain. Energy Rev. **151**, 111530 (2021)
3. Chaudhuri, T., Soh, Y.C., Li, H., Xie, L.: A feedforward neural network based indoor-climate control framework for thermal comfort and energy saving in buildings. Appl. Energy **248**, 44–53 (2019)
4. Chen, Y., Guo, M., Chen, Z., Chen, Z., Ji, Y.: Physical energy and data-driven models in building energy prediction: a review. Energy Rep. **8**, 2656–2671 (2022)
5. Commission, E.: 'fit for 55': delivering the eu's 2030 climate target on the way to climate neutrality. Communication from the Commission to the European Parliament, the European Council, the Council, the European Economic and Social Committee and the Committee of the Regions (2021)
6. Deb, C., Eang, L.S., Yang, J., Santamouris, M.: Forecasting energy consumption of institutional buildings in Singapore. Procedia Eng. **121**, 1734–1740 (2015)
7. Diaz-Mendez, S., Patiño-Carachure, C., Herrera-Castillo, J.: Reducing the energy consumption of an earth-air heat exchanger with a PID control system. Energy Convers. Manage. **77**, 1–6 (2014)
8. Fang, X., Misra, S., Xue, G., Yang, D.: Smart grid-the new and improved power grid: a survey. IEEE Commun. Surv. Tutor. **14**(4), 944–980 (2011)

9. Gouda, M., Danaher, S., Underwood, C.: Thermal comfort based fuzzy logic controller. Build. Serv. Eng. Res. Technol. **22**(4), 237–253 (2001)
10. Harish, V., Kumar, A.: A review on modeling and simulation of building energy systems. Renew. Sustain. Energy Rev. **56**, 1272–1292 (2016)
11. Khalid, R., Javaid, N., Rahim, M.H., Aslam, S., Sher, A.: Fuzzy energy management controller and scheduler for smart homes. Sustain. Comput.: Inform. Syst. **21**, 103–118 (2019)
12. Kuboth, S., Heberle, F., König-Haagen, A., Brüggemann, D.: Economic model predictive control of combined thermal and electric residential building energy systems. Appl. Energy **240**, 372–385 (2019)
13. Labeodan, T., Aduda, K., Boxem, G., Zeiler, W.: On the application of multi-agent systems in buildings for improved building operations, performance and smart grid interaction-a survey. Renew. Sustain. Energy Rev. **50**, 1405–1414 (2015)
14. Lawal, K., Rafsanjani, H.N.: Trends, benefits, risks, and challenges of IoT implementation in residential and commercial buildings. Energy Built Environ. **3**(3), 251–266 (2022)
15. Ma, Y., Borrelli, F., Hencey, B., Coffey, B., Bengea, S., Haves, P.: Model predictive control for the operation of building cooling systems. IEEE Trans. Control Syst. Technol. **20**(3), 796–803 (2011)
16. Mason, K., Grijalva, S.: A review of reinforcement learning for autonomous building energy management. Comput. Electr. Eng. **78**, 300–312 (2019)
17. Mofidi, F., Akbari, H.: Intelligent buildings: an overview. Energy Build. **223**, 110192 (2020)
18. Olu-Ajayi, R., Alaka, H., Sulaimon, I., Sunmola, F., Ajayi, S.: Building energy consumption prediction for residential buildings using deep learning and other machine learning techniques. J. Build. Eng. **45**, 103406 (2022)
19. Parvin, K., Lipu, M.H., Hannan, M., Abdullah, M.A., Jern, K.P., Begum, R., Mansur, M., Muttaqi, K.M., Mahlia, T.I., Dong, Z.Y.: Intelligent controllers and optimization algorithms for building energy management towards achieving sustainable development: challenges and prospects. IEEE Access **9**, 41577–41602 (2021)
20. Shaikh, P.H., Nor, N.B.M., Nallagownden, P., Elamvazuthi, I., Ibrahim, T.: A review on optimized control systems for building energy and comfort management of smart sustainable buildings. Renew. Sustain. Energy Rev. **34**, 409–429 (2014)
21. Somu, N., Raman, M.R.G., Ramamritham, K.: A hybrid model for building energy consumption forecasting using long short term memory networks. Appl. Energy **261**, 114131 (2020)
22. Tabares-Velasco, P.C., Speake, A., Harris, M., Newman, A., Vincent, T., Lanahan, M.: A modeling framework for optimization-based control of a residential building thermostat for time-of-use pricing. Appl. Energy **242**, 1346–1357 (2019)
23. Yu, L., et al.: Deep reinforcement learning for smart home energy management. IEEE Internet Things J. **7**(4), 2751–2762 (2019)

The 12th Workshop on Mining Humanistic Data (MHDW)

Mining Humanistic Data Workshop

12th International Workshop, MHDW 2023, León, Spain, June 14–17, 2023, Proceedings

Preface

The 12th event of the International Mining Humanistic Data Workshop (MHDW 2023) took place in hybrid fashion in León, Spain and over the internet during June 14th to 17th, 2023. The main objective of the conference was to bring together interdisciplinary approaches that focus on the application of innovative as well as existing data matching, fusion and mining as well as knowledge discovery and management techniques to data derived from all areas of Humanistic Sciences. It followed the success of the Crete (Greece 2022), Crete (Greece, 2021), Halkidiki (Greece, 2020), Crete (Greece, 2019), Island of Rhodes (Greece, 2018), Athens (Greece, 2017), Thessaloniki (Greece, 2016), Island of Rhodes (Greece, 2015), Island of Rhodes (Greece, 2014), Halkidiki (Greece, 2013), and Corfu (Greece, 2012) events.

MHDW 2023 received submissions covering a plethora of data and knowledge mining and management techniques, including decision rules/trees, association rules, ontologies and alignments, clustering, filtering, learning, classifier systems, neural networks, and support vector machines, applied to numerous data from various areas of Humanistic Sciences, such as linguistic, historical, behavioral, psychological, artistic, musical, educational, social, etc.

MHDW 2023 would not have succeeded without the deep investment and involvement of the Program Committee members and the external reviewers who contributed to review (16 reviewers) and select the best contributions. Moreover, this event would not exist if authors and contributors did not submit their proposals. We address our special thanks to everyone, authors, reviewers, session chairs, Programme Committee and Organization Committee members involved in the success of MHDW 2023.

The EasyAcademia system was set up for the management of MHDW 2023 to support the submission, review and volume preparation processes. It proved to be a powerful framework. In this respect, special thanks are due to Antonis Papaleonidas for his timely technical support.

We hope that these proceedings will help researchers worldwide to understand and to be aware of recent issues related to mining on humanistic data. We do believe that they will be of major interest for scientists all over the globe and that they will stimulate further research in these domains.

April 2023   Ioannis Karydis

Organization

MHDW 2023 Organising Committee

General Co-chairs

Ioannis Karydis — Ionian University, Greece
Katia Lida Kermanidis — Ionian University, Greece
Spyros Sioutas — University of Patras, Greece

Program Chairs

Andreas Kanavos — Ionian University, Greece
Christos Makris — University of Patras, Greece
Phivos Mylonas — University of West Attica, Greece
Aristidis G. Vrahatis — Ionian University, Greece

Organizing Chair

Andreas Kanavos — Ionian University, Greece

Website and Advertising Chair

Ioannis Karydis — Ionian University, Greece

Program Committee

Christos Didachos — University of Patras, Greece
Georgios Drakopoulos — Ionian University, Greece
Elias Dritsas — University of Patras, Greece
Gregory Gasteratos — Ionian University, Greece
Panagiotis Gratsanis — Ionian University, Greece
Ioannis Hatzilygeroudis — University of Patras, Greece
Eleanna Kafeza — Athens University of Economics and Business, Greece
Sophia Karagiorgou — UBITECH Ltd., Greece
Sotiris Kotsiantis — University of Patras, Greece
Fotis Kounelis — Imperial College London, UK
Manolis Maragoudakis — Ionian University, Greece
Theodor Panagiotakopoulos — Hellenic Open University, Greece
Evaggelos Spyrou — University of Thessaly, Greece
Eleni Vlachou — Ionian University, Greece
Gerasimos Vonitsanos — University of Patras, Greece
Aristidis Vrahatis — Ionian University, Greece

A Framework for Co-creation in Generic Educational Activities Using Swarming

Gregory Gasteratos[(✉)], Eleni Vlachou, Panagiotis Gratsanis,
and Ioannis Karydis

Department of Informatics, Ionian University, 49132 Kerkyra, Greece
{ggasteratos,elvlachou,c20grat,karydis}@ionio.gr

Abstract. The flipped classroom model has become increasingly popular in recent years as it supports students' collaboration leading to co-creation of knowledge. Swarming is a nature-based collaborative solution for complex problems, wherein actors' "collective intelligence" emerges significantly more advanced than the sum of its units. The knapsack problem attempts to select the subset of items with maximum desirability while satisfying a constraint on the selected items. Educationally, the knapsack problem may be mapped as the selection of a subset of literature from a large corpus that is most relevant to a research query, while maintaining some constraint such as time availability, content complexity, etc. In this work we propose a framework that models a generic educational task and maps it to the Knapsack problem to be solved using the Ant Colony Optimisation (ACO) swarming algorithm to take advantage of the co-creational characteristics of the flipped classroom paradigm. Experimentation with alternative solutions to the Knapsack problem indicate their inappropriateness to the requirements of the proposed framework, while experimentation with ACO's key parameters indicates ACO's suitability to the proposed framework.

Keywords: Educational framework · Co-creation · Swarming · Ant Colony Optimisation · Knapsack problem

1 Introduction

In the 21st century, emerging technologies are changing the way we learn [2]. As education continues to evolve into a self-organizing vision, technology continually plays a more significant part in how education is delivered and how is used to provide support for learners' and teachers' processes [12].

The flipped classroom model's popularity has increased in recent years. It's based on the idea that students learn better when actively engaged in the learning process, rather than passively receiving information [25]. Attempting to enhance students' engagement and promote learning in classroom, educators are adopting practices promoting students' autonomy, collaboration, and teamwork [9].

I. Maglogiannis et al. (Eds.): AIAI 2023 Workshops, IFIP AICT 677, pp. 271–283, 2023.
https://doi.org/10.1007/978-3-031-34171-7_21

Although the breadth of educational challenges students need to tackle can be significantly broad, a closer inspection identifies amongst these a small number of generic tasks that are common to a plethora of settings, such as the identification of appropriate educational resources to study. In this work, we focus on this generic task and attempt to model it as a combinatorial optimisation and more specifically, the Knapsack problem [24], that is to select a subset of literature from a large corpus that is most relevant to a specific research question, while maintaining some constraint such as time availability, content complexity, etc.

In this context, swarming methodologies, describing a group of learners working together in a self-organised and decentralised fashion without necessary the presence of a leader/organiser [3], have been shown to be highly effective. Swarming is a nature-based solution that features collaboration and decision-making demonstrated by swarms of animals exhibiting "collective intelligence" or "swarm intelligence" and decision-making in the context of simple rules and local interactions among the animals [15]. One such approach is the Ant Colony Optimisation (ACO) [22], a discrete optimisation approach based on ants' ability to collaborate aiming at the identification of the shortest paths to targets.

1.1 Motivation and Contribution

Despite the obvious complementarity of the key theme of the work, educational task modeling to combinatorial optimisation solved by swarming methods, to the best of our knowledge, existing bibliography is scarce on this amalgamation. The prevailing of the new paradigm of the flipped classroom model, despite its popularity, still requires further exploration. In addition, the collaboration aspect of the flipped classroom model is addressing the ability and use of the capability to create and co-create that still require both further examination. In order to address these challenges, this work proposes a framework that models a generic educational task of finding a subset of literary works, that best meets the task's requirements, in a large corpus, for some constraint, and maps it to the Knapsack problem that is subsequently solved using the ACO swarming algorithm. The key contributions of this work can be summarised as follows:

- modelling of a generic part of numerous educational activities into a combinatorial optimisation,
- proposing a framework that amalgamates the aforementioned modeled educational activity with a collaborative solution based on the swarming methodologies wherein the mapping of the characteristics of the three pillars of the framework are defined,
- experimentation to test the unsuitability of non-swarming solutions to the proposed framework, and
- experimentation to show the suitability of the ACO swarming solution to the proposed framework's theme.

2   Background and Related Work

2.1   Education

In the field of Artificial Intelligence (AI), swarm intelligence has become a critical development direction as an emerging research area that has the potential to revolutionise the way education and learning are being delivered [32].

Wong and Looi [31] introduce the concept of swarm intelligence, for developing adaptive learning systems that can adjust the difficulty of learning materials in accordance with the performance of students. Kurilovas et al. [16] propose an improved swarm-based approach to recommend appropriate learning scenarios based on learners' preferences. [21] argues the limitations of traditional methods of curriculum sequencing that can be overcome by using swarm intelligence.

Swarm intelligence algorithms are increasingly used in research, especially in personalised learning and adaptive assessment. While their use in education is still in early stages, these approaches have shown promising results in improving students' learning outcomes and providing personalised learning experiences.

2.2   Co-creativity

Co-creativity is a concept that has been explored by several researchers in different fields, from education to design, and from arts to technology. At its core, co-creativity refers to collaborative and participatory practices that involve individuals working together to create something new and innovative [18,23].

Early accounts of exploring co-creativity in the context of education [7] addressed the implications of studying collaborative creativity for education and identified the importance of fostering a supportive environment for creativity to thrive. Co-creativity in education is the key theme in [29] where the potential of co-creativity in playful classroom activities is explored. [4] investigated the effectiveness of Collaborative Creativity Learning models in developing scientific creativity skills among secondary school students. In [27], authors explored enhancing skills with augmented reality is emphasising the importance of co-creativity in technology-mediated learning environments.

These examples highlight the versatility and potential of co-creativity as a concept that can be applied across various fields and contexts. Whether in education, design, technology, or the arts, co-creativity can promote, and is ultimately based on, collaboration, participation, and innovation, making it a valuable tool for promoting creative and effective solutions to complex problems.

2.3   Inverted Classroom: A Form of Co-creation

The flipped classroom model is considered a form of co-creation as it involves a collaborative approach to learning between teachers and students. Students receive instructional material to review outside of class allowing them to take ownership of their learning and actively participate in the learning process [1].

During interactive and collaborative activities in the flipped classroom, students can work together to co-create knowledge by sharing their ideas, insights, and perspectives [13]. Teachers can act as facilitators, guiding and supporting students as they work together to make sense of complex concepts and ideas. This collaborative approach to learning can lead to improved learning outcomes for students [14].

In addition to fostering collaboration between students, the flipped classroom model can also encourage co-creation between teachers and students [20]. Teachers can create instructional materials that are more tailored to the needs and interests of their students, while students can provide feedback and contribute their own ideas and insights to the learning process [30].

2.4   Swarming and Ant Colony Optimisation

To develop effective solutions to complex problems, nature-based solutions, such as the principles of "swarm intelligence" are of importance. Swarm intelligence is traced back to the biological study of how insects interact with each other in a self-organised manner [10]. According to Bonabeau et al. [6], social insects, use swarm behavior to coordinate activities that are otherwise too complex for each unit to accomplish. Combining swarm intelligence & algorithmic optimisation techniques has been shown effective in solving complex problems [22].

ACO [22] is a discrete optimisation approach based on the ability of ants to collaborate to identify the shortest paths to targets. The concept behind ACO is the use of artificial ants traversing paths on a graph with nodes being the components of the solution to a challenge. As part of the ACO approach, simulated chemical pheromones are used to attract ants onto better trails. Ants, collaborating, explore randomly and monitor chemicals left by other ants.

2.5   Knapsack Problem

As its name implies, it arises from the problem of filling a fixed-sized knapsack with the most valuable items. The knapsack problem, as defined by Martello and Toth [24], is: "*We are given a set of n items, each item i having an integer profit z_i and an integer weight w_i. The problem is to choose a subset of the items such that their overall profit is maximised, while the overall weight does not exceed a given capacity C.*"

This can be expressed, as per [24], using Equations $max \sum_{i=1}^{n} z_i x_i$ and $\sum_{i=1}^{n} w_i x_i \leq C$ where C is the total knapsack load capacity; z_i is the profit on an object i; w_i is the weight of an object i; C, z_i, and w_i are all integers and positive numbers; and $x_i = 0$ when an object i has not been loaded into a knapsack or $x_i = 1$ when an object i has been loaded into a knapsack.

In this paper, we are focusing on the most commonly used case, the "0-1 knapsack problem", which restricts the number of copies of each item to zero or one. This variation is better suited for our scenario whereby students pick academic papers only once in order to complete a specific task. There are numerous solutions for the knapsack problem [19], ranging from examining all combinations of items, to dynamic programming algorithms to swarming algorithms.

The "Brute-Force" Solution. In order to address the requirements of the 0-1 knapsack problem one might resort to a methodology that evaluates all alternative potential solutions and then keep (one of) the best. This approach requires the non-repeating combination of sampling r of n discrete elements as per Equation $C(n, r) = \frac{n!}{r! * (n-r)!}$.

Moreover, given the requirements of the Knapsack problem to allow one or more elements to be selected, the combinations of all scenarios $\forall r \in [1, n]$ must be considered leading thus to the evaluation of the number of combinations using Equation $\|\mathbf{combinations}\| = \sum_{r=1}^{n} C(n, r)$.

As this method does not utilise any optimisation, the number of combinations it has to examine, even for relatively low numbers of the N elements is significantly high. The number of combinations for one or multiple agents (examining entities of the elements to be included in the knapsack, in a form of parallelisation of the task) when the number of distinct elements and the number of samples are equal for values ranging from 1 to 40, is leading to maximum numbers of combinations reaching values near 10^{12}. As far as the form of parallelisation in the examination processes with multiple agents, the number of concurrent examining agents does indeed significantly effect the number of combinations per agent but given the relative high number of combinations to be examined altogether (and the equal distribution of examinations between them), the combinations per agent still remain quite large.

Accordingly, the "brute-force" solution to the Knapsack problem, despite the fact that it always reaches the best solution(s), becomes prohibitive costly for relatively low numbers of discrete elements in terms of the sheer number of combinations that must be evaluated.

Dynamic Programming Solution. Another way to solve the 0-1 Knapsack problem, is using the Dynamic Programming (DNP) algorithm which works on the principle of using a table to store the answers to solved sub-problems. Whenever a sub-problem is surfaced again, the answer can be looked up in the table rather than having to be computed again. As a result, dynamic programming-designed algorithms are incredibly efficient.

Unfortunately, as per the theme of this work, it cannot be applied on our educational model, i.e. map it to students co-creating solutions by accessing informative resources/papers. Nevertheless, it is used herein as a point of reference to obtain exact solutions, so we can compare the results to other algorithms for the solutions for the knapsack problem, such as the ACOK algorithm, discussed in the sequel (Sect. 2.5).

ACO Algorithm Solution. In this work, to solve the 0-1 knapsack problem, we will employ the ACO algorithm and compare it against the brute force method, as described in Sect. 2.5. Due to the long time the brute force algorithm takes and the fact that the ACO algorithm does not guarantee always a 100% optimal [11] solution, we will be using the aforementioned dynamic programming algorithm, as described in Sect. 2.5, to obtain the exact solution so we have a fixed target to compare against it.

Thus, we utilise a ported version of the standard ACO algorithm tailored for the 0-1 knapsack problem 2.5 (ACOK).

An artificial ant's probabilistic solution building process is biased by pheromones and heuristic variables (α, β) in ACO. The ants' movements are determined by stochastic local decision policies based on two composite parameters, namely, the pheromones and the attractiveness of the path leading to an, also, attractive edge [33]. Each ant incrementally constructs a solution to the problem by moving iteratively in various directions. In the process of completing a solution, the ant changes the pheromone value on the visited items, aiming at pheromone information guiding future ants.

In more detail, each ant moves from one state i to another state j according to a transition probability rule p_j [28], as shown in Equations $p = \frac{\tau_j^\alpha \mu_j^\beta}{\sum_{j \in N_i} \tau_j^\alpha \mu_j^\beta}$, $for\ j \in N_i$ and $p = 0, for\ j \notin N_i$.

The α parameter is responsible for controlling the impact of the pheromone trail τ_j, which is the collective memory of the colony. By increasing the value of α, ants are more likely to follow pheromone trails that other ants have previously followed. Parameter β controls the impact of the heuristic information (attractiveness μ_j), which is local information available to the ants regarding the problem. By increasing β, the ants are more likely to choose paths that appear to be more promising based on the specific characteristics of the problem. The neighbourhood N_i of state i is composed of items that can be used as part of the construction of a partial solution. The attractiveness μ_j refers to the problem-specific heuristic information that is used by the ants to evaluate the desirability of an item from the neighbourhood N_i being added to the N_i solution under construction. z_j is the profit and w_j is the weight of the selected item j. Thus, attractiveness [28] can be expressed as per Equation $\mu = \frac{z_j}{w_j^2}$.

When a solution has been found, each ant deposits an amount Δ_τ of pheromone τ on all the items included in the solution following the pattern using of Equation $\tau = \tau + \Delta\tau$. The amount Δ_τ of pheromone deposited on each item is proportional to the quality of the solution that the ant has found [28]. This is expressed as shown in Equation $\Delta\tau = f(Q) = \frac{1}{1 + \frac{z_{best} - z}{z_{best}}}$.

Finally, a mechanism of evaporation, as far as pheromones are concerned, is incorporated into the process of ACO and respective implementation of algorithms in order to avoid fast convergence to a sub-optimal solution [28]. The strength of evaporation is controlled by the parameter ϱ which represents the evaporation rate. The evaporation is calculated using Equation $\tau = \varrho\tau, \varrho \in (0, 1)$.

3   Proposed Method

This paper introduces and examines a framework for educational scenarios where a teacher/enabler maps an educational task to a distributed and decentralised process during which students cooperate to solve a challenge or, more generally, perform an educational task. As a result, students themselves co-create the solution, thus the solution they develop is a result of their collective output.

In swarm learning, the teacher/enabler plays a different role compared to traditional teaching approaches [17]. The teacher is not necessarily an instructor, but rather more of a facilitator whose primary responsibility is to support and guide students as they work collaboratively in order to learn. The teacher/enabler should first identify the educational task or goal that they want to achieve through their teaching. This could involve defining the learning objectives, outcomes, and/or competencies that they want their students to develop. In examining the integral part of education, i.e. the students, and more specifically a class of students seeking out new knowledge, we observe that it is directly related to the ant colony paradigm and that makes ACO an ideal candidate for a swarming approach for the aforementioned task.

One of the key initial activities of students is identifying information relating to the educational task. To achieve this goal, students are expected to examine sources (proposed by the teacher/enabler or according to will) to gather as much information about the subject in question. Each source is evaluated both by students and peers of its authors. The relative quality of a source depends on how well it meets the student's informational needs. Additionally, students' evaluation of a source requires a thorough examination of the source's content, including its bibliography thus affecting the whole examination process by adding more resources. Moreover, by citing a source within their own work, peers of a source's authors, in addition to providing references where due, they indirectly provide a measurement of evaluation, similarly to PageRank for web-pages [5].

The process of selecting papers that contribute most to the task at hand represents a well-defined problem domain as already discussed in Sect. 2.5, the Knapsack problem that dates back to the early works of the mathematician Tobias Dantzig [8]. To address the mapped educational challenge with the Knapsack problem using the aforementioned swarming solutions, the ACO approach, being a generic approach rather than a specific algorithm, it needs to be tailored to the particular problem under consideration i.e. education. To achieve that we use the Knapsack problem as an intermediary.

As described in Sect. 2.5, the knapsack problem attempts to select the subset of items with maximum desirability while satisfying a constraint of the total weight of the items [26]. Within the context of learning, the knapsack problem can be applied to the selection of resources that address the educational challenge, i.e. to select a subset of resources from a large corpus that is relevant to a specific research question or topic, based on factors such as time availability, reading capacity, and content complexity. For example, given a set of papers with associated relevance scores, citation counts, and a limited amount of time a student has to devote to reading, a student will have to determine the subset of papers that maximises the overall relevance or information gained based on the time limit and reading capacity constraints.

Accordingly, the proposed framework utilises the notions of (a) the Knapsack problem as a generic methodology to identify the best subset of resources that maximise their value while adhering to a (weight) constraint, (b) the ACO swarming algorithm that is inspired from ants for the task of identifying the aforementioned subset, and (c) the educational domain wherein one of the common processes includes the examination of educational resources in order to address an educational need. The fusion of these notions is based on a mapping between their key characteristics, as described in the sequel.

For the pillars educational process and Knapsack problem: educational sources are mapped to items; the number of bibliographic entries within each source are mapped to the item weight; citations received by a source as well as the source's ability to address the informational need are mapped to the desirability of each item; and, the combinations of subset of resources that must be examined to address the educational need are mapped to iterations.

For the pillars Knapsack problem and its ACO swarming approach: items are mapped to locations and/or processes that meet ants' need (e.g. foraging); item weight is mapped to the process of ACO that introduces realism by including constraints; item value is mapped to the desirability of a path; and, iterations are mapped to the paths travelled by ants to meet their need.

For the pillars ACO swarming approach and educational setting: parameter Alpha (α) is mapped to the impact of collective memory on students' decisions; parameter Beta (β) is mapped to the impact of local student information; evaporation rate is mapped to the capability of students to retain a varying persistence collective memory; iterations are mapped to the combinations of subset of resources that must be examined to address the educational need; ants are mapped to students; ants' need is mapped to the educational need/process; and, places that ants meed their need is mapped to the educational resources.

4   Experimental Evaluation

4.1   Experimental Setup

A simulation model was developed in order to test various scenarios using the ACOK algorithm, as well as to run sensitivity tests for the ACOK input parameters to determine their effectiveness. The simulation model was implemented in the .NET framework using C#. The machine characteristics that we run the tests are, Intel Quad Core i7-6820HK CPU @ 2.70 GHz with 16 GB RAM.

In order to have a simulation model that is as realistic as possible, the experiments were conducted using graphs directly obtained from Connected Papers via their REST API. Through Connected Papers, researchers are able to locate relevant academic papers based on the field of study in which they are interested. For the purposes of this work, the graphs experimented on where based on papers that research ICT methodologies for the reduction of risks and vulnerabilities closely related to climate change (e.g. flood risk, risk of fire, erosion, landslides and landslides). This selection was made as a preparation for future application of the proposed framework in various levels of educational institutions in order to promote/educate on issues of the climate crisis.

We tested using a set of three graphs with 20, 30 and 40 papers respectively. For each graph, we run a test scenario with the ACOK algorithm parameters set as follows. Number of Iterations: 5, 10, 100, 1000; Number of Ants: 1, 2, 4, 6, 8, 10, 15, 20, 25, 30, 50, 100; Evaporation Rate: 0.1, 0.2, 0.3, 0.4, 0.5, 0.6, 0.7, 0.8, 0.9, 1; Alpha: 0, 1, 2, 3, 4, 5; and, Beta: 0, 1, 2, 3, 4, 5.

Default Parameter Values. We initially performed a short sensitivity analysis for parameters Alpha (α), Beta (β), and Evaporation Rate (ϱ) that lead to the best performing values of these parameters. Given these results, we selected as the default values for Alpha, Beta and Evaporation Rate to be 1, 2, and 0.8 respectively. In our experimentation process, the Number of Ants never exceeds the value of thirty which maps favourably to the paper's theme of typical number of students in a class. Also, the maximum Number of Iterations to be executed, within which the solution is to be found, is selected to be 10 as, per our theme, most repetitive tasks bigger than these are deemed to become exhausting and boring for the students participating in the experiments.

4.2   Evaluation Results

We performed two experiments: (i) Measure success rate for varying number of ants involved, and (ii) Measure the number of iterations at which the optimal solution found for varying number of items in the graph.

All scenarios have been executed 10 times for each variation of the parameters in order to average out the stochasticity of the heuristic process of the algorithm. The parameters' value ranges used for the ACOK, leading to a resulting dataset of 18,000 entries, are: Alpha: 1; Beta: 2; Evaporation Rate: 0.8; Number of Iterations: 1...10, Number of Ants: 1...30; and, Items in graph:20, 30, 40.

Average Success Rate Per Ant. This experiment involves testing the impact of the number of ants involved on the success rate. That is, the ACOK's average success rate against the exact solution produced by the DNP algorithm, as described in Sect. 2.5. Thus, we measure this as a percentage of the output produced by ACOK against DNP since, as already mentioned, ACO does not always guarantee the exact solution [11] hence the use of DNP.

Thus, the first experiment tests the impact of the number of ants involved in order to find the exact solution. Accordingly, we measure the average percentage of the success rate against DNP's performance.

Examining the results received shown in Fig. 1, we observe that for all three cases and for one ant, all three alternatives of the graph size present the worse success rate of their respective examination. The results increase in an exponential manner as more ants are incorporated into the experiment, reaching at around 90% in average for 30 deployed ants. The result's explanation presents

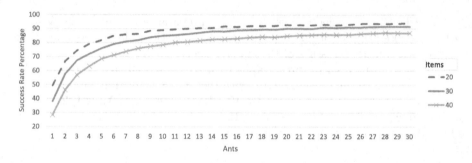

Fig. 1. Average Success Rate per Ant.

as straightforward since the introduction of more ants allows more combinations to be processed within a set number of iterations hence the possibility to find the best solution with higher success rate is also increased. Moreover, we observe that for smaller search spaces, i.e. having less items to process, the success rate is higher than for larger search spaces (i.e. graphs with 20 items as opposed to graphs with 40 items).

Average Number of Iterations the Best Result found at The next experiment concentrates on how the number of ants and number of items in a graph affect the number of iterations needed in order to reach to the optimal solution. Thus, in this experiment we examine the average number of iterations that the optimal solution is found at for varying numbers of ants.

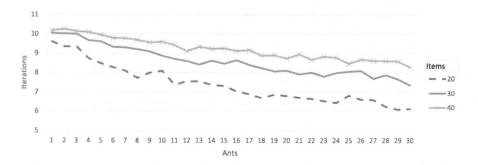

Fig. 2. Average number of iterations the best result found at.

From the results received in this experiment, as shown in Fig. 2, we observe that the maximum number of iterations at which we find the most optimal solution, peaks at around 10 iterations (averaged values). We also observe that as more ants are added to the colony, up to a total of 30, iterations are almost consistently decreasing with the minimum value reaching 6 iterations.

It follows then that as more workers (ants) are being added, the parallelism of the process is increased and thus fewer iterations are required, as expected. Moreover, we observe that the size of the graph, representing the search space, affects proportionately the iteration at which the identification of the most optimal solution is made at, for a given size of workers, again as expected.

5 Conclusions

The meteoric popularity of the flipped classroom model in recent years has been based on its ability to enhance students' engagement and promote learning through students' collaboration in order to address a complex educational task, thus leading to the co-creation of knowledge. Such co-creation of knowledge is also observed in nature-based collaborative solutions, among others, in the form of swarming for efficient and effective tackling of complex problems.

One of the key aspects of the flipped classroom model is the shift of class' time activities to non-class time activities. Students initiate tasks like examining the bibliography outside the classroom thus prompting the generic educational task of the selecting the best subset of educational resources that best addresses a complex educational challenge given constraints, a task efficiently addressed by the Knapsack problem.

Building on the aforementioned aspects of an educational task modeled to combinatorial optimisation solved by swarming methods, in this work we propose a framework that models the generic educational task of identifying a subset of literary works, that best meets the task's requirements, from a large corpus, for some constraint, and maps it to the Knapsack problem that is subsequently solved using the ACO swarming algorithm.

Experimentation with alternative solutions to the Knapsack problem, such as "brute-force" and dynamic programming, indicate their inappropriateness to the requirements of the proposed framework, while experimentation with ACO's sensitivity and key parameters indicate the effectiveness and efficiency of ACO to the proposed framework.

Future plans include the mapping of more generic and specific educational activities to the proposed framework. Moreover, future update of this work includes experimentation with more swarming approaches in order to test their effectiveness and efficiency. Finally, future plans include the application of the proposed framework in various levels of educational institutions in order to promote/educate on issues of the climate crisis.

Acknowledgements. The financial support of the European Union and Greece (Partnership Agreement for the Development Framework 2014–2020) under the Regional Operational Programme Ionian Islands 2014–2020 for the project "Laertis" is gratefully acknowledged.

References

1. Abeysekera, L., Dawson, P.: Motivation and cognitive load in the flipped classroom: definition, rationale and a call for research. High. Educ. Res. Dev. **34**(1) (2015)
2. Ally, M.: Competency profile of the digital and online teacher in future education. Int. Rev. Res. Open Distrib. Learn. **20**(2) (2019)

3. Anderson, C., McMillan, E.: Of ants and men: self-organized teams in human and insect organizations. Emergence **5**(2) (2003)

4. Astutik, S., Susantini, E., Madlazim, M., Nur, M., Supeno, S.: The effectiveness of collaborative creativity learning models on secondary schools scientific creativity skills. Int. J. Instruction **13** (2020)

5. Bianchini, M., Gori, M., Scarselli, F.: Inside PageRank. ACM Trans. Internet Technol. (TOIT) **5**(1) (2005)

6. Bonabeau, E., Dorigo, M., Theraulaz, G., Theraulaz, G.: Swarm intelligence: from natural to artificial systems. No. 1, Oxford University Press (1999)

7. Craft, A.: Studying collaborative creativity: implications for education. Think. Skills Creat. **3** (2008)

8. Dantzig, T., Mazur, J.: Number: The Language of Science (Masterpiece Science ed.) ISBN 9780452288119 (2007)

9. Dillenbourg, P.: What do You Mean by Collaborative Learning? Elsevier, Amsterdam (1999)

10. Garnier, S., Gautrais, J., Theraulaz, G.: The biological principles of swarm intelligence. Swarm Intelligence **1** (2007)

11. Gutjahr, W.J.: ACO algorithms with guaranteed convergence to the optimal solution. Inf. Process. Lett. **82**(3) (2002)

12. Haleem, A., Javaid, M., Qadri, M.A., Suman, R.: Understanding the role of digital technologies in education: a review. Sustain. Oper. Comput. (2022)

13. Hämäläinen, R., Vähäsantanen, K.: Theoretical and pedagogical perspectives on orchestrating creativity and collaborative learning. Educ. Res. Rev. **6**(3) (2011)

14. Hew, K.F., Lo, C.K.: Flipped classroom improves student learning in health professions education: a meta-analysis. BMC Med. Educ. **18** (2018)

15. Ioannou, C.C.: Swarm intelligence in fish? The difficulty in demonstrating distributed and self-organised collective intelligence in (some) animal groups. Behav. Process. **141** (2017)

16. Kurilovas, E., Zilinskiene, I., Dagiene, V.: Recommending suitable learning scenarios according to learners' preferences: an improved swarm based approach. Comput. Hum. Behav. **30** (2014)

17. Limniou, M., Schermbrucker, I., Lyons, M.: Traditional and flipped classroom approaches delivered by two different teachers: the student perspective. Educ. Inf. Technol. **23** (2018)

18. Littleton, K., Mercer, N.: Communication, collaboration, and creativity: How musicians negotiate a collective 'sound'. Musical imaginations: multidisciplinary perspectives on creativity, performance and perception (2012)

19. Martello, S., Toth, P.: Knapsack Problems: Algorithms and Computer Implementations. Wiley, Hoboken (1990). ISBN 978-0471924203

20. Mehring, J.G.: A new pedagogy for the Japanese EFL classroom: instructional redesign with flipped learning. Original Papers **14**(2) (2015)

21. Menai, M.E., Alhunitah, H., Al-Salman, H.: Swarm intelligence to solve the curriculum sequencing problem. Comput. Appl. Eng. Educ. **26**(5) (2018)

22. Merkle, D., Middendorf, M.: Ant colony optimization, marco dorigo, thomas stützle, MIT Press (2004). ISBN 0-262-04219-3 (2006)

23. Paulus, P.B., Dzindolet, M., Kohn, N.W.: Collaborative creativity-group creativity and team innovation. In: Handbook of Organizational Creativity. Elsevier, Amsterdam (2012)

24. Pisinger, D.: Where are the hard knapsack problems? Comput. Oper. Res. **32**(9) (2005)

25. Reidsema, C., Hadgraft, R., Kavanagh, L.: Introduction to the Flipped Classroom. Springer, Singapore (2017). https://doi.org/10.1007/978-981-10-3413-8_1
26. Salkin, H.M., De Kluyver, C.A.: The knapsack problem: a survey. Naval Res. Logist. Q. **22**(1) (1975)
27. Sanabria, J.C., Arámburo-Lizárraga, J.: Enhancing 21st century skills with AR: using the gradual immersion method to develop collaborative creativity. Eurasia J. Math. Sci. Technol. Educ. **13** (2017)
28. Schiff, K., et al.: Ant colony optimization algorithm for the 0-1 knapsack problem. Czasopismo Techniczne **2013**(Automatyka Zeszyt 3-AC (11) 2013) (2013)
29. Schmölz, A.: On co-creativity in playful classroom activities. Creat. Theor. Res. Appl. **4** (2017)
30. Wong, C.C., Kumpulainen, K., Kajamaa, A.: Collaborative creativity among education professionals in a co-design workshop: a multidimensional analysis. Think. Skills Creat. **42** (2021)
31. Wong, L.H., Looi, C.K.: Swarm intelligence: new techniques for adaptive systems to provide learning support. Interact. Learn. Environ. **20**(1) (2012)
32. Zhai, X., et al.: A review of artificial intelligence (AI) in education from 2010 to 2020. Complexity **2021** (2021)
33. Zhao, P., Zhao, P., Zhang, X.: A new ant colony optimization for the knapsack problem. In: 7th International Conference on Computer-Aided Industrial Design and Conceptual Design (2006)

Analyzing User Reviews in the Tourism & Cultural Domain - The Case of the City of Athens, Greece

Tasos Papagiannis[1] , George Ioannou[1] , Konstantinos Michalakis[2] ,
Georgios Alexandridis[3(✉)] , and George Caridakis[2]

[1] School of Computer and Electrical Engineering, National Technical University of
Athens, Zografou, Greece
{tasos,geoioannou}@islab.ntua.gr
[2] Department of Cultural Technology and Communication, University of the Aegean,
Mytilene, Greece
{kmichalak,gcari}@aegean.gr
[3] Department of Digital Industry Technologies, National and Kapodistrian
University of Athens, Psachna, Greece
gealexandri@uoa.gr

Abstract. Tourism is an important economic activity for many countries and the ability of understanding visitor needs as they evolve over time is a priority for all involved stakeholders. The analysis of textual reviews written by travelers on various online platforms may be a valuable tool in this direction. In this work, we showcase the potential of this idea by examining 8 well-known attractions in the City of Athens, Greece. After retrieving the relevant data from two popular online services, we employ a state-of-the-art transformer-based language model for two tasks; the extraction of distinctive keywords and phrases out of the free-text reviews and the assignment of a sentiment score to each review. Based on this information, we can associate certain keywords and phrases with specific sentiment values and monitor their evolution over time, in the context of specific touristic & cultural places. The analysis that follows explores the potential of this idea in more detail.

Keywords: sentiment-analysis · keyword extraction · free-text reviews · language models · transformers

1 Introduction

In many countries, tourism constitutes an important financial sector, displaying a significant potential each year. To better exploit its capacity and further maintain the observed growth rates, it is necessary to interconnect the touristic content with the interests of actual and expected visitors. Nowadays, the vast proliferation of mobile devices and the expansion of high speed data networks has turned tourists into active content creators, who take photos & videos of

I. Maglogiannis et al. (Eds.): AIAI 2023 Workshops, IFIP AICT 677, pp. 284–293, 2023.
https://doi.org/10.1007/978-3-031-34171-7_22

the places they visit, write reviews & recommendations and in general, digitally interact with the cultural & touristic spaces.

As a consequence, vast amounts of relevant data are stored on tourist-based platforms, such as TripAdvisor, map services, such as Google Maps, online social networks, such as Instagram, Facebook and Twitter, as well as on travel blogs, forums etc. The aforementioned data may be of great value to all stakeholders involved in the tourism and cultural domain, ranging from businesses to regulation authorities and policy makers. Indeed, if properly processed, they can provide valuable insight on visitors' interests, preferences, as well as their evolution over time. It is obvious that this information can be very useful to all interested entities in addressing visitor needs and enhance the tourists' cultural experience, so as to meet their expectations. As a result, various tools have been developed over time that crawl the relevant information from the World Wide Web, apply data mining techniques and aggregate results, acting as decision support systems.

In this respect, the current work focuses on the case of the City of Athens in Greece, a place of paramount cultural & historical importance, that attracts thousands of tourists every year. The emphasis is placed on 8 well-known sites and museums with the data being crawled from two popular online platforms; Trip-Advisor, which is tourist-oriented and Google Places, which is more business-oriented and is integrated into Google Maps. After an initial pre-possessing stage, the obtained reviews are fed into transformer-based language models in order to extract the most prominent keywords and phrases for each place. Additionally, the aforementioned language models are used to assign a sentiment score to each textual review [3], which, in turn, is associated with the rating provided by each visitor. Finally, positive and negative reviews are analyzed in order to uncover user/tourist preference and identify key issues, along with their evolution over time.

The rest of this paper is organized as follows; Sect. 2 overviews related work on tourism & cultural spaces-oriented data mining. Section 3 presents the methodology & the approach followed in the current work, while Sect. 4 discusses the obtained results. Finally, the paper concludes in Sect. 5.

2   Related Work

The application of data mining techniques on visitor reviews in the tourism and the cultural domain is an active and interdisciplinary research area [10]. The most common intention, which is also one of the objectives of the current work, is to reason on the aspects of tourist satisfaction [8,12] and explore their connection to other inter-related factors. Of course, the analysis is not limited to attractions but is also directed to hotels [9] and restaurants [18]. It could be argued that the aforementioned feeatures constitute the three most important factors considered by visitors during their stay. Therefore, they play an important role in the hospitality industry, as well as in attraction marketing.

The examined data sources are quite diverse, ranging from travel blogs & tourism-oriented portals to domain-specific online social networks. TripAdvisor, also considered in this work, is the most popular among them, predominately due its specific focus and ease of access (crawling) [1,7]. Other, more rarely used platforms include Yelp, Expedia & Booking [17]. Regarding online social networks, Twitter is a straightforward choice, especially due to its access policy and micro-blogging nature [4]. Researchers from China also prefer Sina Weibo, the Chinese alternative to Twitter [5].

After retrieving the data from the selected sources, most researchers follow a methodology similar to the one described in Sect. 3. Initially, the data are cleaned; HTML tags, URLS, usernames, extra-white space etc are removed, in order to obtain the useful part of the textual review. Then, especially in earlier approaches [15], the text is further pre-possessed, with the removal of stop-words and of very low frequency words. Following, the data are tokenized; that is they are split into words, phrases or any other meaningful elements (tokens). At the final stages, the extracted tokens are lemmatized/stemmed and labeled with part-of-speech taggers prior to further analysis. On the other hand, most state-of-the-art methodologies, directly employ language models after prepossessing [2], an approach followed in this work as well.

Finally, a variety of techniques and methods are used for the actual analysis of the obtained data. These may be simple, descriptive statistics [13], like those presented in Sect. 3. Very often, keyword extraction techniques are considered, an approach followed in the current work as well. In this respect, techniques that identify "topics" in textual data, such as latent Dirichlet allocation [8], are preferred. At a higher level lies text summarization that produces succinct summaries of documents. For example, in [9] a relevant technique was used to identify the most informative sentences in hotel reviews. Lastly, another common modeling technique is sentiment analysis that can help determine visitor attitude towards e.g. attractions [16] or accommodation [9].

3   Methodology

The main objective of the current work is to address knowledge extraction from textual reviews of cultural & touristic places with respect to two different tasks; keyword/phrase extraction and sentiment analysis. For this purpose, the relevant review data are provided to deep learning language models in order to identify possible correlations in-between them and draw an overall insight on visitor opinion regarding specific popular tourist & cultural attractions.

3.1   Data

The data considered in this study are related to 8 well-known cultural places in the City of Athens, Greece and they have been crawled by two popular sources discussed in Sects. 1 and 2; TripAdivor and Google Places. For each place, the reviews and comments of the visitors were extracted, which consisted of ratings (in the 5-star scale), a small comment (review in free-text form), the date of visit and the date the comment was posted. The characteristics of the collected data obtained from TripAdvisor are summarized on Table 1.

Table 1. Characteristics of the TripAdvisor dataset.

Location	Number of reviews	Oldest Review	Newest Review
Acropolis	20, 346	June 6, 2005	January 9, 2023
Acropolis Museum	22, 507	June 21, 2009	February 15, 2023
Ancient Agora of Athens	2, 479	July 24, 2009	February 8, 2023
Benaki Museum	929	June 20, 2005	February 8, 2023
Museum of Cycladic Art	625	October 12, 2005	February 4, 2023
National Archeological Museum	4, 286	April 11, 2007	February 8, 2023
Parthenon	9, 586	January 20, 2006	January 12, 2023
Temple of Hephaestus	2, 225	September 12, 2011	February 8, 2023

In the case of Google Places, the crawling procedure was not as straight-forward, since for each attraction only 1, 000 to 1, 500 reviews were returned, either the most recent or the "most relevant", as determined by the service itself. Despite this fact, we decided to consider this dataset in our analysis as well, in order to identify possible correlations in visitor behavior between the users of the two platforms.

A first observation on the characteristics outlined on Table 1 is that the obtained reviews span a large time period, which in all cases is longer than 10 years and in some cases (the Acropolis, Benaki Museum and the Museum of Cycladic Art) it is close to 20 years (the crawling took place in mid-February, 2023). This is of particular importance, as it allows the ensuing analysis to study the evolution of visitors' beliefs and evaluations over time. Additionally, as it might have been expected, there is an obvious difference in the popularity of places, as quantified by the volume of the relevant reviews. Indeed, the number of reviews of the most popular place (the Acropolis) is two orders of magnitude bigger than those of the least popular place (Museum of Cycladic Art).

The overwhelming majority of the reviews obtained from TripAdvisor were written in the English language. As a consequence, in the data pre-processing stage, we disregarded reviews written in other languages. However, this was not the case for the data originating from Google Places, as it contained reviewers in many languages (e.g. English, Greek, French, German etc.). Nevertheless, given that the dataset obtained from Google Places was considerably smaller and therefore not as representative, we decided to keep the English language reviews in this case as well, for comparison purposes.

The final data pre-processing stage involved an initial "cleaning" of the remaining records (i.e. remove entries with no textual reviews, remove textual reviews with one or two words, etc.). Then, the ensuing data have been provided to the transformer-based language models discussed in the following Subsection.

3.2   Transformer-Based Language Model

For the keyword extraction and sentiment analysis tasks, state-of-the-art transformer-based language models are employed and more specifically, approaches
that are extensions of the Bidirectional Encoder Representations from Transformers (BERT) architecture [6]. One such popular, pre-trained, transformer-
based language model, suitable for Natural Language Processing (NLP) tasks
such as question answering, text classification, and language translation is RoBE-
RTa [11]. Its development involved several key innovations that distinguish it
from its predecessors, like dynamic masking during pre-training, which allowed
the model to learn more effectively from the text data. In this work, a distilled
version of RoBERTa has been considered, with 6 layers, 768 dimension and 12
heads. This is inspired by DistilBERT [14], a distilled version of BERT.

Regarding the keyword extraction task, each review text is initially tokenized
into words and phrases of up to four words, using n-grams of the corresponding length. Then, the ensuing tokens are being fed into the pre-trained model
(RoBERTa) and are assigned to a numerical embedding. The same procedure is
followed for the entire textual review in order to obtain the final representation
(embedding). A comparison is made between the latter embedding and each of
the candidate keyword embeddings, so as to calculate similarities. For this purpose, the cosine similarity metric has been considered and the phrases with a
higher score were denoted as the most relevant keywords.

For the sentiment analysis task, the reviews of both datasets were fed into
a pre-trained DistilBERT-based model in order to quantify visitor opinion and
draw useful insights. This is accompanied by a confidence value of the latter
classification. The confidence values range in $[0, 1]$ and serve as a metric that
measures the overall sentiment of a comment (for negative comments values are
mapped to $[-1, 0]$).

4   Discussion

In this section, the results of the knowledge extraction process are displayed and
reasoned upon, in order to interpret them in a meaningful way. The goal is to
find general patterns in phrasing, as well as patterns regarding the sentiment of
each comment. The analysis will be performed under two different scopes; a long
term one and a seasonal one (e.g. detect periods when reviews are negative, find
patterns concerning the season of the year etc.).

For this purpose, the reviews are grouped by the season they refer to and
their sentiment score (in the $[-1, 1]$ range) is extracted for the corresponding
season. In order to be able to evaluate the credibility of the produced metric,
sentiment scores are scaled to the $[0, 5]$ range and are directly compared with
the users' ratings (stars) for the relevant periods. The sub-figures of Fig. 1 depict
the two metrics based on the reviews of each attraction. The two curves seem to
have similar fluctuations and capture the overall trend per season in most cases.
Also, it seems that the ratings are almost always higher, which shows that even

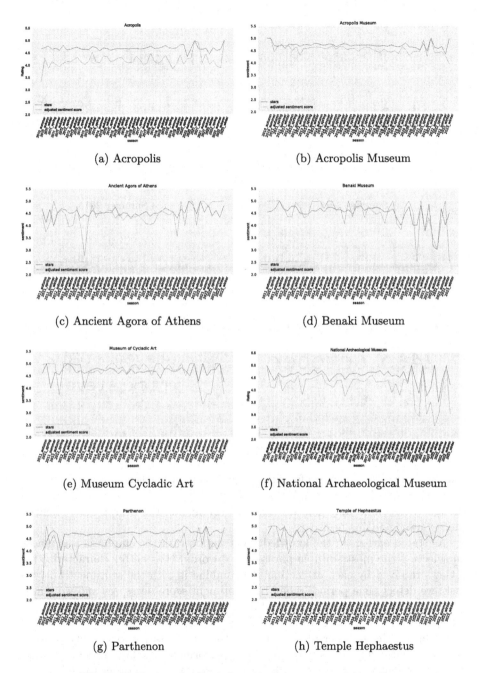

(a) Acropolis

(b) Acropolis Museum

(c) Ancient Agora of Athens

(d) Benaki Museum

(e) Museum Cycladic Art

(f) National Archaeological Museum

(g) Parthenon

(h) Temple Hephaestus

Fig. 1. Ratings and adjusted sentiment scores per attraction.

(a) Summer 2011

(b) Summer 2014

(c) Autumn 2017

(d) Autumn 2021

Fig. 2. Extracted key-phrases for different periods from Parthenon negative reviews.

though the reviews may contain negative comments, the overall assessment of the reviewer remains positive.

As stated earlier, in the knowledge extraction task the emphasis was placed on selecting the most suitable phrases (1–4 words) that better characterize the reviews received by each attraction. To combine it with the sentiment analysis task, we detect time periods when the sentiment score decreases and we search in these particular periods' reviews for negative keywords and phrases.

Specifically, in Fig. 1g we observed a substantial decrease in the sentiment score during the summer of 2011 for Parthenon. In order to identify possible causes, a sentiment analysis step has been performed to isolate negative reviews and subsequently extract knowledge from these reviews, in order to detect possible reasons for this trend. Figure 2a displays the predominant keywords in negative comments for that period, as well as some other later seasons (Figs. 2b to 2d), so as to evaluate the evolution of negative comments overtime.

Regarding the summer of 2011 specifically, we can see various phrases, such as "slippery rocks", "ppl pushing", "broken columns", as well as several references indicating the need for special shoes. Additional conclusions can be drawn for all periods of interest in a similar manner. In this way, knowledge extraction can assist in detecting issues raised by visitors and help the involved parties to address them.

Keyword extraction is also useful for long-term analysis, as seen, for example in Fig. 3 for the Acropolis Museum. It displays some general comments towards this specific attraction, consisting mostly of positive evaluations. An analysis like that is always helpful in quantifying the overall attitude of the people that visited an attraction.

Fig. 3. Most common keywords and phrases for the Acropolis Museum during 2010–2023.

5   Conclusions and Future Work

In this work, an initial analysis of reviews in free-text form, posted on online platforms, of visitors of popular cultural & touristic places in the City of Athens, Greece, has been attempted. To this end, a large and representative dataset of 8 distinctive attractions has been crawled from two popular online services (TripAdvisor and Google Places) that spans several years. After pre-processing, the said dataset has been provided to RoBERTa, a state-of-the-art transformer-based language model, in order to achieve two tasks; keyword/phrase extraction and sentiment analysis. Then, the obtained results have been used to identify visitor opinion, both in a seasonal manner and as a whole. The presented examples showcased the insights that can be drawn from this kind of analysis, as well as its overall potential.

The course of action presented in this work may be extended to other, less popular touristic & cultural attractions in the city of Athens, as well as in the broader Attica region. Of course, the consideration of even more sources, both from online social networks and tourism websites, forums and blogs, is expected to enrich the available datasets and form the basis for further research. Finally, the presented approach can be a part of a larger architecture that constantly collects data from multiple sources and functions as a decision support system for interested parties and policymakers.

Acknowledgements. This research has been co-financed by the European Union and Greek national funds through the Regional Operational Program "ATTICA 2014-2020" of the National Strategic Reference Framework (NSRF) - Research Funding Program: Smart Tourism Recommendations based on Efficient Knowledge Mining on Online Platforms ATTP4-0349847.

References

1. A segmentation of online reviews by language groups: how english and non-english speakers rate hotels differently. Int. J. Hosp. Manage. **48**, 143–149 (2015). https://doi.org/10.1016/j.ijhm.2014.12.007, https://www.sciencedirect.com/science/article/pii/S0278431914001935
2. Arefeva, V., Egger, R.: When BERT started traveling: tourbert-a natural language processing model for the travel industry. Digital **2**(4), 546–559 (2022). https://doi.org/10.3390/digital2040030, https://www.mdpi.com/2673-6470/2/4/30
3. Barbieri, F., Espinosa Anke, L., Camacho-Collados, J.: XLM-T: multilingual language models in Twitter for sentiment analysis and beyond. In: Proceedings of the Thirteenth Language Resources and Evaluation Conference, pp. 258–266. European Language Resources Association, Marseille, France (2022). https://aclanthology.org/2022.lrec-1.27
4. Bordogna, G., Frigerio, L., Cuzzocrea, A., Psaila, G.: Clustering geo-tagged tweets for advanced big data analytics. In: 2016 IEEE International Congress on Big Data (BigData Congress), pp. 42–51 (2016). https://doi.org/10.1109/BigDataCongress.2016.78
5. Cheng, M., Edwards, D.: Social media in tourism: a visual analytic approach. Curr. Issues Tourism **18**(11), 1080–1087 (2015). https://doi.org/10.1080/13683500.2015.1036009
6. Devlin, J., Chang, M., Lee, K., Toutanova, K.: BERT: pre-training of deep bidirectional transformers for language understanding. In: Burstein, J., Doran, C., Solorio, T. (eds.) Proceedings of the 2019 Conference of the North American Chapter of the Association for Computational Linguistics: Human Language Technologies, NAACL-HLT 2019, Minneapolis, MN, USA, June 2–7, 2019, Volume 1 (Long and Short Papers), pp. 4171–4186. Association for Computational Linguistics (2019). https://doi.org/10.18653/v1/n19-1423

7. Fang, B., Ye, Q., Kucukusta, D., Law, R.: Analysis of the perceived value of online tourism reviews: influence of readability and reviewer characteristics. Tourism Manage. **52**, 498–506 (2016). https://doi.org/10.1016/j.tourman.2015.07. 018, https://www.sciencedirect.com/science/article/pii/S0261517715001715

8. Guo, Y., Barnes, S.J., Jia, Q.: Mining meaning from online ratings and reviews: tourist satisfaction analysis using latent dirichlet allocation. Tourism Manage. **59**, 467–483 (2017). https://doi.org/10.1016/j.tourman.2016.09.009, https://www. sciencedirect.com/science/article/pii/S0261517716301698

9. Hu, Y.H., Chen, Y.L., Chou, H.L.: Opinion mining from online hotel reviews - a text summarization approach. Inf. Process. Manage. **53**(2), 436–449 (2017). https://doi.org/10.1016/j.ipm.2016.12.002, https://www.sciencedirect. com/science/article/pii/S0306457316306781

10. Li, J., Xu, L., Tang, L., Wang, S., Li, L.: Big data in tourism research: a literature review. Tourism Manage. **68**, 301–323 (2018). https://doi.org/10. 1016/j.tourman.2018.03.009, https://www.sciencedirect.com/science/article/pii/ S0261517718300591

11. Liu, Y., et al.: Roberta: a robustly optimized BERT pretraining approach. CoRR abs/1907.11692 (2019). http://arxiv.org/abs/1907.11692

12. Liu, Y., Teichert, T., Rossi, M., Li, H., Hu, F.: Big data for big insights: investigating language-specific drivers of hotel satisfaction with 412,784 user-generated reviews. Tourism Manage. **59**, 554–563 (2017). https://doi.org/10. 1016/j.tourman.2016.08.012, https://www.sciencedirect.com/science/article/pii/ S0261517716301534

13. Racherla, P., Friske, W.: Perceived 'usefulness' of online consumer reviews: an exploratory investigation across three services categories. Electron. Commerce Res. Appl. **11**(6), 548–559 (2012). https://doi.org/10.1016/j.elerap.2012.06.003, https://www.sciencedirect.com/science/article/pii/S1567422312000464, information Services in EC

14. Sanh, V., Debut, L., Chaumond, J., Wolf, T.: Distilbert, a distilled version of BERT: smaller, faster, cheaper and lighter. CoRR abs/1910.01108 (2019). http:// arxiv.org/abs/1910.01108

15. Xiang, Z., Schwartz, Z., Gerdes, J.H., Uysal, M.: What can big data and text analytics tell us about hotel guest experience and satisfaction? Int. J. Hosp. Manage. 44, 120–130 (2015). https://doi.org/10.1016/j.ijhm.2014.10.013, https://www. sciencedirect.com/science/article/pii/S0278431914001698

16. Xu, H., Yuan, H., Ma, B., Qian, Y.: Where to go and what to play: towards summarizing popular information from massive tourism blogs. J. Inf. Sci. **41**(6), 830–854 (2015). https://doi.org/10.1177/0165551515603323

17. Xu, X., Li, Y.: The antecedents of customer satisfaction and dissatisfaction toward various types of hotels: a text mining approach. Int. J. Hosp. Manage. **55**, 57–69 (2016). https://doi.org/10.1016/j.ijhm.2016.03.003, https://www.sciencedirect. com/science/article/pii/S0278431916300202

18. Zhang, Y., Cole, S.T.: Dimensions of lodging guest satisfaction among guests with mobility challenges: a mixed-method analysis of web-based texts. Tourism Manage. **53**, 13–27 (2016). https://doi.org/10.1016/j.tourman.2015.09.001, https://www. sciencedirect.com/science/article/pii/S0261517715300054

Applying SCALEX scRNA-Seq Data Integration for Precise Alzheimer's Disease Biomarker Discovery

Aristidis G. Vrahatis[(✉)], Konstantinos Lazaros, Petros Paplomatas,
Marios G. Krokidis, Themis Exarchos, and Panagiotis Vlamos

Bioinformatics and Human Electrophysiology Laboratory, Deparment of Informatics, Ionian
University, 49100 Corfu, Greece
aris.vrahatis@ionio.gr

Abstract. Alzheimer's disease is a complex and devastating neurological disorder, and there is a pressing need to discover effective treatments. Analyses in
specific brain regions can provide valuable insights into the underlying pathology
of the disease. Molecular biology techniques, such as single-cell analysis, can
offer an in-depth analysis of cellular-level changes in the brain in Alzheimer's disease. However, integrating single-cell RNA sequencing (scRNA-seq) data from
different studies can be challenging due to batch effects, which can lead to spu-
rious results. The dominant approach for addressing this issue is SCALEX, an
online single-cell data integration method that projects heterogeneous datasets
into a common cell-embedding space. In this paper, we highlight the impact of
SCALEX in detecting accurate biomarkers in the context of significant genes that
are leading scRNA-seq data. We demonstrate the pitfalls of traditional data integration methods and show the protection offered by SCALEX in preserving the
biological heterogeneity of the sample while minimizing the impact of technical
artifacts introduced by batch effects. Our results show that integrating scRNA-seq
data with SCALEX can lead to more accurate biomarkers and significant genes,
offering insights into the underlying pathology of Alzheimer's disease. These
findings have important implications for the development of new therapies and
treatments for this devastating disease.

Keywords: scRNA-seq integration · SCALEX · Biomarkers · Alzheimer's
Disease

1 Introduction

1.1 Single-Cell Technologies for Alzheimer's Disease

Alzheimer's disease is a neurodegenerative disorder that affects millions of people worldwide, particularly in the aging population. The disease is characterized by the accumula-
tion of amyloid-beta plaques and tau protein tangles in the brain, leading to progressive
cognitive impairment and memory loss. Despite decades of research, there is still no

© IFIP International Federation for Information Processing 2023
Published by Springer Nature Switzerland AG 2023
I. Maglogiannis et al. (Eds.): AIAI 2023 Workshops, IFIP AICT 677, pp. 294–302, 2023.
https://doi.org/10.1007/978-3-031-34171-7_23

effective cure for Alzheimer's disease, and current treatments only offer limited symptomatic relief. One of the major challenges in developing effective treatments is the complexity and heterogeneity of the disease, which involves multiple biological pathways and cell types.

Single-cell RNA sequencing (scRNA-seq) [16, 20] has emerged as a powerful tool for understanding the heterogeneity of Alzheimer's disease [4, 19] and identifying potential biomarkers and therapeutic targets. By analyzing gene expression in individual cells, scRNA-seq can reveal the diversity of cell types and their molecular signatures in the brain, including changes associated with disease progression. This technique allows us for a more detailed understanding of the function and dysfunction of different cell types in Alzheimer's disease. By analyzing gene expression at the single-cell level, researchers can gain insights into why certain cells are more vulnerable to the disease, and how the disease progresses over time. Proper data analysis of scRNA-Seq and snRNA-Seq (single nucleus RNA sequencing) data can significantly enhance our understanding of Alzheimer's disease and aid in the development of new therapies.

However, scRNA-seq data is complex and noisy, and requires careful data integration [14, 18] and analysis to identify reliable biomarkers and understand disease mechanisms. Advanced methods such as SCALEX [13] can help to overcome technical variability and improve the accuracy of biomarker identification.

1.2 Single-Cell Data Integration – A Major Challenge

Single-cell data integration is the process of combining multiple datasets obtained from single-cell experiments to gain a more comprehensive understanding of the biological system under investigation. With the increasing availability of high-throughput single-cell technologies, there is a need to integrate data from multiple sources to identify novel biological insights and reduce technical and biological variability. There are several challenges associated with single-cell data integration, including batch effects, differences in experimental protocols, and technical variability.

Batch effects are a type of technical variability that can arise in single-cell experiments when samples are processed at different times or using different protocols. In single-cell RNA sequencing (scRNA-seq) experiments, batch effects can arise due to differences in library preparation, sequencing, and cell capture. For example, if cells are isolated and processed at different times, there may be differences in the efficiency of cell capture or differences in the quality of the RNA extracted, which can result in batch effects. Similarly, if different sequencing platforms or protocols are used, there may be differences in read depth, sequencing errors, or gene detection rates that can also lead to batch effects.

Batch effects can manifest in various ways in scRNA-seq data, such as differences in the expression of certain genes, the presence of artificial clusters or cell populations, or shifts in the distribution of gene expression levels. To overcome batch effects, several methods have been developed to adjust for batch effects, such as batch correction algorithms, which adjust the data to remove any technical variation associated with the batches. These methods aim to remove batch effects while preserving biological variation, allowing for more accurate biological interpretations and comparisons across samples. Various methods have been developed for data integration [15], such as Seurat [9], Scanpy [11], Harmony [7], and Conos [10].

Meanwhile, in single-cell RNA sequencing (scRNA-seq) experiments, identifying biomarkers through dominant genes is a common task [5]. However, if the scRNA-seq data is not integrated properly, the identified biomarkers may be inaccurate and biased due to the batch effect, which is a technical problem that can arise from processing samples at different times or using different protocols. Batch effects can introduce technical variability that affects the gene expression levels of cells and can lead to the identification of false positive or false negative biomarkers. Therefore, if the integration of single-cell data is not performed correctly, the identified biomarkers may be misleading and not biologically meaningful.

In other words, a bad scRNA data integration can lead to the identification of phenotypically accurate biomarkers that are actually derived from the wrong data and not biologically meaningful, due to the presence of batch effects. Thus, it is essential to perform proper data integration to remove batch effects and ensure the accurate identification of biomarkers from scRNA-seq data. This involves assessing the quality of the data, applying appropriate normalization techniques, and employing reliable data integration methods that can overcome batch effects.

If the integration of single-cell data is not performed correctly, it can lead to erroneous conclusions and misinterpretations of the underlying biology. For example, if batch effects are not properly corrected, it may appear that certain cell types are present in one dataset but not in another, leading to false discoveries or missed opportunities for identifying important cell types.

Additionally, improper data normalization can lead to an overrepresentation of certain genes or features in downstream analyses, potentially biasing the results. In extreme cases, bad data integration can lead to incorrect biological interpretations and wasted resources. Therefore, it is crucial to carefully assess the quality of the data, perform rigorous normalization and feature selection, and choose appropriate data integration methods to ensure reliable and accurate results. Collaboration with experts in bioinformatics and single-cell data analysis can also be helpful in ensuring that the data integration is performed optimally.

2 Methodology – Exploring the Implications of SCALEX Integration

2.1 SCALEX

SCALEX is a single-cell data integration method that uses a VAE (Variational Auto Encoder) [12] framework to project single-cell data onto a low-dimensional space. The key innovation in SCALEX is the use of an asymmetric autoencoder that inputs batch information only to the decoder, not the encoder. This allows the encoder to learn a batch-invariant representation of the data, while the decoder can capture batch-specific variation. The use of a DSBN layer in the decoder further helps to release the encoder from the burden of capturing batch-specific variation, allowing it to focus on capturing the biological signal.

To improve the performance of SCALEX, the authors also employed a mini-batching strategy that samples data from all batches simultaneously, which more closely follows the overall distribution of the input dataset. This strategy includes a Batch Normalization layer in the encoder that adjusts the deviation of each mini-batch and aligns them to the overall input distribution. By using this mini-batching strategy, SCALEX can integrate single-cell data in an online manner, without the need for retraining on new data.

To evaluate the performance of SCALEX, the authors compared it to several test-variants. One variant included an encoder with batch labels as input, which showed similar integration performance to the full SCALEX, but was not capable of integrating data in an online manner. Another variant removed the DSBN layer from the decoder, which resulted in a drop in integration performance. Finally, a variant that used a regular autoencoder instead of a VAE performed the worst among all variants.

Overall, the SCALEX methodology demonstrates an effective approach for online integration of heterogeneous single-cell data using a VAE framework and innovative design choices, such as the asymmetric autoencoder, DSBN layer, and mini-batching strategy. By avoiding the inclusion of batch information in the encoder, SCALEX can learn a batch-invariant representation of the data, allowing for more accurate integration of single-cell data.

2.2 Application to Single-Cell RNA-Seq Data

We applied our method to the scREAD dataset [1], a single-cell RNA-seq database for Alzheimer's disease that includes 23 human and mouse control cell atlases based on 17 scRNA-seq and snRNA-seq datasets. These datasets cover 10 brain regions, two genders, and different ages, totaling 713,640 cells that were redefined into 73 datasets based on species, gender, brain region, disease or control, and age. We focused on the superior frontal gyrus and integrated three datasets with a total of 93,000 cells, including 40,000 healthy and 50,000 diseased cells across five different cell types (macrophages, astrocytes, microglia, etc.).

To the best of our knowledge, this is the first machine learning study to include such a large dataset from the superior frontal gyrus of humans with Alzheimer's disease, integrating several scRNA-seq studies. Our goal was to demonstrate the heterogeneity of significant genes arising without and with SCALEX integration. We compared the results obtained using traditional data integration methods (harmonization) with SCALEX in terms of biomarker detection. Our observations showed that different genes were identified as potential biomarkers using traditional data integration methods compared to SCALEX. This emphasizes the importance of proper data integration, as traditional methods can lead to the identification of wrong gene biomarkers.

More specifically, we employ UMAP [17] to visualize the SCALEX integration in two dimensions and compare its performance against the simple concatenation method for harmonized data provided by the dataset authors. Additionally, we evaluate two state-of-the-art data integration techniques, Scanorama [8] and BBKNN (Batch Balanced KNN) [6]. The 2D visualizations highlight the effectiveness of SCALEX in comparison to the other methods, demonstrating its superior capabilities in data integration. Assessing these visualizations in terms of clustering, we evaluate their performance using the silhouette index, yielding values of 0.7948, 0.2706, 0.3398, and 0.3517 for SCALEX,

Concatenation, Scanorama, and BBKNN, respectively. The high score achieved by SCALEX is reflected in the denser clusters observed in Fig. 1, further emphasizing its superior performance in data integration.

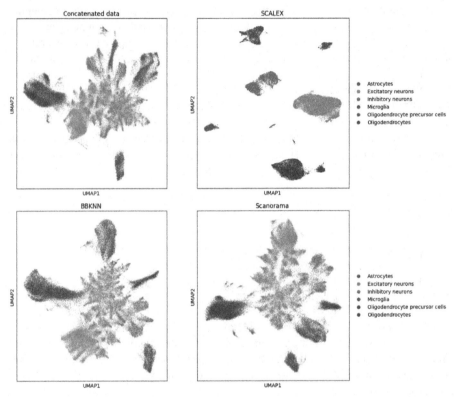

Fig. 1. This UMAP embeddings of our scRNA-seq dataset are displayed, showcasing four different integration methods: the original concatenated integration provided by the dataset authors (top left), SCALEX integration (top right), BBKNN integration (bottom left), and Scanorama integration (bottom right). The UMAP embeddings are color-coded based on cell types. We observe that SCALEX generates denser clusters for each cell type, demonstrating its superior performance in terms of both batch effect removal and preservation of biologically meaningful information.

We also evaluated the effectiveness of SCALEX in identifying the most relevant genes, or potential biomarkers, for Alzheimer's disease research compared to the classical concatenation method. By comparing the significant gene detection performance of the two approaches using XGBoost [2] and ANOVA [3] feature importance methods (see Fig. 2), we aim to demonstrate the benefits of using SCALEX for integrating single-cell RNA sequencing (scRNA-seq) data. The Fig. 2 illustrates the degree to which potentially important disease biomarkers are lost when using the classical concatenation method as compared to the SCALEX approach, emphasizing the advantages of employing SCALEX for a more accurate identification of significant genes in Alzheimer's disease research.

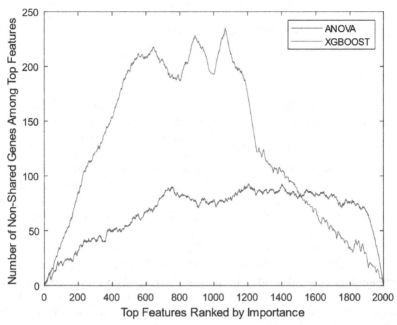

Fig. 2. This figure presents a comparison of significant gene detection between SCALEX and concatenated data integration approaches, utilizing both XGBoost (orange line) and ANOVA (blue line) feature importance methods. The x-axis represents the top 2000 features ranked by importance, while the y-axis indicates the number of non-shared genes between the top features of the concatenated and SCALEX-integrated data. For instance, in the XGBoost plot, at X = 400, Y = 154, which implies that among the top 400 features identified by XGBoost, there are 154 non-shared genes between the two datasets. The graphs highlight the degree to which potentially important disease biomarkers are lost when using the classical concatenation method as compared to the SCALEX approach, for both XGBoost and ANOVA feature selection methods, thereby emphasizing the advantages of employing SCALEX for a more accurate identification of significant genes.

Note here that XGBoost (eXtreme Gradient Boosting) is a popular machine learning algorithm based on decision trees and gradient boosting. In the context of gene expression data, XGBoost can be used to rank the importance of different genes based on their contribution to the predictive accuracy of the model. The XGBoost variable importance score is calculated by considering the frequency and impact of a gene in the decision trees built during the learning process. Highly ranked genes based on their variable importance scores are considered more crucial for the classification or prediction task, providing insights into potential biomarkers and significant genes. Also, analysis of variance (ANOVA) is a statistical test used to compare the means of two or more groups. In the context of differentially expressed genes, ANOVA can be applied to assess the significance of gene expression differences across multiple conditions or groups. The feature importance using ANOVA is based on the F-statistic, which measures the ratio of the between-group variance to the within-group variance. Genes with higher F-statistics indicate a larger expression difference across groups, suggesting their potential importance as biomarkers or significant genes.

3 Discussion

Molecular biology and transcriptomics have significant potential to contribute to our understanding of Alzheimer's disease (AD). Transcriptomic studies can help identify molecular pathways that are disrupted in AD, and highlight potential therapeutic targets. By analyzing gene expression changes in AD brains compared to healthy controls, researchers can gain insights into the underlying molecular mechanisms of the disease. Transcriptomics can also be used to identify biomarkers for AD, which can aid in early diagnosis and monitoring of disease progression. By analyzing gene expression patterns in blood or cerebrospinal fluid, for example, researchers can identify biomarkers that are associated with the disease.

Moreover, transcriptomic studies can aid in drug development for AD by identifying potential drug targets and predicting drug efficacy. By analyzing the gene expression changes induced by candidate drugs in AD models, researchers can assess their potential therapeutic value. AD is a complex disease that affects multiple cell types in the brain. Transcriptomics can help researchers understand the heterogeneity of cell types and their molecular signatures in AD, which can aid in the development of more targeted therapies. Integrating transcriptomic data with other molecular and clinical data can provide a more comprehensive understanding of AD. For example, integrating transcriptomic data with data from imaging or proteomic studies can help identify key molecular pathways and biomarkers associated with disease progression.

The results of this study showed that traditional data integration methods (harmonization) can lead to the identification of different genes as potential biomarkers compared to the SCALEX method. This suggests that the traditional methods may not accurately account for batch effects and other sources of technical variability, leading to false positive or false negative results in biomarker identification.

In contrast, the SCALEX method, which was specifically designed to account for batch effects and reduce technical variability, identified different genes as potential biomarkers compared to the traditional methods. This demonstrates that proper data integration using advanced methods such as SCALEX can improve the accuracy and reliability of biomarker identification in scRNA-seq datasets.

Moreover, the study focused on the superior frontal gyrus, which is an important brain region affected by Alzheimer's disease. The integration of multiple scRNA-seq datasets allowed for a comprehensive analysis of the heterogeneity of gene expression across different cell types and conditions. The large dataset size also provided a powerful resource for identifying potential biomarkers and understanding disease mechanisms.

Regarding the comparisons for the significant gene detection performance between the SCALEX and concatenated data integration approaches, we observed the potential pitfalls and misleading conclusions that can arise from improper data integration without effectively removing batch effects. Inadequate removal of batch effects can lead to the identification of incorrect pathways and erroneous biomarkers, which can have significant consequences for downstream analyses and the development of targeted therapies.

By emphasizing the importance of employing appropriate data integration methods, such as SCALEX, we aim to minimize these risks and facilitate more accurate research outcomes in Alzheimer's disease studies.

In our comparisons we utilized XGBoost variable importance and ANOVA feature importance since they offer distinct methods for ranking genes based on their relevance in gene expression data. XGBoost focuses on the predictive power of genes in a machine learning context, while ANOVA highlights the statistical differences in gene expression levels across multiple conditions or groups. Combining these two approaches can provide a comprehensive understanding of the most important genes for a particular study, contributing to the discovery of potential biomarkers and key genes involved in disease processes.

4 Conclusions

Overall, the discovery of new biomarkers and therapeutic targets for Alzheimer's disease is a pressing need, and scRNA-seq provides a powerful tool for making progress in this area. By integrating large and diverse datasets using advanced methods, researchers can gain new insights into the disease and develop more effective treatments. To ensure the identification of reliable biomarkers, it is crucial to begin with well-preprocessed and clean data as a foundation. In the case of single-cell RNA-seq data, this necessitates effective data integration. SCALEX is a recent tool that has demonstrated remarkable potential in this research area. By applying SCALEX to Alzheimer's disease scRNA-seq data, we showcase the capabilities of this tool and anticipate that it will become a dominant method in the field, paving the way for more accurate and reliable biomarker discovery.

Acknowledgment. This research is funded by the European Union and Greece (Partnership Agreement for the Development Framework 2014–2020) under the Regional Operational Programme Ionian Islands 2014–2020, project title: "Study of Clinical trial protocols with biomarkers that define the evolution of non-genetic neurodegenerative diseases- NEUROTRIAL", project number: 5016089.

References

1. Jiang, J., Cankun, W., Ren, Q., Hongjun, F., Qin, M.: ScREAD: a single-cell RNA-Seq database for alzheimer's disease. IScience **23**(11), 101769 (20 Nov 2020)
2. Chen, T., Guestrin, C.: XGBoost: a scalable tree boosting system. In: Proceedings of the 22nd ACM SIGKDD International Conference on Knowedge Discovery and Data Mining (KDD '16). Association for Computing Machinery, New York,pp. 785–794 (2016). https://doi.org/10.1145/2939672.2939785
3. Lazaros, K., Tasoulis, S., Vrahatis, A., Plagianakos, V.: Feature selection for high dimensional data using supervised machine learning techniques. In: 2022 IEEE International Conference on Big Data (Big Data), Osaka, Japan, pp. 3891–3894 (2022). https://doi.org/10.1109/BigData55660.2022.10020654

4. Mathys, H., Davila-Velderrain, J., Peng, Z., et al.: Single-cell transcriptomic analysis of Alzheimer's disease. Nature **570**, 332–337 (2019). https://doi.org/10.1038/s41586-019-1195-2

5. Paplomatas, P., Krokidis, M.G., Vlamos, P., Vrahatis, A.G.: An ensemble feature selection approach for analysis and modeling of transcriptome data in alzheimer's disease. Appl. Sci. **13**, 2353 (2023). https://doi.org/10.3390/app13042353

6. Polański, K., Young, M.D., Miao, Z., Meyer, K.B.,Teichmann, S.A., Park, J.-E.: BBKNN: fast batch alignment of single cell transcriptomes. Bioinformatics **36**(3), 964–965 February (2020). https://doi.org/10.1093/bioinformatics/btz625

7. Korsunsky, I., Millard, N., Fan, J., et al.: Fast, sensitive and accurate integration of single-cell data with Harmony. Nat. Methods **16**, 1289–1296 (2019). https://doi.org/10.1038/s41592-019-0619-0

8. Hie, B., Bryson, B., Berger, B.: Efficient integration of heterogeneous single-cell transcriptomes using Scanorama. Nat. Biotechnol. **37**, 685–691 (2019). https://doi.org/10.1038/s41587-019-0113-3

9. Butler, A., Hoffman, P., Smibert, P., Papalexi, E., Satija, R.: Integrating single-cell transcriptomic data across different conditions, technologies, and species. Nat. Biotechnol. **36**(5), 411–420 (2018). https://doi.org/10.1038/nbt.4096. Epub 2018 Apr 2. PMID: 29608179; PMCID: PMC6700744

10. Barkas, N., et al.: Joint analysis of heterogeneous single-cell RNA-seq dataset collections. Nat. Methods (2019). https://doi.org/10.1038/s41592-019-0466-z

11. Wolf, F., Angerer, P., Theis, F.: SCANPY: large-scale single-cell gene expression data analysis. Genome Biol. **19**, 15 (2018). https://doi.org/10.1186/s13059-017-1382-0

12. Lopez, R., Regier, J., Cole, M.B., et al.: Deep generative modeling for single-cell transcriptomics. Nat. Methods **15**, 1053–1058 (2018). https://doi.org/10.1038/s41592-018-0229-2

13. Xiong, L., Tian, K., Li, Y., et al.: Online single-cell data integration through projecting heterogeneous datasets into a common cell-embedding space. Nat. Commun. **13**, 6118 (2022). https://doi.org/10.1038/s41467-022-33758-z

14. Argelaguet, R., Cuomo, A.S.E., Stegle, O., et al.: Computational principles and challenges in single-cell data integration. Nat. Biotechnol. **39**, 1202–1215 (2021). https://doi.org/10.1038/s41587-021-00895-7

15. Luecken, M.D., Büttner, M., Chaichoompu, K., et al.: Benchmarking atlas-level data integration in single-cell genomics. Nat. Methods **19**, 41–50 (2022). https://doi.org/10.1038/s41592-021-01336-8

16. Kolodziejczyk, A.A., Kim, J.K., Svensson, V., Marioni, J.C., Teichmann, S.A.: The technology and biology of single-cell RNA sequencing. Mol. Cell **58**, 610–620 (2015)

17. McInnes et al.: UMAP: uniform manifold approximation and projection. J. Open Source Softw. **3**(29), 861 (2018). https://doi.org/10.21105/joss.00861

18. Rautenstrauch, P., Vlot, A.H.C., Saran, S., Ohler, U.: Intricacies of single-cell multi-omics data integration. Trends Genet. **38**(2), 128–139 (2022). https://doi.org/10.1016/j.tig.2021.08.012

19. Wang, M., Song, Wm., Ming, C., et al.: Guidelines for bioinformatics of single-cell sequencing data analysis in Alzheimer's disease: review, recommendation, implementation and application. Mol. Neurodegeneration **17**, 17 (2022). https://doi.org/10.1186/s13024-022-00517-z

20. Chen, G., Ning, B., Shi, T.: Single-cell RNA-seq technologies and related computational data analysis. Front. Genet. **10**, 317 (2019). https://doi.org/10.3389/fgene.2019.00317

Ensemble Machine Learning Models for Breast Cancer Identification

Elias Dritsas[1]([✉]), Maria Trigka[2], and Phivos Mylonas[2]

[1] Department of Electrical and Computer Engineering, University of Patras, Patras, Greece
dritsase@ceid.upatras.gr
[2] Department of Informatics and Computer Engineering, University of West Attica, Egaleo, Greece
{mtrigka,mylonasf}@uniwa.gr

Abstract. The advances in the Machine Learning (ML) domain, from pattern recognition to computational statistical learning, have increased its utility for breast cancer as well by contributing to the screening strategy of diverse risk factors with complex relationships and personalized early prediction. In this work, we focused on Ensemble ML models after using the synthetic minority oversampling technique (SMOTE) with 10-fold cross-validation. Models were compared in terms of precision, accuracy, recall and area under the curve (AUC). After the experimental evaluation, the model that prevailed over the others was the Rotation Forest achieving accuracy, precision and recall equal to 82% and an AUC of 87.4%.

Keywords: Ensemble Models · SMOTE · Machine-Learning · Risk-Prediction · Data Analysis

1 Introduction

Breast cancer develops from the cells of the breast gland tissues. It is the most common type of cancer that occurs in women in both developed and less developed countries. It is the most common malignancy in women with an incidence of 12%, i.e. 1 in 8, and the second most common cause of cancer death after lung cancer [1,26]. Although breast cancer also occurs in men, it is very rare. The incidence of male breast cancer is less than 1% of all breast cancer cases. In 2020, there were 2.3 million women diagnosed with breast cancer and 685000 deaths globally, according to the World Health Organization (WHO) [1,30].

Every woman should be aware of the aggravating factors that increase the risk of developing the disease, the value of prevention, self-examination, and early diagnosis, as well as the effectiveness of modern treatment. Age is a factor in the occurrence of breast cancer, as most cases occur after the age of 50, while it is rare in women under the age of 35. In addition, women who have already been diagnosed with cancer are more likely to develop new cancer in the same

© IFIP International Federation for Information Processing 2023
Published by Springer Nature Switzerland AG 2023
I. Maglogiannis et al. (Eds.): AIAI 2023 Workshops, IFIP AICT 677, pp. 303–311, 2023.
https://doi.org/10.1007/978-3-031-34171-7_24

or the other breast. Also, women in whom menstruation began at the age of fewer than 12 years or stopped at the age of more than 55 years have a relatively increased risk of developing the disease [9,34,44,47]. Obese women have a higher risk of being diagnosed with breast cancer compared to women who maintain a healthy weight. Alcohol consumption and smoking are also aggravating factors as are estrogen and progesterone. Finally, research has shown that women with dense breasts have an increased chance of developing cancer [29,38,39].

In the initial stage, breast cancer shows no symptoms. A palpable mass, change in skin colour, infiltration or discharge may later appear. If a woman does not pay attention to the aforementioned symptoms, then she may show signs of advanced disease, such as red breast (inflammatory cancer), bone pain, and large swelling. The diagnosis of breast cancer in the first stage or even in a pre-cancerous stage is much more due to the awareness of women regarding the preventive control of the breasts with clinical palpation by a doctor, mammography and ultrasound, as well as with self-palpation. Once a suspicious tumour is found, the diagnosis is made by taking material from the tumour for microscopic examination [41,52].

In the second half of the 20th century and up to today, there have been rapid developments in the knowledge and treatment of breast cancer. The introduction of screening healthy women with mammography dramatically changes the profile of the disease and its outcome. New technologies are being added to breast cancer imaging and diagnosis. The discovery of more and more biomarkers decodes the heterogeneity of breast cancer, which is now classified into different groups with different prognostic models and methods. Finally, October 25 is a day that concerns all women, since it is dedicated to their fight against breast cancer [4,26,33].

Machine learning has played an important role in the medical field as it contributes to the early prediction of various diseases complications, such as diabetes (as classification [18,28] or regression task for continuous glucose prediction [6,12]), cholesterol [20,27], hypertension [14,16], chronic obstructive pulmonary disease [11], covid-19 [23], stroke [22], chronic kidney disease [21], cardiovascular diseases [13,24,51], sleep disorders [36,37], lung cancer [19], liver disease [25], and metabolic syndrome [15] etc.

In this research work, we relied on anthropometric data and biochemical indices, which can be collected in routine blood analyses to predict the occurrence of breast cancer. The main contribution of this study lies in the selected models for evaluation. Ensemble machine learning models were assessed based on several predictors that can potentially be used as breast cancer biomarkers. Moreover, from a methodological perspective, before the models' evaluation, we employed the SMOTE [10] technique to render the dataset balanced which, as will be verified in the experiments, favoured the classifiers' performance. Finally, comparing our outcomes with the ones derived from a previous study in the same dataset, it is shown that ensemble methods constitute an alternative and highly efficient solution for breast cancer prediction.

The remainder of the paper is organized as follows. In Sect. 2, a description of the adopted methodology is outlined. Furthermore, in Sect. 3, we discuss related works on the topic under consideration and note the research results. Finally, conclusions and future directions are presented in Sect. 4.

2   Methodology

In this section, the dataset and its characteristics are described, the adopted methodology is noted, the models have been described as well as the evaluation metrics with which the experimental evaluation was carried out.

2.1   Dataset Presentation and Processing

A detailed analysis of the dataset, the adopted methodology for the measurements capturing and the determination of the class label per subject have been made by the authors in [45]. The dataset we relied on comes from the UCI Machine Learning Repository [2]. There are 10 predictors, all quantitative, and a binary dependent variable, indicating the presence or absence of breast cancer. Specifically, the attributes are Age (years), Body Mass Index (BMI) (kg/m^2) that is associated with the subjects' categorization as overweight and obese, Glucose (mg/dL), Insulin (μU/mL), Homeostasis Model Assessment (HOMA), Leptin (ng/mL), Adiponectin (μg/mL), Resistin (ng/mL) and Monocyte Chemoattractant Protein-1 (MCP-1) (pg/dL).

As for the HOMA index, it depends on fasting insulin (microU/L) and fasting glucose (nmol/L) and determines a subject's insulin sensitivity (low values) and resistance (high values). The amount of Leptin is related to body fat and high values occur in obese subjects. Adinopetiny is a factor that regulates glucose levels, fat metabolism, and sensitivity to insulin. Elevated Resistin levels relate to obesity (as indicated by BMI and body fat) and diabetes. The last feature, MCP-1, is associated with cancer progression or metastasis and inflammatory recruitment. Since, from a medical point of view, these features are significant risk factors for breast cancer occurrence monitoring, all of them will be considered as input to prediction models.

The total number of participants is 116, of which 64 (or 55.2%) have been diagnosed with breast cancer and 52 (or 44.8%) have not. Statistical details about the features in the given dataset are illustrated in Table 1.

Here, for data analysis and knowledge extraction, we experimented with a free software tool, the Waikato environment (Weka), widely exploited for data preprocessing and predictive modelling [3]. Concerning data preprocessing, there were no missing values so any data imputation technique wasn't applied. Moreover, investigating the considered features-predictors no outliers were detected. Then, we applied SMOTE technique to make the class distribution uniform. The motivation behind the application of SMOTE is to further improve the classifiers' discrimination ability and sensitivity in identifying both patients and healthy subjects. SMOTE builds iteratively a class-balanced dataset exploiting a portion of the minority class data to make the class distribution 50-50%. SMOTE is preferable since it doesn't create duplicates but new synthetic data [17] using the k-NN method. Given that we worked on Weka, we have used the offered method where $k = 5$. An algorithmic overview of SMOTE is shown in Algorithm 1 where $M = 52$ (the number of instances in the minority class) and $N = 24\%$ (percentage of minority instances that will be used for creating the new instances for

Table 1. Statistical description of the features in the dataset.

Attribute	Description		
	Min	Max	Mean±stdDev
Age	24	89	57.3±16.1
BMI	18.37	38.58	27.58±5.02
Glucose	60	201	97.79±22.52
Insulin	2.432	58.46	10.01±10.07
HOMA	0.467	25.05	2.69±3.64
Leptin	4.311	90.28	26.61±19.18
Adiponectin	1.656	38.04	10.18±6.84
Resistin	3.21	82.1	14.73±12.39
MCP-1	45.843	1698.44	534.65±345.91

class balancing), thus $S = 12$ new instances are created. Note that the statistical description of the balanced dataset was omitted to be referred to since there was no significant difference from the information presented in Table 1.

Algorithm 1. SMOTE

Input: M (minority class sample size), N (% of synthetic minority samples for class balancing), $k = 5$ (number of nearest neighbors), s_{syn} synthetic instance;
Choose randomly a subset S of the minority class data of size $S = \frac{N}{100}M$ (synthetic minority data ratio) such that the class labels are balanced;
for all $s_i \in S$ **do**
   (1) Find the $k = 5$ nearest neighbours;
   (2) Randomly select one of the $k = 5$ NNs, called $\hat{s}_i$;
   (3) Calculate the distance $d_{i,k} = \hat{s}_i - s_i$ between the randomly selected NN $\hat{s}_i$ and the instance s_i;
   (4) The new synthetic instance is generated as $s_{syn} = s_i + \delta d_{i,k}$ (where $\delta = rand(0, 1)$ is a random number between 0 and 1);
end for
Repeat steps number 2-4 until the desired proportion of minority class is met.

2.2 Machine Learning Models and Evaluation Metrics

In this research work, we focused on ensemble models [49], which is a machine learning approach that combines multiple other models in the prediction process. More specifically, the Bagging [35] model was configured to have as a base classifier the Random Forest (RF) [40], the Stacking [50] method was set to combine the base classifiers RF and J48 [46] model, and as a meta classifier the Logistic Regression (LR) [43] model and the Voting [35] method considered the same based models with the stacking, but at the final step averages the probabilities to predict the class (soft voting). Finally, Rotation Forest [48] was set up to use Principal Component Analysis for features transformation and the RF as a base classifier.

To evaluate the performance of ML models, we applied 10-fold cross-validation ensuring also that one class (of either non-patients or patients) is not over-present in the test or train data. Also, we relied on metrics commonly used in the ML field, namely accuracy, precision, recall, and AUC. Note that the final score in each metric is derived by averaging the scores from all folds. The definition of these metrics is based on the confusion matrix consisting of the elements true positive(Tp), true negative (Tn), false positive (Fp) and false-negative (Fn) [31]. Hence, the aforementioned metrics are defined as follows:

- Accuracy:

$$Accuracy = \frac{Tn + Tp}{Tn + Fn + Tp + Fp} \tag{1}$$

- Precision:

$$Precision = \alpha_1 \frac{Tp}{Tp + Fp} + \alpha_2 \frac{Tn}{Tn + Fn} \tag{2}$$

- Recall:

$$Recall = \alpha_1 \frac{Tp}{Tp + Fn} + \alpha_2 \frac{Tn}{Tn + Fp} \tag{3}$$

- To evaluate the distinguishability of a model, the AUC is exploited. It is a metric that varies in $[0, 1]$.

It should be noted that (2), (3) capture the weighted average precision and recall. In both equations, the first term concerns the class "Yes" while the latter relates to the class "No". Generally, if the dataset instances are distributed non-uniformly among the two classes the weights $\alpha_1 = 44.8\%, \alpha_2 = 55.2\%$ will be different and specifically $\alpha_1 \neq \alpha_2 \neq 50\%$. In this study, we have used SMOTE technique to acquire a balanced dataset, therefore, $\alpha_1 = \alpha_2 = 50\%$.

3   Results and Discussion

This section provides a brief overview of the related works on the topic under consideration and notes our experimental results. Observing Table 2, the most common ensemble models are assessed in terms of accuracy, precision, recall and AUC. Also, in the context of our analysis, the selected models were evaluated before and after the application of class balancing using SMOTE. As the results witnessed, the use of SMOTE raised the models' performance metrics by around 5%. The suggested model is Rotation Forest (after SMOTE) which indicated Accuracy, Precision and Recall of 82% and AUC of 87.4%.

Now, let us focus on a recent study that experimented with the same dataset. The proposed model in study [7] is Support Vector Machine (SVM) combined with an extra-trees model for feature selection that performed Accuracy equal to 80.23%, Precision and Recall of 82.71% and 78.57%, correspondingly, and an

Table 2. Performance Evaluation of Ensemble Models.

Ensemble Models	Accuracy		Precision		Recall		AUC	
	Balanced	UnBalanced	Balanced	UnBalanced	Balanced	UnBalanced	Balanced	UnBalanced
Random Forest	0.773	0.724	0.774	0.723	0.773	0.724	0.867	0.807
Voting	0.805	0.698	0.805	0.697	0.805	0.698	0.867	0.800
Bagging	0.804	0.767	0.805	0.768	0.805	0.767	0.870	0.822
Stacking	0.818	0.741	0.816	0.741	0.816	0.741	0.872	0.806
Rotation Forest	0.820	0.775	0.820	0.775	0.820	0.776	0.874	0.824

AUC of 78%. Comparing the prevailing model of work [7] with the suggested model in this study, it is shown the prevalence of ensemble model Rotation Forest against SVM in all metrics.

At this point, we will pay attention to works that study breast cancer exploiting different datasets from the ones considered above. In the paper [8], the authors compared the predictive accuracy of the Naive Bayes (NB) classifier and k-Nearest Neighbour (k-NN) for breast cancer classification using cross-validation. The experimental results showed that the k-NN gives the highest accuracy (97.51%). Moreover, in [5], the authors implemented three machine learning models, namely Decision Tree (DT), Support Vector Machine (SVM), and Artificial Neural Network (ANN), for predicting breast cancer recurrence and comparing them in terms of accuracy, sensitivity and specificity. The SVM model prevailed in all the aforementioned metrics.

Similarly, in [32], the authors compared five supervised ML models, namely SVM, k-NN, RF, ANN and LR. The results revealed that the ANN achieved the highest accuracy, precision, and F1-score of 98.57%, 97.82%, and 98%, respectively, whereas the accuracy of 97.14%, the precision of 95.65%, and F1-score of 97% were obtained by the SVM. Finally, in [42], a performance comparison is performed between SVM, DT, NB, and k-NN models on the Wisconsin Breast Cancer dataset for breast cancer risk prediction using the WEKA tool. The experimental results showed that SVM achieved the highest accuracy of 97.13% with the lowest error rate.

4   Conclusions

In the context of this work, we focused on ensemble ML models, namely RF, Stacking, Bagging, Voting and Rotation Forest, to accurately predict subjects with a high risk of breast cancer occurrence based on critical biochemical indexes. Our models were compared based on the accuracy, precision, recall and AUC metrics to reveal the most suitable one for distinguishing between patients and non-patients. The experimental results showed that the Rotation Forest model prevailed over the others achieving accuracy, precision and recall equal to 82% and an AUC of 87.4% after the SMOTE technique with 10-fold cross-validation. In future work, we intend to follow an alternative path for detecting cancerous tumours by focusing on X-ray images and, thus exploiting efficient processing techniques from Computer Vision, Image Processing and Deep Learning.

Acknowledgements. This research was funded by the European Union and Greece (Partnership Agreement for the Development Framework 2014–2020) under the Regional Operational Programme Ionian Islands 2014–2020, project title: "Indirect costs for project "Smart digital applications and tools for the effective promotion and enhancement of the Ionian Islands bio-diversity" ", project number: 5034557.

References

1. Breast cancer. https://www.who.int/news-room/fact-sheets/detail/breast-cancer. Accessed 1 Apr 2023
2. UCI Ml repository. https://archive.ics.uci.edu/ml/datasets/ Breast+Cancer+Coimbra. Accessed 1 Apr 2023
3. Weka. https://www.weka.io/. Accessed 1 Apr 2023
4. Ahmad, A.: Breast cancer statistics: recent trends. Breast cancer metastasis and drug resistance: challenges and progress, pp. 1–7 (2019)
5. Ahmad, L.G., Eshlaghy, A., Poorebrahimi, A., Ebrahimi, M., Razavi, A., et al.: Using three machine learning techniques for predicting breast cancer recurrence. J. Health Med. Inform. **4**(124), 3 (2013)
6. Alexiou, S., Dritsas, E., Kocsis, O., Moustakas, K., Fakotakis, N.: An approach for personalized continuous glucose prediction with regression trees. In: 2021 6th South-East Europe Design Automation, Computer Engineering, Computer Networks and Social Media Conference (SEEDA-CECNSM), pp. 1–6. IEEE (2021)
7. Alfian, G., et al.: Predicting breast cancer from risk factors using SVM and extra-trees-based feature selection method. Computers **11**(9), 136 (2022)
8. Amrane, M., Oukid, S., Gagaoua, I., Ensari, T.: Breast cancer classification using machine learning. In: 2018 electric electronics, computer science, biomedical engineerings' meeting (EBBT), pp. 1–4. IEEE (2018)
9. Billena, C., et al.: 10-year breast cancer outcomes in women $\leq$ 35 years of age. Int. J Rad. Oncol. Biol. Phys. **109**(4), 1007–1018 (2021)
10. Chawla, N.V., Bowyer, K.W., Hall, L.O., Kegelmeyer, W.P.: Smote: synthetic minority over-sampling technique. J. Artif. Intell. Res. **16**, 321–357 (2002)
11. Dritsas, E., Alexiou, S., Moustakas, K.: COPD severity prediction in elderly with ml techniques. In: Proceedings of the 15th International Conference on PErvasive Technologies Related to Assistive Environments, pp. 185–189 (2022)
12. Dritsas, E., Alexiou, S., Konstantoulas, I., Moustakas, K.: Short-term glucose prediction based on oral glucose tolerance test values. In: HEALTHINF, pp. 249–255 (2022)
13. Dritsas, E., Alexiou, S., Moustakas, K.: Cardiovascular disease risk prediction with supervised machine learning techniques. In: ICT4AWE, pp. 315–321 (2022)
14. Dritsas, E., Alexiou, S., Moustakas, K.: Efficient data-driven machine learning models for hypertension risk prediction. In: 2022 International Conference on INnovations in Intelligent SysTems and Applications (INISTA), pp. 1–6. IEEE (2022)
15. Dritsas, E., Alexiou, S., Moustakas, K.: Metabolic syndrome risk forecasting on elderly with ML techniques. In: Learning and Intelligent Optimization: 16th International Conference, LION 16, Milos Island, Greece, June 5–10, 2022, Revised Selected Papers, pp. 460–466. Springer, Cham (2023). https://doi.org/10.1007/ 978-3-031-24866-5_33

16. Dritsas, E., Fazakis, N., Kocsis, O., Fakotakis, N., Moustakas, K.: Long-term hypertension risk prediction with ML techniques in ELSA database. In: Simos, D.E., Pardalos, P.M., Kotsireas, I.S. (eds.) LION 2021. LNCS, vol. 12931, pp. 113–120. Springer, Cham (2021). https://doi.org/10.1007/978-3-030-92121-7_9

17. Dritsas, E., Fazakis, N., Kocsis, O., Moustakas, K., Fakotakis, N.: Optimal team pairing of elder office employees with machine learning on synthetic data. In: 2021 12th International Conference on Information, Intelligence, Systems & Applications (IISA), pp. 1–4. IEEE (2021)

18. Dritsas, E., Trigka, M.: Data-driven machine-learning methods for diabetes risk prediction. Sensors 22(14), 5304 (2022)

19. Dritsas, E., Trigka, M.: Lung cancer risk prediction with machine learning models. Big Data Cognitive Comput. 6(4), 139 (2022)

20. Dritsas, E., Trigka, M.: Machine learning methods for hypercholesterolemia long-term risk prediction. Sensors 22(14), 5365 (2022)

21. Dritsas, E., Trigka, M.: Machine learning techniques for chronic kidney disease risk prediction. Big Data Cognitive Comput. 6(3), 98 (2022)

22. Dritsas, E., Trigka, M.: Stroke risk prediction with machine learning techniques. Sensors 22(13), 4670 (2022)

23. Dritsas, E., Trigka, M.: Supervised machine learning models to identify early-stage symptoms of sars-cov-2. Sensors 23(1), 40 (2022)

24. Dritsas, E., Trigka, M.: Efficient data-driven machine learning models for cardiovascular diseases risk prediction. Sensors 23(3), 1161 (2023)

25. Dritsas, E., Trigka, M.: Supervised machine learning models for liver disease risk prediction. Computers 12(1), 19 (2023)

26. Fahad Ullah, M.: Breast cancer: current perspectives on the disease status. Breast Cancer Metastasis and Drug Resistance: Challenges and Progress, pp. 51–64 (2019)

27. Fazakis, N., Dritsas, E., Kocsis, O., Fakotakis, N., Moustakas, K.: Long-term cholesterol risk prediction using machine learning techniques in elsa database. In: IJCCI, pp. 445–450 (2021)

28. Fazakis, N., Kocsis, O., Dritsas, E., Alexiou, S., Fakotakis, N., Moustakas, K.: Machine learning tools for long-term type 2 diabetes risk prediction. IEEE Access 9, 103737–103757 (2021)

29. Gordon, P.B.: The impact of dense breasts on the stage of breast cancer at diagnosis: a review and options for supplemental screening. Curr. Oncol. 29(5), 3595–3636 (2022)

30. Gucalp, A., et al.: Male breast cancer: a disease distinct from female breast cancer. Breast Cancer Res. Treat. 173, 37–48 (2019)

31. Hossin, M., Sulaiman, M.N.: A review on evaluation metrics for data classification evaluations. Int. J. Data Mining Knowl. Manage. Process 5(2), 1 (2015)

32. Islam, M.M., Haque, M.R., Iqbal, H., Hasan, M.M., Hasan, M., Kabir, M.N.: Breast cancer prediction: a comparative study using machine learning techniques. SN Comput. Sci. 1, 1–14 (2020)

33. Jafari, S.H., et al.: Breast cancer diagnosis: imaging techniques and biochemical markers. J. Cellular Physiol. 233(7), 5200–5213 (2018)

34. Johansson, A.L., Trewin, C.B., Hjerkind, K.V., Ellingjord-Dale, M., Johannesen, T.B., Ursin, G.: Breast cancer-specific survival by clinical subtype after 7 years follow-up of young and elderly women in a nationwide cohort. Int. J. Cancer 144(6), 1251–1261 (2019)

35. Kabari, L.G., Onwuka, U.C.: Comparison of bagging and voting ensemble machine learning algorithm as a classifier. Int. J. Adv. Res. Comput. Sci. Softw. Eng. 9(3), 19–23 (2019)

36. Konstantoulas, I., Dritsas, E., Moustakas, K.: Sleep quality evaluation in rich information data. In: 2022 13th International Conference on Information, Intelligence, Systems & Applications (IISA), pp. 1–4. IEEE (2022)

37. Konstantoulas, I., Kocsis, O., Dritsas, E., Fakotakis, N., Moustakas, K.: Sleep quality monitoring with human assisted corrections. In: IJCCI, pp. 435–444 (2021)

38. Lee, K., Kruper, L., Dieli-Conwright, C.M., Mortimer, J.E.: The impact of obesity on breast cancer diagnosis and treatment. Curr. Oncol. Rep. **21**, 1–6 (2019)

39. Li, H., et al.: Alcohol consumption, cigarette smoking, and risk of breast cancer for brca1 and brca2 mutation carriers: results from the brca1 and brca2 cohort consortium. Cancer Epidemiol. Biomarkers Prev. **29**(2), 368–378 (2020)

40. Liu, Y., Wang, Y., Zhang, J.: New machine learning algorithm: random forest. In: Liu, B., Ma, M., Chang, J. (eds.) ICICA 2012. LNCS, vol. 7473, pp. 246–252. Springer, Heidelberg (2012). https://doi.org/10.1007/978-3-642-34062-8_32

41. Mokhatri-Hesari, P., Montazeri, A.: Health-related quality of life in breast cancer patients: review of reviews from 2008 to 2018. Health Qual. Life Outcomes **18**, 1–25 (2020)

42. Naji, M.A., El Filali, S., Aarika, K., Benlahmar, E.H., Abdelouhahid, R.A., Debauche, O.: Machine learning algorithms for breast cancer prediction and diagnosis. Procedia Comput. Sci. **191**, 487–492 (2021)

43. Nusinovici, S., et al.: Logistic regression was as good as machine learning for predicting major chronic diseases. J. Clin. Epidemiol. **122**, 56–69 (2020)

44. Olsson, H.L., Olsson, M.L.: The menstrual cycle and risk of breast cancer: a review. Front. Oncol. **10**, 21 (2020)

45. Patrício, M., et al.: Using resistin, glucose, age and BMI to predict the presence of breast cancer. BMC Cancer **18**(1), 1–8 (2018)

46. Posonia, A.M., Vigneshwari, S., Rani, D.J.: Machine learning based diabetes prediction using decision tree j48. In: 2020 3rd International Conference on Intelligent Sustainable Systems (ICISS), pp. 498–502. IEEE (2020)

47. Riggio, A.I., Varley, K.E., Welm, A.L.: The lingering mysteries of metastatic recurrence in breast cancer. British J. Cancer **124**(1), 13–26 (2021)

48. Rodriguez, J.J., Kuncheva, L.I., Alonso, C.J.: Rotation forest: a new classifier ensemble method. IEEE Trans. Pattern Anal. Mach. Intell. **28**(10), 1619–1630 (2006)

49. Sagi, O., Rokach, L.: Ensemble learning: a survey. Wiley Interdisc. Rev.: Data Min. Knowl. Discov **8**(4), e1249 (2018)

50. Satapathy, S.K., Bhoi, A.K., Loganathan, D., Khandelwal, B., Barsocchi, P.: Machine learning with ensemble stacking model for automated sleep staging using dual-channel EEG signal. Biomed. Signal Process. Control **69**, 102898 (2021)

51. Trigka, M., Dritsas, E.: Long-term coronary artery disease risk prediction with machine learning models. Sensors **23**(3), 1193 (2023)

52. Wang, L.: Early diagnosis of breast cancer. Sensors **17**(7), 1572 (2017)

EventMapping: Geoparsing and Geocoding of Twitter Messages in the Greek Language

Gerasimos Razis[1]([⊠]) [iD], Ioannis Maroufidis[2], and Ioannis Anagnostopoulos[1]

[1] Computer Science and Biomedical Informatics Department, University of Thessaly,
35131 Lamia, Greece
{razis,janag}@uth.gr

[2] School of Electrical and Computer Engineering, National Technical University of Athens,
15780 Athens, Greece

Abstract. The rapid development of technology has changed the way people get informed from traditional media to online ones. Governmental accounts emerged on Twitter for rapid broadcasting of information related to real-time events and incidents. However, the accurate definition of locations of those events is a difficult task given the fact that their description is provided in free text with no predefined format for the efficient resolving of geolocation. This paper proposes the EventMapping framework that aims at identifying and extracting geographic information directly from official Greek governmental Twitter accounts and visualizing it on an interactive map. For the purposes of this work, two methodologies are implemented and evaluated. The best approach reached the level of 0.93 in terms of F1-score as far as the geographical term detection is concerned, as well as 93.5% in terms of accuracy on the resolved coordinates. The source-code of our framework is publicly available in open-source format on GitHub.

Keywords: Geographic Information · Language Processing · Text Analysis · Event Extraction · Geocoding · Geoparsing · Map Visualization · Twitter · Greek Language · Emergency Mapping

1 Introduction

The rapid development of technology in the last 20 years has greatly changed the way the Greek public is informed. In particular, the widespread use of the internet and the adoption of smart mobile phones have contributed to the transition from the traditional mass media, such as television and newspapers, to the modern ones, such as online blogs, and social media. According to Kepios[1], an organization investigating people's digital behaviors, at the start of 2023, 84% of the total population in Greece had access to the internet. It is estimated that the average user spends 6 h a day on the internet, 3 h watching TV (broadcasting and streaming), and 2 h on Online Social Networks (OSNs). Searching for information is the main reason that drives Greek users online (86.1%),

---

[1] https://kepios.com/reports.

© IFIP International Federation for Information Processing 2023
Published by Springer Nature Switzerland AG 2023
I. Maglogiannis et al. (Eds.): AIAI 2023 Workshops, IFIP AICT 677, pp. 312–324, 2023.
https://doi.org/10.1007/978-3-031-34171-7_25

filling up spare time is second (67.7%), whereas being updated with the latest events and news comes third (66.5%) [1].

Contrary to other popular OSNs, Twitter focuses almost exclusively on the area of instant broadcasting of information about recent events. Its popularity has led to the creation of governmental accounts, both for individuals and agencies, such as @Potus, the U.S. President, and @DeptofDefense, the U.S. Department of Defense, respectively. The OSNs are often used for managing and reporting emergencies or crises, as the extracted information can be very informative in such events [2, 3] and can be used for a plethora of scenarios, including mapping.

Two important Greek civil protection Twitter accounts are of the Fire Brigade (@Pyrosvestiki) and Hellenic Police (@HellenicPolice). These public agencies post continuous updates on incidents and events regarding their actions and their results. Usually, a textual description of the geographic information where these events took place is present. However, the locations are provided in free text as part of the social message, as either there is no predefined format for posting this type of information in the OSN messages, or the process of embedding this information is complex and requires third-party tools. Moreover, the level of geographic detail is not consistent, as the descriptions of the locations can range from a broad regional unit level to an intersection of roads.

According to Twitter[2], less than 2% of the total tweets are geotagged, namely containing geographical coordinates. However, simply relying on these coordinates is not efficient, as it would be ambiguous whether they intended to describe the location of the event mentioned in the tweet, or simply the author's location at the time of posting the message. These inherent problems make the visualization task challenging, as it requires the development of an automated process for extracting geospatial information from the text of the OSN messages.

As discussed in [4], a subset of information retrieval is information extraction, instances of which are the geocoding, geoparsing, and geotagging. Geocoding involves the transformation of a well-defined textual description of an address into a spatial coordinate. Geoparsing is often applied prior to geocoding and involves the identification of the terms describing a geographic location in a text, prior to their transformation into spatial coordinates. Finally, geotagging is the direct assignment of spatial coordinates into a content item, typically describing its location.

There are two aims of this study. Firstly, we propose a framework for the identification and extraction of terms describing geographic information related to events from the Twitter messages written in Greek of the Fire Brigade and Hellenic Police, while in parallel visualizing these social posts on an interactive map. To this end, two methodologies are implemented and evaluated in detail. Secondly, the source-code of our EventMapping framework, including the methodologies, collected OSN data, extracted geospatial and geocoding information, along with the evaluation results are open-source and available on our GitHub repository[3]. Considering the efforts of the Greek governmental agencies to inform the citizens constantly and accurately about the latest updates and actions, we

---

[2] https://developer.twitter.com/en/docs/tutorials/advanced-filtering-for-geo-data.

[3] https://github.com/jmarou/EventMapping.

believe that our open-source Geographic Information System (GIS) can further improve information and public awareness.

The remainder of this work is organized as follows. In the next section, an overview of the related studies is presented, describing text-based geoparsing and geocoding approaches. In Sect. 3, the architecture of our service is presented along with the data acquisition process. In Sect. 4, we describe in detail the methodologies and processes towards the identification and extraction of terms describing geographic information related to events and their visualization on a map. In Sect. 5, we analytically present and discuss the results of the proposed framework, by providing the evaluation metrics. Finally, in Sect. 6, we present the conclusions of our study by summarizing the outcomes and proposing future directions.

2 Related Work

The research area of extracting terms that describe geographic information from long documents or short OSN posts and inferring their coordinates has attracted high interest. The authors of [4] developed a geoparsing and geotagging framework using the Open-StreetMap database, along with a language model based on tags and multiple gazetteers. Their approach was evaluated against the publicly available DBpedia Spotlight, the GeoNames geographical gazetteer, and the Google Geocoder API using a manually labelled dataset with Twitter content. The proposed algorithm identifies named entities using a combination of the Stanford Part-of-Speech (POS) tagger and a Regular Expression (RegEx) pattern. The derived geolocation is at a high level (city or country), based on lower-level details. The authors experimented with content in various languages; however, the results were better for text written in English.

Another work relying on the DBpedia Spotlight entity recognizer is [5]. The identified parts are then linked to the DBpedia RDF resources, and the geographic information is extracted. Using a machine learning classifier, the erroneous geographic coordinates found in DBpedia are discarded from the pool of candidate results.

The Work in [6] describes a semi-supervised approach for geolocating Twitter posts and classifying them towards US regions, relying on sparse coding and dictionary learning methodologies. If the coordinates cannot be inferred, a multiclass classification takes place to infer the US region and state of the examined tweet.

A methodology for identifying and geolocating emergency-related Twitter messages and representing them on a map is presented in [7]. The study reports the lack of native coordinates in the OSN posts but highlights the existence of textual geographical references. The posts are enhanced with indirect information from their retweets or replies. This work also relies on a POS tagger for extracting candidate geographic terms, and a rule-based RegEx for further increasing the Named Entity Recognition (NER) recall including typical location names of streets, roads, and so on.

Another framework relying on NER for geoparsing unstructured text and returning geographic information is [8]. It is based on the open-source spaCy[4] library for identifying the toponyms and the GeoNames gazetteer for inferring the coordinates. A neural network classifier is applied to the candidate coordinates to derive the final ones.

---

[4] https://spacy.io/.

The authors in [9] relied on Natural Language Processing (NLP) libraries for identifying terms in travel blogs describing geographic areas or places of interest and their spatial relations. GeoNames was used for the geocoding process, whereas the Levenshtein distance metric for associating those terms with the gazetteer's entries.

A study focused exclusively on Greek content is [10], describing a methodology for the semi-automatic geocoding of information found on web pages. Grammar rules were used for identifying the areas in the text where the geographic information is mentioned, whereas external lexicons were employed for correcting spelling mistakes and converting important geographic-related terms into their normalized form. The derived terms were transformed into a standardized format for the geocoding phase, and approximate string matching was used against the predefined database entries. The authors opted to decrease the precision of that process, namely the derived terms to contain more noise, in favor of the recall. Finally, the results were displayed on a map and could be manually corrected.

Another study analyzing Twitter messages mainly in the Greek language with the aim of visualizing on a map the related information is [11]. For the geoparsing task, the grammatical and syntactic rules of the Greek language were considered for the efficient identification of the terms, whereas for the geolocation task a database was used containing descriptive geolocations and their corresponding coordinates.

Similar to many works in the literature, NLP techniques, such as POS tagging, and RegEx, are extensively used in our EventMapping framework as well, and we also relied on a manually annotated dataset for evaluating both our geoparsing, and geocoding tasks. Our research is focused exclusively on content written in Greek and in identifying fine-grained locations (e.g., at a road or crossroad level). Therefore, we cannot use datasets mentioned in the literature that contain geotagged posts due to the complete absence of such detailed information, especially for areas of Greece. Finally, as in [7], our goal is to avoid using pre-loaded data, gazetteer lookups, and training tasks for further improving the accuracy of our framework. The EventMapping service is designed to be lightweight and with minimal dependencies.

Compared to the related literature, our study differs in two important aspects. Firstly, our research is focused exclusively on OSN content written in Greek, a language generally not well-supported by the established NLP tools. Due to that, we opted to release our EventMapping and the described methodologies as an open-source project. Secondly, where possible, our framework can identify fine-grained textual locations (e.g., at a road or crossroad level) in the OSN messages and their resulting coordinates, rather than providing broader-level information (e.g., on a county or region level). Moreover, we do not rely on any offline gazetteers, given that the Greek areas are under-represented and information on a road level is almost entirely absent.

3 EventMapping: Architecture and Data Acquisition

Our proposed EventMapping service consists of multiple interconnected components organized in a three-layered architecture, presented in Fig. 1 along with the external services and relevant data flows. The architectural layers are decoupled to facilitate the future expansion and maintenance of the service, while the implementation and technical dependencies of each layer are kept locally. Specifically, the "Data" layer is represented

316   G. Razis et al.

by the green highlighted rectangle and consists of the dedicated "Persistence Storage" component. This is an SQLite relational database responsible for storing and accessing all relevant data, such as the collected OSN content, the event types, and the geographic location, including the actual coordinates.

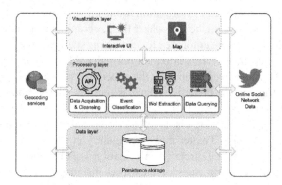

Fig. 1. The three-layered architecture of our service.

The "Processing" layer, represented by the blue highlighted rectangle, is responsible for all business logic, including OSN data collection, cleansing, transformation, querying, extraction, and enrichment tasks. Specifically, the layer was developed using the Python programming language and consists of four components: (a) the "OSN Data Acquisition & Cleansing" component, responsible for retrieving the OSN content, as well as for converting the terms describing geographic information into coordinates leveraging external geocoding services (Sect. 4.3); (b) the "Event Classification" component, where the type of the event described in a tweet is identified (Sect. 4.1); (c) the "WoI Extraction" component, involving the detection of the key terms related to geographic information, referred to as "Words of Interest" (WoIs) (Sect. 4.2); and (d) the "Data Querying" component, handling the database-oriented tasks. All types of data, and especially the spatial information, are converted into the format required by the "Persistence Storage", so that the content can then be visualized on the interactive interface and the map.

Finally, the "Visualization" layer is represented by the grey highlighted rectangle and consists of the "Map" component, responsible for visualizing the OSN events on a map, accessible via the web-based "Interactive User Interface (UI)" component. This layer has been implemented using the ReactJS framework, along with a Leaflet map for presenting the geospatial information and the derived coordinates of the tweets. Flask was used as the main web application framework.

As it can be seen in the right-hand side of Fig. 1, the collected Twitter content is accessible by the appropriate components of all layers, facilitating its parsing, analysis, or enrichment. The latter is achieved through the integration of geocoding services, as seen in the left-hand side of Fig. 1.

The tweets are collected from the official Twitter API. For our EventMapping service, we are only interested in the tweets from the Greek governmental accounts of the Fire Brigade (@Pyrosvestiki) and the Hellenic Police (@HellenicPolice), therefore we relied on the dedicated endpoint returning up to the 3,200 most recent tweets of a specific account, along with their metadata. Despite that the available metadata of each tweet contains the geographical information, this field was not utilized in our work, since neither is populated by the two examined accounts, nor its existence guarantees that it would reflect the location of the announced event and not the location of the author of the post.

The Twitter API returns the data in UTF-8 (Unicode Transformation Format). However, analyzing text to extract the terms related to geospatial information requires it to be in a suitable format. Therefore, the collected original content is pre-processed according to those rules so that the text can be then analyzed by our geospatial information detection methods (Sect. 4). The pre-processing step accepts as input the original text in UTF-8, applies a series of RegEx, and returns its cleansed form in the same encoding.

In the context of our study, a total of 3,741 tweets were collected and analyzed, from the 8th of May 2020 to the 19th of October 2022 from the account of @HellenicPolice, and 3,284 tweets from the 7th of April 2021 to the 20th of October 2022 from the account of @Pyrosvestiki. The raw, pre-processed, translated, and geolocation data are available in the GitHub repository3 of EventMapping.

4 Event Classification and Geographic Terms Identification

In this section, we analytically present the classification process of the events detected in the tweets, the two methodologies implemented toward the identification of WoIs, as well as the three employed geocoding services for transforming the text into the actual coordinates. The experimental results are presented in Sect. 5.

4.1 Event Classification

As already mentioned, prior to processing the tweets for geographical information, these are first categorized according to the described event. Indicative categories are fire updates, search & rescue operations, and arrests. This classification is performed not only for statistical reasons, but also for filtering any events that we know beforehand do not contain geographic information, such as those referencing the suppression of an electronic crime. In case that a tweet is not classified into any of the available categories, it is placed into the default "Miscellaneous" category.

The categories were derived by considering the semi-supervised examination of approximately 3,000 tweets, and the size of each category, namely the number of tweets belonging to it. An indicative indicator for the improvement of categorization is the reduction of the number of tweets belonging to the default category while simultaneously increasing the percentage of correct categorizations. Eventually, a dictionary of terms was created for each category.

For classifying the social content, the original corpus of the tweets was used, along with the authoring government agency account. Each tweet is assumed to belong to a single category, with very few exceptions. The classifier is based on finding terms from a tweet related to each category's dictionary using RegEx.

4.2 Geographic Terms Identification

Once the tweets have been categorized against the described event type, those of the valid categories are analyzed for detecting the WoIs related to geographical information, such as names of streets, cities, and so on. Specifically, two distinct methodologies were implemented, which are analyzed below.

Regular Expression Matching. Our first methodology for detecting WoIs related to geographical information is based on the creation of a complex pattern relying on RegEx, namely language-specific heuristics. According to the evaluation of [4] for a similar task, such approaches lead to superior results in identifying the desired information. Considering that the examined governmental accounts post exclusively in Greek, the derived pattern is based on the main syntactic rules of the Greek language. This pattern consists of two basic "capturing groups".

The first group consists of many alternative words that indicate the existence of toponyms such as "street", "municipality", "in", and so on. The structure of the first group is such that most words are ignored as they do not contribute to the final stage, which is the geocoding (Sect. 4.3). For example, the terms "prefecture of Ilia" and "Ilia" return the same results to most geocoders ("Ilia" is a prefecture of Greece). The second group consists of either contiguous words beginning with a capital letter, or words of one or two letters followed by a period and then contiguous words beginning with a capital letter. Thus, it is possible to identify toponyms such as "N. Makri" ("N" stands for "New"), "L. Alexandras" ("L" stands for "Leoforos", namely "Avenue" in English), or "Ag. Andreas" ("Ag." stands for "Agios", namely "Saint" in English).

However, the aforementioned basic RegEx pattern often returns undesired results, as it detects terms that start with a capital letter but are not toponyms or relate to the location of the event (e.g., denoting where a police station is located). For this purpose, a second pattern was developed for rejecting such cases, based on our findings of how spatial information is described in the posts of the two examined accounts.

NLP on Greek content. The second methodology for detecting WoIs related to geographical information is based on one of the most widespread open-source libraries for NLP spaCy (See footnote 4). The library uses state-of-the-art neural networks for NLP tasks, such as labeling, analysis, NER, and text classification, while offering pre-trained models that users can leverage to train the models on different data sets. According to [12], from an overall viewpoint, NLTK and spaCy have similar results in terms of precision and recall. Moreover, spaCy supports more than 70 languages while offering pre-trained models for 23 languages, including Greek, having been trained on content from news and mass media. In this work, we relied on the most accurate of the available pre-trained model[5] for the Greek language, in terms of f-score.

The OSN text is parsed using that model for the NER task, and the entity categories are assigned to the terms. In our case, we are only interested in the geopolitical entities, represented by the GPE label, such as cities, countries, regions, and states, and not in generic geographical features, represented by the LOC label, such as natural and/or

---

[5] https://spacy.io/models/el#el_core_news_lg.

human-made landmarks and structures. Therefore, the annotated terms are filtered so that only the appropriate entities are extracted. Finally, these terms are concatenated with a blank character, and the resulting string is subjected to the same WoI rejection processing as in the "Regular Expression Matching" method.

4.3 Geocoding Services

Geocoding is the process of converting textual geographical information, such as a pair of coordinates or a toponym, into a location on the earth's surface. The extracted location can then be used for representation on a map or for spatial analysis.

Within our EventMapping framework, the geocoding step is solved by relying on existing geocoding services. For data quality and evaluation reasons, two different services were used, one commercial and one free. These are Esri (ArcGIS Geocoder) and Nominatim (powering OpenStreetMap), respectively. The geocoding process was automatically performed by submitting the requests and retrieving the results using the official APIs of those services.

5 Evaluation Metrics

For evaluation purposes, two datasets were created and manually annotated, consisting of:

- 100 tweets from each Twitter account including all event types for evaluating the event classifier (Sect. 4.1).
- 100 tweets from each Twitter account containing geographical information, for evaluating a) the derived WoIs of the two geographic information extraction methodologies (Sect. 4.2), and b) the final outcome of the framework, namely the corresponding coordinates of the extracted terms.

5.1 Event Classifier Evaluation

As already mentioned in Sect. 4.1, the categories of the events were derived by considering the semi-supervised examination of approximately 3,000 tweets, whereas a dictionary of terms was created for each category. Each tweet is assumed to belong to a single category. The classifier is based on finding terms from a tweet related to each category's dictionary, using RegEx.

For evaluating the event classifier, 100 tweets were selected from each Twitter account including all event types, and their event category was manually assigned. Then, this category was compared against the automatically assigned one. The combination of the categories' dictionaries with the RegEx achieves an accuracy of 98% for both examined governmental Twitter accounts.

5.2 Geographic Information Identification Evaluation

Geographic Term Extraction Evaluation. For evaluating the two geographic information extraction methodologies (Sect. 4.2), 100 tweets were selected from each Twitter account with categories that are likely to contain the location of the described event. For each of these tweets, all terms describing the location of the event were manually identified and stored, separated by a space. Then, these ground truth values were compared against the automatically derived ones (i.e., the WoIs) from the two methodologies using the precision, recall, and F1 metrics.

Precision is defined as the number of WoIs correctly detected by a methodology, namely terms belonging to the ground truth, out of the total WoIs extracted. Recall is defined as the number of WoIs correctly detected by the method, out of the total terms contained in the ground truth. The F1-score is the harmonic mean of precision and recall, representing both metrics in one value. Table 1 presents the results of the evaluation metrics of the two geographic information extraction methodologies, both on an individual account level and combined on all ground truth data.

As the evaluation metrics showcase, the "Regular Expression Matching" methodology outperforms the other approach in all three metrics, which is in line with the findings of [4]. The values of the three metrics are stable and very high for both examined accounts, namely approximately 0.91 for @HellenicPolice and approximately 0.95 for @Pyrosvestiki, while approximately 0.93 overall. This is expected, since the regular expressions are tailor-made rules derived from a) patterns of the main syntactic rules of the Greek language, b) patterns of Greek toponyms, c) the writing patterns of the examined governmental accounts, and d) the exclusion rules for fire brigade or police station locations not being related to the actual location of an event.

The "NLP on Greek content" methodology despite relying on the spaCy library which is trained on Greek content for NLP and NER tasks, in many cases it fails to categorize street names containing people's names as geographic entities (GPE label). The F1 value on the combined dataset is approximately 0.78. The values of the three metrics show minimal variation in the case of @HellenicPolice, approximately 0.82, however greater variation for @Pyrosvestiki, as the Recall (approximately 0.72) is quite reduced compared to Precision (approximately 0.8). This is due to this account sharing street names containing people's names, which spaCy fails to categorize as geographic entities. The results of this methodology have been improved by adding a layer of custom rules for rejecting geospatial abbreviations and undefined areas.

Coordinates Evaluation. The evaluation of the geocoding outcome, namely the corresponding coordinates of the extracted terms denoting geographical information, was performed using the same manually annotated ground truth dataset as in the previous section. For each tweet all terms referring to the location of the event were manually identified. Then, these ground truth values were submitted to Esri's geocoding service, and the returned coordinates were stored. Finally, we compared these ground truth coordinates with the ones derived from the WoIs of the two methodologies.

To this end, a process was implemented that accepted as input two sets of coordinates, one for the ground truth location and one for each of the two methodologies. The aim is to measure the distance between the two points, expressed by their latitude and longitude in WGS 84 geometry. In case that it is less than 200 m, the resulting geolocation of the examined methodology is regarded as correct. This number derives from an empirical evaluation, and balances cases were: (a) only the broad names of cities or regions are mentioned, since all geolocation services return coordinates in a very small radius, (b)

Table 1. The evaluation metrics of the four geographic information extraction methodologies.

Metric / Account	@HellenicPolice	@Pyrsosvestiki	Combined
Regular Expression Matching			
Precision	0.917	0.953	0.935
Recall	0.918	0.958	0.938
F1-score	0.912	0.953	0.933
NLP on Greek content			
Precision	0.827	0.804	0.815
Recall	0.830	0.721	0.776
F1-score	0.824	0.742	0.783

specific names of roads are mentioned with or without additional geographical details, which may span quite a few hundreds of meters.

Table 2 presents the results of the evaluation metrics of the two geographic information extraction methodologies both on an individual account level and combined on all ground truth data.

As the evaluation metrics showcase, the "Regular Expression Matching" methodology outperforms the other approach both on the individual and combined dataset level, with a weighted accuracy of 93.5%. This confirms that it not only identifies the most appropriate WoIs, but also the most important ones in terms of geocoding. Despite that the accuracy of the "NLP on Greek content" methodology on the @HellenicPolice dataset is 82%, it fails to achieve such a score for the @Pyrsosvestiki dataset (62%) leading to a weighted average accuracy of 73%.

As it can be observed from Table 2, the NLP-based solution has a high degree of variation, with low accuracy in the content of @Pyrsosvestiki. This is due to the level of detail provided by the two accounts: @Pyrsosvestiki in most cases reports the location of the event in detail (e.g., at a road or crossroad level), whereas @HellenicPolice usually reports a broader area. The latter is easier to be defined by an NLP approach.

Table 2. The accuracy of the derived coordinates against the ground truth coordinates.

Methodology / Account	@HellenicPolice	@Pyrsosvestiki	Combined
Regular Expression Matching	94%	93%	93.5%
NLP on Greek content	82%	64%	73%

6 Conclusions and Future Work

There are three aims of this study. Firstly, we propose an end-to-end framework for the identification and extraction of terms describing geographic information related to events from the Twitter messages of the Greek Fire Brigade and Hellenic Police, while in parallel visualizing these social posts on an interactive map. To this end, two methodologies are implemented and evaluated in detail. Secondly, the source-code of our EventMapping framework, including all described methodologies, collected OSN data, extracted geospatial and geocoding information, along with the evaluation results are open-source and available on our GitHub repository (See footnote 3). Considering the efforts of the Greek governmental agencies to inform the citizens constantly and accurately about the latest updates and actions, we believe that our open-source GIS can further improve information and public awareness.

The three-layered architecture of our GIS has been developed in an expandable approach so that its maintenance is facilitated, and additional functionality can be effortlessly incorporated. Moreover, each of the individual layers and components handling tasks such as receiving information, processing, storing, and analyzing tweets, as well as the interactive web interface are building blocks that can be used separately in new applications.

The main research contribution of our study is the identification and extraction of terms found in Greek tweets describing geographic information related to events. To this end, two distinct methodologies were implemented, optimized for posts specifically from the examined Greek governmental accounts. The methodologies were thoroughly evaluated (Sect. 5.2) against two manually annotated datasets. It was revealed that the NLP-based solution was outperformed by the rule-based approach. Specifically, the "Regular Expression Matching" methodology achieved the best results, with an F1-score of 0.93, whereas the NLP-based approach achieved an F1-score of 0.78. Moreover, we evaluated the coordinates derived from the extracted terms of these methodologies against the manually annotated ones (Sect. 5.2), and the "Regular Expression Matching" methodology outperformed the other approach with a weighted accuracy of 93.5%. This confirms that it not only identifies the most appropriate terms, but also the most important ones in terms of geocoding.

Compared to the related literature, our study differs in two important aspects. Firstly, our research is focused exclusively on OSN content written in Greek, a language generally not well-supported by the established NLP tools. Due to that, we opted to release our EventMapping and the described methodologies as an open-source project (See footnote 3). Secondly, where possible, our framework can identify fine-grained textual locations (e.g., at a road or crossroad level) in the OSN messages and their resulting coordinates, rather than providing broader-level information (e.g., on a county or region level). Moreover, we do not rely on any offline gazetteers, given that the Greek areas are under-represented and information on a road level is almost entirely absent.

Going forward, our plan is to extend this study in two areas. Firstly, we intend to implement and evaluate two additional methodologies towards the identification of terms describing geographic information. One involves the detection of words starting with a capital letter, based on the grammatical rule of words denoting locations and names, while the second involves the application of a NER on the translated content from Greek to English, since all existing NER systems are trained on English content. Secondly, we aim to introduce the Google Maps geocoding service on top of the examined ones and compare the efficiency of the three geocoding services against a manually annotated dataset.

Acknowledgments. We acknowledge support of this work by the project "Par-ICT CENG: Enhancing ICT research infrastructure in Central Greece to enable processing of Big data from sensor stream, multimedia content, and complex mathematical modeling and simulations" (MIS 5047244) which is implemented under the Action "Reinforcement of the Research and Innovation Infrastructure", funded by the Operational Programme "Competitiveness, Entrepreneurship and Innovation" (NSRF 2014–2020) and co-financed by Greece and the European Union (European Regional Development Fund).

References

1. DataReportal, https://datareportal.com/reports/digital-2023-greece, last accessed February 2023
2. Castillo, C.: Big crisis data: Social Media in Disasters and Time-Critical Situations. Cambridge University Press (2016). https://doi.org/10.1017/CBO9781316476840
3. Avvenuti, M., Cresci, S., Del Vigna, F., Fagni, T., Tesconi, M.: CrisMap: a Big Data Crisis Mapping System Based on Damage Detection and Geoparsing. Inf. Syst. Front. **20**(5), 993–1011 (2018). https://doi.org/10.1007/s10796-018-9833-z
4. Middleton, S., Kordopatis-Zilos, G., Papadopoulos, S., Kompatsiaris, Y.: Location Extraction from Social Media: Geoparsing, Location Disambiguation, and Geotagging. ACM Trans. Inf. Syst. **36**(4), 1–27 (2018). https://doi.org/10.1145/3202662
5. Avvenuti, M., Cresci, S., Nizzoli, L., Tesconi, M.: GSP (Geo-Semantic-Parsing): Geoparsing and Geotagging with Machine Learning on Top of Linked Data. In: Gangemi, A., et al. (eds.) ESWC 2018. LNCS, vol. 10843, pp. 17–32. Springer, Cham (2018). https://doi.org/10.1007/978-3-319-93417-4_2
6. Cha, M., Gwon, Y., Kung, H.: Twitter geolocation and regional classification via sparse coding. In: Ninth International AAAI Conference on Web and Social Media, vol. 9, no. 1, pp. 582–585 (2015). https://doi.org/10.1609/icwsm.v9i1.14664
7. Scalia, G., Francalanci, C., Pernici, B.: CIME: Context-aware geolocation of emergency-related posts. GeoInformatica **26**(1), 125–157 (2021). https://doi.org/10.1007/s10707-021-00446-x
8. Halterman, A.: Mordecai: Full Text Geoparsing and Event Geocoding. Journal of Open Source Software 2(9), (2017). https://doi.org/10.21105/joss.00091
9. Skoumas, G., Pfoser, D., Kyrillidis, A., Sellis, T.: Location Estimation Using Crowdsourced Spatial Relations. ACM Trans. Spatial Algorithms Syst. 2(2), 23 pages (2016). https://doi.org/10.1145/2894745
10. Angel, A., Lontou, C., Pfoser, D., Efentakis, A.: Qualitative geocoding of persistent web pages. In: 16th ACM SIGSPATIAL international conference on Advances in geographic information systems, pp. 1–10. Association for Computing Machinery, New York, NY, USA (2008). https://doi.org/10.1145/1463434.1463460
11. Arapostathis, S.G.: A Methodology for Automatic Acquisition of Flood-event Management Information From Social Media: the Flood in Messinia, South Greece, 2016. Inf. Syst. Front. **23**(5), 1127–1144 (2021). https://doi.org/10.1007/s10796-021-10105-z

12. Schmitt, X., Kubler, S., Robert, J., Papadakis M., LeTraon, Y.: A Replicable Comparison Study of NER Software: StanfordNLP, NLTK, OpenNLP, SpaCy, Gate. In: Sixth International Conference on Social Networks Analysis, Management and Security (SNAMS), pp. 338–343, Granada, Spain (2019). https://doi.org/10.1109/SNAMS.2019.8931850

Extracting Knowledge from Recombinations of SMILES Representations

Christos Didachos[1] and Andreas Kanavos[2(✉)]

[1] Computer Engineering and Informatics Department, University of Patras,
Patras, Greece
christosdidachos@upatras.gr
[2] Department of Informatics, Ionian University, Corfu, Greece
akanavos@ionio.gr

Abstract. The exploitation of all possible combinations of the non-common substructure of compounds using Simplified Molecular-Input Line-Entry System (SMILES) representations is an essential part in terms of accurate chemical information processing. SMILES is a widely used encoding for representing chemical compounds as strings of characters. In our paper, a novel approach, which treats the SMILES strings as a sequence of letters, numbers and symbols in order to extract meaningful knowledge, is presented. It identifies the common substructure between two given SMILES. For the non-common substructure, we extensively search all possible combinations of the string characters of all possible lengths. Finally, for all these character combinations, we accept only those that are chemically correct. So, our approach suggests all possible substructures that may be present for the non-common substructure between two compounds using the atoms that already exist in the initial non-common substructure. This approach can generate all possible fragments that could exist for a given non-common substructure while maintaining the common substructure and could be used in drug discovery and other chemical applications.

Keywords: Knowledge Extraction · Text Mining · Computational Drug Design · De-novo Fragment Design

1 Introduction

Machine learning algorithms can play a crucial role in solving problems related to text mining [3]; it has a great impact in the way we analyze, handle and transform unstructured and structured text data. Taking into consideration the high availability of a plethora of digital information sources (e.g. social media, research publications), machine learning has become a remarkably useful tool of extracting knowledge. This can be extended to the demanding process of discovering and developing new drugs [11, 12, 27].

© IFIP International Federation for Information Processing 2023
Published by Springer Nature Switzerland AG 2023
I. Maglogiannis et al. (Eds.): AIAI 2023 Workshops, IFIP AICT 677, pp. 325–334, 2023.
https://doi.org/10.1007/978-3-031-34171-7_26

Text mining has been involved in a plethora of applications in a variety of fields, including but not limited to healthcare, social media, business, cybersecurity and more. One of the most common applications of text mining is sentiment analysis, also known as opinion mining, which identifies and extracts subjective information from text data, such as opinions and emotions. Obviously, this kind of analysis has been used extensively in marketing and customer service to gain insights into consumer behavior and preferences [20]. Another common application of text mining is topic modeling, which is a kind of statistical modeling and is used to identify the main themes or topics in a collection of documents. However, topic modeling has been extensively used in political science, where it has been used to identify public opinion on a variety of political issues [4].

More to the point, text mining helps in information extraction due to its capability to identify and extract structured information from unstructured text data. This approach is extremely useful in healthcare, as text mining has been used to extract valuable information from Electronic Health Records (EHRs) to improve patient care and outcomes. For example, text mining has been used to detect adverse drug reactions from unstructured EHR data, which can be a valuable tool for healthcare providers to manage in a more efficient way patients' medications and avoid potentially harmful drug interactions [29].

Text mining is being used in the process of drug discovery and development to analyze a lot of unstructured data (scientific literature and electronic health records) in order to extract valuable insights that can aid in drug design. For example, text mining can be used not only to identify potential drugs' targets but even to understand disease mechanisms, and predict drug efficacy and safety (toxicity) [19]. Text mining has also been used to develop predictive models for drug discovery and drug repurposing. For example, a study [13] used text mining approaches to extract information of drug-protein interactions from scientific literature. This approach offered the capability of training machine learning models to predict the bioactivity of new drug candidates.

Our approach designs new compounds, handling SMILES representations [28] as strings, and utilizing statistical methods in order to recombine sets of atoms to create novel compounds. SMILES representations are commonly used to describe chemical compounds in a format which could be more understandable from computers, and consist of a string of characters that represents the chemical structure of a molecule. Treating SMILES as strings offers the ability of easily comparing different compounds and identifying similarities and differences between them [16]. Furthermore, this corresponding method can be applied to Quantitative Structure Activity Relationship (QSAR) modeling [7,26], which is a rapidly evolving technique that investigates the correlation between chemical structure and biological activity in large compound libraries.

In order to design new compounds, we use statistical methods to extract all possible combinations of atoms that exist in a SMILES that can be recombined to form a large variety of new compounds potentially with desirable properties. This approach could be useful in a variety of drug discovery applications, including the design of new anticancer drugs [12]. By applying statistical methods on SMILES representations, it offers the capability of searching for new compounds that may have potential desired bioactivity against specific molecular targets.

The rest of the paper is organized as follows. Section 2 provides the related work for our paper. The material needed for acknowledging the contribution of this paper along with the methods utilized and the dataset used are introduced in Sect. 3. Section 4 presents the research results, and finally, Sect. 5 depicts conclusions and draws directions for future work.

2 Related Work

In silico drug discovery approaches involve generating large molecular libraries using combinatorial techniques, which are then filtered and characterized using computational methods such as QSAR [26] and docking [15]. Another common approach uses metaheuristics such as genetic algorithms to explore the chemical space and identify novel active compounds [24]. These methods rely on generating vast numbers of molecules to discover potential drug candidates, which can then be further analyzed and optimized for their biological functionality.

De novo drug design [17] is a computational approach that involves the in-silico generation of novel chemical compounds with desired properties for drug discovery. Recently, various computational methods have been developed for de novo drug design, including de novo molecular design and de novo fragment design. De novo fragment design is a method to develop potent small-molecule compounds starting from fragments binding weakly to targets [14].

For example, in [21], authors proposed a deep reinforcement learning framework for de novo drug design, which combined deep neural networks with reinforcement learning to generate diverse and chemically valid molecules. They used two different neural networks, the one was responsible to generate feasible SMILES representations, while the second one detected which of the generated SMILES appeared to have desired molecular properties. Sequentially, other research studies have used machine learning approaches such as Recurrent Neural Networks (RNNs), and Generative Adversarial Networks (GANs) in order to computationally design new compounds [10,18,23].

On the other hand, de novo fragment design aims to generate smaller molecular fragments and link them into a larger novel molecule with desired properties. Techniques of detecting common substructures [8] between molecules could be very essential in the de novo fragment design as it offers the capability to detect fragments of a compound that may be essential.

In [1], authors proposed an approach which uses a RNN to detect the basic structure - scaffold of a chemical structure. Sequentially, another model searches the chemical space and suggests new fragments in order to design novel molecules. Our proposed approach not only detects the essential substructure between two compounds, but also calculates all possible atom combinations for each compound in the cluster without introducing new atoms. This ensures that the generated fragments are derived from the existing atoms in the active compounds, maintaining the chemical feasibility.

3   Material and Methods

3.1   SMILES Notation

SMILES representations are a method used to describe the chemical structure of a molecule mostly to create a format that could be used in computational methods. SMILES notations are written as strings of characters, where each character represents a particular atom or bond of the molecule. The notation can be thought of as a linear sequence of atoms, where the order of the atoms in the sequence reflects the connectivity between them.

SMILES encoding provides a simple and standard way of describing simple or even complex chemical structures and is widely used in chemical databases and in ChemInformatic tools for drug discovery [2, 25]. SMILES representations can be generated automatically from the 2D or 3D structure of a molecule or can be set manually by a chemist researcher. Overall, SMILES representations are a powerful tool for chemists and researchers working in the field of drug discovery and development, as they enable the efficient exchange and analysis of chemical information.

Our approach uses the below equation in order to define the number of all possible combinations for a given SMILES string.

$$combinations = \sum_{k=1}^{n} \frac{n!}{k!(n-k)!} \tag{1}$$

where k is the length of each combination and n the length of the string.

3.2   Dataset

Our approach of designing new compounds is based on working with datasets that include compounds represented in SMILES notation and the usage of statistical methods to get all potential combinations. Each dataset of bioactive compounds which are represented in SMILES encoding can be used to design different molecular structures and choose a subset of them for further analysis.

In our case, we selected two compounds with similar structures but different functional groups, which are represented as SMILES strings in following Table 1. These compounds were chosen as they share a common substructure, while having different functional groups at the other end of the molecule. By comparing these compounds and identifying the similarities and differences between their SMILES representations, we are able to leverage the common substructure and generate new compounds by recombining the functional groups in different ways.

Table 1. SMILES Representations

First Compound	CC(=O)O[C@H](CC(=O)[O-])C[N+](C)(C)C
Second Compound	CCC(=O)OC(CC(=O)[O-])C[N+](C)(C)C

This approach could contribute in research fields which are related to drug discovery, as the identification of new compounds with desired functionality is crucial. By working with datasets of SMILES representations and leveraging statistical methods to identify new molecular structures, we can accelerate the process of drug discovery and help identify new compounds that may appear important therapeutic action.

Table 2 reflects some examples of the SMILES representation and presents how the SMILES encoding encodes the chemical structure in terms of atoms and bonds [28].

Table 2. SMILES examples

SMILES	Structure
CC	ethane (CH_3CH_3)
C=C	ethylene ($CH_2 = CH_2$)
COC	dimethyl ether (CH_3OCH_3)
CCO	ethanol (CH_3CH_2OH)
C=O	formaldehyde (CH_2O)
O=C=O	carbon dioxide (CO_2)
O=CO	formic acid ($HCOOH$)
C#N	hydrogen cyanide (HCN)
[H][H]	molecular hydrogen (H_2)

3.3   Methodology

In our approach, we utilize the SMILES representations of two selected compounds, and we aim to design new molecules by recombining the functional groups that are not shared between these two compounds. The first step in our approach is to identify the common substructure between the two SMILES representations, as this may be an essential component of the desired molecule. We achieve this by comparing the SMILES strings character by character, and identifying the longest common subsequence between them. The identification of common substructures between two compounds is critical in drug discovery research. Common substructures provide insights into the stereo-chemistry of compounds, helping researchers understand the key molecular features responsible for the observed biological activity. This knowledge enables rational drug design, guiding the modification of compounds to enhance their potency, selectivity, and safety [9].

Once the common substructure is detected, we then focus on the non-common substructure of the second SMILES string. Sequentially, we use a statistical approach to generate and extract all possible combinations of SMILES characters for this non-common substructure. However, not all combinations of characters will be valid molecules, and so we use the RDKIT framework to check the syntax of each combination and eliminate any that violates the chemical rules.

Our approach ultimately generates a list of all possible recombinations of the non-common substructure (of the two compounds), reserving the common substructure. This process could be characterised as a de novo fragment design approach, which is a method for designing new molecules using a combination of computational and experimental techniques. In de novo fragment design [22], the goal is to design molecules that are structurally distinct from existing compounds, yet possess desirable pharmacological properties. This approach has potential applications in drug discovery, as it can help identify novel lead compounds for further optimization and development.

4 Results

The similarity of the two compounds (similarity based on the SMILES string) is 22.2%. The SequenceMatcher algorithm was used to calculate the similarity of the initial compounds based on their SMILES notation. This ratio, available as a Python class, offers basic information of the structural relevance among the initial compounds [30]. For the non-common substructure, 511 total combinations were checked but only 48 of them were found correct from the perspective of chemical syntax. The structure of the two compounds is represented in Fig. 1, whereas in Fig. 2, a sample of the structures that our approach generated is shown for the non-common substructure.

Figure 1 illustrates the structure of the first two compounds and the non common substructure of them. Specifically, Fig. 1(a) presents the SMILES representation of the first compound, whereas Fig. 1(b) shows the SMILES representation of the second compound and Fig. 1(c) presents the non common substructure between the compounds (a) and (b); actually there were two non-common substructures but for the first one, no meaningful recombination of atoms could exist. All potential atom recombination scenarios have been investigated and examined for the non-common substructure of image Fig. 1(c).

More to the point, Fig. 2 depicts a selection of generated fragments representing the non-common substructure between the two initial compounds. Out of the total of 48 fragments that adhere to the established chemical rules and syntax, only a sample is presented here for illustrative purposes. It should be noted that while the total 48 generate fragments may be syntactically correct, their feasibility in terms of chemical synthesis may vary. Therefore, additional optimization is necessary by a medicinal chemist. Nonetheless, the proposed methods hold promise as a valuable tool for aiding scientists in the field of medicinal chemistry.

5 Conclusions and Future Work

The proposed method generates fragments exploiting all available atom combinations for the non-common substructures. While we ensure that only compounds that appear to be correct as chemical compounds are kept, many of the generated compounds are not feasible or realistic from a synthetic perspective.

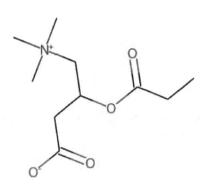

(a) SMILES representation of the first compound

(b) SMILES representation of the second compound

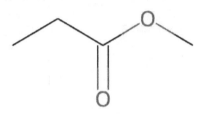

(c) The non-common substructure of the second compound

Fig. 1. Two compounds and the non-common substructure between these compounds.

These unrealistic compounds may be due to various factors, such as synthesis constraints.

One limitation of the proposed method is the required process time as it is undeniably time-consuming, particularly when dealing with longer SMILES strings. However, there is potential for an extension of the current method that draws on the findings of [5,6] to expedite the process. One approach would be to leverage multiple cloud nodes to perform the necessary calculations for all the recombinations, thus allowing for greater parallelization and reducing the overall time required.

A useful extension of our current work could be to develop a set of rules or filters to detect and exclude fragments that are not feasible or realistic. Such filters could be based on chemical or synthetic knowledge and could greatly increase the efficiency and usefulness of the de novo fragment design approach. For example,

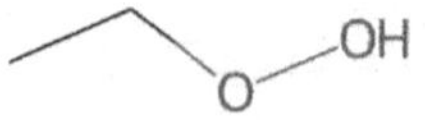

(a) 15th chemical fragment

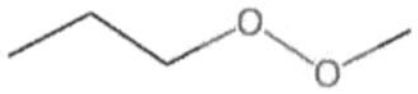

(b) 29th chemical fragment

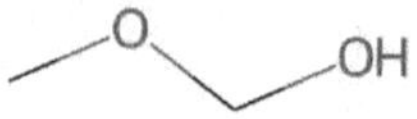

(c) 35th chemical fragment

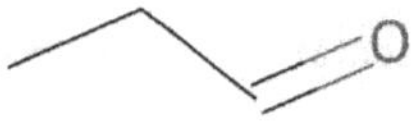

(d) 36th chemical fragment

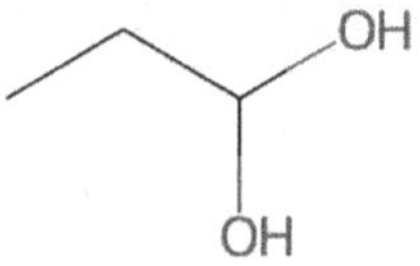

(e) 37th chemical fragment

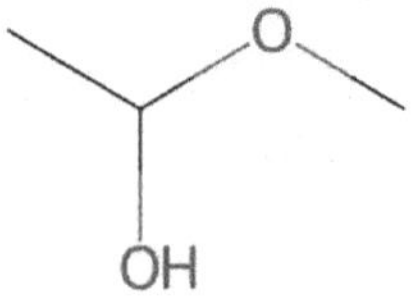

(f) 41th chemical fragment

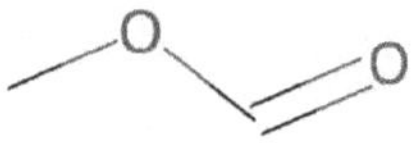

(g) 42th chemical fragment

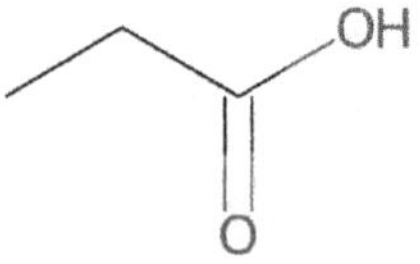

(h) 43th chemical fragment

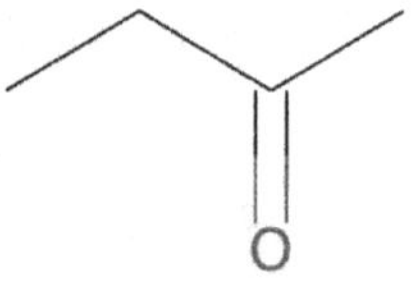

(i) 44th chemical fragment

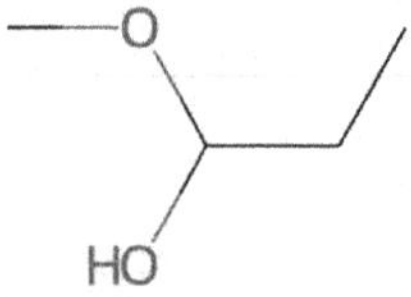

(j) 45th chemical fragment

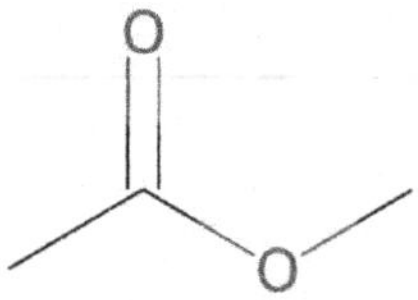

(k) 46th chemical fragment

Fig. 2. Sample of 11 different combinations.

filters could be developed to exclude fragments that violate Lipinski's rule of five or that have a high degree of synthetic difficulty. Overall, the development of such filters could greatly enhance the practicality and applicability of de novo fragment design approaches in drug discovery.

Acknowledgement. This research was co-financed by the European Union and Greek national funds through the "Competitiveness, Entrepreneurship and Innovation" Operational Programme 2014–2020, under the Call "Support for regional excellence"; project title: "Intelligent Research Infrastructure for Shipping, Transport and Supply Chain - ENIRISST+"; MIS code: 5047041.

References

1. Arús-Pous, J., et al.: Smiles-based deep generative scaffold decorator for de-novo drug design. J. Cheminform. **12**(1), 1–18 (2020)
2. Backman, T.W.H., Cao, Y., Girke, T.: Chemmine tools: an online service for analyzing and clustering small molecules. Nucleic Acids Res. **39**(suppl_2), W486–W491 (2011)
3. Baeza-Yates, R.A., Ribeiro-Neto, B.A.: Modern Information Retrieval: The Concepts and Technology Behind Search, 2nd edn. Pearson Education Ltd., Harlow (2011)
4. Blei, D.M., Ng, A.Y., Jordan, M.I.: Latent Dirichlet allocation. J. Mach. Learn. Res. **3**, 993–1022 (2003)
5. Didachos, C., Kintos, D.P., Fousteris, M., Gerogiannis, V.C., Son, L.H., Kanavos, A.: A cloud-based distributed computing approach for extracting molecular descriptors. In: 6th ACM International Conference on Algorithms, Computing and Systems (ICACS), pp. 20:1–20:6 (2022)
6. Didachos, C., Kintos, D.P., Fousteris, M., Mylonas, P., Kanavos, A.: An optimized cloud computing method for extracting molecular descriptors. In: GeNeDis 2022: Genetics, Geriatrics and Neurodegenerative Diseases Research, pp. 165–173 (2021)
7. Dudek, A.Z., Arodz, T., Galvez, J.: Computational methods in developing quantitative structure-activity relationships (QSAR): a review. Comb. Chem. High Throughput Screen. **9**(3), 213–228 (2006)
8. Duesbury, E., Holliday, J.D., Willett, P.: Maximum common subgraph isomorphism algorithms. MATCH Commun. Math. Comput. Chem. **77**(2), 213–232 (2017)
9. Giordano, D., Biancaniello, C., Argenio, M.A., Facchiano, A.: Drug design by pharmacophore and virtual screening approach. Pharmaceuticals **15**(5), 646 (2022)
10. Guimaraes, G.L., Sanchez-Lengeling, B., Outeiral, C., Farias, P.L.C., Aspuru-Guzik, A.: Objective-reinforced generative adversarial networks (organ) for sequence generation models. arXiv preprint arXiv:1705.10843 (2018)
11. Hessler, G., Baringhaus, K.H.: Artificial intelligence in drug design. Molecules **23**(10), 2520 (2018)
12. Lavecchia, A.: Machine-learning approaches in drug discovery: methods and applications. Drug Discov. Today **20**(3), 318–331 (2015)
13. Lavecchia, A., Cerchia, C.: In silico methods to address polypharmacology: current status, applications and future perspectives. Drug Discov. Today **21**(2), 288–298 (2016)
14. Li, Q.: Application of fragment-based drug discovery to versatile targets. Front. Mol. Biosci. **7**, 180 (2020)
15. Lyu, J., et al.: Ultra-large library docking for discovering new chemotypes. Nature **566**(7743), 224–229 (2019)
16. Maggiora, G., Vogt, M., Stumpfe, D., Bajorath, J.: Molecular similarity in medicinal chemistry: miniperspective. J. Med. Chem. **57**(8), 3186–3204 (2014)
17. Mouchlis, V.D., et al.: Advances in de novo drug design: from conventional to machine learning methods. Int. J. Mol. Sci. **22**(4), 1676 (2021)

18. Olivecrona, M., Blaschke, T., Engkvist, O., Chen, H.: Molecular de-novo design through deep reinforcement learning. J. Cheminform. **9**(1), 1–14 (2017)
19. Öztürk, H., Özgür, A., Olmez, E.O.: DeepDTA: deep drug-target binding affinity prediction. Bioinformatics **34**(17), i821–i829 (2018)
20. Pang, B., Lee, L.: Opinion mining and sentiment analysis. Found. Trends Inf. Retr. **2**(1–2), 1–135 (2007)
21. Popova, M., Isayev, O., Tropsha, A.: Deep reinforcement learning for de novo drug design. Sci. Adv. **4**(7), eaap7885 (2018)
22. Rodrigues, T., et al.: De novo fragment design for drug discovery and chemical biology. Angew. Chem. Int. Ed. **54**(50), 15079–15083 (2015)
23. Sanchez-Lengeling, B., Aspuru-Guzik, A.: Inverse molecular design using machine learning: generative models for matter engineering. Science **361**(6400), 360–365 (2018)
24. Schneider, G., Fechner, U.: Computer-based de novo design of drug-like molecules. Nat. Rev. Drug Discov. **4**(8), 649–663 (2005)
25. Stumpfe, D., Bajorath, J.: Similarity searching. Wiley Interdisc. Rev. Comput. Mol. Sci. **1**(2), 260–282 (2011)
26. Tropsha, A.: Best practices for QSAR model development, validation, and exploitation. Mol. Inf. **29**(6–7), 476–488 (2010)
27. Vamathevan, J., et al.: Applications of machine learning in drug discovery and development. Nat. Rev. Drug Discov. **18**(6), 463–477 (2019)
28. Weininger, D.: Smiles, a chemical language and information system. 1. Introduction to methodology and encoding rules. J. Chem. Inf. Comput. Sci. **28**(1), 31–36 (1988)
29. Wu, H.Y., Chiang, C.W., Li, L.: Text mining for drug-drug interaction. Biomed. Lit. Min. 47–75 (2014)
30. Yan, J., Gao, K.: Research and exploration on the construction method of knowledge graph of water field based on text. In: 2nd IEEE ICISCAE, pp. 71–77 (2019)

Forecasting Stock Market Alternations Using Social Media Sentiment Analysis and Regression Techniques

Christina Saravanos[1] and Andreas Kanavos[2(✉)]

[1] Computer Engineering and Informatics Department, University of Patras,
Patras, Greece
saravanou@ceid.upatras.gr
[2] Department of Informatics, Ionian University, Corfu, Greece
akanavos@ionio.gr

Abstract. In recent years, the public opinion is swayed by online social, media and news platforms, such as Twitter, podcasts, and streaming news broadcasts. The public opinion can alter the outcome of various social-economic events, e.g., the volatility of the stock market. This paper presents an overview of forecasting the volatility of the indices of several companies in the U.S. stock market while considering the sentiment and features extracted from the metadata of a tweet and its author's social activity and network. The daily changes in the prices of an index in the U.S. stock market were estimated by applying several regression techniques. The results indicate a strong correlation between the approximated closing prices of the stocks in the U.S. stock market, the sentiment along with the features extracted from a tweet, and its author's activity and network. Finally, the obtained results indicate that the number of attributes did not impact the performance of the applied regression techniques.

Keywords: Knowledge Extraction · Stock Forecasting · Sentiment Analysis · Social Media Analysis · Natural Language Processing (NLP) · Twitter · Regression Techniques

1 Introduction

Nowadays, public opinion is swayed by several online social and media platforms, e.g., social networks and streaming services. Most social networks, such as Facebook, allow their users to upload and comment on a post regarding an event. On the other hand, Twitter endorses its users to upload short-length messages or posts. These posts are referred to as tweets. A tweet comprises 140 characters. Twitter, additionally, endorses its users to interact by replying to or *retweeting* a tweet. Therefore, a tweet will diffuse from its author's social network to the respective networks of its author.

© IFIP International Federation for Information Processing 2023
Published by Springer Nature Switzerland AG 2023
I. Maglogiannis et al. (Eds.): AIAI 2023 Workshops, IFIP AICT 677, pp. 335–346, 2023.
https://doi.org/10.1007/978-3-031-34171-7_27

Furthermore, tweets cover a wide range of subjects. A tweet can either refer to newsworthy events or reflect the opinion or the emotion of their authors regarding a product or service, e.g., the latest MacBook. Most tweets indicate the feelings of their authors towards a subject via certain words, hashtags, punctuation marks, or emojis. As a tweet spreads through millions of social networks, the emotion or the opinion of its author will impact the feelings or the emotion of several millions of users on Twitter.

In recent years, however, several novel techniques have emerged that seek to estimate the fluctuations in the daily prices of an index by relying on the correlation between its historical prices and the sentiment extracted from the respective tweets. The volatility of the index is estimated by either using regression techniques, e.g., linear regression, or deep neural networks such as RNNs [5,8,9,12,17,24].

This paper aims to approximate the volatility of the indices of several companies in the U.S. stock market by relying on the correlation between the daily prices of the indexes, the sentiment, and several features extracted from the respective tweets. The features were extracted from the metadata of a tweet and its author's presence on Twitter. The elicited features indicate the impact of a tweet on its author's social network. In other words, the extracted features hint at the initial impact of the tweet's sentiments on its author's friends and followers. As the tweet diffuses into the social networks of hundreds of users it will impact the emotion and opinions of thousands. The volatility of an index was estimated via regression techniques. The results initially suggest that the daily closing prices and the sentiment are strongly correlated. In addition, the results indicate that the estimated closing prices depend on the previously-mentioned features. Finally, the results suggest that the volume of tweets plays a rather significant role in predicting future closing prices.

The remainder of this paper is organized as follows: Sect. 2 briefly depicts the novel techniques that have recently emerged to forecast the volatility of the stock market by relying on the correlation between the daily closing prices of an index and the emotion extracted from the respective tweets. Section 3 elaborates on the presented scheme, particularly on the extracted features and employed regression techniques. Section 4 comments on the experimental setup and the results that emerged while conducting the experiments. Finally, Sect. 5 draws the final conclusions.

2   Related Work

The volatility of an index in the stock market is affected by several distinct factors, such as the public opinion, the news, and trends. Therefore, predicting the volatility of the stock market is considered an underlying problem.

As the prominence of social network platforms continues to grow, innovative paradigms have been introduced which seek to estimate the volatility of the stock market by relying on regression techniques and the correlation between past prices of an index and the sentiment extracted from several online posts which mention the respective company. These posts have been posted on a social media platform. In [26, 30], the volatility of the Indian and U.S. stock markets was, correspondingly, forecast by, initially, computing the correlation between the past prices of the NSE and the DJIAI indices along the public sentiment extracted from the respective tweets.

Moreover, [1, 10, 27, 31] aspired to predict the future movements of the FTS100, BSE, and the DIJAI indices, respectively, by relying on the interrelationship of the former alternations of the indices and the emotion elicited from the respective tweets as well as the Granger Causality Test. In addition, the future volatility of the stock market in [27, 31] was estimated by employing auto-regression methods such as the Auto-Regressive Moving Average (ARIMA). In [13], however, Gupta et al. proposed a novel paradigm that sought to forecast the volatility of the U.S. stock market by relying on the correlation between the current daily prices of an index and the sentiment excerpted from the respective tweets.

Furthermore, the scheme introduced in [15] extracted features from several social media platforms such as Twitter and Google, the sentiment of thousands of tweets to predict the volatility of the U.S. stock market via a novel regression technique, the Delta Naive Bayes. On the other hand, [18] aspired to estimate possible changes in the future prices of several indices of the U.S. stock market by employing the correlation between the respective previous prices and the emotion extracted from the respective tweets along with several conventional regression techniques, such as RF, KNN, and SVR.

3   Overview of the Presented Scheme

This section elaborates on the forecasting of the volatility in the stock market. The presented scheme comprises three distinct modules. The first module extracts the emotion and several features derived from the tweet and its author's metadata. The second one elicits attributes from public information regarding a company's stock. The tweets and the stock market information were extracted by employing the Twitter and Yahoo! Finance API. Finally, the third module estimates the daily closing price of a company depending on the features provided by the first two components and by employing a regression technique.

3.1   Feature Extraction

This subsection elaborates on the sentiment and the features obtained from the first two modules of the presented scheme. The depicted paradigm relies on the tweets and the daily stock market information acquired from Twitter and Yahoo! Finance API, a platform focused on providing financial news.

3.1.1   Extracting the Sentiment and Features from A Tweet

The first module seeks to extract several features from the content of a tweet and its author's overall presence on Twitter. The attributes obtained from the tweet's metadata and its authors' social activity, as presented in Table 1.

Table 1. Features extracted from Tweet's Metadata and Tweet's Author Profile.

Tweet's Metadata			
IRT	Is Retweet	IRP	Is Reply To
NH	# Hashtags	NU	# URLs
NMU	# Mentioned Users		
Tweet's Author Profile			
NTw	# Tweets	NFoll	# Followers
NFr	# Friends	NL	# Lists
NTU	# URLs used	NTMU	# Users mentioned
NTH	# Hashtags used	NFT	# Favorite Tweets
NTC	# Conversations participated		

Moreover, the first module aims to extract the sentiment from each particular tweet. *Sentiment analysis* consists of a group of techniques that aim to excerpt the sentiment of a tweet towards a product, event, or organization. Sentiment analysis seeks to classify a tweet into one of three sentiments: positive, negative, or neutral by applying either lexicon-based approaches, such as the Natural Language Processing Kit's (NLTK) Vader Analyzer, or supervised learning models such as in [3,16].

NLTK's Vader Analyzer is a lexicon- and rule-based sentiment analysis tool that extracts the sentiment of the tweets via a combination of sentiment lexicons. The sentiment lexicons are a list of lexical features labeled as either positive, negative, or neutral based on their semantic orientation. A polarity score is computed based on the sentiment lexicons [6,23,29,33].

3.1.2   Extracting Stock Market Features
Several stock market features were obtained from the daily public information obtained from Yahoo! Finance and correspond to the number of shares, the opening, closing, and high and low prices of an index in the U.S. stock market. Two additional features, the high/low percentage, and the percentage change, were computed based on the previously-mentioned attributes. The former corresponds to the daily changes between the high and low prices, whereas the latter coincides with the daily alternations between the opening and closing prices of an index.

The two additional features are defined as follows:

$$\text{High/Low Percentage} = \frac{High - Low}{Low} * 100 \tag{1}$$

$$\text{Percentage Change} = \frac{Close - Open}{Open} * 100 \tag{2}$$

where *High*, *Low*, *Close* and *Open* denote the high, low, closing and opening prices of an index in the stock market, respectively.

3.2   Regression Techniques

The volatility of the indices was approximated by employing several regression techniques. Regression models seek to predict the value of the dependent variable, such as the daily closing price, by relying on the independent variables, e.g., the features extracted from the dataset.

Linear Regression (LR) aims to find a relationship between the independent and dependent variables by fitting the data into a linear equation. The relationship between the independent and dependent variables hints at a strong association between the two. Two types of linear regression, *single* and *multivariate linear regression*, are employed depending on the size of the independent variables and the complexity of their relationship with the dependent variables. Both types compute the values of the dependent variable to fit the respective independent or predictor values into a linear model [11, 22, 25].

Moreover, the Support Vector Regression (SVR) algorithm is a non-linear regression approach that seeks to forecast future data points by employing historical samples provided by the dataset. In a high-dimensional feature space, a linear function, referred to as the SVR function aims to create the non-linear relationship between the input and output data, or the predictor and predicted variables [7, 14, 20].

On the other hand, Decision Trees (DTs) are non-parametric models applied to solve either classification or regression problems. A DT consists of a root or parent node, a set of internal and terminal nodes. The dataset is initially allocated at the root node and is subsequently segmented in every internal node. The internal nodes correspond to predictors. The classes or target values that have emerged from several subsequent internal nodes, are assigned to the terminal nodes. The DT regressor relies on applying binary recursive partitioning, i.e., a technique that iteratively splits the dataset into several groups. The regressor partitions the root node into several binary pieces. A binary piece is assigned to a child node. The child node corresponds to an internal node. The regression then selects the child node that either minimizes the sum of squared deviations which emerged from splitting the dataset into two parts or corresponds to the feature with the lowest impurity index. The impurity of a DT is calculated via the *Gini Index*. The dataset splitting is applied on several internal nodes and ends when a node reaches a minimum node size; this node corresponds to a terminal node [19, 32].

Random Forest (RF) is a regression technique that relies on the result and the performance of several DT regressors. The RF scheme is initialized by constructing several hundreds or thousands of de-correlated DT regressors. The DTs are implemented via a randomized subset of predictors to create the random forest. The output of RF is equal to the mean value of the outputs of the DTs. Therefore, RF provides more accurate results in forecasting the future values of a target node than DT. The RF depends heavily on an approach often referred to as *bagging* or *bootstrap aggregation*. *Bagging* seeks to reduce the variance often associated with a regression model to increase the performance of the RF. In addition, bagging decreases the correlation between the implemented DTs by randomly selecting a feature subset from each DT. Therefore, a feature may be employed several times, while others are never selected to train the RF. The random selection of feature subsets is attributed to as *bootstrap*. The selected bootstrap samples are fed into the RF scheme and will result in creating a smaller subset of regressors. The aggregated output of the RF emerges by calculating the mean output of the selected subset of DTs [19, 28].

Finally, the AdaBoost model is an ensemble, iterative paradigm that seeks to create a robust learning-based approach by linearly combining several weak learning algorithms. The learning methods are alluded to as *base learners*. In each iteration, a base learner is called and constructs a weak learning-based paradigm. Thereupon, a weight coefficient is assigned to every learning-based model. The accuracy of the base learners increases by re-calculating their respective weight coefficients. The output of the AdaBoost model emerges by summing the outputs of the learners multiplied by their corresponding weight coefficients [2, 4, 21].

4   Experimental Setup and Results

This section elaborates on the experimental setup and the results that emerged from conducting the experiments. The presented scheme aims to estimate the daily prices of the indices mentioned in Table 2 by relying on the correlation between the features and via the regression techniques described in Sect. 3.

Table 2. The names, the indices and the three most frequent hashtags obtained from the tweets posted from March 22nd to March 31st, 2021 of the companies whose volatility is predicted by the presented scheme.

Company	Stock Index	Three Most Frequent Hashtags
Amazon	AMZN	#amazon, #deals, #sales
Apple	APPL	#Apple, #AppleMusic, #iphone
Delta	DAL	#DAL1669, #AIRBUS, #DAL1038
Google	GOOGL	#google, #DoodleForGoogle, #chrome
Microsoft	MSFT	#windows, #microsoft, #Azure

4.1   Datasets

The daily stock market information of the indices and several thousands of tweets that mention the companies depicted in Table 2 were respectively extracted from the Yahoo! Finance and the Twitter API from March 22nd to March 31st, 2021. The U.S. stock market is closed on the weekends. In other words, the tweets posted on the respective dates were discarded. The presented scheme aims to forecast the volatility of the indices of several companies; therefore, several datasets were created.

4.2   Estimating the Changes of the Daily Closing Prices in the Stock Market

The daily closing prices of the indices of the companies presented in Table 2 from March 22nd to March 31st, 2021 were predicted by applying the techniques mentioned in Sect. 3. Figure 1 illustrates the actual and the respective closing prices of the indices that correspond to Amazon and Delta that emerged from employing the previously - mentioned regression techniques.

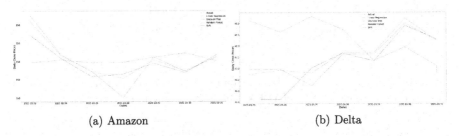

(a) Amazon   (b) Delta

Fig. 1. The actual and estimated daily closing prices of the indices of (a) Amazon and (b) Delta in the U.S. stock markey from March 22nd to March 31st, 2021.

The results depicted in Fig. 1 suggest similar movements between the actual and the estimated daily closing prices of the indices. In several cases, the results indicate that the actual daily closing prices of the indices coincided with the respective estimated prices. Nonetheless, the closing prices that emerged via the SVR deviated from the actual prices of the companies' indices.

Table 3 presents several metrics referring to the total number of tweets and their overall diffusion on Twitter from March 22nd to March 31st, 2021. Figure 1 and Table 3 suggest that as the number of total tweets and their respective diffusion on Twitter increases, the predicted prices coincide with the actual closing prices of the index on Twitter. In a similar manner, a low volume and dispersion of tweets led to the estimated closing prices diverging from the corresponding actual prices in the stock market. Therefore, the volume and diffusion of the tweets play a rather significant role in forecasting the volatility of an index.

The estimated daily closing prices of an index deviated from the respective actual prices due to the high number of features. In several cases, the value of an attribute was equal to zero. Consequently, the sparse dataset led to the curse of dimensionality which led the models to overfit.

4.3   RMSE and MAPE

The accuracy of a regression technique relies on calculating the error between the actual and estimated value of an observation. In most real-world applications,

Table 3. The total number of tweets, retweeted tweets, replied tweets, followers and friends of the tweets' authors extracted from Twitter between March, 22nd to March, 31st, 2021.

Company	Tweets	Retweeted Tweets	Replied Tweets	Followers of Tweets' Authors	Friends of Tweets' Authors
Amazon	51,053	10,817	1,553	443,059,418	577,441
Apple	31,421	23,233	641	181,102,724	636,461
Delta	3,277	1,196	196	77,852,621	66,557
Google	113,659	87,374	1,305	553,284,947	3,085,156
Microsoft	10,065	5,682	283	121,683,430	213,395

the error relies on either the Root Mean Square Error (RMSE) or the Mean Absolute Percentage Error (MAPE), which are defined as:

$$RMSE = \frac{1}{\sum_{i=0}^{N} x_i} * \sqrt{\frac{\sum_{i=0}^{N}(x_i - \hat{x}_i)}{N}} \tag{3}$$

$$MAPE = \frac{1}{N} \sum_{i=1}^{N} \left| \frac{x_i - \hat{x}_i}{x_i} \right| \tag{4}$$

where N, x_i, $\hat{x}_i$ denote the total number of observations, the actual and the estimated value, that emerged from the techniques depicted in Sect. 4 of the ith observation, correspondingly. The RMSE indicates the deviation of the estimated price from the respective actual daily closing price of an index, whereas the MAPE, an accuracy metric, hints at the percentage of change between the predicted and actual closing prices of an index in the market.

Tables 4 and 5 present the RMSE and MAPE which emerged from estimating the indices depicted in Table 2 from March 22nd to March 31st, 2021. The depicted results suggest a similar divergence to the results illustrated in Fig. 1. These results indicate that the MAPE is a better accuracy metric than the RMSE since it points to the actual fluctuation between the actual and predicted

Table 4. RMSE between the companies' actual and approximated close prices in the stock market from March 22nd to March 31st, 2021.

Company	LR	DT	RF	AdaBoost	SVR
Amazon	1.1237e−09	0.4285	0.6720	0.3418	1.5415
Apple	3.2012e−09	0.3149	0.4568	0.2736	2.7477
Delta	1.1254e−10	0.9379	0.7471	1.0724	2.2164
Google	6.2843e−10	0.5052	0.1628	0.2266	1.0376
Microsoft	3.4393e−10	0.5084	0.4738	0.7083	3.2809

Table 5. MAPE between the companies' actual and approximated close prices in the stock market from March 22nd to March 31st, 2021.

Company	LR	DT	RF	AdaBoost	SVR
Amazon	5.6796e−10	0.2330	0.3637	0.1891	0.8425
Apple	2.1637e−09	0.2201	0.3470	0.2042	2.0782
Delta	2.0135e−10	1.2442	1.1789	1.7419	4.1396
Google	5.7707e−10	0.4388	0.1421	0.2127	0.8821
Microsoft	1.2400e−10	0.1619	0.1364	0.2018	1.1091

closing prices of the indices. Finally, the numerical values of the MAPE point to a similar deviation of the actual and approximated closing prices illustrated in Fig. 1.

4.4 Correlation Between Daily Closing Prices and Sentiment Extracted from Tweets

While conducting the experiments, polarity scores, which indicate the sentiment, were extracted from the tweets. The tweets were classified as either positive, neutral, or negative based on the value of their respective polarity scores. Figure 2 illustrates the daily number of positive, neutral, and negative tweets that were posted on Twitter from March 22nd to March 31st, 2021.

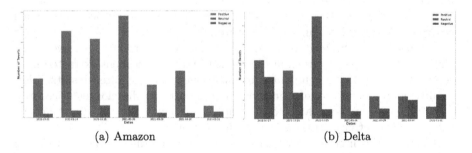

(a) Amazon   (b) Delta

Fig. 2. The daily number of positive, neutral and negative tweets that mention (a) Amazon and (b) Delta posted on Twitter from March 22nd to March 31st, 2021.

Figure 2 and Table 3 cite the overall sentiment and diffusion of the tweets in the social network. The depicted information indicates the impact of the tweets on their authors' friends and followers on Twitter. If a tweet spreads throughout Twitter, then its sentiment will influence the emotion or opinions of thousands. Therefore, the public sentiment will be swayed positively or negatively.

The results and the information depicted in Figs. 1 and 2 respectively suggest that the sentiment extracted from the tweets and the closing prices of the stock market indices are strongly correlated. The illuminated results hint that as the number of positive tweets that mention a company, increases, its stock will be overbought. Therefore, the closing price of the company's index will fall in the stock market. Similarly, the increase in negative tweets that mention a company, will lead to the company's stock being oversold. Thus, the closing price of the company's index will rise.

5   Conclusions and Future Work

This paper presented a scheme that forecasts the volatility of the daily closing prices of stocks, of several companies, in the U.S. stock market via several regression techniques. The advocated paradigm, additionally, relies on the correlation between the past daily closing prices of the respective companies' stocks, the emotion, and several features extracted from the metadata and text of a tweet as well as from the social activity and network of its author on Twitter.

The advocated scheme seeks to forecast the volatility of the stock market by combining the respective past prices, the emotion, and several features regarding the tweet and its author. The changes in the daily closing prices of a company's stock in the U.S. market are approximated by applying several regression techniques. The accuracy of the estimated and the actual closing prices was calculated via the RMSE and the MAPE. The RMSE and the MAPE between the actual and the estimated closing prices that emerged from applying linear regression and SVR are rather low. In other words, the difference between the actual and the estimated prices are close to zero. On the other hand, the RMSE and the MAPE obtained from applying DT, RF, and AdaBoost regression are quite large indicating the presence of noise and curse of dimensionality which occurred due to the vast number of features.

Moreover, the obtained results hint at a strong correlation between the volatility of a company's stock in the market and the sentiment extracted from the tweets in which the companies are mentioned. The acquired results, additionally, point out that the estimated daily changes in the closing prices of a company's stock are correlated to the features extracted from the tweet and its author's social activity on the social media platform.

Regarding the directions for future research, the volatility of the daily closing prices, of a company's stock, can be approximated via the correlation between the respective past prices, the sentiment, and the subjectivity of a tweet. Furthermore, the daily changes in the closing prices can be estimated by applying DL frameworks, such as Convolutional Neural Networks (CNNs) and Generative Adversarial Networks (GANs). In addition, the changeability of the prices in the stock market can be estimated by taking into account the current trends of Twitter, or another social media platform or search engine, such as Google. Finally, features obtained from the social profiles of a user from several other social networks, such as LinkedIn, Facebook, and Reddit, can be concatenated to forecast future changes in a company's price.

Acknowledgement. This research was co-financed by the European Union and Greek national funds through the "Competitiveness, Entrepreneurship and Innovation" Operational Programme 2014–2020, under the Call "Support for regional excellence"; project title: "Intelligent Research Infrastructure for Shipping, Transport and Supply Chain - ENIRISST+"; MIS code: 5047041.

References

1. Ahuja, R., Rastogi, H., Choudhuri, A., Garg, B.: Stock market forecast using sentiment analysis. In: 2nd IEEE International Conference on Computing for Sustainable Global Development (INDIACom), pp. 1008–1010 (2015)
2. Ampomah, E.K., Qin, Z., Nyame, G., Botchey, F.E.: Stock market decision support modeling with tree-based adaboost ensemble machine learning models. Informatica (Slovenia) **44**(4) (2020)
3. Baltas, A., Kanavos, A., Tsakalidis, A.K.: An apache spark implementation for sentiment analysis on twitter data. In: 2nd International Workshop on Algorithmic Aspects of Cloud Computing (ALGOCLOUD), vol. 10230, pp. 15–25 (2016)
4. Barrow, D.K., Crone, S.F.: A comparison of adaboost algorithms for time series forecast combination. Int. J. Forecast. **32**(4), 1103–1119 (2016)
5. Bing, L., Chan, K.C.C., Ou, C.X.: Public sentiment analysis in twitter data for prediction of a company's stock price movements. In: 11th IEEE International Conference on e-Business Engineering (ICEBE), pp. 232–239 (2014)
6. Bonta, V., Kumaresh, N., Janardhan, N.: A comprehensive study on lexicon based approaches for sentiment analysis. Asian J. Comput. Sci. Technol. **8**(S2), 1–6 (2019)
7. Chahboun, S., Maaroufi, M.: Performance comparison of support vector regression, random forest and multiple linear regression to forecast the power of photovoltaic panels. In: 9th IEEE International Renewable and Sustainable Energy Conference (IRSEC), pp. 1–4 (2021)
8. Chicco, D., Warrens, M.J., Jurman, G.: The coefficient of determination r-squared is more informative than smape, mae, mape, mse and rmse in regression analysis evaluation. PeerJ Comput. Sci. **7**, e623 (2021)
9. Das, S., Behera, R.K., Kumar, M., Rath, S.K.: Real-time sentiment analysis of twitter streaming data for stock prediction. Procedia Comput. Sci. **132**, 956–964 (2018)
10. Deveikyte, J., Geman, H., Piccari, C., Provetti, A.: A sentiment analysis approach to the prediction of market volatility. CoRR abs/2012.05906 (2020)
11. Fumo, N., Biswas, M.A.R.: Regression analysis for prediction of residential energy consumption. Renew. Sustain. Energy Rev. **47**, 332–343 (2015)
12. Guo, X., Li, J.: A novel twitter sentiment analysis model with baseline correlation for financial market prediction with improved efficiency. In: 6th IEEE International Conference on Social Networks Analysis, Management and Security (SNAMS), pp. 472–477 (2019)
13. Gupta, R., Chen, M.: Sentiment analysis for stock price prediction. In: 3rd IEEE Conference on Multimedia Information Processing and Retrieval (MIPR), pp. 213–218 (2020)
14. Hu, J., Gao, P., Yao, Y., Xie, X.: Traffic flow forecasting with particle swarm optimization and support vector regression. In: 17th IEEE International Conference on Intelligent Transportation Systems (ITSC), pp. 2267–2268 (2014)

15. Jin, F., Wang, W., Chakraborty, P., Self, N., Chen, F., Ramakrishnan, N.: Tracking multiple social media for stock market event prediction. In: 17th Industrial Conference on Advances in Data Mining (ICDM), vol. 10357, pp. 16–30 (2017)
16. Kanavos, A., Perikos, I., Hatzilygeroudis, I., Tsakalidis, A.K.: Emotional community detection in social networks. Comput. Electr. Eng. **65**, 449–460 (2018)
17. Kanavos, A., Vonitsanos, G., Mohasseb, A., Mylonas, P.: An entropy-based evaluation for sentiment analysis of stock market prices using twitter data. In: 15th IEEE International Workshop on Semantic and Social Media Adaptation and Personalization (SMAP), pp. 1–7 (2020)
18. Khan, W., Ghazanfar, M.A., Azam, M.A., Karami, A., Alyoubi, K.H., Alfakeeh, A.S.: Stock market prediction using machine learning classifiers and social media, news. J. Ambient. Intell. Humaniz. Comput. **13**(7), 3433–3456 (2022)
19. Li, Y., et al.: Random forest regression for online capacity estimation of lithium-ion batteries. Appl. Energy **232**, 197–210 (2018)
20. Lin, K., Lin, Q., Zhou, C., Yao, J.: Time series prediction based on linear regression and SVR. In: 3rd IEEE International Conference on Natural Computation (ICNC), pp. 688–691 (2007)
21. Liu, Q., Wang, X., Huang, X., Yin, X.: Prediction model of rock mass class using classification and regression tree integrated adaboost algorithm based on tbm driving data. Tunn. Undergr. Space Technol. **106**, 103595 (2020)
22. Maulud, D.H., Abdulazeez, A.M.: A review on linear regression comprehensive in machine learning. J. Appl. Sci. Technol. Trends **1**(4), 140–147 (2020)
23. Medhat, W., Hassan, A., Korashy, H.: Sentiment analysis algorithms and applications: a survey. Ain Shams Eng. J. **5**(4), 1093–1113 (2014)
24. Mittal, A., Goel, A.: Stock prediction using twitter sentiment analysis. Standford University, CS229 15, 2352 (2012)
25. Montgomery, D.C., Peck, E.A., Vining, G.G.: Introduction to Linear Regression Analysis. Wiley, Hoboken (2021)
26. Oliveira, N., Cortez, P., Areal, N.: Some experiments on modeling stock market behavior using investor sentiment analysis and posting volume from twitter. In: 3rd ACM International Conference on Web Intelligence, Mining and Semantics (WIMS), p. 31 (2013)
27. Rao, T., Srivastava, S.: Analyzing stock market movements using twitter sentiment analysis. In: International Conference on Advances in Social Networks Analysis and Mining (ASONAM) (2012)
28. Rodriguez-Galiano, V., Sanchez-Castillo, M., Chica-Olmo, M., Chica-Rivas, M.: Machine learning predictive models for mineral prospectivity: an evaluation of neural networks, random forest, regression trees and support vector machines. Ore Geol. Rev. **71**, 804–818 (2015)
29. Sahayak, V., Shete, V., Pathan, A.: Sentiment analysis on twitter data. Int. J. Innovative Res. Adv. Eng. (IJIRAE) **2**(1), 178–183 (2015)
30. Sharma, V., Khemnar, R., Kumari, R., Mohan, B.R.: Time series with sentiment analysis for stock price prediction. In: 2nd IEEE International Conference on Intelligent Communication and Computational Techniques (ICCT), pp. 178–181 (2019)
31. Souza, T.T.P., Kolchyna, O., Treleaven, P.C., Aste, T.: Twitter sentiment analysis applied to finance: a case study in the retail industry. CoRR abs/1507.00784 (2015)
32. Xu, M., Watanachaturaporn, P., Varshney, P.K., Arora, M.K.: Decision tree regression for soft classification of remote sensing data. Remote Sens. Environ. **97**(3), 322–336 (2005)
33. Yao, J.: Automated sentiment analysis of text data with nltk. J. Phys. Conf. Ser. **1187**, 052020 (2019)

Handwritten Word Recognition Using Deep Learning Methods

Vasileios Lagios[1], Isidoros Perikos[1,2](✉), and Ioannis Hatzilygeroudis[1]

[1] Department of Computer Engineering and Informatics, University of Patras, Patras, Greece
{lagios,perikos,ihatz}@ceid.upatras.gr

[2] Computer Technology Institute and Press Diophantus, Patras, Greece

Abstract. The handwriting recognition field has preoccupied the scientific community for several years. The complexity encountered in this sector is due to the fact that each individual has a unique way of writing. Various methods have been examined and evaluated throughout the years, with the sole purpose of achieving sustainable results. The introduction of neural networks, specifically the use of convolutional neural networks (CNN) and recurrent neural networks (RNN), has presented dependable results in the handwriting recognition field. In this paper, we introduce a model that recognizes handwritten words without pre-segmenting the words into characters. The model consists of a CNN for the extraction of features, a RNN for the prediction procedure and a final layer (CTC) for decoding the prediction. We conducted many experiments on the well-known IAM handwriting database and attained an accuracy of 77.22% and a character error rate (CER) of 10.4%.

Keywords: Handwritten Word Recognition · Convolutional Neural Networks · Recurrent Neural Networks · Deep Learning

1 Introduction

Handwritten texts are a common way that people can use to communicate. Generally, a handwritten recognition system is a mechanism that is used for the recognition of handwritten characters, words or texts, even if they come from scanned pictures or in real-time using stylus in an electronic device like tablet. The first option is called offline handwriting recognition and the second one is called online handwriting recognition [6]. In offline handwriting recognition, the input is a two-dimensional image, pixel by pixel, and the output is a sequence of characters. The line continuity of handwriting makes it hard to segment characters for individual recognition. Methods based on isolating the characters of a word, were widely used in the nineties. Now these methods are mostly replaced by the sliding window approach, in which features are extracted from vertical frames of the line image [16]. This method changes the problem to a sequence to sequence transduction one, while potentially encoding the two-dimensional nature of the image with the use of convolutional neural networks [17] or by defining relevant features.

© IFIP International Federation for Information Processing 2023
Published by Springer Nature Switzerland AG 2023
I. Maglogiannis et al. (Eds.): AIAI 2023 Workshops, IFIP AICT 677, pp. 347–358, 2023.
https://doi.org/10.1007/978-3-031-34171-7_28

In this paper, we are going to present a model for offline handwriting recognition. Handwriting recognition acquires special importance in cases such as the authentication of a signature on bank checks, recognition of postal codes in letters and even in cases that have to do with crime, translations and detection of keywords [7] Shankar [18] kumar bhuia. In a world based on data, accurate handwriting recognition is highly desirable.

However, it is a quite challenging task. Recently, researchers have proven that every person has his own and almost unique handwriting type [28] ahmed. Each handwritten character can be written in different styles, lengths or sizes by different writers. Sometimes even the same character can be written in a different style by the same writer in a different period of time. In the level of a word, the difficulty of recognition is even higher. What makes it more difficult is the continuous writing of the characters, the spaces between them and the writing that may not continue a straight line [8, 20].

A HandWritten Recognition system (HWR) is actually an Optical Character Recognition (OCR). OCR is the electronic or mechanical conversion of images of typed, handwritten or printed text into machine-encoded text, whether from a scanned document, a photo of a document, a scene-photo (for example the text on signs and billboards in a landscape photo) or from subtitle text superimposed on an image [23]. In the case of handwritten text it is called Handwritten Recognition (HWR).

A Handwritten recognition system consists of the following stages: pre-processing, segmentation, feature extraction, classification and recognition [9]sharma[10]teddy surya. In the stage of pre-processing what we aim to achieve is the elimination of unwanted features, without however removing any important information. The techniques, applied in this stage, can be applied in every type of image, such as coloured (RGB), grayscale and binary. Due to the fact that these techniques are very costly when applied in coloured pictures, when analyzing handwritten words, we use binary or grayscale images [11]. Effectively we pursue the augmentation of the image's text as well as the preparation of the picture for the next stages, ensuring the model will be able to recognize it better. Segmentation is a process where we isolate the text from the image's background. The techniques that are used are line segmentation, word segmentation and character segmentation [11]. By introducing neural networks, segmentation is now a stage which can be disregarded, since neural networks such as RNN do not require segmented data. Feature extraction is a process where information about an item is collected in order to allow its better classification. In case of recognizing handwritten characters, each character is depicted as a feature sequence [12]. In the next step of the classification, classes with similar properties are created and the inputs are being assigned to a class. In this stage the feature sequence is being predicted. The most traditional classifier in handwriting recognition is neural network.

In our work, the stages of feature extraction and classification are handled by deep neural networks. So, in the recognition process, the prediction given during the classification process, is being decoded, by using a decoder. The usage of neural networks has yielded better results, compared to machine learning algorithms which were used previously [20]. We designed a methodology that relys on Convolutional Neural Networks (CNN) and Recurrent Neural Networks (RNN) for the recognition of handwritten words. CNNs are designed to process two-dimensional data and to extract features. CNNs are able to be successful on multiple writer collections if the training set is large enough.

RNNs are used for classification and time-sequence predictions. Their use in contemporary systems is essential, especially that of the LSTM layers. These layers accumulate data, in time and facilitate an easier retention of previous data in the memory. This renders them appropriate for classification, analysis and time-sequence predictions of unknown time-frame. These layers do not require segmented data. The preferable output of such a network, for decoding the prediction, is the CTC layer, where using a CTC decoder, allows this process to take place. Over the years, several algorithms have been used to perform these processes, but neural networks, in addition to delivering the best results, also facilitate the work of the programmer in that they take him out of the difficult position of finding segmentation techniques, where is a difficult process as well as extracting features manual.

The rest of the paper is organized as follows. Section 2 reviews the related works for handwritten word and text recognition. After that, Sect. 3 introduces the proposed architecture and describes it's functionality. Section 4 presents our experimental results and finally, Sect. 5 concludes the paper and provides directions for future work.

2 Related Work

Several research attempts have been made in the literature for the accurate recognition of handwritten text A detailed overview of methods, systems and approaches can be found in the works presented in [24, 25].

In [3] authors present a method that is a combination of SVM classifiers and nearest neighbor algorithm. Their method encodes the input word image as Fisher Vectors (FV), i.e., as an aggregation of the gradients of a Gaussian Mixture Model (GMM) over some low-level descriptors, SIFT in this case. It then trains a set of linear SVM classifiers, one per each binary attribute contained in a set of word properties. Canonical Correlation Analysis (CCA) is used to link the vector of predicted attributes and the binary attributes vector generated from the actual word. The CCA method finds a common vector subspace where the predicted attributes vector and binary attributes vector are naturally comparable. To find the transcription, a simple nearest neighbor search is made in the transformed lexicon space, which was projected to the common subspace. They achieved 79.99% accuracy and 11.27% CER using the IAM database.

In work presented in [4], authors present a CRNN model with output layer a CTC layer. CNN, which is responsible for features extraction, consists of seven convolutional layers. The first, second, fourth and sixth layers are followed by a max-pooling layer for downsampling, while the third and fifth layers are followed by a batch normalization for reducing internal covariate shift. The RNN consists of two LSTM layers which form a BLSTM. The RNN output is routed to the CTC layer, where the beam search algorithm is used to decode it.

In [5], authors applied dropout layers in Recurrent Neural Network. The input image is divided into blocks of size 2×2 and fed into four LSTM layers which scan the input in different directions indicated by corresponding arrows. The output of each LSTM layer is separately fed into convolutional layers of 6 features with filter size 2×4. This convolutional layer is applied without overlapping nor biases. It can be seen as a subsampling step, with trainable weights rather than a deterministic subsampling function.

The activations of 4 convolutional layers are then summed element-wise and squashed by the hyperbolic tangent (tanh) function. This process is repeated twice with different filter sizes and numbers of features, and the top-most layer is fully-connected instead of convolutional. The final activations are summed vertically and fed into the softmax layer. The output of softmax is processed by Connectionist Temporal Classification (CTC).

In [15], authors proposed a system that consists of three main components: convolutional visual feature extraction, recurrent layers and a transcription layer. For visual feature extraction, they used a convolutional neural network with residual connections. The input to the network is an image tensor of dimensions Wx66x1, where W is a varying image width. The network is comprised of 6 blocks of 2 residual convolution modules, where each residual module is composed of two convolutional layers, a residual connection and batch normalization. Interspersed between the blocks are max pooling operations, which serve to reduce the spatial dimension of the image. To introduce time-dependence between the feature vectors, they applied 3 layers of bi-directional LSTM on the feature vector sequence, with 512 units in each direction. The output of the final LSTM is then projected to transcription layer. They adopt the CTC layer for decoding process. They achieved 79.51% and 88.05% accuracy in IAM and RIMES datasets respectively.

In [19], authors present a model which they called ScrabbleGAN. It's a semi-supervised approach to synthesize handwritten text images that are versatile both in style and lexicon. ScrabbleGAN relies on a novel generative model which can generate images of words with an arbitrary length. They present a fully convolutional handwritten text generation architecture, which allows for arbitrarily long outputs and how to train this generator in a semi-supervised approach. To evaluate their model, they used RIMES, IAM and CVL datasets. They achieved 25.10% and 12.29% WER in IAM and RIMES respectively using the original training data.

In [1], authors proposed a neural network architecture based on a combination of a convolutional neural network (CNN) and an encoder-decoder structure. The convolutional neural network extracts features from all patches of the image. The exported feature sequence is used as input to a sequence to sequence network (LSTM). This network then recognizes the characters of the word. The convolutional network they propose, consists of two convolutional layers followed by the max-pooling function and finally a dropout layer. The encoder is an LSTM network that reads the sequence of features from the convolutional neural network and extracts the correlations between these features. It leads to the decoder which is also an LSTM network which includes an attention mechanism. Their model was trained and evaluated on the IAM database and by using a dictionary they managed to achieve an accuracy of 87%.

Bluche et al. [16] proposed a multidimensional LSTM network with attention. The proposed model comprises an encoder of the 2D image of text, producing feature maps, and a sequential decoder that predicts characters from these maps. The decoder proceeds by combining the feature vectors of the encoded maps into a single vector, used to update an intermediate state and to predict the next character in the sequence. The weights of the linear combination of the feature vectors at every timestep are predicted by an attention network. In this work the attention is implemented with a MDLSTM network. In word level recognition they achieved CER of 12.60% using IAM dataset.

In [3], authors proposed an attention-based sequence-to-sequence model for handwritten word recognition. The proposed architecture has three parts: an encoder, consisting of a CNN and a bi-directional GRU, an attention mechanism devoted to focus on the pertinent features and a decoder formed by a one-directional GRU, able to spell the corresponding word, character by character. It achieved 82.55% accuracy in IAM.

3 Methodology

3.1 Preprocessing

Before we feed the data to the neural network, they go through some pre-processing stage. It is known that the more data a neural network has at its disposal to be trained, the better results it yields. Data augmentation is a technique, which is used to create new and different images from the database's existing images, with the purpose of increasing the database itself. This can be accomplished by applying various transformation techniques. In our case for this purpose, we create random stretches in the already existing data, to increase the database. This technique is applicable only to the training data, and not to the validation data. We also apply a morphological function, the erode from the CV2 library in particular, to erode-increase the lines of the word contained in the image. In conjunction with the morphological function, we also use a technique to increase the contrast of the image. This results in the input data, i.e. the images, being more distinct by the neural network, and therefore it recognizes them better. Finally, we apply the normalization to the data. The purpose of data normalization is to ensure that each input element, in our case the pixels of the image, has a similar input distribution. It is an important step in machine learning, as it makes the models converge faster in the training phase. After the data has passed the pre-processing stage, it is fed to the network.

3.2 Proposed Architecture

The network architecture of CRNN, consists of three components, including the convolutional layers, the recurrent layers, and a transcription layer, from bottom to top. At the bottom of CRNN, the convolutional layers automatically extract a feature sequence from each input image. On top of the convolutional network, a recurrent network is built for making prediction for each frame of the feature sequence, outputted by the convolutional layers. The transcription layer at the top of CRNN is adopted to translate the per-frame predictions by the recurrent layers into a label sequence.

As we know, the levels of a typical CNN model consist of the convolutional layer, the activation function, the pooling layer and the fully connected layer. Bearing that in mind, we removed the fully connected layer, which is being replaced by RNN and we added a batch normalization layer, right after the convolutional layer. This layer is used primarily to accelerate the training procedure and secondarily to avoid overfitting. The CNN is used to extract features and it extracts a feature map which is subsequently used as input for the RNN. The CNN consists of five layers of similar structure. In the convolutional layers, kernels sized 5x5 and 3x3 are used. The 5x5 kernels are used in the first two convolutional layers and in the last three we used the 3x3 kernels. Stride

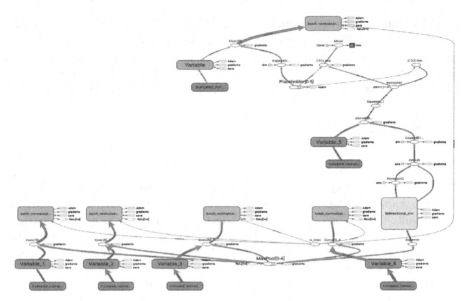

Fig. 1. The overall architecture of the model.

is set to 1. In the last three pooling layers we adopt 1x2 pooling strides instead of the conventional 2x2 strides we utilize in the first two pooling layers (Fig. 1).

This is done in order to create feature maps, with larger latitudes, hence a larger feature sequence. The RNN is responsible for predictions at any time step. We create a bidirectional RNN. Even though RNN are seemingly powerful structures, they are not able to model long term dependencies [13]. For this reason we used LSTM layers which are a modified version of RNN that models long-term dependencies. An LSTM layer is controlled by three gates. The input gate, the forget gate and the output gate. The forget gate allows the network to delete unnecessary information [14]. We used two such layers, which map the feature sequence from both directions. In image-based sequences, contexts from both directions are useful and complementary to each other. The outputs of these two layers are concatenated to get the final output of RNN. The RNN output is a matrix which contains all the possibilities of each character at any time step. This output is then used as input to the transcription layer. Transcription is the process of converting the per-frame predictions made by RNN into a label sequence. Mathematically, transcription is to find the label sequence with the highest probability conditioned on the per-frame predictions. For this reason, a CTC layer has been used. In this layer there are two functions that occur. The loss is being calculated in order to train the model. The loss is being calculated using the way Graves [21] proposed, and it is the negative logarithm of the possibility from the RNN output. Also, the best-path decoder is utilized in order to decode the output given by the RNN. This decoder, simply receives the character with the highest possibility at any time step. It also deletes all the repeated letters, and removes the blank ones in order to give us the final text.

3.3 Training

The model is being trained in order to minimize loss, given the input and label. To train the model the Adam optimizer has been used (which is considered to be the best) with a decay learning rate (a learning rate which is being attenuated in a linear way, during the training). Adam optimizer is simple to implement, computationally efficient, and requires less memory than most of its counterparts. The decay learning rate is preferred over the typical learning rate of a fixed value when the Adam optimizer is applied. In Fig. 2 we see how the loss during training is reduced. The network is trained using Mini-batch Gradient Descent approach. We split the training data into 500 batches. The batch size is set to 50. The loss is calculated for each batch. In this way we make the training of the network easier and faster. The training process stops when there is no improvement of the character error rate for three consecutive epochs.

In Fig. 2 we see how the loss during training is reduced. In the initial stages of training, as is logical the loss receives large values while as the network trains the loss values decrease and in the final stages of training it receives the lowest values.

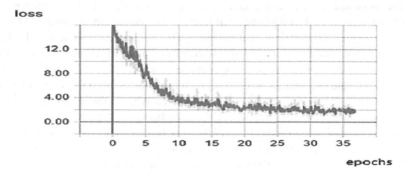

Fig. 2. Loss during training.

We also see that in the initial stages of training the loss decreases at a faster rate than in the final stages of this. This is due to the fact that the learning rate receives on a greater value in the early stages of training, thus enabling greater changes in loss value.

3.4 Formulation of an Online Application

Finally, an application was designed. For the back-end section, Flask framework was utilized. Flask Framework was used for developing the web applications. The homepage of the application displays the navigation bar and two buttons, which allow the selection of the text image that we want the model to recognize. The supported file extensions are PNG and JPG. After selecting the image we want to recognize, we are redirected to the second page, which displays the selected image as well as the text the model has recognized. The user through the "home" option of the navigation bar can perform the above process for as many images as he wishes to recognize. In Fig. 3 the a page of the application is illustrated.

Fig. 3. An example illustration.

The work and all of its components were coded in Python. It is the preferred programming language for developing deep-learning models mainly because its syntax is simpler compared to other programming languages. It is also easier to learn. This led to an increase in its popularity in the last few years and therefore, most machine-learning libraries are based on Python. To implement the network, we used TensorFlow, which allows us to create the network layer by layer. TensorFlow is an end-to-end open source platform for machine learning. It has a comprehensive, flexible ecosystem of tools, libraries and community resources that lets researchers push the state-of-the-art in ML and developers easily build and deploy ML powered applications. Tensorboard was used to visualize the graphs. Other libraries, such as Numpy and cv2, have been utilized, in order to represent the image as a matrix and process the data respectively.

4 Experimental Study

4.1 Dataset

As the IAM Handwritting Dataset is the most popular one for handwritten word and text recognition tasks, we carried out our experiments based on it. The IAM dataset consists of 115.320 isolated and labeled words written by 657 writers. The samples of the dataset are grayscale images, written on a white background and stored in png format.

4.2 Results

We test our system on the IAM English handwriting dataset. We fine-tuned our model on IAM and it achieves CER of 10.4%. Table 1 highlights the results.

The Levenshtein distance is recorded to evaluate the performance of the network after training. Given two strings a, b of length $|a|, |b|$, Levenshtein distance is the amount

Table 1. CER on IAM dataset

Dataset	CER
IAM Handwriting Dataset	10.4%

of transformation it takes to make one sing identical to the other, such as insertions, deletions, and substitutions. It is calculated as illustrated in the following Equations.

$$lev(a, b) = \begin{cases} |a|, \ if \ |b| = 0, \\ |b|, \ if \ |a| = 0, \\ lev(tail(a), tail(b)), \ if a[0] = b[0] \\ 1 + min \begin{cases} lev(tail(a), b) \\ lev(a, tail(b)) \quad otherwise. \\ lev(tail(a), tail(b)) \end{cases} \end{cases}$$

where the *tail* of some string x is a string of all but the first character of x and $x[n]$ is the nth character of the string x, starting with character 0. Note that the first element in the minimum corresponds to deletion (from a to b), the second to insertion and the third to replacement.

For example, the Levenshtein distance between "kitten" and "sitting" is 3, since the following three edits change one into the other, and there is no way to do it with fewer than three edits:

1 **k**itten → **s**itten (substitution of "s" for "k")
2 sitt**e**n → sitt**i**n (substitution of "i" for "e")
3 sittin → sittin**g** (insertion of "g" at the end)

A more intuitive metric taken into account is accuracy. In this paper, the accuracy of the model is calculated as shown in Eq. 2.

$$Accuracy = \frac{(number \ of \ correct \ predictions)}{(number \ of \ total \ predictions)} \tag{1}$$

Because the prediction is made at word level, Eq. 2 is essentially translated as:

$$Word \ Accuracy = \frac{(number \ of \ correct \ word \ predictions)}{(number \ of \ total \ word \ predictions)} \tag{2}$$

and essentially the resulting percentage is the opposite of the Word Error Rate (WER), where WER is the percentage of words that were not correctly recognized.

Table 2 presents the accuracy achieved on IAM English handwriting dataset. It shows that our model recognized correctly the 77.22% of the samples in the dataset. Note, that this is not the best accuracy that was achieved, but the accuracy of the model with the best CER achieved.

In Table 3, methods and results achieved using the IAM handwriting database are reported.

Table 2. Accuracy of our model on IAM dataset.

Dataset	CER	Accuracy
IAM Handwritting Dataset	10.4%	77.22%

Table 3. Comparison with other methods.

Model	CER	Accuracy
Almazan et al. [2]	11.27%	79.99%
Pham et al. [6]	13.92%	68.52%
Bluche et al. [16]	-	76.3%
Gimenez et al	-	74.2%
Mor et al. [15]	-	79.51%
Sueiras et al. [1]	8.8%	76.2%
Bluche et al. [17]	12.6%	-
Fogel et al. [19]	-	74.9%

Table 3 shows the accuracy and CER results of other methods used to recognize handwritten words in the popular IAM dataset. It should be mentioned that some methods trained their model using synthetic data or a lexicon, something that does not happen in our implementation. Also, methods use techniques for line skew and the slant correction in the images like in the work in [1]. We notice that the results we have achieved are close to those of the state of the art methods and in some cases even better.

5   Conclusions

The handwriting recognition field has preoccupied the scientific community for several years. The complexity encountered in this sector is due to the fact that each individual has a unique way of writing. Various methods have been examined and evaluated throughout the years, with the sole purpose of achieving sustainable results. The introduction of neural networks, specifically the use of convolutional neural networks (CNN) and recurrent neural networks (RNN), has presented dependable results in the handwriting recognition field. In this paper, we introduce a model that recognizes handwritten words without pre-segmenting the words into characters. The model consists of a CNN for the extraction of features, a RNN for the prediction procedure and a final layer (CTC) for decoding the prediction. We conducted many experiments on the well-known IAM handwriting database, and attained an accuracy of 77.22% and a character error rate (CER) of 10.4%.

There are many directions for future work. Initially, a bigger scale evaluation will be conducted to shed light on the performance of the methodology and the system developed in additional datasets. Another direction for future work concerns the formulation of ensemble schemas and stacked ensembles and examine their performance on different types of data. This constitutes a main direction for future work.

References

1. Sueiras, J., Ruiz, V., Sanchez, A., Velez, J.F.: Offline continuous handwriting recognition using sequence to sequence neural networks. Neurocomputing **289**, 119–128 (2018). https://doi.org/10.1016/j.neucm.2018.02.008

2. Almazan, J., Gordo, A., Fornes, A., Valveny, E.: Word spotting and recognition with embedded attributes. IEEE Trans. Pattern Anal. Mach. Intell. **12**, 2552–2566 (2014)

3. Kang, L., Toledo, J.I., Riba, P., Villegas, M., Fornés, A., Rusiñol, M.: Convolve, Attend and Spell: An Attention-based Sequence-to-Sequence Model for Handwritten Word Recognition. In: Brox, T., Bruhn, A., Fritz, M. (eds.) GCPR 2018. LNCS, vol. 11269, pp. 459–472. Springer, Cham (2019). https://doi.org/10.1007/978-3-030-12939-2_32

4. Tran, H.-P., Smith, A., Dimla, E.: Offline Handwritten Text Recognition using Convolutional Recurrent Neural Network In: 2019 International Conference on Advanced Computing and Applications (ACOMP) (2019)

5. Pham, V., Bluche, T., Kermorvant, C., Louradour, J.: Dropout Improves Recurrent Neural Networks for Handwriting Recognition In: 2014 14th International Conference on Frontiers in Handwriting Recognition. (2014) https://doi.org/10.1109/icfhr.2014.55

6. Priya, A., Mishra, S., Raj, S., Mandal, S., Datta, S.: Online and offline character recognition: A survey In: Communication and Signal Processing (ICCSP), 2016 International Conference on, pp. 0967–0970, (2016)

7. Shankar Rao, J.: Aditya {Dept of CSE, Andhra University}, Handwriting Recognition – Offline Approach

8. Singla, P., Munjal, S.: A Review On Handwritten Character Recognition Techniques IJIRT 2(11) ISSN: 2349–6002 (2016)

9. Sharma, T. Patnaik, B. Kumar, "Recognition for Handwritten English Letters: A Review", International Journal of Engineering and Innovative Technology (IJEIT), vol. 2, 2013

10. Gunawan, T.S., Mohd Noor, A.F.R., Kartiwi, M.: Development of English Handwritten Recognition Using Deep Neural Network, Indonesian J. Electr. Eng. Comput. Sci. 10(2), p. 562~568, ISSN: 2502–4752 (2018)

11. Hamad, K.A., Kaya, M.: A Detailed Analysis of Optical Character Recognition Technology Int. J. Appl. Mathe., Electron. Comput. ISSN: 2147–82282

12. Pradeep, J., Srinivasan, E., Himavathi, S.: Diagonal based feature extraction for handwritten character recognition system using neural network", InElectronics Computer Technology (ICECT), 2011 3rd International Conference on 8 Apr 2011 4 IEEE, pp. 364–368

13. Hadji, I., Wildes, R.P.: What Do We Understand About Convolutional Networks arXiv:1803.08834v1 [cs.CV] 23 Mar 2018

14. Hochreiter, S., Schmidhuber, J.: Long short-term memory. Neural Computation **9**(8), 1735–1780 (1997)

15. Mor, N., Wolf, L.: Confidence prediction for lexicon-free OCR In: Proceedings of the IEEE Winter Conference on Applications of Computer Vision, pp. 218–225 (2018)

16. Bluche, T., Louradour, J., Messina R., "Scan, attend and read: end-to-end handwritten paragraph recognition with MDLSTM attention", In: Proceedings of the IAPR International Conference on Document Analysis and Recognition, pp. 1050– 1055 (2017)

17. Bluche,T., Ney, H., Kermorvant, C.: Feature Extraction with Convolutional Neural Networks for Handwritten Word Recognition In: 12th International Conference on Document Analysis and Recognition (ICDAR). IEEE, pp. 285–289 (2013)

18. Bhuia, A.K., Das, A., Bhunia, A.K., Kishore, P.S.R., Roy, P.P.: Handwriting Recognition in Low-resource Scripts using Adversarial Learning In: 2019 IEEE/CVF Conference on Computer Vision and Pattern Recognition (CVPR)
19. Fogel, S., Averbuch-Elor, H., Cohen, S., Mazor, S., Litman, R.: ScrabbleGAN:Semi-Supervised Varying Length Handwritten Text Generation In: 2020 IEEE/CVF Conference on Computer Vision and Pattern Recognition (CVPR)
20. Aqab, S., Tariq, M.U.: Handwriting Recognition using Artificial Intelligence Neural Network and Image Processing", (IJACSA) International J. Adv. Comput. Sci. Appl., Vol. 11(7) (2020)
21. Graves, A., Fernandez, S., Gomez, F. J., Schmidhuber, J.: Connectionist temporal classification: Labelling unsegmented sequence data with recurrent neural networks In: Proc. Int.Conf. Mach. Learn.pp. 369–376 (2006)
22. Ahmed, R., Al-Khatib, W.G., Mahmoud, S.: A survey on handwritten documents word spotting. Int. J. Multi. Inf. Retr. 6(1), 31–47 (2017)
23. Memon, J., Sami, M., Khan, R.A., Uddin, M.: Handwritten optical character recognition (OCR): A comprehensive systematic literature review (SLR). IEEE Access 8, 142642–142668 (2020)
24. Baldominos, A., Saez, Y., Isasi, P.: A survey of handwritten character recognition with mnist and emnist. Appl. Sci. 9(15), 3169 (2019)
25. Vashist, P.C., Pandey, A., Tripathi, A.: A comparative study of handwriting recognition techniques. In 2020 International Conference on Computation, Automation and Knowledge Management (ICCAKM) IEEE, pp. 456–461 (2020)

Local Maximal Equality-Free Periodicities

Mai Alzamel[1] [iD], Jacqueline W. Daykin[2,3,4] [iD], Christopher Hampson[5] [iD],
Costas S. Iliopoulos[5] [iD], Zara Lim[5(✉)] [iD], and W. F. Smyth[6]

[1] Computer Science Department, King Saud University, Riyadh, Saudi Arabia
`malzamel@ksu.edu.sa`
[2] LITIS, Normandie University, 76000 Rouen, France
[3] Department of Information Science, Stellenbosch University, Stellenbosch, South Africa
[4] Department of Computer Science, Aberystwyth University, Wales, UK
`jwd6@aber.ac.uk`
[5] Department of Informatics, King's College, London, UK
`{christopher.hampson,csi,zara.lim}@kcl.ac.uk`
[6] Department of Computing and Software, McMaster University, Hamilton, ON, Canada
`smyth@mcmaster.ca`

Abstract. In this paper, we study local maximal antiperiodicities. Given a string X and an integer k, we compute the maximal k-antiperiodicity starting at every position of X; that is, we identify a maximum-length sequence of distinct factors, where each is of length k. The space and time complexity of the algorithm is linear.

Keywords: Antiperiod · Equality-free · Antipower

1 Introduction

Antipowers, antiperiods and the generalised notion of "equality-free" strings can be traced back to applications in genomics and synthetic biology, where DNA strands are artificially constructed to produce novel or disease-resistant proteins [9]. In the construction of such synthetic strands, short strands of DNA (also known as oligo fragments) are produced by DNA synthesis machines; to synthesize longer DNA duplexes, many of these short DNA oligo fragments are assembled together [16]. The assembly of longer DNA sequences has strict regulations, including (i) the length of each strand must be bounded by a given value and (ii) two oligos must not collide (i.e. be too similar) in order to prevent them from hybridising with each other — otherwise it can inhibit proper assembly (see Condon et al. [7,8] for more details). Thus the challenge is to identify which oligos are most suited for self-assembly. It follows that computing the equality-free factors of a string is a generalisation of this problem which can be extended to antipowers and antiperiods, whereby reporting equality-free factors of a string (similarly antiperiodic substrings) would ensure pairs of oligos are not so similar

© IFIP International Federation for Information Processing 2023
Published by Springer Nature Switzerland AG 2023
I. Maglogiannis et al. (Eds.): AIAI 2023 Workshops, IFIP AICT 677, pp. 359–368, 2023.
https://doi.org/10.1007/978-3-031-34171-7_29

as to prevent them from hybridising together. Furthermore, adding a bound on the length of equality-free factors reciprocates the requirement for short oligos.

Condon et al. [7,8] investigated the problem of deciding whether a given string W has an equality-free factorisation of width at most m, where the width is the maximum length of any factor. This problem is also mentioned by Bulteau et al. [5]; furthermore, Bannai et al. [4] investigate the hardness of computing an equality-free factorisation with only palindromes as factors.

Antipowers and antiperiods are more recent variants of powers and periods. Given a string U of length $p \geq 1$, then for any integer $k \geq 1$, the string $X = U^k$ is a power of U of order k with period p. Then $X = U_1U_2...U_k$ is an antipower of order k and antiperiod p if and only if $|U_i| = p$, $1 \leq i \leq k$, and the U_i are pairwise distinct [12]. X is also said to be k-antiperiodic [1].

The notion of powers can be traced back to the early 1900s s by Thue who presented results on strings which do not contain any substrings that are powers [17]. In 2018 Fici et al. [12] coined the term of antipowers, and showed that every infinite string contains either powers or antipowers of any order. Antipowers have been addressed by both combinatiorial and algorithmic communities.

Defant [10] showed that the length of the shortest prefix of the Thue-Morse string which are antipowers grows linearly in k. Gaetz [13] later extended this result to substrings. Burcroff [6] generalised Fici et al.'s results to the avoidability of k antipowers in infinite strings. Badkobeh et al. [3] and Kociumaka et al. [15] have presented algorithmic results, given a string X of length n and a parameter k, all substrings of X that are antipowers of order k can be located in $O(\frac{n^2}{k})$ time and $O(nk \log k + C)$, time respectively, where C is the number of reported fragments.

Alamro et al. [1] originated the definition of an antiperiod, and gave complexity bounds for the offline computation of the minimum antiperiod and all the antiperiods of a word. Their result is based on a weighted level ancestor problem, which has a similar result shown by Kociumaka et al. [14]. Later, Alzamel et al. [2] address the same problems in the online setting.

In this paper, we discuss the *local maximal k-antiperiodicity problem*, which given an input string X and integer k returns each of the maximal substrings of X which are k-antiperiodic with respect to each of the first $n - k + 1$ indexes of X. Note that the length of each k-antiperiodic substring must be a multiple of k, and the last k indices of a string are trivially a local maximal k-antiperiodic substring.

For example, given the string $X = aacbaabc$, and $k = 2$, the local maximal 2-antiperiodic substrings of X are: $X[0..3]$, $X[1..6]$, $X[2..7]$, $X[3..6]$, $X[4..7]$, $X[5..6]$, $X[6..7]$. Of these, the substrings $X[1..6]$ and $X[2..7]$ are the global maximal 2-antiperiodic strings of X (see Fig. 1).

We show that given a string X and an integer k, all of the local maximal k-antiperiodic substrings can be found in $O(n)$ time. The rest of the paper is organised as follows: In Sect. 2, we discuss the preliminaries and definitions. In Sect. 3, we present an overview of our algorithm. In Sect. 4, we discuss the details of our algorithm. In Sect. 5 we perform an analysis on the algorithm, and in Sect. 6 we present our conclusions.

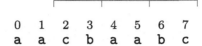

0	1	2	3	4	5	6	7
a	a	c	b	a	a	b	c

Fig. 1. Given the string $X = aacbaabc$, and $k = 2$, the local maximal 2-antiperiodic substrings of X are: $X[0..3]$, $X[1..6]$, $X[2..7]$, $X[3..6]$, $X[4..7]$, $X[5..6]$, $X[6..7]$. Of these, the substrings $X[1..6]$ and $X[2..7]$ are the global maximal 2-antiperiodic strings of X. If the substring $X[2..7]$ was extended $k(= 2)$ indices to the left, the string is no longer antiperiodic, hence the substring $X[2..7]$ is maximal.

2 Preliminaries

A string is a sequence of zero or more symbols from an alphabet Σ. The set of all strings over the alphabet Σ is denoted by Σ^*. We denote a string X of length n by $X[0..n-1] = X[0]..X[n-1]$, where $X[i] \in \Sigma$ for $0 \le i \le n-1$. We denote the length of string X by $|X|$. A string W is a substring or factor of X if $X = UWV$ for $U, V \in \Sigma^*$; we equivalently say that the string W occurs at position $|U| + 1$ of the string X. A string W is a prefix of X if $X = WU$ for $U \in \Sigma^*$. Similarly, W is a suffix of X if $X = UW$ for $U \in \Sigma^*$.

The string XY is a concatenation of two strings X and Y. The concatenations of k copies of X is denoted by X^k. For two strings $X = X[0..n-1]$ and $Y = Y[0..m-1]$ such that $X[n-i..n-1] = Y[0..i-1]$ for some $i \ge 1$, the string $X[0..n-1]Y[i..m]$ is a superposition of X and Y. Let X be a string of length n. We say that a prefix $X[0..p]$, $0 \le p < n-1$, of X is a period of X if $X[i] = X[i+p]$ for all $1 \le i \le n-p$.

An antipower of order k (or k-antipower) is a string obtained by the concatenation of k pairwise-distinct strings of identical length. The antiperiod of a k-antipower of length n is n/k. For $0 \le i \le j \le n-1$, we say that $X[i..j]$ is a maximal k-antiperiodic substring of $X[0..n-1]$ if no longer k-antiperiodic string can be obtained by extending $X[i..j]$ to the left or right. Given a string X of length n, for each index $i \in [0, n-1]$, we say that the local maximal k-antiperiodic substring of $X[i]$ is the maximal k-antiperiodic substring of X beginning at position i. A global maximal k-antiperiodic substring of X is a longest k-antiperiodic substring of X — there may be more than one.

In our algorithm, we make use of the suffix tree data structure. The suffix tree provides a compact representation of the set of suffixes of the string X, in which each leaf node of the tree uniquely corresponds to one of the n suffixes of X, which is determined by following the unique path from the root to the leaf and concatenating the edge labels as they are encountered. To ensure every suffix corresponds uniquely to a leaf node, the string X may be extended by a unique $ character not appearing elsewhere in X. An example suffix tree is shown in Fig. 2.

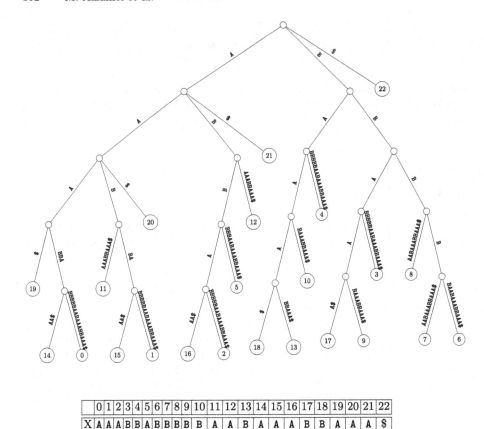

Fig. 2. Suffix tree for the string $X = $ AAABBABBBBBBAABAAABBAAA\$.

3   An Outline of the Algorithm

Given a string X of length n, each of the $n - (k-1)$ local maximal k-antiperiodic substrings can be computed in linear time as follows:

1. Construct the (unordered) suffix tree of X in linear time.
2. Name each k-prefix of every suffix with a unique name.
3. Two equal k-prefixes take the same name, that is to say, all children of a k-prefix get the same name.
4. Store the name of the k-prefix of $X[i]$ in array $A_{(i \mod k)}$.
5. Scan A_i from left-to-right and each name finds the first location of the same name to the right.
6. Identify each local maximal k-antiperiod starting from the rightmost position of each array.
7. The local maximal k-antiperiod starting at index $A[i]$ will be the longest string of first locations.

4   The Algorithm

Given a string X, we first preprocess X to construct its unordered suffix tree, $ST(X)$. Next, we traverse $ST(X)$ to obtain each of the distinct k-prefixes of each suffix, labelling each new k-prefix with a unique label, u_j, as well as each starting index in X of each suffix that u_j labels a prefix of. Each k-prefix is equivalent to the substring obtained by traversing each path of depth k from the root of $ST(X)$.

Next, we initialise $2k$ integer arrays, $A_0, \ldots, A_{k-1}$, and $A'_0, \ldots, A'_j, A'_{k-1}$, where each array is of size $\lfloor (n - j)/k \rfloor$ for $0 \leq j \leq k - 1$. For each $X[i]$ for $i \in [0 \ldots n - k]$, we store the unique label corresponding to the k-prefix starting at index $X[i]$ in array $A_{(i \bmod k)}[\lfloor i/k \rfloor]$. For each $A'_j[i]$ where $i \in [0, \lfloor (n - j)/k \rfloor - 1], 0 \leq j \leq k - 1$, we store the index directly to the left of the next occurrence of the element u_j at $A_j[i]$ in A'_j. If there is no next occurrence, then $A'_j[i] = |A'_j| - 1$. We make the following two observations:

Observation 1. *The local maximal k-antiperiodic substring of $X[i..n - 1]$ is the longest subarray of $A_j[m..|A_j| - 1]$ where each element only occurs exactly once, where $i = mk + j$, for some $j < k$ and $m \geq 0$.*

From Observation 1, each block of k symbols must be distinct to satisfy the antiperiodicity property. Thus, arrays $A'_0, \ldots, A'_{k-1}$ are used to record the next occurrence to the right of the k-prefix at a given index in arrays $A_0, \ldots, A_{k-1}$ so that the end of a k-antiperiodic substring occurs one position to the left of this.

An intuitive approach would be to start from the leftmost position of a string and label the first occurrence of an element as $Head_1$ and label the next occurrence of the same element in the string as $Tail_1$. It would then follow that the local maximal antiperiodic substring is bounded between these two occurrences, however one would also need to check that each of the elements between $Head_1$ and $Tail_1$ do not contain any repetitions within these bounds. We can continue to parse the substring between $Head_1$ and $Tail_1$, labelling each first and second occurrences of elements as $Head_j$ and $Tail_j$ (incrementing the value of j for each new pair). In this instance, the longest string of elements only labelled $Head_j$ (starting from $Head_1$) would correspond to a maximal k-antiperiodic substring. Otherwise, a substring containing an element labelled $Tail_j$ would indicate the repetition of some factor, thus not satisfying the antiperiodicity requirement. In Fig. 3, we note that if there a repeated element between the first pair of indexes labelled $Head_1$ and $Tail_1$, the end of the maximal k-antiperiodic substring would be reduced from the position to the left of $Tail_1$ to the position to the left of $Tail_2$.

Unfortunately, this approach of working left-to-right, has a lot of redundancy as it is possible for reported substrings to be nested in others. For example in Fig. 1, the local maximal 2-antiperiodic substrings starting at $X[1]$, $X[3]$ and $X[5]$ are nested. To avoid re-computing smaller antiperiodic substrings and thereby increasing the runtime of the algorithm, we employ a dynamic programming approach starting from the rightmost position and work right-to-left.

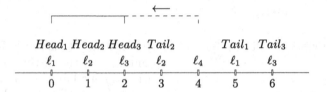

Fig. 3. Given the string $X = \ell_1\ell_2\ell_3\ell_2\ell_4\ell_1\ell_3$ (where each ℓ_i denotes a block of size k), the local maximal k-antiperiodic substring beginning at position 0 is initially upper bounded to position 4 (by the occurrence of $Tail_1$ at position 5). It follows that ℓ_2 at position 1 has a second occurrence at position 3, which is smaller than the index of the upper bound, thus the upper bound is updated to position 2.

To this end, we initialise a new array B_j for each $j = 0, \ldots, k - 1$, where each array is of size $\lfloor (n - j)/k \rfloor$, which will store the position $B_j[i]$ of the first repeated factor that is encountered in A_j starting from position i.

We set $B_j[m_j] = m_j$, where $m_j = |B_j| - 1$ is the index of the last element of B_j, since this final factor of length k is trivially a local maximal k-antiperiodic substring. Next, for all $i = m_j - 1, \ldots, 0$, we set

$$B_j[i] = \min\left(B_j[i + 1], \; A'_j[i] - 1\right), \tag{1}$$

which is to say that the local maximal k-antiperiodic substring starting at position i either terminates in the same position as the local maximal k-antiperiodic substring starting at position $(i + 1)$ (in the case that $B_j[i + 1] \leq A'_j[i]$), or else terminates at one position prior to the factor in position $A'_j[i]$, which by definition, is the next repeat of the factor in position i.

It is straightforward to show that the sequence B_j, as defined by (1), is monotonically increasing, and bounded from below.

Lemma 1. (i) *We have that $B_j[i] \leq B_j[i']$ whenever $i \leq i'$.*
(ii) *We have that $i \leq B_j[i]$ for all $i \leq m_j$.*

Proof. Trivial.

We can then use the sequences B_j to identify the local maximal k-antiperiodic substrings of our input string X using the following theorem.

Theorem 2. *For all $j < k$ and $i = 0, \ldots, m_j$, we have that $A_j[i..B_j[i]]$ is the local maximal k-antiperiodic substring of X of length $k(B_j[i] - (i - 1))$ starting at position $(ik + j)$.*

Proof. Fix $j < k$ and suppose to the contrary that there is some $i \leq m_j$ such that $U = A_j[i..B_j[i]]$ is not the local maximal k-antiperiodic substring of X. Without loss of generality, suppose that i is the largest such value where this contradiction occurs.

– Suppose U is not k-antiperiodic, then there is some $i \leq \ell, \ell' \leq B_j[i]$ such that $A_j[\ell] = A_j[\ell']$. Without loss of generality we may assume that $A_j[\ell']$ is the next repeat of $A_j[\ell]$ after position ℓ. By definition, we have that $A'_j[\ell] = \ell'$, and hence, by (1), we must have that $B_j[\ell] \leq \ell' - 1 < B_j[i]$, contrary to Lemma 1(i).

– Suppose that $B_j[i] \neq m_j$ and that U is not maximal, then U can be extended to a longer k-antiperiodic substring by appending $A_j[\ell + 1]$, where $\ell = B_j[i]$, which is to say that $A_j[\ell + 1] \neq A_j[t]$ for any $t \in \{i, \ldots, \ell\}$.
But then by definition $A'_j[t] > \ell + 1$ for all $t = i, \ldots, \ell$. Moreover, we have that $B_j[\ell + 1] \geq \ell + 1$, by Lemma 1(ii).
It then follows inductively that $B_j[t] \geq \ell + 1$ for all $t = i, \ldots, \ell$. In particular, we have that the contradiction that $B_j[i] \geq \ell + 1 > B_j[i]$, since $\ell = B_j[i]$.

Hence, we must have that $U = A_j[i..B_j[i]]$ is the local maximal k-antiperiodic substring of X, for all $i < m_j$, as required.

Example 1. Consider the string $X = aaabbabbbbbaabaaabbaaa$ and $k = 2$. From the suffix tree of X (displayed in Fig. 2), we obtain each of the distinct 2-prefixes of each suffix as well as their corresponding occurrences (Tables 1, 2 and 3):

Table 1. 2-prefixes of X.

Prefix	Label	Occurrences
aa	u_1	$0, 1, 11, 14, 15, 19, 20$
ab	u_2	$2, 5, 12, 16$
ba	u_3	$4, 10, 13, 18$
bb	u_4	$3, 6, 7, 8, 9, 17$

Each of the arrays, A_0, A'_0, A_1 A'_1 are generated and filled as follows:

Table 2. $j = 0$.

	0	1	2	3	4	5	6	7	8	9	10
A_0	u_1	u_2	u_3	u_4	u_4	u_3	u_2	u_1	u_2	u_3	u_1
A'_0	7	6	5	4	10	9	8	10	10	10	10

Table 3. $j = 1$.

	0	1	2	3	4	5	6	7	8	9
A_1	u_1	u_4	u_2	u_4	u_4	u_1	u_3	u_1	u_4	u_1
A'_1	5	3	9	4	8	7	9	9	9	9

Table 4 reports each of the corresponding instances of $B_j[i]$ for each instance of $A_j[i]$, as well as the corresponding maximal k-antiperiodic substring in X.

The pseudocode for our algorithm is presented in Algorithm 1.

Table 4. Computed instances of $B_j[i]$ for each $A_j[i]$ as well as the corresponding substring of $X = aaabbabbbbbaabaaabbaaa$.

i	$A_0[i]$	$B_0[i]$	max k-antiperiodic substring in X	$A_1[i]$	$B_1[i]$	max k-antiperiodic substring in X
0	aa	$B_0[1]=3$	$X[0..7]$	aa	$B_1[1]=2$	$X[1..6]$
1	ab	$B_0[2]=3$	$X[2..7]$	bb	2	$X[3..6]$
2	ba	$B_0[3]=3$	$X[4..7]$	ab	$B_1[3]=3$	$X[5..8]$
3	bb	3	$X[6..7]$	bb	3	$X[7..8]$
4	bb	$B_0[5]=7$	$X[8..15]$	bb	$B_1[5]=6$	$X[9..14]$
5	ba	$B_0[6]=7$	$X[10..15]$	aa	6	$X[11..14]$
6	ab	7	$X[12..15]$	ba	$B_1[7]=8$	$X[13..18]$
7	aa	9	$X[14..19]$	aa	8	$X[15..18]$
8	ab	10	$X[16..21]$	bb	9	$X[17..20]$
9	ba	10	$X[18..21]$	aa	9	$X[19..20]$
10	aa	10	$X[20..21]$			

Algorithm 1. $FindLocalMaximal\text{-}kAntiperiodicSubstrings$ (X,k)

```
 1: n := length(X)
 2: ST_X := MakeSuffixTree(X)
 3: DkP_dict := GetDistinctkPrefix(ST_X, k)

 4: for j ∈ {0,...,k − 1} do
 5:     Initialise A_j := [ ], A'_j := [ ]

 6: for prefix in DkP_dict do                          ▷ Compute the arrays A_j and A'_j
 7:     last_idx = None
 8:     for pos in DkP_dict[prefix] do
 9:         j := pos%k
10:         idx := ⌊(pos − j)/k⌋
11:         A_j[idx] := prefix
12:         if last_idx ≠ None then
13:             A'_j[last_idx] = idx
14:         last_idx = idx

15: for j ∈ {0,...k − 1} do                             ▷ Compute the Arrays B_j
16:     Initialise B_j := [ ]
17:     i = ⌊(n − j)/k⌋ − 1
18:     B_j[i] := i
19:     i := i − 1
20:     while i ≥ 0 do
21:         B_j[i] := min(B_j[i + 1], A'_j[i] − 1)
22:         i := i − 1

23: Initialise localMaxkAntiPerSubstr := [ ]             ▷ Post-processing
24: for i ∈ {0,..., ⌊n/k⌋} do
25:     for j ∈ {0,...,k} do
26:         start := i · k + j
27:         if start < n then
28:             end := B_j[i] · k + j
29:             localMaxkAntiPerSubstr[i · k + j] := X[start..end]

30: return localMaxkAntiPerSubstr
```

5   Analysis of the Algorithm

Lemma 3. *The length of any maximal k-antiperiodic substring is less than or equal to $|\Sigma|^k \mod k$.*

Proof. Recall that each k-antiperiod of a string must be distinct. As there are $|\Sigma|^k$ possible distinct strings of length k, the longest possible k-antiperiodic string contains every possible distinct substring.

Theorem 4. *Given a string X and integer k, all of the local maximal k-antiperiod substrings of X can be calculated in $\mathcal{O}(n)$ time and $\mathcal{O}(n)$ space.*

Proof. We analyse each step of the algorithm as described in Algorithm 1. In (line 2), we first construct the suffix tree of X, which requires $\mathcal{O}(n)$ time and space to construct [11]. We then create an array with all of the distinct k-prefixes of each suffix in the suffix tree — there are at most $\mathcal{O}(\min\{n-k+1, |\Sigma|^k \mod k\})$ distinct prefixes, and appending each occurrence of each k prefix to the array requires $\mathcal{O}(n)$ time and space.

In (lines 4–5), we initialise $2k$ arrays, $A_0 .. A_{k-1}$ and $A'_0, .. A'_{k-1}$, each of length $\lfloor n - i/k \rfloor = \mathcal{O}(n/k)$, requiring at most $\mathcal{O}(n)$ space and time to construct. The outermost loop in (lines 6–14) is called once for each of the $\mathcal{O}(\min\{n-k+1, |\Sigma|^k \mod k\})$ distinct prefixes in DkP_{dict}. In total, the inner loop in (lines 8–14) collectively loops over all of the $\mathcal{O}(n)$ positions in the string X, with each of the operations performed in (lines 9–14) taking at most $\mathcal{O}(1)$ time (lookup values for j and idx can be pre-computed in $\mathcal{O}(n)$ time and space). The innermost while loop in (lines 20–22) is called collectively once for each of the $\mathcal{O}(n)$ positions in the string X, with the operations performed in (lines 21–22) requiring at most $\mathcal{O}(1)$ time. Finally, the innermost loop in (lines 25–29) loops over all $\mathcal{O}(n)$ positions in the string X, with the operations performed in (lines 24–29) requiring at most $\mathcal{O}(1)$ time. Thus, the overall running time and space of the algorithm is $O(n)$, as required.

6   Conclusions

We show that given a string X and value k, all local maximal k-antiperiodic substrings can be found in $O(n)$ time and space. The algorithm that we presented can be extended to identify the longest (global) k-antiperiodic substring(s) of a given string X and integer k, which can also be identified in $O(n)$ time and space.

A natural generalisation of our problem would be to identify all local maximal k-antiperiodic substrings of a given string for all values of $k = 2, .., n - 1$. Such an algorithm for this problem would take at least $O(n^2)$ time, as the required number of substrings to report are $O(n^2)$. Instead, we leave the following open problem: given a string X, return each of the longest k-antiperiodic substrings for $k = 2, 3, .., n - 1$.

References

1. Alamro, H., Badkobeh, G., Belazzougui, D., Iliopoulos, C.S., Puglisi, S.J.: Computing the antiperiod (s) of a string. In: 30th Annual Symposium on Combinatorial Pattern Matching (CPM 2019). Schloss Dagstuhl-Leibniz-Zentrum fuer Informatik (2019)
2. Alzamel, M., et al.: Online algorithms on antipowers and antiperiods. In: Brisaboa, N.R., Puglisi, S.J. (eds.) String Processing and Information Retrieval, pp. 175–188. Springer International Publishing, Cham (2019)
3. Badkobeh, G., Fici, G., Puglisi, S.J.: Algorithms for anti-powers in strings. Inf. Process. Lett. **137**, 57–60 (2018)
4. Bannai, H., et al.: Diverse palindromic factorization is NP-complete. In: Potapov, I. (ed.) DLT 2015. LNCS, vol. 9168, pp. 85–96. Springer, Cham (2015). https://doi.org/10.1007/978-3-319-21500-6_6
5. Bulteau, L., et al.: Multivariate algorithmics for NP-hard string problems. Bulletin of EATCS 3(114) (2014)
6. Burcroff, A.: (k, λ)-anti-powers and other patterns in words. Electron. J. Comb. 25(P4.41) (2018)
7. Condon, A., Maňuch, J., Thachuk, C.: Complexity of a collision-aware string partition problem and its relation to oligo design for gene synthesis. In: Hu, X., Wang, J. (eds.) COCOON 2008. LNCS, vol. 5092, pp. 265–275. Springer, Heidelberg (2008). https://doi.org/10.1007/978-3-540-69733-6_27
8. Condon, A., Maňuch, J., Thachuk, C.: The complexity of string partitioning. J. Discrete Algorithms **32**, 24–43 (2015)
9. Cox, J.C., Lape, J., Sayed, M.A., Hellinga, H.W.: Protein fabrication automation. Protein Sci. **16**(3), 379–390 (2007)
10. Defant, C.: Anti-power prefixes of the Thue-Morse word. Electron. J. Comb. 24 (2017)
11. Farach, M.: Optimal suffix tree construction with large alphabets. In: Foundations of Computer Science, 1997. Proceedings., 38th Annual Symposium on, pp. 137–143. IEEE (1997)
12. Fici, G., Restivo, A., Silva, M., Zamboni, L.Q.: Anti-powers in infinite words. J. Comb. Theory, Ser. A **157**, 109–119 (2018)
13. Gaetz, M.: Anti-power j-fixes of the thue-morse word. Discrete Math. Theoretical Comput. Sci. 23 (2021)
14. Kociumaka, T., Kubica, M., Radoszewski, J., Rytter, W., Waleń, T.: A linear time algorithm for seeds computation. In: Proceedings of the Twenty-third Annual ACM-SIAM Symposium on Discrete algorithms, pp. 1095–1112. SIAM (2012)
15. Kociumaka, T., Radoszewski, J., Rytter, W., Straszyński, J., Waleń, T., Zuba, W.: Efficient representation and counting of antipower factors in words. Inf. Comput. **286**, 104779 (2022)
16. Stemmer, W.P., Crameri, A., Ha, K.D., Brennan, T.M., Heyneker, H.L.: Single-step assembly of a gene and entire plasmid from large numbers of oligodeoxyribonucleotides. Gene **164**(1), 49–53 (1995)
17. Thue, A.: Uber unendliche zeichenreihen. Norske Vid Selsk. Skr. I Mat-Nat Kl. (Christiana) **7**, 1–22 (1906)

Readability Classification with Wikipedia Data and All-MiniLM Embeddings

Elena Vergou, Ioanna Pagouni, Marios Nanos, and Katia Lida Kermanidis[✉]

Department of Informatics, Ionian University, Corfu, Greece
{elenberg,p19pago,p12nano,kerman}@ionio.gr

Abstract. Evaluating the readability of text has been a critical step in several applications, ranging from text simplification, learning new languages, providing school children with appropriate reading material to conveying important medical information in an easily understandable way. A lot of research has been dedicated to evaluating readability on larger bodies of texts, like articles and paragraphs, but the application on single sentences has received less attention. In this paper, we explore several machine learning techniques - logistic regression, random forest, Naive Bayes, KNN, MLP, XGBoost - on a corpus of sentences from the English and simple English Wikipedia. We build and compare a series of binary readability classifiers using extracted features as well as generated all-MiniLM-L6-v2-based embeddings, and evaluate them against standard classification evaluation metrics. To the authors' knowledge, this is the first time this sentence transformer is used in the task of readability assessment. Overall, we found that the MLP models, with and without embeddings, as well as the Random Forest, outperformed the other machine learning algorithms.

Keywords: Readability classification · Text simplification · Embeddings

1 Introduction

Text simplification refers to the process of converting a given text, whether that is a sentence or a paragraph or even longer text, to a simpler version with higher readability while retaining the original meaning. There are many domains and applications where it's very important to have highly readable material available, as for example in the case of reading material provided to students from lower grades, for students studying foreign languages, where complicated literature text needs to be presented in a clear and simple format so that students can slowly learn and, become familiar with, the language. Another application is the medical field, where it is very important that clear and simple language is used to convey to patients critical, medical information that often contains a lot of medical terms and complicated linguistic items. Another indicative application is culture, where text describing cultural artifacts (e.g. maritime goods or regulations as handled in the ENIRISST + project[1]) is processed for a more intelligent transfer of

---

[1] https://enirisst-plus.gr/.

© IFIP International Federation for Information Processing 2023
Published by Springer Nature Switzerland AG 2023
I. Maglogiannis et al. (Eds.): AIAI 2023 Workshops, IFIP AICT 677, pp. 369–380, 2023.
https://doi.org/10.1007/978-3-031-34171-7_30

cultural axioms. Text simplification is usually accomplished through a mixture of lexical and syntactical changes to the original text. On the lexical side, more complicated words are substituted by simpler, more understandable ones, while on the syntactical side the focus is on simplifying the grammatical and syntactic structure of the text, for example by eliminating subordinate or relative clauses.

A very critical step towards text simplification is the identification of the readability level of a given text. Originally, readability measures in the form of formulae were created based on a few basic metrics, for example number of words, syllables or sentences and their ratios, without any regard towards how word order factors in, or the fact that shorter sentences or words with fewer syllables are not always simpler to understand. More recent approaches, on the other hand, focus on regression or classification algorithms, leveraging several features and exploring non-linearities in the relationship, and use manually classified or graded text corpora. Employing machine learning schemata, these texts are usually either classified as simple or not, or graded along an ordinal scale. In general, typical learning features that have been considered for readability identification fall under a few high-level categories - lexical features (relative word frequencies, text probability based on language models, etc.), syntactic features (sentence length, etc.), discourse features (measures of text cohesion) and semantic features (use of idioms, type of text, etc.).

Unlike previous work, we used a corpus of Wikipedia and Simple Wikipedia sentences, cleaned them, and engineered features and generated embeddings. For the engineered features, multiple surface and part-of-speech (POS) features as well as more traditional readability measures were produced and then fed through a feature selection process to reduce the number of total features and pick the most informative ones for the readability task. Grid search cross validation was used to optimally pick hyperparameters for the models and trained an array of different ML models in order to evaluate comparative performance of different machine learning algorithms and different sources of features - engineered features as well as embeddings based on a recently published pre-trained encoder [15], that offers speed and performance and is tuned for multiple differentuse-cases. Unlike previous work, the state-of-the-art sentence transformer all-MiniLM-L6-v2 was used to generate embeddings for the sentences which were then used as features with several different machine learning models. Also, to the best of our knowledge, the proposed training pipeline and methodology with feature selection and grid search cross validation for the proposed feature set has not been previously used.

2 Related Work

Originally the task of readability assessment was based on readability formulae, with the most popular and widely used ones being the Flesch Reading Ease Score (FRES) [7] and the Flesch-Kincaid readability formula [8]. The FRES uses the average sentence length and the average number of syllables per word in a linear combination and produced an output score between 1 and 100 to evaluate readability, while the Flesch-Kincaid formula uses the same input to produce a grade level. Although these formulae, along with other readability scores, have been considered for the evaluation of text complexity in recent academic research [9], it should be noted that they were designed primarily to be applied at the document rather than the sentence level.

Another approach to readability assessment comes with the use of statistical language models. Instead of feature engineering and creating surface features based on sentence characteristics, like word or syllable counts, a language model is built based on text level distributions where counts of events act as estimates for the probabilities. In an interesting example, the probability of a grade level given a document is estimated based on the convex combination of a sentence distribution model and a unigram language model in [10] with an accuracy of 75%.

With the advances in the NLP field and the gains in computing power, the domain of readability assessment has flourished in academic research in the last two decades with many contributions on both the types of models and algorithms tested as well as the types of features used in modeling readability. In [1], the focus was on the combination of model aspect and embeddings generation, as they did not engineer any features themselves but instead chose to explore different neural network architectures - Recurrent Neural Networks (RNN), Hierarchical Attention Network (HAN), Multi-Head Attention (MHA) and Attention over Bidirectional Context (BCA) - to map the text to a vector representation which was then used in an ordinal regression to predict text complexity, and used pre-trained Glove embeddings in all models. The methodology was applied to graded textbooks and the WeeBit corpus and, based on the Spearman correlation evaluation metric, different models perform better under different circumstances; for example the HAN fared better for entire documents while the RNN did better at the paragraph level. It was also shown that a well trained neural network can generalize well outside the genres of corpora it was trained with.

In [2], the focus was on engineering a set of complex features to use in a Support Vector Machine (SVM) classifier for different grades of text complexity. The text corpus was based on a series of educational articles from the Weekly Reader with 4 different readability grades, augmented with texts from Encyclopedia Britannica and Britannica Elementary as well as CNN articles along with their simplified versions. Statistical language models were leveraged to measure the probability of sequences of co-occurring words and, based on those, new features were engineered, like perplexity, which was then used, along with more traditional features like Flesch-Kincaid score, Average number of syllables per word, Average sentence length, out-of-vocabulary (OOV) rate scores and Parse features, to estimate the complexity of the text with the SVM classifier. The best results were achieved by leveraging together language model-based and more traditional features.

An interesting contribution on the modeling side and the types of models considered, comes from [3], where the authors focused on the exploration of a series of different machine learning models - Random Forests, Decision Trees, Linear Regression, Naïve Bayes, K-Nearest Neighbors (KNN) and Support Vector Machines (SVM) - and their performance as binary classifiers along with the creation of engineered features, like Word and Character counts, Part of Speech counts etc. The methodology was applied to pairs of sentences coming from the English Wikipedia and the Simple English Wikipedia, the best performing model was the Random Forest, and the most important features were specificity and ambiguity. In [4], the authors used a corpus of both, documents and sentences, compared the performance and focused on the syntactic parsing of the sentences to engineer features. They also used lexical and POS features among others.

They observed that when moving from the document-based binary classification to the sentence-based one, accuracy dropped from 90% to 66%.

Most of the research in the last 20 years or so has concentrated on the document or paragraph level, rather than the sentence level. For example, in [11], the authors cast the problem of predicting readability of entire text passages and web pages as a multinomial Naïve Bayes classification task, leveraging multiple language models. In [12] readability assessment is applied to web queries and their resulting summaries and a gradient boosted tree estimates readability. In [13], the authors combine news articles and pairs of sentences from Wikipedia and Simple wikipedia. They break up the text simplification task into its component sub-tasks, the prediction of complexity itself and the complexity explanation, and use adversarial networks to show that leveraging complexity prediction as a first step in a text simplification pipeline reduces their overall error rates. [14] experimented with traditional readability features and more novel ones along with different machine learning approaches, like ranking, classification and regression and reported that the classification model performed best.

3   Data

3.1   Source Data and Data Cleaning

The data used, is based on the Version 2.0 of the dataset made available by D. Kauchak [16], and is made up of a corpus of approximately 167K aligned sentences sourced from the English Wikipedia and the Simple English Wikipedia, downloaded in May 2011. While these aligned sentences are meant to capture the same semantic information, the Simple English Wikipedia articles are a modified, simpler version of the English-language edition of Wikipedia with easier to understand vocabulary, grammar and syntactic structures. The labels used in the binary classification models were 1 for the sentences originating from the Simple English Wikipedia and 0 for the sentences from the English Wikipedia. After combining the two sets of sentences the total number of rows amounted to approximately 334k.

For pre-processing, all sentences of length less than 4 words were discarded, as they represent mostly templates and other assets that are mistakenly included in the corpus. Furthermore, such short sentences cannot meaningfully allow the models to learn patterns of readability. Sentences where the strings.css,.js or MediaWiki appear in the articles title were also dropped, as they were mistakenly included in the corpus and they don't represent real pairs of aligned sentences. After discarding these sentences the dataset contains approximately 331k sentences.

3.2   Feature Engineering and Preparation

With regard to feature preparation and engineering, the Python Natural Language Tool Kit (NLTK) was used to parse the sentences first [17]. A word tokenizer was used based on the Treebank tokenizer, which uses regular expressions, splits contractions, commas and single quotes, and treats punctuation marks as individual tokens. All tokens were then transformed to lower case. The total number of tokens as well as the total number of words (which is equal to the initial number of tokens after removing the number of punctuation marks) were produced as features. The total number of characters, as well as their average and standard deviation per word, were calculated and used as features. The total number of syllables was also computed, as well as the average and standard deviation of the number of syllables per word. A measure of lexical diversity, the Type Token Ratio (TTR), was produced by taking the ratio of the number of unique words to the total number of words, and the same calculation was performed with tokens instead of words.

One of the most widely known readability metrics was used as well - the Flesch-Kincaid reading ease score. The score was calculated based on the weighted average number of words per sentence and the average number of syllables per word with low scores indicating complicated text. Another readability metric was also calculated - the Gunning Fog Score - which is based on the weighted average of the number of words per sentence and the ratio of the number of complex words to the total number of words, where a complex word is defined as a word with 3 or more syllables. In this particular case, since the corpus is made up of sentences, there is only one sentence per observation point. For POS tagging, the NLTK package was leveraged, which uses the Penn Treebank tagset on the entire list of tokens. This generated a list of tuples of tokens and their tags, and then the total number of nouns, adjectives, verbs, pronouns, prepositions and adverbs in the sentence was taken as an individual feature, while grouping all other part-of-speech categories in another feature. To normalize for the different sentence lengths, percentages were calculated and used as features.

In total, the features that were initially calculated were the total number of words, total number of tokens, total number of characters, average number of characters, standard deviation of the total number of characters, total number of syllables, average number of syllables per word, standard deviation of the total number of syllables per word, lexical diversity, Flesch Reading Score, number of number words, the Gunning Fog Score, percentage of verbs, adverbs, nouns, adjectives, pronouns, prepositions, the rest, percentage of verbs, percentage of adverbs, percentage of nouns, percentage of adjectives, percentage of pronouns, percentage of prepositions, percentage of remaining tokens, number of remaining tokens, number of unique tokens, number of unique words, the TTR ratio calculated based on tokens and on words. Since in the feature engineering stage, a lot of similarly calculated features were created, once with tokens and once with words, it is important to add a stage of feature selection so as to reduce the total amount of features used for modeling to a subset that involves the most informative for this task. This reduction in the size of features should help to speed up the computations required for training and reduce the amount of irrelevant or not very helpful features present in the modeling pipelines.

Outside of the engineered features, the Sentence Transformer Python package was used to generate sentence embeddings based on the input sentences that allow the retention of the semantic information in the encodings. The recently pre-trained sentence-transformers/all-MiniLM-L6-v2 transformer model was used, which has been trained on over 1 billion training pairs. It maps sentences to a 384 dimensional dense vector space and it was chosen because of its good balance between average evaluation performance and runtime performance in previously reported work [18].

3.3 Data Splits and Cross Validation

The data was split into train and test using 80% and 20% of the data respectively. Grid search cross validation was used, for estimating the parameters of each model. This technique searches through the space of the cross-product of the set of parameters and, at each iteration, part of the training dataset is held out for validation, while the rest is used to fit the model. Then the average performance over the different folds is used to compare the different configurations of parameters to select the best. Parameter tuning is performed while keeping the test data separate from the training and tuning process. This provides insight on the actual generalization ability of the models on unseen data, and on their ability to avoid over fitting.

3.4 Feature Selection

For feature selection, an XGBoost model was built on the training dataset and the resulting feature weights were used to select a feature subset. Specifically, a binary XGBoost Classifier was trained with maximum depth 4 and 200 estimators (trees), which were selected after trying out different hyperparameters. The resulting weight indicates how useful a feature was in the construction of the boosted decision trees and the more a feature is used to make decisions, the higher is its relative importance. The weight of each feature is calculated as the number of times it appears in the model trees, and then the values are normalized to sum to one. All features with weights over 3% are picked, and are shown in the chart below (Fig. 1).

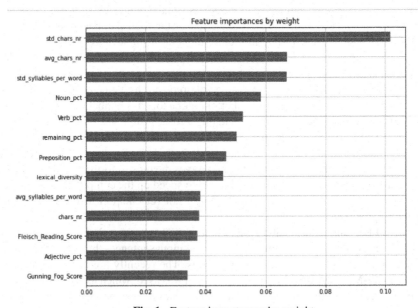

Fig. 1. Feature importances by weight.

4 Model Training and Results

An array of different machine learning models were trained so that the comparative performance can be evaluated for better fit with regard to this particular learning task. The specific modeling algorithms used were chosen based on an examination of other academic papers and literature on the topic of text simplification and readability assessment along with a more general examination of accurate and scalable learning techniques used in industry and academia. All models were run in two different versions - once with embeddings created by the all-MiniLM-L6-v2 encoder, which has not been used before in this task based on our search, and once with the subset of engineered features selected as a result of the feature selection process. The features were also standardized to avoid scale bias as some models are sensitive to it. For the models without embeddings, cross validation was used to pick the best model parameters, and then said parameters were used to train a model on the entire training dataset. The resulting trained model was used to produce inferences on the test dataset and report the evaluation metrics. Four typical classification evaluation metrics were produced - ROC-AUC, accuracy, recall and precision for both classes for both versions, i.e. with and without embeddings.

4.1 Logistic Regression

Logistic regression was used to estimate the probability of a sentence being simple or not. The logistic regression algorithm is based on the logistic function and produces outputs that represent the probability of a sentence belonging to a particular class. Grid search cross validation with precision as the scoring function was used with grid configurations with or without an intercept, and either the L1 or L2 regularization penalties. The L1 and L2 penalties can be leveraged to prevent overfitting of the model to the training data and thus improve the generalization performance to previously unseen data. This can be particularly important when the model has been trained on a domain-specific corpus and is asked to confront a different domain. Grid search cross-validation was used with the 'liblinear' solver and 100 max iterations. The best performance in cross-validation was achieved with the L1 penalty and with an intercept. When using the embeddings as features, cross-validation couldn't be used due to lack of computing power because of large data dimensionality. Maximum iterations of 200 were used along with an intercept, no penalty and the 'sag' solver as it tends to converge faster for high dimensionality data (Fig. 2).

	roc_auc_score	accuracy_score	recall_score_1	precision_score_1	recall_score_0	precision_score_0
LogisticRegression_train	0.60	0.57	0.59	0.57	0.55	0.58
LogisticRegression_test	0.60	0.57	0.59	0.57	0.55	0.58
LogisticRegression_embeddings_train_embeddings	0.61	0.58	0.57	0.58	0.55	0.58
LogisticRegression_embeddings_test_embeddings	0.60	0.58	0.57	0.58	0.55	0.58

Fig. 2. Logistic regression results

4.2 Random Forest

A random forest classifier is an ensemble learning technique that makes use of the output of multiple decision trees to make a classification decision. The engineered features were used and experiments were run with various tree depth limits (4,6,10), estimators, i.e. how many trees we have in the random forest (100,150,200), and maximum number of features considered when looking for the best split - in ('sqrt', 'log2', 3). The best performance was achieved with max depth 6, 200 estimators and max features 'sqrt'. For the embeddings model we also built a model with max depth 6, 200 estimators and max features 'sqrt'(Fig. 3).

	roc_auc_score	accuracy_score	recall_score_1	precision_score_1	recall_score_0	precision_score_0
RandomForestClassifier_train	0.62	0.58	0.60	0.58	0.56	0.58
RandomForestClassifier_test	0.62	0.58	0.60	0.58	0.56	0.59
RandomForestClassifier_embeddings_train_embeddings	0.61	0.57	0.59	0.57	0.56	0.58
RandomForestClassifier_embeddings_test_embeddings	0.54	0.53	0.54	0.53	0.51	0.53

Fig. 3. Random Forest results

4.3 Naïve Bayes

The Naive Bayes classifier makes use of the Bayes' theorem to produce probabilistic estimates of class membership of an instance. Grid search cross-validation was not used for this trainer for both versions with the engineered features and the embeddings (Fig. 4).

	roc_auc_score	accuracy_score	recall_score_1	precision_score_1	recall_score_0	precision_score_0
GaussianNB_train	0.59	0.56	0.60	0.56	0.55	0.58
GaussianNB_test	0.59	0.57	0.60	0.56	0.55	0.58
GaussianNB_embeddings_train_embeddings	0.57	0.55	0.55	0.55	0.55	0.58
GaussianNB_embeddings_test_embeddings	0.56	0.54	0.55	0.54	0.55	0.58

Fig. 4. Naïve Bayes results

4.4 K-Nearest Neighbors

The KNN classifier is a non-parametric machine learning technique that produces inferences by examining the most similar training samples nearest to the inference instance. For the KNN model, grid search cross-validation was used with the engineered features and experiments were run with the number of neighbors between 3 and 5 inclusive. The best performance was achieved with four 4 neighbors and a KNN model was also fit with the embeddings and four neighbors (Fig. 5).

	roc_auc_score	accuracy_score	recall_score_1	precision_score_1	recall_score_0	precision_score_0
knn_train	0.75	0.67	0.46	0.79	0.55	0.58
knn_test	0.49	0.49	0.30	0.48	0.55	0.58
knn_embeddings_train_embeddings	0.62	0.58	0.30	0.68	0.55	0.58
knn_embeddings_test_embeddings	0.28	0.34	0.14	0.23	0.55	0.58

Fig. 5. KNN results

4.5 MLP (Multi-layer Perceptron)

An MLP model is a type of feedforward neural network with at least one hidden layer. In our experiments, grid search cross-validation was used with the engineered features and while using one hidden layer and the adam solver, due to the small dimensionality of the dataset and to avoid an overcomplicated model that could lead to overfit, the size of the hidden layer was used in the grid search, and 50 or 100 neurons were tried. Also, the logistic and tanh activation functions were tried along with different learning rates (0.001, 0.01). As a result of the cross-validation 50 was picked as the number of neurons in the hidden layer along with the logistic activation function and an adapting learning rate starting at 0.001. For the embeddings model, given the higher dimensionality a more complicated architecture was tried with two hidden layers and number of neurons 100 for the first hidden layer and 50 for the second hidden layer The remaining parameters remained the same as in the model with the engineered features (Fig. 6).

	roc_auc_score	accuracy_score	recall_score_1	precision_score_1	recall_score_0	precision_score_0
MLP_train	0.62	0.58	0.52	0.60	0.65	0.57
MLP_test	0.62	0.58	0.52	0.59	0.64	0.57
mlp_embeddings_train_embeddings	0.68	0.62	0.55	0.64	0.69	0.60
mlp_embeddings_test_embeddings	0.63	0.58	0.52	0.60	0.65	0.57

Fig. 6. MLP results

4.6 XGBoost

The XGBoost algorithm is a gradient boosting algorithm that iteratively adds weaker decision trees with a goal to produce a stronger model. For the XGBoost model, cross-validation experiments were run with different learning rates of (0.3, 0.5, 0.7, 1, 1.2), maximum depth of (3, 4, 5, 6) and number of trees in (200, 250, 300). The optimal configuration of parameters as a result of cross validation was a depth of 5, number of trees at 200 and learning rate of 0.3. The same parameters were used for the embeddings model as grid cross validation could not be used with the embeddings model due to lack of computation power (Fig. 7).

	roc_auc_score	accuracy_score	recall_score_1	precision_score_1	recall_score_0	precision_score_0
XGBoost_train	0.68	0.62	0.60	0.62	0.63	0.61
XGBoost_test	0.60	0.57	0.56	0.57	0.58	0.57
XGBoost_embeddings_train_embeddings	0.74	0.67	0.66	0.67	0.68	0.67
XGBoost_embeddings_test_embeddings	0.52	0.51	0.50	0.51	0.51	0.51

Fig. 7. XGBoost results

5 Evaluation

In general, the Logistic Regression, Naive Bayes and MLP models had consistent performance between training and test dataset in the evaluation metrics and for both model versions with and without embeddings, which meant that they didn't overfit the training data and are able to generalize well to unseen data. Overall, the KNN models had the worst generalization ability on unseen data, as evaluation metrics make evident that they tend to overfit the training data.

All model performances were compared also on the test dataset with all dataset versions, both with and without embeddings. In terms of the precision score the highest performance was achieved with the MLP with and without embeddings for the positive class - sentences which come from the Simple English Wikipedia - while for the other class the Random Forest with the manually created features was the top performer. In terms of recall, for the positive class, Naive Bayes and Random Forest with manually created features performed at the top, while for the other class the MLP models with and without embeddings were top performers. In terms of overall accuracy, the two MLP models with and without embeddings as well as the Random Forest model with manually created features were top performers. In terms of ROC AUC the two MLP models with and without embeddings were the best performing models.

Although not exactly comparable due to different data size and features, the academic paper with the closest set-up to ours, [16], reports an accuracy score of 84.14% for their Random Forest model while in this case it's close to 58%, their linear regression model has accuracy of 74.62% while in our case the logistic regression has accuracy of approximately 57%. One of the possible reasons behind the difference in performance is that while the raw source data was the same, the data cleaning process and the resulting number of sentences were different, the features used were different, including the embeddings, the modeling methodology and parameter tuning was different. In our case, even very short sentences were kept - of size 5 or 6 - which could make it harder for the models to pick up on differences, trends and patterns. Also, while in a pair of sentences - one from the English Wikipedia and the other from the Simple English Wikipedia - it's fair to say that one is simpler than the other as this is the starting assumption, over the entire dataset of sentences it might not be the case that each one of the complex sentences is harder than each of the simple sentences (Fig. 8).

	roc_auc_score	accuracy_score	recall_score_1	precision_score_1	recall_score_0	precision_score_0
mlp_embeddings_test_embeddings	0.629	0.583	0.515	0.595	0.651	0.575
MLP_test	0.621	0.582	0.520	0.592	0.644	0.574
RandomForestClassifier_test	0.619	0.582	0.601	0.578	0.563	0.587
LogisticRegression_embeddings_test_embeddings	0.605	0.577	0.567	0.577	0.553	0.578
XGBoost_test	0.604	0.569	0.557	0.569	0.580	0.569
LogisticRegression_test	0.601	0.573	0.544	0.568	0.600	0.577
GaussianNB_test	0.594	0.569	0.604	0.563	0.553	0.578
GaussianNB_embeddings_test_embeddings	0.563	0.540	0.547	0.538	0.553	0.578
RandomForestClassifier_embeddings_test_embeddings	0.541	0.528	0.543	0.526	0.513	0.530
XGBoost_embeddings_test_embeddings	0.519	0.508	0.505	0.506	0.510	0.509
knn_test	0.493	0.487	0.295	0.476	0.553	0.578
knn_embeddings_test_embeddings	0.282	0.343	0.138	0.232	0.553	0.578

Fig. 8. Consolidation and comparison of evaluation metrics by model

6 Conclusions

In this paper several engineered features were explored along with generated embeddings on the task of readability assessment applied on a corpus of English and simple English Wikipedia sentences. A series of different widely used machine learning binary classifiers were separately trained with the engineered features and the all-MiniLM-L6-v2 based embeddings. As a conclusion, it was found that the MLP models with and without embeddings as well as the Random Forest models outperformed the other machine learning algorithms. To the best of our knowledge, this was the first use of the state-of-the-art sentence transformer all-MiniLM-L6-v2 in the field of text simplification to generate embeddings for the sentences to be used as features with several different machine learning models. Also to the best of our knowledge and research this exact training pipeline and methodology with feature selection and grid search cross validation with these features has not been previously used.

As a potential future direction, it would be interesting to continue experimenting with different and more complex neural network architectures as they appeared the most promising. It would also be interesting to try different pre-trained encoders to generate embeddings from the sentences to train classifiers. Another potential future direction would be to experiment with different sentence lengths as in this paper almost all sentences were included and it would be reasonable to assume that smaller sentences might have very few discernable differences between their versions, which would make it harder for a model to learn patterns to discern the two. It would also be interesting to try more experiments with parameter tuning the model trainers. It would be challenging also to expand this research with different datasets sources from various different domains (for example, scientific text, medical text, etc.) and see how the performance changes for the different domains. Also, another idea would be to experiment with an n-gram language model as input to the classifier.

Acknowledgments. This research was co-financed by the European Union and Greek national funds through the "Competitiveness, Entrepreneurship and Innovation" Operational Programme

2014–2020, under the Call "Support for regional excellence"; project title: "Intelligent Research Infrastructure for Shipping, Transport and Supply Chain - ENIRISST+"; MIS code: 5047041.

References

1. Nadeem, F., Ostendorf, M.: Estimating Linguistic Complexity for Science Texts. In: 57th Annual Meeting of the Association for Computational Linguistics. Florence, Italy, pp. 4541–4551 (2019)
2. Schwarm, S., Ostendorf, M.: Reading Level Assessment Using Support Vector Machines and Statistical Language Models. In: 43rd Annal Meeting of the Association for Computational Linguistics (ACL), Michigan, USA, pp. 497–504 (2005)
3. Kauchak, D., Mouradi, O., Pentoney, C., Leroy, G.: Text Simplification Tools: Using Machine Learning to Discover Features that Identify Difficult Text. IEEE Trans. Learn. Technol. 7(3), 276–288 (2014)
4. Vajjala, S., Meurers, D.: Assessing the Relative Reading Level of Sentence Pairs for Text Simplification. In: 13th Conference of the European Chapter of the Association for Computational Linguistics (EACL), Avignon, France, pp. 482–492 (2012)
5. Nisioi, S., Štajner, S., Ponzetto, S.P., Dinu, L. P.: Exploring Neural Text Simplification Models. In: 55th Annual Meeting of the Association for Computational Linguistics (ACL), Vancouver, Canada, pp. 1083–1092 (2017)
6. Saggion, H.: Automatic Text Simplification. Cham, Springer. Switzerland (2017)
7. Flesch, R.: The Art of Readable Writing. Harper, New York (1949)
8. Kincaid, P., Robert P., Fishburne, R., Rogers, L., Chissom, B.S.: Derivation of new readability formulas (Automated Readability Index, Fog count and Flesch Reading Ease Formula) for Navy enlisted personnel. Technical report, Naval Technical Training Command. (1975)https://doi.org/10.1007/978-3-031-02166-4
9. Sander Wubben, S., van den Bosch, A., Krahmer, E.: Sentence simplification by monolingual machine translation. Long Papers. In: 50th Annual Meeting of the Association for Computational Linguistics 1, 1015–1024 (2012)
10. Si, L., Callan, J.: A statistical model for scientific readability. In: 10th International Conference on Information and Knowledge Management, CIKM, pp. 574–576, New York. ACM (2001)
11. Collins-Thompson, K., Callan, J.P.: A language modeling approach to predicting reading difficulty. HLT-NAACL, 193–200 (2004)
12. Kanungo, T., Orr, D.: Predicting the readability of short web summaries. Second ACM International Conference on Web Search and Data Mining, pp. 202–211. ACM (2009)
13. Garbacea, C., Guo, M., Carton, S., Mei, Q.: Explainable Prediction of Text Complexity: The Missing Preliminaries for Text Simplification. In: 57th Annual Meeting of the Association for Computational Linguistics, pp. 2254–2264 (2019)
14. Aluisio, S., Specia, L., Gasperin, C., and Scarton, C.: Readability Assessment for Text Simplification. In: 27th International Conference on Computational Linguistics, pp. 1246–1257 (2018)
15. Hugging Face. (n.d.). Sentence Transformers: all-MiniLM-L6-v2. Retrieved from https://huggingface.co/sentence-transformers/all-MiniLM-L6-v2
16. Kauchak, D.: Data and Code for Automatic Text Simplification. Retrieved from https://cs.pomona.edu/~dkauchak/simplification/
17. Bird, S., Loper, E., Klein, E.: Natural Language Processing with Python. O'Reilly Media Inc. (2009)
18. Sentence Transformers: pre-trained models evaluation https://www.sbert.net/docs/pretrained_models.html

Using Siamese BiLSTM Models for Identifying Text Semantic Similarity

Georgios Fradelos[1], Isidoros Perikos[1,2], and Ioannis Hatzilygeroudis[1(✉)]

[1] Computer Engineering and Informatics Department, University of Patras,
26504 Patras, Greece
up1047143@upnet.gr, {perikos,ihatz}@ceid.upatras.gr
[2] Computer Technology Institute and Press Diophantus, 26504 Patras, Greece

Abstract. The field of Natural Language Processing (NLP) has flourished during the past decades in computer science, and that is largely due to the exponential growth of internet applications, like search engines, social network platforms, chatbots and Internet of Things (IoT). On the other hand, the robotics and human computer interaction fields have been largely connected to NLP development, by exploring ways of human-robot or human-computer communication in natural language. In this work, we deal with the problem of semantic similarity between text passages, which is one of the problems faced in many NLP applications, like human-computer/robot communication through natural language text. More specifically, we developed three deep learning models to face the problem: two variations of the Siamese BiLSTM model and a variation of the Simple BiLST model. We used two different techniques of word embeddings, (a) classic token-to-vec embedding using GloVe, and (b) one implementing the encoder part of the BERT model. Finally, we train and compare each model in terms of performance, through experimental studies on two datasets, MRPC (MSRP) and Quora, and we draw conclusions about the advantages and disadvantages of each one of them. Siamese BERT-BiLSTM model achieves accuracy 83,03% on the Quora dataset, which is comparable to the state of the art.

Keywords: natural language processing · semantic similarity · siamese neural networks · transformers · BERT

1 Introduction

Determining the semantic relationship between texts is one of the most complex and challenging tasks in natural language processing. Social networks, search engines, recommendation systems and plagiarism recognition programs are just a few of the tools that base their operation on recognizing semantic similarity. On the other hand, semantic similarity plays an important role in the field human-machine interaction, where applications of text processing in human-robot or human-computer interaction are necessary [1, 2].

I. Maglogiannis et al. (Eds.): AIAI 2023 Workshops, IFIP AICT 677, pp. 381–392, 2023.
https://doi.org/10.1007/978-3-031-34171-7_31

The main objectives of this work are the study of the techniques proposed in the literature to approach the issue of semantic similarity, research of modern technological tools appropriate for this issue, and finally the practical engagement with the issue through the development of linguistic models capable of recognizing the semantic similarity between texts. In this paper, we propose three neural network models that we train with various datasets to capture the sematic similarity between two short passages of text. We experiment with both Siamese and non-Siamese architectures and we explore the text semantic similarity task both by measuring the similarity between two texts and by capturing the inference between them through classification.

We developed two Siamese architectures that differ in the embedding mechanism that they use. The first and most simple model makes use of an embedding layer that maps the tokens of the textual data to GloVe [3] word embeddings. These sequences are given to a Siamese BiLSTM network. The second Siamese architecture utilizes a BERT encoder [4] instead of a GloVe embedding layer. The encoder takes text as input and produces sequences of vectors. These sequences are then fed to a Siamese BiLSTM network. Both Siamese models consist of the same BiLSTM network, and they only differ in the embedding mechanism. The hidden vectors of the top BiLSTM layers are compared by measuring the Manhattan distance between them to calculate their similarity. The last model we developed is similar to the Siamese-BERT model, although it is a non-Siamese architecture, and it captures natural language inference via 3-way classification. The Siamese architecture with GloVe embeddings achieved an impressive 80.5% validation accuracy on Quora Duplicate Questions Dataset, however, this is a relatively static implementation with restricted practical flexibility. The best result yielded from the non-Siamese architecture using the largest BERT model that we managed to train, due to limited resources, was 87.44% validation accuracy on the SNLI Corpus. The models that use BERT, although demanding in memory and computational resources, are very flexible to use with great development dynamics. The main contributions of this work are a) an extensive literature review in the field of text semantic similarity and b) experimental results for DL models that haven't been used for this task before.

The paper is structured as follows. Section 2 presents related work. Section 3 presents the architectures of the three deep learning models used in the experiments. Section 4 deals with the experimental studies and their results, whereas Sect. 5 concludes the paper.

2   Related Work

In the literature, many works deal with the problem of recognizing and estimating the semantic similarity of texts. In the work presented in [5], Socher et al. use auto-encoders to model representations of local phrases in sentences and then calculate the similarity values of the phrases from the two sentences as features for binary sorting. A model is presented that incorporates the similarities between both single-word characteristics and multi-word phrases, which are extracted from the nodes of the analysis trees. The model is based on two elements. The first is a retrospective neural network (recursive autoencoder/RAE) that learns attribute representations for each node in the tree, the Euclidian distance of which fills a similarity matrix. However, simply extracting aggregate statistics from this table, such as the mean distance or a distance histogram, cannot accurately capture the overall structure of the similarity of the sentences. Therefore, in order to preserve as much of the total information in this comparison as possible, the second part element of the model is then introduced, which is a pooling layer that produces a constant-sized representation. A softmax classifier is then used to categorize sentences as paraphrases or not. RAE architecture with dynamic pooling achieves state-of-the-art performance with 76.8% accuracy and 83.6% F1 score in MSRP.

Hu et al. [6] proposed neural network models (ARC-I), which adopt a convolutional architecture in order to semantically match two sentences, including vision and speech. In order to explore the relationship between the representation of sentences and their matching, they design a new model that can accommodate both the hierarchical synthesis of sentences and the simple-to-comprehensive fusion of the associated patterns of data with the same convergent network architecture. The model is general, does not require prior knowledge of the natural language (e.g. analysis tree) and does not impose any restrictions on the respective tasks. The sentence modeling architecture takes as input the pre-trained word embeddings aligned sequentially and in the order in which the terms appear in the sentence and summarizes their meaning through convolution and pooling layers, until it reaches a fixed vector representation length in the final layer. The convolution in the first level works with sliding-windows, as well as the convulsions in the deeper layers. After each convolution, max-pooling is performed in each window of two units. The first architecture proposed in the article takes a conventional approach. It first finds the representation of each sentence and then compares the representation for the two sentences with a Multi-Layer Perceptron [7]. It is essentially a Siamese architecture. The downside to ARC-I is general to Siamese architectures and lies in ignoring any semantic interaction between the sentences. An additional architecture is proposed, ARC-II, which aims to solve this problem. It has the property of letting two sentences "meet" before creating the individual high-level representations for each one, while maintaining the space for the individual development of the abstraction of each sentence. Both architectures were tested experimentally in paraphrase recognition, sentence completion, and tweet response matching. They achieved an accuracy of 0.696 (ARC-I) and 0.699 (ARC-I I) at Microsoft Research Paraphrase Corpus.

Authors in [8] proposed a Bi-CNN-MI (multigranular interaction features). The model "learns" the representation of each sentence separately through a Siamese deep convolutional neural network ("Bi" denotes a Siamese CNN layout rather than a bidirectional CNN) and computes similarity tables between two sentences at four levels. Each of the levels represents the similarity between unigrams, short n-grams and long n-grams of the sentences and lastly between the sentences themselves. The similarity tables are constructed by measuring the Euclidean distance of the corresponding hidden states of the network and are followed by a dynamic pooling layer. The result of the pooling layer is a vector which is then inserted into a logistic classifier to perform paraphrase detection. Microsoft Research Paraphrase Corpus was used for the experiments where the proposed model achieved 78% accuracy.

Authors in [9] propose a convolutional neural network model consisting of two main levels: modeling input propositions and measuring similarity. The first part learns vector representations of sentences to obtain information from different levels of abstraction, using multiple types of pooling (max, average, etc.), and different convergent filters.

The second part locally compares the representations of the first level using various similarity measurements achieving an accuracy of 78.6% at MRPC. Authors in [10] propose a model that combines CNN and LSTM networks to export three types of features, and then introduces them into a three-tier Multi-Layer Perceptron categorizer. The proposed model achieves an accuracy of 77.7% at MRPC.

Song et al. [11] propose an innovative RNN architecture, the fractional latent topic-based RNN model (FraLT-RNN) that largely retains the overall semantic information of the text. In FraLT-RNN, hierarchical attributes, i.e. word-level and subject-level attributes, as well as sequential word patterns, are integrated into the RNN for text representation via fractional latent topics. First, the fractional latent topic generator is used so that the model can learn the latent subjects according to the latent states of an RNN structure. An attention mechanism for the various topics is then designed to create an attentive vector at the topic level for each latent topic, which measures the perspective of the hidden topic and enhances the interactions between a pair of texts. Finally, hidden topics are checked based on this vector for text representation and similarity calculation. Given a text pair as X and Y, let x and y denote the embedded representations of the word x and y respectively, and assume that the sequential hidden state, as well as each hidden state, corresponds to a word in text X. Next, the text is represented by the method of observing hidden situations. Finally, the degree of similarity is calculated according to the two textual representations and a function of similarity, such as cosine similarity.

Authors in [12] study the subject of Natural Language Inference (NLI) citing a particular LSTM architecture. The model is based on the architecture proposed in [13] and is a neural network model with an observation mechanism for the NLI task but is based on a different idea. Instead of using actual sentence vectors to categorize them, a match-LSTM is developed which does word-to-word matching for each word in the sentence pair. The network can give more emphasis on more semantically important parts and ignore the less important ones. The model 'remembers' the important 'matches' which affect the final prediction. This architecture is called matching-LSTM or mLSTM. The SNLI Corpus is used for the tests, in which the proposed architecture achieves 86.1% accuracy of correct predictions in the testing set.

Authors in [14] propose a series of models for the representation of sentences encoded by GRUs (Gated Recurrent Units). The models are based on the decoder-decoder archi- tecture, however the decoder is replaced by a categorizer that selects the desired sentence from a collection. The model achieves 76.9% accuracy.

Liu et al. [15] propose a Deep fusion LSTM (DF-LSTM) LSTM model with the aim of finding semantic similarity through the prism of textual entailment. The inference of text (or natural language inference), falls within the work of determining the semantic relationship between two sentences. A DF-LSTM consists of two interdependent LSTM networks, each of which models a sequence under the influence of the other. The output of the model is fed to an output level, at which the corresponding degree of similarity is calculated. In addition, researchers are using external memory to increase LSTMs' capacity. This model is compared to other neural networks of the LSTM architecture in two large datasets, one of which is the Stanford Natural Language Inference Corpus (SNLI). DF-LSTM outperformed other LSTMs by 2% in the SNLI Corpus, achieving 84.6% accuracy in the test data.

Vaswani et al. [16] propose an innovative model that follows the architecture of the transformer and is based on attention mechanisms in order to capture the semantic properties of words in vectors. The transformer consists of two parts, the "encoder" and the "decoder". The encoder consists of multiple levels of "multi-head attention mechanisms" followed by a fully connected feed-forward neural network. The decoder is similar to the encoder with an additional multi-head attention level that captures the weights of observing the encoder output. Although this model was originally proposed for the work of machine translation, Devlin et al. [4] used it to create word vectors (BERT embeddings). The model is pre-trained on two tasks: Masked Language Model and Next Sentence Prediction. First, the authors randomly cover a certain percentage of terms (15%) in the corpus and train the linguistic representation model to predict them. To predict the next sentence, the model is trained to predict whether in a pair of sentences, the second one is the next of the first or not. The trained model is then fine-tuned for the individual downstream tasks. The authors report that the model gives state-of-the-art results in 11 works on natural language processing and achieves 89.3% accuracy in the MRPC dataset.

Zhang et al. [17] propose an innovative language model based on BERT which learns linguistic representations in fine-grained manner. The model consists of three parts. A semantic categorizer for data classification, a sequential encoder which uses a pre-trained language model to create vector representations of text input data and semantic tags, and a semantic integration element for combining the representation of a text with the semantic representation of the contexts and the acquisition of the common representation for later works. SemBERT has been evaluated on 11 reference datasets that include natural language inference, question answering, semantic similarity, and text classification. SemBERT achieves state-of-the-art performance at SNLI Corpus and improves semantic perception in GLUE Benchmark and SQuAD 2.0. Studies and analyzes confirm that the introduced explicit semantics is necessary to further improve performance and SemBERT functions effectively and efficiently as a single model of linguistic representation enriched with semantic information.

Parikh et al. [18] propose a simple neural network architecture for natural language inference. Their method utilizes attention mechanisms to break down the problem into separate sub-problems. Researchers take an approach in which they align pieces of the two texts with each other in order to draw semantic information from them. Having as input two propositions, each of which is represented by a vector of attributes, a soft alignment matrix is created primarily using observation mechanisms. This table is then used to break down the desired work into subproblems in order to address them separately. Finally, the results from the solution of the subproblems are combined to extract the final categorization. It achieved 86.8% accuracy in the Stanford Natural Language Inference dataset test data.

In [9] Radford et al. suggest a method that combines unsupervised pre-training and fine-tuning with supervision, for learning universal vector representations of sentences. The proposed model is based on the Transformer architecture [16] and can be used as a general model in various works in the field of natural language processing, through fine-tuning its parameters to the downstream task-specific data. Experimental results show that the proposed method achieves state-of-the-art results by achieving 82% prediction accuracy in Microsoft Research Paraphrase Corpus.

3 Models and Their Architectures

3.1 Vector Space Representations

Through the study of the literature, we came to the development of neural network models, which we will train to recognize the conceptual relationship that characterizes two pieces of text. All language models developed in the context of our work are based on vector space. The models developed in this study represent the pairs of propositions with sequences of vectors, which pass as input to the various models that either measure the distance of these vectors - thus calculating the semantic relation of the corresponding propositions - or categorize the data according to the type of relationship that characterizes them (i.e. whether the two sentences have a common, conflicting, or unrelated meaning). In total, we have developed the following three models:

1. A Siamese BiLSTM model with a token-to-vec vector language representation mechanism using the GloVe collection.
2. A Siamese BiLSTM model integrating the BERT model for vector representation of language data.

The two (Siamese) models take as their inputs the pair of propositions to compare, represent them separately in vector sequences, and estimate their similarity by measuring the distance of the representations of the highest level of BiLSTM networks. The vector space model was applied to the experimental implementations of this study, according to which each word corresponds to a unique vector of size d, e.g. 'Tree': [0.326, 0.543, 0.013,...], which is made in such a way that it contains semantic information about the term. This vector is an instance of the d-dimensional vector space we use, and the d-dimensions of the space define the size of the vectors in it, e.g. if a vector space is $d = 50$ dimensional, each word corresponds to a vector of 50 elements. Thus, we can determine the distance between 2 vectors with different metrics (cosine similarity, Euclidian distance), and draw conclusions about how close or not are, to each other, the concepts of the corresponding words. We call vector space a mathematical structure consisting of a collection of elements called vectors. An example of a vector space is the three-dimensional space in which each of its elements is characterized by 3 values x, y and z. The number of dimensions of the space determines the size of the vectors that belong to it and in applications such as natural language processing we can define vector spaces with more than 3 dimensions e.g. $d = 50$.

3.2 Siamese BiLSTM Model

In the first and simplest implementation, a Siamese BiLSTM network was created that accepts proposal vectors as input using the GloVe collection. In the first stage of implementation, the lexical data is pre-processed. Specifically, the sentences are divided into the tokens from which the punctuation marks and infinitive parts of speech such as 'and', 'or', 'the' and so on are subtracted. Although these terms offer syntactic and semantic coherence in the sentence, they do not contain semantic information; for this reason we remove them to reduce the data volume. Then the suffixes of the inflected parts of speech such as '-ing', '-ed' and so on are removed, and the tenses of the verbs are replaced by the lemmas from which they came from, e.g. 'Went''go'. All these are data without semantic information and therefore we can safely remove them without losing vital semantics information. Finally, we save the processed tokens in a list. The next step is to create a dictionary with all the distinct terms of the processed data (let of number n) to create a matrix of size n × d, where d is the length of the word vectors. For each term of the dictionary, we find in the GloVe thesaurus the vector that corresponds to it and we add it to the register of vectors, so we end up with the final embedding matrix of our model. We end up at the output of the embedding layer taking the final sequences of vector representations of the sentences (sentence embedding sequences). Each sequence corresponds to a sentence, has length λ and each element of the sequence has length $d = 300$. These sequences are given as input to the two-way LSTM network that is trained on them. At each of the LSTM outputs, max pooling is applied to extract their basic characteristics, which pass to a Lambda layer which measures their distance and normalizes it with a sigmoid function within the space [0,1]. Thus, at the output of the network a prediction like '0.54' is generated, which expresses the estimation of the degree of semantic similarity of the sentences.

3.3 Siamese BERT-BiLSTM Model

As a variation of the previously described model, in this model the embedding layer is replaced by the encoder part of BERT. Initially, the input data go through a custom data generator and in batches they pass as separate sequences to the Siamese BERT, which in turn represents them in the semantic vector space. The vector representations of the two sentences then pass as input to the Siamese BiLSTM network, which is trained on them. At each of the LSTM outputs, max pooling is applied to extract their basic characteristics. The two max-pooled vectors pass as input to a Lambda Layer which measures their distance and outputs the final prediction of the model.

4 Experimental Study

4.1 Datasets

The datasets that we used in this study to train and evaluate the proposed models are described in the following.

MRPC (or MSRP) is a dataset created by Microsoft and contains a total of 5801 pairs of sentences that have been collected from online news sources. Each pair of sentences is accompanied by a binary label, which categorizes them as paraphrases or not. '1' defines the sentences that are a paraphrase of each other and therefore have a common semantic meaning, while '0' means that those sentences are not a paraphrase of each other.

Quora is a page on the World Wide Web, where users quote questions of any kind that can be answered by other users of the page. In 2018, the Quora page decided to utilize the volume of data it has collected over its years of operation and published a series of datasets oriented towards natural language processing tasks. One of these datasets is the Quora Duplicate Questions Dataset, which covers the task of semantic similarity of texts and consists of a total of 404,289 pairs of sentences/questions in English. All question pairs are accompanied by a label that indicates whether the two questions are duplicates or not (i.e. if they essentially ask the same thing). '0' means pairs that are not duplicates, so they are not semantically similar, and '1' means those pairs that are duplicates.

4.2 Experimental Setup

The Rectified-Adam optimizer, introduced in 2019 by Liu et al. in [21], was used to model the training. Rectified Adam (RAdam) is a variant of the classic Adam optimization algorithm used extensively in neural network training. The reason we used the RAdam instead of the classic Adam is that catastrophic forgetting was observed during the fine-tuning of the BERT models [22]. In the phenomenon of catastrophic forgetting the following paradox is observed: while the model, during the pre-training, is trained normally, 'learns' a percentage of information and achieves a score, e.g. val_accuracy: 0.65, afterwards, during fine-tuning, this percentage drops almost instantaneously and the model essentially 'forgets' the information it has learned and stops 'learning'. After several tests the problem seems to disappear by replacing the Adam optimizer with the Rectified-Adam which 'stabilizes' the training process. Loss and accuracy metrics were used to evaluate the final performance of the models.

$$\text{Loss: } \sum (Targets - Predictions)^2$$

$$\text{Accuracy: } \frac{True\_positive\_values + True\_negative\_values}{(True\_positive\_values + True\_negative\_values) + (False\_positive\_values + False\_negative\_values)}$$

Accuracy shows the percentage of correct predictions (positive and negative) made by the model, while Loss measures the magnitude of the prediction error.

Each of the developed models was trained separately on the datasets mentioned above. The training process is as follows:

- Processing of the pair of sentences and their numerical coding (integer encoding).
- Representation of those sequences in vector representation of words (GloVe or BERT vector sequences).
- Learning the sequences by the neural network.
- Prediction generation (Distance measurement if it is a Siamese network, categorization if it is simple).
- Comparison of the prediction with the label/error calculation.

4.3 Results

In this subsection, we present the results of the experimental study. For the second Siamese model we implemented two variations. We present the performance results of our models on the above mentioned datasets (Table 1)

Table 1. Results for MRPC and Quora Datasets.

	MRPC			Quora		
	Siamese BiLSTM-GloVe	Siamese BERT-BiLSTM (L = 2, H = 256, A = 4)	Siamese BERT-BiLSTM (L = 8, H = 128, A = 2)	Siamese BiLSTM-GloVe	Siamese BERT-BiLSTM (L = 2, H = 256, A = 4)	Siamese BERT-BiLSTM (L = 8, H = 128, A = 2)
test_accuracy	**0.8055**	0.7856	0.7888	0.8103	**0.8303**	0.8227
test_loss	0.4318	0.4350	0.4216	0.4228	0.3956	0.4067
train_accuracy	0.9118	0.8739	0.8493	0.9333	0.8023	0.7855
train_loss	0.1932	0.2972	0.3356	0.1900	0.4175	0.4463

The best results were achieved by the Siamese BiLSTM-Glove on MRPC (MSRP) dataset, and by the Siamese BERT-BiLSTM (with L = 2, H = 256, A = 4) on the Quora dataset. We used exponential negative Manhattan distance to measure the distance between the two sentences in the Siamese models. The metric that achieved the best results is exponential negative Manhattan distance, and it also contributed to a more stable and predictable training process overall. In the following tables, we compare our results with the results of other attempts on the same datasets (Table 2).

Table 2. Comparative results – MRPC.

Model	Accuracy
MC-QT [23]	0.769
CNN-LSTM [10]	0.770
STN + Fr + De + NLI + L + STP + Par [24]	0.786
CNN [25]	0.8044
Siamese BiLSTM-GloVe (our model)	**0.8055**
FraLT-RNN [11]	0.812
Finetuned Transformer LM [19]	0.820
Transformer Mode [16]	0.893
Hybrid Siamese BiLSTM [29]	0.900

It seems that our models achieved results comparable to the state of the art, especially for the Quora dataset (Table 3).

Table 3. Comparative results - Quora Corpus.

Model	Accuracy
Siamese MALSTM [27]	0.7150
S-ARCNN [28]	0.8146
BERT [26]	0.8223
Siamese BERT-BiLSTM (our model)	**0.8303**
S-CNN [28]	0.8332
Paraphrase-MiniLM-L6-v2 + Siamese MaLSTM [30]	0.9000

5 Discussion and Conclusions

In this study we took a look at the complex topic of text semantic similarity. We developed two Siamese BiLSTM networks. The first Siamese BiLSTM model uses GloVe embedding vectors and achieved 80.5% accuracy on MRPC and 81% accuracy on the Quora Duplicate Questions dataset, both on 'unknown' data. The second Siamese model, instead of GloVe embeddings, utilizes the BERT encoder to produce the embedding sequences of the textual data. After fully training the model (pre-training and fine-tuning) it surpassed the performance of the first model achieving a maximum accuracy of 83% on the Quora dataset. The Siamese GloVe-BiLSTM model although small in size, achieved results that are surprisingly comparable with the other model, given that BERT is a really powerful language model responsible for state-of-the-art performances. The downside of the GloVe-BiLSTM model is that it is static, and incapable of training in multiple datasets over and over, in order to improve its performance. The model that uses BERT, on the other hand, can be trained in multiple datasets making it very flexible and easy to use. Although it is quite demanding in resources (both memory and computational power) due to its large size, and in order to achieve better state-of-the-art results it's necessary to use the large version of it (e.g. $BERT_{LARGE}$). Last but not least, the importance of quality data cannot be overlooked.

Concluding, the task of text semantic similarity is one of the most challenging tasks in Natural Language Processing and Understanding. It is important to emphasize that further research on the subject will provide opportunities for development in the field of NLU (Natural Language Understanding), thus offering innovative solutions that can be used in many practical applications, like text-based human-computer interaction.

References

1. Tellex, S., Gopalan, N., Kress-Gazit, H., Matuszek, C.: Robots That Use Language. Ann. Rev. Control, Robot. Autono. Syst. **3**, 25–55 (2020). https://doi.org/10.1146/annurev-control-101 119-071628
2. Zhang, Y., et al.: Building Natural Language Interfaces Using Natural Language Understanding and Generation: A Case Study on Human-Machine Interaction in Agriculture. Appl. Sci. **12**(22), 11830 (2022). https://doi.org/10.3390/app122211830

3. Pennington, J., Socher, R., Manning, C.D.: GloVe: Global Vectors for Word Representation. In: 2014 conference on empirical methods in natural language processing (EMNLP), Doha, Qatar, (2014)
4. Devlin, J., Chang, M.-W., Lee, K., Toutanova, K.: BERT: Pre-training of deep bidirectional transformers for language understanding. https://arxiv.org/abs/1810.04805. (2018)
5. Socher, R., Huang, E.H., Pennington, J., Ng, C.D.: Manning. Dynamic pooling and unfolding recursive autoencoders for paraphrase detection. In Advances in neural information processing systems. (2011)
6. Hu, B., Lu, Z., Li, H., Chen, Q.: Convolutional neural network architectures for matching natural language sentences. Adv. Neural. Inf. Process. Syst. **27**, 2042–2050 (2014)
7. Bengio, Y.: Learning deep architectures for AI, Montreal. Now Publishers Inc, Canada (2009)
8. Yin, W., Schütze, H.: Convolutional neural network for paraphrase identification. In: Proceedings of the 2015 Conference of the North American Chapter of the Association for Computational Linguistics: Human Language Technologies (2015)
9. He, H., Gimpel, K., Lin, J.: Multi-Perspective Sentence Similarity Modeling with Convolutional Neural. In: Proceedings of the 2015 Conference on Empirical Methods in Natural Language Processing, (2015)
10. Agarwal, B., Ramampiaro, H., Langseth, H., Ruocco, M.: A deep network model for paraphrase detection in short text messages. Inf. Process. Manage. **54**(6), 922–937 (2018)
11. Song, Y., Hu, W., He, L.: Using fractional latent topic to enhance recurrent neural network in text similarity modeling. In: International Conference on Database Systems for Advanced Applications (2019)
12. Wang, S., Jiang, J.: Learning Natural Language Inference with LSTM. In: The 15th Annual Conference of the North American Chapter of the Association for Computational Linguistics: Human Language Technologies, (2016)
13. Rocktäschel, T., Grefenstette, E., Hermann, K.M., Kočiský, T., Blunsom, P.: Reasoning about entailment with neural attention. In ICLR 2016 (2016)
14. Logeswaran, L., Lee, H.:. An efficient framework for learning sentence representations. In: International Conference on Learning Representations (2018)
15. Liu, P., Qiu, X., Chen, J., Huang, X.: Deep fusion LSTMs for text semantic matching. In: Proceedings of ACL 2016, Berlin, Germany, (2016)
16. Vaswani, A., et al.: Attention is all you need. In: Advances in neural information processing systems (2017)
17. Zhang, Z., et al.: Semantics aware BERT for Language Understanding. AAAI-2020 (2020)
18. Parikh, A.P., Täckström, O., Das, D., Uszkoreit, D.: A Decomposable Attention Model for Natural Language Inference. In: MNLP 2016: Conference on Empirical Methods in Natural Language Processing, Austin. Texas, (2016)
19. Radford, A., Narasimhan, K., Salimans, T., Sutskever, I.:Improving language understanding by generative pre-training. (2018)
20. Bowman, S.R., Angeli, G., Potts, C., Manning, C.D: A large annotated corpus for learning natural language inference. In EMNLP, Lisbon, Portugal, (2015)
21. Liu, L., et al.: On the Variance of the Adaptive Learning Rate and Beyond. In: the 8th International Conference on Learning Representations (ICLR 2020) (2019)
22. Chen, S., Hou, Y.,Cui, Y., Che, W., Liu, T., Yu, x.: Recall and learn: Fine-tuning deep pretrained language models with less forgetting. (2020) arXiv preprint arXiv:2004.12651
23. Logeswaran, L., Lee, H.: An efficient framework for learning sentence representations, In: International Conference on Learning Representations. (2018) arXiv:1803.02893 [cs.CL]
24. Subramanian, S., Trischler, A., Bengio, Y., Pal, C.: Learning general purpose distributed sentence representations via large scale multi-task learning. (2018) arXiv:1804.00079 [cs.CL]

25. Zhang, X., Rong, W., Liu, J., Tian, C., Xiong, Z.: Convolution neural network based syntactic and semantic aware paraphrase identification. International Joint Conference on Neural Networks (IJCNN) **2017**, 2158–2163 (2017)

26. Le, H.T., Cao, D.T., Bui, T.H., Luong, L.T., Nguyen, H.Q.: Improve Quora Question Pair Dataset for Question Similarity Task. RIVF International Conference on Computing and Communication Technologies (RIVF), pp. 1–5 (2021)

27. Poksappaiboon, N., Sundarabhogin, N., Tungruethaipak, N., Prom-on, S.: Detecting Text Semantic Similarity by Siamese Neural Networks with MaLSTM in Thai Language. In: Proceedings of the 2nd International Conference on Big Data Analytics and Practices (IBDAP), 07–11 (2021)

28. Han, S., Shi, L., Richie, R., Tsui, F.R.: Building siamese attention-augmented recurrent convolutional neural networks for document similarity scoring. Inf. Sci. **615**, 90–102 (2022)

29. Viji, D., Revathy, S.: A hybrid approach of Weighted Fine-Tuned BERT extraction with deep Siamese Bi – LSTM model for semantic text similarity identification. Multi. Tools Appl **81**, 6131 6157 (2022). https://doi.org/10.1007/s11042-021-11771-6

30. Gontumukkala, S.S.T., Godavarthi, Y.S.V., Gonugunta, B.R.R.T., Gupta, D., Palaniswam, S.: Quora Question Pairs Identification and Insincere Questions Classification. 2022 13th International Conference on Computing Communication and Networking Technologies (ICCCNT), Kharagpur, India, pp. 1–6 (2022) https://doi.org/10.1109/ICCCNT54827.2022.9984492

Water Quality Estimation from IoT Sensors Using a Meta-ensemble

Gregory Davrazos[1](✉) (iD), Theodor Panagiotakopoulos[2,3] (iD),
and Sotiris Kotsiantis[1] (iD)

[1] Department of Mathematics, University of Patras, Patras, Greece
gdavrazo@upatras.gr, sotos@math.upatras.gr
[2] School of Science and Technology, Hellenic Open University, Patras, Greece
panagiotakopoulos@eap.gr
[3] School of Business, University of Nicosia, Nicosia, Cyprus

Abstract. Water quality estimation using machine learning is a type of data analysis process that uses algorithms to identify patterns in large sets of data related to water quality. This can include identifying pollutants and other potential contamination that could negatively impact quality for drinking purposes, recreational activities or other uses. This helps ensure that the safety of water sources and the quality of recreational activities are constantly monitored and maintained. Thus, in this paper, a set of existing machine learning classifiers is applied to Internet of Things (IoT) sensor data on various water quality parameters, and the results are compared. Subsequently, a meta ensemble classifier that utilizes the soft voting technique of the best four previous classifiers is proposed to enhance estimation accuracy. According to results on the majority of the metrics used, this meta ensemble classifier outperforms all previously considered classifiers.

Keywords: Machine learning · Internet of Things · Water quality ·
Meta Ensemble · Soft voting

1 Introduction

Water pollution has nowadays become a universal problem. Besides developed, developing countries are facing water pollution problems. In order to guide the selection of water sources and safeguard water bodies from pollution, water quality standards have been devised. According to Boyd [1] there are many variables for water quality, but depending on the use, only a few variables are selected. For example, drinking water must not include excessive amounts of minerals, poisons, or disease-causing organisms. Other water uses that demand some water quality standards to be met are water use for bathing, recreation, industrial processes, agriculture/aqua culture, etc. Despite the common truth that every human being needs water suitable for drinking to live, there are no common universal standards for drinking water quality. In terms of drinking water quality, there are

© IFIP International Federation for Information Processing 2023
Published by Springer Nature Switzerland AG 2023
I. Maglogiannis et al. (Eds.): AIAI 2023 Workshops, IFIP AICT 677, pp. 393–403, 2023.
https://doi.org/10.1007/978-3-031-34171-7_32

some regulations mostly in the European Union and the United States that require legal compliance from their countries and states respectively, while other countries' drinking quality standards are solely expressed as guidelines or targets. The World Health Organization has recently published an updated edition of guidelines on drinking-water quality [2] to form an authoritative basis for the setting of national regulations and standards for water safety.

Machine learning has been used to a variety of scientific and technological fields, such as education, healthcare, power systems, security, air quality, and shipping [3–7]. Machine learning approaches, have been also used for determining water quality in various settings, seems to outperform traditional techniques because they account for nonlinear relationships among the dependent variables and with lower level of sophistication required for deriving complex experimental equations [8]. These approaches have gained popularity as Internet of Things (IoT) technologies are increasingly deployed over the traditional water grid enabling acquisition of large streams of real-time data end enhancing monitoring, resource utilization and decision making capabilities [9] In order to get reliable and accurate results from machine learning techniques a high-quality training dataset is required. This paper applies various state-of-the-art machine learning models for water quality estimation using a publicly available IoT dataset that contains nine water quality metrics (variables). It also proposes a soft voting meta ensembe model to improve classification results.

The outline of this paper is as follows: In Sect. 2, we present a brief overview of machine learning approaches for evaluating water quality while in Sect. 3 several machine learning classifiers are tested over a freely available dataset and a model based on soft voting of the top-performing algorithms is proposed. Conclusions and discussion for further research end the paper.

2   Overview of Machine Learning Approaches in Water Quality Evaluation

Machine learning algorithms can be used to a variety of applications in evaluating water quality. In the following, we report on recent indicative research work that utilizes simple or more sophisticated machine learning algorithms to estimate water quality.

Kim et. al. [10] explored the application of three machine learning approaches (Random Forest, Cubist Regression Trees, Support Vector Regression) to estimate two water quality indicators in coastal waters on the west coast of South Korea using satellite data. A remote sensing-based multiscale model with machine learning, called CDMIM, was used to monitor water quality changes. This technique encompassed SIASS and SMIR algorithms and was successfully implemented on Lake Nicaragua to predict seasonal changes in water quality [11].

A variety of machine learning approaches, such as Support Vector Regression, Random Forests, Artificial Neural Networks, and Cubist Regression Trees have been used to monitor water quality indicators such as suspended solids, chlorophyll-a, and turbidity in optically complicated coastal waters of Hong

Kong [12]. Along these lines, the research presented in [13] compared the effectiveness of ten machine learning models (Support Vector Machines, Decision Trees, Random Forest, Naïve Bayes, Logistic Regression, k-NN, Linear Discriminant Analysis, Completely-Random Tree, Completely-Random Tree Forest, Deep Cascade Forest) in predicting water quality from Chinese rivers and lakes from 2012 to 2018 on water quality parameters.

A machine learning-based method referred to as PCC-SVM (Pearson correlation coefficient-support vector machine) for detection of cross-connection events in potable-reclaimed water mixtures was proposed in [14]. WDT-ANFIS augmented wavelet denoising technique was proposed to predict water quality parameters at different stations, taking into consideration different amount of inputs. Data from 2009 to 2010 was used to back up WDT-ANFIS and it held a powerful capacity to reliably predict all water quality parameters [15].

Linear regression, Stochastic Gradient Descent, and Ridge regression estimators were used to predict the water quality parameters of lagoons [16]. Different regression algorithms such as linear regression, random forest regression, support vector regression and Gaussian processes regression was used for satellite data and in-situ measurements to assess two water quality parameters of the Valle de Bravo reservoir in Mexico [17].

Two hybrid decision tree-based machine learning models based on Extreme Gradient Boosting (XGBoost) and Random Forest (RF) and incorporating an advanced data denoising technique called Complete Ensemble Empirical Mode Decomposition with Adaptive Noise (CEEMDAN) were created and tested to predict the quality of water more accurately [18].

Four different machine learning models (k-NN, Boosting Decision Trees, Support Vector Machines, Artificial Neural Network) was used to predict recreational water quality in Auckland, New Zealand [19]. Machine Learning models such as Artificial Neural Network, Multiple Linear Regression Decision Tree, Random Forest, Support Vector Regression (SVR), k-Nearest Neighbour (kNN), Stochastic Gradient Descent and Adaptive Boosting (AdaBoost) were developed and tested to effectively predict the quality of irrigation water in the Bouregreg watershed, Morocco [20].

Extra Tree Regression (ETR) model, among other models such as Support Vector Regression and Decision Tree Regression model, yielded better predictions of monthly Water Quality Index (WQI) for the Lam Tsuen River in Hong Kong when the input of BOD, Turbidity and Phosphate concentration were applied in both training and testing phases [21].

UAVs was used to generate hyperspectral data, which was then analyzed using nine different machine-learning algorithms (Adaboost Regression, Gradient Boost Regression Tree, Extreme Gradient Boosting Regression, Catboost Regression, Random Forest, Extremely Randomized Trees, Support Vector Machine, Multi-Layer Perceptron Regression, Elastic Net), to predict two water quality parameters [22]. A stacking approach to predict beach water quality, which was found to be more reliable than individual machine learning models such as Multiple Linear Regression, Partial Least Squares, Sparse Partial Least Squares, Random Forest, Bayesian Networks was presented in [23].

Machine Learning classifiers such as Support Vector Machine, Random Forest, Logistic Regression, Decision Tree, CATBoost, XGBoost, and Multilayer Perceptron were evaluated for predicting water quality for collected data between 2005 and 2014 from various sites in India [24]. For recent comprehensive reviews on machine learning algorithms for evaluating water quality the interested reader is referred to [25, 26].

As the related work shows, the literature on using machine learning algorithms for determining water potability is very limited. Therefore, this work focuses on investigating how state-of-the-art machine learning models perform in this task and proposes a meta-ensemble to improve the water potability estimation performance.

3   Machine Learning Algorithms

In this section we will present the methodology for creating models based on machine learning algorithms for the categorization of water quality.

3.1   Dataset Description

For implementing machine learning algorithms, a dataset available online was used [27]. The water_potability.csv file contains nine water quality independent variables such as pH value, Hardness, Solids (Total dissolved solids - TDS), Chloramines, Sulfate, Conductivity, Organic Carbon, Trihalomethanes (THM), Turbidity for 3276 different water bodies (cases). Potability is the dependent binary variable indicating if water is drinkable (1) or not (0). From 3276 water samples only the 39.01% of them is safe for human consumption with all the rest being unsuitable for humans. Features such as Sulfate, ph, Trihalomethanes contain $781, 491, 162$ missing values respectively. Missing values comprise a common difficulty in data analysis that must be tackled in order not to have biased or incorrect result.

3.2   Preprocessing Phase

All machine learning models used in this study were trained, compared and evaluated using the PyCaret library, which is an open-source low-code machine learning toolkit written in Python [28].

In order for machine learning models to provide precise and insightful results, data preprocessing is an very important step. Our data preprocessing pipeline is depicted in Fig. 1, where LightGBM Classifier [29, 30] was used as the regressor for iterative imputation of missing values. LightGBM is a machine learning algorithm based on Gradient Boosting Decision Tree (GBDT) combined with other algorithms such as Gradient-based One-Side Sampling (GOSS) and Exclusive Feature Bundling (EFB) [29]. LightGBM is an effective iterative method for imputation of missing values due to its high-speed computing power and the ability to handle large datasets. One advantage of using LightGBM for imputation of missing values is that it can automatically identify important features from the data and use them to build accurate imputation models. Since Light-GBM uses gradient-based learning and decision trees, it can also learn from data with high complexity.

Isolation Forest [31] was used as the method for dealing with the outliers. The Isolation Forest is a tree-based anomaly detection technique, as its name suggests. It employs an unsupervised learning methodology to find outliers in the data, which may subsequently be eliminated from the training set. Performance usually improves when the model is retrained on a data set without the outliers. MinMaxScaler [32] was used for data normalization.

As it can be noticed from Fig. 2, features distribution does not deviate significantly from normal distribution so a basic assumption for implementing t-test is satisfied. Before proceeding to develop machine learning models, a t-test for each feature towards the independent variable is performed to decide whether there is a feature that has a statistically significant effect on its own. Figure 3 summarizes the t-test results. The results indicate that no feature has a significant effect on water potability.

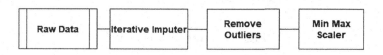

Fig. 1. Data Preprocessing Pipeline

3.3   Machine Learning Models Deployment

After preprocessing, we tested the following machine learning models: Random Forest Classifier [33], Gradient Boosting Classifier (GBM) [34], Light Gradient Boosting Machine (LGBM) [29], Extreme Gradient Boosting (XGBoost) [35], AdaBoost Classifier [36], Decision Tree Classifier [37], Extra Trees Classifier [38], Quadratic Discriminant Analysis [39], Linear Discriminant Analysis [39], k Nearest Neighbors Classifier [40], Naive Bayes [41], Logistic Regression [42], Support Vector Machines - Linear Kernel [43]. A 10-fold cross validation resampling procedure was used for evaluating the performance of the predictive models using the Accuracy, Area Under Curve (AUC), Recall, Precision, F1, Kappa and Matthews Correlation Coefficient (MCC) metrics. The results are shown in descending order with respect to accuracy in Table 1. As it can be observed, the Random Forest Classifier performed better in all metrics but recall and precision, where it had small differences from LGBM and GBM respectively.

We also performed a feature importance analysis based on the Random Forest model [44]. The basic reason for performing this analysis using Random Forests

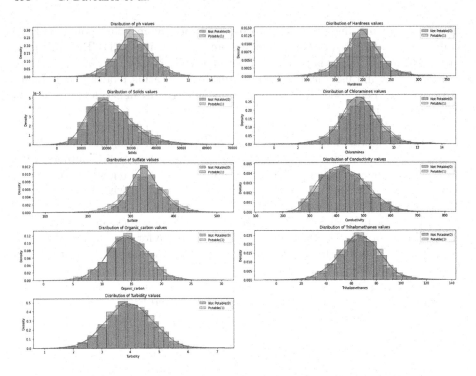

Fig. 2. Feature Distributions

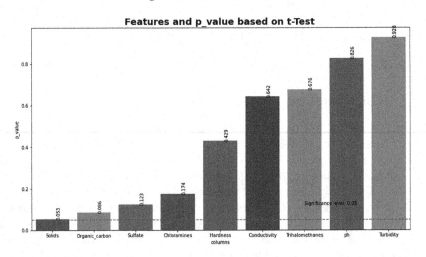

Fig. 3. Results of t-test for Features

is that performed better than all the other examined models (Fig. 4). The feature importance plot according to the Random Forest Classifier is a graphical display of information that helps to explain how much influence each feature has on the model's predictions. The plot shows an individual feature's importance relative to all other features in the dataset, and can help identify which features of the data are most important in predicting a model's outcome. The higher the importance score of a feature, the more influential it is in predicting the outcome. According to this, pH seems to be the most important feature for this machine learning model, although the other features cannot be ignored as the t-test has shown.

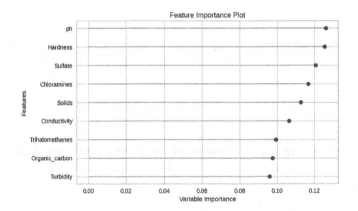

Fig. 4. Feature Importance Plot according to Random Forest Classifier

3.4   Meta Ensemble Model Deployment

Aiming to improve the classification accuracy we constructed a meta ensemble machine learning model featuring a soft voting technique of the four best performing models with respect to accuracy (Random Forest, GBM, LGBM, XGBoost) is proposed (Fig. 5). Soft voting averages the probabilities for each class of the base models so that the class with the highest average probability is selected [45].

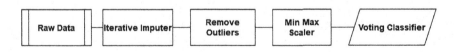

Fig. 5. Meta Ensemble Pipeline Data Processing

Table 1. Metrics for Different Machine Learning Models

Model	Accuracy	AUC	Recall	Precision	F1	Kappa	MCC
Soft Voting MetaEnsemble	**0.8002**	**0.8851**	0.6380	0.8101	**0.7132**	**0.5633**	**0.5732**
Random Forest Classifier	0.7965	0.8726	0.6269	0.8099	0.7057	0.5542	0.5655
Gradient Boosting Classifier	0.7925	0.8742	0.5913	**0.8281**	0.6893	0.5401	0.5578
Light Gradient Boosting Machine	0.7897	0.8770	**0.6498**	0.7760	0.7067	0.5448	0.5505
Extreme Gradient Boosting	0.7851	0.8709	**0.6648**	0.7560	0.7070	0.5384	0.5416
Ada Boost Classifier	0.7391	0.8206	0.4948	0.7541	0.5963	0.4157	0.4366
Decision Tree Classifier	0.7268	0.7146	0.6592	0.6481	0.6531	0.4279	0.4284
Extra Trees Classifier	0.7077	0.7661	0.3795	0.7489	0.5018	0.3257	0.3641
Quadratic Discriminant Analysis	0.6707	0.6825	0.3194	0.6647	0.4278	0.2363	0.2686
K Neighbors Classifier	0.6290	0.6279	0.3937	0.5324	0.4523	0.1816	0.1863
Naive Bayes	0.6213	0.5911	0.2182	0.5339	0.3082	0.1087	0.1291
Logistic Regression	0.6112	0.5040	0.0032	0.2000	0.0062	0.0038	0.0197
Linear Discriminant Analysis	0.6112	0.5040	0.0032	0.2000	0.0062	0.0038	0.0197

As it is shown from Table 1 the meta ensemble model outperformed all sub models with respect to Accuracy, AUC, F1, Kappa and MCC. Only the GBM achieved better precision than the proposed meta ensemble while only LGBM demonstrated better Recall. The ROC curve also verifies the enhanced performance of the meta ensemble (Fig. 6).

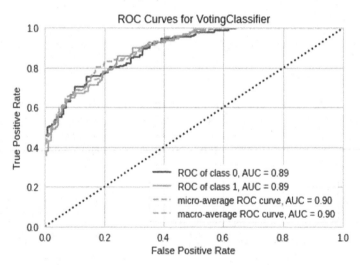

Fig. 6. ROC Curve of MetaEnsemble

4　Conclusions and Future Work

Drinking water quality is an essential human need and greatly affects public health. Machine Learning models possess an inherent ability to quickly and accurately assess water quality by analyzing data collected by IoT sensing devices.

These kind of models could lead to quicker and more effective ways of responding to problems in water systems, providing a better approach for decision making for local authorities and eventually leading to a healthier living environment especially in urban settings. This research study utilizes a water quality dataset available online to deploy various machine learning classifiers and assess and compare their performances. The top four classifiers were combined in a meta enseble using the soft voting technique, which increased the water quality estimation accuracy.

Upon completion of this study a relevant study was discovered [46] that follows a similar methodology over the same dataset. The differences between these two research papers lie on different approaches at the data prepossessing stage which affect the performance of the common machine learning models. Also a Meta Ensemble is proposed in the present paper that outperforms all individual models. As future work, the present study can be modified to forecast water quality in real- time using deep learning models and IoT data or by incorporating the sentiments of local communities in water quality forecasting models.

Acknowledgements. This work was supported by the research project OpenDCO, "Open Data City Officer" (Project No.: 22022-1-CY01-KA220-HED-000089196, Erasmus+ KA2: KA220-HED - Cooperation partnerships in higher education)

References

1. Boyd, C.E.: Water Quality. Springer, Cham (2020). https://doi.org/10.1007/978-3-030-23335-8
2. World Health Organization: guidelines for drinking-water quality. https://www.who.int/publications/i/item/9789240045064. Accessed 25 Mar 2023
3. Jhaveri, R. H. et. al.: A review on machine learning strategies for real-world engineering applications. Mobile Inf. Syst. (2022). https://doi.org/10.1155/2022/1833507
4. Vonitsanos, G., Panagiotakopoulos, T., Kanavos, A., Tsakalidis, A.: Forecasting air flight delays and enabling smart airport services in apache spark. In: Artificial Intelligence Applications and Innovations. AIAI 2021 IFIP WG 12.5 International Workshops, pp. 407–417 (2021). https://doi.org/10.1007/978-3-030-79157-5_33
5. Panagiotakopoulos, T., Kotsiantis, S., Kostopoulos, G., Iatrellis, O., Kameas, A.: Early dropout prediction in MOOCs through supervised learning and hyperparameter optimization. Electronics **10**(14), 1701 (2021). https://doi.org/10.3390/electronics10141701
6. Panagiotakopoulos, T., et al.: Vessel's trim optimization using IoT data and machine learning models. In: 13th International Conference on Information, Intelligence, Systems & Applications (2022). https://doi.org/10.1109/IISA56318.2022.9904361
7. Panagiotou, C., Panagiotakopoulos, T., Kameas, A.: A multi: modal decision making system for an ambient assisted living environment. In: 8th ACM International Conference on Pervasive Technologies Related to Assistive Environments (2015). https://doi.org/10.1145/2769493.2769529
8. Chou, J.-S., Chia-Chun, H., Ha-Son, H.: Determining quality of water in reservoir using machine learning. Ecol. inf. **44**, 57–75 (2018)

9. Panagiotakopoulos, T., Vlachos, D. P., Bakalakos, T. V., Kanavos, A., Kameas, A.: A fiware-based iot framework for smart water distribution management. In: 12th International Conference on Information, Intelligence, Systems & Applications (2021). https://doi.org/10.1109/IISA52424.2021.9555509

10. Kim, Y.H., et. al.: Machine learning approaches to coastal water quality monitoring using GOCI satellite data. GIScience & Remote Sensing, vol. 51, no. 2, pp. 158–174 (2014). https://doi.org/10.1080/15481603.2014.900983

11. Chang, N.-B., Bai, K., Chen, C.-F.: Integrating multisensor satellite data merging and image reconstruction in support of machine learning for better water quality management. J. Environ. Manag. **201**, 227–240 (2017). https://doi.org/10.1016/j.jenvman.2017.06.045

12. Hafeez, S. et. al.: Comparison of machine learning algorithms for retrieval of water quality indicators in Case-II waters: a case study of Hong Kong. Remote Sens., vol. 11, no. 6 (2019). https://doi.org/10.3390/rs11060617

13. Chen, K. et. al.: Comparative analysis of surface water quality prediction performance and identification of key water parameters using different machine learning models based on big data. Water Res. **171** (2020). https://doi.org/10.1016/j.watres.2019.115454

14. Xu, X. et. al.: Real-time detection of potable-reclaimed water pipe cross-connection events by conventional water quality sensors using machine learning methods. J. Environ. Manage. **238**, 201–209 (2019). https://doi.org/10.1016/j.jenvman.2019.02.110

15. Ahmed, N. A. et al.: Machine learning methods for better water quality prediction. J. Hydrol. **578**, 124084 (2019). https://doi.org/10.1016/j.jhydrol.2019.124084

16. Li, Y., et al.: Lagoon water quality monitoring based on digital image analysis and machine learning estimators. Water Res. **172** (2020). https://doi.org/10.1016/j.watres.2020.115471

17. Arias-Rodriguez, L. et. al.: Monitoring water quality of valle de bravo reservoir, mexico, using entire lifespan of meris data and machine learning approaches. Remote Sens. **12**(10), 1586 (2020). https://doi.org/10.3390/rs12101586

18. Lu, H., Ma, X.: Hybrid decision tree-based machine learning models for short-term water quality prediction. Chemosphere **249** (2020). https://doi.org/10.1016/j.chemosphere.2020.126169

19. Xu, T., Coco, G., Neale, M.: A predictive model of recreational water quality based on adaptive synthetic sampling algorithms and machine learning. Water Res. **177**, 115788 (2020). https://doi.org/10.1016/j.watres.2020.115788

20. El Bilali, A., Taleb, A.: Prediction of irrigation water quality parameters using machine learning models in a semi-arid environment. J. Saudi Soc. Agric. Sci. **19**(7), 439–451 (2020). https://doi.org/10.1016/j.jssas.2020.08.001

21. Asadollah, S.B.H.S., et. al.: River water quality index prediction and uncertainty analysis: a comparative study of machine learning models. J. Environ. Chem. Eng. **9**(1) (2021) https://doi.org/10.1016/j.jece.2020.104599

22. Lu, Q. et. al.: Retrieval of water quality from UAV-Borne hyperspectral imagery: a comparative study of machine learning algorithms. Remote Sens. **13**(19), 3928 (2021). https://doi.org/10.3390/rs13193928

23. Wang, L. et. al.: Improving the robustness of beach water quality modeling using an ensemble machine learning approach. Sci. Total Environ. **765**, 142760 (2021). https://doi.org/10.1016/j.scitotenv.2020.142760

24. Nasir, N. et. al.: Water quality classification using machine learning algorithms. J. Water Process. Eng. **48**, 102920 (2022). https://doi.org/10.1016/j.jwpe.2022.102920

25. Tung, T.M., Yaseen, Z.M.: A survey on river water quality modelling using artificial intelligence models: 2000–2020. J. Hydrol. **585**, 124670 (2020). https://doi.org/10.1016/j.jhydrol.2020.124670

26. Mengyuan, Z., et al.: A review of the application of machine learning in water quality evaluation. Eco-Environment & Health (2022)

27. Kadiwal, A.: Water Quality [Dataset]. https://www.kaggle.com/adityakadiwal/water-potability. Accessed 25 Mar 2022

28. Ali, M.: Pycaret: an open source, low-code machine learning library in python, PyCaret version 2.3.5 (2020). https://www.pycaret.org. Accessed 25 Mar 2022

29. Ke, G., et al.: LightGBM: a highly efficient gradient boosting decision tree. Adv. Neural. Inf. Process. Syst. **30**, 3146–3154 (2017)

30. Luo, Y.: Evaluating the state of the art in missing data imputation for clinical data. Brief. Bioinform. **23**(1) (2022). https://doi.org/10.1093/bib/bbab489

31. Liu, F.T., Ting, K.M., Zhou, Z.-H.: Isolation forest. In: 8th IEEE International Conference on Data Mining, Pisa, Italy, pp. 413–422 (2008). https://doi.org/10.1109/ICDM.2008.17

32. Amorim, L.B., Cavalcanti, G.D., Cruz, R.M.: The choice of scaling technique matters for classification performance. Appl. Soft Comput. **133** (2023)

33. Breiman, L.: Random forests. Mach. Learn. **45**(1), 5–32 (2001)

34. Friedman, J.: Greedy function approximation: a gradient boosting machine. Ann. Stat. **29**(5) (2001)

35. Chen, T., Guestrin, C. XgBoost: a scalable tree boosting system. In: Proceedings of the 22nd ACM SIGKDD International Conference on Knowledge Discovery and Data Mining, San Francisco, CA, USA, pp. 785–794 (2016)

36. Freund Y., Schapire, R.E.: A decision-theoretic generalization of on-line learning and an application to boosting. Eur. Conf. Comput. Learn. Theory, 23–37. Barcelona, Spain (2016)

37. Quinlan, J.R.: Induction of decision trees. Mach. Learn. **1**(1), 81–106 (1986)

38. Geurts, P., Ernst, D., Wehenkel, L.: Extremely randomized trees. Mach. Learn. **63**(1), 3–42 (2006)

39. Tharwat, A.: Linear vs quadratic discriminant analysis classifier: a tutorial. Int. J. Appl. Pattern Recogn. **3**(2), 145–180 (2016)

40. Cover, T., Hart, P.: Nearest neighbor pattern classification. IEEE Trans. Inf. Theory **13**(1), 21–27 (1967). https://doi.org/10.1109/TIT.1967.1053964

41. Murphy, K.P.: Naive Bayes classifiers. Univ. British Columbia **18**(60), 1–8 (2006)

42. Kleinbaum, D.G., et al.: Logistic Regression, p. 536. Springer-Verlag, New York (2002)

43. Cortes, C., Vapnik, V.I.: Support vector networks. Mach. Learn. **20**(3), 273–297 (1995)

44. Genuer, R., Poggi, J.-M., Tuleau-Malot, C.: Variable selection using random forests. Pattern Recogn. Lett. **31**(14), 2225–2236 (2010)

45. Sharma, A., Shrimali, V. R., Beyeler, M.: Machine learning for OpenCV 4: intelligent algorithms for building image processing apps using OpenCV 4, Python, and scikit-learn. Packt Publishing Ltd (2019)

46. Kaddoura, S.: Evaluation of machine learning algorithm on drinking water quality for better sustainability. Sustainability **14**(18), 11478 (2022). https://doi.org/10.3390/su141811478

The 1st Workshop on "Visual Analytics Approaches for Complex Problems in Engineering and Biomedicine" (VAA-CP-EB)

Preface

2023 Visual Analytics Approaches for Complex Problems in Engineering and Biomedicine (VAA-CP-EB) Workshop

Many problems today in the fields of biomedicine and engineering involve huge amounts of data, a large number of variables and a high complexity of the underlying processes. Many factors influence their behavior, causing common challenges in diagnosis, prognosis, estimation, anomaly detection, accurate and explainable modeling, timeseries and image analysis or knowledge discovery, just to mention a few.

Machine learning (ML) algorithms allow modeling of complex processes from massive data, and are able to surpass humans in well-defined tasks. However, they are prone to error under changes in the context or in the problem definition. Also, they are often "black box" models, which makes their integration with an expert's domain knowledge difficult. Humans, in turn, although less precise, can work with poorly posed problems, perform well on a wide range of tasks, and are able to find connections and improve responses through an iterative, exploratory process. Aiming to embrace both approaches, Visual Analytics (VA) has emerged in recent years as a powerful paradigm based on the integration of ML and human reasoning by means of data visualization and interaction for complex problem solving.

This special session covered research work that contributes to this paradigm, including applications, algorithms, methods or techniques suitable to support or be part of VA solutions to problems in engineering and biomedicine.

Some example topics included in the VAA-CP-EB 2023 workshop were: ML/AI-powered data visualization, eXplainable Artificial Intelligence (XAI), visualization and/or interaction methods for data analysis, visual analytics of dynamical systems and timeseries, visual analytics in process and biomedical data analysis for knowledge discovery, condition monitoring, anomaly detection, and prognosis and prediction.

Ignacio Díaz Blanco
José María Enguita

Organization of VAA-CP-EB 2023

Workshop Co-chairs

Ignacio Díaz Blanco	University of Oviedo, Spain
José María Enguita	University of Oviedo, Spain

Program Committee

Diego García	Universidad de Oviedo, Spain
Daniel Pérez	Universidad de León, Spain
Ignacio Díaz Blanco	Universidad de Oviedo, Spain
Antonio Morán	Universidad de León, Spain
Pierre Lambert	UCLouvain, Belgium
Antonio José Serrano López	Universitat de València, Spain
Cyril de Bodt	UCLouvain, Belgium
John Lee	UCLouvain, Belgium
Miguel Ángel Prada	Universidad de León, Spain
Emilio Soria Olivas	Universitat de València, Spain
Juan J. Fuertes	Universidad de León, Spain
María Dolores Chiara	Universidad de Oviedo, Spain
Abel Alberto Cuadrado	Universidad de Oviedo, Spain
Antonio Miguel López	Universidad de Oviedo, Spain
José María Enguita	Universidad de Oviedo, Spain
Joan Vila Francés	Universitat de València, Spain

An XAI Approach to Deep Learning Models in the Detection of DCIS

Michele La Ferla$^{(\boxtimes)}$ [iD]

University of Malta, MSD 2080 Msida, Malta
ict-ai@um.edu.mt
http://www.um.edu.mt/ict/ai

Abstract. Deep Learning models have been employed over the past decade to improve the detection of conditions relative to the human body and in relation to breast cancer particularly. However, their application to the clinical domain has been limited even though they improved the detection of breast cancer in women at an early stage. Our contribution attempts to interpret the early detection of breast cancer while enhancing clinicians' confidence in such techniques through the use of eXplainable AI.

We researched the best way to back-propagate a selected CNN model, previously developed in 2017; and adapted in 2019. Our methodology proved that it is possible to uncover the intricacies involved within a model; at neuron level, in converging towards the classification of a mammogram. After conducting a number of tests using five back-propagation methods, we noted that the Deep Taylor Decomposition and the LRP-Epsilon techniques produced the best results. These were obtained on a subset of 20 mammograms chosen at random from the *CBIS-DDSM* dataset. The results showed that XAI can indeed be used as a proof of concept to begin discussions on the implementation of assistive AI systems within the clinical community.

Keywords: Explainable Artificial Intelligence · Layer-wise Relevance Propagation · Deep Taylor Decomposition · LRP-Epsilon · Breast Cancer · Deep Learning · Convolutional Neural Network

1 Introduction

Breast carcinoma is the most common types of tumours among women in the western world, according to WHO reports [19]. As a result, it is very common that many studies have devoted significant time and effort in developing models that can aid radiologists obtain accurate and timely diagnoses of this disease. The mammographic presence of breast cancer can initially be noted through one of the following four methods: by discovering minor distortions of the breast tissue; showing the presence of masses in the breast; through the presence of non-asymmetrical breasts; or through the presence of microcalcifications.

We started our study by collecting information from a questionnaire which was distributed to 12 of the 15 clinical specialists in breast cancer, which Malta

© IFIP International Federation for Information Processing 2023
Published by Springer Nature Switzerland AG 2023
I. Maglogiannis et al. (Eds.): AIAI 2023 Workshops, IFIP AICT 677, pp. 409–420, 2023.
https://doi.org/10.1007/978-3-031-34171-7_33

is currently equipped with. This helped shed light about their practices, as well as their attitudes towards the employment and effectiveness of AI technologies. The similarity of our findings to international literature encouraged us further to pursue our focus on addressing the lack of implementation of assistive AI models in hospitals and also investigate how the introduction of XAI could help clinicians understand how a model classifies between a benign, malignant, or non-tumorous breast tissue.

This was followed by a comparative study between different available datasets to adopt as part of our scientific tests that employed a Convolutional Neural Network (CNN). The *CBIS-DDSM* scanned film mammographic dataset was selected due to its unique features, being that is has been carefully annotated by expert radiologists and has also been extensively used in the deep learning community. Additionally, we used this dataset on an already trained model, due to a lack of computational resources, and to further focus our study on the element of XAI in deep learning.

The results obtained from reverse engineering a CNN model using back-propagation methodologies are discussed further on in this paper and were also presented to the same clinicians interviewed in the initial questionnaire. Optimal results were obtained when using the Deep Taylor Decomposition and LRP-Epsilon techniques. The best performing solution would be a combination of these two techniques to achieve ideal results.

2   Literature Review

In the early 1990 s,s, one of the first datasets on breast cancer was published on the Machine Learning Repository site. This contained information from a total of 699 patients diagnosed with breast cancer. Although very primitive when compared to the mammogram screening image datasets we have today, the dataset has been extensively used in several projects in the following years by utilising its features to predict whether people with similar identifiable traits are more likely to be diagnosed with a tumour. The dataset was curated by the University of Wisconsin hospital in the US and contained data for women who were investigated for breast cancer covering the period between 1989 and 1992 [17].

2.1   Research Studies Involving Deep Learning

Maybe one of the greatest ground-breaking studies made in this research area was the one made by the Google Deepmind team, in collaboration with Cornell University. The research made here involved the creation of the *LYNA* model which helped in the diagnosis of breast cancer through MRI images, which included large pathology images for lymph nodes. The purpose of This study was to identify the presence of a tumour in the lymph nodes around the breast area of female patients. The dataset used in this study involved the analysis of images which have portrayed biopsies from MRI stage procedures in the second stage of a diagnosis and used to develop a deep learning model able to detect a tumour which is at a metastasis stage [18]. While the LYNA model proved to be significantly more effective in detecting breast cancer, the researchers themselves admitted in their study that an accurate model alone does not prove enough to improve the diagnostic work done by pathologists or improve outcomes for breast cancer patients [8]. A very important outcome of this study was that of keeping in mind patient safety using machine learning techniques on patients. Such a model would need to be tested in different scenarios, and use diverse datasets to understand its predictive power. Furthermore, the benefits of such a system whereby medical practitioners used the *LYNA* model had still to be explored. It was still too early to determine whether such an algorithm improved the efficiency of the procedure or diagnostic accuracy. The importance of *LYNA* was however proved in two other studies carried out in 2018 and 2019, respectively [5, 16].

During the NIPS17 conference, one particular study made by Shen et al. contributed significantly to tumour identification using screening mammogram images [13]. This was later improved upon in 2019 by the same researchers [14]. The study initially based its model on the Yaroslav architecture in 2017, but was then tweaked to compare the VGG-16 and ResNet-50 architectures, in an attempt to improve the detection of breast tumours by reading mammograms. The second model modified the first to use a fully convolutional training approach which effectively makes use of the annotations on the curated *CBIS-DDSM* dataset. By using this approach, certain dataset features such as lesion annotations are only needed for the initial training. The inner layers within the model would only require image-level labels, therefore decreasing the reliance on lesion annotations. This was a significant improvement in the radiological field of study, since the availability of annotated mammogram datasets is even to date very limited [14]. The relevance of this project is that it is part of an open-source study which can therefore be used and altered to improve on by other researchers [13]. Shen et al. used the publicly available well-curated *CBIS-DDSM* and inBreast mammographic datasets of scanned film mammography studies to build their model upon [12].

2.2 Developments in XAI

The best approach to consider was that of using Layer-wise Relevance Propagation, which in theory works backwards through the neural network to redistribute the output result back to all the neurons (or pixels) in the input image. The redistribution process can be simplified using formula 1 which uses back propagation from one layer to the previous:

$$R_j = \sum_k \frac{x_j w_{j,k}}{\sum_j x_j w_{j,k} + \epsilon} R_k \tag{1}$$

The function of the formula above is to use neuron activators and weight connections to interpret a deep learning model. This is particularly relevant to ResNet-50 architectures due to their residual properties. x_j takes the value of the activator for the neuron j in any layer of the network. $w_{j,k}$ is used as a weighting given to the connection between neuron j and neuron k in the next one. R_j has the property of the relevance score for each neuron in the first given layer, and R_k is the relevance score for each neuron in the next inner layer [3].

LRP is considered a rather conservative algorithm to backpropagate a deep learning model. This means that in essence the magnitude of any output y is aligned throughout the back-propagation process and is equivalent to the sum of the relevance map R in the input layer. This property is true for any hidden consecutive layers j and k within the neural network and transitivity for the input and output layer [7].

The numerator of the fraction in the formula is the value at which the neuron j can influence the neuron k, which is valid for the linear case of an active ReLU activator. This is split up by the aggregate of contributions in all lower-layer neurons for us to enforce the conservation property. The outer sum over k is a representative of the relevance of the neuron j. It is calculated using the sum of its influence on all neurons k from the following layer and multiplied by the R value of these neurons.

3   Materials and Methods

After developing the initial patch classifier for the NIPS-16 competition Shen et al. moved on to improve on their previous model and built a whole image classifier rather than the previous patch-classifier. The advantage of this is that the new model didn't segment the image into patches but processed the mammogram as a whole. To do this they flattened the heatmap and connected it to the image classification output using a novel idea called fully connected layers. A max-pooling layer followed the fully connected layer and was used to partially eliminate the imbalance brought by the translational invariance which the previous version of the model suffered with [13]. In addition, a shortcut was also introduced between the heatmap and the output layer to facilitate training. The equation used to achieve this result using softmax activation is shown in formula 2.

$$f(z)_j = \frac{e^{z_j}}{\sum_{t=1}^{c} e^{z_t}} \text{ for } j = 1, \ldots, c \tag{2}$$

3.1   Layer-Wise Relevance Propagation

Following the research by Montavon and Binder [3,10], it was found that the Layer-wise Relevance Propagation method is one of the most effective algorithms used to explain and interpret decisions in deep learning networks. Within the ResNet-50 CNN architecture, the explanation given by LRP can be represented through back-propagation utilising those pixels contained in the image in question which influence the outcome as to how the model classifies the image.

The primary benefit of this technique is that it does not conflict with network training, so it could be independently applied to the already trained classifiers in any dataset. Based on a second study by Lehman et al., it is hoped that LRP could provide physicians with the tools not only to interpret mammograms but to alert them to the presence of other co-diseases such as tumours and possible cardiovascular disease [6]. Researchers and medical professionals alike are always enthusiastic to try new methods, particularly those with a lower risk to the patient.

3.2 Deep Taylor Decomposition

Over and above the work done by Montavon and Binder on LRP [9] at the same time, the same authors coined the Deep Taylor decomposition method to better analyse the interpretability of deep learning models. This is an improvement on the original LRP methodology since the authors found a number of constraints, from which one could derive different functions; one of which being Deep Taylor decomposition. If we were to decompose the function f in the equation below in terms of its partial derivatives, the result can be used to approximate the relevance propagation function. The closer x is to x_0, then the better the approximation. This simplifies the Deep Taylor equation to the following one [15].

$$f(x) \approx \sum_{d=1}^{v} \frac{\partial f}{\partial x_{(d)}}(x_0)(x_{(d)} - x_{0(d)}) \mid f(x_0) = 0 \qquad (3)$$

The Deep Taylor decomposition method helps us understand which neurons which contribute to the classification of an image and work best with monochromatic images such as the ones used in mammograms, X-rays and other medical images.

3.3 Comparing the Regions of Interest

The five chosen techniques used for comparison, all formed part of the iNNvestigate library and are the following:

- Deconvolution Network [1]
- Deep Taylor Decomposition [9]
- LRP-Preset A Flat [1]
- LRP-Epsilon [1]
- Guided Backprop [11]

The decision to use these methodologies, in particular, was based on a number of previous studies whereby they were used to interpret medical images; some of which mammograms in particular. Notable among these is the research made by Reyes et al. in 2020 about the interpretability of medical images in radiology. In their attempt to discuss several backpropagation models, the authors compare the Guided Backprop method to others such as gradient-weighted class activation mapping, pointing out that the Guided Backprop methodology performs well when interpreting MRI images of the human brain [11].

4   Results and Discussion

When comparing the five different methodologies we tested to determine the one which interpreted mammograms best, we noticed that the Deep Taylor Decomposition did in most cases perform better than the other four, however, there were instances where the LRP-Epsilon technique gave better results. In the following section, we will go through the different results achieved on the sample subset of 20 mammograms from the *CBIS-DDSM* dataset.

The first notation we may take from the subset used to test the five different methods is that the Guided Backprop and the LRP Preset A-Flat methods are not helpful for our purposes. Starting with the Guided Backprop method, we noticed that this tends to scatter the pixels all over the image, losing the important parts of the mammogram which identify its classification. There were some instances in the subset, where the Guided Backprop method gave certain information about regions in the mammogram where abnormality may occur; such as in 016, 223 and 242; where there is a more dense amount of pixels around particular regions of the mammograms. However, having said that, we found that other methods performed better when attempting to identify tumours in specific regions of a mammogram. We must remember that the dataset chosen contains images of full-breast mammograms. It could therefore be possible to use the Guided Backprop method in detailed sectioned mammograms, to identify the source of cancer.

Similarly, the LRP Preset A-Flat method was found not to be the best method to determine those neurons which contribute most to the classification of a mammogram. For this method, we tested out different betas and epsilon stabilisers, in an attempt to increase the clarity of the output image. The best result we got was when using a beta of 1 and an epsilon stabiliser of 0.07. Once this optimum was determined, all images within the subset which were processed using these values. The results obtained, although improved upon the Guided Backprop method were not sufficient for our purposes. The reason behind this conclusion is that the A-Flat method was able to show the outline of the breast within the mammogram, but failed to highlight those areas where cancer could be found. Nonetheless, there were instances in the subset where abnormalities were detected, pointing to the presence of major metastatic breast cancer; such as in cases 016, 026, 063, 172 and 242. In all instances the A-Flat method enlarged those pixels which showed an abnormality, so it would be beneficial as a first step to identify those mammograms which show a sign of abnormality, but these are also visible to the naked eye, thus not contributing that much to the analysis.

After having analysed and eliminated two of the five options using a visual comparison made using the naked eye, we remained with the LRP Epsilon, DeConvNet and the Deep Taylor Decomposition methods, to help us understand how the neural network classified the mammograms. All three methods provide relevant information about the input images, so our decision and evaluation had to be based on probability. The question we asked ourselves when evaluating the results of these three methods is which of them has the highest probability of identifying abnormalities in a mammogram. Based on the subset

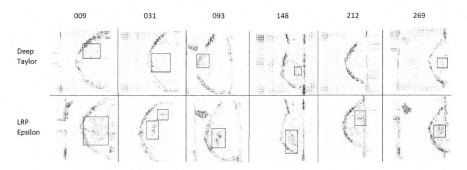

Fig. 1. We gave specific importance to case numbers 009, 031, 093, 148, 212 and 269, which are shown in this order. In these mammograms, the Epsilon method showed clearer pixels than the Deep Taylor Decomposition method, however, that does not mean that they are always better at interpreting mammograms.

of 20 mammograms, we noticed that the Deep Taylor Decomposition method performed better than the other two in 12 of the 20 cases (016, 026, 030, 056, 063, 072, 111, 172, 178, 181, 223 and 259). In another 6 of the 20 images taken in the subset, it was noted that the Epsilon method generated results which visually showed more regions of interest than the ones generated by the Deep Taylor Decomposition. (009, 031, 093, 148, 212 and 269). These can be visualised in Fig. 1. In one particular case; for case no: 131 it was also noted that the image was not clear enough to determine a classification. The results obtained additionally showed that the images being generated by the DeConvNet method were inferior to the ones generated by the Deep Taylor and Epsilon methods. These generated images contained more noise, thus losing pixel-wide information, when it comes to details.

We focused for a moment on those cases where the Epsilon method generated results which showed more regions of interest to the naked eye than when using Deep Taylor Decomposition. Figure 1 shows the results obtained by each of these six cases in particular. The figure shows the results obtained by the Deep Taylor Decomposition method in the first column and the respective result obtained by the Epsilon method to the right. For case 009, The Epsilon results show a larger area which could contribute to the classification of the mammogram. The results obtained by the Deep Taylor Decomposition show a more specific detected area of concern. In this particular case, when comparing to the original mammogram, we noticed that the larger area detected by the Epsilon method could result from the presence of breast milk contained within the lobes of the patient's breast. So in this case, the Deep Taylor Decomposition method proved to be better in identifying the area of a concern than the Epsilon method. When comparing the two methods on case numbers 031 and 223, the Deep Taylor Decomposition found one single large area of concern, while the Epsilon method figured out two separate ones. For case number 093, the Epsilon method again performed better than the Deep Taylor Decomposition one, since it identified a better concerning

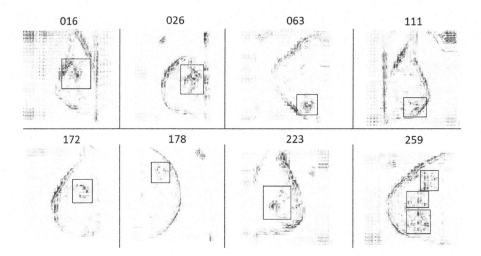

Fig. 2. We used the iNNvestigate library Deep Taylor Decomposition method to identify those areas within a source image which have mostly contributed to the classification of a said mammogram. In the cases shown here, we are identifying those cases where the Deep Taylor Decomposition Method identified instances of malignant breast cancer.

area. In these two instances, we can see that the Epsilon method had superior performance to the Deep Taylor one, highlighting the affected areas in a better way. For cases 148 and 269, we noticed that while the pixels were clearer when using the Epsilon method, the images on the whole gave a better interpretation of the affected areas when using the Deep Taylor Decomposition method.

Based on the results obtained, we were able to understand which areas within a mammogram contribute to its classification into a breast containing, no signs of cancer, having benign cancer or having signs of malignant cancer. It became clear to us that cases no: 016, 026, 063, 111, 172, 178, 223 and 259 for example had a clear signs of malignant cancer. The Deep Taylor Decomposition method was able to successfully show the affected areas of the breast by highlighting them in either blue or red colours. These can be seen in Fig. 2. The same method was also able to define those mammograms which may have a presence of benign breast cancer in case numbers 030, 056, 072, 131, 148, 242 and 269. These can be seen in Fig. 3. This is where the assistance of a radiologist would be needed to help in the diagnosis of such cases. It was also noted that in cases 009, 031, 093 and 181 the Deep Taylor Decomposition method was not able to find any signs of breast cancer; as shown in Fig. 4. Questionable among these is case no: 093, whereby although the Deep Taylor method did not find any abnormalities, the Epsilon method did. This is shown in Fig. 5.

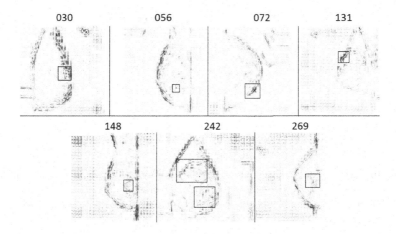

Fig. 3. The Deep Taylor Decomposition method was able to also identify instances of benign breast cancer by highlighting those areas within a mammogram which contribute to its classification by using heatmaps.

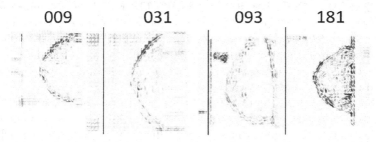

Fig. 4. In some cases, the Deep Taylor Decomposition method we used was not able to identify the presence of breast cancer. While the model took this decision, we still concluded that these mammograms should be interpreted also by a human radiologist.

5   Evaluation

To assist in the evaluation of the developed XAI model, we created a second questionnaire and shared it with the same 12 clinical specialists from Malta who were chosen for the initial questionnaire mentioned in the introduction. This time, the response received involved less participants, but the study was more focused and detailed such that we decided to meet three specialists in breast radiology, and two in breast surgery individually to get a first-hand evaluation from them on the proposed approach and model.

The initial comments we received from the interviewed specialists was that the chosen dataset could have been a better one. Even though the *CBIS-DDSM* dataset is a widely used public dataset of breast mammograms which have been thoroughly curated and annotated by experts in the field, it was noted that the quality of the images was inferior to the ones they were accustomed to. The

Deep Taylor   LRP-Epsilon

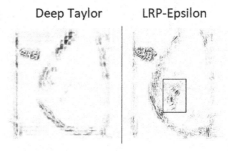

Fig. 5. In one particular case, where the Deep Taylor Decomposition method was unable to detect any areas pertaining to a potential classification of benign or malignant cancer, The Epsilon method was able to identify an area which potentially could contain such signs of cancer.

amount of detail which the *BI-RADS* mammograms go into can therefore be much more than the ones processed by *DICOM* machines, therefore allowing for microcalcifications in the breast to be identified by radiologists in an easier way.

The second point which the clinicians noted was the quality of the mammograms in the *CBIS-DDSM* dataset. In particular case numbers: 072, 056, 063, 148 and 259 were ruled as being unidentifiable, and stating that if they were presented with such mammograms, they would ask for the radiographer to perform a second mammographic test on the patient.

A third point which the clinicians mentioned in the interview was that the *CBIS-DDSM* dataset only displays a one-sided full-size mammogram of each case. Tomosynthethic images have a three dimensional model of each breast, by taking multiple mammographic images of the same breast. Therefore what could be seen as a microcalcification from one facet of the mammogram, could be further viewed from different facets of the same breasts and diagnosed in a better way [4].

6   Conclusions

From the results obtained in the preliminary study made during the summer months of 2020. We can conclude that even though the contribution and involvement of deep learning algorithms were generalised and toned down, the majority of participants who participated in the questionnaire increased their element of trust when the idea of XAI was introduced. The imposition of a back propagation model which highlights those pixels in a deep learning model contributes to its classification, and visualising these areas through a heatmap would indeed provide a better solution to the conventional CNN models. Knowing how a model has classified different mammograms into containing benign, malignant or no signs of a tumour would be beneficial to radiologists who are attempting to diagnose the presence of breast cancer in a patient.

Having said that, it remains a fact that the specialist showed concern around the use of the *CBIS-DDSM* dataset for this study and its lack of detail when compared to the mammograms which the specialists are accustomed to at Mater Dei Hospital. The interviewed participants also commented about the four elements which radiologists look into when studying a mammographic image; being the presence of microcalcifications, an asymmetry between the two breasts, distortion in particular areas and opaqueness of that area.

The combination of a ResNet-50 architectured model together with the Deep Taylor Decomposition methodology has theoretically proved to be a good combination to build a deep learning model and apply backpropagation to it. However, in the scenario set by this study and as expressed by the medical specialists, improvements need to be made to the dataset for a better evaluation of the XAI model. The suggestion given by the radiologists interviewed in the second part of the study was to choose particular mammograms from the *CBIS-DDSM* dataset and run the XAI model against them. This will help evaluate the effectiveness of the XAI model in a better way.

As Ayhan et al. discuss in their paper about guided backdrop methods and their performance in relation to the Deep Taylor decomposition methods, the former seems to generate saliency maps which are better in explaining decisions taken by Deep Learning models. The study concluded that the Guided Backprop method is still in its initial stages when attempting to read from a ResNet-50 model. Therefore classification predictions on medical images cannot be considered conclusive. The reason for this according to Ayhan et. al is due to the restrictions which the Guided Backprop model by design has with ReLU activators. The model should be extended to new architectures beyond the ReLU activator-based models [2]. Nonetheless, the Guided Backprop approach was never employed as a saliency map to reverse engineer mammograms used in breast cancer interpretation. So it remains to be seen whether Guided Backprop can uncover those mammography pixels that contribute the most to the ultimate assessment of benign, cancerous, or normal breast tissue in a future investigation. It is also necessary to demonstrate if this strategy works well with the ResNet-50 patch-classifier models or whether an alternative model should be used to develop a CNN that can successfully diagnose breast cancer.

References

1. Alber, M., et al.: Innvestigate neural networks! J. Mach. Learn. Res. **20**(93), 1–8 (2019)
2. Ayhan, M.S., et al.: Clinical validation of saliency maps for understanding deep neural networks in ophthalmology. medRxiv (2021)
3. Binder, A., Montavon, G., Lapuschkin, S., Müller, K.-R., Samek, W.: Layer-wise relevance propagation for neural networks with local renormalization layers. In: Villa, A.E.P., Masulli, P., Pons Rivero, A.J. (eds.) ICANN 2016. LNCS, vol. 9887, pp. 63–71. Springer, Cham (2016). https://doi.org/10.1007/978-3-319-44781-0_8
4. Ekpo, E., McEntee, M.: Measurement of breast density with digital breast tomosynthesis- a systematic review. British J. Radiol. (2014). https://doi.org/10.1259/bjr.20140460

5. Khan, S., Naveed, I., Jan, Z., Din, I., Rodrigues, J.: A novel deep learning based framework for the detection and classification of breast cancer using transfer learning. Pattern Recogn. Lett. **125**, 1–6 (2019)
6. Lehman, C.D., et al.: Mammographic breast density assessment using deep learning: clinical implementation. Radiology **290**(1), 52–58 (2019). https://doi.org/10.1148/radiol.2018180694
7. Lindwurm, E.: Indepth: layer-wise relevance propagation (2019). https://towardsdatascience.com/indepth-layer-wise-relevance-propagation-340f95deb1ea
8. Liu, Y., et al.: Detecting cancer metastases on gigapixel pathology images (2017)
9. Montavon, G., Binder, A., Lapuschkin, S., Samek, W., Müller, K.-R.: Layer-wise relevance propagation: an overview. In: Samek, W., Montavon, G., Vedaldi, A., Hansen, L.K., Müller, K.-R. (eds.) Explainable AI: Interpreting, Explaining and Visualizing Deep Learning. LNCS (LNAI), vol. 11700, pp. 193–209. Springer, Cham (2019). https://doi.org/10.1007/978-3-030-28954-6_10
10. Montavon, G., Samek, W., Müller, K.R.: Methods for interpreting and understanding deep neural networks. Digital Sig. Process. **73**, 1–15 (2018). https://doi.org/10.1016/j.dsp.2017.10.011
11. Reyes, M., et al.: On the interpretability of artificial intelligence in radiology: challenges and opportunities. Radiol.: Artif. Intell. 2, e190043 (2020). https://doi.org/10.1148/ryai.2020190043
12. Rose, C., Turi, D., Williams, A., Wolstencroft, K., Taylor, C.: University of South Florida digital mammography home page (2006). https://www.eng.usf.edu/cvprg/Mammography/Database.html
13. Shen, L.: Lishen/end2end-all-conv (2019). https://github.com/lishen/end2end-all-conv
14. Shen, L., Margolies, L., Rothstein, J., Fluder, E., McBride, R., Sieh, W.: Deep learning to improve breast cancer detection on screening mammography. Sci. Rep. **9**, 1–12 (2019). https://doi.org/10.1038/s41598-019-48995-4
15. Shiebler, D.: Understanding neural networks with layerwise relevance propagation and deep Taylor series (2017). https://danshiebler.com/2017-04-16-deep-taylor-lrp/
16. Steiner, D., et al.: Impact of deep learning assistance on the histopathologic review of lymph nodes for metastatic breast cancer. Am. J. Surg. Pathol. **42**, 1 (2018). https://doi.org/10.1097/PAS.0000000000001151
17. Street, W.N.: Cancer diagnosis and prognosis via linear-programming-based machine learning. Ph.D. thesis, University of Wisconsin at Madison, USA (1994)
18. Stumpe, M.: Assisting pathologists in detecting cancer with deep learning (2021). https://ai.googleblog.com/2017/03/assisting-pathologists-in-detecting.html
19. WHO: Incidence of female breast cancer per 100000 (2019). https://gateway.euro.who.int/en/indicators/hfa_375-2350-incidence-of-female-breast-cancer-per-100-000/. Accessed 07 Sept 2020

Conditioned Fully Convolutional Denoising Autoencoder for Energy Disaggregation

Diego García[1](✉), Daniel Pérez[2], Panagiotis Papapetrou[3], Ignacio Díaz[1],
Abel A. Cuadrado[1], José Maria Enguita[1], Ana González[1],
and Manuel Domínguez[2]

[1] Department of Electrical Engineering, University of Oviedo, Gijón 33204, Spain
{garciaperdiego,idiaz,cuadradoabel,jmenguita,gonzalezmunana}@uniovi.es
[2] SUPPRESS Research Group, University of León, 24007 León, Spain
{dperl,manuel.dominguez}@unileon.es
[3] Department of Computer and Systems Sciences, Stockholm University, Kista,
Stockholm SE-164 07, Sweden
panagiotis@dsv.su.se

Abstract. Energy management increasingly requires tools to support decisions for improving consumption. This is achieved not only obtaining feedback from current systems but also using prior knowledge about human behaviour. The advances of data-driven models provide techniques like Non-Intrusive Load Monitoring (NILM) which are capable of estimating energy demand of appliances from total consumption. In addition, deep learning models have improved accuracy in energy disaggregation using separated networks for each device. However, the complexity can increase in large facilities and feedback may be impaired for a proper interpretation. In this work, a deep neural network based on a Fully Convolutional denoising AutoEncoder is proposed for energy disaggregation that uses a conditioning input to modulate the estimation aimed to one specific appliance. The model performs a complete disaggregation using a network whose modulation to target the estimation can be steered by the user. Experiments are done using data from a hospital facility and evaluating reconstruction errors and computational efficiency. The results show acceptable errors compared to methods that require various networks and a reduction of the complexity and computational costs, which can allow the user to be integrated into the analysis loop.

Keywords: energy dissagregation · NILM · convolutional neural networks

1 Introduction

Energy efficiency has gained substantial attention not only in the promotion of sustainable products and generation technologies that aim to save energy but also in the study of current systems in order to obtain knowledge about how the

© IFIP International Federation for Information Processing 2023
Published by Springer Nature Switzerland AG 2023
I. Maglogiannis et al. (Eds.): AIAI 2023 Workshops, IFIP AICT 677, pp. 421–433, 2023.
https://doi.org/10.1007/978-3-031-34171-7_34

energy is consumed. Frequently, this consumption is reported as an overview of the total demand in a certain period of time. However, the perception of detailed representations of the energy allows users to obtain feedback that encourages them to take actions to improve overall consumption [9,11].

The development of data-driven models focused on energy disaggregation has provided the capacity to extract detailed information. One kind of these models is known as *Non-Intrusive Load Monitoring* (NILM), where the energy consumption of a facility (commonly residential) is decomposed by estimating the energy demands of specific appliances using only the measurements from the main energy demand. In contrast to other intrusive methods, NILM is able to provide complete energy disaggregation using few measuring devices and, therefore, reducing costs and complexity.

Different solutions for NILM systems have been reviewed in the literature [2,28], mainly using real electrical power data from public datasets [18,21]. Firstly, signatures on total consumption were defined in the seminal work of Hart [14] focusing on transitions between steady-states through finite state machines. Later, other techniques based on *Hidden Markov Models* (HMM) [20] were applied, achieving acceptable results while suffering limitations in computing models for several appliances that include multiple operating states. These results have been remarkably improved thanks to the advancement of *Deep Neural Networks* (DNN) [17,25]. Examples of these architectures are *recurrent neural networks* [19,22], *convolutional neural networks* [5,13] or *denoising autoencoders* [4,13] which are able to extract individual energy consumption accurately. Nevertheless, a set of trained networks are required to disaggregate each individual consumption separately so that the design and computation of these models can be difficult to deploy in complex facilities.

However, it is not only the performance of NILM models that is relevant but also the interpretation of their outcome since they facilitate users to improve the overall efficiency by reducing energy waste thanks to the knowledge gained from NILM feedback [3,31]. In this sense, several solutions have emerged allowing the user to interact with the outcome of NILM models in interactive data visualizations [1,12,29]. Although users are able to manipulate the visualizations and select the sequences of total consumption to be disaggregated, fluid interaction pathways which modulate the behavior of NILM models according to the user's intentions are not commonly supported.

In this article, an alternative perspective of DNN-based NILM models is proposed, where a multi-task approach based on conditioned *Fully Convolutional denoising AutoEncoder* (FCN-dAE) is used to estimate several individual consumptions using a single network, instead of training a DNN model per individual consumption to be disaggregated. The suggested multi-task approach allows users to steer the intermediate activations of the network according to the target individual consumption indicated by a conditioning input. Special layers based on *feature-wise linear modulation* (FiLM) [27] are integrated in our model in order to modulate the intermediate activations from the conditioning input. The multi-task NILM approach allows a fluid integration of the user's intentions in the analysis by steering the energy disagregation model by means of the FiLM modulations and the conditioning input. This facilitates the integration of NILM into interactive applications and provide a more actionable and meaningful feedback to the user.

The remaining sections of the article are organized as follows: in Sect. 2, the DNN-based NILM models are defined; in Sect. 3, the conditioning paradigm and FiLM framework are presented; in Sect. 4, the FiLM approach is adapted to the NILM problem to define the proposed mul-titask FCN-dAE disaggregator; in Sect. 5, the performance, the computational efficiency and the interpretability of the proposed method are evaluated using real energy demand data from a hospital. Finally, the conclusions and future work are presented in Sect. 6.

2   DNN-based NILM Models

In the NILM problem, the disaggregation is computed from a sequence of the whole-facility energy consumption, which is commonly denoted as $\mathbf{P}$. This sequence is the sum of all the appliance-specific loads in the facility:

$$\mathbf{P} = \sum_{m=1}^{N} \mathbf{p}_m \tag{1}$$

where $\mathbf{p}_m$ represents a sequence —with the same length as $\mathbf{P}$— from the m-th individual load and N is equal to the number of individual consumptions of the facility. An *energy disaggregator* D_m is a function that extracts the m-th individual energy consumption from $\mathbf{P}$:

$$D_m : \mathbf{P} \rightarrow \hat{\mathbf{p}}_m \tag{2}$$

Most approaches estimate individual consumptions by means of a set of N disaggregators $\{D_m\}$ $m = 1, 2, \dots, N$. Complex DNN models have been recently proposed as suitable energy disaggregation functions D_m in the literature [4,5,13,16].

All the aforementioned models rely on a previous *windowing operation* that divides the whole sequence of total energy consumption (daily/monthly sequence) into smaller input sequences. This operation is defined by the window length L and the stride M between contiguous windows. The performance of the resulting disaggregators is notably affected by M and L, as they determine the amount of context used to train the energy disaggregators.

Once the windowing operation is applied, the resulting training windows of total and individual consumptions $\{\mathbf{P}^{(i)}, \mathbf{p}_m^{(i)}\}$ are used to minimize the reconstruction loss function $\mathcal{L}$ in order to optimize the parameters θ of the architecture:

$$\theta^* = \arg\min_{\theta} \frac{1}{n} \sum_{i=1}^{n} \mathcal{L}\big(\mathbf{p}_m^{(i)}, D_m(\mathbf{P}^{(i)}, \theta)\big) = \arg\min_{\theta} \frac{1}{n} \sum_{i=1}^{n} \mathcal{L}\big(\mathbf{p}_m^{(i)}, \hat{\mathbf{p}}_m^{(i)}\big) \qquad (3)$$

where $\hat{\mathbf{p}}_m^{(i)}$ is the estimated individual consumption sequence for the i-th training sample and θ^* the optimized weights. Reconstruction error functions, such as RMSE or MSE, are often employed as loss functions in DNN-based NILM models.

After training, each disaggregator D_m estimates individual sequence $\hat{\mathbf{p}}_m$ from a sequence of total consumption $\mathbf{P}$. In practice, this approach entails excessive memory usage and long latencies in the analysis because a total of N DNN-based models must be loaded and executed to obtain all individual consumptions. In addition, interacting with the model, beyond varying the input sequence, is not straightforward.

3   Conditioning Mechanisms for NILM

Recent conditioning techniques for DNN-based models [7,15] can be integrated into the aforementioned NILM models to enhance their computational efficiency and to make them steerable by users. These techniques are able to modulate the intermediate activations of a DNN-based model by means of an auxiliary input or *conditioning input*. Thus, energy disaggregators D_m can be conditioned by adding a user-driven input S_D, as it is shown in Fig. 1.

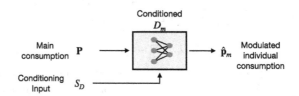

Fig. 1. Conditioning for energy disaggregation.

The intermediate layers are commonly modulated by simple functions such as *biasing* [24], *scaling* [6,15] or *affine* [7,8] transformations. In this regard, *Feature-wise Linear Modulation* (FiLM) [27] is a general-purpose framework to apply affine transformations for modulating the intermediate feature maps of convolution layers from the conditioning input. The affine transformations are applied by means of ad hoc FiLM layers distributed along the DNN to be modulated. The FiLM layer is defined as follows:

$$\text{FiLM}(\mathbf{F}_{j,k}^{(i)}) = \gamma_{j,k}^{(i)} \mathbf{F}_{j,k}^{(i)} + \beta_{j,k}^{(i)} \qquad (4)$$

where the feature map of the j-th convolutional layer and the k-th channel $\mathbf{F}_{j,k}^{(i)}$ computed from i-th input sample is scaled and shifted by means of the parameters $\gamma_{j,k}$ and $\beta_{j,k}$. All $\boldsymbol{\gamma}_j$ and $\boldsymbol{\beta}_j$ corresponding to all FiLM layers are computed from the conditioning input S_D by the functions f_c and h_c, respectively:

$$\boldsymbol{\gamma}_j^{(i)} = f_c(S_D^{(i)}) \qquad \boldsymbol{\beta}_j^{(i)} = h_c(S_D^{(i)}) \tag{5}$$

In practice, an auxiliary neural network or *FiLM generator* is used to approximate f_c and h_c from the conditioning information S_D —both are computed by the same network with two outputs—. The FiLM framework has been able to meaningfully modulate neural networks in complex tasks, such as visual reasoning [27], by adding only a small amount of extra parameters to the main model. Note that FiLM modulations only need two parameters per channel to be conditioned, so that they are independent from the input size and, more importantly, a complete retraining of the network is not necessary in order to change its outcome according to the user's intentions.

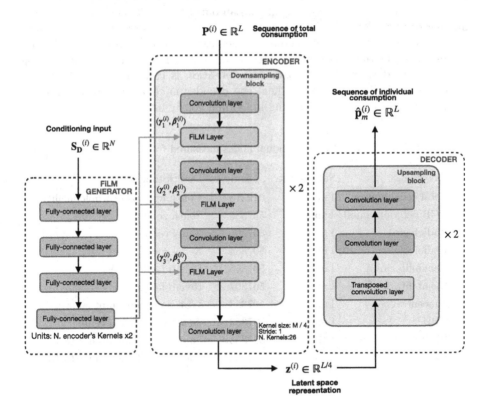

Fig. 2. Multi-task FCN-dAE architecture.

4   Multi-task Fully-Convolutional Denoising Autoencoder

Following the FiLM framework, we propose the conditioned DNN-based model shown in Fig. 2. The conditioned DNN model is based on the architecture *fully-convolutional denoising autoencoder* (FCN-dAE) proposed in [13] and conditioning information S_D is the target individual load to be disaggregated, indicated by the user, thus addressing the NILM problem as a multi-task problem. In the resulting multi-task FCN-dAE (multi FCN-dAE), the estimation of the N individual loads is no longer performed by a set of functions $\{D_m\}$, but a single conditioned NILM model D is able to compute the whole disaggregations.

The target individual consumption should be indicated in S_D using an interpretable format to the user. In this case, the target consumption is specified as a one-hot encoding vector, but more complex formats of S_D, such as attributes related to the individual consumption (e.g., location, type of consumption or any prior knowledge) are also appropriate. Once the S_D is introduced in the model, all the FiLM parameters (γ_j and β_j) are computed by a FiLM generator made of three fully-connected layers and an output fully-connected layer with a number of units equal to the number of affine parameters required.

The computed FiLM parameters are then used for the FiLM layers that modulates all the feature maps of the encoder of the main network. By modulating only the encoder, the latent space representation is conditioned to the target consumption indicated in S_D. Then, the decoder is capable of reconstructing each subspace to the corresponding individual consumption.

Table 1. Description of the individual nodes measured from the hospital facility.

Meter	Sample rate	#samples	Description
Total consumption	1 min	519278	Consumptions of whole facility
CGBT-2.Montante0	1 min	507353	South zone lifts
Radiologia1	1 min	507305	X-ray room 1
Radiologia2	1 min	507354	X-ray room 2
RehabilitacionA	1 min	507355	Rehab facilities A
RehabilitacionB	1 min	507307	Rehab facilities B
Subcentral3	1 min	507353	West zone consumption
CPD	1 min	507353	Server and a data center
Plantas_2-7	1 min	507353	South zone floor from 2 to 7
Plantas_8-13	1 min	507355	South zone floor from 8 to 13

5   Results

The multi-task FCN-dAE approach is evaluated by comparing its performance with other state-of-the-art NILM architectures, such as *denoising AutoEncoders*

[17], *biLSTM* [16] and vanilla FCN-dAE [13]. These models are applied to an non-residential NILM dataset from a hospital complex [13], where the total energy consumption was measured together with 9 individual consumptions. Further details about the measurements of the individual nodes are described in Table 1.

All the models were trained using pairs of sequences of total and individual consumptions $\{\mathbf{P}, \mathbf{p}_m\}$ with length of 1440 minutes ($L = 1440$). For training the proposed multi-task FCN-dAE, the one-hot vectors S_D are also attached to the training sequences. User-defined parameters related to the main architecture (number of layers, number of kernels, initialization, etc.) are the same as the initial FCN-dAE work, except for the latent space dimension which had to be increased to improve the training error. On the other hand, the parameters related to the FiLM generator network were manually adjusted to those that provided the best training error.

After training, the individual consumptions estimated by all the architectures using 1-month test sequence are compared in Table 2, using the MAE and RMSE reconstruction metrics [26].

Table 2. Comparison of disaggregation performance between sequence-to-sequence models and *multi-task FCN-dAE*.

		biLSTM	dAE	FCN-dAE	multi-FCN-dAE
MAE	CGBT-2.Montante0	2.9095	**2.4863**	2.5609	3.2711
	Radiologia1	8.2969	7.0405	**5.9346**	7.3891
	Radiologia2	3.3974	3.1002	**2.7061**	3.2705
	RehabilitacionA	1.4721	**1.2164**	1.2789	1.5251
	RehabilitacionB	3.8967	3.0455	**2.8464**	3.7287
	Subcentral3	2.7142	2.5553	**2.552**	3.3734
	CPD	4.2315	4.3056	3.9156	**2.6909**
	Plantas_2-7	2.4502	2.4512	**2.109**	3.6736
	Plantas_8-13	2.3686	2.5463	**2.0707**	4.5218
RMSE	CGBT-2.Montante0	5.2149	3.5161	**3.4271**	5.318
	Radiologia1	11.6352	9.8098	**8.771**	10.8085
	Radiologia2	6.0392	5.6539	**5.3551**	5.7545
	RehabilitacionA	2.1273	**1.648**	1.6881	2.0971
	RehabilitacionB	6.4429	4.0777	**3.7579**	5.4655
	Subcentral3	3.5735	3.2491	**3.2287**	4.195
	CPD	4.6070	4.6968	4.3564	**3.1575**
	Plantas_2-7	3.1213	3.0926	**2.7183**	4.5093
	Plantas_8-13	3.0489	3.1191	**2.6963**	4.9767

Considering that the proposed multi-task FCN-dAE is built using one network, the performance is close to other methods which use several networks (one disaggregator per each node). Although the DNN-based model using the same baseline (FCN-dAE) architecture shows better overall errors, a comparison of graphical representations of individual nodes extracted, shown in Fig. 3, expose competitive results for the disaggregation of the multi-FCN-dAE method.

Regarding the computational efficiency, the trainable weights of the DNN-based models are shown in Fig. 4a, where the proposed multi-FCN-dAE model needs significantly fewer trainable weights than the rest of architectures. Note that the values shown for the rest of models correspond to the total trainable weights of the set of networks $\{D_m\}$ needed to compute all the individual nodes.

The inference time of predicting the output individual consumption sequence is shown in Fig. 4b, where the proposed model is faster than biLSTM but it is slightly slower than the vanilla FCN-dAE and dAE models. However, it is fast enough (around 20 milliseconds) to consider a change in S_D as a fluid mechanism of interaction [10].

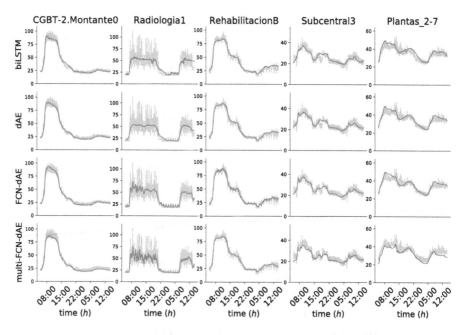

Fig. 3. Several disaggregated individual consumption (blue line) from the hospital complex computed using different DNN-based models compared to ground truth consumptions (gray line). (Color figure online)

5.1   Interpretation of Conditioning Mechanisms

The FiLM conditioning mechanism included in our multi-task FCN-dAE approach is able to adaptively modulate the encoder feature maps according to the target individual consumption, by focusing its attention on those feature maps more related to the target consumption. This modulation is not discrete, but in $\mathbf{S}_D^{(i)}$, one can set *continuous transitions* by drawing trajectories between individual nodes. Figure 5a shows several examples of continuous transitions obtained after introducing the same window $\mathbf{P}^{(i)}$ to the model and several points of a trajectory between two target one-hot encodings in $\mathbf{S}_D$. These transitions insightfully reveal to the user which changes should be applied to the starting individual node to turn it into the end node. This idea is tightly connected to the field of *explainable machine learning*, specially with counterfactual examples [30], since the proposed model is able to reveal which learned features make two sequences from individual nodes different.

The FiLM layer in the encoder also modulates the latent space representation $\mathbf{z}$ on the FCN-dAE latent space — see Fig. 2. In Fig. 5b, $\mathbf{z}$ representation of 300 sequences of main consumptions (each of them conditioned for all available individual nodes) are displayed after being processed by the *Uniform Manifold Approximation and Projection* (UMAP) [23] to visualize a 2D map of the latent space. The UMAP view reveals that the FiLM conditioning divides the latent space into node-specific subspaces, from which the decoder reconstructs the target individual consumption. The location of node-specific clusters in the view also seems to be meaningful, as similar nodes are projected together, and those nodes that are different between each other are mapped aside —see CPD node.

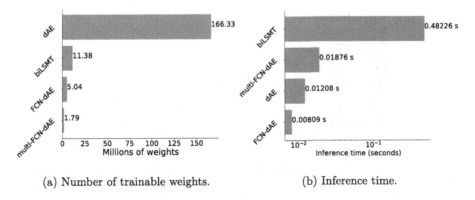

(a) Number of trainable weights.   (b) Inference time.

Fig. 4. Comparison of computational efficiency between suggested multi-task FCN-dAE and sequence-to-sequence DNN-based models.

(a)

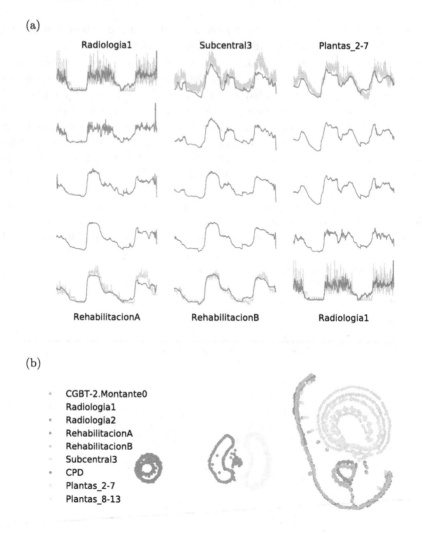

Fig. 5. Interpretability of multi-task FCN-dAE model. (a) Examples of transitions between two individual nodes. (b) UMAP projections of the latent space representation.

6   Conclusions

A conditioned fully convolutional neural network is proposed including an auxiliary input to introduce the condition for the extraction of one specific consumption through *Feature-wise Linear Modulation* technique. This reduces complexity with respect to previous models because of the use of a single conditioned NILM model modulated by determined conditions instead of a network per individual consumption.

Performance is compared between several DNN-based NILM methods using data from a non-residential facility like a hospital complex. The results of the multi-task method are competitive with respect to the rest of models using different specific networks. Moreover, computational efficiency is compared through the number of trainable weights and inference time, showing admissible times to process the output. This reduction of the complexity and computational costs allow the model to be used interactively in an eventual interactive application in order to integrate the user into the analysis loop and thus enhance feedback.

Future work includes the consideration of different types of inputs in auxiliary network for the modulation, the integration into an interactive interface, the effect of the conditioning on the number of training data required for proper training and the study of the generalization capabilities between facilities.

Acknowledgement. This work was supported by the Ministerio de Ciencia e Innovación/Agencia Estatal de Investigación (MCIN/AEI/ 10.13039/501100011033) under grants PID2020-115401GB-I00 and PID2020-117890RB-I00. Data were provided by Hospital of León and SUPPRESS Research Group of University of León within the project DPI2015-69891-C2-1/2-R.

References

1. Aboulian, A., et al.: NILM dashboard: a power system monitor for electromechanical equipment diagnostics. IEEE Trans. Ind. Inf. **15**(3), 1405–1414 (2018)
2. Angelis, G.F., Timplalexis, C., Krinidis, S., Ioannidis, D., Tzovaras, D.: NILM applications: literature review of learning approaches, recent developments and challenges. Energy Build., 111951 (2022)
3. Barker, S., Kalra, S., Irwin, D., Shenoy, P.: NILM redux: the case for emphasizing applications over accuracy. In: NILM-2014 Workshop. Citeseer (2014)
4. Bonfigli, R., Felicetti, A., Principi, E., Fagiani, M., Squartini, S., Piazza, F.: Denoising autoencoders for non-intrusive load monitoring: improvements and comparative evaluation. Energy Build. **158**, 1461–1474 (2018)
5. Chen, K., Zhang, Y., Wang, Q., Hu, J., Fan, H., He, J.: Scale-and context-aware convolutional non-intrusive load monitoring. IEEE Trans. Power Syst. **35**(3), 2362–2373 (2019)
6. Dhingra, B., Liu, H., Yang, Z., Cohen, W.W., Salakhutdinov, R.: Gated-attention readers for text comprehension. arXiv preprint arXiv:1606.01549 (2016)
7. Dumoulin, V., et al.: Feature-wise transformations. Distill (2018). https://doi.org/10.23915/distill.00011, https://distill.pub/2018/feature-wise-transformations
8. Dumoulin, V., Shlens, J., Kudlur, M.: A learned representation for artistic style. arXiv preprint arXiv:1610.07629 (2016)
9. Ehrhardt-Martinez, K., Donnelly, K.A., Laitner, S., et al.: Advanced metering initiatives and residential feedback programs: a meta-review for household electricity-saving opportunities. American Council for an Energy-Efficient Economy Washington, DC (2010)
10. Elmqvist, N., Moere, A.V., Jetter, H.C., Cernea, D., Reiterer, H., Jankun-Kelly, T.: Fluid interaction for information visualization. Inf. Vis. **10**(4), 327–340 (2011)
11. Gans, W., Alberini, A., Longo, A.: Smart meter devices and the effect of feedback on residential electricity consumption: evidence from a natural experiment in Northern Ireland. Energy Econ. **36**, 729–743 (2013)

12. García, D., Díaz, I., Pérez, D., Cuadrado, A.A., Domínguez, M., Morán, A.: Interactive visualization for NILM in large buildings using non-negative matrix factorization. Energy Build. **176**, 95–108 (2018)
13. Garcia-Perez, D., Perez-Lopez, D., Diaz-Blanco, I., Gonzalez-Muniz, A., Dominguez-Gonzalez, M., Vega, A.A.C.: Fully-convolutional denoising autoencoders for NILM in large non-residential buildings. IEEE Trans. Smart Grid **12**(3), 2722–2731 (2020)
14. Hart, G.W.: Nonintrusive appliance load monitoring. Proc. IEEE **80**(12), 1870–1891 (1992)
15. Hu, J., Shen, L., Sun, G.: Squeeze-and-excitation networks. In: Proceedings of the IEEE Conference on Computer Vision and Pattern Recognition, pp. 7132–7141 (2018)
16. Kaselimi, M., Doulamis, N., Voulodimos, A., Protopapadakis, E., Doulamis, A.: Context aware energy disaggregation using adaptive bidirectional LSTM models. IEEE Trans. Smart Grid **11**(4), 3054–3067 (2020)
17. Kelly, J., Knottenbelt, W.: Neural NILM: deep neural networks applied to energy disaggregation. In: Proceedings of the 2nd ACM International Conference on Embedded Systems for Energy-Efficient Built Environments, pp. 55–64 (2015)
18. Kelly, J., Knottenbelt, W.: The UK-DALE dataset, domestic appliance-level electricity demand and whole-house demand from five UK homes. Scientific data **2**(1), 1–14 (2015)
19. Kim, J., Le, T., Kim, H.: Noninstrusive load monitoring based on advanced deep learning and novel signature. Comput. Intell. Neurosci. **2017**, 4216281–4216281 (2017)
20. Kolter, J.Z., Jaakkola, T.: Approximate inference in additive factorial HMMs with application to energy disaggregation. In: Artificial Intelligence and Statistics, pp. 1472–1482 (2012)
21. Makonin, S., Ellert, B., Bajic, I.V., Popowich, F.: Electricity, water, and natural gas consumption of a residential house in Canada from 2012 to 2014. Scientific Data **3**(160037), 1–12 (2016)
22. Mauch, L., Yang, B.: A new approach for supervised power disaggregation by using a deep recurrent LSTM network. In: 2015 IEEE Global Conference on Signal and Information Processing (GlobalSIP), pp. 63–67. IEEE (2015)
23. McInnes, L., Healy, J., Melville, J.: Umap: Uniform manifold approximation and projection for dimension reduction. arXiv preprint arXiv:1802.03426 (2018)
24. Mirza, M., Osindero, S.: Conditional generative adversarial nets. arXiv preprint arXiv:1411.1784 (2014)
25. do Nascimento, P.P.M.: Applications of deep learning techniques on NILM. Diss. Universidade Federal do Rio de Janeiro (2016)
26. Pereira, L., Nunes, N.: Performance evaluation in non-intrusive load monitoring: datasets, metrics, and tools-a review. Wiley Interdisciplinary Reviews: data mining and knowledge discovery **8**(6), e1265 (2018)
27. Perez, E., Strub, F., De Vries, H., Dumoulin, V., Courville, A.: Film: visual reasoning with a general conditioning layer. In: Thirty-Second AAAI Conference on Artificial Intelligence (2018)
28. Schirmer, P.A., Mporas, I.: Non-Intrusive load monitoring: a review. IEEE Transactions on Smart Grid (2022)
29. Völker, B., Pfeifer, M., Scholl, P.M., Becker, B.: A versatile high frequency electricity monitoring framework for our future connected home. In: Afonso, J.L., Monteiro, V., Pinto, J.G. (eds.) SESC 2019. LNICST, vol. 315, pp. 221–231. Springer, Cham (2020). https://doi.org/10.1007/978-3-030-45694-8_17

30. Wang, Z., Samsten, I., Mochaourab, R., Papapetrou, P.: Learning time series coun-terfactuals via latent space representations. In: Soares, C., Torgo, L. (eds.) DS 2021. LNCS (LNAI), vol. 12986, pp. 369–384. Springer, Cham (2021). https://doi.org/10.1007/978-3-030-88942-5_29

31. Zhuang, M., Shahidehpour, M., Li, Z.: An overview of non-intrusive load moni-toring: approaches, business applications, and challenges. In: 2018 International Conference on Power System Technology (POWERCON), pp. 4291–4299. IEEE (2018)

Principal Component Modes of Reservoir Dynamics in Reservoir Computing

José María Enguita[1]([✉])[iD], Ignacio Díaz[1][iD], Diego García[1][iD],
Abel Alberto Cuadrado[1][iD], and José Ramón Rodríguez[2][iD]

[1] Department of Electrical Engineering, University of Oviedo, 33204 Gijón, Spain
{jmenguita,idiaz,garciaperdiego,cuadradoabel}@uniovi.es
[2] SUPPRESS Research Group, University of León, 24007 León, Spain
jrodro@unileon.es
http://isa.uniovi.es/GSDPI/

Abstract. In Reservoir Computing, signals or sequences are fed into a set of interconnected non-linear units (neurons) with capabilities for storing information (reservoir). The reservoir generates an expanded representation of the input, which is subsequently mapped onto the desired output using a trained output layer (readout). However, despite their success in various experimental tasks, the dynamics of the reservoir are not yet well understood. In this paper we introduce a new technique, based on the well known Singular Value Decomposition (SVD), to obtain the main dynamic modes of the reservoir when excited with an input signal. We conduct experiments using Echo State Networks (ESN) to demonstrate the technique's potential and its ability to decompose input signals into Principal Component Modes as expanded by the reservoir. We expect that this approach will open new possibilities in its application to the field of visual analytics in process state visualisation, determination of attribute vectors, and detection of novelties. Furthermore, this technique could serve as a foundation for a better understanding of the reservoir's dynamic state that could help in other areas of research, such as domain shift or continual learning.

Keywords: Reservoir Computing · Echo State Networks · Reservoir Dynamics · Singular Value Decomposition · Visual Analytics

1   Introduction

1.1   Reservoir Computing

Reservoir computing (RC) is a computational framework based on *Recurrent Neural Network* (RNN) models which extends the concept of earlier neural network architectures such as Liquid-State Machines and Echo State Networks [15]. RC is highly effective for processing sequential or temporal data, such as the behaviour of dynamic systems or time series. The input signals are fed into a set

© IFIP International Federation for Information Processing 2023
Published by Springer Nature Switzerland AG 2023
I. Maglogiannis et al. (Eds.): AIAI 2023 Workshops, IFIP AICT 677, pp. 434–445, 2023.
https://doi.org/10.1007/978-3-031-34171-7_35

of interconnected neurons, referred to as the 'reservoir', which generates a high-dimensional expansion [13]. The reservoir contains feedback (recurrent) loops that provide memory and exhibits a complex and highly non-linear dynamic behaviour [9]. A simple readout system is trained to map the internal state of the reservoir to the desired output.

RC systems offer a key advantage over other recurrent neural networks in that they simplify the learning process. Specifically, as the reservoir remains fixed, only the readout layer is trained. This method requires a simple least-squares estimation rather than the more expensive and computationally intensive non-linear optimisation required to train an RNN, reducing the computational cost and facilitating rapid learning. Remarkably, the forecasting capability of RC systems can still be competitive even when dealing with chaotic or spatio-temporally complex problems [1].

Despite all the very convincing experimental results on a variety of tasks, a thorough understanding of the dynamics of the reservoir is still lacking [16]. This contribution aims to extend this understanding by presenting a simple yet effective approach of characterising the reservoir dynamics by means of the *Singular-Value Decomposition* (SVD), which has already been effectively employed in various related applications such as identifying underlying patterns and detecting outliers in time series [10], configuring the weight matrix of a reservoir with specific spectral characteristics [11], and obtaining an optimal low-rank representation of a time series expanded by Dynamic Mode Decomposition [3,4]. In addition, Gallicchio et al. [6] used a similar approach to investigate redundancy in the reservoir.

Our proposal uses the SVD over the evolution in time of the activation values of the neurons in the reservoir when excited by an input signal. We show that this technique yields an interpretable description of the reservoir dynamics and provides a decomposition in terms of principal component modes in a lower-dimensional space.

2   Methods

2.1   Recurrent Neural Networks

Recurrent Neural Networks (RNNs) are rooted on the works by Rumelhart, Hinton and Williams [14] back in 1986. RNNs are a type of artificial neural network in which connections introduce a non-linear feedback by connecting the node outputs with their inputs, thus enabling the network to display temporal dynamic behaviour.

The evolution of the states of the hidden layer neurons $\mathbf{x}(k)$ and the output of the network $\mathbf{y}(k)$ for a given input signal $\mathbf{u}(k)$, follows:

$$\mathbf{x}(k) = f(\mathbf{x}(k-1), \mathbf{u}(k)) \qquad (1)$$
$$\mathbf{y}(k) = h(\mathbf{x}(k)).$$

where f and h are general functions, usually non-linear.

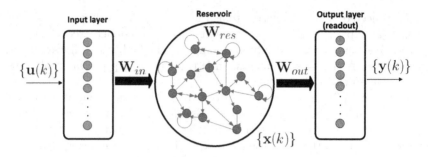

Fig. 1. Representation of an ESN.

2.2 Echo State Networks

Although the methods presented in this paper are general to reservoir computing systems, we implement the results on the well known *Echo State Networks* (ESN) architecture. Nevertheless, it should be easily adapted to other models.

Proposed by Jaeger and Hass back in the beginning of the 21st century [7–9], ESNs use an sparsely connected RNN with random weights as reservoir.

An ESN, in its basic form, allows the modelling of non-linear systems by supervised learning. ESNs, see Fig. 1, are a particular case of equation (1), based on the concept of *non-linear expansion* [13], in which we consider a high-dimensional state vector $\mathbf{x}(k) \in \mathbb{R}^n$, a non-linear model in the state equation and a linear model of the output obtained from the state[1]:

$$\mathbf{x}(k) = \sigma(\mathbf{W}_{res}\,\mathbf{x}(k-1) + \mathbf{W}_{in}\,\mathbf{u}(k)) \tag{2}$$
$$\mathbf{y}(k) = \mathbf{W}_{out}\,\mathbf{x}(k).$$

The model represented by equation (2) includes the reservoir matrix $\mathbf{W}_{res} \in \mathbb{R}^{n \times n}$, the input matrix $\mathbf{W}_{in} \in \mathbb{R}^{n \times p}$, and the output matrix $\mathbf{W}_{out} \in \mathbb{R}^{q \times n}$ as parameters. A non-linear function σ, typically sigmoidal, is used in the state equation, and sparsity is ensured in $\mathbf{W}_{res}$ using a small fraction of the possible feedback connections among nodes. The matrices $\mathbf{W}_{res}$ and $\mathbf{W}_{in}$ are generated with random values, with some modifications applied to bring the system to the edge of stability. Only the matrix $\mathbf{W}_{out}$ is learned to reproduce specific time patterns.

In order for the ESN network to work, the reservoir must satisfy the *echo state property*. This property links the asymptotic characteristics of the excited reservoir dynamics to the driving signal, so that the initial state of the reservoir

---

[1] The original version is given here. Numerous variants exist in the literature incorporating, for example, a bias term added to $\mathbf{u}(k)$, direct effect of $\mathbf{u}(k)$ on the output, feedback term (inclusion of $\mathbf{y}(k)$) in the equation of state, application of a low-pass filter to the states, use of non-linear regression models to obtain $\mathbf{y}(k)$ from $\mathbf{x}(k)$, etc. A detailed description of many of these variants can be found in [12].

is asymptotically 'washed out'. This property is satisfied, for additive-sigmoid neuron reservoirs, if the spectral radius ρ of the reservoir matrix (maximum of the absolute value of its eigenvalues) is less than 1 [2], although some authors reported good results with spectral radius slightly over this value [12].

In the above equations, both $\mathbf{u}(k)$ and $\mathbf{y}(k)$ are vectors because multiple inputs and outputs can be considered. However, to keep the notation simpler and without loss of generality, we will restrict to only single-input and single-output systems for the rest of the paper, so that $\mathbf{y}$ and $\mathbf{u}$ are time series, $u(k)$, $y(k)$ are elements of each series, and $\mathbf{W}_{out} \in \mathbb{R}^{1 \times n}$.

2.3 Analysis of the Reservoir Dynamics

By applying the model in equation (2) recursively, an input or excitation sequence $\mathbf{u}$ generates a sequence of state vectors containing the activation values of the n neurons of the reservoir, $\mathbf{x}(k)$ which, for the case of m samples, can be grouped in a matrix:

$$\mathbf{X} \in \mathbb{R}^{n \times m} = \begin{pmatrix} | & | & & | \\ \mathbf{x}(1) & \mathbf{x}(2) & \cdots & \mathbf{x}(m) \\ | & | & & | \end{pmatrix}. \tag{3}$$

The rows of the matrix $\mathbf{X}$ contain the temporal evolution of the reservoir with a great richness and variety of dynamic behaviours as a response to an input signal. Each state vector $\mathbf{x}(k)$ can be considered an expanded set of descriptors of the dynamics of the input signal at instant k.

In this work, we propose to analyse the dynamics of the reservoir through the SVD of the matrix $\mathbf{X}$:

$$\mathbf{X} = \mathbf{U}\Sigma\mathbf{V}^T = \sigma_1 \mathbf{u}_1 \mathbf{v}_1^T + \ldots \sigma_n \mathbf{u}_n \mathbf{v}_n^T, \tag{4}$$

where $\mathbf{u}_i$ is the i-th column of matrix $\mathbf{U}$, $\mathbf{v}_i^T$ is the i-th row of matrix $\mathbf{V}^T$.

Singular values $\sigma_1, \sigma_2, \ldots, \sigma_n$ represent the weights of the principal modes of $\mathbf{X}$, and may be used as descriptors of the dynamic evolution of the reservoir, when excited by the input signal.

The columns of $\mathbf{U}$ are the eigenvectors of $\mathbf{X}\mathbf{X}^T$, the columns of $\mathbf{V}$ are the eigenvectors of $\mathbf{X}^T\mathbf{X}$. As they are ordered by decreasing values of σ_i, the columns of $\mathbf{U}$ and $\mathbf{V}$ are hierarchically ordered according to the correlation they capture from the columns and rows of $\mathbf{X}$. That's why the former captures the *spatial* correlation (across the n components of the state vector) and the latter the *temporal* correlation (across the m time steps). Both are orthonormal bases for the space to which the columns and rows of $\mathbf{X}$ belong, respectively.

If we select only the r-first singular values, an approximation of $\mathbf{X}$ can be obtained as $\tilde{\mathbf{X}} = \mathbf{U}_r \Sigma_r \mathbf{V}_r^T$. In fact, this is the best rank-r approximation of $\mathbf{X}$ in the L_2-sense, and it provides a reduced-order latent space in which to study the dynamic evolution of the reservoir when the system is excited with an input signal $\mathbf{u}$.

This space can also be projected onto a lower dimension space, such as 2D, for visualisation purposes. This enables enhanced analysis and interpretation of the system's behaviour over time.

2.4   Principal Component Modes

It should be noted that, thus far, the ESN can be analysed for its dynamic behaviour without the need for training. However, a trained ESN can offer interesting possibilities. According to the SVD, in line with (4), the matrix $\mathbf{X}$ can be decomposed in $\mathbf{X}_i = \mathbf{u}_i \sigma_i \mathbf{v}_i^T$, so that $\mathbf{X} = \sum_i \mathbf{X}_i$. The target time series $\mathbf{y}$ is approximated by the ESN using $\mathbf{W}_{out}$ as:

$$\mathbf{y} \approx \mathbf{W}_{out} \mathbf{X} = \mathbf{W}_{out} \sum_i \mathbf{u}_i \sigma_i \mathbf{v}_i^T = \sum_i \alpha_i \mathbf{v}_i^T = \sum_i \mathbf{m}_i, \tag{5}$$

where α_i are scalar values, since $\mathbf{W}_{out} \in \mathbb{R}^{1,n}$, $\mathbf{u}_i \in \mathbb{R}^{n,1}$, and σ_i is a scalar. In sum, taking $\alpha_i = \mathbf{W}_{out} \mathbf{u}_i \sigma_i$ we have that the target time series can be approximated as a sum of *modes* $\mathbf{m}_i$.

The decomposition can also be applied locally on sliding submatrices $\mathbf{X}(k) \in \mathbb{R}^{n \times m'}$, with the columns between k and $k + m' - 1$ of $\mathbf{X}$, to track the evolution of the reservoir when excited by the input signal. This allows to keep track of any variation in the modes $\mathbf{m}_i$, for instance, in process visual monitoring.

There are two primary configurations of operation depending on how the readout is trained:

1. **Autoencoder:** The ESN is trained using the input signal. Then, by utilising the trained readout, the input signal can be decomposed into a hierarchy of dynamic modes as observed by the reservoir:

$$\mathbf{W}_{out}^{AE} = \arg \min_{\mathbf{W}} \|\mathbf{W}\mathbf{X} - \mathbf{u}\| \quad \text{and} \quad \mathbf{m}_i = \mathbf{W}_{out}^{AE} \mathbf{X}_i. \tag{6}$$

2. **Transcoder:** The ESN is trained using the output signal. In this scenario, it is the output signal which is decomposed into its dynamic modes:

$$\mathbf{W}_{out}^{TC} = \arg \min_{\mathbf{W}} \|\mathbf{W}\mathbf{X} - \mathbf{y}\| \quad \text{and} \quad \mathbf{m}_i = \mathbf{W}_{out}^{TC} \mathbf{X}_i. \tag{7}$$

3   Results and Discussion

3.1   Second Order System

In this experiment we simulate a generic second order system:

$$\frac{d^2 y(t)}{dt^2} + 2\zeta\omega_n \frac{dy(t)}{dt} + \omega_n^2 y(t) = K\omega_n^2 u(t), \tag{8}$$

with gain $K = 1$, damping ratio $\zeta = 0.5$ (underdamped) and natural frequency $\omega_n = 1$, for 1200 s seconds. Figure 2 shows an example of hierarchical decomposition in transcoder configuration of the main principal components. The system

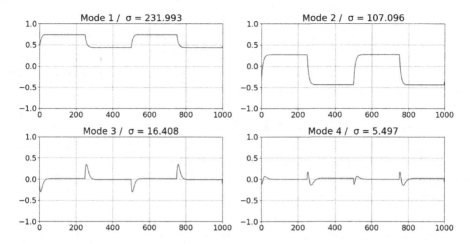

Fig. 2. Plot of the first 4 modes $(\mathbf{m}_1, \ldots, \mathbf{m}_4)$ in which the response of the system to a square signal is decomposed by the ESN. X-axis is time in seconds.

is excited with a square signal and the output is used to train an ESN with 300 neurons in the hidden layer[2]. Figure 3 shows the reconstruction of the output using the first modes in the decomposition.

To analyse the possibilities for local decomposition and tracking, the damping ratio is varied, taking the values 0.2, 0.3, 0.4 and 0.5 during 300 s each. The response to a square signal is shown in Fig. 4.

An ESN is fed with this response signal using a sliding window of size $m' = 800$ samples and a stride value of 20 samples (as we are analysing the reservoir only, the readout doesn't need to be trained). As the ESN has $n = 300$ neurons in its hidden layer, the signal is decomposed into 300 modes, corresponding to the nonzero singular values $\sigma_1, \ldots, \sigma_{300}$, at each step. Projecting these 300-dimensional vectors of singular values into a 2D plot with a simple principal component analysis (PCA) algorithm, the trajectories in the latent space (from the high state of the square signal on the right, to its low state on the left) corresponding to each damping-ratio value can be clearly observed (see Fig. 5, left).

In this example, the input signal has a period of 500 samples. As the window size approaches that value, the trajectories become shorter and better separated until they collapse into 4 distinct positions in the projected map (see Fig. 5, right). Some transition dots still appear in the plot, corresponding to sections where the sliding window partially overlaps with the output of two different system states. These trajectories show the transitions between states, but are, in fact, an artefact of the sliding window mechanism.

---

[2] Other parameters are: $\rho = 0.95$, sparsity $= 0.01$, leaking rate $= 0.025$, input scaling $= 10$ and warm up $= 20$. A bias is added to the inputs.

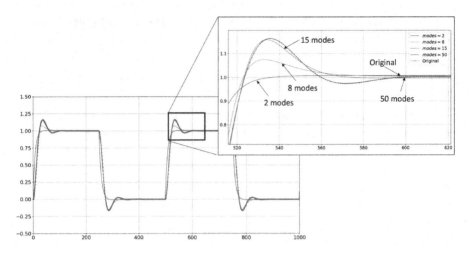

Fig. 3. Reconstruction of the response to a square signal by the ESN using the first 2, 8, 15 and 50 modes (x-axis is time in seconds). The original signal is marked with dots for better reference.

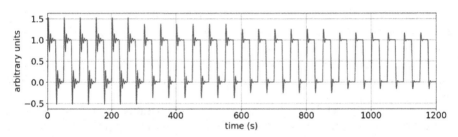

Fig. 4. Response to a square signal. The damping ratio is changed every 300 s, so that $\zeta = 0.2, 0.3, 0.4, 0.5$.

Thanks to the fact that each window corresponds to a single period of the signal, each stride of the window effectively performs a circular shift of the columns of the matrix $\mathbf{X}$. Any row permutation can be represented as $\mathbf{X}_{perm} = \mathbf{X}\mathbf{P}$, where $\mathbf{P}$ is a permutation matrix, therefore orthogonal. If $\mathbf{U}\Sigma\mathbf{V}^T$ is a valid SVD decomposition of $\mathbf{X}$, then $(\mathbf{U}\Sigma\mathbf{V}^T)\mathbf{P} = \mathbf{U}\Sigma(\mathbf{V}^T\mathbf{P})$ is a valid SVD decomposition of $\mathbf{X}_{perm}$. As a result, the singular values remain unchanged, and the rows of matrix $\mathbf{V}^T$ are permuted by $\mathbf{P}$. All values in both $\mathbf{V}^T$ and $\mathbf{U}$ that correspond to non zero singular values remain unaltered, except for a potential change in sign, as both matrices are real.

As a final note in this example, the magnitude of the main singular value, σ_1, can differentiate among the states of the system, as is shown in Fig. 6.

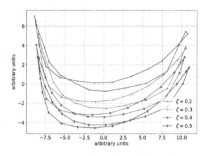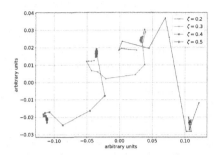

Fig. 5. Latent space trajectories projected to 2D for the different damping ratio values (both axis represent coordinates in the latent space). Left, with a sliding window of size 800 samples (high state of the input signal corresponds to the right and low state to the left). Right, the same trajectories with a window size equal to the period of the signal (500 samples). Four distinct positions, related to the four modes of the system, can be clearly seen.

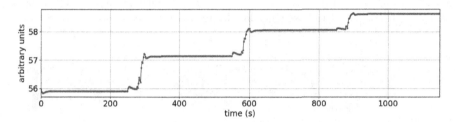

Fig. 6. Plot of the singular value σ_1 when the sliding window size equals the period of the signal. The different dynamics corresponding to different damping ratios can be clearly observed.

3.2 Dynamic Modes of Vibration Signals in an Induction Motor Under Test

For this experiment we used an available dataset [5] containing vibration and current data of a 4kW induction motor with 6306-2Z/C3 bearings that rotates at 1500 rpm (25 Hz) with a supply frequency 50 Hz. This machine has been subjected to nine different tests (Table 1), for which five operating variables have been measured at a sampling frequency of 5000 Hz Hz: three vibrations (measured as accelerations a_c, a_x and a_y) and two phase currents (i_R and i_S). We have selected the horizontal vibration (a_x) for this experiment.

The vibration data were fed into the same ESN as before, but with an input scaling factor of 1. Data were analysed with a sliding window with a length of 1000 samples, and a stride of 100 samples.

The projection of the singular values over a 2D space quickly showed the operation modes and the trajectories indicated how the system varied from one test to the next. This can be seen in Fig. 7. Tests 8 and 9 consisted in gradual variations from one electrical fault state to another, which can be seen in their

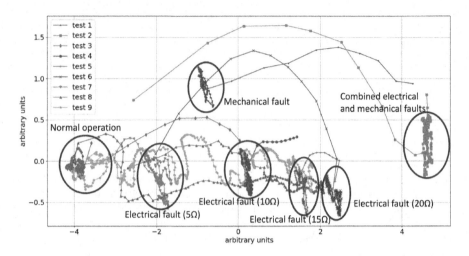

Fig. 7. Latent space trajectories projected to 2D. The different locations of the operational states in tests 1 to 7 were labelled for reference.

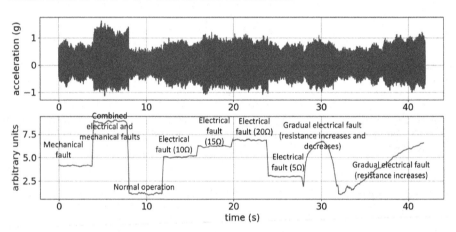

Fig. 8. Top: input signal from the horizontal accelerometer. Bottom: evolution of the singular value σ_2 throughout the tests.

respective trajectories. The former starts at normal operating mode, moves passing through all the electrical fault modes, and gets back to normal operation. The latter, however, starts from normal operation and just moves through all the electrical fault modes. A visual analytics application could help the user to keep track of the operation of the motor just by observing the trajectories. Moreover, the singular value σ_2 is able to differentiate between all the states (see Fig. 8), meaning it could be used for automatic fault diagnosis.

By training the ESN in autoencoder configuration, it is possible to decompose the vibration signal into Principal Component Modes. The result is shown in Fig. 9. A portion of the signal of 200 ms (which equals the used window size) is

Table 1. Description of performed tests.

Number	Performed test	Duration (s)
1	Mechanical fault (eccentric mass on pulley)	4
2	Combined electrical and mechanical fault	4
3	Normal operation	4
4	Electrical fault (15 Ω resistor in phase R)	4
5	Electrical fault (20 Ω resistor in phase R)	4
6	Electrical fault (25 Ω resistor in phase R)	4
7	Electrical fault (5 Ω resistor in phase R)	4
8	Gradual electrical fault (resistance increases and decreases)	4
9	Gradual electrical fault (gradual increase of resistance)	8

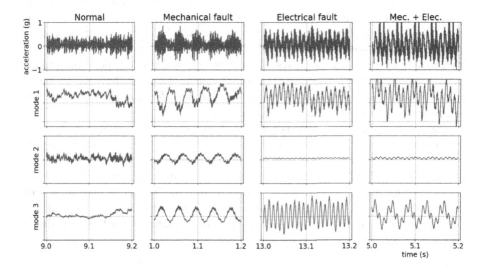

Fig. 9. First Principal Component Modes of the vibration for different tests. A section of 200 ms of the signal (the used window size) at each test segment is displayed. Modes have been centred for clarity.

shown along with the first three modes. Interestingly, mode 3 carries significant information about the vibration caused by each type of fault. It can be observed that mode 3 captures the most representative harmonics of each vibration state. In the case of a mechanical fault, a frequency 25 Hz originating from the eccentric mass is observed, whereas an electrical fault produces a 100 Hz harmonic as a result of electrical asymmetry. It is noteworthy that the combination of both electrical and mechanical faults yields similar proportions of the aforementioned harmonics.

4   Conclusion

The SVD decomposition of the temporal evolution of the reservoir provides valuable information about its dynamic evolution, creating a latent space of dimension $r \leq n$ that can be used to observe trajectories, search for attribute vectors, detect novelties, or project onto a visualisation space to apply visual analytics techniques. Unlike Fourier analysis, which uses an imposed basis of sine wave signals, the SVD performs a decomposition into *principal* components, those that contain the most energy, potentially resulting in more relevant and interpretable information.

This idea can be applied to quasi-periodic signals or variant systems, as long as the echo state property is fulfilled. This does not result in any additional restrictions, as such property must be fulfilled for the ESN to function properly.

Training the output layer of the network is not a requirement, however, if this layer is trained, it becomes possible to reconstruct the principal modes of the temporal series dynamics from the reservoir's perspective. Two different modes have been defined: the *autoencoder* configuration, where the network is trained with the input signal itself, and the *transcoder* configuration, where the network is trained to learn a dynamical system between the input excitation and a target output signal. In both cases, the obtained information can be used in multiple ways, such as searching for the principal modes for monitoring, predictive maintenance, or novelty detection in a process.

Although its main purpose is analytical, we believe that this technique can also serve as a basis for developing new methods that allow analysing the dynamic characteristics of the reservoir and determining its suitability for specific problems. Moreover, the location of the operating point in the latent space or the information obtained from certain principal modes can be used to address other research issues in this type of networks, such as domain shift or continual learning, both of which are topics of interest in the field of machine learning in general and in reservoir computing in particular.

Acknowledgements. This work was supported by the Ministerio de Ciencia e Innovación / Agencia Estatal de Investigación (MCIN/AEI/ 10.13039/ 501100011033) grant [PID2020-115401GB-I00].

References

1. Bollt, E.: On explaining the surprising success of reservoir computing forecaster of chaos? The universal machine learning dynamical system with contrast to VAR and DMD. Chaos: Interdisc. J. Nonlinear Sci. **31**, 013108 (2021). https://doi.org/10.1063/5.0024890. http://aip.scitation.org/doi/10.1063/5.0024890
2. Buehner, M., Young, P.: A tighter bound for the echo state property. IEEE Trans. Neural Netw. **17**, 820–824 (2006). https://doi.org/10.1109/TNN.2006.872357
3. Dylewsky, D., Barajas-Solano, D., Ma, T., Tartakovsky, A.M., Kutz, J.N.: Stochastically forced ensemble dynamic mode decomposition for forecasting and analysis of near-periodic systems. IEEE Access **10**, 33440–33448 (2022). https://doi.org/10.1109/ACCESS.2022.3161438

4. Dylewsky, D., Kaiser, E., Brunton, S.L., Kutz, J.N.: Principal component trajectories for modeling spectrally continuous dynamics as forced linear systems. Phys. Rev. E **105**, 015312 (2022). https://doi.org/10.1103/PHYSREVE.105. 015312/FIGURES/10/MEDIUM. https://journals.aps.org/pre/abstract/10.1103/ PhysRevE.105.015312

5. Díaz Blanco, I., Cuadrado Vega, A.A., Muñiz, A.G., García Pérez, D.: Dataicann: datos de vibración y corriente de un motor de inducción. https://digibuo.uniovi. es/dspace/handle/10651/53461 (2019)

6. Gallicchio, C., Micheli, A.: A Markovian characterization of redundancy in echo state networks by PCA. In: Proceedings of the 18th European Symposium on Artificial Neural Networks, Computational Intelligence and Machine Learning (ESANN-2010), pp. 321–326 (2010)

7. Jaeger, H.: The "echo state" approach to analysing and training recurrent neural networks. GMD Report 148, GMD - German National Research Institute for Computer Science (2001). http://www.faculty.jacobs-university.de/hjaeger/pubs/ EchoStatesTechRep.pdf

8. Jaeger, H.: Echo state network. Scholarpedia **2**(9), 2330 (2007)

9. Jaeger, H., Haas, H.: Harnessing nonlinearity: Predicting chaotic systems and saving energy in wireless communication. Science **304**, 78–80 2004). https://doi.org/ 10.1126/science.1091277. https://www.science.org/doi/10.1126/science.1091277

10. Khoshrou, A., Pauwels, E.J.: Data-driven pattern identification and outlier detection in time series. Adv. Intell. Syst. Comput. **858**, 471–484 (2018). https://doi. org/10.1007/978-3-030-01174-1-35. http://arxiv.org/abs/1807.03386

11. Li, F., Wang, X., Li, Y.: Effects of singular value spectrum on the performance of echo state network. Neurocomputing **358**, 414–423 (2019). https://doi. org/10.1016/j.neucom.2019.05.068. https://linkinghub.elsevier.com/retrieve/pii/ S092523121930774X

12. Lukoševičius, M.: A practical guide to applying echo state networks. In: Montavon, G., Orr, G.B., Müller, K.-R. (eds.) Neural Networks: Tricks of the Trade. LNCS, vol. 7700, pp. 659–686. Springer, Heidelberg (2012). https://doi.org/10.1007/978-3-642-35289-8_36

13. Lukoševičius, M., Jaeger, H.: Reservoir computing approaches to recurrent neural network training. Comput. Sci. Rev. **3**(3), 127–149 (2009)

14. Rumelhart, D.E., Hinton, G.E., Williams, R.J.: Learning representations by back-propagating errors. Nature **323**, 533–536 (1986). https://doi.org/10.1038/ 323533a0. https://www.nature.com/articles/323533a0

15. Tanaka, G., et al.: Recent advances in physical reservoir computing: a review. Neural Netw. **115**, 100–123 (2019). https://doi.org/10.1016/J.NEUNET.2019.03. 005

16. Verstraeten, D., Schrauwen, B.: On the quantification of dynamics in reservoir computing. In: Alippi, C., Polycarpou, M., Panayiotou, C., Ellinas, G. (eds.) ICANN 2009. LNCS, vol. 5768, pp. 985–994. Springer, Heidelberg (2009). https://doi.org/ 10.1007/978-3-642-04274-4_101

Visual Analytics Tools for the Study of Complex Problems in Engineering and Biomedicine

Ignacio Díaz$^{(\boxtimes)}$ (ID), José M. Enguita(ID), Abel A. Cuadrado(ID), Diego García(ID), and Ana González(ID)

Department of Electrical Engineering, University of Oviedo, Edificio Torres Quevedo, módulo 2, Campus de Gijón, Oviedo 33204, Spain
{idiaz,jmenguita,cuadradoabel,garciaperdiego,gonzalezmunana}@uniovi.es

Abstract. In this article, we present the main lines of an ongoing research project funded by the Spanish government. The project proposes research on visual analytics techniques for solving complex problems in engineering and biomedicine. We outline the characteristics of complex problems that make it difficult for machine learning approaches to tackle them. Next, we present the benefits of solutions that exploit the synergy between machine learning and data visualization through interactive mechanisms for solving such problems. Finally, we briefly present the approaches being worked on in this project to achieve the objectives and the results achieved so far. We hope that these ideas and approaches will serve as inspiration for other projects or applications in the field.

Keywords: Visual analytics · engineering applications · biomedicine

1 Introduction

Many problems today in the fields of biomedicine (genomics [1,26], epidemiological studies, analysis of clinical data [25], etc.) and engineering (complex systems with many sensors and data sources [2,40]) involve huge amounts of data, a large number of variables and a high complexity, with many factors influencing their behavior. Unlike classical approaches, based on first-principles models, data carry detailed and updated information and can be processed to produce models and useful knowledge. Machine learning (ML) algorithms allow the analysis of massive data, being able to surpass humans in well-defined tasks, such as the analysis of a tumor in an X-ray image or making a fault diagnosis of a bearing from vibration data. However, ML algorithms have significant limitations in many data analysis problems today. They are prone to error in the presence of minimal changes in context or the definition of the problem. Also, they are often

This work was supported by the Ministerio de Ciencia e Innovación / Agencia Estatal de Investigación (MCIN/AEI/ 10.13039/501100011033) grant [PID2020-115401GB-I00].

I. Maglogiannis et al. (Eds.): AIAI 2023 Workshops, IFIP AICT 677, pp. 446–457, 2023.
https://doi.org/10.1007/978-3-031-34171-7_36

"black box" models, making their integration with related domain knowledge difficult and being, in consequence, less reliable [42]. However, humans, although less precise, can work with poorly posed problems, perform well on a wide range of tasks, and are able to find connections and improve responses through an iterative and exploratory process. This suggests a "third way", based on the efficient use of interaction mechanisms between humans and ML algorithms to create hybrid "ML-human" problem-solving processes that can potentially allow a great improvement over "human" or "ML" only approaches.

Within this context, we need data analysis tools that allow a quick, effective and intuitive analysis about the behavior of the system under study (e.g., a disease, an epidemic, or an industrial process) in different scenarios, such as different medical treatments, clinical conditions, patient groups, or for different process parameters or setpoint values in the case of an industrial process, as well as to support decisions and the development of protocols. The tools developed must be easily reproducible, able to be implemented in a short time, applicable to new scenarios, and must be able to carry out a multilevel analysis which allows to move smoothly from a "big picture" of the problem, towards the detail and the obtaining of quantitative information. Finally, they should allow to be powered by ML algorithms, which can reveal hidden patterns in the data and be able to integrate that information in a visual and intuitive way.

1.1   Hypotheses

Complex Nature of Today's Problems. Complex problems arising in the analysis of biomedical data, including gene expression and clinical or epidemiological data, as well as in engineering fields such as industrial process supervision and energy efficiency management, are highly multifactorial and multidomain in nature, for which commonly we do not have a comprehensive understanding. This makes them problems that most often cannot be posed in terms of canned operations achievable by machine learning algorithms or other automated approaches alone, since most of the times a precise formulation is not available. The question, then, is how to pose them as closed problems since, once this is achieved, we can deploy powerful numerical methods to get precise answers.

Need of Human-ML Hybrid Approaches for Today's Challenges. As the complexity, size and dimensionality grows, the problem definition becomes a nontrivial task, requiring the combination of the user's expert knowledge with data analytics methods. Despite the fact that ML algorithms allow analysis of massive data, outperforming humans in well-defined tasks, they are prone to failure under changes in the context or the problem statement. At the same time, humans can perform well under ill-posed problems and in a vast range of tasks, find connections and improve answers by means of an iterative and exploratory cognitive process. So, data visualization and well-designed interaction mechanisms between humans and ML algorithms leading to an "ML-human" hybrid problem-solving process can, in consequence, result in a vast improvement over "human" or "ML" approaches alone.

2   Methods and Techniques

2.1   Main Architectural Approach

We propose to apply the above idea, centered on the user, emphasizing the iterative and exploratory character, innate to human learning, and exploiting the efficiency of the visual and motor system in pattern analysis. The solutions and approaches we will work on will be based on the search for synergies between data visualization techniques, ML algorithms and interaction mechanisms, allowing the user to steer the analysis process and formulate new questions based on the answers he gets on the way.

Inspired by [39], the workflow of the visual cognition process aimed at in our proposal which takes place during a problem analysis task is described in Fig 1.

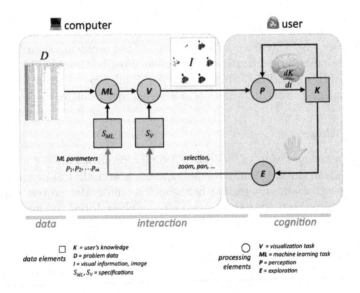

Fig. 1. Analysis workflow

During the analysis, the increment $\frac{dK}{dt}$ of the user's knowledge depends both on the visual information I that he perceives through the perception P, and the user's current knowledge K itself, which modulates the perception, that is, $\frac{dK}{dt} = P(I, K)$. Based on her knowledge, the user modifies the view through interactive exploration, E, which involves interaction (zoom, selection or pan), or more advanced methods, such as the reconfiguration of ML algorithms steering parameters $p_1, p_2, \ldots, p_n$. Note that the interaction takes place at two levels, visualization and ML, implying that the user has control on what he sees but also on the formulated questions and their answers provided by ML. We hypothesize that particularly this fact is key to speed up the quest for a proper problem formulation under weakly posed scenarios.

2.2   Interactive Data Cubes

Interactive data cubes (iHistograms) [9] allow the user to analyze datasets with several attributes (columns), organizing samples (rows) internally as a hypercube, where each side is an attribute and each cell contains samples with a combination of attribute values. By defining filters for a set of attributes, the histogram of the remaining samples, conditioned to the filtering operation, is shown in real time, allowing the user to explore different scenarios interactively. Aggregated values can also be represented, such as the mean or the sum, which allow the generation of statistics of the type "average of deaths by age for COVID-19 patients treated with dexamethasone", and instantly, "on the fly", modify the filters (e.g., change dexamethasone by remdesivir, or consider both drugs administered simultaneously) through drag and drop gestures. Two working demos and videos can be checked at http://isa.uniovi.es/GSDPI/dpi2015.html.

2.3   Morphing Projections

Morphing Projections (MP) [11,13], are based on the use of continuous transitions (*morphing* operations) between several basis views, each of which represents items (e.g., patients) spatially organized according to different criteria, such as age, sex, value of a clinical variable, or administered dose of a drug. Transitions let the user keep a mental model of the data between views, which allows different aspects of the data to be connected. In addition, it makes possible to define new views by "mixing" two or more basis views, resulting in a spatial rearrangement of the data according to a mixed criterion (e.g., men-old, women-young...). The combination of morphing and other interaction elements such as zoom, detail and multiple selection results in an immersive interface that enables the user to link and combine information in unprecedented ways. Videos and a playable demo app can be checked at http://isa.uniovi.es/GSDPI/morphingProjections. html.

2.4   Dimensionality Reduction Techniques

Dimensionality reduction (DR) techniques consist in obtaining a mapping between a large number of variables that describe the state of a system and a small set of "latent" variables or factors that explain the possible modes of variation of the system's states. In biomedical applications, latent factors could summarize the evolution of a disease from numerous clinical data (sensors, lab values, medication, etc.), opening ways to determine biomarkers, health indicators, and treatments, as well as elaborating a taxonomy of variants of this disease using the factors to generate insightful data visualizations. In industrial engineering problems the factors could summarize the process states from multiple sensor measurements, allowing, for instance, to build visual maps of its operating conditions useful to improve process efficiency or to build indices showing degradation. This idea can be taken further by integrating latent factors into visual analytics tools (morphing projections and interactive data cubes), making it possible, for instance, to represent maps of the patients' conditions on a disease and allowing exploratory analysis in combination with other data such as treatments or other relevant information. Interactive exploration could also help in finding combinations of factors that allow to determine potential biomarkers of medically relevant properties about the patient's condition that serve as a basis for generating diagnostic or medication protocols. In engineering processes, the latent variables could allow to develop virtual sensors to estimate non-measured variables or more abstract quantities such as efficiency or quality. These are unexplored topics that will be subject of research in this project.

3   Proposal

Our proposal will seek for approaches that exploit the synergies between the three techniques mentioned above and novel ML-based methods, resulting in visual analytics models pursuing the following abilities: 1) the interpretability of a complex data set from the ML output; 2) interactively exploring latent spaces obtained from modern DR techniques; and 3) novelty detection.

3.1   Interpretability from Machine Learning

An important weakness of ML methods is their black-box nature. ML algorithms, in their basic philosophy, learn a model from input/output data sets and later, in the inference phase, take new inputs to predict their outcomes (e.g., a classification result or an estimation). This inference is done without any user intervention, and no explanation is provided. This produces a lack of confidence in the results, which is a major drawback, for instance, in medicine as a paradigmatic example, but also in any industrial area that involves economical or personal consequences. Explainable ML —and the closed topic of interpretable ML— [24, 35, 37] has arisen in last years as a branch that looks for designing ML algorithms having the user in mind, providing her with complementary information that "explains" or suggests the pathway taken for the inference results and also providing ways for the user to "tune" the ML behavior according to interpretable parameters. We outline below three ways —see Fig. 2—that will inspire our research in this topic:

- *Visualization of the ML output.* The most naive (yet effective) way to get meaning from ML is probably to visualize its outcome for a number of samples. Its effectiveness can be potentiated with a good visualization design, using a meaningful layout of the samples (e.g., according to a context variable, such as sex, age, or a similarity-based arrangement using DR) and proper channels to convey the information of the ML output (e.g., color scales, size, etc.).
- *Introspection in ML models*, that is, "reverse engineering" the model by getting out information stored in its parameters and transforming it into a human readable format by means of visualization or natural text generation. This

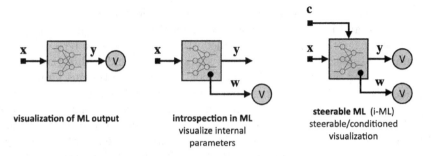

Fig. 2. Different approaches for interpretability in ML. V=visualization, $\mathbf{x}$ = input, $\mathbf{y}$ = output, $\mathbf{w}$ = internal model weights, $\mathbf{c}$ = conditioning parameters.

approach is not new. An example are SOM component planes ([29] and many other later related works). A recent work about visualizing deep convolutional networks has been presented by the researchers of this group [22]. The possibilities of this approach in industrial processes and biomedical applications are unexplored as far as we know and will be object of research in this project.
- *Steering ML models.* In the typical workflow of DR visualization, interaction often takes place *after* DR computation. The user typically sets an initial configuration, runs it until convergence and, after N iterations, the results are visualized. The user can later reconfigure this visualization or run the DR algorithm again with a different parameterization. However, interaction can go far beyond if we allow the user to take complete control of the DR algorithm during convergence and visualize the intermediate projections, resulting in interactive dimensionality reduction, iDR [10] [16], which suits the concept outlined in Fig. 1. Using DR algorithms based on iterative approximation, such as the SNE (stochastic neighbor embedding), the visualization of intermediate projections produces a smoothly varying layout that reveals the changes in the relationships between the samples in terms of the chosen parameters (e.g., redefining the weights of the variables used in computing the similarities). The result is a visualization that changes dynamically - an animated transition- that allows the user to track the changes in the projection that results from changes in the formulation of the problem, such as changes in the input data samples, or in the weights of the input attributes. Working demos of this approach, developed in a former Spanish research-funded project (DPI2015-69891-C2-2-R grant), can be seen in iDR visualization: map of vibration states and other demos in the project page http://isa.uniovi.es/GSDPI/dpi2015.html.

3.2   Explanatory Power of Latent Spaces

Many high-dimensional datasets, such as images of human faces, gene expression patterns, or power demand profiles, can be approximately explained by a reduced number of latent factors by means of DR methods. Latent spaces summarize the modes of data variability and can provide human-tractable ways for visualization and interaction of high-dimensional data. As suggested in [3] certain directions in the latent spaces, called *attribute vectors*, can be associated to meaningful abstract concepts (such as a "smiling" or a "gender" direction in a map of faces). Using manifold learning methods to obtain continuous latent spaces (*t*-SNE [31], UMAP [32], deep autoencoders [23], etc.) this idea can be transferred to the genomics data analysis domain to discover explanatory directions with biomedical relevance [28,30]. For instance, looking for directions revealing the stages of tumors could reveal what genes are involved in the cancer progression. Interestingly, we expect to find parallelisms of this idea in industrial process analysis to design health indicators or understand the causes of process degradation by finding directions of faults in the latent space.

3.3 Novelty Detection

Anomaly detection consists in finding those patterns in data that do not conform to expected normal behavior. Such patterns, commonly known as anomalies or outliers, represent deviations from the normal behavior, so their detection is not only of great value, but is often critical in a wide variety of applications, such as intrusion detection, fraud detection, medical anomaly detection or industrial damage detection [5]. In the context of industrial processes, anomaly detection is a topic of great importance, since both detection and diagnosis of faults are crucial to optimize and guarantee safety in the operation of machines, leading to higher productivity and process efficiency, with benefits such as reduced operating costs, longer operating life or improved process uptime [34]. In biomedical data analysis, novelty scores have been used to develop test of pluripotency in human cells [33]. In [38] novelty detection was used to perform high-content screening, allowing the discovery of rare phenotypes without user training. In [41], the authors propose a confidence-aware anomaly detection (CAAD) model able to achieve a rapid and accurate detection of viral pneumonia (reporting also radiologist-level results in COVID-19 cases) from chest X-rays, combining deep learning (DL) feature extraction stage, anomaly detection based on one-class SVM, and a confidence prediction score.

A common approach in the literature is to detect anomalies by means of residual analysis (instances with large residual errors are more likely to be anomalies) [36], using dimensionality reduction techniques to generate them, such as SOM, which has been studied by our research group in former projects and published in several papers [6–8,18,21]. In recent years, new techniques have emerged, but their potential has yet to be explored. This is the case of the *variational autoencoder* (VAE), which has become one of the most successful unsupervised learning algorithms, showing promising results in encoding and reconstructing data in the field of computer vision [27]. Also, regression models aiming to replicate the system dynamics (e.g., virtual sensors providing a redundant analytic estimation of a real sensor measurement) can be used for this purpose as a source of analytical redundancy.

4   Methodology

The planned project work packages (WPx) to achieve the objectives are summarized as follows:

WP1 Interaction and Data Visualization. This task aims at integrating the principles of MP and interactive data cubes, carrying out research on potential ways to extend the idea with the ML techniques studied in the other tasks. We propose to extend the MP approach described in [13] with full **F**ilter, **G**roup-by and **A**ggregation (FGA) operations found in the interactive data cubes presented in [9]. Attention will be given to the individual possibilities of these operations. For example, filters can be applied to a MP view using a 2D lasso and grouping can be done using ML clustering algorithms. Aggregation operations involve computing a summary value from the elements of a group and basic aggregations include count, average, sum, and max. However, ML algorithms can be used to compute more elaborate outputs such as classification, novelty or saliency of items within a group, or making a prediction or prognosis.

WP2 Dimensionality Reduction Approaches. This task will aim to evaluate potential advantages of recent developments in DR, with a special focus on the explanatory power of latent variables and their efficient integration within interactive data visualization tools to contribute to problem understanding. It will focus on novel *methods* (e.g. deep autoencoders, manifold learning algorithms), exploring their ability to disentangle complex data; *interpretability* by studying the explanatory power of latent variables; and in the possibilities of *integration* in interactive data visualization interfaces.

WP3 Novelty Detection. This task will involve research in ML methods to detect salient or abnormal data suitable for engineering and biomedical data analysis, and how they can be integrated in interactive data visualization approaches to boost discovery of relevant knowledge. We will research on methods based on the principle of *analytical redundancy*, building first a model of the data, and then comparing the actual sample with its reconstruction by the model, resulting in *residuals*, which convey information highly related to the degree of novelty or saliency of the data. The visualization of residuals within an interactive tool, allowing the user to confront them with other problem attributes providing context information, is expected to be a powerful way to generate valuable knowledge.

WP4 Other ML Approaches. This task will involve research in ways of integrating other ML methods (mainly regression and classification algorithms) in the visual analytics tools to improve interpretation and quantitative assessment of data.

WP5 Applications. Finally, this task will evaluate, by means of data analysis, case studies and demo applications, the suitability and potential of the methods and techniques proposed in the project on real problems from the process engineering and biomedical domains.

4.1   Project Achievements up to Date

Development of Health Indicators (WP3, WP5). A novel method harnessing the disentangling capability of variational autoencoders (VAE) was proposed in [19] to generate effective health indicators. The core idea implies using the latent reconstruction error, which is the error in reconstructing data from the latent space of an autoencoder, as a health indicator. The approach was tested on three different datasets and was compared to other state-of-the-art approaches. It was found that the proposed approach outperformed conventional approaches in terms of quality metrics, and that it is suitable for VA-based monitoring of the condition of machinery.

Anomaly Detection and Componentwise Characterization (WP3, WP5). A variational autoencoder (VAE) and a classifier were used in [20] to detect anomalies in engineering systems at two levels: a global one, that indicates the nature (normal/faulty) of the samples, and a detailed analysis showing anomalies of individual components in each sample. The ability to visualize anomalies for individual process features (components) provides an explainable diagnostic of the anomaly decision.

Visualization of Time Series Using ESN (WP2, WP4, WP5). *Echo State Networks* (ESN) are used in [14] to characterize time series of processes using an autoregressive model of the reservoir states, and proposes a visualization method based on a principal component analysis (PCA) projection of the regression matrix, that can be used for the exploratory analysis of processes with dynamics as well as for monitoring their condition.

Morphing Projections for Cancer Genomics Research (WP1, WP5). Visual analytics techniques helped also in gene expression analysis as part of a study of hypoxia mechanisms in certain cancer types [4]. Several t-SNE projections of cancer samples using different sets of genes were used to visualize the relative positions in a similarity map of samples with three different mutations of pheochromocytoma-paraganglioma. Additionally, a sorted visualization of a gene expression matrix (samples, genes) was produced by using 1D-DR projections, which facilitated the visual identification of relevant patterns.

Dual Interactive Visualization Gene Expression Data (WP2, WP5). We presented two applications of interactive DR for exploratory analysis of gene expression data. One of them produces two lively-updated projections, a sample map and a gene map, by rendering intermediate results of a t-SNE, [15]. The other combines the sample and gene view with a heatmap visualization of the gene expression map, [12]. In both applications the user can condition the projections "on the fly" by subsets of genes or samples, so updated views reveal co-expression patterns for different cancer types or gene groups.

Visual Analytics of COVID-19 Clinical Data During the First Wave in Spain (WP1, WP5). We presented in [17] a visual analytics approach that uses the morphing projections technique to combine the visualization of a t-SNE projection of clinical time series, with views of other clinical or patient's information. The proposed approach is demonstrated on an application case study of COVID-19 clinical information taken during the first wave.

Interactive Visualization of Cell Movement in Cancer Samples (WP2). A 2D map has been used as a tool for the analysis of cellular motility in cancer processes, using a deep autoencoder preceded by a manual feature extraction stage based on the extraction of the velocity field and the *Histogram of Oriented Optical Flow* (HOOF) of the working videos. The exploration of the obtained map has allowed to identify different patterns of movement in the cells, providing therefore a preliminary evaluation of the working samples, which represents a valuable starting point for further analysis. Videos showing the proposed approach can be found in the project page http://isa.uniovi.es/GSDPI/pid2020-es.html.

References

1. (many authors): Pan-cancer analysis of whole genomes. Nature **578**(7793), 82–93 (2020)
2. Belhadi, A., Zkik, K., Cherrafi, A., Sha'ri, M.Y., et al.: Understanding big data analytics for manufacturing processes: insights from literature review and multiple case studies. Comput. Indust. Eng. **137**, 106099 (2019)
3. Carter, S., Nielsen, M.: Using artificial intelligence to augment human intelligence. Distill **2**(12), e9 (2017)
4. Celada, L., et al.: Differential hif2α protein expression in human carotid body and adrenal medulla under physiologic and tumorigenic conditions. Cancers **14**(12), 2986 (2022)
5. Chandola, V., Banerjee, A., Kumar, V.: Anomaly detection: a survey. ACM Comput. Surv. (CSUR) **41**(3), 1–58 (2009)
6. Díaz, I., Cuadrado, A.A., Diez, A.B., Domínguez, M., Fuertes, J.J., Prada, M.A.: Visualization of changes in process dynamics using self-organizing maps. In: Diamantaras, K., Duch, W., Iliadis, L.S. (eds.) ICANN 2010. LNCS, vol. 6353, pp. 343–352. Springer, Heidelberg (2010). https://doi.org/10.1007/978-3-642-15822-3_42
7. Díaz, I., Hollmen, J.: Residual generation and visualization for understanding novel process conditions. In: Proceedings of the International Joint Conference on Neural Networks (IJCNN 2002), vol. 3, pp. 2070–2075. Honolulu, Hawaii (USA) (2002)
8. Díaz, I., Cuadrado, A.A., Diez, A.B., Loredo, L.R., Carrera, F.O., Rodríguez, J.A.: Visual predictive maintenance tool based on SOM projection techniques. Revue de Metallurgie-Cahiers d Informations Tech. **103**(3), 307–315 (2003). https://doi.org/10.1051/metal:2003179
9. Díaz, I., Cuadrado, A.A., Pérez, D., Domínguez, M., Alonso, S., Prada, M.A.: Energy analytics in public buildings using interactive histograms. Energy Build. **134**(1), 94–104 (2017). https://doi.org/10.1016/j.enbuild.2016.10.026

10. Díaz, I., Cuadrado, A.A., Pérez, D., García, F.J., Verleysen, M.: Interactive dimensionality reduction for visual analytics. In: European Symposium on Artificial Neural Networks, Computational Intelligence and Machine Learning. Bruges, Belgium (2014)
11. Díaz, I., Domínguez, M., Cuadrado, A.A., Diez, A.B., Fuertes, J.J.: Morphingprojections: Interactive visualization of electric power demand time series. In: Meyer, M., (Editors), T.W. (eds.) Eurographics Conference on Visualization (EuroVis) (2012), pp. 121–125. Viena (Austria) (2012)
12. Díaz, I., et al.: Exploratory analysis of the gene expression matrix based on dual conditional dimensionality reduction. IEEE J. Biomed. Health Inform. **PP**, 1–10 (2023). https://doi.org/10.1109/JBHI.2023.3264029
13. Díaz, I., et al.: Morphing Projections: a new visual technique for fast and interactive large-scale analysis of biomedical datasets. Bioinformatics **37**(11), 1571–1580 (2020). https://doi.org/10.1093/bioinformatics/btaa989
14. Díaz, I., Enguita, J.M., García, D., Cuadrado, A.A., González, A., Domínguez, M.: Modelado de series temporales mediante echo state networks para aplicaciones de analítica visual. In: XVII Simposio CEA de Control Inteligente. CEA-IFAC, CEA-IFAC (2022)
15. Blanco, I.D., et al.: Interactive dual projections for gene expression analysis. In: ESANN 2022 Proceedings, pp. 439–444 (2022)
16. Endert, A., et al.: The state of the art in integrating machine learning into visual analytics. Comput. Graph. Forum **36**(8), 458–486 (2017). https://doi.org/10.1111/cgf.13092
17. Enguita-Gonzalez, J.M., et al.: Interactive visual analytics for medical data: application to covid-19 clinical information during the first wave. In: ESANN 2022 Proceedings, pp. 451–456 (2022)
18. Fuertes, J.J., Domínguez, M., Reguera, P., Prada, M.A., Díaz, I., Cuadrado, A.A.: Visual dynamic model based on self-organizing maps for supervision and fault detection in industrial processes. Eng. Appl. Artif. Intell. **23**(1), 8–17 (2010). https://doi.org/10.1016/j.engappai.2009.06.001
19. González-Muñiz, A., Díaz, I., Cuadrado, A.A., García-Pérez, D.: Health indicator for machine condition monitoring built in the latent space of a deep autoencoder. Reliability Eng. Syst. Safety **224**, 108482 (2022)
20. González-Muñiz, A., Díaz, I., Cuadrado, A.A., García-Pérez, D., Pérez, D.: Two-step residual-error based approach for anomaly detection in engineering systems using variational autoencoders. Comput. Electr. Eng. **101**, 108065 (2022)
21. González, D., Cuadrado, A.A., Díaz, I., García, F.J., Diez, A.B., Fuertes, J.J.: Visual analysis of residuals from data-based models in complex industrial processes. Int. J. Modern Phys. B **26**(25), 1–9 (2012). https://doi.org/10.1142/S0217979212460022
22. González-Muñiz, A., Díaz, I., Cuadrado, A.A.: DCNN for condition monitoring and fault detection in rotating machines and its contribution to the understanding of machine nature. Heliyon **6**(2), e03395 (2020). https://doi.org/10.1016/j.heliyon.2020.e03395
23. Goodfellow, I., Bengio, Y., Courville, A.: Deep learning. MIT press (2016)
24. Holzinger, A., Langs, G., Denk, H., Zatloukal, K., Müller, H.: Causability and explainability of artificial intelligence in medicine. Wiley Interdiscip. Rev.: Data Min. Knowl. Disc. **9**(4), e1312 (2019)
25. Hospitales, H.: Covid data save lives (2022). https://www.hmhospitales.com/coronavirus/covid-data-save-lives

26. Hutter, C., Zenklusen, J.C.: The cancer genome atlas: creating lasting value beyond its data. Cell **173**(2), 283–285 (2018)
27. Kingma, D.P., Welling, M.: Auto-encoding variational Bayes. arXiv preprint arXiv:1312.6114 (2013)
28. Kobak, D., Berens, P.: The art of using t-SNE for single-cell transcriptomics. Nat. Commun. **10**(1), 1–14 (2019)
29. Kohonen, T.: Self-Organizing Maps, Springer Series in Information Sciences, vol. 30. New York, third extended edition edn, Springer, Berlin, Heidelberg (2001). https://doi.org/10.1007/978-3-642-56927-2
30. Liu, Y., Jun, E., Li, Q., Heer, J.: Latent space cartography: visual analysis of vector space embeddings. Comput. Graph. Forum **38**(3), 67–78 (2019). https://doi.org/10.1111/cgf.13672
31. Van der Maaten, L., Hinton, G.: Visualizing data using t-SNE. J. Mach. Learn. Res. **9**(11), 2579–2605 (2008)
32. McInnes, L., Healy, J., Melville, J.: UMAP: uniform manifold approximation and projection for dimension reduction. arXiv preprint arXiv:1802.03426 (2018)
33. Müller, F.J., et al.: A bioinformatic assay for pluripotency in human cells. Nat. Methods **8**(4), 315–317 (2011)
34. Mobley, R.K.: An introduction to predictive maintenance. Elsevier (2002)
35. Murdoch, W.J., Singh, C., Kumbier, K., Abbasi-Asl, R., Yu, B.: Definitions, methods, and applications in interpretable machine learning. Proc. Natl. Acad. Sci. **116**(44), 22071–22080 (2019)
36. Pimentel, M.A., Clifton, D.A., Clifton, L., Tarassenko, L.: A review of novelty detection. Signal Process. **99**, 215–249 (2014)
37. Roscher, R., Bohn, B., Duarte, M.F., Garcke, J.: Explainable machine learning for scientific insights and discoveries. IEEE Access **8**, 42200–42216 (2020)
38. Sommer, C., Hoefler, R., Samwer, M., Gerlich, D.W.: A deep learning and novelty detection framework for rapid phenotyping in high-content screening. Mol. Biol. Cell **28**(23), 3428–3436 (2017)
39. Van Wijk, J.: The value of visualization. In: 16th IEEE Visualization 2005 (VIS 2005). IEEE Computer Society (2005)
40. Wang, J., Xu, C., Zhang, J., Zhong, R.: Big data analytics for intelligent manufacturing systems: a review. J. Manuf. Syst. **62**, 738–752 (2022)
41. Zhang, J., et al.: Viral pneumonia screening on chest X-ray images using confidence-aware anomaly detection. arXiv preprint arXiv:2003.12338 (2020)
42. Zihni, E., et al.: Opening the black box of artificial intelligence for clinical decision support: a study predicting stroke outcome. PLoS ONE **15**(4), e0231166 (2020)

Visualizing Cell Motility Patterns from Time Lapse Videos with Interactive 2D Maps Generated with Deep Autoencoders

Ana González[1] , José María Enguita[1] , Ignacio Díaz[1]([✉]) , Diego García[1] ,
Abel Alberto Cuadrado[1] , Nuria Valdés[2] , and María D. Chiara[3,4]

[1] Department of Electrical Engineering, University of Oviedo, Gijón 33204, Spain
{jmenguita,idiaz,garciaperdiego,cuadradoabel}@uniovi.es
[2] Department of Internal Medicine, Section of Endocrinology and Nutrition, Hospital
Universitario de Cabueñes, Gijón 33204, Spain
nvaldes@fis.hca.es
[3] Institute of Sanitary Research of the Principado de Asturias, Hospital Universitario
Central de Asturias, Oviedo 33011, Spain
mdchiara.uo@uniovi.es
[4] CIBERONC (Network of Biomedical Research in Cancer), Madrid 28029, Spain

Abstract. Cell motility, the ability of cells to move, is crucial in a
wide range of biological processes; for instance, in cancer, it is directly
related to metastasis. However, it is a complex phenomenon which is
not well-understood yet, and studies are mainly done by human observation, which is subjective and error-prone. We intend to provide an
automated mechanism to analyze the movement patterns that occur in
in-vitro cell cultures, which can be registered by time lapse microscopy.
Our approach, which is still a work in progress, utilizes an interactive 2D
map that organizes motility patterns based on their similarity, enabling
exploratory analysis. We extract the velocity fields that represent the cell
displacements between consecutive frames and use a deep convolutional
autoencoder to project a characterization of short video sequences of
smaller parts of the original videos into a 10D latent space. The samples
(small videos) are visualized in a 2D map using the *Uniform Manifold
Approximation and Projection* (UMAP). The possibilities and extent of
our method are showcased through a small interactive application that
allows to explore all the types of cell motility patterns present in the
training videos on a 2D map.

Keywords: Deep autencoders · Cell motility analysis · Deep
learning · UMAP visualization · Cancer metastasis

1 Introduction

Cell motility refers to the ability of cells to move spontaneously and independently, and represents a crucial dynamic process in a wide range of biological

© IFIP International Federation for Information Processing 2023
Published by Springer Nature Switzerland AG 2023
I. Maglogiannis et al. (Eds.): AIAI 2023 Workshops, IFIP AICT 677, pp. 458–468, 2023.
https://doi.org/10.1007/978-3-031-34171-7_37

processes. In cancer, this movement is related to cell survival and, therefore, to metastasis, which currently represents one of the great challenges in the clinical treatment of cancer. However, cell motility is a complex phenomenon, affected by the physiological context, cell type, cell morphology and cell-cell interactions. Moreover, cells can move in amoeboid, mesenchymal or epithelial modes, as individuals or in groups, etc. and can even dynamically switch between different modes in response to changing environments [22]. There is therefore great interest in studying the mechanisms underlying all types of cell motility, with the ultimate goal of identifying therapies that increase the motility of beneficial cells and block the spread of harmful cells [21].

In this context, advances in microscopy have played a key role in the study of cellular processes, as they have facilitated the acquisition of images and videos of the cell cultures of interest, making it possible to analyze their evolution over time. As a result, large datasets are generated, the exploration of which could provide intuition about new hypotheses or lines of research in the study of cell motility. However, the manual exploration of these datasets —which may contain hundreds, thousands or even millions of images— is very time-consuming for the researcher, for whom the task of finding relationships of interest in such a vast amount of data is enormously complex.

In this article, which reflects an ongoing work, we propose to explore a dataset of cell test videos by projecting them into a low-dimensional space using a combination of a deep autoencoder and the *Uniform Manifold Approximation and Projection* (UMAP) [17]. As shown below, the results of the research have demonstrated that the generated 2D map allows the identification of different patterns of cell movement, thus providing a preliminary assessment of the working samples, which represents a valuable starting point for further analysis. These results also demonstrate the potential for the qualitative characterization of cell movement, which can be potentially associated to underlying biological processes related to cancer or other conditions with biomedical relevance, thus establishing an interesting line of future work.

2   Methods and Techniques

2.1   Time Lapse Microscope Videos

The dataset consists of five cell-culture videos, characterized by very low — almost non-existent— levels of succinate dehydrogenase B (SDHB). Reduced expression or activity of SDHB, usually as a consequence of mutations in the gene that encodes it, has been described in the literature as being associated with the pathogenesis of numerous renal carcinomas [6,7,14,28,29]. There is therefore great interest in the study of this protein, in search of a better understanding of its involvement in carcinogenesis and the progression of this type of tumor. Cell movement could play a key role in the development of these processes, so we propose an exploration of working videos focused on the analysis of cell motility.

2.2   Video Preprocessing: Velocity Fields

Processing videos for valuable information about cell movement is a complex task. Therefore, data pre-processing is recommended to extract relevant information from the videos to feed the deep model, thus simplifying —and guiding— its learning. In particular, we calculated the velocity field of the cells, since it provides a detailed description of their motion and is a common approach in the analysis of cell motility [3,13]. For this purpose, Gunnar Farnebäck's optical flow algorithm [8], available in the OpenCV-Python library, was used[1].

It is worth noting that optical flow algorithms have only recently started to be used in the cellular domain, but they have already proven to be able to provide more accurate and robust velocity fields than other state-of-the-art techniques, such as those based on particle image velocimetry *(Particle Image Velocimetry, PIV)* [9,26], or MATLAB[TM] imregdemons algorithm [23,25]. "Video 1" (see appendix with videos) shows a visualisation of the velocity field obtained for one of the working videos.

As shown in Table 1a, the starting dataset contains 5 videos, of 539 frames each that, in turn, have a size of 2000×2000 pixels, where for each pixel the gray level is known. After the calculation of the velocity fields, a new set is available (Table 1b), where for each pixel, we have four variables: the horizontal and vertical components of the velocity (u, v) and the position of the pixel in the image (x, y). The velocity fields were then subjected to post-processing, which, as can be seen in Table 1c, modified the number of frames as well as their size. Based on the recommendation of the research group that provided the data[2], the first 360 frames of each video were retained for the study, while the remaining frames were discarded due to their high cell density and lack of representativeness of the process's state. Secondly, the fields were decimated (with square windows of 4 × 4 size and without overlapping), in order to reduce the size of the set and thus facilitate its processing. Also, the edges (top and bottom) of the fields were discarded, as they correspond to the strips (top and bottom) of the frames, which do not contain any cellular information. As a result, the field of each frame was reduced from a size of 2000×2000 to one of 355×500.

2.3   Video Feature Extraction

We performed an additional feature extraction process to obtain a representative descriptor of the velocity fields. In particular, we used the *Histogram of Oriented Optical Flow (HOOF)* technique [4], shown in Fig. 1. These histograms have been shown in the literature to have great potential as movement descriptors in a variety of applications [5,15,24], also with recent uses in the study of cell

---

[1] The algorithm was implemented with Object Tracking of OpenCV-Python, using the following parameters: pyr_scale = 0.5, levels = 3, winsize = 60, iterations = 3, poly_n = 5, poly_sigma = 1.1, flags = cv2.OPTFLOW_FARNEBACK_ GAUSSIAN.

[2] Head and Neck research group from the Instituto de Investigación Sanitaria del Principado de Asturias (ISPA, https://www.ispasturias.es).

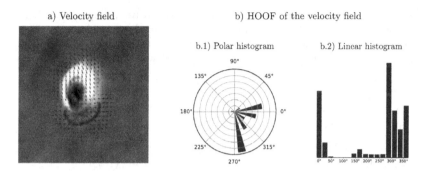

a) Velocity field   b) HOOF of the velocity field

b.1) Polar histogram   b.2) Linear histogram

Fig. 1. Example of a HOOF for a working window. A window is shown in (a), along with its corresponding velocity field. In (b) the HOOF of the velocity field is shown with different representations: in terms of a polar histogram (b.1) and in terms of a linear histogram (b.2). In this example a HOOF of 16 *bins* was generated.

motility [10]. In our case, we divided the working frames into 24 windows —of size 75×75 and with no overlapping— and we calculated a 16-element HOOF for each of them. The dimensions of the resulting dataset are given in Table 1d. It must be noted that other descriptors of the vector fields —such as classical rotational or divergence operators— could be used and will be subject of future work.

Importantly, the samples in this dataset contain valuable information about the displacement of cells within each window. However, the HOOF information is limited to the displacement experienced between two consecutive frames. In order to obtain samples with a greater temporal context for the evolution of the cells, we concatenated —for each window— the current HOOF with the HOOFs of the next 15 frames, resulting in the final working package (Table 1e) consisting of 41280 samples —5×344×24 samples— of size 16×16.

Finally, this dataset was normalized using a *min-max* scale [19] with range [0, 1], divided randomly into two subsets: training (70%, 28896 samples) and test (30%, 12384 samples), for the training and evaluation of the deep autoencoder presented in Sect. 2.4.

2.4   2D Map of the Cell Motility Dataset

Each of the 41,280 samples describes locally the type of cellular movement contained in a small video of 16 frames of 75×75 pixels each, using a 16×16 matrix of HOOF of features (16 HOOF descriptors $\times$ 16 frames), equivalent to 256 dimensions. To visually represent the types of movement of the samples, organized spatially by similarities, a dimensionality reduction method is proposed to project the samples onto a 2D space for visualization.

For that purpose, a two-step dimension reduction was used: first, the original dimension of the dataset was reduced from 256D to a latent space with a lower dimensionality by means of a deep autoencoder. Next, the data were

Table 1. Cell motility dataset (a) and datasets derived from its preprocessing (b, c, d, e). The # of samples of each dataset is expressed as: a) # of videos × # of frames × frame width × frame height; b, c) # of videos × # of frames × field width × field height; d, e) # of videos × # of frames × # of windows.

Dataset	# of samples	Size of the samples
a) Starting data	$(5\times539\times2000\times2000)$	(1)
b) Velocity fields	$(5\times539\times2000\times2000)$	(4)
c) Post-processed velocity fields	$(5\times360\times355\times500)$	(4)
d) HOOF	$(5\times360\times24)$	(16)
e) HOOF temporal	$(5\times344\times24)$	(16×16)

projected from the latent space to a 2D visualization space using a neighbor embedding technique. As shown in other research works [2,16], the success of this combination is due to the fact that it exploits: on one hand, the ability of deep autoencoders to generate low-dimensional, disentangled latent representations of the data; and, on the other hand, the ability of the neighbor embedding techniques to provide compact, visualizable (2D) representations of such latent representations with good separability properties, which makes them especially useful in clustering applications. In this case, we used the UMAP technique, as proposed in other works in the literature [1,18,27]. In line with these works, the results obtained demonstrate that, even though the high dimensionality of the data makes it difficult to capture its structure in a two-dimensional space, it is possible to generate quality 2D maps with meaning about the processes thanks to the combination of both DR techniques.

After trying several dimensionalities for the latent space, the autoencoder training showed poorer reconstruction results when trained with dimensionalities below 10D, so we decided to keep this number of dimensions for the latent space, followed by the 2D projection step.

The autoencoder was trained using the gradient descent algorithm [20] combined with the ADAM optimizer [11]. The number of epochs, the size of the *mini-batch* and the architecture are detailed in Table 2. This table shows that the autoencoder trained with the cell motility dataset contains convolutional and subsampling layers as recommended in the literature for 2D data processing [12]. Regarding the activation functions, the ReLU function was used in all the layers except in the output layer and in the bottleneck of the model, where a linear activation function was used. For the training of the UMAP model, after testing several configurations, a number of 5 neighbors and a minimum distance of 0.5 were chosen since they were found to provide a good distribution of the different types of cell motility.

Regarding the choice of hyperparameters for the autoencoder (number of layers, number of neurons in the layers, number of epochs, size of the "mini-batch", etc.), we ran different ranges of experiments and chosen those hyperparameters with which the model showed the lowest reconstruction error. The reconstruc-

Table 2. Architecture of the *deep autoencoder*. All the layers are dense, except the following: Conv2D (2D convolutional layer), MaxPooling2D (subsampling by max value), Flatten (unidimensional conversion layer), Reshape (multidimensional conversion layer), Conv2DTranspose (deconvolution layer). The convolutional and subsampling layers were configured with a null *(padding)* and a *(stride)* of 1, except in the first deconvolution layer, for which a stride of 2 was used.

# of epochs	Size of *mini-batch*	# of layers	# neurons in layers		
			Encoder	Bottleneck	Decoder
600	1000	15	(16×16×1, 14×14×8 Conv2D, 12×12×4 Conv2D, 10×10×2 Conv2D, 5×5×2 MaxPooling2D, 50 Flatten, 20)	(10)	(20, 50, 5×5×2 Reshape, 12×12×2 Conv2DTranspose, 14×14×4 Conv2DTranspose, 16×16×8 Conv2DTranspose, 16×16×1 Conv2D)

tion error has been evaluated on the test subset, while the model was fed with the training subset.

2.5   Interactive Visualization

In order to demonstrate the capability of the approach proposed in this article for distributing and clustering different cellular movement patterns across a 2D map, the proposed processing was integrated into an interactive application, solely for demonstrative purposes, that is shown in Fig. 3 and can be watched in "video 2" of the appendix of Sect. 5. The application allows for the representation of three views for each sample: 1) its projection on the 2D map; 2) a representative heatmap of 16 × 16 pixels with the value of 16 HOOF descriptors for the 16 frames; and 3) the original video clip. As shown in "video 2", using this application the different movement patterns on the map, including translation, rotation, crawling, among others, can be identified and are spatially organized along the map in a coherent manner.

3   Results and Discussion

Figure 2 shows the map obtained after a dimensionality reduction done with the proposed mapping obtained with the combination of the deep autoencoder and UMAP. The combination of both approaches provides a regularized representation of the data, which also presents a good separability of the different cell motility patterns.

As shown in Fig. 4, the exploration of the map allows to find different patterns of movement in the data, represented in color in the figure (it should be noted that the map has not been fully explored yet, given the large volume of samples to be handled; unexplored samples are shown in gray color).

In detail, zones with absence or presence of cells, zones where rotation or displacement movements predominate, zones of interaction between cells, etc. were identified. Therefore, the map provided a compact and meaningful representation of the data, whose semantics could be explored interactively. Finally,

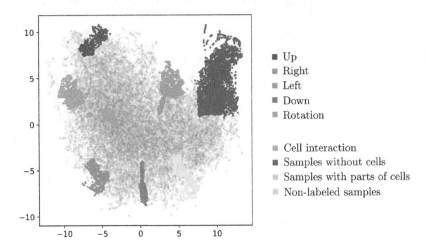

Fig. 2. 2D map of the cell motility types using a deep autoencoder + UMAP

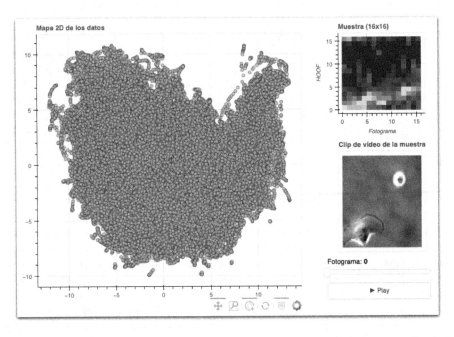

Fig. 3. Interactive visualization of the cell motility map. The primary visualization consists of a 2D scatter plot that displays the projected samples (mini videos). On the right side of the plot, there is a heatmap that shows the HOOF description of the currently selected sample. Below the heatmap, there is an animated view of the selected sample.

an overall animation of the map is shown in "video 3", where several example samples were included for each of the motility patterns identified.

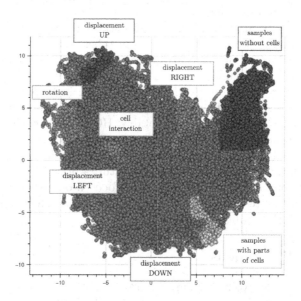

Fig. 4. Cell motility map labeled by movement patterns (samples that have not been labeled are presented in gray).

4   Conclusions

In this article, we have introduced a novel approach for automatically detecting relevant patterns of movement in cell cultures using deep autoencoders. Although this work represents a preliminary study, the results demonstrate significant potential. Notably, the interactive visualization of the latent space illustrates the autoencoder's ability to classify different movement patterns and represents a robust preliminary step in their automated processing.

The 2D map of the data not only serves as a valuable tool for exploring the dataset, but also provides evidence for the potential of cell motility analysis approaches in investigating cancer processes. In particular, the resulting map enables the identification of potential avenues for future research into the mechanisms linking the SDHB protein to the development and evolution of renal carcinomas. For instance, the map permits the analysis of behavioral differences between cell cultures exhibiting low levels of SDHB (i.e., the working dataset) and other cultures of varying nature (e.g., control cultures or cultures with normal SDHB levels) by projecting them onto the map.

Furthermore, the identification of distinct motility zones on the 2D map also provides an opportunity to explore other lines of interest for future research related to unsupervised sample labeling. Such labeling could enable a comprehensive analysis of the dataset, by excluding samples with no relevant information (i.e., samples without cells) or by focusing exclusively on specific patterns of interest present on the map.

However, certain limitations exist in this study. Firstly, the analyzed videos pertain to a specific problem, and images in other contexts may differ significantly. Although we do not anticipate this to pose a challenge for the adaptation of the described technique, no tests have been performed to validate this assumption. Secondly, the use of HOOF for extracting movement features in each mini-video also presents certain limitations, which could explain why some patterns are not classified correctly. Notably, HOOF does not account well for patterns with local symmetries in the directionality, which suggests that alternative methods could potentially enhance the results. Exploring the applicability of other descriptors is an interesting line of future work.

As a final note, although this article has focused on a specific problem, the applications of this technique can extend to numerous different fields in which the analysis of cell motility is critical.

5   Appendix: Videos

video 1. https://www.youtube.com/watch?v=gisz0Px4k_8 → Velocity fields

video 2. https://www.youtube.com/watch?v=zVWGxsjtvsg → Interactive visualization of cell motility dataset

video 3. https://www.youtube.com/watch?v=dZoB_2Wi9Co → Patterns of movement in the cell motility map

Acknowledgments. This work was supported by the Ministerio de Ciencia e Innovación / Agencia Estatal de Investigación (MCIN/AEI/ 10.13039/501100011033) grant [PID2020-115401GB-I00]. The authors would also like to thank the financial support provided by the Principado de Asturias government through the predoctoral grant "Severo Ochoa".

References

1. Ali, M., Jones, M.W., Xie, X., Williams, M.: Timecluster: dimension reduction applied to temporal data for visual analytics. Vis. Comput. **35**(6), 1013–1026 (2019)
2. Allaoui, M., Aissa, N.E.H.S.B., Belghith, A.B., Kherfi, M.L.: A machine learning-based tool for exploring covid-19 scientific literature. In: 2021 International Conference on Recent Advances in Mathematics and Informatics (ICRAMI), pp. 1–7. IEEE (2021)
3. Camley, B.A., Rappel, W.J.: Physical models of collective cell motility: from cell to tissue. J. Phys. D Appl. Phys. **50**(11), 113002 (2017)
4. Chaudhry, R., Ravichandran, A., Hager, G., Vidal, R.: Histograms of oriented optical flow and binet-cauchy kernels on nonlinear dynamical systems for the recognition of human actions. In: 2009 IEEE Conference on Computer Vision and Pattern Recognition, pp. 1932–1939. IEEE (2009)

5. Colque, R.V.H.M., Caetano, C., de Andrade, M.T.L., Schwartz, W.R.: Histograms of optical flow orientation and magnitude and entropy to detect anomalous events in videos. IEEE Trans. Circuits Syst. Video Technol. **27**(3), 673–682 (2016)
6. Cornejo, K.M., et al.: Succinate dehydrogenase B: a new prognostic biomarker in clear cell renal cell carcinoma. Hum. Pathol. **46**(6), 820–826 (2015)
7. Fang, Z., Sun, Q., Yang, H., Zheng, J.: SDHB suppresses the tumorigenesis and development of ccRCC by inhibiting glycolysis. Front. Oncol. **11**, 639408 (2021)
8. Farnebäck, G.: Two-frame motion estimation based on polynomial expansion. In: Bigun, J., Gustavsson, T. (eds.) SCIA 2003. LNCS, vol. 2749, pp. 363–370. Springer, Heidelberg (2003). https://doi.org/10.1007/3-540-45103-X_50
9. Hoshikawa, E., et al.: Cells/colony motion of oral keratinocytes determined by non-invasive and quantitative measurement using optical flow predicts epithelial regenerative capacity. Sci. Rep. **11**(1), 1–12 (2021)
10. Huang, Y., Hao, L., Li, H., Liu, Z., Wang, P.: Quantitative analysis of intracellular motility based on optical flow model. J. Healthcare Eng. **2017**, 1848314 (2017)
11. Kingma, D.P., Ba, J.: Adam: A method for stochastic optimization. arXiv preprint arXiv:1412.6980 (2014)
12. Krizhevsky, A., Sutskever, I., Hinton, G.E.: ImageNet classification with deep convolutional neural networks. Advances in Neural Information Processing Systems 25 (2012)
13. Ladoux, B., Mège, R.M.: Mechanobiology of collective cell behaviours. Nat. Rev. Mol. Cell Biol. **18**(12), 743–757 (2017)
14. Linehan, W.M., et al.: The metabolic basis of kidney cancer. Cancer Discov. **9**(8), 1006–1021 (2019)
15. Liu, Y.J., Zhang, J.K., Yan, W.J., Wang, S.J., Zhao, G., Fu, X.: A main directional mean optical flow feature for spontaneous micro-expression recognition. IEEE Trans. Affect. Comput. **7**(4), 299–310 (2015)
16. McConville, R., Santos-Rodriguez, R., Piechocki, R.J., Craddock, I.: N2d:(not too) deep clustering via clustering the local manifold of an autoencoded embedding. In: 2020 25th International Conference on Pattern Recognition (ICPR), pp. 5145–5152. IEEE (2021)
17. McInnes, L., Healy, J., Melville, J.: UMAP: uniform manifold approximation and projection for dimension reduction. arXiv preprint arXiv:1802.03426 (2018)
18. Morehead, A., Chantapakul, W., Cheng, J.: Semi-supervised graph learning meets dimensionality reduction. arXiv preprint arXiv:2203.12522 (2022)
19. Patterson, J., Gibson, A.: Deep learning: a practitioner's approach. O'Reilly Media, Inc. (2017)
20. Ruder, S.: An overview of gradient descent optimization algorithms. arXiv preprint arXiv:1609.04747 (2016)
21. Stuelten, C.H., Parent, C.A., Montell, D.J.: Cell motility in cancer invasion and metastasis: insights from simple model organisms. Nat. Rev. Cancer **18**(5), 296–312 (2018)
22. Te Boekhorst, V., Preziosi, L., Friedl, P.: Plasticity of cell migration in vivo and in silico. Annu. Rev. Cell Dev. Biol. **32**(1), 491–526 (2016)
23. Thirion, J.P.: Image matching as a diffusion process: an analogy with Maxwell's demons. Med. Image Anal. **2**(3), 243–260 (1998). https://doi.org/10.1016/S1361-8415(98)80022-4
24. Verburg, M., Menkovski, V.: Micro-expression detection in long videos using optical flow and recurrent neural networks. In: 2019 14th IEEE International Conference on Automatic Face & Gesture Recognition (FG 2019), pp. 1–6. IEEE (2019)

25. Vercauteren, T., Pennec, X., Perchant, A., Ayache, N.: Diffeomorphic demons: Efficient non-parametric image registration. NeuroImage **45**(1, Supplement 1), S61–S72 (2009). https://doi.org/10.1016/j.neuroimage.2008.10.040. https://www.sciencedirect.com/science/article/pii/S1053811908011683, mathematics in Brain Imaging

26. Vig, D.K., Hamby, A.E., Wolgemuth, C.W.: On the quantification of cellular velocity fields. Biophys. J . **110**(7), 1469–1475 (2016)

27. Wang, Y., Yu, Z., Wang, Z.: A temporal clustering method fusing deep convolutional autoencoders and dimensionality reduction methods and its application in air quality visualization. Chemom. Intell. Lab. Syst. **227**, 104607 (2022)

28. Yang, J., et al.: Functional deficiency of succinate dehydrogenase promotes tumorigenesis and development of clear cell renal cell carcinoma through weakening of ferroptosis. Bioengineered **13**(4), 11187–11207 (2022)

29. Yong, C., Stewart, G.D., Frezza, C.: Oncometabolites in renal cancer. Nat. Rev. Nephrol. **16**(3), 156–172 (2020)

Author Index

A

Agapiou, George   55, 118, 168
Alexandridis, Georgios   284
Alzamel, Mai   359
Anagnostopoulos, Christos-Nikolaos   183, 195, 207, 219, 231, 242, 254
Anagnostopoulos, Ioannis   312
Anastasopoulos, Markos   66, 139
Anastassova, Margarita   91
Antonopoulos, Angelos   32
Arvanitis, Konstantinos I.   183
Arvanitozisis, Dimitrios   91

B

Beerten, Robbert   151
Belesioti, Maria   106
Bellesini, Francesco   91
Bolzmacher, Christian   91
Bouilland, Stephane   91
Brodimas, Dimitrios   126

C

Caridakis, George   284
Chanclou, Philippe   151
Chartsias, Kostas   151
Chartsias, Panteleimon Konstantinos   66, 139
Chatzinotas, Symeon   32
Chawla, Ashima   17
Chiara, María D.   458
Chochliouros, Ioannis P.   17, 91, 106, 118, 126, 151
Christofi, Loizos   17
Ciornei, Irina   126
Corsi, Antonello   91
Cuadrado, Abel Alberto   421, 434, 446, 458
Cugat, Diego   91

D

D'Ostilio, Paride   91
Davrazos, Gregory   393
Daykin, Jacqueline W.   359

D (continued)

Denazis, Spyros   66
Diagourtas, Dimitris   17
Díaz, Ignacio   421, 434, 446, 458
Didachos, Christos   325
Dimara, Asimina   183, 195, 207, 219, 231, 242, 254
Dimas, Panagiotis   106
Domínguez, Manuel   421
Dritsas, Elias   303

E

Engin, Ihsan Bal   91
Enguita, José María   421, 434, 446, 458
Exarchos, Themis   294

F

Fiore, Marco   32
Flegkas, Paris   66, 139
Fradelos, Georgios   381
Fraternali, Piero   195

G

García, Diego   421, 434, 446, 458
Gardikis, Georgios   17, 91
Gasteratos, Gregory   271
Gavrielides, Andreas   55, 118, 168
Giannakeas, Nikolaos   45
González, Ana   421, 446, 458
Gonzalez, Roberto   151
Gonzalez, Sergio Luis Herrera   195
Gratsanis, Panagiotis   271
Guevara, Andrea P.   151
Gutiérrez, Jesús   139

H

Hampson, Christopher   359
Harris, Philip   32
Hatzilygeroudis, Ioannis   347, 381
Hristov, Georgi   126

I

Ibañez, Francisco   17
Iliopoulos, Costas S.   359
Imeri, Adnan   91
Ioannidis, Dimosthenis   183, 195, 207, 219,
    231, 242, 254
Ioannou, George   284

K

Kalafatakis, Konstantinos   45
Kanavos, Andreas   325, 335
Karatzia, Kanela   183
Karatzinis, Georgios   207, 231, 254
Karydis, Ioannis   271
Kermanidis, Katia Lida   369
Klitis, Charalambos   151
Kołakowski, Robert   32, 77
Kosmatopoulos, Elias   207, 231, 254
Kostopoulos, Alexandros   17
Kotis, Konstantinos   242
Kotsiantis, Sotiris   393
Kourtis, Michail -Alexandros   91
Krinidis, Stelios   183, 195, 207, 219, 231,
    242, 254
Kritharidis, Dimitrios   17, 66, 151
Krokidis, Marios G.   294
Ksentini, Adlen   17

L

La Ferla, Michele   409
Lagios, Vasileios   347
Lampros, Theodoros   45
Lazarakis, Fotis   32
Lazaros, Konstantinos   294
Lendinez, Adrian   55
Lessi, Christina C.   55, 91, 118, 151, 168
Lessis, Konstantinos C.   118
Li, Dayou   55, 168
Lim, Zara   359
Lin, Chih-Kuang   32
Litke, Antonis   91
Liu, Enjie   168
Lyberopoulos, George   66, 139

M

Makris, Nikos   66, 139
Marin-Perez, Rafael   195
Markakis, Albertos   91
Maroufidis, Ioannis   312

Martinopoulou, Efstathia   195
Mayrargue, Sylvie   17
Mesodiakaki, Agapi   32
Mesogiti, Ioanna   66, 139
Michailidis, Iakovos   207, 231, 254
Michalakis, Konstantinos   284
Millet, Marta   91
Montanera, Enric Pages   106
Mosahebfard, Mohammadreza   32
Mourad, Alain   17
Mylonas, Phivos   303

N

Nanos, Marios   369
Nicholson, Didier   17
Nitzold, Walter   17
Ntontin, Konstantinos   32

O

O'Meara, Jimmy   17

P

Pagouni, Ioanna   369
Panagiotakopoulos, Theodor   393
Papagiannis, Tasos   284
Papaioannou, Alexios   183, 207, 219, 231,
    242
Papaioannou, Panagiotis   66
Papapetrou, Panagiotis   421
Paplomatas, Petros   294
Pappas, Nikolaos   32
Pérez, Daniel   421
Perikos, Isidoros   347, 381
Politi, Christina   66, 139
Pollin, Sofie   17
Porcu, Daniele   126
Psaromanolakis, N.   66

Q

Qiu, Renxi   55, 118, 168
Quarato, Lucrezia Maria   91

R

Rahman, Md Arifur   17, 151
Ramantas, Kostas   17
Rantopoulos, Michalis   126
Razis, Gerasimos   312
Rodríguez, José Ramón   434

S

Samarati, Pierangela   151
Sanchez, Enrique Areizaga   91
Santiago, Ana Rita   32
Saravanos, Christina   335
Segado, Juan Andres Sanchez   195
Setaki, Fotini   66, 139
Shangov, Daniel   126
Siddiqui, Shuaib   17
Skianis, Charalabos   106
Smyth, W. F.   359
Sofianopoulos, Manolis   106
Sophocleous, Marios   55
Soumplis, Polyzois   151
Špaňhel, Jakub   55
Spiliopoulou, Anastasia S.   17, 91
Stamatis, Konstantinos   66, 139
Stefanopoulou, Aliki   207, 231, 254

T

Tavernier, Wouter   91
Tcholtchev, Nikolay   91
Teran, Jesus Gutierrez   66
Theodoropoulou, Eleni   66, 139
Theodorou, Vasileios   17, 66
Tomaszewski, Lechosław   32, 77
Trakadas, Panagiotis   91
Tranoris, Christos   66, 139
Trigka, Maria   303
Tsiouris, George   118
Tsipouras, Markos   45
Tsita, Anastasia   195

Tzallas, Alexandros   45
Tzanakaki, Anna   66, 139
Tzanis, Nikolaos   126
Tzitziou, Georgia   219
Tzouvaras, Christos   183, 219, 242
Tzovaras, Dimitrios   183, 195, 207, 219, 231, 242, 254

V

Valdés, Nuria   458
Vardakas, John   17, 151
Varvarigos, Emmanuel   151
Vasilopoulos, Vasileios Georgios   254
Velkov, Atanas   126
Vergou, Elena   369
Verikoukis, Christos   17, 151
Vlachou, Eleni   271
Vlamos, Panagiotis   294
Vrahatis, Aristidis G.   294

W

Watts, Simon   32

X

Xenakis, Christos   91
Xezonaki, Maria-Evgenia   66
Xilouris, George   91

Z

Zahariadis, Theodore   106
Zaharis, Zaharias   91
Zarakovitis, Charilaos   91

Printed in the United States
by Baker & Taylor Publisher Services